ASPECTS OF POLITICAL IDEAS AND INSTITUTIONS IN ANCIENT INDIA

Aspects of Political Ideas and Institutions in Ancient India

RAM SHARAN SHARMA

MOTILAL BANARSIDASS PUBLISHERS
PRIVATE LIMITED • DELHI

4th Reprint: Delhi, 2018
Fifth Revised Edition: Delhi, 2005
First Edition: Delhi, 1959

ISBN: 978-81-208-0827-0 (Cloth)
ISBN: 978-81-208-0898-0 (Paper)

MOTILAL BANARSIDASS
41 U.A. Bungalow Road, Jawahar Nagar, Delhi 110 007
1 B, Jyoti Studio Compound, Kennedy Bridge, Nana Chowk, Mumbai 400 007
203 Royapettah High Road, Mylapore, Chennai 600 004
236, 9th Main III Block, Jayanagar, Bengaluru 560 011
8 Camac Street, Kolkata 700 017
Ashok Rajpath, Patna 800 004
Chowk, Varanasi 221 001

Printed in India

by RP Jain at NAB Printing Unit,
A-44, Naraina Industrial Area, Phase I, New Delhi–110028
and published by JP Jain for Motilal Banarsidass Publishers (P) Ltd,
41 U.A. Bungalow Road, Jawahar Nagar, Delhi-110007

भवत्यधर्मो धर्मो हि धर्माधर्मावुभावपि ।
कारणाद्देशकालस्य देशकालः स तादृशः ॥

शान्ति पर्व, ७९।३१

In response to the demands of time and place what is proper may become improper, and what is improper may become proper.

Śānti Parva, 79.31

PREFACE TO THE FIFTH EDITION

In 2004 I published a paper entitled from *Jana* to *Janapadaniveśa* in Professor Sukumari Bhattacharji Felicitation Volume. For the fourth edition of *Aspects* I have made some changes in this paper. This has to be included as an Appendix to chapters on Stages in Ancient Indian Polity. This may further explain developments in ancient Indian political structure.

Patna R.S. SHARMA

17 *November* 2004

PREFACE TO THE THIRD EDITION

The second edition of the book appeared in 1968, and has been out of print for the last fifteen years. During the last two decades Indian historians have not given as much attention to polity as to society and economy, though some Indianists from abroad have taken interest in the subject. In this study recent researches of importance have been surveyed. Five chapters and an appendix, bearing mainly on the problems of state formation and the nature of the central authority exercised at various stages have been added. The relevance of kin-ordered formations to the construction of polity has been considered. Whether rituals and religion divorced from social and economic processes independently influenced the development of polity has also been investigated.

The bibliography has been updated to include important publications in English on the subject. In preparing it as well as the body of the book I have received help from Mr. Mritunjay Kumar, Mr. M.C. Joshi, Dr. Madhusudan Mishra, Dr. Sita Ram Roy, Mr. P.N. Sahay, and Dr. B.P. Sahu who has also prepared the index. I extend my sincere thanks to them.

Patna
April 1991

R.S. SHARMA

PREFACE TO THE SECOND EDITION

The reviews and criticisms of the book in the first edition have been taken into account. In addition to minor alterations and additions in the chapters that have been retained, a few major changes have been made. Since the chapters on Land Revenue System in the Pre-Maurya Period and Origins of Feudalism contain considerable matter on early economy they have been taken out. New chapters on Sources and Method, *Sabhā* and *Samiti*, the Sātavāhana Polity, the Gupta Polity and Stages in Ancient Indian Polity have been inserted. I have however added only as much as is based on fresh survey or investigation.

I wish to acknowledge the help given by Dr. Mrs. Suvira Jaiswal, Mr. Jagannath Mishra, Dr. Sitaram Rai and Mr. P.C. Ray. My thanks are due to Dr. D.N. Jha, who has helped me with the correction of the proofs and the preparation of the index.

Department of History
Patna University
May 1968

R. S. SHARMA

PREFACE TO THE FIRST EDITION

In 1951, when Political Thought and Administration in Ancient India was introduced as a special paper at the M.A. stage in History at the Patna University, I began a more careful study of the subject for lecturing to my students. In course of my pursuit I discovered that in spite of two dozen monographs on the subject there was scope for new lines of enquiry. The following pages, therefore, embody the results of that investigation and are intended to focus light only on those problems which are considered rather obscure or need to be studied *de novo.* About one-half of this book has already been published in the form of articles. But for the purpose of the present work those essays have been re-touched, edited and brought into some sort of relation with the additional material, both in form and substance. The chapters dealing exclusively with political ideas have been put at the beginning, and the others have been arranged in chronological order. In the case of the discussion of the origins of feudalism, its economic aspects, though not quite relevant to the theme of the book, have also been taken into account. Although the book as it has emerged, can hardly be regarded a coherent study of the subject, it is not without some connecting threads and assumptions.

In the preparation of the book I have received valuable help and guidance from Professor A.L. Basham, who kindly went through more than half of the matter in 1955-7. I must express my sense of gratitude to Dr. Yogendra Mishra, who has saved me from several slips and errors in the preparation of the press copy. I also must thank Mr. Surendra Gopal, Mr. Chandra Shekhar Prasad Singh, Dr. Upendra Thakur and several other friends and students, who have helped me in different ways. My thanks are due to Mrs. Suvira Jaiswal and Dwijendra Narayan Jha, who have assisted me in preparing the index, and to Dr. Dev Raj Chanana for his help in the correction of the proofs. Finally, I have to thank my wife, Mrs. Malina Sharma, who cheerfully put up with all domestic worries and enabled me to devote my time to the present study.

R. S. SHARMA

ABBREVIATIONS

AA	*Aeschylus and Athens* by George Thomson.
AI	*Ancient India*, Delhi.
AB	*Aitareya Brāhmaṇa.*
Amara	*Amarakośa.*
Āp. ŚS	*Āpastamba Śrautasūtra.*
AŚ	*Arthaśāstra of Kauṭilya*, ed. R. Shamasastry.
ASIR	*Archaeological Survey of India, Reports.*
ASR	*Archaeological Survey, Reports.*
ASS	Ānandāśrama Sanskrit Series, Bombay.
AV	*Atharva Veda.*
Baudh.	*Baudhāyana Dharmasūtra.*
B. C. Law Vol.	*B.C. Law Volume*, Part II, Ed. D.R. Bhandarkar and others.
BI	*Bibliothca Indica*, Calcutta.
Bṛ	*Bṛhaspati Smṛti.*
Bṛ. Ār. Up.	*Bṛhadāraṇyaka Upaniṣad.*
BSOAS	*Bulletin of the School of Oriental and African Studies*, London.
CCIM	*Catalogue of the Coins in the Indian Museum*, Calcutta, i.
Cal.	Calcutta Edition of the *Mahābhārata.*
Chā. Up.	*Chāndogya Upaniṣad.*
CHI	*Cambridge History of India*, Ed. E.J. Rapson.
CII	*Corpus Inscriptionum Indicarum.*
CIS	*Contributions to Indian Sociology*, Delhi.
Cr. Edn.	Critical Edition of the *Mahābhārata* published by the Bhandarkar Oriental Research Institute, Poona.
DN	*Dīgha Nikāya.*
Ed.	Edited by, Edition.
EI	*Epigraphia Indica*, Calcutta and Delhi.
Gaut. Dh. S.	*Gautama Dharmasūtra.*
GOS	Gaikawad Oriental Series.
HCIP	*History and Culture of the Indian People*, Ed. R.C. Majumdar.

Hist. Dhs.	*History of Dharmaśāstra* by P.V. Kane.
HOS	*Harvard Oriental Series.*
HPT	*Hindu Political Theories* by U.N. Ghoshal.
IA	*Indian Antiquary*, Bombay.
IC	*Indian Culture*, Calcutta.
IHQ	*Indian Historical Quarterly*, Calcutta.
IHR	*Indian Historical Review*, New Delhi.
JA	*Journal Asiatique*, Paris.
JAOS	*Journal of the American Oriental Society*, Baltimore.
JASB	*Journal of the Asiatic Society of Bengal*, Calcutta.
JAHRS	*Journal of Andhra Historical Society*, Rajahmundry.
Jāt.	*Jātaka.*
JBBRAS	*Journal of the Bombay Branch of the Royal Asiatic Society*, Bombay.
JBORS	*Journal of the Bihar and Orissa Research Society*, Patna.
JDL	*Journal of Department of Letters*, Calcutta.
JESHO	*Journal of the Economic and Social History of the Orient*, Leiden.
JGJRA	*Journal of the Ganganatha Jha Research Institute*, Allahabad.
JIH	*Journal of Indian History*, Trivandrum.
JNSI	*Journal of Numismatic Society of India*, Varanasi.
JOR	*Journal of Oriental Research*, Madras.
JRAS	*Journal of the Royal Asiatic Society of Great Britain and Ireland*, London.
JRASB	*Journal of the Royal Asiatic Society of Bengal*, Calcutta.
KNS	*Kāmandaka Nītisāra.*
Kāma S.	*Kāmasūtra.*
Kātyā.	*Kātyāyana Smṛti.*
KS	*Kāṭhaka Saṃhitā.*
KŚS	*Kātyāyana Śrautasūtra.*
Manu	*Manu Smṛti.*
Mārk. P.	*Mārkaṇḍeya Purāṇa.*
MASI	*Memoirs of Archaeological Survey of India.*
Mbh.	*Mahābhārata.*
Milinda	*Milindapañho.*
MS	*Maitryāṇī Saṃhitā.*
Nār.	*Nārada Smṛti.*

NS	New Series.
OUP	Oxford University Press.
Pā	*Pāṇini's Grammar.*
PB	*Pañcaviṃśa Brāhmaṇa.*
PGS	*Pāraskara Gṛhyasūtra.*
Pat.	Patañjali's *Mahābhāṣya.*
P.E.	Pillar Edict of Aśoka.
PHAI	*Political History of Ancient India* by H.C. Raychaudhuri.
Proc. IHC	*Proceedings of Indian History Congress.*
PTS	Pali Text Society, London.
Rām.	*Rāmāyaṇa.*
R.E.	Rock Edict of Aśoka.
RV	*Ṛg Veda.*
ŚB	*Śatapatha Brāhmaṇa.*
SBB	*Sacred Books of the Buddhists*, London.
SBE	*Sacred Books of the East*, London.
SE	Southern Edition of the *Mahābhārata* (also indicated as Kumb.)
SED	*Sanskrit-English Dictionary* by M. Monier-Williams.
Sel. Inscrr.	*Select Inscriptions*, i, by D.C. Sircar.
ŚNS	*Śukranītisāra.*
ŚP	*Śānti Parva.*
Śūdras	*Śūdras in Ancient India* by R.S. Sharma.
TB	*Taittirīya Brāhmaṇa.*
TGS	T. Gaṇapati Śāstri's editions of the *Arthaśāstra.*
Tr.	Translated by, Translation.
TS	*Taittirīya Saṃhitā.*
Vā. P.	*Vāyu Purāṇa.*
Vas. Dh. S.	*Vasiṣṭha Dharmasūtra.*
VI	*Vedic Index.*
Vin.	*Vinaya Piṭaka.*
Viṣṇu	*Viṣṇu Smṛti.*
VS	*Vājasaneyi Saṃhitā.*
Yāj.	*Yājñavalkya Smṛti.*
ZDMG	*Zeitschrift der Deutschen Mörgenlandischen Gesellschaft*, Berlin.

Roman Equivalents of Nāgarī Letters

अ	a	ए	e	क्	k	च्	c
आ	ā	ऐ	ai	ख्	kh	छ्	ch
इ	i	ओ	o	ग्	g	ज	j
ई	ī	औ	au	घ्	gh	झ्	jh
उ	u	ऋ	ṛ	ङ्	ṅ	ञ्	ñ
ऊ	ū						
ट्	ṭ	त्	t	प्	p	य	y
ठ्	ṭh	थ्	th	फ्	ph	र	r
ड्	ḍ	द्	d	ब्	b	ल्	l
ढ्	ḍh	ध्	dh	भ्	bh	व्	v
ण	ṇ	न	n	म्	m	श्	ś

ष्	ṣ	Anusvāra (.)-ṃ
स्	s	Visarga (:)-ḥ
ह	h	

CONTENTS

Preface to the Fifth Edition vii
Preface to the Third Edition viii
Preface to the Second Edition ix
Preface to the First Edition x
Abbreviations xi
Roman equivalents of Nāgarī letters xv
Introduction xxiii

CHAPTER

I Historiography of Ancient Indian Polity up to 1930 1
Imperialist approach versus nationalist ideology 1; Merits and limitations of the nationalist approach 12

II Sources and Method 15
Vedic texts 15; Dharmasūtras and Smṛtis 16; Epics and Purāṇas 18; Kauṭilya and Kāmandaka 20; Buddhist and Jain texts 23; Coins and inscriptions 25; Greek and Chinese accounts 28; Comparison and coordination 30

III The Saptāṅga Theory of the State 31
Analysis of the seven elements 31; Comparison with Greek and modern concepts of the state 38; Calamities affecting the elements 41; Relative importance of the elements 43; The "organic" theory of the state 47

IV Theories of Property, Family and Varṇa Regarding the Origin of the State 49
Main features of the state of nature 49; Origin of the social institutions and state 51; Kingless society 55; Duties of the king and the origin of the state 57

V The Contract Theory of the Origin of the State: An Historical Survey 63
Evidence of the Brāhmaṇas 63; Evidence of the *Dīgha Nikāya* 64; Kauṭilya's views 68; Evidence of the *Mahāvastu* 69; Evidence of the *Śānti Parva* 71; Buddhist and brāhmaṇical attitudes 75

VI Theory of "Oriental Despotism": A Socio-Economic Critique 77

Ecological and psychological explanations 77; Role of irrigation 78; Royal ownership of land 79; Self-sufficiency of village 82; Presence of the exploiting class 85; Motivated generalisations 86

VII Vidatha: The Earliest Folk-Assembly of the Indo-Āryans 87

References and interpretations 87; Woman membership 88; Deliberative and distributive functions 91; Military nature 93; Religious functions 94; Collective nature of sacrifice 98; Composition and antiquity 101; Earliest assembly 103

VIII Sabhā and Samiti 105

I Sabhā: Constitution 105; Functions 107; Sabhā and the king 109

II Samiti: Composition 111; Functions 112

III Relation between the Sabhā and the Samiti: Similarities 116; Differences 117

IX The Vedic Gaṇa and the Origin of the Post-Vedic Republics 119

Variations in the meaning of the term *gaṇa* 119; Tribal and military character of the Vedic *gaṇa* 120; Functions of the Vedic *gaṇa* 122; Nature of the composition and functions of the Vedic *gaṇa* 126; Origin of the post-Vedic republics 130; Reaction of the deprived chiefs 131

X The Early Pariṣad 133

Vedic references 133; Epic and Purāṇic evidence regarding the military character of the *pariṣad* 135; Size and composition of the *pariṣad* 137; Changes in later Vedic and post-Vedic times 139

XI Ratnahavīṃṣi Ceremony 143

Analysis of the *ratnin* lists 143; Specificities of the *Satapatha Brāhmaṇa* list 151; Political organisation as known from the *ratnin* lists 153

XII Tribal and Primitive Aspects of the Later Vedic Polity 159

Social and political implications of the *rājasūya* 159;

Devasūhavīṃṣi ceremony 159; Other rituals of the rājasūya 161; Cow-raid and game of dice 163; Chariot-race and other *vājapeya* rituals 164; Review of the coronation rituals 167

XIII Kin-conflicts and Rise of Hierarchy in Later Vedic Times 171

Conflict between the chief and his kinsmen 171; Help from the brāhmaṇas 173; Conflict and the rise of the varṇa system 175; Increasing power of the ruling chiefs 177; Lineage and tributes 179; Kin-based fighting hosts 181; Erosion of the kinship and rise of the proto-state 182

XIV From Gopati to Bhūpati: Changing Position of the King 185

Meaning of *rājan* 185; Viśpati and other terms used for the chief 187; Post-Vedic terms for the king 190; Gupta and post-Gupta terms for royal ownership of land 191

XV Taxation and State Formation in Northern India in Pre-Maurya Times 197

Relative place of treasury and coercion in the state 197; Material conditions and the availability of surplus 199; Regular collection of land revenue 203; Machinery for revenue collection 209; *Rājabhoggam* and *bhogagāma* 212; Increasing taxes and growth of non-kin state apparatus 217; Taxes and professional soldiers in different kingdoms 223; Advent of taxation and emergence of the state 226

XVI Varṇa in Relation to Law and Politics (c.B.C. 600-A.D.500) 233

Varṇa and the origin of the state 233; Varṇa in relation to kingship 235; Varṇa in relation to army and bureaucracy 237; Varṇa element in the *pariṣad*, the *paura* and *jānapada* 241; Varṇa justice and legislation 243; Dominance of the two upper varṇas 247; Exclusion of the two lower varṇas 250

XVII Religion and Politics in the Arthaśāstra of Kauṭilya 253

I Influence of religion on the policy of the state: Internal and external policy 253; Attitude towards the brāhmaṇas and brāhmaṇical religion 255; Ideas on the divinity of kingship 259; Attitude towards the heterodox sects 261; Non- and anti-religious aspects of the state 263

II Superstition and Politics: Raising money through superstitious devices 266; Superstitions and external policy 268; Deliberate use of superstitions 271

XVIII The Sātavāhana Polity 275

Background of state formation 275; Traces of the Aśokan system 276; Amātyas and other officers 277; Financial system 278; Artisans and merchants in local administration 279; Matrilineal traces in polity 281; Rural administration 284; Fiscal and administrative immunities 287; General appraisal 289

XIX The Kuṣāṇa Polity 291

Background of the polity 291; Grandiloquent titles of the king 291; Feudatory political system 294; Dual governorship 295; Military system 296; Village administration 299; Forms of land tenure 300; *Devaputra*, *devakula* and divinity of the king 301

XX Kuṣāṇa Elements in the Gupta Polity 311

Introductory 311; Divinity and royal titles 312; Use of cavalry 313; Continuity of Kuṣāṇa officials 315; Guild system 317; Feudatory practice 318

XXI The Gupta Polity 321

Economic and political background 321; Features of kingship 322; Ministers and high officers 323; Military system 327; Taxation 328; Provincial and district administration 330; Town administration 334; Law and Justice 336; Feudal elements 339

XXII Stages in Ancient Indian Polity: Vedic and Post-Vedic 349

I The Ṛg Vedic Phase: Tribal Military Democracy

Material and social background 349; Tribal kingship 352; Tributes and lack of regular army 355; Few officers 356

II The Later Vedic Phase: Transition to Class and Territorial Government

Material and social set-up 357; Rise of territorial kingship 359; Tributes, officers and kin-based army 361; Towards the state system 362

III The Pre-Maurya Phase: Territorial Monarchies and Tribal Oligarchies

Material developments in eastern U.P. and Bihar 363; Officials, taxes and army in monarchies 364; Nature of oligarchies/republics 367

XXIII Stages in Ancient Indian Polity: Maurya and Later 371

I The Maurya Phase: Centralised Bureaucratic Interlude

Economic and political background 371; Exaltation of state power and elaboration of bureaucracy 372; Army and criminal administration 374; Urban and rural administration 375; Central control in a large area 377

II The Post-Maurya phase: Divinity and Decentralisation

Material and social setting 378; Elements of decentralisation 379; Autonomous towns 380; Fiscal and military system 382; Divine aspects of the kingship 384

III The Gupta Phase: Proto-Feudal Polity

Economic and political background 386; Army and taxes 387; Local administration 388; Administration of justice 389; Feudatories 390; Landed beneficiaries 391-392

Appendix to Chapter XXIII: I 392

Pooling of resources 392; Provision for controlling departmental heads 393; *Maṇḍala* theory not typical of Maurya times 394; Extent of state control as known from Megasthenes and Aśokan inscriptions 395; Material background of the state control 399; Concepts of empire and bureaucracy 401

Appendix to Chapters XXII and XXIII: I (a) From Jana to Janapadaniveśa 403
Jana 403; Janapada 403; Janapadin 404; Mahājanapada 405; Janapadaniveśa 405; Evidence from Aśokan Inscriptions 408; Conclusion 408

XXIV Recapitulation 411
Ancient India's contribution to the theories of the state 411; Vedic communal assemblies 411; Varṇa and polity 412; Main phases in ancient Indian polity 413

Bibliography 415

General Index 431

A Pāli, Sanskrit and Allied Terms 446

B Authorities 456

INTRODUCTION

The first edition of this book was based on some pieces I had written in 1950-54. My study was particularly influenced by the ideas generated by historical materialism. In collecting, analysing and interpreting the evidence I relied on *Ancient Society* by Henry Morgan and *The Origin of the Family, Private Property and the State* by Fredrick Engels. My approach enabled me to understand better the origin, growth and nature of the state in ancient India and also the history of its organs. Drekmeier, a political scientist, who adopted a sociological framework in his *Early Kingship and Community* (1962), found many of such findings acceptable. He underlined the primitive and tribal character of ancient rituals and institutions connected with polity. On the other hand although the importance given by me to the treatment of the *vidatha* was recognised by J.P. Sharma in his *Republics in Ancient India* (1965), he considered it to be a religious body and ignored the undifferentiated character of functions performed by the kin-ordered institutions of a pre-class Vedic society. However, came to be regarded as an important Vedic assembly along with the *vidatha* the *sabhā* and *samiti* by many scholars including A.S. Altekar.

A.S. Altekar's *State and Government in Ancient India* has been a popular textbook. Published in 1949, it has undergone three editions, and the third edition (1958) was reprinted in 1972 and 1977. Although he generally admired ancient institutions, in the third edition he did take note of some unorthodox researches which were stimulated by anthropological and other ideas. He referred to the role of the family and property in explaining the origin of the state. In his view the "institution of the family with the notion of family and property thus played its own part in the origin of the State."[1] He also states that "the state in the early Vedic period was still tribal"[2] and that the Vedic tribes had a for a long time no permanent territorial basis for their states.[3] These views are sound though Altekar and scholars of his generation were neither interested in the definitions of kin-

1. 1958 edn., p. 36.
2. Ibid., p. 43.
3. Ibid.

ordered collectivities such as clan, tribes, etc., nor in the stages and processes of state formation and polity evolution. Altekar also gave some attention to the discussion of the character of the *vidatha*.[1] His concern with problems of social injustice is evident.[2] A revivalist and Hindu nationalist, he blames both the state and society for perpetuating an inequitious social system.[3] However he singles out society for castigation and does not examine the linkage between the state and the dominant social classes. He defends the disabilities of the śūdras and untouchables on the ground that they "believed that they were born in their particular caste as a natural result of certain sins committed by them in past lives"[4]. Altekar also discovered "a welfare state"[5] which was the case with K.A. Nilakanta Sastri[6] and even A.L. Basham.[7] He not only tried to demonstrate the state's effort to establish harmonious relationship between castes and social classes,[8] but also put up the ideal of the Vedic kings and of the ancient republics[9] before modern citizens. He did not investigate whether these 'ideals' were the products of certain social situations. Altekar was deeply religious, but he did not adopt a consistent position on the role of religion in ancient Indian polity. He finds "considerable force in the view that the ancient Indian state was theocratic to a great extent."[10] However, he does not accept Willoughby's view that in all early Asiatic monarchies the rulers claimed a divine right to control the affairs of the state.[11] He asserts that religion and philosophical dogmas and concepts

1. Ibid., p. 141.
2. Ibid., pp. 49-51, 385.
3. Ibid., p. 385.
4. Ibid.
5. Ibid., p. 60.
6. *Proceedings of the 16th Session of the All-India Oriental Conference*, Lucknow, 1951, pp. 67-68.
7. A.L. Basham, foreword to John W. Spellman, *Political Theory of Ancient India*, Oxford, 1964, p. vi. After the attainment of independence by India in 1947 Altekar saw the possibility of trying limited monarchy by the princely states on Vedic lines and implicitly regretted that it could not be done (Ibid., p. 38). Also see K.N. Mishra, *State Sponsored Public Welfare Plans in the Mahabharata*, Varanasi, 1972.
8. Altekar, op.cit., pp. 350, 325-26.
9. Ibid., pp. 379-21.
10. Op.cit., p. 53.
11. Ibid., pp. 94-95.

did not deeply influence Hindu political thought, practice and institutions.[1]

As in the earlier phase, Ghoshal's contribution in the post-independence period is marked by impeccable scholarship. In his, *A History of Hindu Public Life* (1957) and *A History of Political Ideas Ancient and Medieval* (1959) he elaborates the points made in his earlier publications and documents them so carefully that it is difficult to detect any error. His analysis is more or less on the lines of Western liberal writings on the history of political thought which he taught for long in Calcutta. Though associated for many years with a journal called *Greater India*, Ghoshal is not swayed by Hindu chauvinism. He substantially adds to our information on political ideas and institutions but does not *try* to link them to social and economic developments; he considered such an exercise to be 'speculative.'[2] Apart from his repetitive and involved style of writing, Ghoshal creates some problem because of the methods he adopts in using the sources. For example, he ascribes the major part of the Kauṭilyan material to pre-Maurya times on the ground that Kauṭilya frequently quotes from masters of political thought who preceded him. Unfortunately the writings of these teachers have not been discovered so far, and many of them may have been Kauṭilya's senior contemporaries. The more one examines the *Arthaśāstra* the more difficult it becomes to use its major part even for Maurya times.[3]

The *Mahābhārata* continues to attract a good many researchers. In recent years at least four dissertations on political ideas and institutions in the *Mahābhārata* have appeared.[4] They certainly systematise much information bearing on ancient Indian polity.[5]

1. Ibid., p. 57.
2. This is what he told me in a discussion in Patna when he stayed with me in 1957.
3. R. Trautman identifies several strata in the *Arthaśāstra* on the basis of computerised mannerism in style. S.C. Mishra's inscriptional analysis of the text reveals four strata, the latest of which tallies with the inscriptional use of the terms in the 11th-12th centuries. See S.C. Mishra, "An Inscriptional Approach to the Arthaśāstra of Kauṭilya", Ph.D. Thesis, University of Delhi, 1984.
4. S.L. Pande, *Bhīsma Kā Rājadharma*, Lucknow, 1955; Premkumari Dikshit, *Mahābhārata mein Rājavyavasthā*, Lucknow, 1970; B.P. Roy, *Political Ideas and Institutions in the Mahabharata*, Calcutta, 1975; N.K.P. Sinha, *Political Ideas and Ideals in the Mahabharata (A Study of first two Parvans)*, New Delhi, 1976.
5. B.P. Roy, op.cit.

Formerly more emphasis was placed on the *rājadharma* section of the *Śānti Parva*, but now references found in the *Sabhā*, *Anuśāsana* and other parvas are also used for research in polity which is seen in the perspective of political science.[1] These studies, however, ignore stratification in the text and do not situate references in the context of time, place and social evolution. Rituals surviving till today contain vestiges of various stages of evolution; and legends as well as descriptive and didactic portions in the *Mahābhārata* reflect ideas and practices prevalent in different regions and periods. A tentative explanatory framework for handling the epic material has been provided by us elsewhere.[2] But further progress in the field will depend on a more critical reconstruction of the Critical Edition text.[3]

Western Indologists of the nineteenth and the early twentieth centuries popularised the stereotypes of oriental despotism and the hold of religion and spiritualism.[4] These came under heavy attack, largely justified, from Indian scholars. After India attained independence, the West developed a kind of neo-orientalism based on sociology. As a concession to the independent republican status of India, Western historians and Indologists modified the idea of perpetual despotism, but they placed undue emphasis on the role of religion, particularly rituals, and on the divinity of kingship.[5]

J. Gonda overemphasises the role of religion in the formation of kingship in ancient India.[6] The sources he uses to argue his case are unrelated, distant in time and place though they show some superficial continuity in tradition. Gonda frequently states that the honour shown to a sovereign is similar to the marks of

1. N.K.P. Sinha, op.cit.
2. R.S. Sharma, *Material Culture and Social Formations in Ancient India*, Delhi, 1983, ch. VIII.
3. An attempt has been made in this direction by Keshavram K. Shashtree, (*The Jaya-Samhitā*, i.e., *the Ur-Mahābhārata*, vols. I and II, Gujarat Research Society, Ahmedabad, 1977), but it is difficult to agree with the criteria he has adopted for selecting original 8800 verses constituting the *Jaya*.
4. Infra, ch. 1.
5. J.W. Spellman, *Political Theory in Ancient India*, 1964; J. Gonda, *Ancient Indian Kingship from the Religious Point of View*, Leiden, 1969; J.C. Heesterman, *Inner Conflict of Indian Tradition*, Delhi, 1985.
6. *Ancient Indian Kingship from the Religious Point of View*, Leiden, 1969.

veneration conferred on the images of the gods.[1] The fact that gods are conceived after the pattern of chiefs and kings and are given the latter's attributes and qualities does not strike him. Similarly he repeatedly asserts that in India divinity of king has always been accepted by the masses.[2] But the *Arthaśāstra* of Kauṭilya clearly shows that superstitious ideas about the miraculous powers of the king are deliberately propagated by the ruling class. Bāṇabhaṭṭa exposes the hollowness of the mass belief in royal divinity.[3]

Though Gonda's etymological and philological study of ancient Sanskrit terms from the angle of comparative religion is valuable, his decontexualised approach obscures the changing meanings of terms. For instance, the translation of *dharma* as religion or even moral order would not suit all the Sanskrit passages. In fact most allusions in which the king is called the upholder of the *dharma* or in which he is called *dharmaparavartaka*[4] (promoter or advancer of *dharma* according to Gonda) refer to the varṇa-based social order in which the brāhmaṇas and kṣatriyas either lived respectively on the gifts and taxes collected from the peasants (mainly the vaiśyas) or on śūdra labour. But Gonda completely misses this significance of *dharma*. He sees decay of *dharma* causing fatal losses in welfare and happiness though really it means mixing of the varṇas and upsetting of the society structured in favour of the two higher orders.

Gonda's pupil J.C. Heesterman overstresses the part played by ritual and tradition in the formation of polity. Some of his interpretations of the Vedic rituals are acceptable.[5] However it is not sufficiently realised that political power was made acceptable to people through rituals, legends, genealogies, marriage alliances, hierarchical ideology and various other means. Further, the fact that the Brāhmaṇas, Śrautasūtras, Gṛhyasūtras and some other texts deal with rituals should not create the impression that all Indian history is rituals. The inference of social and economic processes from archaeological and anthropological sources is equally important. Rituals and traditions may

1. Ibid., p. 56.
2. Ibid., pp. 1-2, 15, 24, 67, 86, 127, 132, 138-39.
3. See *Śakanāsopadeśa* in *Kādambarī*.
4. Ibid., p. 70.
5. J.C. Heesterman, *The Ancient Indian Royal Consecration*, The Hague, 1957.

have their roots in reality but are usually manipulated by dominant social groups to serve their interests. Heesterman, who rules out any broad-based struggle of the Indian against the colonial rule and thinks that they fought between themselves and not with the Raj,[1] emphasises fragmentation and atomisation in Indian history. But we have instances of both local and pan-Indian supralocal political formations. The ancient Indian king in his view was primarily interested in mastering his senses (*indriya-jaya*) though real history shows more interest in territorial conquest and administration. He thinks that the king derives his ultimate authority from the brāhmaṇa who is a renouncer. The theory that the eternal and transcendant values of renunciation were meant for the guidance of the state[2] hardly worked in practice. The brāhmaṇas opposed the renunciatory religions of the Buddha and Mahāvīra, and prescribed renunciation only for the fourth stage (*āśrama*) of life which rarely materialised. The brāhmaṇas were an integral part of the varṇa divided society which they regulated with the help of the kṣatriyas. They occasionally quarreled, but they together lived on the gifts, taxes, tributes and presents provided by artisans, peasants and other sections of society. Towards the end of the ancient period the brāhmaṇas were given substantial land grants, and rituals were reoriented.

The French scholar Robert Lingat, who has produced "a work of outstanding merit" on *dharma* or law,[3] takes a balanced view of the divinity of kingship as well as the relation between the temporal and spiritual power (*brahma* and *kṣatra*). He considers *dharma* "essentially, a rule of interdependence founded on a hierarchy corresponding to the nature of things and necessary for the maintenance of social order".[4] The king is considered indispensable to the social order,[5] in which "religious aspirations do not monopolise all human activity".[6] We may add that this social order is varṇa-divided and male-dominated, and its laws regarding person and property help the higher varṇas.

1. Ibid., *Inner Conflict of Tradition in India*, Delhi, 1985, p. 176.
2. Ibid., pp. 43, 155, 160, 177.
3. *The Classical Law of India*, translated from French with additions by J. Duncan M. Derrett, University of California, 1973, p. xi.
4. Ibid., p. 211.
5. Ibid., p. 207.
6. Ibid., p. 5.

That the *puruṣārthas*, namely, *artha*, *dharma*, *kāma* and *mokṣa* shaped ancient political ideas and institutions is also held by some Indian writers. Ideas do shape the course of history, but there is nothing to show that the fourfold aims of life or the *puruṣārthas* determined the development of society. Such ideas hardly appear in Vedic times; nor do they figure in early Buddhist texts. They assume importance only in Gupta and post-Gupta times, especially in the Purāṇas. Initially only *artha*, *dharma* and *kāma* appear, and can be connected with the institutions of the family, property and varṇa. The idea of *mokṣa* or salvation linked to renunciation is tagged on to the original three ideals. What is really needed is an explanation of the origin and development of these ideals in the context of time, place and social milieu. How far ancient rulers, priests and others were influenced by the relative importance of such ideals in their policies and actions also requires investigation.

The establishment of the Republic of India in 1950 made some impact on researchers. It was no longer necessary to make a case for the existence of republics in ancient India, as was forcefully done by K.P. Jayaswal under the colonial rule, but to think of steps for the preservation of the Indian Republic. In this context A.S. Altekar finds it necessary to understand the causes of the disappearance of the republics in ancient India.[1] He adumberates the seven conditions laid down for the success of the Vajji republic and recommends that "Modern India may carve on the gate of the Parliament the Buddha's prophesy"[2] about the decline or survival of that republic. The subject of the republics therefore assumed greater importance in the post-independence period than the study of limited monarchy. Republics in the popular notion came to be confounded with democratic governments, and this idea also influenced researchers. Thus in his book *Republics in Ancient India* (1963) J.P. Sharma discusses at length the various popular assemblies including the *vidatha* in Vedic times. Another book on the subject[3] makes a descriptive study of the republics and adds very little to what K.P. Jayaswal has written. The conclusion that the republics of today do not differ from those of ancient times in their

1. Op. cit., p. 378.
2. Ibid., p. 379.
3. Shobha Mukherji, *The Republican Trends in Ancient India*, Delhi, 1969.

essentials is naive.[1] S.N. Mishra has collected exhaustive data on the *gaṇa-rājya* and its different interpretations.[2] But except Ghoshal writers on polity hardly emphasise the clan or the oligarchical character of the republics that were set up in post-Vedic times.

Thus the questions which exercise the minds of scholars are not entirely new. Neither the influence of colonialism nor that of nationalism has been completely eliminated from writings on ancient Indian polity. The stress on spiritualism, which first appeared in the nineteenth century and the early twentieth century, is given a new form. Some writers, both Western and Indian, still consider religion to be an autonomous factor that influences the formation of the state and kingship and makes for permanent divisiveness.

Influenced by historical materialism D.D. Kosambi made a penetrating study of ancient Indian society,[3] but he did not give attention to polity. Karl Marx formulated primitive communist, ancient, slave, Germanic, Asiatic, feudal and capitalist modes of production.[4] Now the Asiatic mode is also applied to Latin American countries, and certain Marxist anthropologists advance the concepts of the 'African', 'lineage', 'domestic', 'foraging' and some other modes of production, but none of these has won any general acceptance.[5] Taking the cue from the lineage mode of production Romila Thapar[6] underlines the point that members of senior lineages claim special shares from those of junior lineages in Vedic times. But how patrilineages and genealogies are formed and manipulated and whether achievements determine seniority and ascriptive claims to spoils and shares in produce has to be investigated.[7]

1. Ibid., p. 205.
2. *Ancient Indian Republics from the Earliest Times to the Sixth Century* A.D., Lucknow, 1976.
3. *An Introduction to the Study of Indian History*, Bombay, 1956.
4. Karl Marx, *Pre-Capitalist Economic Formations*, ed. and introduction, E. Hobsbawm, London, 1964; *The Grundrisse*, ed. M. Nicolaus, Penguin, Harmondsworth, 1973, p. 472 ff.
5. 'Mathew Sprigg in *Marxist Perspectives in Archaeology*, Cambridge, 1984, pp. 4-5.
6. *From Lineage to State*, Delhi, 1984.
7. During the last 30 years lineage studies have hardly gone beyond the Goros of Africa, and are confined to a few French anthropologists.

In the light of historical materialism we propose to look at ancient political ideas and institutions in relation to socio-economic processes. We will consider various modes of production including the tribal and the post-tribal. Insights derived from recent studies of tribal societies and archaeological discoveries will be used to explain the significance of rituals and institutions in ancient India. But in exploring the linkage between economy and polity historically we would not ignore comparisons with the ancient institutions of Asia and Europe.[1]

1. Pre-industrial India is considered similar to pre-industrial Europe and not to pre-colonial Africa in respect of the family and systems of marriage in Jack Goody, *The Oriental, the Ancient and the Primitive*, Cambridge University Press, 1990. This also applies to ancient political institutions in several cases.

CHAPTER I

HISTORIOGRAPHY OF ANCIENT INDIAN POLITY UP TO 1930

The first serious attempt at the study of India's past, on the part of both the Western as well as Indian scholars, began after the revolt of 1857-59.[1] A perusal of some introductions to the *Sacred Books of the East* reveals the motive underlying this great venture extending over years. It was felt by the British rulers that the revolt was due to lack of their knowledge of Indian religion, manners, customs and history. Further, the people could not be won over to Christianity and consequently to the empire unless the missionaries acquired an idea of the vulnerable points in their social structure. According to Max Müller, to the missionary an accurate knowledge of the sacred books was as indispensable as the knowledge of the enemy's country to a general.[2] In their study of the ancient history of India, Western scholars reached two important conclusions, which can be summed up in the words of Max Müller. In 1859 he wrote that the Indians are a nation of philosophers and Indian intellect is lacking in political or material speculation, and that the Indians never knew the feeling of nationality.[3] We do not know whether Max Müller drew upon the famous dictum of Aristotle that oriental rule is autocratic in character. But his idea was the stock-in-trade of the great European historians who wrote in the 18th and 19th centuries. Thus Gibbon pointed out that all oriental history is "one unceasing record of valour, greatness, degeneracy and decay". Green stated that "the empires of the East are, in the main, tax-collecting institutions. They exercise coercive power on their subjects of the most violent kind...(and) do not impose laws as distinct from particular and occasional commands."[4]

1. Although the establishment of the Asiatic Society of Bengal in 1784 marks the starting point of Western interest in ancient Indian studies the number of books that were published till 1859 was small. Max Müller, *A History of Ancient Sanskrit Literature*, p. 1.
2. *SBE*, i, pt. I, Preface, p. xl.
3. Max Müller, op.cit., p. 16.
4. Quoted in Beni Prasad, *The State in Ancient India*, p. 498.

Similar ideas continued to find expression in the work of eminent orientalists. Writing in 1898 Sénart stated that India never attained to the idea either of the state or of the fatherland,[1] and that it could not evolve any political constitution, even in conception.[2]

Such a view about India's past history and polity was obviously dominated by imperialist ideology. Its practical implications in the existing set-up were dangerous to the demand for self-government in India. If Indians were essentially philosophers, absorbed in the problems of the spiritual world, it followed that their material world should be managed for them by their imperialist masters. If Indians were accustomed to autocratic rule and never had any idea of nationhood, state or self-government, it was in keeping with their tradition that they should be ruled autocratically by the British Governor-General and Viceroy.

This colonialist ideology regarding ancient history and particularly the nature of the early Indian polity came as a challenge to Indian scholarship and to the few foreign scholars who were yet unaffected by imperialist ideology. In 1889, controverting Max Müller who had said that "to the Greek, existence is full of life and reality, to the Hindu it is a dream and delusion"[3], the great American savant Hopkins pointed out that the religious element did not penetrate deeply into the vast mass of unpriestly classes.[4] But the biggest response to this challenge came from the Indian scholars themselves. During the last three decades of the 19th century Bhagwan Lal Indraji, R.G. Bhandarkar, R.L. Mitra and B.G. Tilak, most of whom actively associated themselves with the political and social movements of their time, tried to prove the falsity of the imperialist ideology. By their researches into the manifold aspects of the past history of their country they tried to build a powerful case for the political and social progress of the country in their own times. Since then the study of India's past was mainly guided by the nationalist ideology. This point can be especially illustrated by presenting a rapid survey of research on ancient Indian polity.

1. *Caste in India*, p. 198.
2. Ibid., p. 212.
3. *A History of Ancient Sanskrit Literature*, p. 18.
4. "Position of the Ruling Caste etc.", *JAOS*, xiii, 182.

Just as there were two phases, moderate and radical, in the growth of the nationalist movement, so also there were two such phases in the progress of research on ancient Indian polity. It is well-known that the chief demand of the Indian nationalist movement in its earlier stages was to curtail the powers of the autocratic Viceroy by introducing a popular element at the Centre and in the Provincial Governments. Hence in 1887 R.C. Dutt wrote an article on the "Civilisation in the Brāhmaṇa Period", in which he tried to show that in ancient times the king did justice to all.[1] He was followed by Purnendu Narayan Singh, who, in an article in 1894, strongly countered the statement of Sir Auckland Colvin that "the British have taught for the first time that the end and aim of rule is the welfare of the people, and not the personal aggrandisement of the sovereign." He argued that such an idea is due to the ignorance of the system of government in ancient India which, in his opinion, was limited monarchy.[2]

The strong nationalist movement that followed the partition of Bengal in 1905 gave further impetus to research in ancient Indian polity. Curzon's homily on the oriental character, his autocratic measures for the partition of Bengal, and his attack on the elected element in the Calcutta Corporation could not but influence the course of research on ancient polity. In an article written in 1907 A.C. Das repeated with greater emphasis the view of the previous scholars that "it is a mistake to suppose that the Hindus have been accustomed to an autocratic form of government, and that the popular element never existed as a distinct force in the country." He further said that "it was not Absolute but Limited Monarchy that flourished in Ancient India."[3] Perhaps by way of indirect suggestion that Curzon's attack on the elected element in the Calcutta Corporation was unwarranted, in another essay of the same year Das pointed out that "Local Self-Government existed in Ancient India even in a better form than that in which it exists at present under British rule."[4] Four years later, S.K. Aiyangar in his thesis on Coḷa Administration brought to light the working of elected village

1. *Calcutta Review*, xxxv (1887), 266.
2. Ibid., xcviii (1894), 301.
3. "Limited Monarchy in Ancient India", *Modern Review*, ii (1907), 346ff.
4. Ibid.

panchayats, exercising all functions in early mediaeval times under the Colas.[1]

The nationalist movement stimulated the search for ancient manuscripts, resulting in the discovery of the *Arthaśāstra* of Kauṭilya in 1905 and its publication by Shamasastry in 1909. The discovery was an epoch-making event in the history of the study of ancient Indian polity, for it provided valuable raw material which could be utilised in yielding "political precedents for modern controversies."[2] This was an important factor which contributed to many critical and descriptive studies of the ancient Indian polity.[3]

The period from 1905 was a period of extremist politics. Extremists, who did not believe in constitutional methods for the attainment of slow reforms, set up a net-work of revolutionary societies in Bengal and Maharashtra. The movement was coloured by the spirit of Hindu revivalism. The very names of these societies betray their love for past culture. For instance the Anushilan Samiti, which was set up in 1905 and had about 550 branches by 1907, means the society for the promotion of culture and learning. It is legitimate to suspect that, although wedded to the cult of violence, it must have published certain research tracts of which we are unaware. These societies created a revolutionary temper in the country and prepared the minds of many intellectuals for the complete independence of their motherland. It was through them that the word Swaraj got the widest currency. As interpreted by a left-wing paper it means "self-taxation, self-legislation and self-administration."[4] It is not known whether K.P. Jayaswal was in any way connected with these societies, but the fact that he was made to resign his post in the postgraduate teaching department of Calcutta University by the Bengal Government in 1912-3 might suggest that he was considered a potential contributor to the "seminaries of sedition."[5] It is to the late K.P. Jayaswal that Indology owes its greatest work on ancient Indian polity. His articles contributed

1. *Ancient India*, pp. 158-91.
2. K.V. Rangaswami Aiyangar, *Some Aspects of Ancient Indian Polity*, p. 87.
3. An up-to-date bibliography is found in R.P. Kangle, *The Kauṭilīya Arthaśāstra*, Part III, University of Bombay, 1965.
4. Quoted in Hiren Mukerjee, *India Struggles for Freedom*, p. 88.
5. *Hindu Polity*, p. xxv.

to *Modern Review* between 1912 and 1915—which appeared later in the form of his famous book *Hindu Polity* in 1924—were really pioneer works, as later admitted by D.R. Bhandarkar, R.C. Majumdar, B.K. Sarkar and other scholars who followed him. For the first time he showed the importance of republics in ancient Indian history. He tried to prove that the ancient Hindu political system was partly of republics of the Athenian type, and of constitutional monarchies such as that of Great Britain. There were popular assemblies such as the *paura* and *jānapada*, acting as checks on the powers of the king. According to him these organisations were more advanced than any thing which modern Switzerland or the United States can boast of. At the end of his study Jayaswal concluded: "The constitutional progress made by the Hindus has probably not been equalled much less surpassed by any polity of antiquity." And finally, he expressed the undying hope of a patriot that the "Golden Age of his polity lies not only in the past but in the Future."[1] The implications of his research are clear. His conclusions present the first solid ideological case for complete independence and a republican form of Government in India. It is because of this that no thesis on ancient Indian history has been so frequently quoted as *Hindu Polity*. It became the Bible of the Indian nationalists. Meet any educated old man and he knows about *Hindu Polity*.

Jayaswal was followed by a host of scholars, who flooded *Modern Review*, *Hindustan Review* and *Indian Antiquary* with a spate of articles and wrote a number of theses. In many ways the period between 1916 and 1925, coinciding with post-war nationalist and revolutionary movements sweeping over Europe and Asia, marked the peak of our nationalist movement. No other period of the present century has produced so many research works on ancient Indian polity as this period of nine years. Leaving aside the articles, the number of monographs on Hindu political theories and institutions would come to more than a dozen. It is not possible to notice the ideological basis of all works, but we can examine the important ones to find out the main trends.

To begin with works of a general nature on polity, P.N. Banerjea

1. Ibid., p. 366.

in his *Public Administration in Ancient India*, published in 1916, points out that the "ancient system of government may thus be called constitutional monarchy." It was "Sachivatantra".[1] He further says that not only in monarchies but also in republican states the popular assemblies were important in ancient times.[2] In the same year K.V. Rangaswami Aiyangar brought out *Some Aspects of Ancient Indian Polity*, which was based on his lectures delivered in 1914. In his work the author deprecates the tendency to look into the armoury of "our" ancient polity for weapons to be used in the arena of modern political controversies.[3] But at the same time he points out that the undermining of the "current" belief that ancient Indian institutions and political theory were unprogressive will long form a vital condition of a successful, historical study of ancient Indian polity.[4] In his book *Corporate Life in Ancient India* (1918) even a trained historian such as R.C. Majumdar admits that he was led to this line of inquiry through the importance of "the spirit of co-operation" in the present highly developed stage of civilization.[5] In his opening lines in the introduction he says that "India at present is very backward in this particular aspect of culture, but the following pages are intended to show that things were quite different in the past." It pains him to find that it required great effort to believe that political institutions "which we are accustomed to look upon as of western growth had also flourished in India long ago."[6] At the same time he assails the commonly held view that India was only absorbed in religion. His researches are intended to show that "religion did not engross the whole or even an undue proportion of the public attention." A similar view is expressed by Shamasastry in his book *Evolution of Indian Polity* (1920). He asserts that neither during the Vedic period nor in the times of Kauṭilya divine birth or right of kings seems to have been thought of.[7] Coming to the next publication,

1. Ibid., p. 51.
2. Ibid., p. 97.
3. K.V. Rangaswami Aiyangar, *Some Aspects of Ancient Indian Polity*, pp. 3-4. Although the 1935 edition of this book has been consulted, it does not mean any difference in matter except for footnotes and appendices.
4. K.V. Rangaswami Aiyangar, op.cit., p. 65.
5. Introduction, p. i.
6. *Corporate Life in Ancient India*, p. 122.
7. Ibid., p. 145.

Aspects of Ancient Indian Polity by N.N. Law (1921), Keith says in his foreword that the development of a keen interest in the history of Indian theories of polity is one of the gratifying consequences of the awakening of political aspirations in India.[1] The longest chapter (IX) in the book is "The Religious Aspects of Ancient Hindu Polity." While concluding it, Law states that "there were wide and various fields of political actions in which the Hindu showed considerable judgment and acumen undelegated by the force of beliefs."[2] By 1922 B.K. Sarkar was ready with his *Political Institutions and Theories of the Hindus.* In its preface he claims that on fundamental points the volume delivers "a frontal attack on the traditional Western prejudices regarding Asia, such as are concentrated in Hegel, Cousion, Max Müller, Maine, Janet, Smith, Willoughby and Hutington."[3] He deplores that the "servile and degenerate Asia of to-day" should be compared with Asia which was the leader of humanity's progress.[4] Repudiating the suggestion of the influence of religion on politics he says that "Hindu states were thoroughly secular."[5] In *Development of Hindu Polity and Political Theories* (1927) N.C. Bandyopadhay asserts that the ancient Indian king could neither claim divinity nor possessed any prerogatives.[6] In his opinion the views of thinkers who justify the expulsion or destruction of a tyrant disprove the theory of divinity.[7]

In 1923 there appeared *A History of Hindu Political Theories* by U.N. Ghoshal.[8] He ably refutes the view of Max Müller and Bloomfield that Hindus, because of certain inherent tendencies in their character, could not conceive of the idea of the state and that there is no provision for the interest of the state in their scheme. His main targets of attack are Western writers of history of political thought such as Janet, Dunning and Willoughby. He questions Janet's estimate that the sole

1. *Aspects of Ancient Indian Polity,* p. iv.
2. Ibid., p. 218.
3. P. viii.
4. P. 9.
5. P. 13.
6. P. 94.
7. P. 294.
8. This book has been more than doubled in size and has been re-issued in 1959 under the title *A History of Indian Political Ideas* which is a good reference book for details but does not add substantially to the original work.

city for the Indian sages is the city divine. This, says Ghoshal, when tested in the light of sober fact, will appear no more than a half truth.[1] Dunning states that the Āryans in India could never develop Political Science as an independent branch of knowledge and free it from its theological and metaphysical environment as the European Āryans did, while Willoughby thinks that because of their supreme faith in the divine creation they were never impelled to enquire into the *rationale* of their institutions.[2] Rejecting this view Ghoshal says that the chief characteristic of the Buddhist political thought is "bold and avowed appeal to human reason."[3] Moreover, he asserts that the Indian states, contrary to the usual view, were not modelled after a uniform pattern, that of despotic monarchy.[4]

In his lectures *Some Aspects of Ancient Hindu Polity* delivered in 1925, D.R. Bhandarkar again quotes the same views of Dunning, Max Müller and Bloomfield in order to refute them. In case of Dunning he makes allowance for the fact that he had no direct knowledge of orientalia. But he sees no justification for the statement of oriental scholars such as Max Müller and Bloomfield, who hold that the Indian never knew the feeling of nationality and that his heart never trembled in the expectation of national applause.[5] He points out that particularly after the discovery of the *Arthaśāstra* "it is no longer correct to assert that the Hindu mind did not conduce to the development of political theories, and that the Indians never set up politics as an independent branch of knowledge."[6] While discussing the rules of business in the republican assembly he is apprehensive lest his conclusions are regarded "as prompted by patriotic bias."[7]

The high watermark of the nationalist ideology finding reflection in research on polity can be traced in V.R.R. Dikshitar. His work *Hindu Administrative Institutions*, which he took up as his thesis in 1923 and completed in 1927, goes rather too far

1. *A History of Indian Political Ideas*, p. 5.
2. Ibid., p. 8.
3. Ibid., p. 9.
4. Introduction, p. 2.
5. P. 2.
6. P. 3.
7. P. 77.

in singing the glories of our past institutions. He regards Hindu polity as almost modern. Strongly rebutting the view that patriotism was not a phenomenon realised in ancient India, he argues that "the oneness of the country and the ideal of every monarch to make a *digvijaya* and achieve sole rule over the world extending from the Cape Comorin to the Himalayas indicate beyond doubt the existence of a strong nationalist feeling in the country." And then he quotes the famous verse *jananī janmabhūmiśca svargādapi garīyasī.*[1] His concluding lines carry exactly the same sense as those of Jayaswal. He says that, though every nation evolved its own polity, no polity had the inherent vitality that Hindu polity possessed. At the end of his work he repeats the robust optimism of Jayaswal that "the Golden Age of his (Hindu) Polity lies not in the past but in the future."[2]

Thus a review of general works on polity during 1916-25 reveals a marked tendency to place an ideological weapon in the hands of Indian nationalists. The same is the case with certain special works such as those on Local Self-Government and International Law in Ancient India. R.K. Mookerji's *Local Government in Ancient India* seeks to modify the opinion of such critics as declare that "In ancient India there was nothing of the nature of a political institution between the village and central government."[3] Like other scholars, Mookerji also feels that to see endless repetitions of autocratic and theocratic institutions in Indian history is a great source of of historical misinterpretation.[4] He claims that the study of ancient Indian local institutions will point the way to the lines of development on which reconstruction should proceed. On the other hand, "to the people it will bring a new inspiration, a fresh stimulus to national self-respect that will look back with pride on the record of institutions which gave them at once the blessings of self-rule and a means of self-preservation amidst adverse political conditions."[5]

Similar sentiments are expressed in P.N. Banerjea's work

1. P. 78.
2. P. 384, bracketted portion ours.
3. P. 316.
4. Introduction, p. xiii.
5. Pp. 21-22.

International Law and Custom in Ancient India (1920). Banerjea says that imbued with imperialistic ideas Hall considers International Law as a "favoured monopoly" of the European family of nations.[1] He complains that even a considerate publicist such as Lawrence regards the Indian troops as "semi-civilized or imperfectly civilized troops" and that he recommends their use against border tribes and in warfare with people of the same degree of education as themselves.[2] The object of Banerjea's thesis is "to establish the apparently incredible fact that *the ancient Indians had a definite knowledge of the rules of International Law according to which they regard their international conduct.*"[3] S.V. Viswanath's *International Law in Ancient India* institutes a comparison between the First World War, which was waged in contravention of the accepted laws of nations and in defiance of all notions of international morality laying its hand on combatants and non-combatants alike,[4] and the wars in ancient India, which were fought according to the rules of *Dharmayuddha* and in which wholesale destruction and devastation was forbidden.[5]

Between 1925 and 1930 the number of works on ancient polity was comparatively fewer than what it was between 1916 and 1925. In 1927 N.C. Bandyopadhay brought out two books *Development of Hindu Polity and Political Theories* and *Kauṭilya.* While in the former he tried to demolish the belief that India was the birthplace and the peculiar habitation of despotic power, in the latter he concluded that Kauṭilya "dreams the prospect of a truly 'national king' who was to merge even his identity with customs and language."[6] But Beni Prasad, who published his two books *State in Ancient India* and *Government in Ancient India* about the same time, sounded a word of warning against reading too much of modern ideas into ancient institutions. Nevertheless, to prove the superiority of early Indian institutions over the Greek and Roman systems he said that in ancient India there was no aristocracy in the Greek or Roman

1. *JDL*, i (1920), p. 202.
2. Ibid., p. 203.
3. Ibid.
4. Pp. 3-4.
5. P. 126.
6. P. 298.

sense. Caste forbade a combination of office, wealth and prestige of birth as in other countries.[1] In 1931 S.K. Aiyangar published his *Evolution of Hindu Administrative Institutions in South India* "for an understanding of the native Indian theory of government so that there may be a correct apprehension of the constitutional needs of the country."[2] He flatters himself with the idea that the ancient "administration seems to have made a clear, but close approach to these ideals which modern democracy is making an effort at realising."[3] An important work of specific nature published in 1929 was *Contributions to the History of the Hindu Revenue System* of U.N. Ghoshal. Therein he states that the principles of taxation formulated in early times "surpass the achievements of classical antiquity and tend to approach the ideas of European thinkers in the 18th and early 19th centuries."[4] In his opinion the view that taxes are the king's dues for the service of protection is identical with the similar doctrine of 17th and 18th century Europe.[5]

Thus a reviewer of Dikshitar's *Hindu Administrative Institutions* in 1929 rightly pointed out that "the general trend of the works during the last fifteen years has been to show that the government of the country in ancient days was not irresponsible, that there was public opinion with recognised channels for the expression thereof, that public opinion was respected in almost all cases by the powers, that it could grow at times so powerful as to lead to the abdication or dethronement of the ruler, and so on."[6] There is no doubt that this whole series of research works on the history of political theories and institutions was written with a purpose. It was meant to bring grist to the nationalist mill and to sustain the nationalist movement. After 1930 there set in a stagnation in research, and few works on polity were produced in the following twenty years or so. The books that appeared during this period mostly covered the old ground.

Here let us pause and consider the merits and limitations of

1. *The State in Ancient India*, pp. 7-8.
2. Ibid., p. v.
3. P. 379.
4. P. 14.
5. P. 17.
6. *JIH*, viii (1929), p. 405.

the nationalist and revivalist line of approach to the study of India's past polity. Its one great result was that by presenting an encouraging picture of the past it filled the people with great self-confidence. As a scholar of Hindu polity says in 1922, "the nationalist movement of Young India which has won recognition as a world force in international politics since August 7, 1905, is receiving a conscious guidance and direction from the solid results of unquestionable antiquarian investigation."[1] This knowledge of ancient polity gave tongue to those who advocated self-government and independence of India. If they had self-government in the past, there was no reason why they should not have it in the present. Secondly, this ideology produced splendid research works, and certain inferences regarding the prevalence of limited monarchy, republics, local self-government and international law in ancient India came to be accepted by nearly all scholars, in spite of the dissenting note of V. Smith that it was not safe to rely on the admonitions of the early sages about the ideal king.

But this nationalist ideology had also its limitations. First, while it did serve to rouse the educated middle class against alien rule, it hardly appealed to conscious intellectuals interested in the masses of peasants and workers who were being drawn into the national struggle from 1920 onward. By a fulsome adoration of ancient Hindu institutions it tended to antagonise the Muslims, though this was not done deliberately. Secondly, it gave us a false sense of past values. It glossed over the fact that, whether it was monarchy or republic, the two upper varṇas dominated the two lower varṇas, who were generally excluded from all political offices. It also ignored the fact that one fundamental feature of our legislation was that it worked in the interests of the upper varṇas. It did not pay attention to the fact that the ruling class consciously exploited religion for the promotion of their political interests. It never took into consideration the fact that wealth and political offices went hand in hand.

Thirdly, many Indian scholars fought shy of the religious aspects of ancient Indian polity and, as if to cover a sense of guilt, took too much pains to prove the secular character of the

1. B.K. Sarkar, *The Political Institutions and Theories of the Hindus*, p. 4.

ancient Indian state, little realising that even in the Western world the first completely secular state did not come into existence until 1783 and that India was not the only country where religion influenced political ideas and actions.[1]

Fourthly, in its craze for proving the superiority of our ancient institutions over those of the ancient West it hardly tried to examine them in the light of the evolution of primitive tribes as known from anthropology or in the light of the early institutions of other Indo-European peoples. Because of these limitations it appears that the possibilities of research in ancient Indian polity on purely nationalistic lines have been almost exhausted. We are in need of an objective approach free from cheap generalisations.

1. The religious aspect has been emphasised recently in several publications, as has been shown by us in our Introduction.

CHAPTER II

SOURCES AND METHOD

Until we come to the first law-books known as Dharmasūtras the main source for the study of ancient Indian political ideas and institutions is provided by the Vedic literature. The earliest Vedic manuscripts are not older than the 10th century A.D., and inscriptional evidence for writing in India between the 17th and 3rd century B.C. is wanting. But some Ṛg Vedic gods are mentioned in the Mitannian inscription of the 14th century B.C., and the great reverential attitude to the *Ṛg Veda* leading to its correct recitation and consequent oral preservation suggests that it was compiled, at least orally, around 1200 B.C. or so. However, even the fidelity towards its recitation did not prevent its inflation at the beginning and end, which is a common feature of many other ancient Indian texts. Therefore in using the *Ṛg Veda* for the study of tribal assemblies such as *sabhā*, *samiti*, *vidatha*, *gaṇa*, etc., or social categories such as brāhmaṇa, kṣatriya, etc., or of references to *rājan* and its synonyms one has to be wary about their occurrences in BKS I & X, which were added to the main body later. Perhaps it would be better to use BK X for the post-Ṛg Vedic period. The area covered by the Ṛg Vedic references is generally taken to be Afghanistan and the Punjab or the land of five rivers, but some tribal institutional practices may have their counterparts in other ancient Indo-European texts which were composed in Greece or Iran. A study of such parallels prevalent in different countries might help to trace the elements of common heritage in the Vedic public life.

The later Vedic texts were compiled in western U.P., in the land of Kuru and Pañcāla. To the *Ṛg Veda*, a book of prayers, these add rituals which have to be rationalised for reconstructing the polity of the period *c*. B.C. 1000-500. The various collections (*saṃhitās*) of the *Yajus*, Black and White, are a storehouse of rituals, public and private. In using them however one has to take account of the various strata of the same text such as the *Taittirīya Saṃhitā*, whose sections from 19 to 40 were composed much later.

In the Brāhmaṇas rituals are supplemented by a few explanations and speculations regarding the origin of kingship. The two texts that are useful for our purpose are the *Aitareya Brāhmaṇa* and the *Śatapatha Brāhmaṇa*, but their date cannot be pushed much beyond 700 B.C. or so. The geographical area of the later text also includes eastern U.P. and north Bihar, west of the Gandak. The form of political organisation deducible from the rituals in the Saṃhitās and Brāhmaṇas would be generally true of U.P., although the area down to the Narmada river in the south seems to have come within the pale of āryanisation, and forms of government mentioned in the *Aitareya Brāhmaṇa* may apply to this area.

Upaniṣads are regarded as philosophical works, but the origin of kingship and similar themes do not interest them. Incidental references to *samiti* and tribal identities throw some light on later Vedic polity, although the texts in which they occur cannot be taken much beyond 500 B.C.

Because of the publication of the comprehensive word-index to the Vedic literature by the Vishweswarananda Institute, Hoshiarpur, it is not difficult to look up terms of institutional import. But caution has to be exercised in consulting those Brāhmaṇas, Upaniṣads, and Śrautasūtras which are compiled after 500 B.C. and even in the early centuries of the Christian era.

Vedic literature being mainly religious in nature, it becomes a little difficult to isolate facts of polity from it. The Dharmasūtras, or the earliest law-books written in prose during the period *c.* 500-200 B.C. do not present this difficulty. Of the four law-books those of Āpastamba and Baudhāyana seem to have been the oldest, and not of Gautama as is generally supposed; the law-book of Vasiṣṭha is also a later work.

The Dharmasūtras are the earliest texts dealing with the duties of the king and the four varṇas or social orders and provide laws regarding taxation and the protection of property, family and person. They offer the first systematic exposition of the brāhmaṇical view of the social and political order. It is an idealised picture, which can be partly corrected with reference to the Greek accounts and early Pāli texts.

The Dharmasūtras—also known as Dharmaśāstras which cover all kinds of legal texts including commentaries—developed into the Smṛtis, written in verse. The oldest and most well-known of the Smṛtis is that of Manu, also called *Manu-Saṃhitā* or *Mānava-Dharmaśāstra*. About a century ago Bühler assigned it to 200 B.C.—A.D. 200, and later Jayaswal thought it to be a product of the Śuṅga period on the ground that it exalts the position of the brāhmaṇas and accords divine sanction to kingship. But its style and contents suggest its final compilation in the second century A.D. or later. For our purpose the subject of *rājadharma* treated in Chapter VII of this text is most valuable. It not only deals with the duties of the king but also lays down the principles of taxation and points out the importance of the coercive authority symbolised by the term *daṇḍa*. The *Viṣṇu Smṛti*, seems to have been composed in the same period, and shows a developed legal structure in its treatment of the problem of inheritance.

The *Yājñavalkya Smṛti*, assignable to the period *c.* A.D. 200-400, arranges the material of Manu in a more concise and systematic manner. It has many provisions in common with the *Arthaśāstra* of Kauṭilya from which it evidently borrowed. With its commentary *Mitākṣarā* written by Vijñāneśvara in the 11th century it came to form the basis of the Hindu civil law.

But the three completely legal texts are the Smṛtis of Nārada, Bṛhaspati and Kātyāyana. The first two belong to the 5th century A.D. and the last probably to the sixth century A.D. Nārada uses the term *dīnāra*, which appears in inscriptions from the second century A.D. on and helps to fix his date. Bṛhaspati may be a little later. His book forms a landmark in legal history, for he treats the law under 18 titles, of which 14 may be placed under civil and 4 under criminal law. Only the *vyavahāra khaṇḍa* of Kātyāyana has been recovered, which shows that it is exclusively a work on civil law; it also lays down detailed judicial procedure.

The study of the Smṛtis is beset with two difficulties. In the first place they repeat the same idea and statement *ad nauseam*. This is because most later Smṛtis such as Yājñavalkya, Nārada and Bṛhaspati are based on Manu, and explain and amplify his provisions on different topics. This creates an impression of very little development in ancient Indian polity in the first six centuries of the Christian era. But a careful study of the variations on different subjects will surely help dispel this notion. Secondly, the ideas of commentators who continued their work till the 18th century or even later are fathered on the original law-givers. There are as many as seven commentators on Manu ranging from the 9th to the 16th century, and they naturally interpret the original in the light of conditions in their times and areas. This creates a false image of Manu's times, and will have to be borne in mind in relation to all the other Smṛtis.

If we can steer clear of these two difficulties the Smṛtis give us a good idea of the royal functions, position of ministers or advisers known variously as *mantrin*, *saciva*, *amātya*, *pārṣada* and *sabhya*, and also of interstate relations. Above all they enlighten us about the judicial machinery and the type of law that was administered by it. Manu and Yājñavalkya contain sections on expiations and ethical code which will not be regarded as law from the modern point of view, but Nārada, Bṛhaspati and Kātyāyana are almost exclusively legal texts.

The Smṛti portions are also found in the epics and Purāṇas. The idea that there was an epic period will have to be discarded in the study of political ideas and organisation. It is difficult to use the material drawn from the *Mahābhārata* for one particular period, for its narrative portion looks back to as early as the 10th century B.C. and didactic and descriptive portions belong to as late as the 4th century A.D. Originally this epic consisted of 8,800 ślokas, then had 24,000 ślokas, and was finally inflated to 1,00,000 ślokas, which number is mentioned in a Gupta inscription, though the Critical Edition now consists of nearly 78,000 ślokas. Three *parvas*, the *Sabhā*, the *Śānti* and the *Anuśāsana*, are useful for the history of political ideas and practice. The date of the compilation of the first cannot be pushed beyond the first century B.C. The *Anuśāsana* was probably compiled at about the same time as the *Śānti*. Undoubtedly the *rājadharma* section of the *Śānti Parva* is the most important for our purpose, and it has many verses in common with the law-book of Manu, particularly in regard to the divinity of the king, pretensions of the brāhmaṇas and the importance of *daṇḍa*. The *rājadharma* section is mainly didactic and seems to have been inserted in the Book of Peace some time in the first four centuries of the Christian era. It mentions the Greeks, Śakas, and especially the Pahlavas or the Parthians who ruled in north-western India in the first century A.D., and therefore it cannot be earlier than that date. Hence it would be wrong to use its material, as has been usually done so far, for the study of the political institutions of the later Vedic or the post-Vedic period. Even its treatment of the constitution and working of the *gaṇa* may not apply to post-Vedic times except in very general terms. As regards the *saptāṅga* theory, the royal functions, the composition of the council of ministers, the rules of war, the sources and principles of taxation, all these reflect the state of affairs in the early centuries of the Christian era. Speculations on the origin of kingship constitute the most fertile and original portion in the *rājadharma* section of the *Śānti Parva*. These provide the first reasoned brāhmaṇical justification for the royal office which symbolised state power.

The younger epic *Rāmāyaṇa*, which has also been critically edited, though not as well as the *Mahābhārata*, is neither so bulky nor so useful for our study. An earlier version mentioned in some Jain and Buddhist texts of the early Christian era consisted of 12,000 verses, and the earliest contained 6,000 verses; now it consists of 24,000 verses. Though the major part of the text was compiled by Gupta times, additions were made to it even around the twelfth century. What forcibly strikes about its contents is its description of a kingless (*arājaka*) state. It also tells us about the duties of the king, his officials, and other political institutions. But they appear to have been an idealised and simplified version of the Gupta political institutions.

The Purāṇas belong to the same category as the epics, and contain considerable didactic sections dwelling upon royal functions and other allied subjects. Several Purāṇas, such as the *Vāyu* and *Matsya* (also mentioned in the *Mahābhārata*), were completed by Gupta times, and furnish theoretical background to the political institutions of the period.

In recent times several theses have been written on political ideas in the *Mahābhārata*, and some of them have been published. But since they follow the pattern set by Hopkins in the 1880's in his article on the position of the ruling caste they add a few more details but do not advance our knowledge. Similarly the attempt to attribute the institutions known from the *Rāmāyaṇa* to the early history of Kosala or to reconstruct Rāmāyaṇic polity in a historical vacuum is misplaced. Political thought in the Purāṇas has received some attention, but the only worthwhile exercise has been a work on the *Agni Purāṇa*,[1] which does not fall within the period of our study.

The Dharmasūtras, Smṛtis, epics and Purāṇas represent a tradition which is religious and out and out brāhmaṇical. A somewhat different tradition is embodied in the *Arthaśāstra* of Kauṭilya, which is more practical and less influenced by religious considerations. Because of its being the earliest and basic specimen of its type this text has given rise to an enormous corpus of literature. Perhaps no question in ancient India has been so hotly debated as the date and authenticity of this work. Indian scholars generally place it in the Maurya period, and European scholars four or five centuries later. But in any case there is no basis for using the *Arthaśastra* material for the pre-Maurya period.[2] The text as we have it does not seem to have been a homogeneous work written at one time and place. Although most of the book is written in prose following the *sūtra* style prevalent till the first century B.C. or so, its portions in verse were inserted later. The discussion of its style is better left to language specialists, but it would be fruitful to disentangle the various strata of the text from one another on the basis of style. As regards language the contrast between the Aśokan Prākrit and the Kauṭilyan Sanskrit is obvious. The political organisation outlined by Kauṭilya is different from the system indicated by Aśoka's inscriptions. While Kauṭilya emphasises centralisation Aśoka tends towards decentralisation. The typical Aśokan officials such as *dharmamahāmātra*, *rājuka*, *prādeśika*, *prativedaka*, etc., are not mentioned in the *Arthaśāstra*. *Mahāmātras* appear as the most important functionaries in Aśokan inscriptions, but only their office *mahāmātrīyam* occurs once in the *Arthaśāstra* which nowhere indicates their functions. Of course a minor Aśokan official called *yukta* is known to Kauṭilya but that does not prove much. The same holds good of the Aśokan administrative unit called *āhāra*. On the other hand, many terms of fiscal and administrative import mentioned in the *Arthaśāstra* appear in inscriptions, particularly in grants of the second and later centuries A.D. *Bhoga*, *praṇaya*, *viṣṭi* and *parihāra* (and

1. B. B. Mishra, *Polity in the Agni Purāṇa*, Calcutta, 1965.
2. This has been done in U. N. Ghoshal, *A History of Indian Public Life*, II, Bombay, 1966.

taradeya?) occurring in inscriptions of the Deccan and western India find place in the *Arthaśāstra*; of these *parihāra*, which means exemptions from taxes on the land granted to beneficiaries, is a significant term found frequently in Sātavāhana inscriptions. Similarly the *amātya*, who emerges as the most important functionary in Śaka and Sātavāhana epigraphs, occupies the same place in the *Arthaśāstra* of Kauṭilya. The epigraphic evidence would, therefore, suggest that Kauṭilya's *Arthaśāstra* was elaborated in the first century A.D. Several revenue terms and names of officers mentioned in the *Arthaśāstra* first appear in the inscriptions of the sixth and seventh centuries and even of the eleventh-twelfth centuries.[1]

But some similarity of the royal control of economic activities noted by Megasthenes to that recommended by Kauṭilya suggests that BK II, which deals with the duties of superintendents, has some genuine Maurya touch about it; this may be also true of BKS III and IV, which deal with civil and criminal law. However, the sections which treat interstate relations and war seem to be fairly well developed, and we do not know where to place them. Of course the term *skandhāvāra*, military camp, occupies the same prominent place in BK I of the *Arthaśāstra* as it does in Sātavāhana and later inscriptions.

Since all the contents of the *Arthaśāstra* do not seem to belong to the same period their summary is not of much use to the historian. Divided into 15 *adhikaraṇas* and 180 *prakaraṇas* the text embraces economics, sociology, politics, etc. However, the major portion is devoted to the problems of administration. It deals with the seven elements of the kingdom; training, duties and vices of the king; recruitment and duties of the *amātyas* and *mantrins*; civil and criminal administration; and guilds and corporations. Republics form the theme of one whole chapter. Further, the text enunciates the principles of interstate relations and describes the military organisation. It suggests methods to win wars and acquire popularity in the conquered territories. A distinguishing feature of its contents is the exaltation of the central authority and the assignment of many social and economic functions to the king.

On the basis of its contents the *Arthaśāstra* of Kauṭilya cannot

1. S. C. Mishra, *An Inscriptional Approach to the Study of the Arthaśāstra of Kauṭilya*, Delhi University Ph.D. Thesis, 1986.

be regarded as a textbook of political science in the modern sense of the term. It is not exactly of the same type as the *Republic* of Plato or the *Politics* of Aristotle. Its practical character shows that it is closer to the latter. The two Greek classics are not exclusive works on political science; so also is the case with the *Arthaśāstra* of Kauṭilya. But undoubtedly a good part of the work is concerned with politics. And what is further important is that Kauṭilya makes a deliberate and conscious attempt to free politics from the influence of religion and morality. Indeed he goes against their principles to achieve political objectives.

Thus the *Arthaśāstra* is not only a treatise on the science of wealth as its name indicates but also a treatise on political science called *daṇḍanīti*. Kauṭilya quotes from five schools and thirteen individual writers, which shows that this branch was quite well established in his time. Some of these authors are also mentioned in the *Śānti Parva*. It is a pity that the works of the predecessors of Kauṭilya have not been discovered so far, and the few fragments attributed to them by Kauṭilya are too inadequate to form a clear picture of political beliefs in pre-Kauṭilyan times.[1]

Kauṭilya's immediate successors are unknown, but he had quite a few in early mediaeval times which does not fall within the scope of the present study. We might however mention the *Kāmandaka Nītisāra* compiled around A.D. 800. Kāmandaka clearly acknowledges his debt to Kauṭilya, whose material he digests in a systematic manner so that this borrowing appears better organised than its source. Repetitions of Kauṭilya's views merely suggest that his school continued to enjoy authority and influence in later times, but for new developments in the period of Kāmandaka we will have to take note of the variants occurring in his text. Some of these relate to the army and interstate relations.

The second *Nītisāra*, that of Śukra, has been heavily drawn upon by modern writers[2] with consequent increase in the size of their textbooks on early Indian polity. But in view of convincing arguments supporting the early 19th century compilation of this text[3] this temptation will have to be resisted.

1. This has been attempted in U.N. Ghoshal, *A History of Indian Political Ideas*, Ch. V.
2. An important example is A. S. Altekar, *State and Government in Ancient India*.
3. Lallanji Gopal, *BSOAS*, xxx.

For whom was the literature on polity meant? Surely not for the common people, and not even for members of the priestly class who might have produced it. The prevalent form of government being monarchy, texts on polity were written for the instruction and training of the princes in the art of government. Kauṭilya has a whole section on the education of the prince, similar to the scheme of Plato's education in the *Republic* which is meant for members of the guardian class. Kāmandaka states that his book is addressed to the king (*bhumīśvaraṃ prati*).

Since the Dharmaśāstra literature was produced to cover *dharma*, and the Arthaśāstra to cover *artha* it is natural to look for differences between the two schools. The Dharmaśāstra generally tends to exalt the authority of the brāhmaṇas and lays stress on the rules which govern the social and political order. On the other hand, the Arthaśāstra seems to exalt the authority of the king and emphasises the rules which govern the political and economic structure. The first type of literature sounds theoretical; the second appears to be practical. But beyond this it is not possible to exaggerate the divergence between the two, for both share a common outlook and ideology regarding the varṇa-divided society and represent the king as its upholder.

As regards the nature of contents on polity and political ideas the early Pāli canonical texts present a somewhat different picture. Although they took final shape in Sri Lanka in the first century B.C. and their references to monarchies and republics probably look back upon affairs in Magadha and Kosala in the age of the Buddha. This is perhaps true of the situation of the various states and their mutual relations. But allusions to their internal constitutions will have to be taken with a grain of salt. The *Mahāvagga* and *Cullavagga* portions of the *Vinaya Piṭaka*, or Book of Discipline, provide rich data on the organisation of the Buddhist church. It is argued that the rules and regulations which governed the conduct of the monks collectively were adopted from the republican states of the time of the Buddha. Reasonable as this hypothesis may appear, we have to find out how far the original rules were modified and adjusted to the needs of a religious organisation.

Unless we take recourse to Greek accounts and Pāṇini we do

not have any firmly dated contemporary sources for the study of republican institutions in pre-Maurya times. The Jātakas, Buddhist birth stories, on the basis of which the Licchavi constitution is constructed, in their present form are not older than the second century B.C. Primarily folktales, they speak of the duties of the king, administration of justice, varṇas and *jātis* and economic activities. There could be some justification for using their narrative portion for an earlier period, but certainly not for reconstructing the Śākya constitution on the basis of the commentaries compiled in Sri Lanka in the 5th century A.D. As in the case of the Dharmaśāstra literature a line will have to be drawn between the structure found in the early texts and the superstructure raised by the later commentators.

The *Dīgha Nikāya*, containing the teachings of the Buddha, gives the earliest systematic speculations regarding the origin of the kingship or the state and of the social orders. This appears as a part of the story of the creation in the *Ambaṭṭhasutta*. The entire text may be placed in the third century B.C. It shows that systematic theories of the origin of the state were propounded only when the state had become a well-established institution. Later Buddhist texts such as the *Mahāvastu*, ascribable to the first century B.C. and written in hybrid-Sanskrit, embellish, and add to, the original story of the origin of kingship, but the nucleus remains unaltered.

The Jain Prakrit texts, finally compiled in Valabhī in the sixth century A.D., embody some useful material, but its chronological order is far from settled. Some of the earliest doctrinal texts, such as the *Uttarādhyayanasūtra*, contain the oldest part of the Jain canon from the linguistic and literary points of view. Their poems containing parables, similes and dialogues have their parallels in the Jātakas and the *Śānti Parva*. In this type of literature we may pick up incidental references to the system of administration. The Jain Purāṇas compiled in the 8th and 9th centuries A.D. narrate the story of creation, which conjectures about the origin of the state and the castes; especially the picture of pre-state society is fairly detailed in these works. However, the material supplied by the Jain Prakrit works has not found any place in modern textbooks on early Indian polity. The only Jain text which has been used so far for this purpose is the

Nītivākyāmṛta by a Jain author Somadeva Sūri, who wrote it in Sanskrit in the 10th century A.D. But it is heavily indebted to earlier brāhmaṇical texts from which it quotes generously. Nevertheless, it belongs to the series on *Nītisāra* and as a text on polity can be profitably used for the early mediaeval period.

A survey of indigenous literary sources might include Pāṇini's grammar of about the 5th century B.C. and Patañjali's commentary of about the second century B.C. The first is valuable for grammatical illustrations referring to contemporary republics, and the second for sidelights on the mode of administration in post-Maurya times. A similar use can also be made of the *Bṛhatsaṃhitā* of Varāhamihira for the late Gupta period. But references from books on grammar and astronomy or astrology cannot form the basis of the study of the polity of any period; they can only supplement our knowledge.

The native literary source material presents several difficulties. First, many of these, especially the Jain texts, are not critically edited; so the danger of being misled by interpolations is always there. Secondly, they are mostly didactic which makes it difficult to find out the real position about the system of administration although they reflect political ideas and theories. Thirdly, even in the case of texts such as the *Arthaśāstra* of Kauṭilya we do not feel sure of the time and place to which they belong. Nonetheless, by and large, ancient native literary sources provide the theoretical aspect of ancient political institutions.

The practical aspect can be derived from the study of archaeology, coins and inscriptions, which are comparatively free from the disadvantages enumerated above. Apparently the archaeology of a region and period can be only remotely linked up with its political structure. But the discovery of settled rural communities or of the urban complex can certainly do something to check the inferences drawn from literary sources. Thus large and effective imperial organisation presupposes substantial material remains. Further, evidence of the existence of towns on a large scale in a period would point to the need for urban administration.

The earliest Indian coins, called the punch-marked and ascribed to the fifth-second centuries B.C., suggest that in post-Vedic and Maurya times taxes could be collected in cash and disbursed as salaries. Punch-marked coins with certain common symbols are found in a large area. They are considered 'imperial' coins and attributed to the Mauryas, whose central authority may have been helped by monetisation. From the post-Maurya period onwards coins become more useful for the study of polity. The titles of kings mentioned on the Kuṣāṇa coins disclose the connection between religion and politics. Coins show that some of the states were dedicated to gods, as for instance the state of the Kuṇīndas. Some contemporary coins do not mention the names of the kings but of the tribes or the peoples such as the Mālavas and Yaudheyas, which suggests that these were republican states. The Gupta coins also give some information; some titles and legends occurring on them enable us to determine the nature of kingship and administration. Evidently on account of lack of space much material cannot be put on the coins, but whatever little occurs there is important for administrative history.

What is provided by the coins on a very small scale is done by inscriptions on a large scale. The first Indian inscriptions to be deciphered are those of Aśoka. Engraved on rocks and pillars generally in Prakrit language and Brāhmī character[1] throughout the length and breadth of his empire, these are royal commands or proclamations for regulating social, religious and administrative behaviour. Many of these edicts are called *dharma* inscriptions, but they do not deal with what is regarded as purely religious matters in modern times. They are mainly concerned with such questions as the relation between the king and the *parisā* (*pariṣad*), judicial administration, the functions of high royal officers such as the *rājukas* and *mahāmātras*, and the paternal ideal of kingship. Although most Aśokan officials are not mentioned in the *Arthaśāstra* of Kauṭilya, the broad fact about the wide state control suggested by Megasthenes and Kauṭilya can be inferred from records issued by Aśoka in the early part of his reign. The fact that Aśokan inscriptions appear on important highways suggests improved communications facilitating imperial control.

The post-Maurya and Gupta inscriptions fall into two wide categories—private and official. Private inscriptions are mainly donation records which, though short, generally describe the official position of the donors. Written in both Brāhmī and

1. Some inscriptions were also written in Kharoṣṭhī, Aramaic and Greek characters.

Kharoṣṭhī these records give incidental information about the administrative machinery of the period.

Official inscriptions include a few eulogistic records called *praśastis*, but generally comprise land charters which are donation records. The former celebrate the all-round achievements of the princes, their victories, their endowments, etc. To this category belong the Hathigumpha Inscription of Khāravela and the Allahabad Inscription of Samudra Gupta. The first recounts the events of Khāravela's reign year by year and speaks of his education, coronation, and favours showered upon the urban and rural population (*paura-jānapada*). The second enlightens us about the relation between Samudra Gupta and the various categories of the conquered princes and peoples who were treated as vassals and tributaries.

By far the most important class of the official inscriptions are the land charters which began with the Sātavāhanas during the second century A.D. The process continued on a large scale down to the 13th-14th centuries, when it began to be undermined by the Turkish Muslim conquest and later by the introduction of paper. Although mostly religious, the contents of these grants vary from period to period and region to region. These grants often mention the fiscal and administrative units, enumerate the sources of revenue, and also the officers who were informed of the land donations. The royal proclamations of Aśoka are addressed only to two or three functionaries consisting of the provincial governor called *kumāra* or the *āryaputra* and of the high officials called *mahāmātras*. The Sātavāhana royal charters are invariably addressed to the *amātyas*. But from the Gupta period onwards the number of officers mentioned in the land charters goes on steadily multiplying till it counts nearly three dozen in the Pāla land charters of early mediaeval times. Of course the fiscal and administrative terms used in inscriptions baffle attempts at easy interpretations, but from the second century A.D. onwards they are our only sure guide to the system of taxation and administration. If Gupta inscriptions are read along with the Smṛtis of the period, they give us a fairly good picture of the Gupta polity.

Even when not dated, inscriptions can be placed within narrow chronological brackets on palaeographic grounds, and hence their value for the study of the ancient polity is far greater than that of the law-books. The technical epigraphic terms of fiscal and administrative import can very well help determine the dates of the various strata of the *Arthaśāstra* of Kauṭilya, of the Dharmaśāstra and allied literature. Some of these terms such as *praṇaya, viṣṭi, hiraṇya, parihāra, dīnāra, sāndhivigrahika, karaṇika,* etc., may be treated as date indicators and the literary texts in which they figure may be regarded as closer to the period of the corresponding inscriptions. Although the *Indian Epigraphical Glossary* by D. C. Sircar does not always indicate the first occurrence and the precise location of such terms, it is a handy and useful compendium for tracing them. If the *History of Dharmaśāstra* by P. V. Kane and the *Dharmakośa* by L. S. Joshi are consulted together with the *Glossary*, we may obtain dependable data.

The present survey will not be complete without some reference to Greek and Chinese accounts, which embody valuable data on the system of administration. Historians of Alexander the Great, who was not considered important enough to be mentioned in any contemporary or even later ancient Indian source, have left detailed accounts of his Indian campaigns (326-325 B.C.), some describing the internal constitutions of the states which faced him in the Punjab and Sind. Although Greek writers show a tendency to read city-state constitution in some of these states, without doubt several republics flourished in north-western India in the 4th century B.C. But for the study of the Maurya system of administration the account of Megasthenes, who lived as an ambassador in the court of Candragupta Maurya at Pāṭaliputra, is invaluable. Although his *Indika* has not been recovered so far and the fragments quoted by later authors are not always considered reliable by classical writers such as Arrian, his is the only account that can be firmly dated. Since the dating of the *Arthaśāstra* of Kauṭilya is not free from doubt the citations from Megasthenes form our only datable and direct source for the administration of the founder of the Maurya empire. They describe the daily routine of the king, the main functions of councillors, and also of magistrates controlling irrigation and other activities. They also outline the municipal administration of Pāṭaliputra and the military organisation of the empire. Influenced by Greek conditions they report the fall of monarchies and the rise of democratic states. The Greek and

Latin accounts of the post-Maurya period are mainly useful for economic history.

The Chinese accounts are helpful for the Gupta and post-Gupta periods. Although both Fa-hsien and Hsüan Tsang were primarily interested in the fortunes of Buddhism in India they notice a few facts about administration. Fa-hsien, who visited India in A.D. 399-414 in the reign of Candra Gupta II, speaks of the system of government in Madhyadeśa or U. P. and western Bihar. He also mentions the mode of payment to the attendants and bodyguards of the king. But this Chinese traveller does not in any way refer directly to the Gupta king or his empire, as Hsüan Tsang does in the case of Harṣavardhana. The account of Hsüan Tsang, who visited India in A.D. 629-41, is more detailed and specific. He speaks in glowing terms of the system of government set up by his patron and gives exaggerated figures about his military strength. All the same Hsüan Tsang is the only important source from which we get an idea of the fiscal and military systems of Harṣa.

Indian scholars, most of whom do not know Greek or Chinese, have to depend on English translations which are now a century old and hence badly in need of revision. The crucial passages in Greek accounts relating to the ownership of land or royal share of produce have been variously rendered. Similarly Fa-hsien's passage on the mode of payment to officials has been translated in three different ways. So in all such cases the exact translation will have to be settled. We have also to consider the intellectual horizon of the Greek and Chinese writers who tended to project the administrative practices of their respective countries on to the Indian system and also of the 19th century translators and introduction writers who did not have the advantage of the Indological knowledge that has accumulated since then.

Governmental practices in native Hindu states recorded by census superintendents, anthropologists, missionaries and others in the 19th or even in the early 20th century may be of some use in interpreting the measures recommended by the Dharmaśāstra. Since India has been a country of long survivals some ancient customs have been made to continue till recent times. A typical example is the practice of settling caste promotions and demotions by the Hindu kings in Nepal and Orissa, which reminds us of the Dharmaśāstra rule that the king is the upholder of the varṇa system, and, according to the *Arthaśāstra* of Kauṭilya, even its promulgator. Some of the old administrative titles and terms such as amātya, nāyaka, sāmanta, chaudhuri (from *caurodharaṇika*), mahāpātra, daṇḍausī (from *daṇḍapāśika*), koṭhārī (from *koṣṭhāgārika*), veṭh (from *viṣṭi*), etc., still current particularly in the outlying provinces where the Indo-Persian system of administration did not make any serious impact, are as old as Gupta times if not earlier. Some knowledge of the family traditions of the holders of these titles might give hints of the original functions assigned to them.

Our survey will show that students of ancient Indian political ideas and institutions have not to bother so much about the dearth of material as about its indifferent and unreliable nature. Unfortunately much of the original stuff is taken for granted although in many cases its time, place and authenticity are riddled with uncertainties. This is true of literary texts, and it substantially alters the picture if the Brāhmaṇas are placed before 1000 B.C., the whole of the *Mahābhārata* is used for pre-Maurya times and the *Śukranītisāra* for the period A.D. 600-1200.[1] We cannot get a clear idea of development in political thought and administration unless we attempt a periodwise co-ordination between the literary and the epigraphic sources. But before this is done the typical portion of a text or an inscription will have to be determined. It is easy to locate the typical part of an inscription by weeding out the preamble and the conventional, but it is difficult to find out what is typical of a Smṛti, Purāṇa or a Nītiśāstra, for most of these are compendia quoting profusely and indiscriminately from earlier texts. Unless the typical in such texts is isolated—as has been done in the case of the *Agni Purāṇa*—students of polity would not be able to put them to any critical use. Finally, we want to stress the obvious that Indian literary texts can be mainly used for the history of political theories. But the history of administration and state formation can be reconstructed in the first place from coins and inscriptions, secondly from foreign accounts; thirdly from comparisons with the ancient institutions of Asia and Europe, fourthly from a study of the primitive tribes,[2] and finally from survivals in modern times.

1. This has been generally done in Altekar, *State and Government in Ancient India.*
2. Pre-industrial India is considered similar to pre-industrial Europe and not to the pre-colonial Africa in respect of the family and systems of marriage in Jack Goody, *The Oriental, the Ancient and the Primitive*, Cambridge University, Press, 1990.

CHAPTER III

THE SAPTĀṄGA THEORY OF THE STATE

Despite considerable theorising in regard to rituals in later Vedic collections and the Brāhmaṇas, we neither find any definition of the state either in this literature nor in the early law-books, the Dharmasūtras. This was due to the fact that this institution was not established on a firm footing so far. It is only after the rise of the well-organised states of Kosala and Magadha in the age of the Buddha that the state is defined for the first time in the *Arthaśāstra* of Kauṭilya as consisting of seven elements, a definition which becomes an axiom in the later sources. The *Sarasvatīvilāsa*, a text of the 16th century A.D.[1], ascribes the seven-element definition to Gautama from whom it quotes[2], but this cannot be traced in his law-book. Besides, as has been shown by the present writer elsewhere, this work seems to have been much tampered with and, therefore, compiled at a later date.[3] Although some elements such as *rājā*, *amātya*, *viṣaya*, etc., are mentioned in some early Dharmasūtras, it is for the first time in Kauṭilya that we get the complete definition of the state.

The seven elements enumerated by Kauṭilya are *svāmī*, *amātya*, *janapada*, *durga*, *kośa*, *daṇḍa* and *mitra*.[4] These seven elements are mentioned in most texts dealing with polity[5], although in some cases the synonyms of some elements differ. The *Viṣṇu-dharmottara Purāṇa*, a work of about the fifth century A.D.[6], however, mentions two new elements *sāma* (pacification) and *dāna* (charity) respectively in place of *svāmī* and *amātya*.[7] Perhaps we can explain this variation in the context of interstate relations

1. Kane, *Hist. Dhs.*, i, 413.
2. Ibid., iii, 17 fn. 20.
3. *Śūdras*, pp. 83-84.
4. *AŚ*, VI.1.
5. *Manu*, IX.294; *ŚP*, 69.62-3, the term used in the constituted text is *saptātmakaṃ rājyam*; *Viṣṇu*, III.33; *Yāj.*, I.353; *ŚNS*, i, 61; *Agni Purāṇa* quoted in Jagdish Lal Shastri, *Political Thought in the Purāṇas*, p. 48, *Mārk. P.* quoted op. cit., p. 23; *Kālikā P.* quoted op. cit., p. 115.
6. R. C. Hazra, *Studies in the Upapurāṇas*, i. 212. The text may belong to the 8th century.
7. Extract quoted in Shastri, op. cit., p. 163.

in which this statement is made. Apparently the two elements fit ill with the other, and there is no doubt that the seven element definition of the state as given by Kauṭilya was almost universally accepted as the standard connotation of the state. Even the *Viṣṇudharmottara Purāṇa* reproduces this definition at another place.[1] A difference, however, is found in some manuscripts of the *Śānti Parva*, which uses the term *aṣṭāṅgika rājya* (eight element state) in the Critical Edition,[2] but the eighth element is not mentioned anywhere.

Of the seven elements the *Arthaśāstra* does not define *amātya* and *durga* in the section where it deals with all the other elements; these two are treated separately. But on the whole the treatment of the seven elements in this text is thorough and systematic, and we have no parallel to this in the other texts. As we will notice, the subsequent texts have something different to say on the mutual relations of these elements, otherwise they do not add anything of substance to the Kauṭilyan definition. Hence for the analysis of the seven elements we have to fall back on Kauṭilya.

Svāmī, which means head or master, is mentioned as such by all the sources.[3] Perhaps it refers to the element of headship in both monarchies and republics, for in discussing the calamities affecting the *rājā* Kauṭilya mentions the weakness of *vairājya*, non-monarchical state.[4] For the first time the term *svāmī* is used in the Śaka inscriptions. It is significant that for the head of the state none of the texts uses the term *rājā* which literally means noble or ruler; rather they prefer the term *svāmī*[5], which means master. Nevertheless, since the term is first used by Kauṭilya, its significance may better be appreciated with reference to his other ideas. The intention is to stress the sense of possession exercised by the head, who occupies a very exalted position in the scheme of Kauṭilya. Kauṭilya dilates at some length on the qualities requisite for the *svāmī*. In his opinion the *svāmī* should be endowed with qualities flowing from noble birth, wisdom, enthusiasm and personal ability.[6] The qualities of noble

1. Ibid., p. 153.
2. 122. 8.
3. *AŚ*, VI.1; *Manu*, IX.294; *Viṣṇu*, III.33; *ŚP*, 69.62-63; *Yāj.*, I.353.
4. *AŚ* VIII.2.
5. *ŚP*, 69.62, however, uses the term *ātmā* which stands for *rājā*.
6. *abhigāmikā guṇāḥ, prajñā guṇāḥ, utsāhaguṇāḥ* and *ātmasampat*. *AŚ*, VI.1.

birth deserve special mention, for this does not envisage the possibility of men of humble origins being raised to kingship.

The second element *amātya* is also mentioned as such in all the texts. The usual translation of *amātya* as minister may convey the wrong impression that they were intended to act as ministers, whose number was small. But even in a later text such as the *Śānti Parva* the number of the *amātyas* is put at thirty-seven, and they are distinguished from the *mantrins* whose number is prescribed at eight.[1] In the *Arthaśāstra* the *amātyas* constitute a regular cadre of service from which all high officers such as the chief priest, ministers, collectors, treasurers, officers engaged in civil and criminal administration, officers in charge of harem, envoys and the superintendents of various departments are to be recruited.[2]

When Kauṭilya thinks of a council of *amātyas*, he bears in mind the distinction between the *mantrins* and the *amātyas*. In the case of the former he puts the limit at three or four, but in the case of the latter he states that their number should depend upon the capacity to employ them.[3] In stating the requisite qualifications of the *amātyas*, Kauṭilya advises that all can be appointed *amātyas* in deference to the needs of time, place and work, but this formula cannot apply to the *mantrins*.[4] Here he quotes the views of seven thinkers, two of whom prefer claims based on hereditary posts and qualities of noble lineage.[5]

Since the *amātya* of Kauṭilya is identical with the Pāli *amacca*, we can better appreciate his position and functions on the basis of the early Pāli texts. The Jātakas show that the *amātyas* were employed in hundreds, acting as village headmen, supervisors of sale transactions, judges, guides in worldly and spiritual matters, surveyors, etc.[6] Most references show that the *amaccas* were appointed to act as judges and magistrates to administer lawsuits (*vohāra*) and trials (*viniccaya*).[7] The suggestion that they formed

1. The passage, which provides for a body of 36 *amātyas*, occurs in the Calcutta edition (*ŚP*, 85. 7-11), and not in the Critical Ed. which refers only to eight *mantrins* (*ŚP*, 85.7-10).
2. I.9-10, 16.
3. Ibid.
4. *AŚ*, I.8.
5. Kauṇapadanta and Bāhudantīputra, Ibid.
6. Fick, *Social Organisation of North-Eastern India*, pp. 144-49.
7. *Jat.*, ii, 2, 181; iii, 105; v. 228.

a class of knights[1] is hardly supported by early Buddhist texts; on the other hand, they seem to have been commonly officers of a general nature rather than ministers or knights. In the beginning they seem to have been friends, companions and courtiers of the king, probably related to him. But gradually they became his officers, which development perhaps began in pre-Maurya times and crystallized in Maurya times. Kauṭilya's view of the *amātyas* is almost compatible with their position in the Jātakas. He assigns them agricultural operations, fortifications, welfare of the territory, prevention of adversities, punishment of the criminals, collection of royal dues, etc.[2] Thus it would appear that the *amātyas* stand for the governmental machinery. Kāmandaka also takes the *amātyas* in a generic sense, but he seems to identify them with the *sacivas* for in laying down qualifications the two terms are used without any discrimination.[3] The *amātyas* are, however, different from the *mantrins*, who are charged with the duty of advising the king and safeguarding the counsel (*mantra*).[4] The difference between the two is clearly brought out in a passage, which states that the king, living in his capital, equipped with treasury and army, should think of the good of his kingdom together with his *mantrins* and *amātyas*.[5] In post-Maurya times *amātyas* were known as *sacivas*, and, as would appear from the use of the terms *mati-saciva* and *karma-saciva* in the inscription of Rudradāman,[6] formed a general cadre of officers from amongst whom high functionaries were recruited.

The third element *janapada*, which primarily means tribal settlement, is mentioned as *rāṣṭra* in two post-Maurya texts[7] and as simply *jana* in a law-book of the Gupta period.[8] The term *rāṣṭra*

1. R. N. Mehta, *Pre-Buddhist India*, p. 136.
2. *janapadasya karmasiddhayaḥ svataḥ parataśca yogakṣemasādhanaṃ vyasanapratīkāraḥ śūnyaniveśopacayau daṇḍakarānugrahaścetI. AŚ*, VIII.1.
3. *KNS*, IV.25-27, 34.
4. Ibid., 30-31.
5. Ibid., VIII.1.
6. *Sel. Inscrr.*, II, no. 67, 1.17.
7. *Manu*, IX.294; *Viṣṇu*, III.33, *ŚP*, 69, 62-63, where the *saptāṅga* state is defined, uses the term *janapada*, but in another context, where all the other six elements are mentioned (*ŚP*, 60.3-4), the term *rāṣṭra* is used. Kāmandaka sometimes uses the term *rāṣṭra* (IV.50).
8. *Yāj.*, I.353.

clearly conveys the meaning of territory, but *jana* certainly means population. The nature of *janapada* defined in the *Arthaśāstra* indicates that both territory and population are intended to be covered by this expression. It is said that the territory should have a good climate, should provide grazable land for cattle and should yield grain with little labour. Further, it should be inhabited by industrious peasants who are capable of bearing the burden of taxes and punishments. Finally, it should contain intelligent masters and be predominantly populated by members of the lower classes, and its people should be loyal and devoted.[1] Kāmandaka amplifies this statement by adding that the territory should be inhabited by śūdras, artisans, traders and hard-working and enterprising peasants.[2] Two Purāṇas of the Gupta period state that the king should live in a country which is mostly populated by vaiśyas and śūdras, a few brāhmaṇas but many hired labourers. Thus all the sources, which indicate the nature of population, emphasise that it should mainly consist of the producing masses.[3] Usually they do not prescribe the size of the territory or the number of population, although in connection with the settlement of the new territories Kauṭilya states that the village should comprise one hundred to five hundred families, and that the *sthānīya*, which is the largest unit in the *janapada*, should consist of eight hundred villages.[4]

The fourth element mentioned by Kauṭilya is *durga*, which is called *pura* in Manu and occupies the third place there.[5] The expression *durga* is understood in the sense of fortress.[6] But as a synonym of *pura*, it should be understood in the sense of fortified capital, which meaning can also be inferred from the two independent sections *durgavidhāna* and *durganiveśa* provided by

1. *daṇḍakarasahaḥ karmaśīlakarṣako'bāliśasvāmyavaravarṇaprāyo bhakta-śucimanuṣya iti janapadasampat*. *AŚ*, VI.1.
2. *śūdrakāruvaṇikprāyo mahārambhakṛṣībalaḥ*. IV.54. This passage is literally reproduced in the *Agni Purāṇa*, 239.26.
3. *vaiśyaśūdrajanaprāyamanāhāryaṃ tathā paraiḥ, kiñcidbrāhmaṇasaṃyuk-taṃ bahukarmakaraṃ tathā*. *Matsya P.* quoted on p. 11 and *Viṣṇudhar-mottara P.* on p. 139 of J. L. Shastri, op. cit. This passage is literally reproduced in the *Agni P.*, 222.1-2. Cf. *Mārk, P.*, 49.47.
4. *AŚ*, II. 1.
5. IX. 294.It is also called *pura* in *ŚP*, 69. 63.
6. Altekar, *State and Government in Ancient India*, p. 44.

Kauṭilya. The first refers to the construction of fortresses[1], and the second to the planning and layout of the capital.[2] The distinction between the *janapada* and the *pura* seems to have been made out in the *Śānti Parva*, the former indicating the countryside and the latter the capital.[3] The section on *durga-niveśa* specifies the characteristics of a *durga*, referred to by Kauṭilya when he discusses the features of the other elements.[4] In the planning of the capital, which is to be built at a central place, areas are to be set apart for members of the different varṇas and for artisans as well as gods.[5] It is to be noticed that artisans such as those dealing with wool, thread, bamboo, hide, weapons, etc., workers in metal and gems, and the various guilds are especially mentioned in this connection.[6] Thus the artisan class is considered valuable, probably because of its use for defence and contribution to state income.

Kośa or treasury appears as the fifth element in Kauṭilya and other sources. According to Kauṭilya the treasure accumulated by righteous and legitimate means should be retained by the king or should be amassed by him in the same manner.[7] Filled with gold, silver, precious jewels and gems, the treasury should be able to stand the strain of expenditure during times of adversity, such as famines, etc.[8] Kauṭilya states that without treasury it is not possible to maintain the army and to keep it loyal.[9] This is a clear recognition of the vital link between the two elements of the state, although he also makes a broader assertion that all activities depend upon finance.[10]

Daṇḍa, or coercive power mainly in the form of army, is mentioned as the sixth element, and is sometimes bracketed with *kośa*.[11] This element consists, according to Kauṭilya, of hereditary, hired, forest and corporation soldiers comprising infantry,

1. *AŚ*, II.3.
2. Ibid., II.4.
3. *ŚP*, 69.63.
4. *AŚ*, VI.1.
5. Ibid., II.4.
6. Ibid.
7. Ibid., VI.1.
8. Ibid.
9. Ibid., VIII.1.
10. Ibid.
11. *KNS*, VIII.1.

chariots, elephants and cavalry. But in treating the subject of *daṇḍa* the *Śānti Parva* states that the army comprises elephants, horses, chariots, infantry, boats, forced labour, indigenous and hired soldiers, and therefore describes it as *aṣṭāṅga bala.*[1] The characteristics of *daṇḍa* are enumerated by Kauṭilya at several places. Kṣatriyas are considered to be the most excellent material for the army,[2] which suits the function of fighting assigned to them by all brāhmaṇical and Buddhist texts. In times of emergency Manu allows the brāhmaṇas and vaiśyas to bear arms but not the śūdras.[3] Kauṭilya, however, recommends the enlistment of vaiśyas and śūdras into the army on considerations of their numerical strength.[4] Besides, according to him the army should be hereditary and loyal; their sons and wives should be contented with the maintenance received from the state; they should be equipped with all the necessary provisions at the time of invasion; they should be invincible, patient, skilled in work, indifferent to losses and gains, and should act as desired by the king.[5]

The seventh and the last element mentioned by Kauṭilya is *mitra,* who is also known as *suhṛt* in several other texts. According to Kauṭilya the ally should be hereditary, not artificial, one with whom there is no possibility of rupture and one who is ready to come to help when occasion demands it.[6] In contrast the enemy is defined as one who is greedy, unjust, licentious, evildoer, etc.[7]

The definition of the state, as expounded above, is still more exclusively the product of brāhmaṇical school than the contract theory which is the product of the Buddhist school; the latter nowhere refers to the *saptāṅga* theory of the state. In the Buddhist view taxes form the only distinctive feature of the state. Here we may quote from a Buddhist source, which is ascribed to the Maurya period. "And whoever among men gets his rents from village or lands know this, O Vāseṭṭha—is a king and no

1. *ŚP*, 121.43.
2. *AŚ*, VI.1.
3. VIII.348.
4. *AŚ*, IX.2.
5. Ibid., VI.1.
6. Ibid.
7. Ibid.

brâhmaṇa."[1] This statement suggests the importance of *kośa* to the *rājan*, but the other five elements are not mentioned.

Whatever may be the deficiency in the Buddhist school, the definition of the (state) *rājya*, which literally means the act of ruling or sovereignty, must be regarded as a unique contribution of the early Indian thought to the history of political theory. Although Plato and Aristotle speculate on the origin of the state, they never define it as sharply and clearly as is the case with early Indian thinkers. In this sense Kauṭilya furnishes us as full and complete a definition of the state as was possible in ancient times. The Greek thinkers hardly discuss the constituent elements of the state. Plato makes some attempt at this in the *Republic*. His philosopher may be compared to the *svāmī*, his warriors to the *daṇḍa*, and his artisans and husbandmen in some measure to the *janapada*. Aristotle gives the impression that the households and citizens constitute the state, and in laying down the material conditions of his ideal state he fixes the size of the city and the limit of the population. But none of these gives as full a definition of the state as is found in Kauṭilya. Keith complains that it would be melancholy if the *Arthaśāstra* were the best that India could show as against the *Republic* of Plato or the *Politics* of Aristotle[2], but in respect of the definition of the state there is no basis for such a criticism; on the contrary Kauṭilya surpasses the Greek philosophers in this field.

It has been generally recognised that the modern constituents of the state such as sovereignty, government, territory and population are covered respectively by the elements of *svāmī*, *amātya* and *janapada* in the *saptāṅga* theory of the state. Perhaps it is difficult to identify sovereignty with the head, who is required by the lawgivers to govern according to the canons of *dharma*. But there can be no doubt about the identification of the other elements. We may add that in modern times unless a state receives the recognition from the other states, its *de jure* status is not established. Perhaps this element in the modern state may be compared to *mitra* (ally), although the object in ancient times was to secure allies and not recognition from other states. It is said that population does not find any place in the *saptāṅga* theory

1. *yo hi koci manussesu gāmaṃ raṭṭañ ca bhuñjati evaṃ vāseṭṭha jānāhi, rājā eso, na brāhmaṇo. Sutta Nipāta*, no. 619.
2. *History of Sanskrit Literature*, Preface, p. xviii.

because it was too evident to be mentioned.[1] But, as has been shown earlier, at least in one text *jana* or population is unequivocally mentioned as an element in the structure of the state.[2] In the other texts the term *janapada* clearly stands for inhabited territory. On the contrary there is no place for army, taxation, capital and ally in the modern definition of the state. Perhaps the elements of army and taxation are covered by the concept of sovereign power, which exercises the function of coercion and tax-collection. Since these ingredients are not clearly mentioned in the modern definition, it sounds to be abstract in contrast to the ancient definition, which was concrete and eminently practical. In the ancient definition no attempt was made to cover the reality by the use of abstruse phrases, which often obscure the real meaning.

In so far as the practical and concrete nature of the state is concerned, its ancient Indian definition is strikingly similar in several respects to the definition of the state set forth by Engels, who emphasises the class character of the state. In his opinion public officials, who are divorced from society and who compel obedience from the people by means of exceptional laws, form an organ of the state.[3] The officials, who are looked upon as organs of society standing over society,[4] may be compared to the *amātyas*, represented as a class of nobles from whom high officers of the government are to be recruited. As has been shown elsewhere, according to the brāhmaṇical law-books there is hardly any scope for the recruitment of high functionaries from the common people.[5]

Another organ of the state, according to Engels, is a public power distinct from the mass of the people.[6] This is composed not only of armed men, but also of material accessories such as prisons and institutions of coercion of all kinds, of which gentile society knows nothing.[7] The counterpart of this public power in the ancient Indian definition is *daṇḍa*, which, as noticed earlier,

1. Altekar, *State and Government in Ancient India*, p. 45.
2. *Yāj*, I.353.
3. *Origin of the Family, Property and State*, p. 244.
4. Ibid.
5. Infra, Ch. XVI.
6. *Origin of the Family, Property and State*, p. 244.
7. Ibid., pp. 242-43.

could be wielded normally by the kṣatriyas and in exceptional circumstances by members of the other varṇas. Kauṭilya's view that the territory inhabited by the armed people should be considered defective clearly implies that the people should be kept disarmed. Megasthenes informs us that peasants, who formed the bulk of population, had nothing to do with arms, which were borne by the members of the fighting class.[1]

Further, according to Engels, in order to maintain this public power, contributions from citizens become necessary, giving rise to taxes.[2] This may be compared to the *kośa*, without which, in the opinion of Kauṭilya, the army cannot be maintained. Thus at least in three respects there is remarkable similarity between the Kauṭilyan and the Marxist conception of the state. This is because both schools stress that theory should reflect practice. They come to grips with the realities of political life and are not lost in the claptrap of empty forms.

Kauṭilya's only departure from reality seems to be in excluding the priest from the organs of the state. The priest, who plays an important part in later Vedic polity and enjoys a weighty position in the law-books and even in the work of Kauṭilya, does not find place in the elements of the state. This is taken as Kauṭilya's distinct service to the cause of political theory.[3] But in his chapter on the description of the seven elements of the state Kāmandaka lays down the qualifications of the chief priest (*purohita*) and astrologer (*jyotiṣī*) immediately after those of the *mantrins*,[4] showing thereby that these two occupy very prominent positions among the *mantrins* who in their turn enjoy the same status among the *sacivas* or *amātyas*. Much cannot be made of the omission of the priest from the *saptāṅga* list, for the brāhmaṇas as a class seem to have been covered by *amātya*, kṣatriyas by *daṇḍa*, and the vaiśya and the rest of the folk by the terms *pura* and *rāṣṭra*.[5] The priest continues to hold an important position in later times, for in the *Śānti Parva* the *ṛtvik*, *purohita* and *ācārya* are mentioned along with the *rāṣṭra*, *rājā*, *kośa*, *daṇḍa*, *durga* and *manṭrins*. In this text the question

1. *Megasthenes*, XXXIII. McCrindle, *Megasthenes and Arrian*, pp. 83-85.
2. Engels, op. cit., p. 243.
3. Ghoshal, *Hindu Political Theories*, p. 88.
4. IV.31-34.
5. Hopkins, *Mutual Relation of the Four Castes*, pp. 11-12.

is asked: what leads to the prosperity of the king and kingdom, city people and servants, and how the king should deal with treasury, army, capital, ministers, priests and teachers.[1]

An important theoretical contribution made by Kauṭilya in connection with the discussion of the seven elements of the state is his exposition of the nature of calamities affecting the various *prakṛtis*. He quotes the view of some unnamed teacher, in whose opinion, of the calamities affecting the *svāmī amātya, janapada, durga, kośa, daṇḍa* and *mitra*, the calamity of each preceding one is more serious than that of the one immediately following. He also quotes the opinion of those teachers who think that the calamity befalling the succeeding element is more serious than the calamity befalling the preceding one. Kauṭilya upholds the first view, which means that the calamity affecting the *svāmī* is more important than that affecting the *amātya*, the one affecting the *amātya* is more important than that affecting the *janapada* and so on.[2] This, as will be shown presently, enables us to find out the relative importance of various elements according to Kauṭilya. But what is more important, in this connection Kauṭilya throws light on the nature of calamities affecting the king, territory, capital, treasury, army and ally. The king may be addicted to wine drinking, gambling or women; he may thus fall a prey to moral diseases. The weakness of the territory lies in its being mainly inhabited by armed people, and that of the capital in its being mainly inhabited by agriculturists.[3] Kauṭilya also states that the people (*prakṛti*) may be weakened by quarrels amongst themselves, but this may be ended by arresting the leaders.[4]

Finance may be undermined by natural calamities such as drought, flood and famine, and man-made calamities such as the oppressions of the collector, provision of remission of taxes in favour of leaders, false accounts of revenue, etc.[5] The army

1. *kena svid vardhate rāṣṭraṃ rājā kena vivardhate, kena pauraśca bhṛtyaśca vardhante bharatarṣabha. kośaṃ daṇḍaṃ ca durgaṃ ca sahāyānmantriṇ-astathā ṛtvikpurohitācāryān kīdṛśān varjayennṛpaḥ. ŚP*, 60.3-4.
2. *AŚ*, VIII.1.
3. *karṣakaprāye* [*durge*] *tu durgavyasanam āyudhīyaprāye tu janapade janapa-davyasanamiti. AŚ*, VIII.1. The meaning of the first part of this passage is somewhat obscure.
4. *AŚ*, VIII.4.
5. Ibid.

may be rendered weak by disloyal and treacherous elements or neutralised either by those who are not paid or are guided by their wives.[1] Allies may be purchased by others or may be indifferent to the fate of their friends.[2] The remedy for these ills is suggested by Kauṭilya in some cases. The general inference seems to be that the king should stand on guard against these weaknesses. He should try to understand the nature of calamities affecting a part of the elements or two elements. In the opinion of Kauṭilya even if two elements are affected by calamities, the project can be accomplished provided the other elements are in a serviceable condition. But if the calamity affecting even one element is such as may overwhelm the remaining elements, it should be considered a very serious affair,[3] and obviously the king should take note of it.

Kauṭilya's treatment of the calamities affecting the different elements of the state reminds us of Aristotle's exposition of the causes of instability in the state. Aristotle points out certain general causes affecting the state as a whole and also specific causes affecting particular types of government. The chief cause according to him is the struggle between the rich and poor, of which we hardly get any indication in Kauṭilya's discussion. As regards the remedy, Kauṭilya enjoins the king to be vigilant, a solution characteristic of the exalted position he assigns the king in his system. But Aristotle recommends that a balance should be maintained between the forces of democracy and oligarchy.

The *Arthaśāstra* exposition of the calamities affecting the various elements of the state is to a large extent summarised in verse by the *Agni Purāṇa*, a work of the 9th century A.D.[4] Although the total space devoted to this topic in this text is much less[5] than that given in the *Arthaśāstra*, the Purāṇa refers to the weakness of the *sacivas* who, in its opinion, may suffer from sloth, indecision, arrogance, intoxication or insanity and double-dealing.[6] We may note that the weakness of the *amātya* is not

1. Ibid., VIII.5.
2. Ibid.
3. Ibid., VIII.1.
4. R. C. Hazra, *Studies in the Upapurāṇas*, i, 209. Cf. B. B. Mishra. *Polity in the Agni Purāṇa*, p. 24.
5. *Agni P.* (ASS), 241.26-34.
6. Ibid., 241. 26-27.

discussed by Kauṭilya, who also, does not elaborate the weak points of the *durga*. The *Agni Purāṇa*, however, states that the fortified capital may be weakened by its ruined walls, ditches, and mechanical contrivances, lack of defence and deficiency in army.[1] In regard to the weakness of the army, this Purāṇa merely versifies the statement made by Kauṭilya, mostly retaining the same words.[2] But in dealing with the infirmities of the different elements this text gives the largest space to weak points in the army, suggesting thereby that in the period and place represented by the *Agni Purāṇa* the greatest weight was attached to the apparatus of coercion.

Kauṭilya's exposition of the weaknesses of the elements of the state also throws light on the mutual relation of these organs,—a topic which is not discussed in such detail by any other ancient thinker. Bhāradvāja argues that ministers are the mainstay of government; they initiate all important measures, and hence they should be considered to be the most important.[3] But, in the opinion of Kauṭilya, of all the elements (*prakṛtis*) the king is the most important. If the king is endowed with sufficient qualities, he can equip the other elements with those qualities. But if he is wanting in desirable qualifications the qualities of the other *prakṛtis* avail nothing;[4] on the contrary they are destroyed. The king appoints ministers, and superintendents, who take measures of relief against calamities befalling the other *prakṛtis*.[5] Even when he is powerless, he is the symbol of the state. He is the standard of sovereignty to rally loyalty and hold the realm together.[6] The whole position can be summed up in the epigrammatic sentence of Kauṭilya who states that the king is the state[7], which reminds us of the famous statement of Louis XIV "L etat, c'est moi." It is typical of the predominantly

1. Ibid., 241.28.
2. Ibid., 241.30-33.
3. *AŚ*, VIII.1.
4. Ibid., VI.1.
5. *AŚ*, VIII.1.
6. Ibid., V.6.
7. *rājā rajyamiti prakṛtisaṃkṣepaḥ*. *AŚ*, VIII.2. In his comment to this passage Gaṇapati Śāstri holds that it refers to two elements, namely, *rājā* and *rājyā* (*TGS*, iii), a view which has also been accepted by Ghoshal, *A History of Indian Political Ideas*, p. 137, fn. 7. But this interpretation is hardly supported by the contents of the section in which the passage occurs.

monarchical constitution in ancient India and especially of the completely monarchical attitude of Kauṭilya that the greatest importance is attached to kingship. In spite of weakening in royal power in later periods, the concept of the importance of the king repeatedly occurs in the Purāṇas of Gupta times. They assert that the king is the basis of the *saptāṅga* state, and hence of all the elements he should be preserved most, so that he might preserve the other six elements.[1]

As regards the other elements Kauṭilya argues that the preceding element is more important than the succeeding. For instance, the *amātya* is more important than the *janapada*[2], and the *janapada* more important than the *durga, kośa* and *daṇḍa*. But there is no doubt that in the opinion of Kauṭilya the king is the most vital of all elements, and even their basis.

In post-Maurya and Gupta times we notice a change in the attitude of political thinkers towards the relative value of the seven elements. Manu finds it impossible to state categorically that anyone of the seven elements excels the others in merit, but that at different times a different element acquires importance over others, since that particular element is, in the particular circumstances, capable of accomplishing the purpose in hand.[3] There is, however, some contradiction in Manu's statement, for earlier he states that the preceding element is more important than the succeeding element.[4] But this contradiction is not noticeable in the *Śānti Parva*[5], which confirms the statement of Manu. A similar position is taken up by Kāmandaka, who states that each of the seven elements is complementary to the others.[6] Such a view can be contrasted with that of Kauṭilya, who seems to underrate other elements and attaches the greatest weight to the *svāmī*. While Manu indicates a stage of transition when the central authority seems to be important and unimportant, the *Śānti*

1. *saptāṅgasyāpi rājyasya mūlaṃ svāmī prakīrtitaḥ. tanmūlatvāttathāṅgānāṃ sa tu rakṣyaḥ prayatnataḥ. Mārk P.* quoted on p. 23 and *Viṣṇudharmattara P.* on p. 153 of J. L. Shastri, op. cit.
2. *amātyamūlāḥ sarvārambhāḥ. AŚ*, VIII.1.
3. *Manu*, IX.297.
4. Ibid., IX.295.
5. Extract quoted in Kane, *Hist. Dhs.*, iii, 18, fn. 21.
6. *parasparopakārīdaṃ saptāṅgaṃ rājyamucyate.* IV. This passage is literally reproduced in *Agni P.*, Ch. 239; and also in *Matsya P.* quoted in Kane, *Hist. Dhs.*, ii, 18, fn. 21.

Parva and Kāmandaka clearly reflect a state of affairs when, in spite of the prevailing monarchical type, central power receded into the background. This change in attitude towards the king can only be explained on the basis of post-Maurya and Gupta political and administrative developments, which show the rise of feudatories and the beginnings of the feudalisation of the state apparatus, ultimately leading to the decline of royal power.[1]

Probably because of the growing forces of disorder in post-Maurya times Manu and the *Śānti Parva* emphasise the importance of coercive power or force. Manu looks upon *daṇḍa* as the real king, leader (*netā*) and administrator (*śāsitā*); it is the *daṇḍa* which governs the people, protects all and is the custodian of *dharma*.[2] If the king does not exercise coercive power, the strong devour the weak in the same manner as the fish are fried.[3] The *Śānti Parva* states that it does not behove a kṣatriya to remain without coercive power, for neither he nor his subjects can enjoy prosperity.[4] We learn how Jambudvīpa, Krauñcadvīpa, Śakadvīpa, Bhadrāśva and other lands were subjugated by force (*daṇḍa*).[5] At least forty-eight verses in chapter 15 of the *Book of Peace* dilate on the importance of *daṇḍa*, some of these being the literal reproductions of the verses in Manu. Herein the functioning of *daṇḍa* is considered identical with the whole social order based on the varṇas, āśramas, marriage system, irrigation arrangements, workers, subjects, etc. The burden of several verses is that, if the *daṇḍa* abrogates its functions (*yadi daṇḍo na pālayet*), it will disturb all the aforesaid elements in society.[6] In chapter 121, where the problem is discussed again, it is stressed that the *daṇḍa* forms the organ and source of the state, which is represented as a body-politic consisting of seven elements and eight organs (*aṣṭāṅga*), but the meaning of the term *aṣṭāṅga* is not clear.[7] The importance of *daṇḍa* is further evident from the use of the term *daṇḍanīti* or the "mode of force or punishment",

1. R.S. Sharma, *Indian Feudalism*, Ch. I.
2. *Manu*, VII.17-18; the same in ms. D7S of *ŚP*. Fascicule 19, p. 620.
3. Ibid., VII.20; the same in ms. D7S of *ŚP*, Fascicule 19. p. 620.
4. *nādaṇḍaḥ kṣatriyo bhāti nādaṇḍo bhūtimaśnute, nādaṇḍasya prajā rājñaḥ sukhamedhanti bhārata. ŚP*, 14.14.
5. *ŚP*, 14.21-25.
6. Ibid., 15.37-45.
7. *saptaprakṛti cāṣṭāṅgaṃ śarīramiha yadviduḥ, rājyasya daṇḍa evāṅgaṃ daṇḍaḥ prabhava eva ca. ŚP*, 121.46.

to the treatment of which this text devotes the whole of chapter 70.[1] Both Manu and the *Śānti Parva,* however, enjoin that force should be exercised according to law. In enforcing his authority the king should take into account the precepts of the *śāstras* and the advice of the ministers according to Manu, and the *vyavahāra* based on the Veda and *dharma* according to the *Śānti Parva.*[2] Although the importance of *daṇḍa* in the two texts is not discussed in the context where the seven elements are mentioned, there is no doubt that they attach great weight to this element. In the case of Yājñavalkya, whose law-book seems to have been compiled towards the beginning of the Gupta period, the value of *daṇḍa* is stressed immediately after the enumeration of seven elements. It is stated that having obtained the seven-element state the king should use his authority (*daṇḍa*) in punishing the wicked, for *dharma* was created in the form of *daṇḍa* by Brahmā in ancient times.[3] The next five verses in the law-book deal with the usefulness of coercive power.[4] Thus the element of *daṇḍa* seems to have assumed considerable significance in post-Maurya times, when centrifugal forces had been set in motion on account of foreign invasions and internal uprisings.[5]

Perhaps the same factor also explains the "organic" theory of the state, which is not much in evidence in Kauṭilya. The only indication of the integration of the various elements in Kauṭilya is the view that a serious distress affecting one element might overtake the remainder. In ordinary course even two organs of the state may get into trouble, and still the state can function presumably because of the efficiency of the *svāmī.* But Manu expresses the close interrelation of the organs in clear terms. First, for the first time he and the *Śānti Parva* use the term *aṅga,* which implies that the organs are comparable to the limbs of the body.[6] Secondly, he compares the organs to the three staves

1. In ms. D7S the importance of *daṇḍa* is further emphasised in about 40 verses inserted after *ŚP,* 14.14 (Fascicule 19, pp. 619-20) and in 24 verses inserted after *ŚP,* 95.4 (Fascicule 19, pp. 629-30).
2. *Manu,* VII.31; *ŚP,* 121.50-54.
3. *tadavāpya nṛpo daṇḍaṃ durvṛtteṣu nipātayet, dharmo hi daṇḍarūpeṇa brahmaṇā nirmitaḥ purā.* I.353-54.
4. I.355-59.
5. *caṇḍālamlecchajātīnāṃ daṇḍena ca nivāraṇam.* Ms D7S of *ŚP,* Fascicule 19, p. 630.
6. *Manu,* IX.294; *ŚP,* 69.63 in ms. Ds.

of a *saṃnyāsin,* well-knit together so as to form a single staff.[1] More emphatic on this question is the view of Kāmandaka, according to whom even if one organ is defective it will endanger the normal functioning of the whole state, and so the impaired organ should be repaired.[2] The most clear enunciation of the organic theory of the state is found in Śukra, who compares the different parts of the state with those of the human body[3], but this very late work cannot be used for the ancient period.

There seems to be one basic difference between the ancient Indian concept and the modern organic view of the state which was expounded in the nineteenth century by Herbert Spencer (1820-1903). His object seems to have been to underline the unity of the industrial state, for he compares the industrial organisation to the elementary organ, commercial (distributive) organisation to the circulatory organ, political organisation to the nervo-motor organs, and the legislature to the cerebrum in man. On the other hand, the organic conception of the state in ancient India was intended to stress the importance of the different elements in relation to the head of the state. It seems that the emphasis on the importance of the other elements was due to the growing independence of the hereditary *amātyas* and *daṇḍanāyakas.* Since this tendency is not strong in the Maurya period, Kauṭilya does not clearly advocate the organic view of the state. But this view is more clearly expounded by the Greek thinkers Plato and Aristotle, who were the near contemporaries of Kauṭilya. Plato compares the state to the natural body of a man. He points out that when a finger is hurt the whole body feels the pain, so also when a member of the state is hurt all suffer likewise. In his opinion that state is the best in which the unity is that of the natural man. Aristotle cannot conceive of the part of the state unless he has conceived of the whole to which the part belongs. As a hand is not a hand unless it is attached to the body, so man is not man unless he is the member of a state. Comparing the state with the body, he further points out that the exaggeration of any part of the state is like the exaggeration of a part of the body. Thus the Greek theory

1. IX.296.
2. IV.2.
3. *dṛgamātyaḥ suhṛcchrotraṃ mukhaṃ keśo balaṃ manaḥ hastau pādau durgarāṣṭrau rājyāṅgāni smṛtāni hi. Śukra,* 1.62.

implies that no organ of the state should be allowed to assume undue proportions and to function as a state within the state. The idea is, therefore, to emphasise the unity of the state, which was jeopardised by the perpetual struggle between the democratic and oligarchical elements in the Greek cities. But in spite of the fact that the practical scheme of Kauṭilya provides for a very much centralised and well-knit state apparatus, this is not so much reflected in his theoretical discussions.

The review of the *saptāṅga* theory of the state shows that it not only bears some resemblance to the modern definition of the state, but also possesses certain basic elements typical of the theory of the state expounded by Engels. Perhaps its resemblance to the modern organic view of the state can be explained on the ground that in the interests of the ruling class in all ages attempts have been made to underline the unity of the state. But, if we apply the term modern to the concept of the state in Western democracies, we notice that the modern definition is characterised by that abstraction and abstruseness which are wanting in its ancient counterpart. Hence it would be too much to say that the ancient Indian conception of the state is "surprisingly modern"[1] in character.

1. *HCIP*, ii, 307.

Chapter IV

THEORIES OF PROPERTY, FAMILY AND VARṆA REGARDING THE ORIGIN OF THE STATE

The origin of the state has been studied with reference to the state of nature depicted in the Buddhist sources,[1] but no attempt has been made to present a complete picture of the pre-state society on the basis of all the sources including the Purāṇas, the *Mahābhārata*, and Jain traditions.[2] A comparative examination of these sources not only furnishes an idea of the early 'state of nature', but also sheds new light on the circumstances which led to the origin of the state.

Although the pictures differ in detail from one another, four essential characteristics of the early state of nature stand out clearly. First, the earliest means of subsistence was the fruits and roots of trees. The description of a *kalpavṛkṣa* as the main source of the livelihood of the people is a very common affair in brāhmaṇical and Jain traditions.[3] The Buddhist traditions refer to wild creepers (*vanalatā*) and some sort of roots (*bhūmiparpaṭaka*) as the earliest means of subsistence.[4] It is natural that in the earliest state of his life, which generally corresponds to the Kṛta age of the Purāṇas and epics, man should have lived as a food gatherer and not as a food producer. This is supported by anthropology and is true of the people of the palaeolithic age.[5] As Morgan points out, the first livelihood was "natural subsis-

1. Ghoshal, *HPT*, pp. 118-20; Bhandarkar, *Carmichael Lectures*, 1918, pp. 115-22; Bandhyopadhaya, *Development of Hindu Polity and Political Theories*, pp. 275-77; Banerjea, *Public Administration in Ancient India*, pp. 34ff.; Beni Prasad, *Theory of Government in Ancient India*, pp. 235-36; Dikshitar, *Hindu Administrative Institutions*, pp. 17-18; Altekar, *State and Government in Ancient India*, pp. 12-14.
2. *Mārk. P.*, Ch. 49; *Vāyu P.*, i, Ch. 8; *Kūrma P.*, Ch. 29; *Brahma. P.*, Ch. 5; *Viṣṇu P.*, Bk. I, Ch. 6; *Brahmāṇḍa P.*, Chs. 29-31; *Padma Carita*, Ch. 3; *Tibetan Dulva* quoted in Rockhill, *The Life of the Buddha*, pp. 2-9; *Mahāvastu*, i, 340-48; *Dīgha Nikāya*, Aggañña Sutta; *ŚP*, Chs. 59, 67, 69 and 206.
3. *Vāyu P.*, i, VIII.84; *Padma Carita*, 111.55.
4. *Mahāvastu*, i, 340-41.
5. Childe, *Man Makes Himself*, Ch. IV.

tence upon fruits and roots on a restricted habitat."[1] Nobody could then conceive that the fruits and trees belonged exclusively to him. It was a period of savagery, when "a passion for its (property's) possession had scarcely been formed in their (men's) minds, because the thing itself scarcely existed. It was left to the then distant period of civilization to develop into full vitality that greed of gain (*studiam lucri*), which is now such a commanding force in the human mind."[2]

Second, probably there was nothing like the institution of family based on the supremacy of man over woman. Except in the *Mahābhārata*, the traditions about the state of nature give no clear indication of the origin of the monogamous family, in which the father becomes supreme and all the domestic activities centre round the wife. As the *Śānti Parva* states: "A householder's home, even if filled with sons, grandsons, daughters-in-law and servants, is regarded empty if destitute of the housewife. One's house is not one's home; only one's wife is one's home."[3] But how did this home originate? The epic and Purāṇic traditions state that formerly there existed a state of promiscuity when children could be produced merely by *saṃkalpa*, the desire to cohabit. In the Kṛta age there was neither mating (*maiṭhuna*) nor recognised monogamous marriage system (*dvandva*).[4] The *Śānti Parva* informs us that in the land of the Uttarakurus the institution of marriage did not exist. This is also supported by the *Aṭānaṭiya-sutta* in the *Dīgha Nikāya*, which refers to the land of Kuru in these words: "There do men live calling no goods their own. Nor as their chattels any womenkind."[5]

Third, it is clearly stated in the Purāṇas that there were no varṇas in the Kṛta age. In their account of the earliest life of

1. Morgan, *Ancient Society*, p. 20.
2. Ibid., p. 27.
3. *ŚP*, 144.5-6; *Mbh.*, 1.4.9-12.
4. *na caiṣāṃ maithuno dharmo babhūva bharatarṣabha, saṃkalpādeva caiteṣām apatyam upapadyate. dvāpare maithuno dharmasteṣāmapi janādhipa, tathākaliyuge rājan dvandvamābedire janāḥ. ŚP*, 207, 38-41; *tāsāṃ viśuddhāt saṃkalpājjāyante mithunāḥ prajāḥ. Vāyu P.*, i, VIII.57. The interpretation of the crucial passage of the *ŚP* follows that of Dange, *India from Primitive Communism to Slavery*, p. 67. Bachofen was the first modern scholar to bring to light traces of promiscuous intercourse in historical and religious traditions.
5. *ŚP* (Bombay ed.), 102.26; *SBB*, iv, 192.

mankind[1] the Buddhist sources also do not mention the division of the people into social classes.

Fourth, the statements in the *Śānti Parva* make it clear that in the early stage of human society the institution of the state did not exist.[2] According to Kauṭilya in certain lands called *vairājya* there was no kingly office, and the people thereof had no sense of thine and mine.[3] This implies that the absence of the ruler coincided with the lack of private property.

Primitive societies existing in modern times show that the institutions of property, family and class (or caste) are hardly to be found in the earliest stage of the man's life. It is not just a mere coincidence that according to ancient texts, in the absence of these institutions, the state also did not exist. As will be shown later, there was a vital connection between the existence of these institutions and the rise of the state. Although people living without these institutions cannot be called civilised, they are credited with a harmonious life free from cares, anxieties and greed.[4] The main characteristics of this state of nature, which find place in almost all the classical sources and are broadly supported by anthropological evidence,[5] must have some basis in the existing facts. Hence it would not be correct to dismiss the state of nature[6] as fanciful, although people may not have been happy.

But this 'harmonious' tenor of life was destroyed by the discovery of the art of cultivation,[7] which enabled people to produce more than they could consume. There began the tendency to store rice,[8] and people "appropriated to themselves

1. *Vāyu P.*, i, VIII.60; *Mahāvastu*, i, 340-46; *SBB*, iv, 62-67; Rockhill, *The Life of the Buddha*, pp. 2-6.
2. *na vai rājyaṃ na rājāsīnna daṇḍo na ca dāṇḍikaḥ. ŚP*, 59.14.
3. *vairājyaṃ tu jīvataḥ parasyācchidya "naitanmama" iti manyamānaḥ. AŚ*, VIII.2. The sense of this passage has been given above on the basis of Jayaswal, *Hindu Polity*, p. 83.
4. *Vāyu P.*, i, VIII.48-49, 52, 62, 65; *viśakāssattvabahulā ekāntabahulāstathā...tā vai niṣkāmacariṇyo nityaṃ muditamānasāḥ. Kūrma P.*, Ch. 29.
5. Childe, *Man Makes Himself*, Ch. VI.
6. Banerjea, *Public Administration in Ancient India*, pp. 33-34.
7. *Vāyu, P.*, i, VIII.128.142-45, 154; *Mārk P.*, Ch. 49, 51; 60 and 74; *tasmin vanalate antarhite taṃ śāliṃ akaṇaṃ atuṣaṃ surabhitaṇḍulaphalam āharamāharantā ciraṃ dīrghamadhvānaṃ tiṣṭhensu. Mahāvastu*, i, 342.
8. Rockill, *The Life of the Buddha*, p. 5; *SBB*. iv, 86; *Mahāvastu*, i, 343.

by force and violence rivers, fields, hills, trees, shrubs and plants."[1] For the first time they established their separate houses, which required the sanction of law. Rice fields were divided, and boundaries were set up round them saying: "This is thine, this is mine."[2] But when people began to snatch away the rice of others without their consent, there arose the necessity of some authority which would protect their respective fields. And that led to the creation of the office of the *mahākhattiya* or protector of the fields.[3]

The Buddhist sources not only emphasise the importance of the rise of private property in the origin of the state but also vaguely refer to the role of the family in this connection. They inform us that when sexual congress began between man and woman, in order to conceal their sin they built houses (or huts).[4] Probably one house was meant for one pair. According to the *Tibetan Dulva* this was the first appearance of division by houses (or families?) in the world, and this division was made lawful or not lawful according to the king's decision.[5] At one place the *Śānti Parva* refers to the rise of *dvandva* or monogamous family in the Kali age but does not connect it with the rise of the state.[6]

The importance of varṇas (social classes) in the rise of the state is chiefly dealt with in the Purāṇas. According to them when the means of subsistence had been provided, people were divided into four varṇas. Brāhmaṇas were meant for praying, kṣatriyas for fighting, vaiśyas for producing and śūdras for manual tasks. Apparently this division worked in favour of those who fought and prayed, and was resented by the conscious producers. Therefore, at one place the *Vāyu Purāṇa* states that the duties of the castes were settled but they did not fulfil their respective duties and came into mutual conflict.[7] "Having become aware of this fact the Lord Brahmā prescribed criminal

1. *tatstāḥ paryyagṛhṇanta nadīkṣetrāṇi parvatān.* *Vāyu P.*, i, VIII.31, *Mārk, P.*, 49.62; *Kūrma P.*, Ch. 29.
2. *The Life of the Buddha*, pp. 5-6; *SBB*, iv, 87.
3. *The Life of the Buddha*, pp. 6-7; *SBB*, iv, 88; *Mahāvastu*, i, 347-48.
4. *Mahāvastu*, i, 343; *SBB*, iv, 85; *The Life of the Buddha*, p. 4.
5. *The Life of the Buddha*, p. 5.
6. 207.40.
7. *varṇadharmairjīvantyo vyarudhyanta parasparam...* *Vāyu P.*, i, VIII.155 60; cf. *Padma Carita*, III.240.

justice (*daṇḍa*) and war as the profession of the kṣatriya."[1] An analogous account of the origin of the state is given at another place in the same text. It states that Brahmā established the *varṇāśrama* institution, but the people did not observe their respective duties and came into clash with one another. Therefore, they approached Manu, who produced the first two kings namely Priyavrata and Uttānapāda. Henceforth the kings came to be vested with *daṇḍa*, the rod of authority.[2] Therefore in the Purāṇic view the state arose to check the mutual struggle between the different varṇas. Obviously this anticipates the theory of Engels that "the state came into existence owing to the necessity of curbing class-antagonisms."[3]

In the *Śānti Parva*, which seems to present a synthesis of the speculations, the part played by all the three institutions, property, family and varṇa, in the origin of the state can be seen at one place. The circumstances that led to the creation of the state are set forth clearly: "The wealth of one is snatched away by two, that of those two is snatched away by many acting together. He who is not a slave is made slave. Women, again, are forcibly abducted. For these reasons the gods created kings for protecting the people."[4] And when the people made a compact to put an end to such a state of affairs, its two main conditions were that they should throw out those who abducted other people's wives or robbed other's wealth.[5] Besides, the compact was made to "inspire confidence amongst all varṇas."[6] In order to place the agreement on a permanent footing they went out in search of a king. They were prepared to give him a certain share of their own property and beautiful maidens in marriage.[7] The result would be that the king would have a vital and permanent interest not only in the preservation of his

1. *brahmā tamarthaṃ buddhvā yāthātathyena vai prabhuḥ, kṣatriyāṇāṃbalaṃ daṇḍaṃ yuddhamājivamādiśat. Vāyu P.*, i, VIII.161.
2. *varṇāśramavyavasthānaṃ teṣāṃ brahmā tathākarot. punaḥ prajāstu tu mohāttān dharmānna hyapālayan, parasparavirodheṇa manuntāḥ punaranvayuḥ...priyavratottānapadau prathamantau mahīpatī, tataḥ prabhṛti rājānḥa utpannā daṇḍadhāriṇaḥ... Vāyu P.*, i, 57.55-58.
3. F. Engels, *The Origin of Family, Private Property and the State*, p. 244.
4. *ŚP*, 67.14-15.
5. Ibid., 67.17-18.
6. Ibid., 67.19.
7. Ibid., 67.23-24.

property and family but also of those of his subjects. It was on such conditions that Manu finally accepted the kingship. The Purāṇic tradition also credits the first traditional king Manu Svāyambhuva with the establishment of the varṇas and the moral rules.[1]

Besides Manu, Pṛthu is represented as the first traditional king by the epic and Purāṇic traditions.[2] They inform us that one of the main complaints of the people was that dishonest men seized the property of their neighbours. When Pṛthu was consecrated, he removed the grievances of the people.[3] At the time of his coronation, the first king Pṛthu assured the people in these words: "I shall establish the *svadharma*, *varṇadharma* and *āśrama-dharma*, and enforce them with the rod of punishment."[4] It is further said that the first king was equally honoured by all the four varṇas.[5]

In this connection the Dharmaśāstras contain two stray references, which may be relevant to the study of our problem. Nārada and Bṛhaspati, although the lawgivers of Gupta times, seem to have retained the memories of the old golden age, its destruction and the consequent rise of *vyavahāra* (justice or *daṇḍa*),—the chief instrument of the state authority. For example, Nārada speculates upon the origin of *vyavahāra* in these words: "When mortals were being bent on doing their duty alone and habitually veracious, there existed neither *vyavahāra* nor hatred, nor selfishness. The practice of duty having died out, *vyavahāra* has been introduced; and the king has been appointed to decide lawsuits because he has authority to punish." Bṛhaspati also expresses identical views. According to him in former ages men were strictly virtuous and devoid of mischievous propensities. Only when avarice and malice had taken possession of them, *vyavahāra* was established.[6] It is tempting to suggest that the

1. *paramparāgataṃ dharmaṃ smārtañcācāralakṣanam, varṇāśramācārayantaṃ manuḥ svāyambhuvo' bravīta. Vāyu P.*, i, 4.57.41.
2. *ŚP*, 59.125.
3. *Viṣṇu P.*, Bk. I, Ch. XIII.
4. *Samarāṅgaṇa Sūtradhāra*, VIII.
5. *Brahma P.*, V.116-21.
6. *dharmaikatānāḥ puruṣāstadāsan satyavādinaḥ tadā na vyavahāro'bhunna, dveṣo nāpimatsaraḥ naṣṭe dharme manuṣyeṣu vyavahāraḥ pravarttate.* Nārada. *dharmapradhānāḥ puruṣāḥ pūrvamāsanna hiṃsakāḥ, lobhadveṣābhibhutānāṃvyavahāraḥ pravarttate.* Bṛhaspati. Quoted in *Vīramitrodaya*, p. 4.

good old days of Nārada and Bṛhaspati, when everything was considered all right, correspond to the Kṛta age or the period of the state of nature described in Buddhist and Jain sources. The fact that the golden age disappeared due to the advent of "selfishness", "avarice", "hatred", and "malice" probably refers to the rise of private property, family and varṇa, which naturally give rise to feelings of greed and mutual hatred. If that be the interpretation of the references in question, we may suggest that *vyavahāra*, the principal apparatus of the state power, arose to protect the institutions of property, family, and social classes which created the feelings of mutual hatred and selfishness.

Direct references to the origin of the state cited above throw sufficient light on the importance of property, the family and caste in this respect, but certain indirect evidence may also be examined. One line of approach may be: what would happen if the state did not exist? The one recurrent theme in the *Śānti Parva*, the *Ayodhyā Kāṇḍa* and the *Viṣṇudharmottara Purāṇa*, which contain long descriptions of *arājaka* (kingless) states, is that the family and property would not be safe in such a state.[1] It is stated that if the king did not exercise the duty of protection: "Nobody, then, with reference to any article in his possession would be able to say—this is mine. Wives, sons, food and other kinds of property would not then exist."[2] Once the state was established on a firm basis, it came to be regarded as the greatest safeguard of one's wife and property. Therefore, it was wisely laid down that one should first select a king in whose dominion to live; then should he select a wife, and then earn wealth. If there be no king, what would become of his wife and wealth?[3] Naturally in such a case, the strong would forcibly appropriate the possession of the weak.[4] Bhandarkar has quoted five passages, which suggest that the kingly office arose to protect the weak against the strong.[5] Possibly it may not be correct to

1. *ŚP*, Ch. 68; *Ayodhyā Kāṇḍa*, Ch. 67; *Viṣṇudharmottara P.*, Bk. II. Ch. 11 quoted in Jagdish Lal Shastri, *Political Thought in the Purāṇas*, pp. 120-21.
2. *ŚP*, 68.15, 33; cf. *Ayodhyā Kāṇḍa*, 67.10-11, 31; *Viṣṇudharmottara P.*, Bk. II. Ch. 11.14 quoted in Shastri, *Political Thought in the Purāṇas*, p. 121.
3. *rājānaṃ prathamaṃ vindet tato bhāryāṃ tato dhanam, rājanyasati lokasya kuto bhāryā kuto dhanam.* *ŚP*, 57.46.
4. *ŚP*, 68.14.
5. Bhandarkar, op. cit., pp. 115-18.

interpret the "weak" as poor and "strong" as rich. But there are certain references which give the impression that the kingly office was meant to support the haves against the combined attacks of have-nots. It is apprehended that in the absence of the royal protection the wicked men would forcibly siege the vehicles, robes, ornaments and precious stones, and other kinds of property belonging to others.[1] Obviously only the privileged could own such items of property. It is also said that, if the king does not protect, the wealthy would have to encounter death, confinement and persecution.[2] In such a situation two persons combining together snatch the wealth of one, and many acting in concert rob the two.[3] The *Ayodhyā Kāṇḍa* informs us that in a kingless state the wealthy feel insecure, and they cannot sleep keeping their door open.[4] In this connection it would be of interest to quote from the story of Vena and Pṛthu from the *Viṣṇu Purāṇa.* When the enraged sages extinguished the life of Vena, the whole atmosphere was surcharged with dust on all sides. As the sages wanted to know the reason of such a change, the people said: "Due to the kingdom being kingless the poor have turned thieves and have begun looting the property of others. O sages, it is on account of the depredations of these thieves, who swiftly usurp the wealth of others, that this great storm of dust is being raised."[5]

Furthermore, it is stated that under anarchical conditions all restrictions about marriage and intercourse come to an end, and the institution of marriage ceases to exist[6]; it is not possible to give away daughter in marriage in the normal way in a kingless state.[7] Besides, in the absence of the king the *varṇavyavasthā* (the system of social divisions) is destroyed and an intermixture

1. *ŚP*, 68.16.
2. *ŚP*, 68.19.
3. *ŚP*, 90.39-40.
4. Shastri, *Political Thought in the Purāṇas*
5. *tataśca munayo reṇuṃ dadṛśuḥ sarvato dvija, kimetaditi cāsannānpāpracchuste janāṃstadā. ākhyātaṃ ca janaisteśāṃ corabhūtairarājake, rāṣṭre tu lokairārabdhaṃ parasvādānāmāturaiḥ. teṣāmudīrṇavegānāṃ corāṇāṃ munisattamāḥ, sumahān dṛśyate reṇuḥ paravittāphāriṇām. Viṣṇu P.*, Bk. 1. Ch. 13.30-32.
6. *ŚP*, 68.21-22.
7. *arājakeṣu rāṣṭreṣu naiva kanyā pradīyate. Viṣṇudharmottara P.* quoted in *Political Thought in the Purāṇas*, p. 120.

of castes take place.[1] Exactly the same consequences follow if *daṇḍa*, the coercive power of the state, disappears. It is pointed out that it was by means of *daṇḍa* that the misappropriation of other people's possessions was stopped and that is why it was called *vyavahāra*. But once when it disappeared, the results were disastrous. "There were no restraints in the matter of the union of the sexes. All idea of property ceased. All creatures began to rob..."[2] Thus it can be argued that, since the absence of the ruler or *daṇḍa* is regarded in the classical tradition as a great menace to the institutions of property, the family and caste, the state arose out of the necessity to protect them.

The chief functions of the king also can throw light on the purpose for which his office was created. One of the main duties of the king was the protection of private property by punishing the thief, and that of the family by punishing the adulterers. So great was the responsibility for protecting property that it was incumbent on the king to restore to a subject the stolen wealth at any cost.[3] That the king was intimately connected with the protection and probably with the distribution of wealth was the popular notion, which can be inferred from a passage of the *Pañcatantra*. It states that the person who desires wealth should approach the king.[4] The Tamil classic *Tirukkuṟaḷ* also defines the king as one who is capable of acquiring, preserving and distributing wealth.[5] The old law-books suggest that only the authority of the state could assure "seven modes" of acquiring and "three titles" to property.[6] A king of strict rule is described as one who cherishes the poor.[7] But there is also some evidence to the contrary. It is ordained that the king should always honour those of his subjects that are rich because in every kingdom the wealthy constitute an estate. Further, there is no doubt that a wealthy person is the foremost of men.[8]

1. *ŚP*, 68.29.
2. *ŚP*, 121.13: cf *Manu*, VII. 20-34.
3. *ŚP*, 75.10; *Āpastamba Dharmasūtra*, II.10, 27.4; *Agni P.* quoted on pp. 43 and 67 and *Viṣṇudharmottara Purāṇa* quoted on pp. 147-48 of Shastri, *Political Thought in the Purāṇas.*
4. *Pañcatantra*, p. 104.
5. Dikshitar's Translation, p. 81.
6. *Vasiṣṭha*, XVI.10; *Manu*, X.115.
7. *ŚP*, 139.97.
8. *dhaninaḥ pujayennityaṃ yānācchādanabhojanaiḥ... aṅgametanmahadrājñāṃ dhanino nāma bhārata, kakudaṃ sarvabhūtānāṃ dhanastho nātra saṃśayaḥ.* *ŚP*, 88.26-30. Cf. Critical Ed. 89. 25-26 which has been preferred here.

The preservation of the family and the prevention of adultery was another great responsibility of the king. Manu enumerates eighteen offences into which the king should look. Out of them ten offences are connected with property and two with family.[1] Similarly Kātyāyana lists ten wrongs deserving attention by the king. Out of them five are connected with property and one with the family.[2] It is only natural that most of the offences against the state should be linked with questions of property because it was thought that poverty lies at the root of all evils and the poor are always full of vices.[3] It was recognised that the poor people can resort to all sorts of crimes.[4] Kātyāyana feels especially concerned that there should be sudden accession of riches to indigent men.[5] Out of seven conditions, which the Buddha laid down for the success of the Vajji state, two can be said to be related to property and the family. One condition was that the Vajjis should act in accordance with the *vajjidharma* as established in the old days. If the term *vajjidharma* is explained in the light of the extract from the *Aṭṭakaṭhā* quoted in the *Dīgha Nikāya,* it means that the thief should be punished according to law.[6] A second condition clearly enjoins that they should not detain among them by force or abduction women or girls belonging to them.[7] Especially according to the Buddhist sources the punishment of thieves was one of the primary charges of the king, and the thief could be summarily killed at the order of the king either by hanging or by the removal of his skin, flesh, bones, etc.[8]

The Buddhist sources, however, do not refer to the maintenance of the varṇas, which according to the brāhmaṇical sources was one of the most notable functions of the king. Practically all important sources state that the duty of the king was to uphold

1. *Manu,* VIII.4-7.
2. Verses 947-48.
3. *Mṛcchakaṭika,* I.8-15, 36, 53; III.24, 27; IV.5; V.8-9; X.16, etc.
4. *kiṃ citraṃ yadi nirdhano'pi puruṣaḥ pāpaṃ na kuryāt kvacit. Garuḍa P.* cited in *Political Thought in the Purāṇas,* p. 101.
5. Verses 849-50.
6. *Dīgha Nikāya* (Hindi), pp. 118-19.
7. Ibid., p. 118.
8. Ibid. pp. 201, 204, cf. p. 236.

the observance of the respective duties of the four varṇas.[1] According to the *Rāmāyaṇa* under the ideal rule of Daśaratha members of the different castes pursued their respective avocations.[2] As will be shown later,[3] inscriptions provide solid evidence about the obligation of the king to preserve the varṇa system.

Of the ancient Indian lawgivers, Manu laid special emphasis on the preservation of the caste or varṇa system by the king. In his view the kingdom prospers only so long as the purity of castes is maintained, otherwise it perishes together with its inhabitants.[4] Almost the same idea is expressed by Plato in his *Republic*. To quote him: "Any meddlesome intercharge between the three classes would be most mischievous to the state and would properly be described as the height of villainy."[5] At one place Manu declares that only those who live like Āryans deserve the protection of the king.[6] This is also corroborated by the *Bṛhannāradīya Purāṇa*, a work of about the 9th century A.D.,[7] which lays special emphasis on the protection of the first three varṇas.[8] Generally the maintenance of the caste system was considered an indispensable element of *dharma*, for according to Kāmandaka if *dharma* is violated by the members of the state, there is bound to be a *pralaya* or dissolution of the whole social order.[9]

It appears that the existence of the state or the ruler was so completely identified with the maintenance of the institutions of property, the family and the varṇa system that the *Śānti Parvà* provides the same punishment for a person guilty of arson, theft, or the cohabitation of women which may lead to intermixture of castes, as is prescribed for the person guilty of compassing

1. *AŚ*, III.1; *Kāmandaka Nītisāra*, XIII.41, 58; *Bṛhaspati AŚ*, III.18; *Manu*, VII.17, 35; *Kātyāyana*; Verses 949-50; *ŚP*, 57.15, 53.27; 56.12, 77. 11-17; *Brahma P.*, 222.103; *Viṣṇu P.*, Bk., III. Ch. 8; *Matsya P.* quoted on p. 5, *Agni P.* quoted on p. 49, *Mārkaṇḍeya P.* quoted on p. 81 and *Vāyu P.* quoted on p. 153 of Shastri *Political Thought in the Purāṇas.*
2. *Bāla Kāṇḍa*, VI.17, 19.
3. Infra, Ch. XVI.
4. *Manu*, X.61; cf. *Śukranītisāra*, IV.1.215-16.
5. *The Republic*, iii, 434.
6. IX.253.
7. R. C. Hazra, *Studies in the Upapurāṇas*, i, 344.
8. *Bṛhannāradiya P.*, 104.62.
9. 11.34.

the death of the king.[1] Such a conception of the king's duties continued to persist till medieval times. For instance, the *Abhilaṣitārthacintāmaṇi* of Someśvaradeva (beginning of the 12th century A.D.) also lays emphasis on the similar duties of the king as the preventer of thefts and immoral activities,[2] and the defender of the *vraṇāśrama* system.[3]

Consistent with the view of the basic function of the state expressed above it is natural that the Hindu political thinkers should make sins of violating the laws of property and family inherent in the very nature of man. According to Kāmandaka men are by nature subject to passions and are covetors of one another's wealth and wives.[4] Manu holds that rare is the man pure or sinless. In his opinion people are prone to interfering with the rights of others and violating morals and manners.[5] Thus if the violation of the laws of property and the family are considered to be the innate natural weaknesses of man, it follows that the state should be created as a natural necessity to restrain these evils.

The king in ancient India is commonly described as the upholder of *dharma.* The Buddhist sources also hold before him the ideal of *dharmadhvaja*, *dharmaketu* and *dharmādhipati.*[6] What the *dharma* meant in the case of the Vajjis has been explained above.[7] But what were the concrete contents of the brāhmaṇical *dharma* which the king was asked to uphold? This may be known from the Dharmaśāstras, the law-books to be followed by the kings. They contain elaborate chapters on property laws, marriage relations and caste system. The *Śānti Parva*, which describes *dharma* as resting upon the king,[8] refers to the consequences of its disappearance in these words: "When sinfulness is not restrained no one can, according to the rights of property as laid down in the scripture, say—this thing is mine

1. 85.22.
2. *corebhyo mānyakebhyaśca tathaivrthādhikāritaḥ coraissāhasikaiscāḍhyaiḥ durācāraistathā paraiḥ.* Verse 157.
3. *pūjanaṃ suraviprāṇāṃ varṇāśramanirīkṣaṇam māraṇaṃ taskarādīnāmātmarakṣāvidhikramam.* Verses 710-11.
4. II.42.
5. VII.21-22, 24.
6. *Dīgha Nikāya* (Hindi), p. 234.
7. Supra, p. 58.
8. 90.5.

and this is not mine. When sinfulness prevails in the world, men cannot own and enjoy their own wives, animals, fields and houses."[1] It is also stated that *dharma* is meant to aid the acquisition and preservation of wealth; if *adharma* increases it causes a confusion of castes.[2] In the address of the sages to the tyrannical king Vena, *dharma* is explained in similar terms. They warn him that *dharma* is the greatest friend of men of all castes. If the king renounces *dharma*, nobody's wife, wealth or house would be his own. According to Kauṭilya when all *dharmas* perish, the king becomes the promulgator of the *dharma* for the establishment of the fourfold varṇa system and the protection of morality.[3] Therefore, in concrete terms the king's maintenance of *dharma* signified nothing but the defence of the social order based on the family, property and caste. The ideal set forth for the realisation of the king also reflects the purpose of the kingly office. The dominant ideal that moved the kings in ancient India was the attainment of *dharma, artha* and *kāma*. If the term *artha* is taken in the sense of enjoyment of property, the term *kāma* in the sense of the enjoyment of family life and the term *dharma* in the sense of the maintenance of the legal system, it would be clear that in the *trivarga* ideal also the conceptions of property, family and caste dominated. It may, however, be noted that according to some ancient Indian traditions *artha* (property) lay at the basis of the *trivarga* ideal, and without this it was not possible to achieve the other two objectives.[4]

From whatever point of view we study the problem of the origin of the state—the circumstances in the state of nature leading to the rise of the state, the conditions obtaining in a kingless community, the chief duties of the king, the implication of the upholding of *dharma* by the king, the ideal to be followed by him—it is difficult to avoid the conclusion that in the opinion of early thinkers and lawgivers property, family and varṇa played the primary and vital role in the rise of the state in ancient India.

1. *ŚP*, 90.9-10.
2. Ibid., 90.17, 35.
3. *AŚ*, III.1.
4. *dhanavān dharmamāpnoti dhanavān kāmamaśnute. Agni P.* quoted on p. 42 and *Viṣṇudharmottara P.* quoted on p. 145 of Shastri, *Political Thought in the Purāṇas. tyajanti mitrāṇi dhanairvihīnaṃ putrāśca dārāśca suhṛjjanāśca. Garuḍa P.* quoted on p. 92 of Shastri, *Political Thought in the Purāṇas.*

Chapter V

THE CONTRACT THEORY OF THE ORIGIN OF THE STATE : AN HISTORICAL SURVEY

Attempts have been made to find out the counterparts of the Western theories of the origin of the state in ancient Indian texts, but this has been done without much care for the age and the historical background of their sources. The task is rendered difficult because of the uncertainties which hang over many texts in regard to their dates and contents. Any attempt at the reconstruction of the history of a political theory, such as the contract theory of the origin of the state, will be provisional in nature. In doing so we have to fall back upon the generally accepted chronology of the texts, which include the Brāhmaṇas, the *Dīgha Nikāya*, the *Arthaśāstra* of Kauṭilya, the *Mahāvastu* and the *rājadharma* section of the *Śānti Parva*. This chronological order is, however, not followed by some scholars, who take up the *Śānti Parva* evidence first and follow it up with the data from the *Dīgha Nikāya* and Kauṭilya.[1] But the *rājadharma* section of the *Śānti Parva* cannot be placed earlier than the first century A.D. It is significant that Chapter 67 deals with the contract theory of the origin of the state and Chapter 65 (verse 13) refers to the Pahlavas (Parthians).

The first faint traces of the contract theory of the origin of the state are to be found in two Brāhmaṇas, which refer to the origin of kingship through election among the gods on account of the compelling necessity of carrying on successful war against the Asuras.[2] In one Brāhmaṇa this idea is further developed in connection with the great coronation ceremony of Indra. It is stated that headed by Prajāpati the gods said to one another

1. Altekar, *State* and *Government in Ancient India*, p. 27ff. Beni Prasad's *The Theory of Government in Ancient India* suffers from complete lack of historical perspective inasmuch as it treats the didactic material in the epic first and follows it up with Manu, Arthaśāstras, Dharmaśāstras, Buddhist and Jain sources, etc.
2. *AB*, I.14, 23; *TB*, I.5.9.

that amongst them Indra was "the most vigorous, the most strong, the most perfect, the best in carrying out any work." So they decided to install him in kingship and accordingly to perform his *mahābhiṣeka*, in which he was consecrated for different forms of royalty.[1] Obviously election implies some sort of consent on the part of the electors as well as the elect, but their mutual obligations are not specified in the text. Nevertheless, since necessities of war form the background of election in which stress is laid on the physical qualities of the king,[2] the obligations of obedience on the part of the subjects and that of command and protection on the part of the king are implicit in the transaction. How far this speculation represents the real nature of kingship in the later Vedic period is difficult to say. The election in divine society may be regarded as a reflection of the practice in early Vedic tribal society, for the coronation ceremonies suggest that by the end of the Vedic period kingship had been fairly established on hereditary basis. It is said that the Brāhmaṇas anticipate in some measure the celebrated theory of Social Contract of later times.[3] But if we take a narrow view of social contract, it means that people agree amongst themselves to respect the family and property of one another and thus lay the foundations of society. This idea is not advanced in the Brāhmaṇas, which seem to visualise some kind of political contract.

Although the contract theory of the origin of the state is anticipated by early brāhmaṇical literature, the first clear and developed exposition of this theory is found in the Buddhist canonical text *Dīgha Nikāya*, where the story of creation reminds us of the ideal state of Rousseau followed by the state of nature as depicted by Hobbes. We may summarise the main stages in this story, which is related by the Buddha to refute the brāhmaṇa's claim for precedence over members of all the other social classes. It is said that there was a time when people were perfect, and lived in a state of happiness and tranquillity. This perfect state lasted for ages, but at last the pristine purity declined and there set in rottenness. Differences of sex manifested themselves, and there appeared distinctions of colour. In a word, heavenly life

1. *AB*, VIII.12-17.
2. Cf. *HPT*, p. 43.
3. Ibid.

degenerated into earthly life. Now shelter, food and drink were required. People gradually entered into a series of agreements among themselves and set up the institutions of the family and property. But this gave rise to a new set of problems, for there appeared theft and other forms of unsocial conduct. Therefore, people assembled and agreed to choose as chief a person who was "the best favoured, the most attractive and the most capable." On their request he consented "to be indignant at that where one should be rightly indignant, to censure that which should be rightly censured, to banish him who deserves to be banished."[1] In return they agreed to contribute to him a portion of their paddy. The individual, who was thus elected, came to hold in a serial order three titles: (*i*) *mahāsammata*, (*ii*) *khattiya*, and (*iii*) *rājā*. According to the text the first means one chosen by the whole people; the second means the lord of the fields; the third means one who charms the people by means of *dharma*.[2]

The speculation made in the *Dīgha Nikāya* is the product of an advanced stage of social development when the tribal society had broken up, giving rise to clash of interests between men and women, between peoples of different races and colours, and between people of unequal wealth. This idea was adumberated in the middle Ganga plains, where paddy was the basis of the economy of the people. Although excavations at Hastināpura take back the existence of paddy in north-east India to about the eighth century B.C.,[3] it was only in the age of the Buddha that it had come to be widely cultivated. It is significant that the text does not refer to any other grain except paddy, which was clearly the main crop in the eastern regions. The story of creation gives the impression that one of the chief sources of discord was the hoarding of rice by some people over and above what they required for their consumption, and, what is worse, the stealing of rice fields[4], the repeated occurrence of which is regarded to be an important factor leading to the election of the chief. But this political compact is preceded by the establishment of a social compact, which markedly distinguishes the Buddhist contract theory from the one which can be inferred from the Brāhmaṇas.

1. *DN*, iii, 93f.; tr. *SBB*, iv, 88f.
2. Ibid.
3. *Ancient India*, No. 10 & 11 (1954-5), pp. 131-34.
4. *DN*, iii, 89-92.

However, the idea of social contract is not presented as sharply as we find it in the *Śānti Parva.*[1] In the *Dīgha Nikāya* it is evolved in stages, which first refer to the creation of family and then to that of private property. The obligation to respect the family and private rice fields of one another is implied but never stated.[2] But there is no doubt that the idea of social compact accounts for far greater space than that of political compact in the present text.[3]

Political compact as developed in the *Dīgha Nikāya* not only lays a different type of emphasis on the qualifications for election as king but also clearly states the obligations of the two parties. The stress is shifted from the qualities of vigour and strength, as mentioned in the *Aitareya Brāhmaṇa,* to that of beauty, popularity, attractiveness and ability. In other words, physical qualities of aesthetic type are coupled with those of head and heart, which change is obviously due to the Buddhist bias against the use of force and violence. When evil acts are committed the king expresses his displeasure by showing indignation and making censure, but what concrete shape is given to these two is not known. The only definite form of punishment is the banishment of the guilty. Thus on the whole the obligation of the head of the state is negative; he steps in only when people break the established laws. The fanciful etymological explanation of the titles of the elected chief throws further light on the nature of obligations supposed to be carried out by him. The title *khaṭṭiya,* which means the lord of fields, suggests that the primary duty of the king is to protect the plots of one against being encroached upon by the other. Further, the title indicates that the king derives his power over land as the representative of the community, which was considered as the owner of land in Vedic times.[4] The first indication of effectual royal ownership over land is to be found in pre-Maurya times, when the early Pāli texts furnish us instances of land grants made by the king to the brāhmaṇas in north-eastern India. Accordingly the contractual relation between the king and the people reflects the proprietary right of

1. Infra. pp. 71-75.
2. *DN,* iii, 89-92.
3. Ibid.
4. It seems that no land could be given away without the consent of the *viś* (community). *CHI,* i, 118.

the oligarchy over land. The interpretation of the title *rājā* imposes on the king the positive obligation of charming or pleasing the people. What practical form this should take is not indicated;[1] nor is this specified at the place where the mutual duties of the king and the people are recorded.

In contrast to several obligations of the king, the people are assigned only one duty, namely, to pay a part of their paddy as contribution to the king. The rate of taxation is not prescribed, but the contemporary law-book of Baudhāyana lays down that the king should protect the people in return for one-sixth of the produce.[2] Thus the idea of protection in lieu of taxation was current in the brāhmaṇical circles of pre-Maurya times also. But it is difficult to say whether the brāhmaṇas borrowed it from the Buddhists or *vice versa*. The probable origin of the contractual idea should be sought in the existing political organisation, in which payment of taxes had been made obligatory on the people with the beginning of the Post-Vedic period so that traditions refer to the fleeing of the villagers on account of oppressive taxation.[3]

Originally the agreement takes place between a single kṣatriya on the one hand and the people on the other, but at a later stage it is extended to the kṣatriyas as a class. Towards the end of the story of creation in the *Dīgha Nikāya* it is stated that thus took place the origin of the social circles of the nobles, *khattiya-maṇḍala*.[4] Thus what is described here is not merely the contract between the primordial kṣatriya ruler and the people but the one between the ruling class comprising the kṣatriya oligarchs on the one hand and the non-kṣatriya people on the other. This obviously is intended to justify and strengthen the rule of oligarchies, which existed in the middle Gangetic plains in the age of the Buddha, by giving them the cloak of popular support and thus sanctioning payment of regular taxes by the people. It is characteristic of the Buddhist theory of contract that it applies

1. The Buddhist ruler Aśoka enjoins his *rājukas* not only to award punishments but also to confer rewards upon his subjects.
2. I.10.18-19.
3. The Jātaka tradition that the people of Dakṣiṇa-Pañcāla fled away to the kingdom of Uttara-Pañcāla on account of too much oppression of their king is recorded in the *Divyāvadāna*, pp. 435-37.
4. *DN*, iii. 93; tr. *SBB*, iii, 88.

not to a single individual who is the head of the state, as we find it in the case of the theory of the brāhmaṇical *Śānti Parva* or in that of Rousseau, but to individuals who constitute the ruling class.

The obligations imposed on the ruler in our text are impressive, and may lead us to think that they are in line with the republican outlook of the age and the reformist attitude of Buddhism in social and religious matters. But Ghoshal rightly holds that there is no evidence to confirm the impression that this theory was used to exert some measure of popular control on royal power.[1] On the contrary, the long account of the disturbed and miserable life of the people is intended to serve as a justification for the kṣatriya rule, monarchical or oligarchical, flourishing in the time of the Buddha. The only limitation proposed on the power of the ruler in the Buddhist contract theory is that he should act according to the Norm or *dharma,* but this does not directly form part of the contract theory. At one place it is stated that the *rājā* pleases the people in accordance with *dharma.*[2] The closing passage of the present account relates that the origin of the *khattiya-maṇḍala*, namely, the ruling oligarchy, took place according to *dharma*, justice or righteousness.[3] Thus, as in the case of Plato's *Republic*, the state is conceived as the fructification of the idea of *dharma* or justice.

The earliest brāhmaṇical exposition of the contract theory of the origin of the state in clear terms occurs in the *Arthaśāstra* of Kauṭilya. Just as in the *Dīgha Nikāya* this theory is propounded incidentally in connection with the refutation of the brāhmaṇa's claim to social supremacy, similarly in the *Arthaśāstra* it is expounded casually in the course of a talk amongst the spies about the nature of royal power.[4] It cannot be regarded as a deliberate and thought-out exposition, as is the case with the theoretical discussion of the seven elements of the state. Nevertheless, in to the terms of contract it introduces certain new elements which are absent in the *Dīgha Nikāya.* It states that overtaken by a state of anarchy the people elected Manu Vaivasvata as their king and undertook to pay 1/6 of their grain, and 1/10 of their articles of

1. *HPT*, p. 121.
2. *DN*, iii, 93.
3. Ibid.
4. *AŚ*, I.13.

merchandise in addition to a portion of their gold. In return for these taxes the king guaranteed social welfare to the people by undertaking to suppress acts of mischief, afflicting the guilty with taxes and coercion. Even the inhabitants of the forest were required to give him 1/6 of the forest produce. This account of the origin of the state closes with the moral that the king should not be disregarded.

The Kauṭilyan speculation is in keeping with an advanced economy, when the different kinds of grain were produced so that the king laid claim not only to an unspecified part of paddy but also to a fixed part of all kinds of grain produce. Similarly trade had been established as a regular source of income to the state, for both Megasthenes and Kauṭilya refer to officers regulating trade in this period. Besides, mining was a thriving industry in the Maurya age; probably on account of this, provision is made for payment of a part of *hiraṇya*, which covers not only gold but also includes similar other precious metals. Finally, the fact that even the inhabitants of the forest are not exempted from taxes is an indication of the comprehensive character of the Kauṭilyan state. Thus taken as a whole the first three taxes, namely, those in grain, commodities and metals, reflect the developed economy of the Maurya period, and all the four taxes mentioned in the terms of contract made between the mythical Manu and the people betray to some extent the elaborate taxation system and the increasingly acquisitive character of the Maurya state.

The contractual origin of kingship in the *Arthaśāstra* is not intended to impose limitations on royal power. On the contrary the obligations put upon the people are burdensome and are designed to strengthen royal authority. This point is clearly brought out towards the close of the passage which describes the contract theory of the origin of kingship. It is argued that the king, who assures security and well-being to his subjects by eliminating wrongful acts through coercion and taxes, should never be disregarded. Hence Kauṭilya's contract theory is purported to buttress royal power as that of Hobbes, rather than to limit it as that of Locke.

The next stage in the history of the contract theory of the origin of the state is indicated by the *Mahāvastu*, a biography of the Buddha written in the first century B.C. in, what is regarded by some scholars, Buddhist-Hybrid Sanskrit. Such is the force of sectarian tradition in ancient India that although this biography seems to have been removed from the *Dīgha Nikāya* by about three hundred years, in expounding the contract theory of the origin of kingship, it reproduces the greater part of the story of creation recorded in the earlier text. It refers to the ideal state of life in the beginning followed by degeneration leading to the establishment of the family and property by a series of agreements, finally cemented by the foundation of the state as a result of the election of the most gracious and mighty as the king, who is known as the *mahāsammata*.[1] But there are some significant differences in regard to the terms of contract, which are enlarged by this text directly and indirectly. On the request of the people the king undertakes not only to punish those who deserve punishment, but also, what is a new obligation, to cherish those who deserve to be cherished. This element of rewarding the good is not noticeable in the earlier speculations, although Aśoka underlines it in his instructions to his officers. Perhaps the idea owes its origin to the Buddhist ruler, but we do not know whether it was actually practised unless it be the various kinds of donations made to the religious sects and priests. At any rate the obligation of the king to reward the good is directly stated in this text. Further, the two new titles applied to the king in the present source give some indication of his other obligations. The king is designated *mūrdhnābhiṣikta* (consecrated head), for he properly protects and carefully guards his people.[2] He is called *jānapadasthāmavīryaprāpta* (one who has attained the security of his realm), for he is established among the people of the town and countryside as their parents.[3] Curiously enough the title *rājā* in this text is explained as suggesting that the king is entitled to a share in the produce of paddy.[4] This title, therefore, indicates the right of the king rather than his duty towards the people, whose obligation towards the king is stipulated earlier in very clear terms. In return for this pledge on the part of the king the people promise to pay him one-sixth of the produce of

1. *Mahāvastu*, i, 343ff.
2. *samyak rakṣati paripāleti mūrdhnābhiṣiktaḥ...sañjñā udapāsi*. Ibid. i, 348.
3. *mātāpitṛsamo naigamajānapadeṣu tti jānapadasthāmavīryaprāpto ti sañjñā udapāsi*. Ibid.
4. Ibid.

the paddy fields, a rate which is specified in the *Dīgha Nikāya* and is in consonance with that given by Kauṭilya. Although it is a period of thriving trade and the king is represented as attending to the interests of the inhabitants of the urban and rural areas, there is no mention of taxes on commodities. This is explicable if we assume that in a biography of the Buddha the writer tries to be faithful to the conditions of the age when the great teacher lived. But even the *Mahāvastu* unwittingly reflects the political practices of the time when it was compiled. For it gives us the genealogy of the successor of the first elected king Sammata for several generations,[1] suggesting thereby that once a person came to power he tried to perpetuate his line. It is also because of this that the element of election is retained, for the brāhmaṇical chapters on polity in Manu and the *Śānti Parva*, compiled in the period when hereditary monarchy had become the rule, do not refer to the election of the king.

Regarding the origin of kingship, the *Śānti Parva* contains two speculations, both of which may be interpreted as embodying elements of the contract theory of the origin of the state. We do not know whether these two suppositions were incorporated into the section on *rājadharma* at the same time, for, as will be shown later, their objects seem to have been widely divergent. The first occurs in the 59th chapter, which begins with a long discussion on the importance of *daṇḍa* and *daṇḍanīti*. It is stated there that Viṣṇu created a son born out of his mind to undertake the responsibility of administration, but he and several of his descendants renounced the world ultimately leading to the tyrannical rule of Vena.[2] The sages (*ṛṣis*) put an end to the life of this ruler, and created out of his right thigh Pṛthu, who was the eighth in descent from Viṣṇu. By means of a contract, the sages clearly laid down the conditions on which Pṛthu Vainya would hold the throne. The sages asked him to swear that he would rule according to the principles of *daṇḍanīti*, that he would consider the brāhmaṇas above punishment and that he would save the world from the intermixture of castes.[3] At this Pṛthu promised the deities headed by the *ṛṣis* that he would always worship the highly blessed brāhmaṇas, the bull among

1. Ibid.
2. *ŚP*, 59.94-99.
3. Ibid., 59.100-14.

men.[1] Earlier he had assured that he would do whatever is proper and in accordance with the science of polity.[2]

Although the contract does not take place with the original ruler, the writer seems to convey that real kingship began with Pṛthu, after whom the world (*pṛthivī*) was named. It is significant that the contract does not take place with the people but with the brāhmaṇas, who claim special privileges and protection from the king. There is nothing to prove the contention of Jayaswal that to the royal oath the people pronounced 'Amen' (*evamastu*).[3] The pledge is clearly administered by the deities and the great sages *paramarṣayaḥ*[4], who speak 'Amen' when it has been taken by the king.[5] By no stretch of imagination can they be considered as representing the whole people. King Pṛthu does not repeat the whole oath, but he states it in unequivocal terms that he would always respect the brāhmaṇas. This theoretical recognition of the special position of the brāhmaṇas in the contract is a measure of their increasing importance in post-Maurya and Gupta times, when several brāhmaṇical dynasties such as those of the Śuṅgas, Kaṇvas, Sātavāhanas, Vākāṭakas, etc., were ruling in the country and brāhmaṇism had reasserted itself, ultimately leading to its efflorescence under the Guptas. In the same context, by way of further explanation we are given a fanciful etymological derivation of the term kṣatriya, which is interpreted to mean one who protects the brāhmaṇas from wounds.[6] The only concession to royal obligation towards the people is contained in a similar elucidation of the term *rājā*, which is interpreted to mean one who delights the subjects.[7]

The second speculation regarding the origin of the state occurring in the 67th chapter of the *Śānti Parva* can be clearly taken as envisaging the contract theory of the origin of the state. It embodies theories of both social and political contract. It is stated that in ancient days when anarchy was rampant, people made an agreement among themselves. According to this they

1. Ibid., 59.115.
2. Ibid., 59.108.
3. *Hindu Polity*, p. 225.
4. *ŚP*, 59.109.
5. Ibid., 59.128.
6. Ibid.
7. Ibid., 59.127.

undertook to abandon one who speaks much, is cruel in acts, encroaches on other's property, and violates woman's chastity. Clearly this was a social agreement to maintain the institutions of family and property, an agreement which is not recorded in the Buddhist texts in such lucid terms.

The next stage in the rise of the state is indicated by the formulation of political compact. It is stated that the people did not observe the contract (*samaya*), with the result that they fell on very bad days. And hence they approached Brahmā for a lord (*īśvara*) whom they would together worship and who would, therefore, protect them. Brahmā asked Manu to undertake the work of governing them, but he refused because it would be an onerous task to rule over the wicked and untruthful people. The people, however, overcame his reluctance by promising to pay him 1/50 of the cattle, 1/50 of gold and 1/10 of grain for increasing his treasury (*kośavardhanam*).[1] They further promised that those who would become the foremost in the use of weapons would follow Manu like the deities following Indra.[2] In return they sought the protection of the king and further assured that one-fourth of spiritual merit, which the subjects protected by the king would earn, would accrue to the king. Manu agreed and with a great army started for the conquest of all the quarters.

The important element common to the two theories in the *Śānti Parva* is the fact that none of them, unlike the Buddhist theory, refers to the election of the king. On the contrary, they ascribe the origin of kingship to divine agencies such as Viṣṇu and Brahmā. Thus the element of election, which is noticeable in the Brāhmaṇas and Kauṭilya, is eliminated in the *Śānti Parva*. In this sense the theories of the origin of the king may be regarded as anti-popular in origin.[3] There is, however, clear difference of objective between the two theories in the present text. While the earlier theory is intended to place limitations on the power of the king in the interests of the priestly class, the latter is calculated to emphasise the power of the king. This can be inferred from the context, in which the evils arising out of the kinglessness are enumerated in detail. Moreover, the obligations imposed on the subjects are very many in contrast to

1. *ŚP*, 67.19-23.
2. Ibid., 67.24.
3. *HPT*, p. 173.

those imposed on the king. Out of the taxes mentioned in this text two are in gold and grain, also found in Kauṭilya. But the tax on commodities in Kauṭilya is paralleled by the tax on cattle wealth here.[1] What is more important here, we have a new tax promised to the king, namely the king's share in the spiritual merit earned by his subjects. We do not know whether it refers to the merit earned by the brāhmaṇas in particular. But this second speculation, which seems to justify royal power, was probably the product of some kṣatriya school in contrast to the first speculation, which, since it stresses the brāhmaṇical power, may have been the product of some brāhmaṇa school.

A striking element in the second speculation on contract in the *Śānti Parva* is the provision for military service by the best warriors among the people. Some other readings of the relevant verses of this source also refer to the people's offer of a beautiful maiden to the king, although this does not occur in the Critical Edition of the *Mahābhārata*. These remind us of the obligations of the vassals of Samudra Gupta. At any rate it is clear that the provision for military service reflects some semi-feudal practice of the Gupta period. From the viewpoint of the ancient Indian definition of the state, the second contract theory should be regarded as a fairly adequate theory on the origin of the state. It involves the king and people, who respectively correspond to the *svāmī* and the *janapada*. The people's obligations to pay taxes and render military service to the king clearly imply the presence of the elements of *kośa* and *daṇḍa*. Thus four important elements of the state out of seven can be distinctly discerned in the statement of the contract theory of the origin of the state in the 67th chapter of the *Śānti Parva*.

Although the Gupta period was prolific in the production of varied types of literature, it cannot boast of any fruitful contribution to the contract theory of the origin of the state, unless it be the chapters on this topic in the *Śānti Parva*, which may have been finally compiled during this period. The two lawgivers, Nārada and Bṛhaspati, speak of an ideal state of affairs in the beginning followed by social chaos leading to the estab-

1. As to gold and animals the rate is exactly the same as in Manu, but the rate of one-tenth in grain is much lower than in the *Arthaśāstra* and *Mahāvastu*, and might reflect an earlier practice.

lishment of government.[1] But they do not throw any light on the contract theory of the origin of the state.

Our survey would show that the Buddhist texts attach more weight to the contract theory of the origin of the state and discuss it in a more systematic fashion. But it would be too much to say, as Ghoshal does, that "the Buddhist theory of contract virtually exists as an isolated phenomenon in the history of political thought."[2] We have seen how the germs of this theory are found in the Brāhmaṇas, and its developed forms in the *Śānti Parva*. Ghoshal himself admits that the principle of taxation in return for protection is one of the root ideas of Hindu political philosophy.[3] He holds that the Kauṭilyan theory is a brāhmaṇised adaptation of the Buddhist theory of contract.[4] Such a possibility cannot be altogether ignored, but there is no evidence of exchange of ideas between the two schools or of the Kauṭilyan borrowing from the *Dīgha Nikāya*. We do not know whether the theory elaborated in the *Śānti Parva* (Ch. 67) owes anything to Buddhist influence, although the very term *Book of Peace* smacks of the spirit of non-violence. At any rate it is evident that in this text the contract theory is more systematic and elaborate than what we find in the *Dīgha Nikāya*, with the result that the two stages of social and political compact are clearly defined here.

The contract theory of the origin of the state should be regarded as an original contribution of ancient Indian thinkers to political thought, for even the Greek thinkers Plato and Aristotle, who had established political science practically as an independent discipline, did not think in terms of contract between the king and the people. Plato points out in the *Republic* that when even three or four people come together for the satisfaction of their mutual needs that leads to the rise of the state. This, therefore, implies some idea of social compact. In the *Laws*, however, while enunciating his view of history, Plato states that in the beginning people lived at peace in a natural age. Then he refers to degeneration leading to the rise of the kingdom. But after the laws had been established and the state created, in

1. *Nārada* (*SBE*), I.1-2; *Bṛhaspati* (*SBE*), I.1.
2. *HPT*, p. 121.
3. Ibid., pp. 120-21.
4. Ibid., p. 135.

each of the Dorian kingdoms people took oath in accordance with the common laws equally binding on the rulers and ruled.[1] Thus the oath followed the rise of the state and was not a preceding condition of its rise, and hence it cannot be interpreted as implying the contract theory of the origin of the state. Perhaps the origin of the contract theory in India may be attributed to the prevalence of oligarchical rule in the age of the Buddha, although Hobbes, Locke and Rousseau conceived of this theory under monarchical rule, either with the object of justifying it or with that of limiting or overthrowing it.

1. *Laws* (The Loeb Classical Library), i, 191.

CHAPTER VI

THEORY OF "ORIENTAL DESPOTISM": A SOCIO-ECONOMIC CRITIQUE

The pedigree of the idea of oriental despotism in Europe can be traced back to Plato and Aristotle. But it was only when the mercantilist and first-generation industrial powers had acquired colonies in India and other parts of Asia that the idea was popularised. Amongst others it is found in the writings of Adam Smith, Montesquieu, Richard Jones and Hegel, and was propagated by James Mill. They talked not only of oriental despotism but also of the unchanging east. Montesquieu postulates immutability of laws, customs, manners and religion in the eastern countries,[1] and Hegel speaks of unchanging Hindus,[2] their one unbroken superstition,[3] and stationary China and India.[4] Evidently the idea of oriental despotism coupled with the unchanging character of the east infected not only the western orientalists of the second half of the nineteenth and early twentieth centuries but also Karl Marx and Frederick Engels. What Marx and Engels really did was to discuss the different features of oriental despotism in their scattered writings and to link them up with the Asiatic mode of production, which was put forth as a reasoned explanation for oriental despotism. It would be however wrong to attribute to the two thinkers any systematic and well-thought out formulation of the Asiatic mode, for they kept on shifting their views not only on its components such as irrigation, absence of private property in land, autarchic villages, lack of towns, etc. but also on their relative importance. The problem of oriental despotism can be studied by isolating and analysing these ingredients and by examining their applicability to ancient India.

We may begin with an ecological explanation of oriental despotism given by Montesquieu. As he puts it: "In Asia they

1. *The Spirit of the Laws*, p. 225.
2. *Philosophy of History*, p. 154.
3. Ibid., p. 167.
4. Ibid., p. 173.

have always had great empires; in Europe these could never subsist. Asia has larger plains; it is cut out into much more extensive divisions by mountains and seas;...Power in Asia ought, then, to be always despotic; for if their slavery was not severe they would make a division inconsistent with the nature of the country."[1] This geographical factor leading to despotism cannot be applied to India. India, unlike Egypt, is not the gift of one river. Geographically several viable territorial units could be formed in pre-industrial India, and its history attests this process. If there are many units one would act as a check on the other. Montesquieu buttresses his theory of oriental despotism by emphasising the unchanging character of laws, customs, manners and religion of India. He states that the Indians easily succumb to all kinds of impressions,[2] and once an impression is formed it cannot be easily wiped out. There is no change in laws, customs and manners because the Indians are indolent in both body and mind, and hence prone to inaction.[3] This again in attributed to the excessive heat of the climate, which deprives the body of all vigour and strength.[4] Montesquieu's ecological explanations of the inaction and submissiveness of the Indians should not detain us long.

But another explanation which is both ecological and sociological deserves more attention. The need for irrigation in arid zones is sometimes put forward as the main cause of oriental despotism.[5] It is stated that irrigation facilities could not be organised by individual families or local authorities but only by a strong central authority. The point has been developed in the theory of hydraulic despotism. Irrigation maintenance required a large number of officers so that bureaucracy became an important element in the Asiatic mode of production or of oriental despotism. The applicability of irrigation theory to medieval India has been rightly questioned.[6] Even theoretically irrigation is not considered to be a monocausal explanation for centralisation and despotism by anthropologists and archaeolo-

1. *The Spirit of Laws*, i, 269.
2. Ibid., ii, 224-25.
3. Ibid., 225.
4. Ibid., 224.
5. Karl Marx, *Historical Writings*, i, 593.
6. Irfan Habib, "An Examination of Wittfogel's Theory of Oriental Despotism", *Studies in Asian History*, pp. 378-92.

gists who have examined its relevance in non-Indian contexts.[1] This has led some recent exponents of this theory to revise their stand,[2] and consider irrigation as one of the several factors leading to centralisation.

Only the north-western part of the Indian subcontinent is arid, otherwise its major part has plenty of rain, which certainly must have been greater in ancient times when there was not much of deforestation. Irrigation would be needed still, but it could be a communal, provincial and central responsibility as was the case under the Mauryas. There is nothing to show that a large bureaucracy developed in Maurya times in response to the needs of irrigation. Kauṭilya mentions about 30 departmental heads and eighteen high officers, all of whom are needed for looking after various economic and administrative activities, but none is provided for irrigation. That governors of Saurashtra took steps to repair the embankment of the Sudarśana lake under the Mauryas, Rudradāman and the Guptas shows that irrigation was also a provincial responsibility. Evidence of family and communal construction of irrigation works is not lacking.[3]

Basing his argument on Colebrooke's *Digest of Hindu Law*, which emphasises the sovereign's proprietary right to the land on the strength of conquest, Richard Jones (1830-31) made the point that right from brāhmaṇical times the sovereign had the right to the ownership of all the land[4] and that all subordinate peasant (ryot) rights were either rendered precarious on account of constant wars or else were completely nullified by the king who was the strongest person.[5] Since everybody depended for his livelihood on the sovereign who was the sole proprietor of land this perpetuated Asiatic despotism, which did not have any intermediate and independent classes.[6] The thread was resumed

1. William P. Mitchell, "The Hydraulic Hypothesis: A Reappraisal", *Current Anthropology*, xiv (Dec. 1973), pp. 532-34.
2. Steward, who advanced the irrigation hypothesis in 1949 (Wittfogel first did it in 1955), revised it later. Ibid. p. 532, fn. 2. For critique of Wittfogel's hydraulic despotism see Barry Hindess and Paul Q. Hirst, *Pre-Capitalist Modes of Production*, pp. 207-20; Brendan O'Leary, *The Asiatic Mode of Production*, Ch. 6.
3. R. S. Sharma, *Perspectives in Social and Economic History of Early India*, Ch. XI.
4. Rev. Richard Jones, *An Essay on the Distribution of Wealth and on the Sources of Taxation*, p. 114.
5. Ibid., pp. 114-15.
6. Ibid., p. 113.

by Karl Marx, who at the initial stage accepted Bernier's theory regarding royal proprietorship of all land in India. Marx looked upon the absence of private property in land as the key to the understanding of the Asian system.[1] Later he came to stress the communal ownership of land, and eventually he seems to have realised that the question was not so simple. It has been ably shown that Marx recognised three forms of land tenure in India: (i) communal property, the "original form" of tenure which had survived in certain Indian villages; (ii) "Private property" in the region south of the Krishna which had not come under British rule; and (iii) feudal property in areas such as Oudh, where tax-collectors had developed into feudal land-holders on account of weakness in the central government.[2] Of these the first two relate to ancient India, and there is some evidence for them in both texts and inscriptions.[3] However, in early medieval times there is strong evidence for the royal ownership of land[4] as well as some kind of feudal property in land.

Evidence for royal ownership of land in ancient times is weak. Under the all-powerful Kauṭilyan state royal ownership seems to have been enforced only in the waste lands in which new rural settlements were founded and peasants allotted arable lands for lifetime. However, the situation began to change in Maharashtra in the second century A.D. and over a considerable part of the country in the Gupta period. The royal right to grant land was extended to cultivable areas situated in the personal domain of the king. The term *rājakaṃ khetam* (cultivable land under the king's possession) occurs as early as the second century in a Sātavāhana grant.[5] Eventually the grants were extended to revenue-paying lands held by the peasants, so that the superior rights of the king covered all the three categories of land—waste, royal domain and revenue-paying (the last two belonging to the cultivable category).

1. *Capital*, iii, 771-72.
2. R.A.L.H. Gunawardana, "The Analysis of Pre-Colonial Social Formations in Asia in the Writings of Karl Marx", *The Indian Historical Review*, ii (1976), 377.
3. R.S. Sharma, *Indian Feudalism*: c. 300-1200, Ch IV.
4. Ibid.
5. D.C. Sircar, *Select Inscriptions*. Bk. II, no. 84, line 4.

The first important indication of the process by which the king claims ownership of the soil is found in Manu, who calls the king *mahīpati* or lord of the earth;[1] later Kātyāyana calls him *bhūsvāmin* or owner of the earth.[2] The synonyms for the term king found in Sanskrit and Jaina Sanskrit kāvyas are significant. The terms *kṣitīndra*, *kṣitīśa*, *kṣitipati*, *urvīpati*, *pṛthvīpati*, *vasudheśvara*, *mahībhuk*, *mahīpati*, etc. represent him more as the lord of the land than the protector or lord of the people. The practice becomes common in early medieval law-books, which emphasise royal lordship over the land. The literary texts of early medieval times make the point that earth is like wife to the king, meant for enjoyment. Hence the principle of possession and enjoyment rather than that of royal service, sovereignty and protection becomes the basis of the king's claim to taxes, both proper and improper, in this period.

Royal ownership of arable and revenue-paying lands in early medieval times is supported by the fact that the king claimed *bhoga*, *bhogakara* or *rājakīya bhoga*.[3] Initially *bhoga* stood for periodical supplies of fuel, flowers, fruits and similar other things by the peasants to the king; then gradually it came to include eight or eleven types of *bhoga* embracing the enjoyment of all possible agrarian resources.[4] The absence of *bhoga* in Kauṭilya's enumeration of taxes to be collected from the rural areas is as striking as that of Kauṭilya's *sitā* (income from crown lands directly cultivated by the king's agents) in the land grants. *Bhoga* is invariably used in the sense of possession or enjoyment and repeatedly mentioned in the Smṛtis in that sense either singly or in combination with other terms. It is, therefore, most likely that the king demanded *bhoga* from the peasant on the plea that the land lay within his overall possession (*bhoga*/*bhukti*).

But in addition to royal rights in land there developed in early medieval times feudal property in land. The king's dominion over the soil was limited by the intermediate landlords he created. In the earliest grants the royal right to revenues was transferred, but in later grants the royal right to the enjoyment

1. VIII. 39.
2. Verse 16.
3. For references see U.N. Ghoshal, *Contributions to the History of the Hindu Revenue System*, p. 394.
4. Ibid.

of all agrarian resources was transferred. What is more significant, the beneficiaries were given the right of evicting the existing cultivators and getting the lands enjoyed and cultivated by others. Naturally royal charters called *śāsanas* were bound to lead to land disputes between the beneficiaries and peasants, and in such cases the king respected his charters. Medieval legal texts enjoin that in trying a suit if there are differences between *dharma* (law), *vyavahāra* (agreement), *carita* (custom) and *śāsana*, the last should override all the three other sources of authority.[1] Most probably this rule applied to land disputes which arose out of peasant claims to the benefice lands. These could be decided mainly on the strength of royal charters or *śāsanas* and not so much on the basis of the other types of titles to the land. All the religious and secular beneficiaries who were granted lands by the king developed their own rights in these lands, as distinct from those of the king and peasants. So the fact that the king becomes the greatest landowner in the early medieval phase does not lead to royal despotism for his power is restricted by the lesser landlords he creates and by the revenue officials who turn into hereditary landlords. The king could possibly intervene in an effective manner in the conflict between the peasants and beneficiaries, or between rival beneficiaries. And then there were remnants of communal rights. Conflicts between these different types of land rights would pose problems for the stability of government. It is held that the combination of sovereignty and ownership of land in the person of the king led to oriental despotism. But there is nothing to show that this happened either in ancient or medieval India, for royal ownership had to contend with feudal property and peasant property.

An important ingredient of, and explanation for, oriental despotism, is the self-sufficiency of villages which led to the unchanging character of Indian society presided over by a despot. The idea was first advanced by Hegel. Hegel speaks of a fixed and immutable arrangement, subject to no one's will, existing in the villages, with the result that all political resolutions become matters of indifference to the common Hindu, "for his

1. *Kātyāyana* quoted in Laxman Shastri Joshi, *Dharmakośa*, vol. i, Pt. I, p. 103; Hārita quoted ibid., p. 106; cf. Bṛhaspati quoted ibid., p. 99. To me it appears that a similar verse in *AŚ*, III.1 is a later insertion.

lot is unchanged". The arrangement may be described in his words:

> "The whole income belonging to every village is, as already stated, divided into two parts, of which one belongs to the Rajah, the other to the cultivators; but proportionate shares are also received by the Provost of the place, the Judge, the Water-Surveyor, the Brahmin who superintends religious worship, the Astrologer (who is also a Brahmin, and announces the days of good and ill-omen), the Smith, the Carpenter, the Potter, the Washerman, the Barber, the Physician, the Dancing Girls, the Musician, the Poet."[1]

As is well-known, on this basis as well as on the basis of the early 19th century reports of some British officials, Karl Marx developed the theory of the self-sufficiency and autarchy of villages based on a happy combination of crafts and agriculture, which freed them from economic dependence on the outside world. Artisans did not have any 'market' outside their village. These microcosms led passive and vegetative life, and were incapable of combining horizontally with the result that the oriental despot reigned supreme over them.[2] Recently the theory has been taken over by anthropologists and refined into the *jajmānī* system. But it would be wrong to postulate that the Indian social structure was based on this system from ancient times. Only in the Maurya period some kind of oriental despotism with a sizeable bureaucracy can be noticed, but the system was not exclusively based on the taxes collected from peasants living in self-sufficient villages. The contribution of state production carried on with the help of slaves and wage labour in farms and elsewhere seems to have been significant. Although the surplus was collected from the countryside which also included state farms (*sītā*), urban settlements (*durga*) inhabited by artisans and traders formed a good source of income. In fact far more sources of taxes are mentioned under the urban head than under the rural head. These were supplemented by income from mining activities (*khani*).[3] The detailed laws of Kauṭilya

1. Hegel, *Philosophy of History*, p. 154.
2. Karl Marx, *Historical Writings*, i, pp. 594-96; *Capital*, i, pp. 357-58.
3. *AŚ*, II.6.

agains the undesirable activities of artisans[1] (*kāruka-rakṣaṇam*) and traders[2] (*vaidehaka-rakṣaṇam*) underline the importance of artisanal production. Obviously the commodities produced by state artisans and by guilds of artisans were used not only by people living in towns but also in the countryside.

Generally speaking till Gupta times artisans and traders were mostly associated with towns, as would appear from Kauṭilya's plan regarding the foundation of cities. In the settled, developed areas clusters of villages seem to have existed around towns which satisfied their artisanal and other needs such as cloth, oil, salt and agricultural implements in return for raw material, food-grains, and cash payment. Kauṭilya provides for the establishment of various types of urban centres in the midst of villages. The theory that in India towns were princely camps superimposed upon a predominantly agricultural population without having any organic relation with it may not apply to ancient times. The continued existence of a good number of towns in north India from the fifth century B.C. to the third century A.D. and even later cannot be doubted. Archaeology, inscriptions and classical texts refer to several towns in western India, all connected with crafts and commerce, in the two centuries before and after Christ. Merchants from the Deccan evince a sense of pride in their cities inasmuch as they mention them along with their names. The decline of trade and towns seems to have started in Gupta times and become marked in the post-Gupta phase.[3] It is in this period that we notice many princely military camps called *skandhāvāras*, nine of the Pālas and twenty-one of the Candellas, from where land charters were issued.

With the decline of trade and towns in early medieval times artisans dispersed to the countryside and contributed to the formation of autarchic villages. A good deal of peasant needs was supplied by village artisans who were remunerated at each harvest in fixed quantities of foodgrains. Big temples, and landed magnates, living on rents collected from the peasant tenants, obtained the services of artisans in return for grants of land, with the result that artisans lost mobility and became encumbered

1. Ibid., IV.1.
2. Ibid., IV.2.
3. For details see, R.S. Sharma, *Urban Decay in India* (*c.* 300-*c.* 1000).

with agriculture. Thus in early medieval times villagers obtained what they needed through the *jajmānī* system. However all economic activities were not exhausted by this system, and occasional market fairs (*haṭṭa*) run by pedlars were held to meet the needs of the countryside. The *jajmānī* system, therefore, has neither been typical of India in all ages and all periods, nor all-pervasive even in medieval times. Self-sufficient units seem to have originated and proliferated in medieval times, but they do not seem to have been so passive as they are depicted.

The concept of Asiatic despotism presupposes the absence of an exploiting class apart from the king and his bureaucracy.[1] Even those who argue for the limiting role of *dharma* ignore its class character. In the ancient Indian system the king was a member of the warrior-noble order. To us it seems that the exploiting orders were symbolised by *brahma* (priests) and *kṣatra* (warrior-nobles). The two upper orders may not have been in effective possession of land, the chief means of production, but the varṇa system was devised in such a way that taxes and tributes collected from the peasants, artisans and traders could be used to maintain them. The fact that the two upper orders did not have to pay taxes in the age of the Buddha is significant. Naturally the two orders were allied to the king for the protection of the rights and privileges conferred on them by the varṇa system as against the vaiśyas and śūdras. The two upper orders were opposed to the king when their rights and privileges were threatened from above. But by and large the texts stress the collaboration between these two. Constitutionally there may not have been a check on royal authority except the body of the brāhmaṇas which was called to interpret *dharma*, but socially the king dare not ignore the power behind the throne. The Asiatic stereotype suggests the helplessness of the rural population in the face of royal despotism, but the Buddhist and brāhmaṇical texts mention several popular revolts led by the brāhmaṇas against the king. In the early Christian centuries slowly emerges a class of landed magnates, mostly brāhmaṇas, as a result of land grants. In post-Gupta times they were supplemented by secular grantees. Although the landed beneficiaries do not seem to have formed a well-articulated class, they did constitute an important segment

1. For a theoretical critique see Hindess and Hirst, *Pre-Capitalist Modes of Production*, pp. 197-99.

of the ruling order and certainly a check on the power of the king.

The reason why the theory of oriental despotism was propounded by most western scholars is evident to students of the colonial history of India. It was meant to serve as a garb for colonial aggression. A disappointed French patriot and orientalist called Anquetil-Duperron writes: "Despotism is the government in these countries, where the sovereign declares himself the proprietor of all the goods of his subjects: let us become that sovereign, and we will be the master of all the lands of Hindustan. Such is the reasoning of avid greed, concealed behind a facade of pretexts which must be demolished."[1] Obviously in adopting the theory of oriental despotism Karl Marx was deeply influenced by Hegel and by colonialist writers on India. But significantly enough he tried to explain oriental despotism in terms of the mode of production and not in terms of the psychological make-up of the Hindus, as was done by Montesquieu and Hegel.

Ours is a preliminary examination of the socio-economic assumptions underlying the theory of 'oriental despotism' in the light of the existing historical evidence from early India.[2] We have touched upon such features as irrigation, royal ownership of land, self-sufficient villages, lack of towns, absence of intermediate classes, etc. It appears that generalisations regarding despotism in ancient India not only overreached the existing evidence but were even motivated. Of course it is easy to criticise theories of oriental despotism propounded in the 18th and 19th centuries on account of subsequent advance in historical research. But the theory is not yet a dead horse, and is now being resurrected by injecting a dose of religion into it. However our understanding can advance if we examine the social and economic formations in early India. In this respect credit must be given to Karl Marx for posing the problem of Asiatic despotism in quite a different manner and thus making us think about the socio-economic bases of the state in India and other parts of Asia in ancient times. If orientalists, who have the advantage of keeping very close to the sources, get interested in the larger aspects of 'despotism', they can make an effective contribution to the subject.

1. *Legislation Orientale* (1778), p. 178 quoted in Perry Anderson, *Lineages of the Absolutist State*, pp. 465-66, fn. 9.
2. A detailed and convincing refutation of the theory of 'oriental despotism' appears in Brenden O'Leary, *The Asiatic Mode of Production*, Chs. 6 and 7.

CHAPTER VII

VIDATHA: THE EARLIEST FOLK* ASSEMBLY OF THE INDO-ĀRYANS

Although much has been written to elucidate the nature of the Vedic assemblies *sabhā* and *samiti*, scant attention has been paid to the study of the *vidatha*, an important Vedic institution.[1] Its importance will appear from the fact that, while the terms *sabhā* and *samiti* are mentioned respectively only eight and nine times in the *Ṛg Veda*, the term *vidatha* is mentioned 122 times. Similarly in the *Atharva Veda* the terms *sabhā* and *samiti* occur respectively seventeen and thirteen times, but the term *vidatha* occurs twenty-two times.

There are ten occurrences of the term *vidatha* in the *Vājasaneyi Saṃhitā*, twenty-one in the Brāhmaṇas, and one in the *Taittirīya Āraṇyaka*. The Vedic literature is replete with references to the *vidatha*, but those to the *sabhā* and *samiti* are few and far between. Moreover, references to the *sabhā* and *samiti* are few in the *Ṛg Veda*, but there is a relative increase in their number in the *Atharva Veda* in the same way as there is a relative decrease in the number of the occurrences of the term *vidatha* in it. This shows that as an institution the *vidatha* was more important in the Ṛg Vedic period, and the *sabhā* and *samiti* gained prominence during the period of the later Saṃhitās. Numerous mentions of *vidatha* in the earliest literature lend to it a significance which needs careful examination.

There are about half a dozen views regarding the meaning and interpretation of the word *vidatha*.[2] Since the word can be derived from the root *vid*, which means respectively to know, to consider, to possess and to exist,[3] it has been possible to ascribe the meaning of knowledge, possession (or house according to Bloomfield) and assembly to it. Oldenberg derives the term

*The term folk may be understood as a kin-based community.

1. In *HCIP*, i, *The Vedic Age*, the term *vidatha* is not even mentioned.
2. They have been summarised in *Vedic Index*, ii, 296 and U.N. Ghoshal, *History of Hindu Public Life*, Pt. I, p. 28.
3. *vid jñāne, vid vicāraṇe vidlṛlābhe, vid sattāyām. Śabdakalpadruma*, iv, 386.

vidatha from the root *vi-dhā* and thinks its original meaning to be "distribution, disposition and ordinance", and its derivative meaning "sacrifice".

Vedic scholars tend to emphasise one or the other meaning of the term *vidatha* and to impose the same on all passages. But in view of the undifferentiated nature of the functions of the primitive assemblies a proper course would be to fall in line with Roth, who seems to make a synthesis of various views and concludes that the *vidatha* was an assembly meant for secular, religious and military purposes. Following him Jayaswal thinks that the *vidatha* was probably "the parent folk assembly from which the *sabhā, samiti* and *senā* differentiated".[1] Although there is no direct evidence to establish the institutional connection between the *vidatha* on the one hand, and the *sabhā* and *samiti* on the other, a scrutiny of the mass of the occurrences of the term in different contexts would show prominent traces of the earliest clan or tribal[2] assembly in the *vidatha.* Assuming broad similarity between the life of the primitive people known to anthropology and that of ancient people known to history we may elucidate and supplement the obscure references to the *vidatha* in the Vedic literature and try to understand its composition and functions.

As regards its composition the one salient feature, which distinguishes the *vidatha* from the *sabhā* and *samiti,* is the frequent association of woman with it. The *Ṛg Veda* only once indicates the connection of woman with the *sabhā.* She is described as worthy of going to the *sabhā.*[3] There is little to show that she sat on the *samiti.* Even in respect of the *sabhā* the *Maitrāyaṇī Saṃhitā* shows that she ceased to attend it in later times.[4] But the Ṛk and Atharvan collections, taken together, furnish at least seven references, attesting not only woman's attendance in the *vidatha* but also her participation in its deliberations, although no such reference occurs in the Brāhmaṇas. The *Ṛg Veda* informs us that the *yoṣā* went to the *vidatha.*[5] Grown-up men are

1. Jayaswal, *Hindu Polity*, p. 21.
2. In the early Vedic context the tribe may be understood as a large kin-based group consisting primarily of pastoralists; the clan may be considered a small kin-based group in the same set-up.
3. *RV*, 1.167.3.
4. *MS*, IV.7.41.
5. *gúhā cárantī mánuṣo ná yóṣā sabhā́vatī vidathyèva sáṃ vāk. RV*, 1.167-3.

described as installing strong and social maiden for the sake of good in the *vidatha*.[1] It appears that the woman member was not a mute participant in the affairs of the assembly. Thus Sūryā is instructed to speak to the assembled people in the *vidatha*.[2] We learn further that women took part in the deliberations of the *vidatha*. A desire is expressed in the marriage ceremony that the bride may not only figure as a housewife but having control she may speak to the *vidatha* (council).[3] Again it is said that she may speak to the *vidatha* in her advanced age.[4]

This should not be taken to mean that woman got decided preference over man. Even with regard to man the same desire of speaking to the *vidatha* (council) in advanced age is repeated.[5] So in the deliberative functions of the *vidatha* woman enjoyed an equal voice with man. References, therefore, make it clear that the meeting of this body was attended by women as well, and that it was a sort of assembly. Sometimes in these cases the term *vidatha* has been understood in the sense of house, but there does not seem to be much sense in desiring for woman's speaking in the house and still less sense in man's speaking there. Further, at one place, the bride is asked to come to the house (*gṛha*) and speak in the *vidatha*,[6] which distinguishes the one from the other. Therefore, probably in all these references the *vidatha* means a family council. It may be compared to the council of the Iroquois,[7] which generally served as "the democratic assembly of all adult male and female members of the gens, all with equal voice"[8]. In this respect the *vidatha* was completely different from the earliest known Greek, Roman and German popular as-

1. *ásthāpayanta yuvatíṃ yúvānaḥ śubhé nímiślāṃ vidátheṣu pajrā́m. RV*, 1.167.6. Here the *vidatha* may mean house.
2. *gṛhā́n gaccha gṛhápatnī yáthā́so vaśínī tváṃ vidátham ā vadāsi. RV*, X.85.26.
3. *AV*, XIV.1.20 repeats exactly the same hymn as *RV*, X. 85. 26.
4. *enā́ pályā tanvàṃ sáṃsrjasvā́dhā jívrī vidátham ā vadāthaḥ. RV*,X.85.27; *AV*, XIV.1.21. There is a slight variation in the *AV* hymn.
5. *AV*, VIII.1.6.
6. *RV*, X.85.26.
7. A league of five (later six) tribes which inhabited New York State.
8. F. Engels, *The Origin of the Family, Private Property and the State*, p. 126. Among the Andaman islanders "the affairs of the community are regulated entirely by the older men and women." Radcliff Brown, *Andaman Islanders*, p. 44, quoted in Landtman, *Origin of the Inequality of Social Classes*, p. 312.

semblies, in which woman did not find any place. But the old Welsh laws, of not later than the eleventh century A.D., show that woman had the right to vote at the popular assemblies.[1] So far as the Indo-Āryans are concerned, if we assume that matriarchy preceded patriarchy at some early stage, the *vidatha* appears as an institution of the highest antiquity.

By citing certain passages from the *Maitrāyaṇī Saṃhitā* (iv.7.4: 97.15) and *Aitareya Brāhmaṇa* (iii. 24.7-*Gopatha Br.*, ii.3.22) Bloomfield seeks to prove that even in early times woman had nothing to do with public assembly or life and that she did not attend the *sabhā*.[2] But these passages are the products of a later period, when the patriarchal society had been established on a firm footing and woman was fast losing her old importance. As such they cannot apply to the earliest period represented by the Ṛk and Atharvan collections. In subsequent times women were relegated to the background in the conduct of public affairs. Still the *vidatha* tradition of woman's share in public affairs can be traced in the place given to her in the list of the ratnins. The list given in the *Taittirīya Brāhmaṇa* (1.7.3) consists of twelve ratnins, of whom three, namely, *mahiṣī*, *vāvātā* and *parivṛkti* are women. It seems that in this case one-fourth of those whose voice and support counts in the consecration of the king consists of women.

In the early stage of social development most institutions were tribal in nature. The tribal element is to be found in the case of the *sabhā* and *samiti*. While the corresponding words for *sabhā* in several Indo-European languages mean the assembly of the kin,[3] there is a clear reference to the *viś* sitting in the *samiti*.[4] As regards the *vidatha* there is no direct proof of its kin-based character. In one passage, however, the people assembled in the *vidathas* are described as praising Agni's splendour and Maruts' might in *gaṇas*.[5] This seems to suggest that people assembled in kin-based groups. The tribal nature of the *gaṇa* is evident

1. Engels, op. cit., p. 188.
2. *JAOS*, xix, 14.
3. Brugmann, *Comparative Grammar of the Indo-Germanic Languages*, i, 395.
4. *RV*, X.173.1.
5. *vrā́taṃvrāṭaṃ gaṇáṃgaṇaṃ suśastíbhir agnérbhā́maṃ marútām ója īmahe, pṛ́ṣadaśvāso anavabhrárādhaso gántāro yajñáṃ vidátheṣu dhī́rāḥ. RV*, III.26.6.

from the fact that the Maruts, who are repeatedly mentioned in the *Ṛg Veda* and *Atharva Veda* as a *gaṇa* and according to a later source number sixty-three,[1] are described as the sons of Rudra. Therefore, the association of the *gaṇas* with the *vidatha* shows indirectly the latter's clan character, a feature which does not appear to be unlikely in the earliest phase of human history.

Since the *vidatha* was an assembly, there are references to its deliberative functions. We learn that people aspired for talking big there.[2] The householder prayed for warding off death so that living he could speak to the council.[3] It seems that in the deliberations of the *vidatha* advanced age received some weightage, a characteristic which is generally found in primitive assemblies. Remarkably enough the function of debate appears to have been exercised by the Vedic assemblies, the *vidatha*, the *sabhā* and *samiti*, but is not to be found in the early popular assemblies of the other Indo-European peoples.

What was the subject of deliberations can be known only vaguely. According to Oldenberg one of the meanings of the term *vidatha* is the "act of disposing of any business" or the like. This meaning appears in well-known passages "may be with valiant men mightily raise our voice at the determining (of ordinance)"[4]. There seems to be some sense in this, for Mitra-Varuṇa are described as directing the thoughts of the three gatherings in the sky, air and earth. They are described as strengthening the law.[5] At another place Agni, who comes to the *vidatha*, is described as an ordainer.[6] This shows that as an assembly it probably made laws and ordinances for the regulation of the affairs of the tribe. We may, therefore, presume that the *vidatha* transacted the tribal business which is typical of primitive assemblies.

Again in the opinion of Oldenberg another meaning of the term *vidatha* is distribution,[7] for which we find some basis in the texts. According to a passage from the kernel of the *Ṛg Veda* members summoned in the *vidatha* are instructed to be present on

1. *ŚB*, II.5.1.12.
2. *AV*, XIII.3.24.
3. *AV*, XII.2.30; VII.1.6.
4. *SBE*, xlvi, 26.
5. *RV*, VII.66.10.
6. *RV*, III.14.1.
7. *SBE*, xlvi, 26.

the occasion of the distribution of whatever is produced daily by Savitṛ.[1] At another place Agni is described as the liberal distributor of produces in the *vidatha*.[2] It is worthy of remark that the distribution of produces was an important function of the primitive assemblies. Till recent times there prevailed among the tribal people the practice that whatever game was obtained by an individual was not solely appropriated by him but shared together with his neighbours.[3] We can, therefore, well presume that the people assembled in the *vidatha* made distribution of what they procured as food. Another reference of almost the same kind suggests a tendency towards individual accumulation. A sacrificer is described as moving with his chariot "first in rank and wealth, munificent and lauded in assemblies (*vidatheṣu*)"[4]. In this respect the *vidatha* stands in sharp contrast to the *sabhā* and *samiti*, of the distributive functions of which we have no instance. In the case of the Vedic *gaṇa*, however, we have a reference, which suggests communal appropriation of the wealth captured in war.[5]

How this distribution was made in the *vidatha* is not clear. Probably the only reference, which hints at the nature of distribution effected, is the one which states that the *dhīras* (brave) in the assemblies do not diminish the portions due to the mighty Agni.[6] This may indicate two things. Either the portions were offered to the gods first and then distributed among the members or they were distributed among the gods there. Whatever might be the mode of distribution this much is beyond doubt that one who was mighty in the *vidatha* received more share. This hints at unequal distribution.

Probably most Ṛg Vedic references to the *vidatha*, as many as about two dozen, point to its military nature. Some of them show that an important subject for discussion in the assembly was the exploits of the heroes. The *vidatha* discussed the conquer-

1. *yádádya deváḥ savitā́ suvā́ti syā́māsya ratnínovibhāgé. RV*, VII.40.1.
2. *tvám agne rā́jā váruṇo...tvám aryamā sátpatir yásya saṃbhújaṃ tvám áṃśo vidáthe deva bhājayúḥ. RV*, II.1.4.
3. Will Durant, *The Story of Civilization*, i, 17.
4. *sá revā́n yāti prathamó ráthena vasudā́vā vidátheṣu praśastáḥ. RV*, II.27.12.
5. Infra, Ch. IX.
6. *ágne yahvásya táva bhāgadhéyaṃ ná prá minanti vidátheṣu dhī́rāḥ. RV*, III.28.4.

ing might of Agni,[1] and invocations made to the various gods describe the *vidatha* as full of heroes. There are at least twenty-one hymns in the *Ṛg Veda* which end with the verse "with brave sons (or heroes) in the assembly (*vidatha*) may we speak about"[2]. In these passages the word for son, namely *vīra*, came to be identical with *brave one*, which betrays the military nature of the Vedic tribe in which sons were valued because of their usefulness in war. The main military function of the *vidatha* may have been to conduct the tribal war against the hostile tribes, a phenomenon which was natural in the earliest stage of the Indo-Āryan history. It is well-known that primitive tribes consider themselves in a state of perpetual war with a tribe with which they have not concluded terms of peace. That is why members of the Iroquois gens were bound to give one another assistance, protection and particularly support in avenging injuries inflicted by outsiders.[3]

That the *vidatha* conducted its military operations under some war chief can possibly be inferred from several passages. At one place Indra is called the might of the *vidatha*, and at another the lord of heroes leading the people to the *vidatha*.[4] Pūṣan is described as the hero of the *vidatha*, and Agni's will is represented like that of a sovereign in an assembly.[5] These divine chiefs seem to have been the reflections of human chiefs. How the chief was appointed is difficult to determine. However two references show that Agni, frequently described as the priest, was elected in the *vidatha*. According to one passage Agni, the *hotṛ* priest who makes the assembly full, is elected at sacrificial offerings by the great and small alike.[6] Another passage states that the arrangers elect Agni as their priest in the sacred gatherings.[7] The sense of consent in accepting Agni as priest is found in another hymn, which declares that gods and men have made Agni their chief support.[8]

1. *RV*, VI.8.1.
2. *bṛhád vadema vidáthe suvī́rāḥ. RV*, II.1.16; 2.13; 11.21; 13.13; 14.12; 15.10; 16.9; 17.9; 18.9; 19.9; 20.9; 23.19; 24.16; 27.17; 28.11; 29.7; 33.15; 35.15; I.117.25; II.12.15; VIII.48.14.
3. F. Engels, op. cit., p. 124.
4. *pátiṃ dákṣasya vidáthasya. RV*, I.56.2; 130.I.
5. *RV*, VII.36.8; IV.21.2.
6. *medhākārắṃ vidáthasya prasā́danaṃ agníṃ hótāraṃ paribhū́tamaṃ matím, támíd árbhe havī́ṣyā́samānámit támínmahé vṛṇate nā́nyáṃ tvát. RV*, X.91.8.
7. *tvā́mídátra vṛṇate tvāyávo hótāram agne vidátheṣu vedhásaḥ. RV*, X.91.9.
8. *RV*, X.92.2.

Thus it is obvious that Agni, the chief priest, was elected in the *vidatha*. We have no indication how Indra was made the hero or the war chief of the *vidatha*. But generally in primitive societies no distinction can be made between the war chief and the priest, in many cases the same person combining both offices. The evidence in ancient India is not strong but not altogether wanting. We have the case of Viśvāmitra, a rājanya of the Bharata and Kauśika families,[1] who acted as the priest of king Sudās[2] and as *hotṛ* priest at a sacrifice of Hariścandra.[3] Similarly Devāpi, the priest of king Śantanu,[4] is represented by Yāska[5] as the elder brother of Śantanu. All this might suggest that at one stage in Vedic India also the functions of the chief and the priest were exercised by the same person. Hence it would not be untenable to hold that the war chief was also elected by the people assembled in the *vidatha*. This is further corroborated by anthropological evidence. For the council of the Iroquois gens, which was a "democratic assembly" consisting of all men and women members, elected and deposed the *sachems* and chiefs, and it also elected the Keepers of Faith who exercised religious functions.[6] Had there been no real election of the war chiefs in the *vidatha* in early times, the tradition would not have been carried down to the age of the *samiti* and continued in the form of various formalities observed in the coronation ceremonies described in the Brāhmaṇas.[7]

In point of number, next to its military nature, references point to the religious character of the *vidatha*. Its religious aspect appeared so predominant and all-pervading to Śāyaṇa that he explained the term *vidatha* as *yajña* or sacrifice. But it would be as improper to equate *vidatha* with *yajña* in all Vedic passages on this basis as to equate the *samiti* with battle[8] or sacrifice on the basis of Yāska.[9] The meaning of sacrifice assigned to *vidatha*

1. *RV*, III.53.9-12.
2. *RV*, III.53.11.
3. *AB*, VII.16.
4. *RV*, X.98.7.
5. *Nirukta*, II.10.
6. Lewis H. Morgan, *Ancient Society*, p. 85.
7. Infra., Ch. XII.
8. *Nighaṇṭu*, II.17.
9. Quoted in Bandyopadhaya, *Development of Hindu Polity and Political Theories*, pp. 118-19.

may be true of some passages, but it cannot suit other passages in which *vidatha* and *yajña* are put as exclusive and independent terms.[1] For instance, in a passage Heaven and Earth are praised with sacrifices (*yajñaiḥ*) in the assemblies (*vidatheṣu*).[2] In another passage, Indra and Varuṇa are invoked "to make our sacrifice (*yajñam*) fair amid the assemblies (*vidatheṣu*)."[3] These passages, which distinguish between *vidatha* and *yajña*, can be supplemented by some others of a similar type.[4] In this connection we may take into account the arguments, by which Bloomfield rejects the meaning of the term *vidatha* as sacrifice.[5] But, as will be shown later, his assertion that the *vidatha* was the patriarchal house does not seem to be convincing. Meanwhile we may stress that in all cases it would not be correct to render the term *vidatha* as sacrifice.

This is not to argue against its religious character, which is inextricably mixed with the worldly aspects of the *vidatha*. The institution undoubtedly provided common ground to clans and tribes for the worship of their gods. Agni, who is described as going on his embassy between both the gathering places (*vidathas*) of heaven and earth, seems to have been the centre of this worship.[6] People assembled in the gathering place also worshipped Indra, Mitra-Varuṇa, Viśvedevas and other gods.[7] It is significant that the worship performed in the *vidatha* is conducted in a collective manner, and blessings are sought for all the people. People seem to extend joint invitation to the gods for attending their sacrifices. For instance, the Maruts are invited to refresh themselves in 'our' *vidatha*.[8] There is no manifestation of the desire of adding to one's wealth and progeny at the cost of others. Thus Savitṛ, who is invited to come to '*our synod*', is invoked to gladden '*all our people*' through '*our*

1. Griffith, whose translation has been generally accepted in this chapter, translates *vidatha* variously as synod, assembly, gathering and sacrifice. Whitney, renders it as council.
2. *prádyā́vā yajñaiḥ pṛthiví ṛtāvṛ́dhā mahí stuṣe vidátheṣu prácetasā*. *RV*, I.159.1.
3. *kṛtáṃ no yajñáṃ vidátheṣu*...*RV*, VII.84.3.
4. *RV*, III.4.5; 26.6.
5. *JAOS*, xli, 204-6.
6. *RV*, VIII.39.1.
7. *RV*, III.1.18; 14.1; I.130.1; 153.3.
8. *asmā́kam adyá vidáthesu barhíḥ á vītáye sadata pipriyāṇáḥ*. *RV*, VII.57.2.

hymn'.[1] Likewise, when Agni is being lauded in the assembly he is asked to "give us wealth with stores of heroes and mighty strength in food and noble offspring".[2] In another passage, Indra is invoked to bless the people assembled in the *vidatha* with wealth.[3]

Most allusions to the *vidatha* from the *Atharva Veda* show that this institution continued to function primarily as a religious body in subsequent times. In this text gods are regarded as its maintainers,[4] and they are invoked in its meeting.[5] In one passage it is regarded as a heaven gaining instrument,[6] and Agni acts as its *hotṛ* priest.[7]

Gods were worshipped in two ways. One was the common method of inviting them to sit on the sacred grass and to request them to share in the food and banquet provided by the assembly. Agni is asked to enjoy the sacrificial cake in the *vidatha*;[8] similarly the Maruts are asked to accept sacrifices offered there.[9] Generally these were collective offerings made to the deity, and in this sense, the *vidatha* served as a sacrificial institution. The second method of worshipping gods was to sing their praises in the assembly. In some cases the sacred food offered to the god takes the form of praises.[10] Several references indicate that the *vidatha* was the scene of singing. Singers assembled there and sang prayers in honour of the gods. Indra, the might of the *vidatha*, received in large measure the songs of praise.[11] Agni, who filled the *vidatha* hall, conserved the holy acts of the singers.[12] The gods were besung in the *vidatha*, so that they

1. *ā́ na iḷābhirvidáthe suśastí viśvā́naraḥ savitā́ devá etu, ápi yáthā yuvāno mátsathā no víśvaṃ jágadabhipitvé manīṣā́. RV*, I.186.1.
2. *vidáthe mánma śaṃsi, asmé agne saṃyádvīrā́ṃ bṛhántaṃ kṣumántaṃ bā́jaṃ svapatyáṃ rayī́ṃ dāḥ. RV*, II.4.8.
3. *asmábhyaṃ tádvaso dānā́ya rā́dhaḥ sámarthayasva bahú te vasavyàṃ, índra yáccitrā́ṃ śravasyā́ ánu dyū́nvṛhádvadema vidáthe suvī́rāḥ. RV*, II.13.13.
4. *AV*, VII.73 (77).4.
5. *AV*, VIII.3.19.
6. *AV*, XVII.1.15.
7. *AV*, XVIII.1.20.
8. *RV*, III.28.4.
9. *RV*, III.26.4; I.166.2.
10. *RV*, 1.186.1.
11. *sthūrásya rāyó bṛható yá ī́śe támuṣṭavāma vidátheṣvíndraṃ. RV*, IV.21.4.
12. *RV*, X.122.8; II.4.8.

might be merciful to the devotees.[1] Such being the importance of singing, priests were invoked to assume the role of singers to inspire the people in the assemblies.[2]

The *vidatha* was not only the scene of singing but probably also of drinking and sports. Soma is described as "driving the drops, at our assemblies", which shows that the people enjoyed the *soma* drink in the *vidatha.*[3] It is said that the Maruts play sports in their gatherings,[4] which were evidently conceived on the basis of gatherings of human beings. This suggests that the *vidatha* served as the playground for the people assembled there. Besides, it was an assembly in which the clansmen discussed the virtues of horse,[5] similarly as they dilated upon the virtues of cow in the *sabhā*. They also sang about the merits of the chariot wrought by Vibhvan.[6] All this shows that the *vidatha* met in a homely atmosphere, and was in line with kin-ordered assemblies which are marked by singing and playing and the observance of festivals and religious ceremonies.

As a key to the understanding of the sacred character of the *vidatha* we may refer in particular to the religious functions of the early assemblies of the Indo-European peoples. Each of the thirty curies, which together constituted the sovereign tribal assembly of Rome, had its peculiar worship and chapel.[7] But in course of time some of these tribal assemblies lost their worldly functions to other institutions and retained only their religious character. Speaking of tribal assemblies in Sweden, Chadwick says: "They appear to have been primarily religious gatherings, of the great annual sacrifices at the chief national sanctuary. It is more than probable that such was the case also with the assemblies of the ancient Germans."[8]

Bloomfield does not accept the collective nature of sacrifice

1. *AV*, I.13.4; V.12.7.
2. *RV*, X.110.7.
3. *RV*, IX.97.56.
4. *krī́ḍanti krīḍā́ vidátheṣu ghṛ́ṣvayaḥ, nákṣanti rudrā́ ávasā namasvínam....* *RV*, I.166.2.
5. *RV*, I.162.1.
6. *vibhvataṣṭó vidátheṣu pravā́cyo yáṃ devāsó'vathā sá vícarṣaṇiḥ. RV*, IV.36.5.
7. William Smith, *A Smaller History of Rome from the Earliest Times to the Death of Trajan*, p. 18.
8. H. Munro Chadwick, *The Heroic Age*, p. 169.

associated with the *vidatha* and tries to show that it means the patriarchal house which served as the home of the Vedic sacrifice.[1] Accepting the conclusions of Barth[2] and Keith[3] he assumes that in the Vedic age sacrifice was a strictly private affair, the individual *yajamāna* kindling the sacred fire in his own house and performing the sacrifice. As such he concludes that the public nature of the *vidatha* sacrifice would not be in consistence with the prevalence of the individual type of sacrifice. But Bloomfield's basic assumption is only partly correct. There are reasons to suppose that during the Vedic period there existed public sacrifice alongside the individual sacrifice, and that the former was older than the latter. As shown above, public (in the sense of tribal) sacrifice prevailed among other Indo-European peoples. Therefore, it would be only natural to expect it in the Vedic literature, particularly in the *Ṛg Veda*, the earliest monument of the Indo-European letters. The presumption in favour of such a sacrifice is further strengthened by anthropological evidence, which bears testimony to the prevalence of communal (tribal) sacrifice in the earliest stage of social evolution.

As regards internal evidence in the Vedic literature one may cite several passages, indicating the tribal functioning of the people not only in worldly life[4] but also its reflection in religious life. The kernel of the *Ṛg Veda* (namely BK II to VII) contains numerous passages, in which prayers are addressed to the gods in chorus by the worshippers. Since sacrifice in the Vedic period is indispensably accompanied by prayer,[5] there is no reason why it should not be of collective nature. In respect of sacrifice in general we may refer to two Ṛg Vedic passages, which indicate its tribal nature. According to one passage men kindle the signal of sacrifice and the race of men (*mānuṣo janaḥ*) invites Agni to the solemn rite.[6] Similarly (another passage states that the tribesmen dear to Indra (*priyaḥ janaḥ*) present oblations

1. *JAOS*, xix, 14ff.
2. Barth, *Religions of India*, p. 50.
3. Keith, *Religion and Philosophy of the Vedas*, p. 290.
4. This has been ably done by a host of scholars such as K.P. Jayaswal, R.C. Majumdar, N.C. Bandyopadhaya and U.N. Ghoshal in their pioneer works on communal life in ancient India.
5. P.S. Deshmukh, *Religion in Vedic Literature*, p. 144.
6. *sajóśastvā divó náro yajñásya ketúm indhate yáddhasyá mā́nuṣo jánaḥ-sumnāyúr juhvé adhvaré.* *RV*, VI.2.3.

to him and are his friends.[1] These passages do not mention any individual sacrificer, and it is obvious that the word *jana* used in them stands for the tribe or the clan. At several places in the *Ṛg Veda* the word *yajamāna* is used in plural, which suggests that more than one sacrificer participated in some religious rites. In one passage Sarasvatī is requested to give food and wealth to the "present sacrificers"[2].

With regard to specific Vedic sacrifices it may be pointed out that the domestic *gṛhya* rites are of a strictly private nature, but of that there is hardly any trace in the earliest collection of hymns. Most Vedic sacrifices of later times provide for only one *yajamāna*, although some stipulate for more than one priest. Nevertheless, the *sattra* sacrifice, which was not conducted by one *yajamāna* but several and in which the merit of performance belonged collectively to them,[3] may be regarded as a clear and specific case of the prevalence of collective (tribal) sacrifice during the Vedic period. In the opinion of Tilak the *sattras* are "the oldest of the Vedic sacrifices"[4].

Although no description of the *sattra* is given in the early Vedic literature, what we know about it from later sources seems to confirm the opinion of Tilak. First, there are no separate priests but the *yajamānas* themselves act as priests.[5] This betokens an early stage of social development when the division of labour had not given rise to a separate class of priests. Secondly, the generally prevalent view about the sacrificers seems to be that only members of the same *gotra* (clan) could perform this sacrifice.[6] This furnishes a clear example of the tribal sacrifices, which are known to have been practised among primitive tribes. Thirdly, the term *sattra* in its different forms occurs over fifty times in the Ṛg Veda, and according to Tilak its meaning is *yajña*. The primitive character of the *sattra* gives no ground for doubting its antiquity. Had it been a priestly inven-

1. *RV*, VII.20.8.
2. *RV*, X.17.9.
3. Keith, op. cit., pp. 290. 349. S.A. Dange has brought to bear a new point of view on the analysis of the communal characteristics of the *sattra* in his book *India from Primitive Communism to Slavery*, pp. 41-43.
4. B.G. Tilak, *The Arctic Home in the Vedas*, p. 193.
5. *Jaimini Pūrvamīmāṃsāsūtra*. X.6.45-60.
6. The view of the ancient ritualists, *i.e.* Gāṇagāri, Āśvalāyana and Jaimini are quoted in Kane, *History of Dharmaśāstra*, ii, 1241.

tion of later times it would have provided some measure either to fill the pockets of the priests at the cost of the lay sacrificers or to increase their social pre-eminence, but of such developments there is no indication in this sacrifice.[1]

Curiously enough the *sattra*, which is noted for its collective (tribal) character and antiquity, escaped the notice of Bloomfield. He, however, suspects that there may be something of either communal or national worship hidden away in the folds of the horse sacrifice.[2] We may add that an examination of some ceremonies of the *vājapeya* and *rājasūya* sacrifices would also bear out his suspicion. Thus in the chariot-race ceremony of the former, and in the cattle-raid and dice-playing ceremonies of the latter, the king (sacrificer) participates as one of the numerous competitors, and in one case there is clear evidence of competitors being described as clansmen.[3] These ceremonies clearly betray elements of communal functioning in these sacrifices. In the context of these traces of communal sacrifice it would be unfair to dismiss Hillebrandt's proofs for the existence of tribal sacrifices in the Vedic period as a "poor substitute for the evidence which should be forthcoming"[4]. An important work on this line has been done by B.N. Datta, who, on the basis of the analysis of the Ṛg Vedic hymns composed by the *ṛṣis* of different clans in honour of different deities, concludes that originally a particular tribe or clan was the votary of a special god.[5] This is a very strong proof of the existence of the tribal or collective sacrifice in the earliest period. Hence Bloomfield's theory regarding the absence of collective sacrifices during the Vedic period is undoubtedly open to question.

Above all, as shown previously, in the large mass of the occurrences of the term *vidatha* it is not the individual who aspires for brave sons and wealth but a number of people assembled together. Lastly, the meaning of patriarchal house assigned to this term by Bloomfield runs counter to its interpretations given in the lexicons. The *Nighaṇṭu* explains it as sacrifice and the

1. Ghoshal, op. cit., p. 3.
2. *JAOS*, xlviii, 200.
3. Infra, Ch. XII.
4. Keith, op. cit., p. 290.
5. B.N. Datta, *Dialectics of Hindu Ritualism*, i, pp. 110-14.

Nirukta as both sacrifice and assembly,[1] but none interprets it in the sense of house.

In conclusion it may be stated that there is evidence of both communal and tribal life, religious and worldly, as well as patriarchal family life in the early Vedic period. The institution of the *vidatha*, however, seems to be in tune with the former type of life. The use of words in the *Ṛg Veda* does not supply much direct proof of strictly monogamous patriarchal family life. The term *kula*, which indicates such a life, is not used at all in the *Ṛg Veda*; the term *kulapā* in the sense of family head is used only once. Although *gṛha* or household is used nearly 90 times, the terms for tribe, namely, *jana* and *viś*, are mentioned there respectively about 275 and 171 times. This can be taken as sufficient proof of the importance of the tribal and communal life during the early Vedic period. And it is probably this aspect of life which manifests itself in its manifold ramifications in the *vidatha*.

Similarly it may not be quite correct to exaggerate the fact that the *vidatha* was a council of the wise or a spiritual body. There are, of course, some references to this aspect. We learn that there existed in heaven the synods (*vidathas*) of the wise.[2] It is not known whether the term *vidathya*, like *sabheya*, was used as a title of distinction.[3] But one or two stray references are not adequate to establish the general nature of the *vidatha* as the council of the wise. It is far more probable is that it was a popular assembly in the beginning, but in course of time it came to be confined to a few people, and its membership, like that of the Anglo-Saxon national council Witenagemot, came to be regarded as a mark of distinction.

An important point for consideration is whether the rājanyas and brāhmaṇas, who tended to establish themselves as the ruling class in the period of the later Saṃhitas and Brāhmaṇas, attended the *vidatha*. References suggest the presence of the priest generally called the *hotṛ*, but priests or brāhmaṇas as a class are not associated with this institution. Although the people present in the *vidatha* address Indra and Varuṇa as rājan, there is no refe-

1. *Nirukta*, IX.3; *Nighaṇṭu*, III.17.
2. *RV*, III.1.2.
3. *sādanyàṃ vidathyàṃ sabhéyaṃ pitṛśrávaṇaṃ yó dádāśadasmai*, *RV*, I.91. 20.

rence to the presence of rājans in that assembly. In one passage the term *vidathya* is applied to the *samrāṭ* or the great king, which shows that the chief also attended the *vidatha*.[1] In another passage we find the use of the term "king in the assembly" (*vidatheṣu saṁrāṭ*).[2] But the rājanyas or brāhmaṇas hardly act as members of the *vidatha*, as they do in the case of the *sabhā* and *samiti*. Ludwig has made several convincing citations to prove the high social status of the members of the *sabhā*. On the basis of *RV*, X.97.6. Ghoshal suggests that the rājas (princes) were the most distinguished members of the *samiti*, which evidently contained also a popular element.[3] But it is difficult to accept the view that *vidatha* primarily means the assembly, especially of the *maghavans* (rich men) and brāhmaṇas.[4] In interpreting *RV*, II.27.12 Zimmer takes the *vidatha* to be a smaller assembly than the *samiti*, which may give the impression that it was aristocratic in nature. There is no doubt that the passage in question refers to some rich and munificent people, riding on chariots, attending the *vidatha*, which may suggest the beginnings of social differentiation. Besides, neither the passage cited above throws any light on the relative numerical strength of the *samiti* and the *vidatha* nor is this discussed anywhere else in the Vedic literature. Indeed there is more proof of the rise of aristocratic elements in the case of the *sabhā* and *samiti*, particularly in that of the former, than in the case of the *vidatha*. Hence if any hypothesis can be built on negative evidence, we may suggest that the early *vidatha* was probably a typical institution of the period when the tribe had not broken into classes such as brāhmaṇas and kṣatriyas.

In the light of what has been stated above it may be of some interest to examine the problem of the antiquity of the *vidatha* in relation to two other Vedic institutions, the *sabhā* and *samiti*. The primitive character of the *vidatha* is evident from the undifferentiated nature of its functions. That nature it shares with both the Vedic assemblies. What makes it more primitive is the distributive functions or common consumption of the produces, which presupposes common efforts to collect or produce food.

1. *RV*, IV.21.2.
2. *RV*, III.55.7.
3. Ghoshal, *History of Hindu Public Life*, Pt. I, p.17.
4. Ludwig quoted in *VI*, ii, 296.

This, according to the evidence of anthropology, can be found only in the most primitive tribal organisation. Secondly, the participation of woman in its deliberations places it earlier in point of time than the other Vedic institutions. Women are generally more important than men in the pre-plough agricultural stage, especially in the horticultural stage. Thirdly, the absence of any clear and definite evidence of class distinctions in the *vidatha* vouches for its antiquity. Lastly, we may also consider the bearing of comparative philology on this problem. The term *sabhā* has its parallel in some Indo-European languages, so also the term *vidatha* has its equivalent in Gothic, an important Indo-European language. Although its parallel does not find place in any of the dictionaries, according to the rules of philology the term *vidatha* can be reduced to the Gothic word *vitoth*, which means law.[1] It may be noted that both these words can be derived from the root '*vid*'[2]. We may add that in the opinion of Oldenberg the term *vidatha* means ordinance, and according to Roth it means order.[3] It is not surprising that its deliberative functions should invest it with the meaning of law.

Thus a consideration of the nature of the composition and functions of the *vidatha* and the existence of its corresponding equivalent in Gothic tend to support the hypothesis that the *vidatha* was the earliest collective institution of the Indo-Āryans. Since some of its features, the association of woman and distributive functions, are not prominent in the early assemblies of the Indo-European peoples, the *vidatha* may have been a common collective organisation of the speakers of the Indo-European language before they branched off into different subdivisions. At any rate it seems to have been the oldest Indo-Āryan kin-based assembly.

A study of all the available references reveals that the *vidatha* was the earliest folk assembly of the Indo-Āryans attended by both men and women, performing all kinds of functions, economic, military, religious and social. It answered the needs of a primitive society which hardly knew division of labour or domination of man over woman, and which probably shared its

1. August Fick, *Indogermanischen Wörterbuch*, p. 189. I have consulted S.K. Chatterjee and T. Chaudhury on this point.
2. August Fick, *Indogermanischen Wörterbuch*, p. 189.
3. Quoted in *VI*, ii.296.

subsistence in common. It seems that the keystone of the *vidatha* system was co-operation. Tribesmen gathered in this assembly fought together, sang together, prayed together, played together and deliberated together without any discrimination of sex. We find hints at the beginnings of social differentiation, but the position of the chief seems to be elective. The *vidatha* reminds us of Morgan's view of the council of the gens, which was "the great feature of ancient society, Asiatic, European, and American from the institution of the gens in savagery to civilization. It was the instrument of government as well as the supreme authority over the gens, the tribe and the confederacy."[1]

1. Lewis H. Morgan, op. cit., pp. 84-5. For different views on the subject see Altekar, *State and Government in Ancient India* (1958), p. 141, fn. 1; J.P. Sharma, "The question of the Vidatha in Vedic India", *JRAS* 1965, Pts. 1 and 2, pp. 43-56; and J.W. Spellman, *Political Theory of Ancient India*, p. 96.

CHAPTER VIII

SABHĀ AND SAMITI

(I) *Sabhā*

The term *sabhā* is mentioned eight times in the *Ṛg Veda* and denotes both the people in conclave and the hall which was the venue of their meeting. In the second sense it is also used in later texts. The collections of the *Yajus* speak of sins being committed in the village, the forest or the *sabhā*,[1] which evidently appears here in the sense of some place. We also hear of the *sabhāpāla*,[2] who represents the guardian of the assembly hall.

Who constituted the *sabhā*? The term *sabheya* applied to the *vipra*[3] indicates that when it was convened for administrative purposes, it was a gathering of the elect, namely of the brāhmaṇas and the elders. One late Ṛg Vedic reference[4] speaks of woman as *sabhāvatī*, worthy of going to the *sabhā*, which shows that woman members attended this body.

Since the practice obtained in only very primitive assemblies the association of woman with the *sabhā* indicates its greater antiquity, which is also suggested by the fact that in contrast to the term *samiti* the term *sabhā* has several corresponding words in Indo-European languages. Perhaps Hopkins first pointed out the antiquity of the *sabhā* and compared it with the German *sippe*.[5] It has been now established that the word *sabhā* (cf. Indo-European *s(u)ebho*) is derived from a root closely associated with Old European *sub(b)*, Old High German *sipp(e)a*, Gothic *sibja*, and Mid German *sippe*—all meaning an association of the kin, tribe, family or the clan. It is rightly suggested by Bandyopadhaya that probably the early *sabhās* in India also were of the same type.[6] In other words, they were kin-based assemblies. The popular and primitive character of the *sabhā* is also betrayed by the homely nature of its functions. Like a primitive assembly

1. *VS*, III.45, XX.17.
2. *TB*, III.7.4.5-6.
3. *RV*, II.24.13.
4. I.167.3.
5. "Position of the Ruling Caste etc.", *JAOS*, xiii. 148.
6. *Development of Hindu Polity and Political Theories*, p. 110.

which does not know of any differentiation of functions, members of the *sabhā* debated over the domestication of cattle, played dice and offered prayers and sacrifices.

But subsequently the *sabhā* came to assume a mainly patriarchal and aristocratic character. Woman attended it in the earlier period, but the practice stopped in later Vedic times.[1] In connection with the Draupadī episode reference is made to the immemorial custom according to which women do not attend the *sabhā*. The very term came to mean a body of men shining together, which suggests that those who sat on it were supposed to be men of distinction. Several passages are cited by Ludwig to prove the high social status of members of the *sabhā*. One Ṛg Vedic passage refers to the votaries of Indra, who are rich in horses, chariots and kine, and who receive wealth and go to the *sabhā*,[2] a second refers to the prominence conferred on the member of the *sabhā* (*sabhāsada*) by Yaśas,[3] and a third speaks of the assemblages (not in the context of the *sabhā*) of the well-born or *sujātāḥ*[4] around Agni; according to Sāyaṇa these include priests and their clients but the text shows that they are *suvīras*. A few other references are cited by Bandyopadhaya. For instance, the *Atharva Veda* states that "princes come together" presumably to make the assembly complete.[5] According to a passage of the *Ṛg Veda*,[6] worshippers ask for sons skilled in household affairs and prominent in the *sabhā* and sacrifice. The term used is *sabheya*, which means worthy of sitting on the *sabhā*. Another passage from the *Ṛg Veda* speaks of *sabheya vipras*, which shows that the *sabhā* was attended by priests. So even the early Vedic texts do not have much to support the clan character of the *sabhā*; on the other hand they reflect the presence of people of high social rank. Men of learning, bearing, and character made their mark here, and were, therefore, called *sabheya* and *sabhāsaha*. Speeches worthy of the body are referred to in several passages of the *Ṛg Veda*.[7] The *Śatapatha Brāhmaṇa* speaks of Soma as

1. *VI*, ii, 427.
2. VIII.4.9.
3. X.71.10.
4. VII.1.4.
5. XIX. 57.2.
6. I.91.20.
7. II.24.13.

an overlord holding a court to which under-kings are flocking together. This shows that the royal court was attended by chiefs in later Vedic times. It is suggested that it was attended by the elders or fathers,[1] although this is not supported by any passage from Vedic literature.

The original, clan character of the *sabhā* was undermined in the age of the *Ṛg Veda*. It may have been a clan assembly in the period when there were no developed classes, not much distinction between the rich and the poor and no stability in the office of the chief. But as economic inequalities and social classes developed and as the king emerged to be the principal factor in the political system of the day, his person came to be associated with men of position and the elders, whose counsel commanded weight and authority with the community.[2] Those who possessed cows, horse and chariots constituted the dominant group, standing over dispossessed and impoverished fellow tribesmen who could not sit on the *sabhā*. Evidently power belonged to the horse- and chariot-owning aristocracy, whose members made up the *sabhā*. "These formed his advisory body, and the king came to be dependent on their advice and counsel. The evolution of this body was similar to that of the council of chiefs among the Teutons, to the Senate among the Romans and the Witanagemut among the Anglo-Saxons."[3]

The earliest references do not give prominence to the political character of the *sabhā*. On the other hand, a passage from the *Ṛg Veda* speaks of the *sabhā* as a dicing and gambling assembly.[4] If a later tradition be accepted as a guide, the *sabhā* was also used for popular amusements such as dancing and music. This is natural because primitive people do not make any distinction between sport, politics and religion. The *sabhā* was also associated with popular practices of witchcraft and magic. For example it is said in one of the passages from the *Atharva Veda*[5]: "What witchcraft they have made for that in the *sabhā*, I take that back again."

The *sabhā* discussed pastoral affairs. Cattle being one of the

1. Jayaswal, *Hindu Polity* (1924), p. 18.
2. Bandyopadhaya, op. cit., p. 113.
3. Ibid.
4. X.34.6.
5. V.31.6.

main sources of the livelihood of the people, it delighted in dwelling on the excellences of the kine.[1] People expressed their anxiety for the fattening of the lean cattle. They showered praises upon the kine and recalled their vigour with gusto in the meeting.[2]

Religious activities were not altogether absent in the *sabhā*. Its members invoked Indra to protect the *sabhā* and the *sabhāsads*. When this body met, a sacrifice was offered on behalf of the assembly, the fire used being called *sabhya*.

The *sabhā* performed political and administrative functions. Several references show that the *sabhā* exercised judicial functions, a fact which has been stressed by several writers. A late passage from the *Ṛg Veda* has been taken to represent *sabhā* as a body which removes the stain attaching to a person by means of accusation.[3] In the *puruṣamedha* sacrifice the *sabhācara* is dedicated as a victim to Dharma. Dharma means justice, and hence the authors of the *Vedic Index* see in *sabhācara* a member of the law-court, perhaps as one of those who sit to decide cases.[4] They also take *sabhāsad* to refer to the assessors who decided legal cases in the assembly. They further remark: "It is also possible that the *sabhāsads*, perhaps the heads of the families, were expected to be present at the *sabhā* oftener than the ordinary man; the meetings of the assembly for justice may have been more frequent than for general discussion and decision." They point out that the judicial functions of the *sabhā* were exercised not by the whole assembly but by a standing committee of the same.[5] Further evidence of the *sabhā* acting as a judicial body has been adduced by Jayaswal. The *sabhā* is called the 'trouble' and 'vehemence',[6] implying that it brought trouble to those who violated the law. Sometimes we hear of sharp repartees and offensive speeches, as thieves and criminals were dragged before the *sabhā*, and it seems that the richest and the most influential men had to submit to the decisions

1. *RV*, VI.28.6.
2. *AV*, IV.21.6.
3. *RV*, X.71.10.
4. *VI*, ii, 427-28.
5. *VI*, ii, 428.
6. *Pāraskara Gṛhyasūtra*, tr. H. Oldenberg, SBE, xxix, 362.

of their peers assembled here.[1] All such allusions clearly point to the judicial functions of the *sabhā*.

The *Maitryāṇi Saṃhitā* mentions *sabhā* in the sense of the court house of the village judge, the *grāmyavādin*, who is referred to in all the collections of the *Yajus*. Furthermore, in ancient mythology Yama, who was regarded as the king and judge of the departed, is described as having a *sabhā* and a number of *sabhāsads*. A passage from the *Atharva Veda* speaks of Yama's *sabhāsads* dividing among themselves 1/16 of hopes fulfilled or pious deeds[2] done on the earth. We have, therefore, no doubt that the *sabhā* had judicial functions to discharge, although most references to this aspect belong to later Vedic times. In any case Jayaswal's statement that the *sabhā* was a national judicature[3] is not sound, for there may have been several clan *sabhās*.

The judicial character of the *sabhā* continued even to later times. The Jātakas preserve an old memorial verse which says that the *sabhā* which has no good people (*santa*) is no *sabhā* and that the people who do not speak out the *dharma* (justice) are not good people, and that those who avoid personal sentiments and speak out the *dharma* are called the good people.[4] Moreover, the term *sabhāsad* in the sense of the assessor continued down to the times of the Dharmasūtras and Smṛtis, which lay down qualifications for their election. "In the legal literature, the *sabhā* is a court or judicial assembly presided over by the king as chief judge, and only the councillors, judges and police officers take part as men of authority over witnesses and accused."[5]

Both the earlier and the later references testify to the royal presence in the *sabhā*. Although some passages hint at the king's election by the *samiti*, we have no such reference to his election by the *sabhā*. But the king definitely attended the *sabhā* in Vedic times. Probably in earlier times he did not regularly preside over the *sabhā*, for the *sabhāpati*, lord of the assembly, is separately mentioned in the collections of the *Yajus*. But in later times he

1. *AV*, VII.12.3.
2. III.29.1.
3. Jayaswal, *Hindu Polity*, p. 18.
4. *Jāt.*, v.509 quoted and explained in Jayaswal, *Hindu Polity*, p. 19 and fn. 8.
5. Hopkins, *JAOS*, xiii, 148.

presided over its deliberations. Two references in the *Chāndogya Upaniṣad*[1] show that the king maintained his own *sabhā*. A notable piece of evidence is furnished by the *Śatapatha Brāhmaṇa*,[2] which describes Soma as an overlord holding a court, to which under-kings are flocking together. This reminds us of the numerous rājās sitting in the Licchavi assembly and claiming equality in rank and position.

The king considered the advice of the *sabhā* to be of supreme importance and could not possibly do without the support of its members, who spoke and hotly discussed proposals. This is clearly conveyed by the tenor and spirit of an *Atharva Veda* passage,[3] which, according to Bandyopadhaya, were presumably uttered by a king.

> "In concord may Prajāpati's two daughters *sabhā* and *samiti* protect me. May, everyman I meet, respect and aid me. Fair be my words, oh, my fathers, at the meetings.
>
> We know thy name, oh, *sabhā*, thy name is interchange of talk. Let all the company who join the *sabhā* agree with me.
>
> Of the men seated here, I make the splendour and lore my own. Indra make me conspicuous in all this gathered company."

If such a prayer was offered by the king it is manifest that he could not ignore the support of the *sabhā*, which was evidently a debating and deliberative body. Prayer was made in the *sabhā* for co-operation and for avoiding discord. It seems that the resolution passed by the *sabhā* was binding on all. The *Atharva Veda* calls this body *nariṣṭā*,[4] which Sāyaṇa explains as the resolution of the many that cannot be broken or violated. From this Jayaswal infers that the resolution of the *sabhā* was considered binding on all and inviolable.[5] But the term *nariṣṭā* has been taken to mean interchange of talk by Griffith and sports by Whitney.[6] However, Sāyaṇa's interpretation of the term is supported by the character of the assembly of the Homeric age. In

1. V.3.6; VIII.14.1.
2. *tasya rājānaḥ sabhāgāḥ*. III.3.3.14.
3. VII.12.1-3 (on the basis of Griffith's tr.).
4. *AV*, VII.12.2.
5. *Hindu Polity*, p. 19.
6. *HOS*, vii, 397.

Heroic Greece also the decision of the meeting was supreme and final. As Schomann says in his *Antiquities of Greece*, "whenever a matter is discussed that requires the co-operation of the people for its execution, Homer gives no indication of any means by which the people could be forced to it against their will."[1]

The nature of the *sabhā* in the epic traditions is discussed by Hopkins. He states: "In the Epic we find the *sabhā* to be an assembly of any sort. It may be a judicial one, a court of law; it may be a royal one, the king's court; it may be a social gathering for pleasure; and finally it may, in its older meaning, be a political assembly."[2] Although it is difficult to assign this material to any particular period, it suggests the continuity of the later Vedic tradition.

II. Samiti

Significantly the *samiti* appears in those portions of the *Ṛg Veda* which are considered to be the latest; all the six references we have come from Books I and X. This would mean that the *samiti* assumed importance only towards the end of the Ṛg Vedic period or even later. But with the *sabhā* the position is different; four references belong to the earlier portions of the *Ṛg Veda* and four to its later portions. So the *samiti* does not seem to be older than the *sabhā*. The two bodies are mentioned together four times in the *Atharva Veda*, and every time *sabhā* appears first and *samiti* next. This again suggests that the *sabhā* is older than the *samiti*. It is generally recognised that the early *samiti* was a folk assembly in which people of the tribe gathered for transacting tribal business. According to Ludwig the *samiti* was a more comprehensive conference including not only all the common people (*viṣāḥ*) but also the brāhmaṇas and the rich patrons known as *maghavan*. Possibly it was a general tribal assembly corresponding to the Agora of Homeric times. It met for discharging tribal business, and was presided over by the king, whose presence in the assembly is clearly indicated. The phrase "*samiti* of the Pañcālas" suggests that it was a tribal body. A reference in the *Atharva Veda* shows that women also attended it,[3] but this is not as clear as in regard to the *sabhā*.

1. Quoted in Engels, *Origin of the Family, Property and State* (Moscow ed.), p. 150.
2. *JAOS*, xiii, 148.
3. *AV*, VIII.10.5.

In later times the chiefs or the *rājans* also attended the *samiti*. They were the most distinguished members of this body, which evidently contained also popular elements.[1] Jayaswal thinks that the composition of the *samiti* was based on some principle of representation, and that the town and the village were probably represented by its *grāmaṇī*,[2] but the available evidence does not support it.

The functions of the *samiti* embraced several non-political activities. In the later Vedic period the *samiti* discussed philosophical questions. When Śvetaketu completed his education and claimed complete knowledge of the philosophic literature, he presented himself before the *samiti* of the Pañcālas. Pravāhaṇa Jaivali, the *rājanya* who presided over the assembly of the Pañcāla people, put to him five philosophic questions, none of which the presumptous young man could answer. At this Jaivali remarked "How could anybody who did not know these things say that he had been educated?"[3] Here we find the *samiti* acting as a gathering of scholars to test the knowledge of educated persons.

The *samiti* was concerned with religious ceremonies and prayers. Prayers were made for reaching common agreements there. It has also something to do with the offerings made to the gods. Thus in one of the hymns Agni is invoked in the *samiti* to enjoy the portions offered to him as oblations. It is also desired that the divine *samiti* may take place among the gods also.[4]

It is suggested by Bandyopadhaya[5] that the *samiti* had some military functions also, for commentators take the term to mean war or battle array. Yāska assigns to this word the meaning of battle,[6] which is also associated with it in classical literature.[7] Further, Sāyaṇa translates the word *samiti* by *yuddha* or *saṃgrāma*.[8] We may add that a reference in the *Atharva Veda* suggests that the *samiti* was identical with the tribal military

1. Ghoshal, *History of Public Life*, i, 17.
2. Op.cit., p. 15.
3. Br. *Ār. Up.*, *VI.* 2; *Chā. Up.*, V.3.
4. *AV*, XVIII.1.26.
5. P. 119.
6. *Nirukta*, II.107.
7. *Amara*, II.8.107.
8. Comm. on *RV*, X.97, 6 (what is physician among herbs, so is king in the *samiti*.)

unit *grāma* whose collection was called *saṃgrāma*.[1] The *samiti's* association with fighting is corroborated by a comparative study of the early Indo-European institutions. In the early Greek, Roman and German assemblies fighting and voting went side by side. The freemen of the Homeric age assembled in military array and decided important questions.[2] Tacitus states that the armed freemen of the German tribe assembled under their chief in a gathering and took decisions on peace and war. "If his sentiments displease them, they reject them with murmurs; if they are satisfied they brandish their spears. The most complimentary form of assent is to express approbation with their weapons."[3] The Roman assembly (comitia centuriata) definitely served as a military body. All this would imply the use of the *samiti* for military purposes.

But the political functions of the *samiti* are far more prominent. References suggest that the king was elected and re-elected by the *samiti*. Zimmer pointed out long ago that the election of the king in case of elective monarchies was carried only by the *viś* who assembled in the *samiti*. He thinks a passage in the *Ṛg Veda* (X.166.4) probably refers to an influential candidate for the throne, wishing to carry through his will in the teeth of the *samiti*. Zimmer infers the elective function of the *samiti* from a passage of the *Atharva Veda*[4] and is supported by Jayaswal. But the passage in question refers to the choosing of the king by his clansmen (*viśaḥ*). However, as Ghoshal thinks, there is nothing improbable in the election of the king in special cases by the *samiti*.

That it was the duty of the king to attend the meeting of the *samiti* is demonstrated by the use of the simile "like a true king going to the *samiti*." Several passages speak of kings having been present at meetings of the *samiti* and guiding its deliberations;[5] the kings of the Pañcālas or Videhas are prominent

1. The expression *ye saṃgrāmā samitayaḥ* (*AV*, XII.1.56) is taken to mean by Jayaswal the villages which assembled together in the *samitis* (*Hindu Polity*, p. 15), but his citation (ibid.) that Śaryāta Mānava wandered about with his *grāma* (*ŚB*, IV.1.5.2.7) clearly shows that in the beginning the *grāma* was not a settled unit but a clan band led by its chief.
2. Sidgwick, pp. 34-36 quoted in Bandyopadhaya, op. cit., p. 119.
3. *The Complete Works of Tacitus*, (tr., A.J. Church and W.J. Brodrib), Germany and its Tribes, Fragment 11 (p. 714).
4. III.4.2.
5. *RV*, IX.92.6; *Chā. Up*., V.3.

examples. The *samiti* was considered to be a great asset to the king. A king prays for the destruction of his rivals and claims to have mastered their thought (*citta*), their way of life (*vrata*), their *samiti*.[1] It was such an integral part of the early Vedic polity that a king without a *samiti* was not even to be thought of. What a forest was to the buffalo, what a pitcher was to the Soma juice, what a sacrificer was to the priest, so was the *samiti* to the king.[2] It was the main prop, without which the royal power could not be conceived to have subsisted. After coronation the priest utters a formula to establish the king on his throne and make the *samiti* loyal to him.[3] In a hymn the brāhmaṇa priest utters a curse on those kṣatriya rulers who destroy the cattle of brāhmaṇas. In that context he alludes to the catastrophe befalling the *rāṣṭra* or the kingdom of tyrannical kṣatriya rulers. It is said that the rain of Mitra-Varuṇa does not fall on him who wrongs the priest. The *samiti* (the popular gathering and hence loyalty) does not submit to him, and he wins no friend to do his will.[4]

Perhaps the clansmen (*viś*) who met in the assembly exercised control over the public land. A reference in the *Śatapatha Brāhmaṇa*[5] clearly points to the right of control possessed by the popular assembly. The passage says "To whomsoever the kṣatriya with the approval of the *viś* grants a settlement, that is properly given." According to Ghoshal it seems to mean that the king's gift of folk or public land with the consent of the people was in accordance with the tribal or customary law. Although this reference does not speak of the *samiti*, the clansmen evidently discussed the distribution of land when they met together in that body. "The Homeric evidence shows clearly that while power or privilege was in the gift of the king, land was in the gift of the people, who bestowed on their leaders, in reward for military service, estates which differed from others in that they were not assigned by lot to tribe or clan, but by special gift to an individual."[6]

1. *RV*, X.166.4.
2. *RV*, IX.92.6. Incidentally it shows that in the age of the *Ṛg Veda* buffaloes had not been domesticated by the newcomers.
3. *AV*, VI.88.3.
4. Ibid., V.19.15.
5. VII. 1.1.4.
6. Quoted in Thomson, *Aeschylus and Athens*, p. 40.

Both the *Ṛg Veda* and *Atharva Veda* stress the need for concord in the *samiti*. In a prayer for agreement in the assembly the poet says that the counsel or the *mantra* be common, the *samiti* be common, the *manas* or the mind be common and their thoughts (*citta*) be united. They strove to reach common agreement in the *samiti*.[1] Desire is expressed for the same *mantra*, the same *samiti* and the same *vrata*.[2] The insistence on unanimity is in accord with the practice obtaining in primitive communities. Thus "among the Iroquois the final decisions had to be unanimous, as was also the case with many of the decisions of the German mark communities."[3] This unanimity was however reached in the *samiti* after a good deal of debate. All the prayers and ceremonies, charms and counter-charms were directed to one end alone—to get the better of one's rival in debate, to induce the members present to accept his view of the case, to make his speech pleasant to members and to bend the minds of those who are of different views.[4]

The *samiti* was a great deliberative body. It carried on active discussions to achieve concord. "May deliberations be one-pointed; discussions to the same intent; and resolutions to the same effect. Oh Rājā Soma, sow the seeds of agreement among them,"[5] so says a prayer. The speaker wanted to prove himself "brilliant, not to be contradicted" in the *samiti*. Apparently the chief was expected to conduct the deliberations in such a manner so as to bring about a consensus of opinion in this assembly. Charms and spells were prescribed to secure concord and harmony.[6]

That the *samiti* enjoyed immense powers is made clear by the references. But it would be stretching the evidence to say that the *samiti* was a sovereign body from the constitutional point of view, as is stated by Jayaswal.[7] It may have wielded supreme powers in the earlier stage, but it did not retain them till the end of the Vedic period. The *samiti* cannot be taken as the exact

1. *RV*, X.191.3.
2. *AV*, VI.64.2 (Whitney's tr, p. 329).
3. Engels, *Origin of the Family, Property and State*, p. 132.
4. R.C. Majumdar, *Corporate Life in Ancient India*, pp. 125-26.
5. *AV*, VI.88.3.
6. Ibid., III.30.
7. *Hindu Polity*, pp. 12-13.

counterpart of the sovereign popular assembly described by Tacitus in the ancient German constitution.

III. Relation between the Sabhā and the Samiti

The distinction between the *sabhā* and the *samiti* cannot be made out with precision. In the beginning probably there was no difference between the structure and the functions of the two bodies, a fact which seems to be true of the relation between the Homeric assembly and the council. In the opinion of Vedic people both originated from the same source; they were daughters of Prajāpati. A passage from the *Atharva Veda* shows that both were mobile units, led by chiefs who kept moving along with their force.[1] According to Chadwick there is some evidence "to indicate that council and assembly were not very clearly distinguished."[2] Probably the only difference was that the *sabhā* performed judicial functions which the *samiti* did not. Later the *sabhā* tended to be a small, aristocratic body, and it became a court of the king, but the *samiti* passed out of existence. Jayaswal thinks that in later times the *pariṣad* took the place of the *samiti*. But this can be said of the *sabhā* as well. Again, in contrast with the *sabhā* the *samiti* also fought wars. However, both the bodies were not without some religious functions although these are not prominent. According to Chadwick tribal assemblies in Sweden appear to have been primarily religious gatherings for the great annual sacrifices at the chief national sanctuary. It is more than probable however that such was the case also with the assemblies of the ancient Germans.[3] This can be said to some extent of both the *sabhā* and the *samiti*.

Opinions differ regarding the nature of the *sabhā* and the *samiti*. According to Hillebrandt there can be no distinction between the *sabhā* and the *samiti*; the two indicate the same thing. But the *sabhā* and the *samiti* are clearly mentioned at least four times in the *Atharva Veda* as the two daughters of Prajāpati. According to Bloomfield[4] the *sabhā* was the place of assembly which also served as a centre for social gathering. In his view the *sabhā* generally means a public assembly. Zimmer

1. *AV*, XV.9.
2. *The Heroic Age*, 384.
3. Ibid., p. 369.
4. *JAOS*, xix, 13, 18.

looks upon the *sabhā* as the village assembly. On this basis R.C. Majumdar takes it to be a local assembly in contrast with the *samiti* which he regards as the central assembly. But the king or the chief attended the *sabhā*, which appears to be more than a local clan assembly. Further in several collections of the *Yajus* the *sabhā* is mentioned along with the village and *araṇya*.[1] If that be so it can be as well equated with *araṇya* and can be described as an assembly of the forest.

The commonly accepted view about the mutual relation of these two Vedic institutions is one initiated by Ludwig. According to him the *samiti* was the assembly of the whole people, and the *sabhā* was an analogue of the Homeric council of elders. The latter was a select body to which great men of the tribe (*maghavan*) alone would go to take counsel with the king. Jayaswal practically concurs with this opinion. He states that the *sabhā* was also a popular body, but it was "the standing and stationary body of selected men working under the authority of the *samiti*." N.C. Bandyopadhaya also thinks more or less on the same lines, but Ghoshal holds that like the *samiti* the *sabhā* was also a folk assembly. In our opinion the *sabhā* did not retain its kin-ordered, popular character throughout the Vedic age. It may have been a tribal, popular body at some stage in the beginning, but it became an aristocratic, non-tribal body later. However the *samiti* retained its popular character even in later Vedic times.

1. *VI*, II.426, fn. 4.

CHAPTER IX

THE VEDIC GAṆA AND THE ORIGIN OF THE POST-VEDIC REPUBLICS

K.P. Jayaswal, who did pioneer work in bringing the ancient Indian republics to prominent notice in the framework of Indian history writing, observed the following about their origin: "The hymns of the *Ṛik* and *Atharvan*, the view of the *Mahābhārata* and the tradition which Megasthenes heard in India in the 4th century B.C., all point to the fact that republican form of government in India came *long after monarchy*, and *after the early Vedic* age."[1]

Gaṇa, the technical word for the republic, is found at forty-six places in the *Ṛg Veda*, at nine places in the *Atharva Veda*, and at several places in the Brāhmaṇas. In most cases it has been interpreted in the sense of "assembly" or "troops". For a few years after 1910 there raged a controversy as to the meaning of this term. In explaining the phrase *Mālava gaṇa*, Fleet translated it as tribe. Jayaswal translated it as an assembly or government by assembly and was supported by F.W. Thomas. But in the chronological order both the interpretations may be correct. It may be noted that in Vedic texts the Maruts are repeatedly described as a *gaṇa*.[2] Since they were the sons of Rudra, their *gaṇa* in this sense was a clan unit. Later this meaning tended to be obsolete. In the *Mālava gaṇa* the term Mālava did not indicate all the people of the Mālava state, and the same was the case with the Kṣudrakas.[3] Patañjali states that the slaves and serfs of the Mālavas and the Kṣudrakas should not be known as *Mālavya* and *Kṣaudrakya*, but these terms should be applied to only the children of tribesmen, presumably with full rights.[4] This is a clear indication that the Mālava and Kṣudraka

1. *Hindu Polity*, p. 23; italics ours.
2. *RV*, I.64,12; V.52.13-4; 53.10; 56.1; 58.1-2; VI.16.24; X.36.7; 77.1; III.32.2; VII.58.1; IX.96,17; *AV*, XIII.4.8; IV.13: 4; *ŚB*, V.4.3.17.
3. *Kāśikā* on *Pāṇini*, V.3.114.
4. *idaṃ tarhi kṣaudrakāṇāmapatyaṃ mālavānāmapatyaṃ ityatrāpi prāpnoti kṣaudrakyo mālavya iti. naitat teṣāṃ dāse vā bhavati karmakare vā.* Patañjali on *Pāṇini*. IV.1.168.

republics were based on slavery and serfdom. Altogether the two references imply that the slaves and serfs of these republics corresponded to the vaiśyas and śūdras. It is further known that slaves and hired agricultural labourers in the republican states of the Mallas and Koliyas were excluded from the exercise of political power, which was monopolised by the clan chiefs. Such a sharp class distinction is not to be found in the tribal *gaṇa* of the Vedic age.

A study of the references to the *gaṇa* in early and later Vedic literature would show that it was a sort of gentile organization, chiefly of the Indo-Āryans. It is incorrect to state that the Latin *gens*, which was a group of families descended in the male line from a common ancestor, and the Greek *genos*, are the Indo-European equivalents for the Sanskrit *gaṇa*.[1] The term *gaṇa* cannot be derived from the root *jan* which means to beget. It comes from the root *gaṇ* which means to count. Although literally the term *gaṇa* does not mean a tribe but an artificial collection of people not necessarily belonging to the same tribe, it appears that in most cases in the Vedic literature this term is used in the sense of a tribal or clan solidarity.

The tribal character of the Vedic *gaṇa* is evident from what we know about the Maruts. They are described as sons of Rudra numbering either forty-nine[2] or sixty-three divided into seven groups, each consisting of nine.[3] There are several references to the *gaṇas* of the Devas in Vedic literature.[4] The Purāṇic and epic literature, which records our earliest traditional history, makes copious allusions to the *gaṇas* of gods and demons. It is needless to add that they were nothing but the reflections of the *gaṇa* organization existing in human society. In every case members of the *gaṇa* are represented as having the same ancestor. It is noteworthy that several of the *gaṇas* mentioned in these traditions bear metronymics. For instance, there existed the *gaṇa* of the Ādityas descended from Aditi.[5] Further, references in the *Mahābhārata* relating to the exploits of Skanda or Kārttikeya

1. S.A. Dange, *India from Primitive Communism to Slavery*, p. 61.
2. *ekonapañcāśanmaruto vibhaktā api gaṇarūpeṇaiva vartante. Tāṇḍya Mahābrāhmaṇa*, XIX.14.2.
3. *ŚB*, II.5.1.12; *RV*, VIII.96.9; *TB*, I.6.2.3.
4. *gaṇáṃdevā́nāṃ ṛbhavaḥ suhastāḥ. RV*, IV.35.3; *TB*, II.8.6.4; *ŚB*, XIII. 2.8.4.
5. *Ādi Parva*, 60.36-39.

inform us that he went to fight against the Daityas accompanied by seven *gaṇas* of mothers.[1] At another place, in a section on the eulogy of his mothers, we come across the names of over a hundred mothers who form a number of *gaṇas*.[2] The mythical references to their role in the destruction of the *gaṇas* of enemies indicate their fighting character.[3] It would not be correct to take mothers in the literal sense of the term. Obviously they stand for adult women who could take part in the battle. Such a tradition is found among the Oraons, who hold a festival to commemorate an event in which their women drove out the enemy. The idea that only men can fight is so deeply embedded in our minds that only with great effort can we conceive of military assemblies of women, who accompanied Skanda in his march against the Daityas. The earliest division of labour known to prehistory is on the basis of sex, in which cattle breeding, hunting and fighting fell to the share of man, and cooking and pre-plough agriculture to that of woman. The epic myth perhaps refers to the horticulturist stage of society, when women were more important than men. Although it does not record a historical fact, such a myth could not have been possibly conceived without some basis in the life of early times. Skanda, with whom the women *gaṇas* are associated, may have been a later god, but the story of the fight between Devas and Asuras is as old as the Vedic period. Moreover, although not forming a part of the main narrative, these references seem to have recorded the old traditions, and are not included in the didactic sections of the epic. All this may lead us to suppose that women were also associated with the Vedic *gaṇa*, although no direct proof exists in the Vedic literature. There are seven references in early Vedic texts to the association of woman with the *vidatha*,[4] but none in the case of the *gaṇa*.

There is no doubt that the tribal *gaṇa* acted also as an assembly. Griffith translates this term at several places in the *Ṛg Veda* as an assembly of gods or men. The Vedic references are

1. *saptamātṛgaṇāścaiva samājagmurviśāmpate*...*Śalya Parva* (Kumbakonam edn.), 45.29; 47.33-34.
2. *śṛṇu mātṛgaṇān rājankumārānucarānimān, kirtyamānān mayā vīra sapatnagaṇasūdanān. yaśasvinīnāṃ mātṛīnāṃ śṛṇu nāmāni bhārata, yābhirvyaptāstrayo lokā kalyāṇibhiścabhāgaśaḥ.* Critical Edn., IX.45.1-2 ff.
3. Ibid.
4. Supra, pp. 88-89.

silent on the deliberative aspect of the *gaṇa* which can be inferred from a Purāṇic reference. On one occasion the sages assembled on the Meru mountains passed a resolution (*samaya*), as a result of which all the sages with their *gaṇa* assembled for the transaction of some business.[1] This might suggest that the resolution had been adopted earlier by a *gaṇa* of sages, although the term *gaṇa* is not mentioned in that connection.

In Roman assemblies fighting and voting went together. That may have been the case with the *gaṇa*; to its military character there are numerous references. The *Ṛk* and *Atharvan* collections repeatedly mention the strong and vigorous *gaṇas* of Maruts in the sense of the army and troops,[2] at times under the command of the Sun or Indra.[3] Heroes are described as marching in *gaṇas* or companies.[4] The troops of Maruts are called to the rescue of man.[5] The *gaṇas* seem to have been well equipped with swift steeds and well provided with weapons.[6] It seems that their equipment consisted of bows, arrows and quivers.[7] What is known about the relations between primitive tribes suggests that these tribal republics were always hostile to one another and in a perpetual state of warfare. We learn, for example, that Bṛhaspati destroyed the obstructive Vala with the loud-shouting *gaṇa* and drove away the cattle. At another place Pūṣan is invoked to lead the *gaṇa* of men that longs for kine to win the spoil.[8] On the analogy of the gentile organization of primitive and early peoples, the *gaṇa* appears to be a self-acting armed organization, every member of which bore arms. Since neither the *Ṛg Veda* nor the *Atharva Veda* restricts war to a nobility or its retainers,[9] every

1. *Vāyu P.* (ASS), 61.12-14. Unless specified otherwise, the BI edn. of the *Vāyu Purāṇa* has been used in this book.
2. *yúvā sá mā́ruto gaṇástveṣáratho ánedyaḥ, śubhaṃ yā́vā́pratiṣkutaḥ. RV*, V.61.13.
3. *AV*, XIII.4.8, *yā́ṃ ábhajo marúta indra sóme yé tvā́m ávardhannábhavan gaṇás te*...*RV*, III.35.9.
4. *ródasi ā́ vadatā gaṇaṣriyo nṛṣā́caḥ śūrāḥ śávasā́himanyavaḥ, ā́ bandhúreṣvamá tirná darśatā́ vidyúnná tasthau maruto ráthesu vaḥ. RV*, I.64.9.
5. *trā́yantāmimáṃ devā́strāyantāṃ marútāṃ gaṇā́ḥ. AV*, IV.13.4.
6. *ubhā́ sá várā prátyeti bhā́ti ca yádīm gaṇám bhájate suprayā́vabhiḥ. RV*, V. 44.12; VI.52.14.
7. *RV*, X.103.3; *AV*, XIX.13.4.
8. *imáṃ ca no gavéṣaṇaṃ sātáve siṣadho gaṇám. RV*, VI.56.5.
9. *VI*, ii, 251.

member of the popular assembly such as the *sabhā*, *samiti*, *vidatha* and *gaṇa* could take up arms. The remnant of such an organization is found later in the ten *āyudhajīvī saṅghas* of Pāṇini and four *vārtāśastropajīvī saṅghas* of Kauṭilya. The latter term probably indicated that these republics had not evolved permanent class divisions, in which only the ruling class possessed the power of arms as against the disarmed mass of the ruled class. Hence it would appear that the Vedic *gaṇa* was an armed organization of the whole clan or tribe.

The leader of the *gaṇa*, at one place known as *gaṇasya rājā*, is generally called *gaṇapati*. Indra[1], Marut[2], Bṛhaspati[3] and Brahmaṇaspati[4], particularly the last three, are repeatedly described as *gaṇapati*. At least in one reference in the *Ṛg Veda*, the leader of the *gaṇa* is given the title of *rājan*.[5] In the *Aitareya Brāhmaṇa* the king is invoked as *gaṇānāmpati*.[6] Brahmaṇaspati, who at several places is called *gaṇapati*, is also described as the supreme king of prayers.[7] The appellation of *rājan* for *gaṇapati* may suggest that gradually the latter transformed himself into the position of a chief. Whether the *gaṇapati* was selected by members of the *gaṇa* is nowhere indicated in the texts. The *vidatha* elected its priest, but there is no such reference in the case of the *gaṇa*.[8] Anthropological analogies and the practices of the Greek tribes strengthen the hypothesis that the *gaṇapati* was elected. Certainly there is no reference to the hereditary nature of his office. Clearly his most important function was to lead his band for the capture of cattle, which formed the chief spoils of war. It is stated that the *gaṇas* were always anxious to win wealth for themselves.[9]

The spoils captured by the members of the *gaṇa* were not directly appropriated by them in their individual capacity. It was

1. *RV*, X.113.9.
2. *TB*, III.11.4.2.
3. *gaṇā́nāṃ tvā gaṇápatiṃ havāmahe...jyeṣṭharā́jaṃ bráhmaṇāṃ brahmaṇaspata ā́ naḥ*. *RV*, II.23.1.
4. *AB*, I.21.
5. *RV*, X.34.12.
6. *AB*, IX.6.
7. *RV*, II.23.1.
8. Supra, p. 93.
9. *yácciddhí te gaṇā́ imé chadáyanti madháttaye, pári cidváṣṭayo dadhurdádato rā́dho áhrayaṃ sújāte aśvasūnṛte*. *RV*, V.79.5.

obligatory on them to surrender all such booty to their chief. A person speaks to the great captain of the mighty army who was the *gaṇa's* royal leader in these words: "To him I show my ten extended fingers. I speak the truth. No wealth am I withholding."[1] It seems that the *gaṇapati* distributed equal shares among them. This is suggested by the following passage of the *Atharva Veda* included according to Sāyaṇa in the *gaṇakarmāṇi* (duties of the *gaṇa*). "Having superiors (*jyāsvant*), intentful, be ye not divided, accomplishing together, moving on with joint labour (*sadhura*); come hither speaking what is agreeable to one another. I make you united (*sadhrīcīna*), like-minded. Your drinking (*prapā*) be the same, in common your share of food; in the same harness (*yoktra*) do I join (*yuj*) you together; worship ye Agni united, like spokes about a nave."[2] If this is taken as evidence of what happened in a *gaṇa*, it implies common acquisition and distribution, as is found in other tribal societies. Evidently the tribesmen laboured together and shared their produce in common. We do not know whether the *gaṇapati* received any special share in booty, although such a share called 'geras' was given to the leader of early Greek tribes.[3] It is likely that by means of special shares the chief went on accumulating spoils of war till there was a qualitative change in the character of his office, making him into a hereditary *rājan*, ruling with the help of priests and nobles.

In the republics of the time of the Buddha there appears a well organized machinery consisting of *rājan*, *uparājan*, *senāpati*, *bhāṇḍāgārika*, etc. But the Vedic *gaṇa* does not know of any public officer except the *gaṇapati*. Whether this functionary received any other form of remuneration in addition to his share in the spoils of war is not clear. There is no mention of any form of compulsory taxes paid by the members of the *gaṇa* to its leader. The Marut *gaṇa* is invoked to accept voluntary offerings made by the worshippers.[4] The *Baudhāyana Gṛhyasūtra*, in its section on *baliharaṇam*, has a ritual regarding offerings. With the recitation of the formula *gaṇebhyaḥ svāhā* and

1. *yó vaḥ senānī́rmaható gaṇásya rā́jā vrā́tasya prathamó babhū́va, tásmai kṛṇomi ná dhánā ruṇadhmi daśā́hám prā́cīstádṛtám vadāmi.* *RV*, X.34.12.
2. *AV*, III.30.5-6 (Whitney's Translation). Bloomfield gives a slightly different translation. S.A. Dange draws attention to this passage (op. cit., p. 140).
3. George Thomson, *Studies in Ancient Greek Society*, pp. 329-33.
4. *áccha ṛṣe mā́rutaṃ gaṇáṃ dānā́ mitráṃ ná yaṣáṇā* *RV*, V.52.14.

gaṇapatibhyaḥ svāhā voluntary religious offerings are made to the *gaṇa* and its leader.[1] Similarly the Vedic phrase *gaṇānāṃ gaṇapatiṃ havāmahe* is proof of religious offerings made to the *gaṇapati*. Proceeding on the assumption that these rituals are past social practices put in a religious garb, it would appear that the *gaṇapati* in human society received voluntary gifts out of love and affection for his leadership in war, a fact which is supported by the prevalence of a similar practice among primitive tribes. What was offered voluntarily to the *gaṇa* and its leader in the early period became a mandatory payment when the tribal *gaṇa* was transformed into a monarchy in the surplus producing agricultural stage.

The post-Vedic *gaṇas* are described as settled on a fixed territory, but the Ṛg Vedic *gaṇas* seem to be in a nomadic and migratory state, engaged in perpetual warfare for the possession of cattle. Perhaps the economic basis of the Ṛg Vedic *gaṇas* was the rearing of cattle, which constituted their chief form of wealth. It would thus appear that these *gaṇas* were not rooted in the soil of any particular territory but moved from place to place with their herds of cattle. There is no mention of the capture of agricultural produce or of land, which alone could ensure a stable economy. Later, in the *Śatapatha Brāhmaṇa*, the Maruts are described as peasants. Again, in the *Taittirīya Brāhmaṇa* Marut is described as grain, which is named *Māruta* after him.[2] Thus it seems that in the period represented by the Brāhmaṇas members of the *gaṇas* practised the art of cultivation.

References indicate that the *gaṇa* also served as a kind of religious assembly. At one place Agni is invoked not to fail its members, who pray and worship. He is further asked to bring all the gods so that they might give riches to the members of the *gaṇa*.[3]

There is also mention of drinking and singing in the *gaṇa*. The *gaṇa* of the Maruts is referred to as drinking heavily.[4] Indra is invited to drink *soma* in the assembly of gods.[5] Bṛhaspati is

1. II.8.9.
2. *māruta eṣa bhavati. annaṃ vai marutaḥ. TB*, 1.7.7.3.
3. *ágne yāhí dūtyàṃ mā́ riṣanyo devā́ṃ acchā brahmakṛ́tā gaṇéna...devā́n ratnadhéyāya víśvān. RV*, VII.9.5.
4. *ādityā́n mā́rútaṃ gaṇā́ṃ. prá vo bhriyanta índavo matsarā́ mādayṇávaḥ drapsā́ mádhvaścamūṣádaḥ. RV*, I.14.3.4.
5. *RV*, VI.41.1.

referred to as singing or providing songs for the *gaṇa*.[1] There are several references to the singing of Maruts. In one reference their *gaṇas* are asked to sing to Parjanya.[2] In another they are described as singing and drinking the *soma* juice in a rejoicing mood.[3] It is also stated that Soma enters the hearts of all the company who sing.[4] Again, worshippers are asked to begin the song seated in the *gaṇa*, and Indra is invoked to give strength for sacrifice to one who sings.[5] Probably from the singing function of the *gaṇa* the term *gaṇaka*, meaning one who is an expert in the knowledge of sound (*svaramaṇḍala*, etc.), is derived.[6] The term *gaṇikā* may have been derived from *gaṇaka*. The epic evidence for the existence of matriarchal *gaṇas* may suggest that in early times women also figured in the *gaṇa*, and hence came to be known as *gaṇikās* in later times. But dancing women, though unknown to the early *gaṇa*, are associated with the *gaṇarājya* of the Licchavis during the sixth century B.C.[7]

The Vedic *gaṇa* clearly shows the absence of class distinctions. Maruts, the typical example of the *gaṇa* society, are described as the *viśvaḥ* or people.[8] In later Vedic texts they are repeatedly described as peasants, whose *gaṇas* consist of troops of seven each.[9] Even the earliest reference shows that they are sixtythree in number, divided into nine *gaṇas* of seven each.[10] This grouping gives no indication of class divisions based on labour. The Purāṇic traditions refer to the *gaṇas* of kṣatriyas. We are told that the Dhārṣṭaka Kṣattra comprised a *gaṇa* of three thousand kṣatriyas,[11] and that Nābhāga owed his power to the backing of a thousand kṣatriyas.[12] Moreover, the kṣatriya clan of Haihayas

1. *sá suṣṭúbhā sá ṛ́kvatā gaṇéna valáṃ ruroja phaligáṃ rávena. RV*, IV.50.5.
2. *gaṇā́stvópa gāyantu mā́rutāḥ parjanyaghoṣíṇaḥ pṛ́thak. AV*, IV.15.4.
3. *ágne marúdbhiḥ śubháyabhirṛ́kvabhiḥ sómaṃ piba mandasānó gaṇaśribhiḥ. RV*, V.61.8.
4. *RV*, IX.32.3.
5. *RV*, VI.41.1.
6. *vīṇāvādakaṃ gaṇakaṃ gītāya. TB*, III.4.15.
7. Āmrapālī, the famous dancer in the Licchavi state, was courted by the rājās, and was so important as to serve as host to the Buddha.
8. *ŚB*, II.5.1.12.
9. Ibid., V.4.3.17.
10. *RV*, VIII.96.8 with the commentary of Sāyaṇa.
11. *Vāyu P.* (ASS), 88.4-5.
12. Ibid., 86.3.

consisted of five *gaṇas*.[1] All this might suggest that the *gaṇa* type of organization was peculiar to the kṣatriyas, but probably some Vedic clans were called kṣatriyas in later traditions because of their warlike character. At any rate it is clear that in Vedic times the same *gaṇa* did not consist of kṣatriyas and other elements. Therefore, in all probability, the Vedic *gaṇa* was not characterized by any *varṇa* distinction. If credence is given to the Purāṇic tradition, the period of the Vedic *gaṇa* may be taken as corresponding to the Kṛta age when the varṇa system did not exist. The *Śānti Parva* states that the members of the *gaṇa* are equal in terms of birth and family, but not in terms of bravery, wisdom and money.[2] In the tribal stage of society there could have been little inequality, particularly in respect of wealth, and hence equality by birth may have been the most significant factor in the early *gaṇa*. Later authorities define the *gaṇa* as a collection of families, of which there does not seem to be any indication in the early Vedic *gaṇa*. If the early Vedic *gaṇa* was a family, it was a large extended family amounting to a clan.

Whether the *gaṇa* was a pre-Āryan institution is open to question. Early traditions associate it with the Devas as well as the Asuras. The *Vāyu Purāṇa* describes and names the *gaṇas* of Devas.[3] The *Ādi Parva* enumerates six *gaṇas* of gods, namely, those of Rudras, Sādhyas, Maruts, Vasus, Ādityas and Guhyakas, prayers to whom emancipate mankind from all sins.[4] The Vedic association of the *gaṇa* with well-known Āryan gods such as Bṛhaspati, Indra (who is mentioned in a fourteenth century B.C. Mitanni inscription[5]), and especially Marut who is also mentioned as Maruttash[6] in a Kassite inscription of about the eighteenth century B.C., indicates that this form of kin-ordered organization obtained among the Āryans. On the other hand, many epic and

1. Ibid., 94.51-52.
2. *jātyā ca sadṛśāḥ sarve kulena sadṛśastathā na tu śauryeṇa buddhyā vā rūpa-dravyeṇa vā punaḥ. bhedāccaiva pramādācca nāmyante ripubhirgaṇaḥ... ŚP*, 1.8.30-31. It is difficult to accept the translation of Beng. edn. quoted by Jayaswal. The words *tu* and *punaḥ* connect these two verses and do not separate them, as has been done by K. M. Ganguly.
3. ii, 3.2-3.
4. *trayastriṃśata ityete devāsteśāmahaṃ tava, anvayaṃ sampravakṣyāmi pakṣaiśca kulato gaṇān. Ādi P.*, 60.36ff.
5. H.R. Hall, *The Ancient History of the Near East*, p. 201.
6. Ibid., p. 202, fn. 1.

Purāṇic references to this institution are associated with Śiva who is called *gaṇādhyakṣa*[1], with his son Skanda, with Bhūtas,[2] and above all with women. The *Vāyu Purāṇa* mentions the *gaṇas* of Yakṣas, Gandharvas, Kinnaras, Vidyādharas, who are described as the progeny of Kaśyapa.[3] We learn about the Saiṃhikeya *gaṇa* of Daityas who were ten thousand strong,[4] and the numerous *gaṇas* of Mlecchas who inhabited the various parts of Jambūdvīpa such as Aṅga, Śaṅkha and Varāha dvīpas.[5] All this may suggest that the *gaṇa* form of organization also prevailed among the non-Āryans. Absence of a parallel word in Indo-European languages may lend force to the hypothesis that it was typically an Indian institution unaffected by Āryan influences. In sharp contrast to the *vidatha*, which became obsolete both as an organization and as a term in the post-Vedic period, the *gaṇa* continued into post-Vedic times.

The study of ancient Indian institutions such as *sabhā*, *samiti*, etc. is vitiated by the attempt to concentrate on their purely political aspects divorced from their other dimensions. Since primitive institutions hardly admit of differentiation of functions, social and political, for a correct appraisal of their nature we need to examine their various aspects in interrelation with one another. Seen in this light, the Vedic *gaṇa* was probably another primitive tribal democracy combining in itself the military, distributive, religious and social activities of early man. Although there is no direct evidence of the election of the chief or the *gaṇapati*, it seems that there were no public officials, no taxes, no classes and no army apart from the *gaṇa* army. In other words, the Vedic *gaṇa* was primarily a tribal republic. By the end of the Ṛg Vedic period we come across tribal republics of other varieties. A passage[6], which refers to kings or chiefs sitting together in an assembly, has been rightly interpreted to imply that some tribes had no hereditary chief, but were governed

1. *Mbh.* (Kumbakonam edn.), X.7.8.
2. *Bhāgavata P.*, II.6.13; XII.10.14. The Purāṇic statement that Sagara destroyed the five *gaṇas* of Yavanas, Pāradas, Kāmbojas, Pahlavas and Śakas refers to a much later tradition.
3. *Vāyu P.*, ii. 8.11ff.
4. Ibid., 7.17-21.
5. Ibid., no. 477, App. quoted in Patil, *Cultural History from the Vāyu Purāṇa*, p. 174.
6. *RV*, X.97.6.

directly by the tribal council. As in some oligarchic clans, the title of the *rājā* was taken by all the great men of the tribe, who governed it through a folk-moot.[1] Accordingly Jayaswal's view that the republic came *after the early Vedic age* and *after monarchy*[2] can be true of some post-Vedic class divided republican states but not of the early tribal solidarities marked by a good deal of kin-based equality between its members. The tribal republic passed into the monarchical state, a trend supported by anthropological evidence.[3]

The first and nearest attempt at the classification of the types of government or chieftainship is found in the *Aitareya Brāhmaṇa*, where the terms *svarājya* and *vairājya* are used in the sense of power structures which did not have one-man rule. The regions which are credited with the two types of government[4] suggest that a good portion of India, namely West and North, was ruled by various types of chieftains or tribal 'democracies', which were transformed into or superseded by monarchies. Thus the two trans-Himalayan tribes,[5] Uttarakurus and Uttaramadras, are described as having a *vairājya* form of government,[6] but when they migrated to the Indian plains they established monarchies[7] or strong chiefdoms. Again, when monarchy or chiefdom was dissolved, it made way for an artificial republic. The record of this process seems to have been preserved in the tradition quoted by Arrian from Megasthenes, who states that the republican form of government was thrice established.[8] Although the Purāṇic traditions record the existence of *gaṇas*,

1. Basham, *Wonder That Was India*, p. 33.
2. Our italics.
3. "Among the most primitive races tribal authority is exercised almost universally in the democratic form of a general council, while governments representing the monarchic principles are almost entirely absent among peoples usually relegated to the lowest group. We regard this as a very remarkable fact concerning primitive social organization, and it has in most cases only been mentioned in passing in theoretical literature." G. Landtman, *The Origin of the Inequality of the Social Classes*, pp. 309-10, cf. pp. 310-16.
4. *AB*, VIII.14.
5. B.C. Law, *India as Described in Early Texts of Buddhism and Jainism*, p. 89.
6. *AB*, VIII.14.
7. B. C. Law, op. cit., pp. 89.93-96.
8. Arrian, IX, McCrindle, *India as Described by Megasthenes and Arrian*, p. 208.

they do not tell us anything about subsequent changes in their constitution. They refer to a *gaṇa* of a thousand kṣatriyas headed by Nābhāga, who might be identical with sage Nābhāka mentioned in the *Ṛg Veda.* But the descendants of Nābhāga are not mentioned by the Purāṇas. Patil argues that since the Nābhāgas were a republican tribe, the Purāṇas did not care to preserve their genealogy.[1] Nevertheless, if a reference in an inscription of Aśoka[2] is taken as referring to the Nābhāgas, it will appear that they continued to exist as a republican tribe for a long period. All this would suggest that the tribal republic was followed by monarchy and not *vice versa.*

The origin of the post-Vedic republics is discussed in a general way by D.R. Bhandarkar. On the basis of a passage of the *Bṛhadāraṇyaka Upaniṣad* along with the commentary of Sāyaṇācārya, referred to him by R.C. Majumdar, he argues that since "the crucial passage speaks of *gaṇas* only in the case of Vaiśyas and not of Brāhmaṇas, Kṣatriyas or Śūdras, it appears that we had commercial *gaṇas* (*i.e.* śreṇis) first among the Vaiśyas before there were political *gaṇas* among the Kṣatriyas."[3] He further states that just as the political *gaṇas* are divided into *kulas* or families, so also the commercial *gaṇas* are divided into *kulas*, as is known from the seals discovered at Bhiṭā and Basārh.[4] As has been shown earlier, the *gaṇa* was well-known in its political and social aspects as early as the Vedic period, when there was not even the faintest idea of its commercial character. Moreover, it is needless to add that in the beginning only the functions of agriculture (*kṛṣi*) and rearing of cattle (*paśupālana*) were assigned to the vaiśya; (*vāṇijya*) was a later development. Hence the hypothesis of Bhandarkar regarding the origin of the *gaṇa* has no basis in fact.

The real causes of the origin of the territorial, socially stratified republics of the post-Vedic period have to be sought in the widespread reaction against the pattern of life as evolved in the later Vedic period. On the social plane the new movement sought to do away with the growing class and sex distinctions, as well as expensive and superstitious religious practices involv-

1. *Cultural History from the Vāyu Purāṇa*, p. 53.
2. *R. E.* XIII.
3. D.R. Bhandarkar, *Carmichael Lectures*, 1918, pp. 169-70.
4. Ibid., p. 170.

ing the senseless destruction of cattle wealth which hampered agriculture. On the political plane it wanted to do away with the hereditary kingship or chiefdom based on brāhmaṇical ideology and denial of all rights to the masses of the people. For lack of a new programme, the leaders of the new movement modelled their ideals on the basis of the past tribal solidarities when there were no varṇa distinctions, no domination of the brāhmaṇas and kṣatriyas over the tribal masses and no coercive authority of the king depriving the overwhelming majority of the tribal peasants and others of the surplus and the right to the kin-based equality.

If we consider the brāhmaṇical and Buddhist traditions together, Videha and Vaiśālī would appear as the two main examples of monarchies transformed into republics. It is difficult to accept this inference because of the absence of signs of habitation in these two areas before 700 B.C. These may have been breakaway states from the parent stock,[1] which had occupied some other areas in earlier times. Deprived of power over peasants and share in their produce, some adventurous clan chiefs may have set up oligarchies. In early Vedic times they obtained a portion of the spoils of war and tributes collected from the non-Āryans, but when heads of the conquering clans settled down as permanent princes, claiming to receive all revenues from settled peasants, Āryans and non-Āryans, other members of the clan were denigraded and dispossessed. They naturally resented the situation in which one of them emerged as the sole recipient of taxes and the undisputed organiser of war. The leading members of the clan, therefore, demanded the right to collect taxes from peasants and the right to bear arms and maintain their army, howsoever small in size. The polity that emerged as a result of this skin conflict was of the old tribal military democracy type in form. In substance it was essentially oligarchical,[2] because in the Licchavi state the vast mass of the non-rājās, slaves, hired labourers, etc., had no place in the republican assembly.[3]

1. Romila Thapar, *A History of India* (Pelican) i, 50-51.
2. Ruben thinks that each member of the oligarchy was the proprietor of a landed estate (*Kunwar Mohammad Ashraf*, p. 23), but of real ownership the oligarchs show no consciousness nor do they give any evidence in action.
3. Apparently dispossessed people were excluded from Vedic assemblies, but their number was very small and social stratification had just started.

Jayaswal thinks that the religious *saṅghas* were created on the pattern of political *saṅghas*,[1] but both of them seem to have been created on the model of the kin-based *gaṇas*, which did not have class distinction. It seems to be particularly true of the early Jain religious order, which bears the same name *gaṇa*, with Mahāvīra as its *gaṇī* or leader, and nine among his prominent disciples as *gaṇadharas* or sectional leaders.[2] It was to recapture the past glory of kin-based equality in the simple tribal *gaṇas* that there arose the desire to overthrow the new forms of state and society. In doing so it was not possible to cancel the socio-political development of centuries at one stroke, and hence success was only partial. Kingship or strong chiefdom was dissolved and republics with small chiefs were set up, but the stratified patriarchal society, bureaucracy, taxation system and an army for the coercion of the people remained. The tribal republic, which probably guaranteed an equal share of food and equal rights to all its members, existed in the pastoral stage and perhaps in an agricultural economy which did not go much beyond the needs of subsistence. It could not be resurrected in its pristine glory in the age of the Buddha when the peasants made considerable surplus available because of the use of the iron ploughshare-based agriculture and the practice of paddy transplantation. The new edition of the old tribal collectives was the 'distorted' republics of the Licchavis, Śākyas, etc., with all the paraphernalia of monarchical state apparatus under the control of the kṣatriyas and the brāhmaṇas.[3]

1. K.P. Jayaswal, op.cit., p. 42.
2. Mrs. S. Stevenson, *The Heart of Jainism*, p. 61.
3. In the post-Vedic *saṅgha-gaṇa* the "Kṣatriya aristocracy ranked higher in the social scale than the Brāhmaṇas and the gahapatis, not to speak of inferior classes", Ghoshal, *Indian Culture*, xii, 6.

CHAPTER X

THE EARLY PARIṢAD

The nature of the later *pariṣad,* which is mentioned in the *Arthaśāstra,* Aśokan inscriptions and the Dharmaśāstras,[1] is fairly well-known, but our knowledge of the early *pariṣad* is deficient. We can, however, form some idea of it on the basis of references in the *Ṛg Veda*, the *Atharva Veda*, later Vedic literature and its frequent mention in the narrative portions of the *Mahābhārata* and the Purāṇas. Although the epic and Purāṇic evidence cannot be considered as reliable as the Vedic evidence, it cannot be altogether discarded.

In a passage occurring in the *Ṛg Veda* Indra is celebrated for destroying with his thunderbolt the *pariṣadas* (companions) of the Asuras who obstruct rain.[2] This suggests that under the leadership of Indra, the Āryans fought against the organised bands of the pre-Āryans. A reference from the later portion of the same text shows that the *pariṣadvāns* (associates) of god Vasu desired to slay the son of Nṛṣad.[3] These references indicate the primitive military character of the *pariṣad,* mentioned in the case of the Āryans as well as non-Āryans. Two other references throw some light on the nature of property, collectively owned by the members of this body. In a prayer, belonging to the early portion of the *Ṛg Veda* and reproduced by the *Atharva Veda*, the gods are described as "making us a conclave (*pariṣad*) rich in kine."[4] Sāyaṇa explains the terms *gavyaṃ pariṣadantaḥ* as *gosaṅgham*, and so Griffith translates it as a "herd of cattle". But since the term *gavyaṃ* occurs as the adjective of *pariṣad,* the correct meaning seems to be 'an assembly rich in kine'[4], a feature which is not uncommon to an early assembly. Another passage from the Ṛk collection states that the wealth of the foe belongs to the *pariṣad*, and, in that connection, it expresses the

1. K.P. Jayaswal, *Hindu Polity*, Chs. XXX and XXXI; R.K. Mookerji, *Aśoka*, p. 148; V.R.R. Dikshitar, *Mauryan Polity*, pp. 133-34; A.S. Altekar, *Source of Hindu Dharma*, Ch. VI.
2. *vívájreṇa pariṣádo jaghāna. RV*, III.33.7.
3. *RV*, X.61.13.
4. *gávyaṃ pariṣádanto agman. RV*, IV.2.17; *AV*, XVIII.3.22.

desire of the people to be "masters of permanent riches."[1] In other words the booty is not confined to the leader but claimed collectively by the whole group which he leads. All this would suggest that the *pariṣad* owned kine and spoils of war in common.

In the *Yajur Veda* the epithet *pariṣadya* applied to Agni may point to his presence in the *pariṣad*.[2] This is corroborated by a Purāṇic reference, in which Pariṣatpavamāna is the name of a descendant of Agni.[3] As in the case of the *vidatha*, the fire-god was supposed to grace the *pariṣad* with his presence. This indicates that among the Āryans the *pariṣad* also functioned as a religious assembly, in which they offered worship to Agni. A later Brāhmaṇa mentions *daivī pariṣad* (divine assembly) along with the *sabhā* and *saṃsad*,[4] which also mean assembly. Clearly the divine assembly was a reflection of the worldly assembly prevalent among the Āryans. This is counterbalanced, however, by another reference, in which Ahirbudhnya, a form of Rudra (and therefore probably pre-Āryan), is represented as *pariṣadya*, which term is explained by Sāyaṇa as (*sabhāyogya*) worthy of attending the *sabhā*.[5] A passage from a later Brāhmaṇa suggests that the *pariṣad* was a royal assembly, in which members evinced anxiety for scoring victory over their opponent in debate. In the reference one party declares: "I am a supporter of the king and you are the supporter of a kingless state,"[6] which implies that it was not without a tough fight that the smaller chief and other clansmen submitted to a big chief. Perhaps it indicates the process by which the king was gaining his foothold in the early *pariṣad* with the help of his supporters.

The few references that are found in the early Vedic literature do not give any direct evidence of the tribal character of the

1. *pariṣádyaṃ hi áraṇasya rékṇo nítyasya rāyáḥ pátayaḥ syāma. RV*, VII.4.7. The translation of the term *pariṣadyaṃ* by Wilson and Griffith seems to be faulty. It should mean "belonging to the *pariṣad*", a meaning which is in keeping with the military and tribal nature of early assembly.
2. *VS*, V.32.
3. *Brahmāṇḍa P.*, II.12.22.
4. *Jaimini Upaniṣad Br.*, II.11.13-14.
5. *TB*, III.1.2.9.
6. *parṣadi rājani cottaravādī bhavatyuttaravādī bhavati. Sāmavidhāna Br.*, II.7.5. The passage has been interpreted on the basis of Sāyaṇa's commentary.

early *pariṣad*, but the oft-quoted *Śatapatha Brāhmaṇa* passage relating to the *pariṣad* of the Pañcālas shows that it was primarily their clan assembly presided over by the king or the chief.[1] The epic and Purāṇic references point not only to the tribal but also to the military and partly matriarchal character of the *pariṣad*. It has been shown that Ahirbudhnya, a form of Rudra, is called *pariṣadya*, but in the *Mahābhārata*, Skanda, the son of Śiva, is associated with the *pāriṣadas* (obviously the members of the *pariṣad*) at numerous places. Śiva, who is described as *gaṇādhyakṣa*, is also called *pāriṣadpriya*, one who loves the company of the members of the *pariṣad*.[2] There is some evidence that *pāriṣadas* (companions) were the kins of their leader Skanda. These fearful and curious-looking comrades represented as the male children of Skanda were born as a result of the striking of his thunder.[3] The gist of the myth seems to be that Skanda and his followers belonged to the same clan. In this sense the relation of the *pāriṣadas* to Skanda is similar to that of the Marutgaṇas with their father Rudra. Their tribal character can be further inferred from the statement that clad in diverse kinds of skins the *pāriṣadas* speak diverse languages and different provincial dialects.[4] They can be thus compared to primitive peoples, among whom every tribe has its own dialect—its basis being not territorial. The hypothesis about the tribal character is further strengthened by the comparison of their faces to various kinds of animals and birds such as cocks, dogs, wolves, hares, camels, sheep, jackals, etc.[5] Such associations with animals probably disclose their totemic origin. Since the totems of primitive tribes owed their origin to the sources of their food supply,[6] in many cases the edible species of animals might suggest totemic and tribal connections. It may, however, be noted that in the long list of animals and birds connected with the *pāriṣadas* horse, which is generally associated with the Āryans, is conspicuous by its absence.

1. *Chāndogya Up.*, V.3; *Bṛhadāraṇyaka Up.* VI.2; *ŚB* XIV.9. 1.1.
2. *Mbh.*, X.7.8. If not otherwise specified the edition used in this chapter is Kumbakonam.
3. *skandapāriṣadān...vajraprahārāt skandasya jajñur...Mbh.* (Chitrasala Press), III.228.1.
4. *Mbh.* (Cal.), IX.45.102.
5. Ibid., IX.46.79-88.
6. George Thomson, *Studies in Ancient Greek Society*, p. 37.

The military character of the *pariṣad* indicated by Vedic references is confirmed by epic and Purāṇic evidence. In the *Matsya Purāṇa* the *Śiva-gaṇas* with awkward forms, who fought against the Asuras, are described as *pārṣadas*.[1] Numerous references in the *Mahābhārața* speak of the *pāriṣadas* as "fearful people equipped with uplifted weapons" of various kinds. The same expression *pārisadairghorainānāpraharaṇodyataiḥ* is used at several places.[2] At the time of his investiture with the rank of generalissimo for fighting against the Asuras, Skanda or Kārttikeya is supplied with mighty soldiers (*pāriṣadas*) by Brahmā, Pūṣan and Vindhya.[3] Invariably represented as mighty and impetuous fighters, the *pāriṣadas* made over to Skanda are portrayed as armed with terrible weapons and fighting with large pieces of stones (*mahāpāṣāṇayodhinaḥ*)[4]. Passionately fond of battle this is the one hobby in which they take great delight. They were so brave that even the foremost among the gods were no match for them.[5] Perhaps even in times of peace they continued their predatory activities against the Āryan people, for they are stigmatised as stealing the life of little children.[6]

Although several gods had their own *pāriṣadas*, who were lent to Skanda in the fight against the Daityas, generally speaking the *pariṣad* was led by Śiva or Skanda. A whole chapter in the *Śalya Parva* deals with the *pāriṣadas* under the leadership of Skanda.[7] It informs us that, accompanied by them and the members of the matriarchal *gaṇas*, he proceeded for the destruction of the Daityas.[8] How was Skanda made their leader? There is perhaps some indication that he was elected. First, recognising him as their leader the gods willingly furnished him with their *pāriṣadas*. Secondly, when Skanda was born, persons of different varṇas sought his protection and came to be called *pāriṣadas* by the brāhmaṇas.[9] All this indicates willing acceptance of his leader-

1. V.R.R. Dikshitar, *Purāṇic Index*, ii, 321. Both the terms *pārṣada* and *pāriṣada* are used in the sense of companion.
2. *Mbh.* (Chitrashala Press), III.109.3, 272.78.
3. *Mbh.*, IX.46, 23-26, 44, 49.51.
4. Ibid., IX. 46. 108, 111-14, 49-50.
5. Ibid., IX.45.95.
6. *Mbh.* (Chitrashala Press), III.228.2.
7. Ch. 46.
8. *Mbh.* (Cal.), IX.47.53-54.
9. *Mbh.* (Chitrashala Press), III.225.31.

ship by his followers, although the second reference reflects a period of anarchy when irrespective of varṇa considerations people offered their allegiance to some lord, and hence it might suggest a developed stage of myth-making, perhaps in post-Maurya times. This lateness, however, cannot be ascribed to some other references to the *pariṣad.* In later times the *pariṣad* is always associated with the king, but the early epic or Purāṇic references hardly make mention of any king having his *pariṣad.* We may, therefore, presume that when the commander was elevated to the position of the king or the chief the *pāriṣads,* whose number fell down, assumed the character of councillors in peace rather than comrades-in-arms.

There is some idea about the size of the early *pāriṣad.* The tradition of a large *pariṣad,* of 1000 members, is preserved both in the *Arthaśāstra* of Kauṭilya and the *Rāmāyaṇa.*[1] In connection with the presentation of fighting companions (*pāriṣadadāna*) made by different gods it is said that they were joined by other such comrades as came in thousands.[2] An early law-book states that those who are without *mantra* (sacred counsel) and *vrata* (vow), even if accompanied by thousands of companions, cannot shine in the *pariṣad.*[3] These statements give sufficient indication of the big size of this assembly in earlier times.

In post-Vedic times the *mantripariṣad* in particular and the *pariṣad* in general shows no trace of having any woman member. But the use of the term *pāriṣadī* suggests otherwise in the case of the early *pariṣad.* In formulas accompanying the water offerings to ancestors, oblations have to be made not only to the *pārṣadas* of Brahmā, Rudra, Vighna, Skanda, Viṣṇu, Vaivasvat (either Yama or Manu) and Dhanvantari but also to their wives and *pārṣadis* (lady companions).[4] This leaves no doubt that at one time women were also regarded as members of the *pariṣad.* There can be little question about the antiquity of the formulas referring to *pārṣadīs,* for they occur in the second book of Baudhāyana, considered as a part of the original Dharmasūtra.[5] In point of time this might suggest the situation existing towards the end of

1. Jayaswal, op. cit., p. 302.
2. *sahasrasaḥ pārisadāḥ kumāramupatasthire. Mbh.* (Cal.), IX.46.78.
3. *Baudhāyana Dharmasūtra*, I.1.16.
4. Ibid., II.5.12; also in ms. O given in Appendix I.
5. Ibid., Ed. E. Hultzsch, Introduction, pp. ix-x.

the Vedic period. The practice of having woman members of the *pariṣad*, however, was perhaps confined to the peninsular India to which Baudhāyana belonged, and where even in later times matrilineal traces persisted. Thus the association of woman with the *pāriṣad* cannot be denied, although it has to be admitted that the evidence on this point is not as strong as on her membership of the *vidatha* and *sabhā*.

Something can be said about the relation between the *pariṣad* and *gaṇa* on the basis of post-Vedic sources. Some of the references do not suggest any difference between the two. The *Śiva-gaṇas* fighting against the Asuras are described as *pārṣadas*; which implies that in later times the *gaṇa* and *pariṣad* are considered identical in this case. In the epic and Purāṇic references both of them are generally associated with Śiva; the *gaṇa* is frequently referred to as the assembly of the Maruts, the sons of Śiva. The *pariṣad* and *gaṇa* are placed on the same footing in connection with voluntary offerings, which are made to the former just after the *gaṇa* and *gaṇapati*.[1] Further, the enumeration of about a hundred matriarchal *gaṇas* may indicate woman membership[2] in the case of the *gaṇa*, a feature which is probably also true of the *pariṣad*. The statement that Skanda proceeded to fight against the Asuras accompanied by the *pāriṣadas* and the mother *gaṇas*[3] suggests some distinction between the two institutions, but its exact nature is nowhere clearly stated.

All this would indicate that the early *pariṣad* was a tribal military assembly, partly matriarchal and partly patriarchal. It had hardly anything to do with the king and brāhmaṇas, who came to dominate it in later times. Proceeding on the assumption that matriarchy played an important part in some earlier stages of the development of society and that the evolution of kingship and varṇa society could take place only by the end of the Vedic period, the early *pariṣad* may be regarded as an institution of Vedic times. But how do we account for comparatively rare references to it in the *Ṛg Veda*? First, out of the four references to the *pariṣad* in this collection, three occur in what is regarded as its kernel, which is sufficient proof of its antiquity. Second, paucity of data in Vedic literature may have been due

1. *Baudhāyana Gṛhyasūtra*, II.8.9.
2. *Mbh.*, IX.47.
3. Ibid., IX.47.54.

to the non-Vedic character of the *pariṣad*, which can be inferred from its association with Śiva and Skanda and the absence of horse in the list of its totems. Non-Vedic, pre-Āryan practices and institutions naturally found their way into the epic and Purāṇic traditions in post-Maurya and Gupta times, for in course of the preceding centuries elements of non-Āryan culture had been sufficiently imbibed by the Āryans. Third, the *Mahābhārata* references, which occur chiefly in connection with the exploits of Śiva or Skanda, although not forming part of the main narrative, undoubtedly record the tradition of earliest times. They rarely occur in the didactic or Smṛti sections of the epic and the Purāṇas, as is the case with the exposition of the *rājadharma* (duties of the king) in the *Śānti Parva*. The epic and the Purāṇic traditions can be utilised for constructing the earliest dynastic history provided they are supported by Vedic and archaeological evidence. Similarly they may be tapped for the study of the earliest social and political institutions provided they are supported by Vedic and anthropological evidence.

In judging the character of the early *pariṣad* on the basis of two sets of evidence, Vedic and post-Vedic, there is always the danger of slipping into the chronological fallacy. But the relevant references can convey some meaning only if they are examined according to the methodology of Pargiter, namely, the coincidence between the Vedic and epic-Purāṇic material. Apart from the independent value of the epic references to the *pariṣad*, their broad agreement in several respects with the Vedic counterpart imparts to them some measure of authenticity. This shows that in its essentials there is hardly any difference between the Vedic and the epic *pariṣad*. Both the sources show that it was a tribal military assembly. But as will be indicated later, there is a world of difference between the structure and functions of the *pariṣad* as known from the early Vedic and epic sources and the one as known from the Jātakas, Kauṭilya's *Arthaśāstra*, Aśokan inscriptions and the Dharmaśāstras.

The transitional phase in the history of the *pariṣad* can be ascribed to the period represented by the Upaniṣads and Gṛhyasutras. It seems that, on account of the growth of varṇas and state power towards the close of the later Vedic period, the *pariṣad* tended to become partly an academy and partly a royal council dominated by the priests, who functioned as teachers and advisers. The academic character of this institution is suggested by references in some Upaniṣads and one Gṛhyasūtra. According to the latter the *pariṣad* is a seminary in which the pupil sits near the teacher.[1] The evidence that it functioned as a royal council is provided by the *Pāraskara Gṛhyasūtra,* wherein the *pariṣad* is represented as conducting debate under the chairmanship of its *Īśāna* (president). We further learn that in the course of debate members not only desired to prove themselves superior and brilliant over others but also tried to disarm the wrath of the president and win his favour.[2] The commentary of Harihara to a passage of the same source shows that this body was attended mainly by the brāhmaṇas,[3] but perhaps this reflects the composition of the *pariṣad* in the age of the commentator rather than in that of the text.

That the *pariṣad* acted as a royal council and its members exercised enormous influence upon the king is known from Pāṇini's grammar, in which the king is called *pariṣadbala.* The same source indicates that the *pariṣad* did not confine itself to one function, the same body performing social, academic and political functions.[4] Although Pāṇini does not throw any light on the composition of this body, either as a royal council or as a literary academy, the *pariṣad* seems to have been a small and distinguished body. Nobody could be a member of the *pariṣad* (*pāriṣad* or *pāriṣadya*) unless he was duly qualified or eligible for it.[5] Thus towards the close of the Vedic period the character of the *pariṣad* had undergone a qualitative change. The name remained the same, but its connotation became different.

The new character of the *pariṣad* stabilised during the pre-Maurya period. In the early brāhmaṇical law-books the *pariṣad* took on the character of a body of legal experts. The *pariṣad* as known to the Dharmasūtras was an institution engaged in teaching and intellectual discussions, but its learned members were now inclined more towards law than teaching. In respect of its structure, the relevant passages from the Dharmasūtras

1. *Khadira Gṛhyasūtra,* III.1.25; *Gobhila Gṛhyasūtra* (*SBE*), III.2.50.
2. *PGS,* III.13.4.5.
3. Ibid.
4. V.S. Agrawala, *India as Known to Pāṇini,* p. 399. For academic functions of the *pariṣad* see op. cit., pp. 297-98.
5. Ibid., p. 399.

justify the statement that it was essentially a council of the priests.[1] Baudhāyana, Gautama and Vasiṣṭha describe its composition more or less in similar terms.[2] Baudhāyana clearly states that the ten members of the *pariṣad* should be *viprās*[3] (brāhmaṇas). The details of qualifications laid down for the membership of the *pariṣad* in other references too leave no doubt that it was to be formed mainly of the priests.

The process by which the *pariṣad* was reduced to the position of a small body dominated by the brāhmaṇas can be linked up with the break-up of the old tribal society into varṇas and the emergence of the brāhmaṇas as one of the two upper dominant classes. The supremacy which the brāhmaṇas enjoyed from the end of the Vedic period[4] onwards is naturally reflected in the composition of the *pariṣad* outlined in the brāhmaṇical law-books.

The process of reduction in the size of the *pariṣad* was probably gradual. It is possible that in between the small *pariṣad* of the Dharmasūtras, Kauṭilya's *Arthaśāstra* and Aśokan inscriptions on the one hand, and the early *pariṣad* on the other, intervened an intermediate *pariṣad* of comparatively bigger size corresponding to the *parisā* of the Jātakas or to the council of thirty-seven amâtyas in the *Śānti Parva.*[5] Perhaps Kauṭilya's quotation of the views of old thinkers that the *pariṣad* should consist respectively of twenty, sixteen or twelve members refers to such an intermediate stage.[6] At any rate the *mantri-pariṣad* mentioned in Kauṭilya, or the legal *pariṣad* of the brāhmaṇas, was basically different from the early *pariṣad*, to which we cannot attach any constitutional or political significance as we do to the *sabhā* and *samiti.*

1. E.W. Hopkins, "Social and Military Position of the Ruling Caste etc.", *JAOS*, xiii, 148.
2. *Baudh.*, 1. 1.8.9; *Gautama*, XXVIII.50-51; *Vas. Dh. S.*, III.20.
3. *Baudh.*, 1. 1.8.9.
4. Cf. U.N. Ghoshal, "The Status of Brāhmaṇas in the Dharmasūtras", *IHQ*, xxiii, pp. 83-92. H.C. Ray, "Position of the Brāhmaṇas in the Arthaśāstra", *Proceedings of the All-India Oriental Conference*, 1924.
5. R.N. Mehta, *Pre-Buddhist India*, p. 135.
6. *AŚ*, I.15.

CHAPTER XI

RATNAHAVĪṂṢI CEREMONY

Perhaps no other single ritual throws so much light on the political organization of the Āryans in the later Vedic period as the *ratnahavīṃṣī* ceremony, which forms a part of the *rājasūya* coronation sacrifice. In commenting upon its importance we have to acknowledge our debt to Weber, Jayaswal and Ghoshal, who have given sufficient thought to the examination of the later Vedic texts bearing on this subject.[1] But there is still some scope for the further study of the problem, if we bear in mind the regional differences in the composition of the source material, the economic background of the period, the comparative study of the early institutions of the other Indo-European peoples, and the difficulty of interpreting the exact functions of the ratnins (jewel holders).

According to the *ratnahavīṃṣi* ceremony the sacrificing king went to the house of each ratnin and offered oblations to the appropriate deity there. The names of these ratnins are mentioned in five texts, on the basis of which Ghoshal has prepared a chart,[2] which is reproduced on page 144 with some modification.

Jayaswal enumerates eleven ratnins,[3] but the names which occur in one list do not find mention in another list, with the result that the total number of the persons whose houses are visited by the king for offering oblations to various gods comes to fifteen. As regards the order and mention of their names, we observe a marked difference between the various other texts of the *Yajus* on the one hand and the *Śatapatha Brāhmaṇa* on the other. The list in the *Taittirīya Brāhmaṇa*, however, is more in conformity with that given in the Saṃhitās of the *Yajus*. Leaving aside the differences with the list of the *Śatapatha Brāhmaṇa* for later consideration, let us, as a whole, examine the lists which seem to have been prepared in the land of the Kuru-Pañcāla.

1. Jayaswal, *Hindu Polity*, pp. 200-5; Ghoshal, *Historiography and Other Essays*, pp. 249-54.
2. Ghoshal, op. cit., facing p. 249. Actually these are not known as ratnins in the *KŚ* and *TS*; this appellation is applied to them later in the *TB* and *ŚB*.
3. Op. cit., pp. 201-3.

LIST OF RATNINS AT THE RATNAHAVĪṂṢI

TS, I.8.9	*MS*, II.6.5; IV.3	*KS*, XV.4	*TB*, I.7.3ff.	*ŚB*, V.3.1ff.
1. brahman	1. brahman	1. purohita for Bṛhaspati	1. brahman	1. senānī
2. rājanya	2. rājanya	2. rājā for Indra	2. rājanya	2. purohita
3. mahisī	3. mahiṣī	3. mahiṣī for Aditi	3. mahiṣī	3. sacrificer
4. parivṛkti	4. parivṛkti	4. parivṛkti for Naiṛta	4. vāvātā	4. mahiṣī
5. senānī	5. senānī	5. senānī for Agni	5. parivṛktī	5. sūta
6. sūta	6. saṃgrahītṛ	6. saṃgrahītṛ for Aśvins	6. senānī	6. grāmaṇī
7. grāmaṇī	7. kṣattṛ	7. ksattṛ for Savitar	7. sūta	7. kṣattṛ
8. kṣattṛ	8. sūta	8. sūta for Varuṇa	8. grāmaṇī	8. saṃgrahītṛ
9. saṃgrahītṛ	9. vaiśyagrāmaṇī	9. vaisya-grāmaṇī for Marut	9. kṣattṛ	9. bhāgadugha
10. bhāgadugha	10. bhāgadugha	10. bhāgadugha for Pūṣan	10. samgrahītṛ	10. akṣāvāpa
11. akṣāvāpa	11. & 12. takṣan and rathakāra	11. akṣāvāpa	11. bhāgadugha	11. govikartana
	13. & 14. akṣāvāpa and govikarta	12. govyaccha for Rudra	12. akṣāvāpa	12. pālāgala
				13. parivṛkti (not mentioned as ratnin.)

That the *rājasūya* sacrifice was performed in this land is evident from the formula of bepsrinkling, according to which the people to be ruled by the king are represented to be Bharatas, Kurus and Pañcālas.[1] Therefore the institution of the ratnins probably functioned in Madhyadeśa. Barring some changes which occurred when the Āryans moved further east into Videha, this institution, as would appear from the evidence of the *Śatapatha Brāhmaṇa*, continued to exist till the end of the Vedic period.

If we accept the contention of von Schroeder, who regards *Maitrāyaṇī* and *Kāṭhaka* Saṃhitās earlier in point of time,[2] it would appear that the earliest list as given in the former text consists of fourteen ratnins. At the head of the list stands the brāhmaṇa, who occupies this position in three texts and also in a fourth where he is known as the *purohita*, a title applied to him in the *Śatapatha Brāhmaṇa*, where he occupies the second position. The brāhmaṇa, at whose house the pap is to be offered by the king to Bṛhaspati, the chief priest of the gods, obviously represents the newly organized priestly class. It has been argued with great force of logic that the brāhmaṇas were pre-Āryan priests. The fact that they stand at the head of the ratnins speaks not only of their ingenuity in ingratiating themselves into the favour of the conquerors but also of the great tolerance shown by the newcomers.

The second name in four texts is that of the rājanya, with the difference that he is mentioned as rājā in one text. If we accept the interpretation of the *Śatapatha Brāhmaṇa* and *Kāṭhaka Saṃhitā* this ratnin would appear to be the king himself, but it sounds strange that the king's name should get the third place in the *Śatapatha* and the second place in other texts. It is almost clear that the rājanya, at whose house the oblation is to be made to Indra, the warrior *par excellence*, represents the warrior class of the kṣatriyas formed by the close kinsmen of the king.

The third name in all the lists, excepting that of the *Śatapatha Brāhmaṇa*, is that of the *mahiṣī*. The term literally means the chief queen, which shows that the king or the chief married several women. Jayaswal thinks that the queen is provided here to complete the spiritual self of the king-elect.[3] But the explana-

1. *TS*, I.8.10; Keith, *HOS*, xviii, p. xciii.
2. *HOS*, xviii, pp. xci-iv.
3. *Hindu Polity*, p. 201.

tion given in the *Śatapatha Brāhmaṇa* does not warrant this assumption. Probably the *mahiṣī*, at whose house oblation is to be offered to Aditi, represents the goddess Earth, which, like a milch cow and mother, sustains men and fulfils all their desires.[1] This would indicate the importance of the matriarchal element in later Vedic polity, a point which is also supported by the mention of the two other queens as ratnins.

The fourth name in three Saṃhitās and the fifth name in one Brāhmaṇa is that of the *parivṛkti*. She is not formally included in the list of the ratnins in the *Śatapatha Brāhmaṇa*, but, after the enumeration of the ratnins, appears as a discarded wife who has no son and whom the king visits in order to free himself from the evil that might overtake him.[2] Although the object stated here is not to secure the support of such a wife, there can be no doubt that she was considered capable of causing harm to the king. Unlike the other ratnins, she was not thought to be a source of positive help to the ruler, but a source of opposition which had to be disarmed. We may add that the *vāvātā* or the favourite wife is mentioned as a ratnin only in the *Taittirīya Brāhmaṇa*, where she occupies the fourth place and is followed by the *parivṛkti*.

The fifth name in three Saṃhitās is that of the *senānī*, who is assigned the fifth place in four texts, the sixth place in the *Jaiminīya Brāhmaṇa* and the first place in the *Śatapatha Brāhmaṇa*. Originally the *senānī* seems to have been the leader of the host, but in the *Śatapatha Brāhmaṇa* he seems to have functioned as the commander-in-chief.[3] Sāyaṇa's characterization of the *senānī* as śūdra suggests that the right to fight was neither confined to the kṣatriya nor denied to the śūdra.

So far we have arranged the five ratnins in the order in which they seem to have been placed by most texts. But it is difficult to arrange the remaining ratnins in any definite order of importance. None the less, we can examine the position of these six ratnins, namely, *sūta*, *grāmaṇī*, *ksattṛ*, *saṃgrahītṛ*, *bhāgadugha* and *akṣāvāpa*, who are common to all the lists.

The *sūta* is taken by several writers in the sense of a court minstrel or chronicler.[4] This interpretation suits the epic *sūta*,

1. V.3.1.4.
2. V.3.1.13.
3. V.3.1.1.
4. Ghoshal, op. cit., chart facing p. 249.

but the fact that oblation at his house is offered to Varuṇa for which the sacrificial fee of a horse is prescribed shows that this celebrity was a charioteer.[1] In another reference this functionary is considered identical with the *sthapati*[2], who may be taken variously as governor, chief, architect, master-builder, carpenter and wheelwright.[3] Of these the meanings of governor[4] and chief judge[5] have been preferred. But in view of the association of the *sūta* with chariot, the meaning wheelwright would better suit the context. Probably the *sūta* functioned both as charioteer and wheelmaker, and was honoured as a craft specialist. But. on account of his association with manual labour, in later times he fell in esteem. However his importance in the earlier period was well recognised; in the *Atharva Veda* he and the *grāmaṇī* figure among those whom the newly consecrated king wishes to make his support (*upastins*).[6]

The *grāmaṇī* is mentioned as *vaiśya-gramaṇī* in two Saṃhitās which indicates that he was the head of the people (*viś*) living in the village. It is suggested that he was a hereditary territorial proprietor living in the capital,[7] but there is nothing to show that he always lived at the capital. We should think that the kingdoms of the Bharatas, Kurus and Pañcālas was not so large as to render the movement of the rulers difficult in their respective states. The exact functions of the *grāmaṇī* are difficult to determine. In all likelihood he continued the old practice of leading little groups of people to the battlefield, in addition to which he may have acquired functions of a general supervisory nature over the villagers. Jayaswal thinks that the *grāmaṇī* was also the head of the township,[8] but urban life had not developed on any considerable scale during the later Vedic period. Similarly the conjecture that royal dues were received through the *grāmaṇī*[9] does not seem to have been well founded.

To the *kṣattr* are assigned the meanings of carver and chamber-

1. *ŚB*, V.3.1.5.
2. Ibid., V.4.4.17-18.
3. s. v. *sthapati*. Monier-Williams, *Sansk-Eng. Dictionary*.
4. Eggeling, *SBE.*, xli, 111.
5. Ghoshal, *Historiography and Other Essays*, p.272.
6. *AV*, III.5.7.
7. Eggeling, *SBE*, xli, p. 61, fn.
8. *Hindu Polity*, p. 202.
9. *CHI*, i, 117.

lain.[1] But the term also means distributor which better suits the context, for in tribal societies distribution of booty, produce and tributes was an important function of the chief. It is significant that the *kṣattṛ* is associated with God Savitā, the objects produced daily by whom are distributed in the *vidatha.*[2] In later times he lost in position like the *sūta* and came to be condemned as a mixed caste.

There is also difference of opinion about the position of the *saṃgrahītṛ*, who is regarded as the master of treasury by Jayaswal on the basis of later commentators.[3] According to Jayaswal in the *Arthaśāstra* this office-bearer is called *sannidhātā*. The literal meaning of the term is the custodian of the store as well as the holder of the reins or the driver.[4] Probably this ratnin should be understood in the sense of a charioteer of an inferior kind in contrast to the *sūta* who acts as a *sārathi* to the chief warrior. In the ritual of the cattle raid the chariot plays such a vital part[5] that great weight is given to different kinds of people associated with the making and moving of the chariot. That the *saṃgrahītṛ* was a charioteer can be also inferred from the fact that at his house oblation is to be offered to the Aśvins[6], who are represented as swift moving gods in the sky having horse as their means of conveyance (*vāhana*).

Though somewhat low in various lists a very significant ratnin mentioned is the *bhāgadugha*. At one place this term is taken in the sense of the distributor of shares,[7] an attribute applied to Pūṣan. In the age of the *Ṛg Veda* the people did not pay fixed taxes to the king but brought him voluntary presents. This continued largely in later Vedic times. Since at the house of the *bhāgadugha* oblation is offered to Pūṣan,[8] the god of cattle, the *bhāgadugha* may have disbursed cattle and cereals among those

1. Keith, *HOS*, xviii, 120; Jayaswal, op.cit., p. 202; Ghoshal *Historiography and Other Essays*, chart facing page 249. For its Pali equivalent *khatta* see *DN*, *i*, 112.
2. *RV*, VII.40.1.
3. *Hindu Polity*, p. 202.
4. Ibid., fn. 12.
5. *ŚB*, V.4.3.
6. Ibid., V.3.1.8.
7. *SBE*, xli, 63, fn. 1 on SB, I.1.2.17. Rau (*Staat und Gesellschaft in Alter Indisschen*, pp. 110-11 with fns.) holds that he was a server of food.
8. ŚB, V.3.1.9.

who served the king or the chief and also among others on ceremonial occasions.

The eleventh ratnin common to all the lists is the *akṣāvāpa*. The literal meaning of the term is dice thrower. But it is argued that for the king to approach the officer in charge of gambling seems to be something very extraordinary, and hence on the basis of the *akṣaśālā* mentioned in the *Arthaśāstra* of Kauṭilya this ratnin is interpreted as the officer in charge of state accounts.[1] But, as suggested earlier, later evidence cannot be always used in elucidating the duties of the functionaries of the later Vedic period. The *akṣāvāpa* may have been a dice thrower, for in this connection reference is made to the gaming board and dice.[2] The dice may have been used in distributing shares by lot, and the *akṣāvāpa* may have been a distributor of land plots for sowing.[3] He may be compared to a similar officer called *kṣetrasādha* in the *Ṛg Veda*.[4] Till recent times land was periodically distributed among the members of the Lushai tribe in Mizoram. The old tradition of distributing land by lot is still used in north Bihar villages in partitioning the landed property between brothers.

Finally, we have to consider the remaining four ratnins, whose names occur in one list or the other, thus taking the total to fifteen. Of these the name of the *govikartana* occurs with variation in three lists, *govikarta* in the *Maitrāyaṇi* and *gavyaccha* in the *Kāṭhaka* editions of the *Yajus*, and *gavikartana* in the *Śatapatha Brāhmaṇa*. The literal meaning of the term is butcher or the killer of the cows. And hence this officer has been understood in the sense of chief huntsman.[5] The theory that this officer corresponds to Megasthenes' officer being in charge of the huntsmen who cleared the land of wild beasts and fowls which devoured the seeds[6] seems to be without any basis. He may have acted as the keeper of the games and forests. Perhaps his duty was to get sufficient game for the royal or chiefly household, showing thereby that hunting still continued as an important occupation of the people and that beef was one of

1. Jayaswal, op.cit., pp. 202-3.
2. *ŚB*, V.3.1.10.
3. s. v. *avāpa, SED.*
4. s. v. *kṣetrasādha*, ibid.
5. Ghoshal, *Historiography and Other Essays*, the chart facing p. 249.
6. Jayaswal, op.cit., p. 203.

the chief items in their food. The *govikartan* may have arranged the distribution of beef, mutton, etc.

The two other ratnins, *takṣan* and *rathakāra*, are mentioned in two Saṃhitās of the *Yajus*. There can be hardly any dispute about their meaning; one stands for the carpenter and the other for the chariot maker. The fact that all kinds of metals are prescribed as the sacrificial fee in the ceremonies performed at their homes shows that they owed their importance to their association with metal working.[1] It seems that the *rathakāra* and *takṣan* owed their positions to their original membership of the Āryan tribes, which had gradually broken up into varṇas, since in the *Atharva Veda* the *rathakāra* and the *karmāra* (whose place is now taken by the *takṣan*) are clearly described as part of the *viś* (people) round the king[2] or the chief. Their inclusion in the two *Yajus* collections therefore should not be viewed as a priestly manipulation but as recognition of their importance to the chief. That the experts in crafts enjoyed high position in primitive societies cannot be denied.[3]

The *pālāgala* should be considered as the last in the list of the ratnins, for his name occurs in the *Śatapatha Brāhmaṇa*, which was composed towards the end of the later Vedic period. He acted as a messenger carrying errands from place to place.[4] We may note that messengers play an important part in the political organisation of primitive tribes in Australia. They are used by the headmen, councils and other groups in authority to communicate to particular individuals, local groups, or tribes information about holding a meeting, a ceremony or a communal feast, or organising an expedition for blood-revenge.[5] On this analogy, although the *pālāgala* was considered a śūdra, his importance in the political organisation of the later Vedic period cannot be underestimated. The name *pālāgala* does not appear to be Āryan but most probably stands for some aboriginal tribe living in Videha, which marked the easternmost expansion of the Āryans in the age represented by the *Śatapatha Brāhmaṇa*. This can also be inferred from the use of the term *pālāgalī*, condem-

1. *MS*, II. 6, 5; *Ap. ŚS*, XVIII.10.17.
2. III.5.6.
3. Alexander Goldenweiser, *Anthropology*, p. 386.
4. *ŚB*, V.3.1.11.
5. Alexander Goldenweiser, op. cit., p. 380.

ned as a śūdra wife,[1] who may have been wedded from the aboriginal people. Incidentally the sacrificial fee of a skin-covered bow, leather quivers, and a red turban, for the courier[2] suggests that he was equipped with these weapons in order to defend himself on the way against unfriendly elements.

The inclusion of the *pālāgala* in the rank of the ratnins is a striking feature of the *Śatapatha Brāhmaṇa* list. So is the elevation of the *senānī* to the top of the list of the ratnins. This also can be explained on the basis of regional differences. Although the Āryan expansion in Videha is attributed by the *Śatapatha Brāhmaṇa* to the pioneering efforts of Videgha Māthava, and Agni Vaiśvānara who seems to have cleared the forests by burning it,[3] it is reasonable to think that such expansion involved wars with the result that the *senānī* or the military leader came to the forefront. Although the *Śatapatha Brāhmaṇa* has many passages testifying to the pretensions of the brāhmaṇas, who claim the immunity of their property, it gives the impression that the kṣatriyas were asserting themselves not only in the political field, but, what is more significant, also in the intellectual field which was considered to be the monopoly of the brāhmaṇas. Several kṣatriya rulers mentioned in that text and the concurrent stories of the Upaniṣads, namely, Aśvapati Kaikeya, Pravāhaṇa Jaivali, Vaideha Janaka and Ajātaśatru of Kāśī, are noted for their philosophic attainments, disputing with and instructing the priests in philosophy.[4] It is no wonder then that the *senānī*, who represents the warrior class, is placed at the head of the ratnins and the *purohita* is given the second place in the present text. The lack of internal consistency in the *Śatapatha Brāhmaṇa* in this respect can be explained by presuming a later redaction of this text in the brāhmaṇical interests.

Another indication of the growing military and patriarchal atmosphere in which this Brāhmaṇa seems to have been composed is to be found in the complete omission of the *vāvātā* from the list of ratnins and the mention of the *parivṛkti* not as a regular ratnin but at the end of the formal enumeration of all the

1. *Śūdras*, p. 50.
2. *ŚB*, V.3.1.11.
3. Ibid., 1.4.1.10-17; cf. *SBE*, xii, pp. xli-iii.
4. *CHI*, i, 113.

ratnins. This indicates gradual deterioration in the position of women of which we get more evidence in post-Vedic times.

Lastly, we might take into account the omission of the *rathakāra* and *takṣan* from the list of the ratnins in the *Śatapatha Brāhmaṇa*. This should be taken as proof of the growing contempt of the brāhmaṇas and kṣatriyas for the artisans engaged in manual labour. The next step is to be found in pre-Maurya times when the *rathakāra* is condemned as a mixed caste in the Dharmasūtras and as a follower of *hīna sippa* (low trade) in the early Pāli texts. The origins of this contempt can be traced back to the age of the *Śatapatha Brāhmaṇa* when social differentiation caused by the division of labour tended to be stratified into varṇas. Thus the ratnin list as given in the present text is richer in content and more elaborate in regard to the functions of the ratnins, and shows a transition from a partly tribal and matriarchal society into a completely class and patriarchal society.

An interesting anthropological explanation of the *ratnahavīṃṣi* ceremony has been given by Heesterman. In his opinion this ceremony is based on the idea of marriage and rebirth, which is most clearly represented by the group of royal consorts, who act as wombs.[1] He thinks that the charioteers and the representatives of the four varṇas can also be connected with the idea of the embryonic covers.[2] But this interpretation is not consistent with the explanations of the rituals given in the Saṃhitās or the Brāhmaṇas. Further, by the later Vedic period the institutions of wife and mother had been so well established that the very idea of entering the wombs of his wives and thus treating them as his so many mothers must be regarded as extremely reprehensible and repulsive not only to the royal sacrificer but also to the brāhmaṇa priests. Heesterman contends that the names of the ratnins do not provide us with any clue to the actual organization of the government.[3] He points out that royal consorts, governmental or household dignitaries, and artisans are incoherently mixed up in the list.[4] But at the early stage, when life had not been so much compartmentalized and purely governmental functions were not completely differentiated from

1. *The Ancient Indian Royal Consecration*, p. 55.
2. Ibid., p. 56.
3. Ibid., p. 53.
4. Ibid.

other functions, there is nothing incongruous about the lumping together of several functionaries. Several passages convey in no uncertain terms the political importance of the personages whom the king or the chief visited in the *ratnahavīṃṣi* ceremony. It is repeatedly stated that the king regards the ratnins as the sustainers of his realm, a point which has been stressed by several writers.[1] The ratnins are described as the givers and takers of the kingdom (*rāṣṭrasya pradātāraḥ, ete pādātāraḥ*).[2] The *Maitrāyaṇi Saṃhitā* calls them "limbs of the ruling power"[3] (*kṣatrasya vā etānyaṅgāni*), which expression anticipates the seven limbs of the state mentioned by Manu and other authorities. The same text adds that, if the ratnins become vigorous and energetic, the state also becomes vigorous and energetic.[4] The formula recited at the house of most ratnins states that the king is consecrated for the sake of the ratnin and that he makes the ratnin his faithful follower.[5] That the *purohita*, the *rājanya*, the *mahiṣī*, the *sūta*, the *grāmaṇī*, the *kṣattṛ* and the *saṃgrahītṛ* were persons of distinction is also corroborated by a source which has nothing to do with the *ratnahavīṃṣi* ceremony. These are described as persons who consecrate the king, and together sustain the kingship.[6] The functionaries, who are called ratnins in the ceremony, also figure as important personages in another ritual of the *rājasūya* sacrifice, the passing round of the sacrificial sword in the game of dice. The *White Yajus* school mentions *sūta* and *grāmaṇī*, to whom the sword has to be passed round in order to make them ultimately subordinate to the king.[7] In this connection a text of the *Black Yajus* school states that the sword is passed on to the *purohita*, who hands it over to the ratnins. Finally it goes to the *akṣāvāpa*, who prepares the gaming ground with it.[8] Although only two ratnins are specifically mentioned in this context, three others, namely the *saṃgrahītṛ*, the *bhāgadugha* and the *kṣattṛ*, are

1. Jayaswal, *Hindu Polity*, pp. 203-4; Ghoshal, *Historiography and Other Essays*, pp. 250-51.
2. *TB*, 1.7.3.
3. *MS*, IV.9.8.
4. *...yasya vā etānyojasvīni bhavanti tadrāṣṭramojasvi bhavati...yasya vā tāni tejasvīni bhavanti tadrāṣṭraṃ tejasvī bhavati.* Ibid.
5. *ŚB*, V.3.1.12.
6. *PB*, XIX.1.4.
7. *ŚB*, V.4.4.15-19.
8. *Ap. ŚS*, XVIII.18.14-16.

invited by the king, at the end of the ceremony of the game of dice, to act as witnesses.[1]

Survivals of old rituals are still to be found in Hindu society. On the occasion of the *upanayana* ceremony the boy has to visit the house of his family potter where he offers oblations to the wheel and also that of his family oilman whose pressing mill he has to worship. This practice is also followed by the girl on the occasion of her marriage. From this it would be too much to conclude that these artisans are responsible for the management of the client's family. But at the same time it is abundantly clear that the ritual concerns only those artisans with whom the family members have dealings in their daily life, and surely in pre-industrial rural society no peasant family can carry on without the assistance of these artisans. Such an inference can reasonably be also drawn from similar rituals in Vedic times. Functional relations between the chief and his employees and dependants were validated by the *ratnahavīṃṣi* ceremony. The ratnins whom the king or the chief visited certainly formed his household entourage and administrative machinery, between the two of which it is difficult to draw a line in later Vedic polity.

But it is difficult to speak in terms of the high constitutional position of the ratnins,[2] for there was hardly anything like constitution in the modern sense. Jayaswal describes the ratnins as high functionaries of the state,[3] which seems to be correct in so far as the object of the jewel offering ceremony was to secure the support and allegiance of the ratnins to the king. We may add that the ritual also presupposed the support of the gods, to whom oblations were offered at the house of the ratnins. In the case of the *parivṛkti* the oblation was offered not to secure the support of the god but to ward off the evil associated with that queen and the god Nirṛti. At any rate the negative importance of the discarded queen cannot be questioned. Perhaps it is not possible to push the distinction between the officers of higher grade and those of lower grade too far,[4] for in the texts the allegiance of every functionary is considered to be equally

1. Ibid., XVIII.19.6. These three functionaries are also mentioned by Bhaṭṭabhāskara Miśra in his comment on *TS*, 1.8.16.
2. Ghoshal, op. cit., p. 255, fn.
3. Op. cit., p. 203.
4. Cf. Ghoshal, op. cit., p. 255, fn.

important for the king. Nevertheless some sort of precedence is observed in the official hierarchy.

It seems that the ratnins, eleven of whom are common to all the lists and twelve to the majority of them, formed a kind of king's council. The number may have varied from area to area, for the *rājasūya* ceremony was practised in the kingdoms of the Bharatas, the Kurus and the Pañcālas. The geographical horizon of the *Śatapatha Brāhmaṇa* suggests that it was also practised in Videha, where the number of the ratnins seems to have been twelve though the *parivṛkti* was not included in the list of regular ratnins. It is striking that the practice of having a council of twelve prevailed among several Indo-European peoples. According to Chadwick, there is some evidence for councils consisting of a fixed number of men, namely twelve, whose position may have differed somewhat from the ordinary members of the court. The Old Saxons had a council of twelve which met annually, but they had no king. Such a council of twelve existed in Sweden in traditional and historical times. Some Indo-European gods too were credited with possessing a council of twelve which performed judicial and sacrificial duties; there is the legend of the twelve Frisian judges.[1] Councils of twelve are known to have existed among the Celts and other European peoples.[2] Excepting the Homeric people the council of twelve was an institution common to many Āryan peoples, and therefore Chadwick considers this type to be of great antiquity.[3] Most probably before their separation the Indo-Europeans possessed such an institution, which they continued to retain even when they had settled down as independent peoples in Europe and India. In view of this supporting evidence from the institutions of the other cognate peoples it appears that the eleven, and in most cases the twelve, ratnins of the later Vedic period may have functioned as a council of elders for advising and helping the king or the chief; the *sabhā* was too big a body to help him in conducting the day-to-day affairs of the state. "It might naturally be expected that the authority of the council would make itself felt most on the occasion of the king's death", on the succession of a new ruler to the throne.[4]

1. *The Heroic Age*, p. 370.
2. Ibid.
3. Ibid.
4. Ibid., p. 371.

It is this which explains the king's going to the ratnins at the time of his accession to power.

But in those days it was difficult to distinguish between the members of the council on the one hand and the high functionaries or officers of the state on the other. Apparently the ratnins show the beginnings of bureaucracy, the most developed form of which is to be found in the *Arthaśāstra* of Kauṭilya. However, the number of officials known from the *ratnahavīṃṣi* indicates a more developed administrative organization than what we find in earlier times. Although the *Ṛg Veda* does not know the ratnins as such, certain high personages such as *rājanya, purohita, senānī, sūta, grāmaṇī* are mentioned there. But in the later Vedic period we come across half a dozen new functionaries, some of whom seem to have been recruited from the pre-Āryans. Since disbursement of shares was an important function of the chief or the king, at least two ratnins were entrusted with distribution. It seems that the tributes received by the chief or the king were pooled together and then distributed by the *bhāgadugha* and the *akṣāvāpa*. The *bhāgadugha* was an officer in charge of distribution and so was the *akṣāvāpa*. Although some officers of the state were concerned with religion, sports and cattle, which recalls the undifferentiated nature of the tribal life, others performed functions which would be regarded as properly governmental. It can be said that the ratnins were "differentiated organs of government", not to be found in the early stage. It appears that the old tribal assemblies were found inadequate to deal with the problems which had cropped up on account of the expansion of the Vedic communities, with the result that the chiefdom needed more officials, as different from the people, to manage its own affairs.

The existence of numerous officials, some of non-Āryan extraction, indicates that the kingdom tended to be non-tribal and had become predominantly territorial. The territorial character of the state can also be inferred from the use of the term *rāṣṭra* in the sense of kingdom at several places.[1] Each of the ratnins lived in his house, which is another indication of the well established settlements in the state. Fixed habitations of the peasants paved the way for the collection of frequent tributes.

However, the functions of the ratnins do not suggest much

1. *MS*, IV.3.8; *TB*, I.7.3.

progress in tax collection and exercise of coercion. On the other hand, the *kṣattṛ*, *bhāgadugha*, *akṣāvāpa* and *govikartan* seem to be concerned with the distribution of game, cereals, cattle and various types of booty and tribute brought by the chief. Frequent distribution would keep alive the element of egalitarianism and would hamper the process of state formation.

How the ratnins were appointed is difficult to say. According to Jayaswal they were high functionaries of the state selected on the principle of class and caste representation.[1] For the greater part of the later Vedic period the institution of caste had not been well established, but it cannot be denied that almost all the emerging varṇas and important social groups were associated with the work of government. In some cases even the representative character of the ratnin can be inferred. Thus the *vaiśya-grāmaṇī* represented the *viś* or the village, the headship of which he enjoyed. Possibly the headman may have been elected because of personal qualities and seniority in age, if we accept the analogy from primitive societies. Since the varṇas of several ratnins such as *kṣattṛ*, *saṃgrahītṛ*, *akṣāvāpa*, etc., cannot be identified, it is very difficult to find out the varṇa ratio among the ratnins. Some ratnins were undoubtedly of śūdra origin or were condemned as such. But, as has been shown elsewhere, all the śūdra ratnins cannot be proved to have been non-Āryans[2], and hence it is wrong to hold that the śūdra ratnins represented only the conquered helots, as is done by Jayaswal.[3]

What is remarkable about the ratnin list is that it also included women. In some lists two, and in other three, ratnins happen to be women, who are wives of the king. The fact that out of about a dozen ratnins associated with the state ceremony women occupy two or three places reminds us of the age of the *Ṛg Veda* when women took part in the deliberations of the *vidatha* and, to some extent, even in those of the *sabhā*. In post-Vedic times they gradually came to lose their importance, a process which had begun in the later Vedic period because of the practice of polygamy. The king or the chief had at least three wives in this period; the *mahiṣī* enjoyed the highest legal status, the *vāvātā*'s position was based on favour and love shown to her,

1. *Hindu Polity*, p. 203.
2. *Śūdras*, p. 51.
3. *Hindu Polity*, p. 204.

and the *parivṛkti* was practically discarded on account of her barrenness. The ritual shows that the legal status of the *mahiṣī* was not yet established on a firm footing, and that the other wives of the king could challenge her position, for the other two could not be ignored on this occasion of great political importance.

Our discussion would show that the *ratnahaviṃṣī* ritual was the product of a developed political, social, and economic organisation in which tribal and matriarchal elements were being submerged by class, territorial, and patriarchal elements, leading to the emergence of differentiated organs of government in the later Vedic period. In spite of priestly support the power structure was predominantly military in character, for as many as half a dozen functionaries were associated with military work.

CHAPTER XII

TRIBAL AND PRIMITIVE ASPECTS OF THE LATER VEDIC POLITY

Our chief source for the study of the later Vedic polity is the coronation rituals, but the attempt to look for elements of contractual or constitutional monarchy in the Vedic period[1] has vitiated our understanding of the significance of several ceremonies in the *rājasūya* and *vājapeya* sacrifices. This, to some extent, has been counterbalanced by Ghoshal's study of these rituals.[2] A study of the *rājasūya* by Heesterman underestimates its social and political implications[3], which were brought to light by Weber and treated further by several Indian scholars. Heesterman claims to have studied the problem against the Vedic view of the world, but his completely anthropological and idealistic approach makes him present a distorted picture. The correct position may be known from an examination of these Vedic ceremonies in the light of comparative anthropology and parallel rituals prevalent among the other branches of the Indo-European peoples. The present study, therefore, will be confined to primitive and tribal aspects of the later Vedic polity as known from the rituals but will not completely ignore the new social factors. Excepting the *ratnahavīṃṣi* ceremony, which presupposes a developed society based on differentiation of functions and settlement in a fixed territory, other rituals such as the *devasūhavīṃṣi* (offerings to gods acting as divine quickeners), sprinkling ceremony, the ceremony of vesting sovereignty, the mimic cow raid, the chariot race and the game of dice can be interpreted in this light.

In the *devasūhavīṃṣi* ceremony, according to all the texts, a desire is expressed for different kinds of authority, two of which, namely *kṣatra* and *jānarājya*, are mentioned by all the authorities.[4] The first means chiefdom or simple authority over the people,

1. Jayaswal, *Hindu Polity*, pp. 219-20.
2. *Historiography and Other Essays*, Essay XIII.
3. J.C. Heesterman, *The Ancient Indian Royal Consecration*, pp. 4-5 and fn. 2.
4. *VS*, IX.40; *MS*, II.6.6; *TS*, I.8.10; *ṚS*, XV.5.

but the second has variously been interpreted as man-rule, rule over the people, and national rule. Ghoshal thinks that it means rule over the whole folk as distinguished from rule over a single tribe.[1] But the use of the term *pañcajanāḥ* in the Vedic literature in the sense of five tribes is well-known. Hence *jānarājya* probably means the desire for rule over the tribe to which the king belongs. We need not examine the terms indicating other forms of authority, which the sacrificer wishes to obtain. It is significant that nowhere any desire is expressed for territorial sovereignty. The invocation formula describes the king as the son of such a man and the son of such a woman.[2] In one text, however, he appears only as the son of such a man.[3] Although the formula indicates the human origin of Vedic kingship, it also suggests matrilineal influences in Vedic society. Not only the name of the father is given, but the name of the mother also is mentioned. The formula therefore demonstrates that mother is as important as father. This ceremony is concluded by the priests by presenting the sacrificer to the assembled tribesman with the following words:

"This is your king, ye (people), Soma is the king of us Brāhmaṇas."

For the term people we have variants such as the Kurus, Pañcālas, Bharatas, etc.[4] This shows that the basis of the kingship is not fully territorial but tribal. The brāhmaṇas are excluded from the control of the king. It implies that, though they may form part of the tribe, they are raised above the common tribesmen: Or it might suggest that since the brāhmaṇas do not belong to the original Vedic people they are exempted from the authority of the king; this might indicate the non-Āryan origin of the brāhmaṇas for which a case has been made by several scholars.[5] The theory that Soma is identical with the king and hence the crucial passage does not refer to the special position of the brāhmaṇas[6] cannot be accepted; several other

1. Op. cit., p. 257.
2. *VS*, IX.40; *MS*, II.6.6.
3. *TS*, I.8.10.
4. *VS*, IX.40; *KS*, XV.7; *MS*, II.6.9; cf. *TS*, I.8.10; *TB*, 1.7.4 uses the term Bharatas.
5. Pargiter, *Ancient Indian Historical Tradition*, p. 306ff; Kosambi, *An Introduction to the Study of Indian History*, pp. 97-98.
6. Heesterman, op. cit., pp. 75-77.

passages indicate the privileged status of the brāhmaṇas. The *Śatapatha Brāhmaṇa* clearly states that the brāhmaṇa is not to be lived upon by the king.[1] Therefore, it would be wrong to think that the passage means the glorification of the royal sacrificer and not the independence of the brāhmaṇa.[2]

An important ceremony in the *rājasūya* sacrifice is the *abhiṣecanīyam*, in which the king is sprinkled over by the representatives of the three upper classes and the *janya*, who is interpreted variously as a śūdra, a member of the hostile tribe, king's rival or a man of aristocratic birth or a foreign ally.[3] The origin of the practice of sprinkling seems to have been shrouded in mystery.[4] But it seems that this rite corresponds to that of purification prescribed in almost all important *saṃskāras* (rituals) laid down in the Gṛhyasūtras. We do not know how far this idea is connected with that of the renewal of life. At any rate, according to primitive methods of purification, the novices are washed in water or blood; they bathe in a stream or in the sea, or are scorched in front of fire.[5]

The sprinkling ceremony is followed by the investiture ritual, in which the priest invests the prince with a strong bow with three arrows and the prince is asked to protect the people.[6] The bow is described as the noble man's strength, and in the opinion of a Brāhmaṇa the weapon is handed to the king in order to endow him with strength and thereby make him fit for consecration.[7] This ritual may have been derived from the hunting ceremony practised among primitive tribes at the time of the initiation of a person into manhood when he uses the bow. It appears that the bow, the symbol of sustenance for the hunter, becomes the symbol of power and protection for the sacrificer who is initiated into kingship.

Next the king or the chief is announced to the deities and then to the people by name, parentage and tribe.[8] The fact that he

1. V.3.3.12.
2. Heesterman, op. cit., pp. 77-78.
3. Jayaswal, *Hindu Poliy*, p. 208; Ghoshal, op. cit., p. 267.
4. Bandyopadhaya, *Development of Hindu Polity and Political Theories*, p. 174.
5. George Thomson, AA, p. 99.
6. *VS*, X.8-9; *ŚB*, V.3.5.27-30
7. *ŚB*, V.3.5.30.
8. *TS*, I.8.12; *KS*, XV.7; *MS*, II.6.9; *TB*, I.7-7; *KŚS* XV.94-96.

is announced by his tribe is explained by Kātyāyana as indicating the tribal basis of the later Vedic kingship. In the opinion of this commentator the king was the "king of the people as the territory was not fixed but fluctuating."[1] This is also evident from the fact that the proclamation was made: "Oh people, this is your king."[2] All these references indicate the tribal character of the Vedic state. However there is a passage in the *Taittirīya Saṃhitā* in which the king is announced "in this tribe (*viś*), in this kingdom (*rāṣṭra*)."[3] This might imply that the tribe and the chiefship were now considered identical. Although the chiefship was regarded territorial in nature, its tribal character still persisted and the chief was identified by his tribe. Significantly enough the compilers of the later Vedic texts were conscious of the gradual transformation of the Vedic chiefship from the tribal to the territorial stage. This can be inferred from a passage, which states that by partial performance of a ritual the king or the chief attains the people (*viś*), but not the kingdom; on the other hand he attains both by its full performance.[4] But the following ceremony, in which the king mounts the four quarters and the zenith, symbolises his sovereignty over those regions.[5] It implies the conception of territorial sovereignty. This sovereignty was further accompanied by the assertion of royal authority over people of the emerging social classes, for in the accompanying formula brāhmaṇas, kṣatriyas and vaiśyas, and some others whose identity it is difficult to establish, are invoked to extend their protection to the sacrificer.[6] This ceremony clearly indicates the political influence of the three higher classes, whose emergence tended to strongly undermine the tribal character of the state in later Vedic times.

The *rājasūya* sacrifice provides a curious ceremony in which the priest silently strikes the king with sticks on the back.[7] Some regard it as the height of priestly authority,[8] others think that

1. *yasyāśca jāte rājā bhavati, deśasyānavasthitatvat. KŚS*, XV.96-97.
2. *ŚB*, V.3.3.12. Here the name of the people, *viz.* Kurus, Pañcālas and Bharatas, is inserted in other texts such as *Āp. ŚS*, XVIII.12.7.
3. I.8.12.
4. ...*ubhe eva viśaṃ ca rāṣṭraṃ cā'vagacchati. TS*, II.3.1.
5. *VS*. X.10-14; *TS*, I.8.13; *KS*, XV.7; *MS*, II.6.10.
6. Ibid.
7. *ŚB*, V.4.4.7.
8. Weber, *Über den Rājasuya*, p. 63 quoted in Ghoshal, op.cit., p. 2 fn. 37.

by this the king is brought under the laws;[1] still others hold that the ceremony signifies the king's purification or acquisition of special privileges,[2] such as royal immunity from punishment. There is support for the last view in some texts. The *Śatapatha Brāhmaṇa* makes it clear that through this process the king is made exempt from judicial punishment.[3] Another later text states that thereby the king is purified of his sin and carried beyond death.[4] The ritual was probably meant to judge the physical competence of the candidate. It can be better understood if we take into account the practices prevalent among tribal peoples. The savage Timmes of Sierraleone, who elect their king, reserve to themselves the right of beating him on the eve of his coronation; and they avail themselves of this constitutional privilege with such hearty goodwill that sometimes the unhappy monarch does not long survive his elevation to the throne.[5] It seems that the practice was meant to test the physical endurance of the king. We may also refer to an analogous rite among the Spartans. As Nilson points out, the flagellation of the Spartan boys "was once a rite in which the boys were struck with the sacred bough, which conferred strength and good luck".[6] In other words, it seems to have been a rite of initiation. Thus originally the ceremony of beating was either a rite of initiation or a test to find out the power of endurance in the tribal chief. In later Vedic times the priests used this ritual to assert their power over the king though they interpreted it as the king's exemption from the operation of law.

The tribal and primitive character of the rituals is more in evidence in the ceremonies of cow raid, game of dice and chariot race. These seem to have been originally prescribed as ordeals for establishing the qualifications of the sacrificer for kingship or chieftainship. In the ceremony of cow raid the king is allowed to take away a herd of kine from the house of a friend. The *Śatapatha Brāhmaṇa* states that the sacrificer takes more than a hundred cows from his relative, using his chariot for the purpose

1. Jayaswal, *Hindu Polity*, p. 217.
2. Ghoshal, op.cit., p. 269.
3. V.4.4.7.
4. *KŚS*, XV.191-92.
5. Frazer, *The Golden Bough*, p. 176.
6. Quoted in Thomson, AA, p. 437.

and "conquering by the impulse of Maruts."[1] It comments that the Maruts are the clansmen, and it is by his clan that the chieftain wins what he desires to win.[2] According to the same source the king or the chief presents to his relatives just as many cows as he takes from them or more;[3] the sacrificer returns the cows because he is not capable of a cruel deed.[4] The ritual of the *Black Yajus* recommends a sham fight, in which the king discharges the arrows at a rājanya posted with bow in hand and thus overpowers him.[5] The whole ceremony, therefore, means defeating the kinsman in the cow raid and then reinstating him in his position by an act of grace. The ceremony of cow raid reminds us of an old test prevalent among the tribal people. Primarily this must have meant the ability to capture cows from the enemies, of which we have many instances in the Vedic period, the very term *gaviṣṭi* having the secondary meaning of war. In the present ritual, however, cows are not taken from the inimical tribes but from the kinsmen, the idea being to assert the chiefly or royal power over the rival from the same clan. Evidently it is a mimic cow raid, for the contestant is deliberately made to win. But there is no doubt that originally the chief's or the king's success in the cow raid exhibited in him those qualities which distinguished the early chiefs in the cattle forays.

Another such rite prescribed in the *rājasūya* ceremony is the game of dice. According to this a cow is staked on the gaming ground by a kinsmen of the king, who wins the stake from him.[6] It is suggested that this symbolises the assertion of the royal sacrificer's rule over the common freeman.[7] But the game of dice should be seen as a method to distribute shares in food, cattle and other objects in kin-ordered societies. The chief manipulated the lot system in such a manner so that he might get a larger share. The game of dice was therefore intended to test the sagacity of the chief at the time of election. Since election to

1. V.4.3.1.-8.
2. V. 4.3.8.
3. V.4.3.12.
4. Ibid.
5. *SBE*, xli, 100. fn. 1.
6. Heesterman (op.cit., p. 156) thinks that the real stake at the game is the king himself, although the ritual leaves no doubt that the real stake is the cow; in any case the king's success is ritually ensured.
7. Ghoshal, *Historiography and Other Essays*, p. 272.

chiefship or kingship was confined only to the members of the clan, the king's competitor in this game is described as his *sajāta*.[1] Actually this might refer to the state of affairs existing in the earlier period. But although chiefship had become hereditary now, election was continued in the coronation ceremony to credentialise the chief in the eyes of the large community.

Of such tests as imply the election of the chief at some early stage, the chariot race occupies an important place. It forms a part of the *vājapeya* sacrifice, by performing which a brāhmaṇa becomes the chief priest and a kṣatriya attains universal sovereignty. In the race the royal sacrificer competes with sixteen others, the total number of the chariots being seventeen.[2] The chariots start with the beating of drums and raising of war cries. A rājanya shoots an arrow for fixing the goal of the race. Commenting on this the *Śatapatha Brāhmaṇa* states that the rājanya is "most manifestly of Prajāpati"; hence while being one he rules over many.[3] This may rightly be taken as an early statement of the doctrine of the divinity of the king, which is not generally supported by the other Vedic texts.

Heesterman thinks that chariot races and other games were intended to regenerate productive forces in the cosmos and renew the world,[4] although the passages quoted by him nowhere mention this purpose. The general theory that many rituals in primitive society were saturated with the ideas of rebirth and reproduction may also apply to Vedic society. Reproduction of labour power was necessary to keep the society going. But we may miss the real significance of the chariot race if we look at it only from that point of view. The chariot race, the product of a developed social stage, seems to have been a later version of an older test for proving the competitor's superiority in valour and physical power; it was intended to detect the military qualities of the candidate for the post of the king or the chief of the tribe. The victory cries raised in connection with this rite make it clear that it was the reflection of the actual practice in military campaigns.[5] Remarkably enough chariot race as a rite prevailed

1. *VS*, X.29; *ŚB*, V.4.4.19-23; *KŚS*, XV.197-205.
2. *ŚB*, V.1.5.6-10.
3. *ŚB*, V.1.5.13-14.
4. *The Ancient Indian Royal Consecration*, p. 133.
5. Heesterman, op. cit., p. 137.

not only among several primitive peoples but also in prehistoric Greece. In that country initiation into kingship was effected by a competitive ordeal, which was originally a foot race and later became a chariot race. In this race the winner was acclaimed the god king of the year.[1] According to tradition the earliest games at Olympia were held by Endymion, who set his sons to run a race for the kingdom.[2] Influences of this tradition continued to persist in later times. Even in historical times the Olympian victor was regarded with superstitious veneration and invested with honours that might be described as royal or divine. At Olympia he was crowned with olive. On his return to his native city he was dressed in purple and drawn by white horses in a triumphal procession passing through a breach in the walls.[3] Probably the ceremony of chariot race was inherited by the Vedic Āryans from the original stock of the Indo-Europeans, who used this method in the selection of their chief. In India also the race was undoubtedly used for this purpose, for at the very beginning of the *vājapeya* sacrifice it is stated that the kingdom belongs to him who wins the race.[4] But later it became a mock race in which the form continued but the substance had departed; for the king was deliberately made to win this race.

The concluding portion of the *vājapeya* sacrifice also points to the tribal aspects of the Vedic polity. After the king ascends the throne he is addressed thus: "Thee for tilling! Thee for peaceful dwelling!—Thee, for wealth!—Thee for thrift!"[5] This according to the *Śatapatha Brāhmaṇa* implies that the king is placed on the throne for the welfare of the people.[6] In other words, the supreme power was vested in one man; the purpose of the gift was promotion of agriculture and well-being of the people. It may be noted that the tribal chief of an agricultural society was meant for performing similar duties. Agricultural society, due to slow, arduous and uncertain nature of agricultural processes, is characterized by an extensive development of magic. Out of such a society eventually there emerges the god-king with the

1. Thomson, AA, p. 118.
2. Fraser, *The Golden Bough*, p. 156.
3. Thomson, AA, p. 118.
4. *ajimeva asmin ajāmahai. sa yo na ujjeṣyati tasya na idaṃ bhaviṣyatīti ŚB*, V.1.1.3.
5. *ŚB*, V.2.1.25.
6. Ibid.

special function of promoting by mimetic magic the annual sequence from seed-time to harvest.[1] This may not have been the case in Vedic India where the king had not yet acquired the status of God, but at any rate we notice striking similarity in respect of the ruler's obligations, which were not confined to the maintenance of law and order.

The formula addressed on the occasion of the *vājapeya* sacrifice to the king reminds us of the coronation oath in the *aindra mahābhiṣeka* ceremony. Herein the king and the priest pledge mutually to each other to observe a certain code of conduct. The king repeats the following oath which is administered to him by the priest:

"From the night of my birth to that of my death, for the space between these two, my sacrifice, my gifts, my place, my good deeds, my life, and my offspring mayest thou take, if I play thee false."[2]

Jayaswal rightly points out that the oath is contractual in nature,[3] but there is nothing to show that the pledge was given to the people as a whole. He thinks that the oath was made to the officiating priest, who represented the whole community.[4] But by no stretch of imagination a member of one social class, however, pre-eminent, can be taken as representing the interests of all the other social classes. In the beginning the oath may have been made by the chief in relation to the whole tribe. We have examples of such oaths in primitive societies. The Mexican kings, when they mounted the throne, swore that they would make the sun shine, the clouds give rain, the river flow, and the earth bring forth fruits in abundance.[5] Although the present oath is dissimilar, it may have been administered by the tribe to the chief. But as the tribe disintegrated into classes and the priests emerged as important a class as the warriors themselves, the king transferred his pledge to the priests to whose ideological support he owed his power.

The rituals shed some light on the nature of the office of the king. Here the *Aitareya Brāhmaṇa* furnishes contradictory

1. Thomson, AA, p. 22.
2. *AB*, VIII.15 (Keith's tr.).
3. Op. cit., p. 210.
4. Ibid., p. 211.
5. Frazer, op. cit., p. 87.

evidence. According to one school if enjoyment of the kingdom is desired for the lifetime of the king-elect only the first syllable *bhūḥ* is to be pronounced, if for two generations *bhūr bhuvaḥ*, if for three generations *bhūr bhuvaḥ svaḥ*, namely, the complete formula was to be repeated.[1] In the same source there also occurs the phrase *rājānaṃ rājapitaram*,[2] which indicates hereditary kingship for two generations. Thus according to this Brāhmaṇa the maximum period up to which a family could rule covered three generations. But the *Śatapatha Brāhmaṇa* mentions dynasties of kings who ruled successively for ten generations. The two sets of evidence can be reconciled only by presuming that in the beginning the tenure lasted only for a limited period, and then in course of time it became hereditary. Limited tenure is supported by the practice among primitive and ancient tribes. Among several tribes the tenure of the ruler lasts for a year, and when it expires the king or the chief is re-crowned. An historical instance can be found in the case of Babylon, whose kings used to take the hand of Marduk annually.[3] But the tenure lasted for a longer period in Greece where at the end of every eight years the king's sacred powers needed to be renewed by intercourse with the godhead, without which he would have forfeited the right to the throne.[4] What was obviously a ritual in later times may have been a reality in earlier days. This might be also true of the formulas quoted from the *Aitareya Brāhmaṇa*.

A general review of the coronation rituals suggests that coronation was essentially a form of initiation, a more imposing version of the initiation of the tribal man into manhood or chieftainship. The rituals repeatedly advance the idea of rebirth, which shows that with the king's accession to the throne began a new phase of his life, implying a complete break with his past. Further, the ordeals prescribed on the occasion of coronation are similar to those prescribed for testing the physical power of the tribal man and the chief at the time of initiation. As we know, in the selection of a man for succession to the throne in early society physical strength and beauty held a prominent

1. *AB*, VIII.7; according to Weber (*Ind. Stud.*, ix, 335) this passage refers to the sacrificer, his son and grandson.
2. Ibid., VIII.12.
3. Frazer, *The Golden Bough*, p. 281.
4. Ibid., pp. 279-80.

place.[1] Some ordeals such as the chariot race seem to have been common to the other branches of the Indo-Europeans, who first used horses more for yoking to the chariots than for riding. But the ordeals of cow raid and the game of dice seem to be of Indian origin. Though these ordeals do not indicate the prominent tribal character of kingship in the later Vedic period, when they were retained only as a matter of form, yet they show that the chief was elected in the earlier period.

Since in some ordeals the competitors of the king or the chief were of equal birth (*sajāta*) we may reasonably conjecture that originally the king was elected by the members of his own clan. Further evidence of the tribal character of early kingship is born out by the fact that the king is identified by the *viś* and is formally announced to the *viś*. But by the end of the later Vedic period the tribal character of kingship had considerably corroded. Several rites imply the territorial jurisdiction of the king, and two rites explicitly refer to this aspect of the later Vedic kingship. The great solvent of the old tribal order was the rise of social classes based on the differentiation of functions. The warriors claimed tributes and the priests claimed gifts from the peasants or the vaiśyas. In several ceremonies the participants are not described as the representatives of the tribe, but as brāhmaṇas, kṣatriyas, vaiśyas, and in some cases even śūdras. Finally, the names of officials mentioned in the ratnahaviṃṣi ceremony indicate that the old tribal equality was being shattered not only by the elevation of some members of the tribe to higher position over the others but also by the recruitment of non-Vedic people into the ranks of the Vedic community. Hence there does not seem to be much support for the view that monarchy was generally tribal in the later Vedic period.[2] The class and the territorial aspects of the polity of the period were equally important.

1. Ibid., p. 156.
2. Cf. Ghoshal, *Historiography and Other Essays*, p. 289.

Chapter XIII

KIN CONFLICTS AND RISE OF HIERARCHY IN LATER VEDIC TIMES

The sense of chief's power in later Vedic texts is conveyed by the use of various terms such as *rājan*, *rājanya*, *rājanya-bandhu*, *kṣatra* and *kṣatriya*, not to speak of the ten types of chieftainships enumerated in the *Aitareya Brāhmaṇa*.[1] The term *rājanya* is a dimunitive of the term *rājan* and means the chief's close kinsmen. The number of rājanyas was larger than that of the rajas. *Rājanya* and *kṣatriya* are interchangeable, and at several places *rājanya* is called *kṣatra*.[2] *Kṣatra* means authority or power. Those who possessed power could be included in the kṣatriya group so that Marutta Āvikṣita, an *āyogava* of non-Vedic origin, could also be consecrated.[3] However, once the kṣatriya category came into being eventually it came to constitute a kind of kin-ordered group. Interestingly in later times on the basis of his functions the kṣatriya was fancifully defined as one who protected people from injuries (*kṣatra*).

In the Vedic texts the kṣatriya appears not as a varṇa member but singly or as the kṣatriya par excellence; he appears as a supreme chief, and in this context the rituals show the perpetual struggle between the *kṣatra*/kṣatriya and the *viś*/vaiśya. That the kṣatra was differentiated out of the viś can be clearly inferred from a rite in the *sautrāmaṇi* ceremony of the Soma sacrifice. It is stated that through the offering of the milk to the gods and the fathers the sacrificer secures the Soma drink, and through the *surā* liquor food. Further, milk symbolises the chieftaincy, and *surā* liquor the peasantry or clan. It is stated that he first purifies the *surā* liquor and then the milk; he thus produces the chieftaincy out of the clan or the peasantry,[4] although sometimes the *kṣatra* is said to have been produced out of the brāhmaṇa.[5]

1. VIII.6. These are wrongly considered to be ten types of the state.
2. *ŚB*, XII.7.3.12.
3. R. S. Sharma, *Śūdras*, p. 60.
4. *viśo hi kṣatram jāyate*. *ŚB*, XII.7.3.8.
5. *ŚB*, XI.7.3.12; It is a part of the general myth that all the four varṇas were created out of the different organs of the Creator.

Later Vedic rituals show several types of conflict in the tribal structure. One lay between the central chief or the raja and numerous dispersed similar clan chiefs or rajas. The cow raid prescribed for the *rājasūya* refers to a sham fight between the raja and the rājanya at whom the arrows are discharged by the 'king' who comes out victorious. As will be shown, the central chief was elected by various clan chiefs or lineage chiefs. Further, interests of the central chief and his close kinsmen, i.e. the rājanyas through whom he collected tributes from kinsmen, were both identical and divergent. Above all, polarisation appears between the rājanyas and the *viś*, i.e. between the kin aristocracy who helped the raja on the one hand and the ordinary kinsmen who worked as peasants on the other. A perpetual tug of war went on within the kinship structure between the rājanya or the *kṣatra* and his ordinary kinsmen comprising peasants over the collection of tribute. The raja or the chief protected his people as well as collected tributes from them. He also distributed a part of the tributes on ceremonial occasions, but a major portion went to priests and not to ordinary kinsmen. His function as tribute collector conflicted with his function as protector and distributor. Therefore the chief or the raja is called both *viśāmpati/viśpati* and also *viśāmattā*.[1]

In the dominant ideological ethos of later Vedic texts the idea of distinction between the chiefs (*rājā, rājanya, kṣatra, kṣatriya*) on the one hand and the *viś* or the clan peasantry on the other was the uppermost in the minds of the emerging orders of priests and warriors. All kinds of imageries are used to draw a line between the two. The first is deer, the second barley; the first is horse, the second the other animals; the first is Soma, the second the other plants; the first is milk, the second *surā*; the first is the brick possessed of prayers, the second the space-filling bricks; the first is a large ladle, the second a small ladle; the first is Indra, the second the Maruts; the first is a large grass and the second a small grass; and so on. These imageries were familiarised by the priests so that the tribute-paying peasants could accept the domination of the rājanyas/kṣatriyas and the brāhmaṇas.

The *Atharva Veda*[2] and the *Taittirīya Saṃhitā*,[3] a text of the

1. *TS*, 1.8.15 with comm. quoted in *SBE*. XLI. p. 100 fn. 1.
2. *AV*, I.9.3.
3. *TS*, II.3.9.1; II.2.11.5.

Yajus collection, contains many prayers and rituals attesting a state of perpetual conflict between the *yajamāna* (sacrificer) and his kinsmen called the *sajāta*. As an ambitious aspirant for chiefship the sacrificer tries to establish his hegemony over his kinsmen in order to control the *grāma* of which the *sajātas* are members. *Grāma* might mean a fighting group or even a village in the agricultural context of later Vedic times. Rituals are performed to subordinate the kinsmen and also to win their support through prayers to a god of harmony called Manasdeva. In these rituals the *yajamāna* is identical with Indra,[1] who is evidently the same as the kṣatriya or the *rājanya*. The subdued *sajāta* is called *viś* and is identified with the Maruts or All-Gods (Viśvedewas),[2] who represent the *viś* in the divine world. Later texts such as the Brāhmaṇas provide numerous rituals meant for establishing the control of the kṣatriya/*rājanya* and the brāhmaṇa over the *viś* or the tribal peasantry.[3]

Serious attempts were made to establish the varṇa system. By the end of the Vedic period the vaiśya is ideologically reduced to the position of one who has to pay tribute, one who is meant for being devoured by others, and one who is meant for being oppressed by others.[4] The raja or the chief secured tributes and submission from the vaiśya not only with the ritualistic and ideological support of the brāhmaṇas, but what is more important, with the coercion-based support of his own close kinsmen called the rājanyas, who acted as important functionaries[5] and were skilled in archery and mighty chariot-fighters.

To cope with the perpetual conflict within the kin structure the chief seems to have invoked and enlisted the help of elements from outside. Such an element could be the priests or the brāhmaṇas, who were recruited from both Vedic and non-Vedic groups. The chief sought and obtained ritualistic and ideological support from the priests. The Niṣāda, Āyogava and Ambaṣṭha chiefs seem to have been subjugated and absorbed in Vedic

1. *TS*, VII.1.1.4.
2. *TS*, II.2.11.4; 1.6.4; 3.9.2.
3. Bijoy Kumar Chaudhary, of K.P. Jayaswal Research Institute, Patna, gives many instances in "Kinship Relations and Social Hierarchy in the Vedic Period" (unpublished).
4. The vaiśya is called *anyasya balikṛta anyasyādya* and *yathakāmajyeya* in *AB*, VII, 29.
5. *tasmād rajanyena adhyakṣena vaiśyam ghnanti*, *KS*, XXVIII.4.

society with priestly help. Similarly some artisans also belonged to clans outside the kin structure of the chief. The chief also tried to secure the support of people from other clans who were obviously subjugated by him with the help of his close kinsmen. This can be said on the analogy of the Maruts who are considered the gods of the peasantry or common clansmen. The Maruts are regarded to be sons of Rudra,[1] but they became the companions of Indra and are called *Indrasakhā*.[2] It is obvious that people outside his own clan were preferred by Indra for his support. This practice would also be adopted by rajas in Vedic society. Thus it would appear that the chief and the kin aristocracy managed to obtain support from outside the kin structure in order to resolve the conflict within it.

The attempt to reduce the *viś* or the ordinary kinsmen to the position of subordination and exploitation and to raise the kṣatriya and brāhmaṇa to superordination is evident in many passages of the *Śatapatha Brāhmaṇa*. Its rituals give a good idea of the anxiety and efforts of the priests and tribal chiefs to gather gifts/tributes for their support, for which it was found necessary to promote the elements leading to the emergence of the varṇa system.

In the context of Soma as the 'king' it is stated that when the kṣatriya occupies a higher position, the *viś* serve him as subjects (*prajā*) from a lower position.[3] The ritual regarding bricklaying is explained repeatedly. The object always is to make the chieftain (*kṣatra*) more powerful and to subordinate the *viś* to him. Further, the peasants or the *viś* are to be kept divided in speech (*pṛthagvādinī*) and in consciousness (*nānācetasa*)[4], so that they may not be able to resist the demand of the *kṣatra* for regular tributes and perpetual submission.

Further evidence of the need to secure the obedience of the peasant clansmen to the ruling chief, i.e. of the *viś* to the *kṣatra*, is found in the rituals of the *aśvamedha*. Of the animals to be sacrificed the horse is called *kṣatra* and the other animals are

1. *RV*, 1.38.7; they are called Rudrīyas.
2. The epithet *marutvat* (accompanied by the Maruts is considered characteristic of Indra. A.A. Macdonell, *Vedic Mythology*, p. 57; the term *marudgaṇa* or attended by the Marut host is also applied to Indra, *Ibid.*
3. *ŚB*, III.9.3.7; see *SBE*, XXVI, p. 228, fn. 2.
4. Ibid., VIII.7.2.3.

called *viś*. Appropriate invitation and offering formulas have to be used while sacrificing the horse and other animals to the deities. If this is not done, then the peasantry becomes equal and refractory (*pratyudyaminī*) to the chieftain and the sacrificer loses his longevity. But if the priests do everything in the prescribed manner, the *viś* becomes obedient and subservient to the *kṣatra*.[1] All this shows the necessity of subjugating the refractory peasant who refuses to surrender his freedom and position of equality to the chief.

A ritual in the *vājapeya* coronation ceremony shows that both the *rājanya* and the *vaiśya* were treated as the rivals of the sacrificer who wanted to be crowned. A *vaiśya* or a *rājanya* from a rival chariot, which evidently loses the chariot race, sits down on the northern tip of the altar. A cup of *surā* or liquor is presented to the *rājanya* or the vaiśya in order to buy him for the sacrificer. What happens to the *rājanya* as a result of this presentation is not clear. But in doing so the priest (*neṣṭṛ*) smites the vaiśya with "untruth, misery and darkness". On the other hand, he presents a cup of honey with the golden vessel to the brāhmaṇa which confers immortal life on the recepient.[2] At any rate the need of keeping the vaiśyas in a state of misery and ignorance was realised by the priests and chiefs. In the context of the *sautrāmaṇi* it is stated that the cups of milk are taken first and then the cups of *surā*, by which the peasantry or the *viś* is made obedient to the *kṣatra*.[3] It is further stated that Soma stands for the nobility and the other plants stand for the common people. The *viś* constitutes the kṣatriya's food; the plants constitute the food of Soma.[4]

In the early Vedic age inter-tribal and intra-tribal conflict gave rise to the śūdra order.[5] The conflict centred round the possession of cattle and distribution of booty including women slaves. The struggle became more varied and intense in the settled agricultural phase during later Vedic times. It went on in the Aryan/ Vedic kin structure and also within the embroynic or proto-varṇa system which arose as a consequence of this struggle.

1. Ibid., XIII.2.2.15.
2. Ibid., V.1.5.28.
3. Ibid., XII.7.3.12.
4. Ibid., III.3.2.8.
5. R.S. Sharma, *Śūdras*, pp. 9-45.

Division between mental and physical labour and continuous struggle within the Vedic and non-Vedic kin structures led to the formation of the four varṇas, which appear clearly in the *Śatapatha Brāhmaṇa*[1] and other later texts. The division of society into four varṇas is broadly recognised, but it is not legalised and well defined in later Vedic texts. In many passages rājanya and not kṣatriya is used; similarly *arya* and not vaiśya is used, and sometimes the term *vaiśya* also occurs. Śūdra appears in all such passages, but in the tribal milieu he is made a participant in several important Vedic sacrifices; this is reversed in the early law-books in which he is deprived of all such participation.

Rituals indicate conflict between the rājanya and the *viś* in which the brāhmaṇa or some other types of priests intervene on the part of the former. In many rituals the rājanya and brāhmaṇa combine against the *viś* and the śūdra. U.N. Ghoshal cites numerous instances to demonstrate the dominance of the *brahma* and *kṣatra* in later Vedic society, their mutual antagonism and their close political alliance.[2] Prayers for the protection of the two upper varṇas appear in the Yajus collections[3] and in the Brāhmaṇas.[4] It is stated that the brāhmaṇa and the kṣatriya enclose the vaiśya and the śūdra.[5] Further, those who are neither kṣatriya nor *purohita* (priest) are incomplete.[6] In a later version of the *rājasūya* rite the vaiśya and śūdra are excluded from the game of dice.[7] However the *Aitareya Brāhmaṇa* shows that the raja tried to bring under control not only the vaiśyas and the śūdras but also the brāhmaṇas; there is no mention of the rājanya and the kṣatriya in this context. Rituals also reflect the process of conflict between the kṣatriyas and rājanyas, possibly between the non-kin king and the old kin aristocracy for a share in cereals and cattle collected from the *viś* and the labour power to be supplied by śūdras and women slaves.

Although it lay in the interests of the kṣatriyas and brāhmaṇas to combine against the vaiśyas and śūdras the two carried on a

1. *V.* 5.4.9.
2. *Hindu Public Life*, Pt. 1, pp. 73-80.
3. *Kānva Saṃhitā*, XX.2.
4. *ŚB*, III.5.2.11; III.6.1.17-18; IX.4.1.7.8.
5. Ibid., V.4.4.12-13.
6. Ibid., VI.6.3.12-13.
7. R.S. Sharma, *Śūdras*, p. 57.

protracted mutual struggle. We have the famous story of Paraśurāma who destroyed the kṣatriyas repeatedly. F.E. Pargiter highlights this conflict. It seems that the main issue involved in the conflict in the emerging varṇa society was the question of social supremacy linked with that of sharing gifts and tributes. The kṣatriya claim to knowledge and their reaction against the cult of sacrifice certainly meant reaction against the flow of numerous and continuous gifts to the priests. Eventually the struggle ended in the recognition of the ritualistic leadership of the brāhmaṇas by the kṣatriyas and the recognition of the political leadership of the kṣatriyas by the brāhmaṇas.

The end product of the various types of conflict in Vedic times seems to have been the rise of the varṇa system, according to which the domination of the brāhmaṇas and kṣatriyas came to be recognised by the vaiśyas and śūdras. The raja or the chief had to identify himself with this system and to uphold dharma. Ritualistic and ideological devices were developed to support the varṇa and political power in later Vedic times, and the two were strengthened and formalised by the legal superstructure raised in post-Vedic times.

The brāhmaṇas played a pivotal part in strengthening the authority of the rājanyas/kṣatriyas along with whom they enjoyed a position of domination and superiority over the vaiśyas and śūdras. Together with the chiefs they appear as "eaters of the peasantry" and masters of the labouring class called the śūdra. How the non-Vedic brāhmaṇas joined hands with the Vedic rājanyas is not clear, but the dominance of the priests is visible. Later Vedic texts mention as many as seventeen classes of priests of whom brāhmaṇa is the only one. Eventually the brāhmaṇa claims half of all the *dakṣinā* and he succeeds in superseding all the other classes of priests.[1] In no other Indo-European society the priestly stratum enjoyed such authority as it did in Vedic society. More importantly, it played a crucial role in bolstering the power and privileges of political leadership at the cost of the common peasantry through the invention, elaboration and explanation of rituals.

Perpetual wars strengthened the power of the ruling chiefs. The fight between the gods and the asuras, i.e. the *devāsura*

1. R.S. Sharma, *Material Culture*, etc., p. 82. Supersession needs investigation.

saṃgrāma, is the most important story in the *Śatapatha Brāhmaṇa*.[1] The gods were divided into four factions: Agni led the Vasus, Soma led the Rudras, Varuṇa led the Ādityas and Indra led the Maruts. So the Asura-Rākṣasa came in between them. In order to overcome the Asuras, all the gods yielded to the excellence of Indra and made him their chief. It was decided that the kinsmen should not fall out. Now a higher chief presided over several chiefs. The role of war in strengthening the chief's power may also be inferred from the institution of the *aśvamedha* sacrifice.[2] It is needless to add that the chief used a good part of the booty to strengthen his power as well as that of his loyal followers.

The advent of iron may have added to the authority of the chiefs in this period. In the initial stage it was used mainly for purposes of war. Spear heads and arrow heads have been found in large numbers at excavated Painted Grey Ware sites of 1000 B.C.—500 B.C. in Haryana, Western U.P. and the adjoining areas.[3] As heads of various clans or tribes the chiefs may have exercised special authority over the use of the metals. When iron came into use they may have monopolised weapons made of it. The arrow heads and spear heads discovered in excavations may have mostly belonged to the clan chiefs or elders. It seems that the smiths and the chariot-makers were especially attached to the emerging warrior class. As an artisan engaged in fabricating the war material, the *rathakāra* held a special position, as shown by his role in coronation ceremonies.

On the basis of some anthropological findings[4] it is argued that as members of senior lineages in Vedic society the rājanyas were entitled to receive tributes from the *viś* or ordinary kinsmen who were relegated to the ranks of junior lineages.[5] Although the genealogical superiority of the rājanya over the *viś* is not advanced as a ground for claiming tributes in the rituals we have

1. *ŚB*, III, 4.2.2-3; *AB*, I.24.
2. *ŚB*, XIII.
3. R.S. Sharma, *Material Culture*, etc., pp. 60-61.
4. P.P. Rey, "The Lineage Mode of Production", *Critique of Anthropology*, 1975, no. 3 has some stimulating ideas, but his attempt to treat age and sex conflict as exploitation and class struggle has been sharply criticised by several anthropologists including C. Meillasoux. Aidan Southhall, op.cit., pp. 181 and 192, fn. 162.
5. Romila Thapar, *Lineage to State*.

discussed, the matter deserves attention. In our opinion forcible methods adopted by the descendants of the elected chiefs led to social distancing which was frozen into genealogical ideology at a much later stage. In the kin-based groups distinctions appeared on the basis of age, skill and experience in procuring subsistence, ability to lead in wars and so on. Elders naturally had more experience in procuring sources of livelihood. If they combined it with skill, physical bravery, etc., they could become chiefs. The great coronation of Indra tells us that he was elected raja because he was "the most vigorous, the most strong, the most perfect and the best in carrying out any work".[1] This may apply to the early Vedic stage. We have references to the election of the raja or the chief in the later portions of the *Ṛg Veda*[2] and also in the *Atharva Veda*.[3] In the early Vedic stage the *viś* or the kinsmen assembled in the *samiti* elected raja, who became the protector of his people or the *viśpati* or the *viśāmpati* and received voluntary gifts called *bali* from them. In the next stage, or in later Vedic times, the raja tried to strengthen his power with the help of his close blood relations called rājanyas who consequently came to be demarcated and distinguished from the *viś*. The rājanyas were skilled in archery and the use of chariots, and were engaged in fighting, collecting *bali* and maintaining order. The king (chief) also enlisted the support of the brāhmaṇas and some non-Vedic chiefs and artisans. Certain *rājakartṛs* or king makers, who were not necessarily his kinsmen, elected the raja. In the third stage the rajas elected the raja, i.e. the chiefs elected the great chief. "To whomsoever the chiefs agree to entrust the chiefdom he becomes the chief and not he over whom they do not agree."[4] This passage recurs repeatedly in the *Śatapatha Brāhmaṇa*. Finally the great chief would try to retain all powers and privileges in his family. The *Aitareya Brāhmaṇa* prescribes formulas for securing chiefly office for one, two or three generations.[5] The *Śatapatha Brāhmaṇa* speaks of the ten generation chieftainship,[6] but power would not necessarily go to

1. *AB*, VIII, 12-17.
2. X. 166.4.
3. III. 4.2.
4. *yasmai vā rājāno rāiyam anumanyante sa rājā bhavati na sa yasmai na.* IX.3.4.5; IX.4.1.1 and 13; IX.4.3.12.
5. VIII.7.
6. XII.9.3.4.

the eldest son; the eldest could be superseded in favour of the dearest son.

Various types of chiefs tried to perpetuate the functions and privileges acquired by them. In the agricultural state it meant the continuation of divorce between production and management, between mental labour and physical labour. The privileges of the interest group and their withdrawal from primary production came to be maintained through the device of seniority, heredity and primogeniture, not to speak of numerous rituals. Many of these methods were sanctified by rituals, which were invented, elaborated and frequently performed by the priests.

In the beginning unequal access to resources or whatever little surplus was available was based on achievement, which brought gain, prestige, power and influence. This is found in many tribal societies. In the case of the Lushais[1] knowledgeable farmers called the Ramhuals were asked to look for good lands for *jhum* cultivation. When they succeeded they were allowed first choice of fields to cultivate. In course of time what was derived from achievement and experience would be based on heredity and mythical/ritualistic considerations. This could have also happened with the rājanyas/kṣatriyas as well as with the brāhmaṇas.

Apart from the rise of a strong chief, we have clear evidence of the emergence of a well-defined territory over which a chief ruled. The idea of territoriality is conveyed by the use of the term *rāsṭra* or *janapada*, which occurs in later Vedic texts. The chief belongs not only to his clan but also to the territory.[2] The Bhārata battle was fought for chieftainship over territory. It raised the issue of control over the Kuru land or the power to raise tributes from it. Whether this power should go to the senior line or to the senior son of the junior line in the Kuru family was the issue. The war dealt a heavy blow to the values and principles generated by the institution of kinship. It brought victory to those who really had the physical capacity, to those who were more attached to territory and to the values of varṇa society than to the clan loyalities.

The territorial element had come to the fore, but the system of

1. N.E. Parry, *A Monograph on Lushai Customs and Ceremonies*, pp. 7-8.
2. *TS*, 1.8.12; II.3.1; *ŚB*, IX.4.11.

taxation was not well established. Tributes were collected forcibly. No indications of any assessment nor of any regular collection nor of any apparatus for fiscal purposes are found. The *bhāgadugha* was a distributor of shares and not a collector of taxes. Puṣan is *bhāgadugha* in relation to the gods for he places with his hands the food before them.[1] Once cereals and cattle were collected as tributes or booty, they may have been distributed to the close kinsmen and non-kin functionaries attached to the chief, for distribution was an important function of the chief.

The Vedic *senā* was a kin-based host which comprised the *viś*. The Maruts, who numbered variously 36, 37 and 49, and were considered *viś* or peasants in divine society, formed a fighting host.[2] The Kuru king was surrounded by 64 everready warriors who were his sons and grandsons.[3] When the Pañcāla king performed a rite there arose 6033 Turvasa warriors clad in male; the Turvasas were one of the five clans of the Pañcālas.[4] These numbers may be conventional; but the kin-based ties of the warriors are clear. The *aśvamedha* sacrifice required a large army to protect the horse. There is nothing to show that this army was recruited on the basis of payment; on the other hand it consisted of both kṣatriyas and the *viś*[5] who constituted the ordinary kinsmen. The *Mahābhārata* shows that the kin-based units did not work because of their conflict within the emerging varṇa order. The story of war between the Kauravas and Pāṇḍavas does not show the presence of a state system although we hear of huge numbers of people fighting in the war. They were not paid soldiers but the kinsmen and relations of both the parties. The main soldiery of the Pāṇḍavas consisted of the Yādava contingents supplied by their relation Kṛṣṇa.

It seems that all able-bodied males of the clan or the tribe bore arms in times of war. In later Vedic times the *viś*/vaiśya was identical with *bala* or force, which signified that the whole clan or the kin-based group could be mobilised at the time of war. But in post-Vedic times the vaiśya became identical with

1. *ŚB*, I.1.2.17.
2. Ibid., V.4.3.47. A.A. Macdonell, *Vedic Mythology*, pp. 77-81.
3. *AB*, III.48.
4. H.C. Raychaudhuri, *Political History of Ancient India*, p. 66.
5. *ŚB*, IV.3.3.15; V.4.3.8.

bali or tax, and the *bala* or force became an organ of the state, and the function of fighting came to be confined to the kṣatriyas. Without regular taxes professional soldiery could not be raised and maintained. The *rājanyas* were trained fighters. There was some differentiation between the rank and file of the army on the one hand and the captains on the other. The captains used chariots and weapons, but ordinary kinsmen used sticks or *lāṭhīs*. The bond of kinship was still visible because both the captains and the common soldiers ate from the same plate.

Of course we have a good number of public functionaries in later Vedic times, and as many as twelve of them called *ratnins* or jewel holders can be counted. Some of them seem to have been artisan members of the dominant clan to which the chief belonged. Though they worked under the direction of the chief yet their formal consent to the coronation of the chief was considered essential. Many of these functionaries did not belong to the kin group of the raja; they seem to have been recruited from and fused into wider tribes from non-Vedic kin groups. This shows that the ties of kinship were being heavily undermined at the lower level and secondary kin ties were being developed at the higher level. In the later Vedic power hierarchy the respective positions of the brāhmaṇa, raja, raja's brother and others are known.

By the end of the Vedic period the ranks of the brāhmaṇa and the rājanya tended to become hereditary. The qualities associated with the priest and the warrior were attributed to their birth so that we have an element of genealogical ideology. It is desired that the brāhmaṇa be born in the brahman (priestly office or order) so that he may be endowed with spiritual luster (*brahmavarcas*), and the rājanya be born in the royal office or order (*rāṣṭra*) so that he may be heroic, skilled in archery, sure of his mark and a mighty car-fighter.[1] All this is supposed to have happened in older days (*purā*), which implies that in subsequent times the brāhmaṇa and the rājanya had to acquire their respective qualities after they were born. The genealogical myth was still not very strong.

The power of the chief was immeasurably strengthened because of the tendency to make his position hereditary. Initially sacri-

1. Ibid., XIII.2.1.1-2. The version given above is based on the translation of Julius Eggeling in *SBE*, XLIV, p. 294 with fn. 2.

fices may have been used by the chief to distribute the presents and the tributes collected and received from defeated tribes, chiefs and also from his clansmen. But if we consider the praise of gifts or *dāna-stuti* appearing prominently in a late part of the *Ṛg Veda* it will appear that a major portion of what the chief or the king possessed was made over to the priests who sang praises in support of his chiefly power. Continuous unequal distribution of cattle, horses, women slaves and other resources strengthened the ranks of priests and warrior chiefs. Later Vedic sacrifices allude to times when chiefs were frequently elected. References to the election of the king also occur in the Jātakas. But once the chiefs managed to stabilise their position and privileges by making it hereditary they did not need frequent validations which provided occasions for sharing of the surplus. Towards the end of the Vedic period the Upaniṣads show a strong reaction against sacrifices led by the kṣatriyas and in later centuries led by the Buddhists.

All in all the later Vedic power structure had assumed a character which was that of a proto-state. This society stood at the threshhold of the formation of the state which originated in settlements inhabited by agriculturists. Sustained attempts were made to collect tributes from a reluctant peasantry consisting of the chief's kinsmen and others. In the absence of a regular flow of taxes a professional army was lacking. The distance between the chief and his kinsmen was still not very wide. Occasionally the king lent hand to the plough and ate from the same plate with ordinary soldiers mobilised from his kin.

The state could not assume a full-fledged shape because the surplus available from agriculture was still marginal. Agriculture carried with the wooden ploughshare in the upper Ganga plains could create a subsistence economy and not a large surplus producing economy. The Vedic people produced the rainy season crop of rice called *ṣaṣṭika*, which ripens in sixty days.[1] They did not know the practice of transplantation. A term called *plāśuka*[2] used in the *Śatapatha Brāhmaṇa* is interpreted to mean transplantation in later times. But it seems that wet rice cultivation was not known in the period represented by the ritualistic

1. *VI*, ii, p. 345.
2. The term literally means 'rapidly growing up again', s.v. *plāśuka*, Monier-Williams, *Sanskrit-English Dictionary*.

texts called the Brāhmaṇas. Cattle slaughter on a large scale hindered agriculture. Though iron may have helped the chiefs in their wars, it was not being used widely for purposes of agriculture. These limitation notwithstanding, a few organs associated with the state assumed recognisable forms.

CHAPTER XIV

FROM GOPATI TO BHŪPATI: CHANGING POSITION OF THE KING

The frequent use of the term *rājan* in Vedic texts creates the illusion that in Vedic times kingship was a well-established institution. But the term *rājan* seems to have a tribal origin. It is derived from an Indo-European stem, which means to proceed in a straight line for the selection of some site for settlement or religious structure.[1] In *rex*, the Latin counterpart of *rājan*, we must see not so much the 'sovereign' as the one who traces out the line, the way which must be followed, which also represents what is right.[2] Although in Sanskrit the term *rājan* is generally derived from the root *rāj* (to shine) or the root *rañj/raj* (to grow red, to paint, to decorate, to charm),[3] according to *Naighuṇṭa* II.14 the root also means to go.[4] The meaning ascribed to this term by the *Naighuṇṭa* is closer to a similar meaning assigned to the verb *orego* in Greek which is translated as 'stretch, stretch out'.[5] It may be noted that the meaning 'to go' attributed to *raj/rañj* by the *Naighuṇṭa* is nearer to *rāji*, which is used in the sense of line in the *Śatapatha Brāhmaṇa*[6] and is probably derived from the root *rāj/rāñj*.[7] In view of the interpretation of the terms *raj/rañj* and consequently *rājan* suggested above, the commonly held view, based on the moralist/idealistic meanings of the term *rājan* given in classical Sanskrit, that the *rājan* was meant to please the people, has to be generally discarded for Vedic times. Even if we base *rājan* on the root *rāj* (to shine)[8] it would mean one who shines among many which would justify his being a ruler. Apparently he shines not only because of his good physique

1. Emile Benveniste, *Indo-European Language and Society*, pp. 311-12.
2. Ibid. p. 312.
3. M. Monier-Williams, *Sanskrit-English Dictionary* s.v. *rañj* or *raj*.
4. Ibid.
5. Benveniste, op.cit., p. 309.
6. s.v. *rāji*, *SED*.
7. Ibid.
8. s.v. *rāj*, *SED*.

and military accomplishments but also because of his qualities of head and heart which all combine to get him accepted as leader of the tribe.

Whether we derive the term *rājan* from *raj/rañj* or from *rāj*, in our understanding originally it meant a tribal leader and not a prince or ruler, as is generally made out. On the basis of Indo-European analogies[1] if we accept the meaning of *rājan* as one who draws a line for the selection of a settlement site or a religious structure, it would appear that the earliest Ṛg Vedic *rājan* was a tribal leader who combined the functions of both priest and warlord. The case of Devapī and Śantanu suggests this. We learn from the *Nirukta* that *Devāpi* acted as domestic priest (*purohita*) for his younger brother Śantanu, who had anointed himself king, and thus obtained rain for him.[2] That the *rājan* was a tribal leader is also supported by the term *janasya gopā*[3] or *gopati*[4] applied to him. Both these terms literally mean cowherd, and came to be applied to the *rājan* because it was his duty to protect and look after the *jana* or tribe. In the *Ṛg Veda* the term *janarājan* is also used.[5] The Ṛg Vedic *pañcajanāḥ* or the five tribes are well-known. The term *jana* occurs about 275 times[6] in the *Ṛg Veda* which hardly leaves any doubt that it reflects a predominantly tribal society. The term *jana* evidently stood for tribe comprising several clans, and even when the tribe broke into smaller kin-based units or gradually into social classes in later Vedic times the term *janeśvara* was occasionally used for the king as we learn from the kernel of the *Mahābhārata*,[7] and also from the *Rāmāyaṇa*.[8]

Another important term indicating the tribal character of the Vedic King was *viśpati*.[9] Although it is argued that the term

1. Beneveniste, op. cit., pp. 311-12.
2. A.A. Macdonell and A.B. Keith, *Vedic Index of Names and Subjects*, i, 377.
3. Ibid., i. 269 and fn. 2.
4. Soma is called *gopati janasya* 'protector of the people'. *RV*, IX.35.5. Ibid.
5. s.v. *jana* (*RV*, I.53.9), *SED*.
6. Infra, ch. XXI.
7. *The Jaya-Saṃhitā*, i.e. *The Ur-Mahābhārata*, i, redacted by Keshavram K. Shastree, Gujarat Research Society (Ahmedabad, 1977), [henceforth *JS*], I.124.1; 187.15.
8. *VI*, ii, 308.
9. Ibid. with fns. 6-9.

means either the head of a canton or of dewelling, in our opinion it really means head of a clan comprising kinsmen. This can be inferred from several passages in which the king clearly appears as 'lord/or protector?/ of the subject-people'[1] [or just people]. We may add that the term *viś* occurs about 170 times in the *Ṛg Veda.*[2] Although the word is taken to mean the clan and settlement,[3] in our opinion the former meaning suits many passages. In any case the Vedic term *viśpati* is nothing but an earlier form of *viśāmpati* found in the epics. In the kernel of the *Mahābhārata* we come across this term at many places mostly in the vocative case (*viśāmpate*).[4] Although in the epic it may mean lord of the people, really the term evokes the tribal and archaic nature of the kingship. *Viśpati* may be compared with *viṭpati,* which is translated as 'chief of men', a king or prince, and is found in the *Mahābhārata.*[5] It may be noted that the term *viśām* is also compounded with *nāthaḥ* or *Īśvaraḥ* which in the *Śatapatha Brāhmaṇa* and later texts[6] convey the same meaning as *viśāmpati.* The use of *viśāmpati, viṭpati, viśāmattā* or *viśāmīśvaraḥ* in later Vedic and post-Vedic texts suggest that ordinarily the *viśpati* was the head of a clan in the *Ṛg Veda* and not the lord of a settlement, although when the clan settled at a place the later meaning naturally came to be attached to it, as it happened in the case of *grāmaṇi.*

A few other terms indicating headship of large kin-based segments were not necessarily attached to the king, but they indicate a stage in the evolution of the tribal kingship. For example *vrātapaḥ,*[7] i.e. protector or lord of the *vrāta,* was evidently a tribal leader of the same category as *rājan. Vrāta* in the sense of a military flock[8] seems to have been a kin-based unit, for in Vedic times army regiments were made of such segments. The term *pañcavrātas,*[9] i.e. five races of men, can be compared

1. *VI,* ii, 305-06.
2. Infra, ch. XXI.
3. *VI,* ii, 305-06.
4. *JS,* I.127.15; 145.4; 152.11; 176.33; 187.20, 22; 188.4; 192.17; 194.113, 18; 196.23; 197.25; 198.13; 205.5.
5. s.v. *viṭ, SED.*
6. s.v. *viś, SED.*
7. s.v. *vrāta. SED.*
8. Ibid.
9. Ibid.

to *pañcajanas* or five tribes. This would suggest that the *vrāta* was identical with the *jana*. But we cannot guess the size of the *vrāta* in relation to the *gaṇa*, for in a passage which speaks of military mobilisation *vrātas* precede the *gaṇas*.[1] The leader of a *gaṇa* is called *gaṇapati*, who at one place is also called *rājan*.[2] The *gaṇapati*, who appears frequently even in the *Ṛg Veda* and later Vedic texts,[3] was most probably a tribal leader.[4] This may be also true of *gaṇeśvara* mentioned in the epics,[5] which may have preserved some memory of the past.

Towards the end of the Vedic period we come across terms which stress the territorial and tribute-collecting aspects of the kingship or the chiefdom. Coronation rituals show a conflict between the tribal and territorial roles, because the territory was fixed and the tribe kept on moving.[6] But gradually the king got established in the *rāṣṭra*, which term is derived from the root *raj*.[7] In the tenth book of the *Ṛg Veda* the king is asked to uphold the *rāṣṭra*;[8] the term *janapada* does not find any place in the Veda. However in a Brāhmaṇa we come across the term *rāṣṭra-gopa*, applied to the *purohita* in the sense of the protector of a kingdom,[9] and we find *raṣṭrapati*, 'lord of a kingdom' in another *Brāhmaṇa*.[10] *Raṣṭrabhṛt* is applied to the king, in the sense of a sustainer of the kingdom in the *Śatapatha Brāhmaṇa*.[11] The same text also uses the term *rāṣṭrin* or 'possessing or occupying a kingdom'. A Purāṇa has the term *rāṣṭrapāla*[12] or protector of the kingdom.

Though *janapada* in the sense of a community is used in several Brāhmaṇas,[13] later Vedic texts hardly use any term which might

1. *RV*, III.26.6. In our opinion the *vrāyta* belonged to an alien *vrāta* in the same way as a *janya* belonged to an alien *jana*.
2. *AB*, IX.6.
3. RV, II.13.1, X.113.9; *TB*, III.11.4.2. *AB*, I.21.
4. *RV*, II.23.1.
5. s.v. *gaṇa*, *SED*.
6. Infra, ch. XXI.
7. s.v. *rāṣṭra*. *SED*.
8. *RV*, X.173.1-2, The term *rāṣṭra* is however mentioned even in earlier portions of the *RV*, *VI*, ii, 223.
9. *AB*, VIII.25 quoted in VI, ii, 223.
10. s.v. *rāṣṭrapati*, *SED*.
11. VII.1.1.4.
12. s.v. *rāṣṭra*, *SED*.
13. Ibid.

indicate the protection or lordship of a *janapada* by the king. Such terms however appear in the kernel of the *Mahābhārata*, which might apply to later Vedic times. We hear of *janapadeśvara*[1] and *janapadasya īśa*.[2] In the sense of king the *Rāmāyaṇa* mentions *janapadādhipa*[3] and Pāṇini mentions *janapadin*.[4]

In later Vedic times the protection of territory by the king is suggested by such terms as *rāṣṭrapati*, *rāṣṭrabhṛt*, etc., but only a few words indicate his tribute-collecting functions. *Bali*, voluntary offering made to a prince or god,[5] forms part of the compound *balihṛt*,[6] tribute-giving princes and tribes in the *Ṛg Veda*. But in later texts a term which indicates forcible collection of taxes from clansmen, i.e. *viśāmattā*,[7] eater of the peasant people, is applied to the king. This role comes into conflict with his protective obligations, which once extending to the whole tribal community, is restricted to the brāhmaṇas.[8] *Bhoja* is another term, used in Vedic texts, to express the tribute-enjoying aspect of the kingship. It is however also used to denote a liberal, bountiful person.[9] In the *Aitareya Brāhmaṇa*, which is one of the youngest Brāhmaṇas composed around 600 B.C., *bhaujya*, derived from *bhoja*, appears as a form of rulership.[10]

The king has to 'eat' and yet protect the people. As numerous later Vedic rituals show; the tribal peasantry resists the acquisitive attempts of the king or the chief[11] and apparently demands protection. The dichotomy arising out of such a situation is solved in the iron ploughshare-based, class-divided society of post-Vedic times when the law-books (Dharmasūtras) enunciate

1. *JS*, I.177.21.
2. Ibid., I.148.3.
3. II.63.48 quoted in *SED*, p. 410, col. 2.
4. IV.3.100 quoted ibid.
5. *RV*, I.70.9, V.1.10.
6. *RV*, VII.6.5, X.173.6.
7. *AB*, VIII.17.
8. In the same passage of the *AB*, (VIII.17) the king is called *brāhmaṇānāṃ goptā*.
9. s.v. *bhoja*, *SED*.
10. *Ait.Br.* quoted in *SED*, p. 768, col. 2.
11. *TS*., VIII.7.1.12, X.4.3.22, XII.7.3.15. Several instances of strife between the *viś* and *kṣatra* are quoted in *VI*, ii, 307, fn.12. The problem has been discussed in my *Material Culture and Social Formations in Ancient India*, ch. V.

the principle that the king receives taxes as wages for the protection he affords to the people.[1] In post-Vedic and classical texts a large number of terms stress the tax-enjoying aspects of the kingship. These are, for example, *baliṣaḍbhāghārin*[2] *bhāgabhuj*,[3] *ṣaḍbhāgabhāk*,[4] *ṣaṣṭhavṛtti*,[5] etc.

In post-Vedic times when tribes broke into individual peasant households under *gahapatis* on a large scale, especially in the middle Gangetic plains, and tribal identities were overshadowed by household peasant production units headed by patriarchs and distinguished by occupational groups the king assumed new titles to emphasise his lordship over all category of people in general. Such titles as *nṛpa*,[6] *nṛpati*,[7] *nareśvara*,[8] *narendra*,[9] *narādhipa*,[10] *manujādhipa*,[11] etc., came into prominence. It is significant that the terms used for the protective aspect of the king come to mean lordship or authority. This can be said of the word *pati* found in *nṛpati*. In general most terms used for the king emphasise his lordship or sovereignity. For instance the term *nareśa* stands for the person who disciplines (*īś*) the people (*nara*).

The division of society into varṇas or social classes in which the two upper classes performed non-productive and managerial and the two lower classes productive functions came also to be reflected in the use of the synonyms and designations for the king. The duties of the varṇas were laid down in the Dharmaśāstras, which made the king the defender and upholder and even promulgator of dharma or law. Hence the title *dharmamahārāja* and *dharmapravartaka*[12] came to be applied to him. *Dharmarāja* was applied not only to Yudhiṣṭhira, but inscriptions of the early

1. P.V. Kane, *History of Dharmasāstra*, iii (second edn. Poona, 1973), pp. 27, 189.
2. Manu, VIII.308.
3. *Markaṇḍeya Purāṇa* quoted in s.v. *bhāgabhuj*, *SED*.
4. Manu VIII.305.
5. Monier-Williams, *Śakuntalā*, p. 187 quoted in s.v. *ṣaṣṭhavṛtti*, *SED*.
6. *JS*, I.176.13, 108.4, 12.
7. *JS*, I 180, 5, 205.16.
8. *JS*, I 127, II, 175.14.
9. Manu quoted in s.v. *narendra*, *SED*.
10. *JS*, I 118.4, 136.8, 144.20, 180.4, 197.9, 200.3, 214.1.
11. *JS*, I.174.12.
12. Kauṭilyaś *Arthaśāstra*, III.I. The title occurs in a verse probably interpolated in the *AŚ*.

centuries of the Christian era show that it was adopted as a proper name by several kings.[1] Royal epithets stressing the defence of the varṇa system appear in inscriptions as early as the second century A.D.[2] and become common thereafter. After the Kali social crisis, inferable from the Purāṇic passages of about the last quarter of the third and the first quarter of the fourth century A.D., this aspect comes out prominently in inscriptions of the 4th-6th centuries and becomes conventional in later epigraphs. Siṃhavarman, a Pallava king, is described as *kaliyuga-doṣāvasanna-dharmoddharaṇa-sannaddha*,[3] i.e. keenly engaged in salvaging the dharma beset by the evils of the Kali age. Several kings are described as engaged in the maintenance of the varṇa system.

The most interesting development in the history of the synonyms used for the king appearing in Gupta and post-Gupta times is the one which regularly attributes to him the protection/lordship/sovereignty/ownership of the earth or land. Manu states that the king is entitled to taxes because he protects the people and because he is *mahīpati*[4] or the lord of the earth. The term *mahīpati* may be translated as the protector of the earth but the term *bhūmeradhipati* (lord of the soil) is also used by Manu.[5] The idea of territorial lordship appears in earlier texts[6] also, but it is only, around the second century A.D. or a little later that it is linked to the king's claims for taxes. The position is further clarified and made unequivocal by Kātyāyana, a lawgiver of about the sixth century A.D. His law-book does not refer to royal protection as the basis of taxation. According to him the king is entitled to one-fourth of the produce as tax because he is *bhūsvāmin*.[7] Here we have to appreciate the difference between *mahīpati* and

1. D.C. Sircar, *Select Inscriptions*, BK II, No. 9, line 2. As a proper name it occurs in ibid. BK III, No. 71-B, lines 5-6. The term *dharmasthita* is used by several (Buddhist?) Kuṣāna princes (ibid., 2nd edn, pp. 110, 128). However *dharmarāja* occurs as an epithet of Aśoka in the second century A.D. (ibid p. 528).
2. Gautamīputra Śātakarni is called *vininvatita-cātūvaṇa-saṃkarasa*. *Select Inscriptions*, BK II, no. 8 line 6.
3. *Sel. Inscri.*, BK III, no. 67, line 13.
4. VIII.39, cf. VII.182.
5. VIII.439.
6. Several instances of this can be produced from the *Jaya Saṃhitā*.
7. P.V. Kane. ed., verse 16.

bhūsvāmin. *Svāmin* is a legal term used in the law-books, and therefore *bhūsvāmin* indicates legal ownership of land by the king different from mere lordship or sovereignity indicated by numerous terms found even in pre-Gupta records.[1] The formation of the term *svāmin* from *sv+min*[2] does not help us, although the word *sva* and its corresponding terms in the sense of a bond of kinship or sentiment are found in several Indo-European languages.[3] The sense of belongingness as well as the sense of self is implied by it. *Svāmin* may have been a combination of three terms such as *sva+āma+in*, which would mean ownership of raw material or resources.[4] Whatever may be its derivation the term *svāmin* is hardly found in pre-Maurya texts. It occurs frequently in Kauṭilya in opposition to *dāsa* and *bhṛtya*.[5] The legal sense of ownership is clearly conveyed by the use of the term at various places in BK III of the *Arthaśāstra*. More importantly, it becomes in BK VI a synonym of the king or sovereign in the enumeration of the seven elements of the state by Kauṭilya.[6] But this portion of the *Arthaśāstra* may be a late addition, and it is not clear whether the king, who is called master or owner, enjoys ownership of land. The term *svāmin* is also used in the Junagadh inscription of Rudradāman around A.D. 150.[7] It again appears in inscriptions of Andhra Pradesh during the fourth century A.D.[8] Although in all such cases the designation *svāmin* given to the king is intended to stress his possession of the realm, it is nowhere specifically connected with the royal ownership of land. But this idea seems to have been implicit and without doubt the law-book of Kātyāyana makes it explicit.

The fact that the king was called *bhūsvāmin* was a legal recognition of the royal ownership of land. On the other hand, rules of the

1. *bhūmipa*, JS, I.175.13; *mahīpati*, I.130.9, 177.8, 194.16 *vasudhādhipa*, I.125.29.
2. s.v. *svāmin*, *SED*.
3. Benveniste, op.cit., pp. 269-72.
4. In a discussion with me Professor R.C. Pandeya derives *svāmin* from *sv+āmi+n*. i.e. one who possesses plenty of paddy.
5. *AŚ*, III.13.
6. Ibid. VI.I. BK VI however is considered to be a late portion of the *Arthaśāstra*. A similar enumeration of seven elements of the state beginning with *svāmin* is made in *Amarakośa*, II.8.
7. Sel. Inscrr., BK II, no. 67 line 4.
8. Ibid. no. 104-A, lines 2-4; no. 104-8, line 3.

partition of landed property in the Gupta law-books[1] show that peasants were in actual possession of land. This created a kind of legal duality and conundrum which Śabara Svāmī tried to solve in his commentary on Jaimini's *Mīmāṃsā*. Jaimini's view that land belonged to all and not to the king[2] reflected an earlier state of affairs around 400 B.C., and naturally it was questioned by Śabara in Gupta times when the situation had materially changed. Śabara Svāmī took the position that the king enjoyed as much control and ownership over the land as others did over it.[3] In a way both Nārada and Kātyāyana speak of both royal ownership of land and individual possession of land and try to strike a balance between the two.

In addition to Kātyāyana's clear enunciation of the royal ownership of land, Gupta and post-Gupta *kāvyas* and inscriptions contain a large number of terms which emphasize royal control and possession over land in a manner in which it is not done in earlier texts. These are, for example, *avanīśa, avanīndra, kṣitipati, kṣitīndra, kṣitīśa, kṣiteradhipa, pārthiva, prabhurbhuvaḥ, pṛthivīnātha, bhūpa, bhūpati, bhūbhuj, bhūmīśvara, mahīpati, mahīpāla, mahīndra, mahīmahendra, urvīpati, vasudhādhipa, vasudheśvara, sāmantabhūmīśvara*.[4] Some such synonyms as bear the suffix *pa, pati* and *pāla* indicate merely protection or lordship. Some others indicating authority over or possession of land occur and find place in the kernel of the *Mahābhārata*,[5] but the fact of their inclusion in the *Jaya Saṃhitā* makes the authority of the concerned passages suspect. The old epithets which represent the king as chief protector of men were not discarded but swamped by the new synonyms and designations which stressed his ownership and enjoyment of land.

Numerous terms indicating royal enjoyment and ownership of land appear in inscriptions and in Jain and brāhmaṇical texts of early medieval times. The literary texts make the point that earth

1. Laxman Shastri Joshi, ed., *Dharmakośa*, i, 1251-52, 1201 and 1207.
2. VI.7.3. quoted in *Dharmakośa*, i, 793.
3. Commentary on VI.7.3 quoted ibid.
4. Such synonyms as *pārthiva, bhūpa, mahīkṣita, mahībhuk, cakravartī sārvabhauma* are found in *Amarakośa*, II.8.
5. *mahīkṣita, JS*, I.55.26, 179.8, 196.17, 205.1; *vasudhādhipa*, I.125.29; *pārthiva*, I.127.17, 180.7; 192.6, 23, etc.; *pṛthivīpati*, I.133.14; *pārthivendra*, I.180.8; *bhūmipa*, I.175.13. *mahīpa*, I.180.1; *mahīpati*, I.130.9, 177.8, 194.16, 205.14.

is like wife to the king, meant for enjoyment. But the king did not come to acquire land all of a sudden. It was a long process. There is no doubt that in an early stage of social development the kings were agriculturists. Pṛthu Vainya, the first appointed king who gave the name *pṛthivī* to the area over which he ruled, is credited with the invention of agriculture.[1] The epics tell us that Janaka of Videha lent his band to the plough, and that a proposal was made to Duryodhana for tilling the sacrificial ground. With the use of land for agricultural purposes the king or the chief may have been allotted the best piece of land by the community in recognition of his military, administrative and other qualities, just as he was given the lion's share in the booty and the best horse, elephant, etc. Till recent times when a zamindar rāja visited his tenantry, his tenants would occasionally present to him the best piece of land in the village for providing him with the paddy of the best quality. Although we have not been able to trace instances of land allotments made by the tribe/community to the king or the chief in ancient Indian texts, the tradition of his ploughing the land continued in the form of *vappamaṅgaḷa* mentioned in the Pāli texts.[2] The ploughing ritual is still performed annually by the Buddhist king of Thailand.

In addition to land gifts from the community land grabbing in war and leadership in clearing the alluvial river basins and other types of land may have added to royal landed property. Further when the tribes settled as enlarged and integrated communities, tribal chiefs known as *rājan* came to symbolise in their person the tribal authority over land. For a long time this authority was confined to the grant of waste land by the king, but he would also make grants out of *rājakaṃ khetam* (cultivable lands under the king's possession).[3] Royal ownership of arable and revenue paying lands in early medieval times is supported by the fact that the king claimed *bhoga*, *bhogakara* or *rājakīya bhoga*.[4]

As a result of the factors indicated above by the beginning of the medieval period the situation seems to have materially

1. s.v. *Pṛithī*, *SED*.
2. T.W. Rhys Davids & William Stede, The PTS *Pali-English Dictionary*, s.v. *vappamaṅgala*.
3. *Sel. Inscrr.*, i, BK II, no. 84, line 4.
4. References are discussed in U.N. Ghoshal, *Contributions to the History of the Hindu Revenue System*, p. 394.

changed, and the king who was head/protector of his tribe (*janasya gopati*) emerged legally and ideologically as the sole landowner or *bhūsvāmin*, commonly known as *bhūpati*. The stages in the long process which eventually resulted in transferring landownership to the king are not clear, but an analysis of the terms and epithets used for the king certainly enable us to identify the changes in his position from *gopati* to *bhūpati*. In his new capacity he made land grants to his officers and supporters but only with the formal consent of the leading members of the community. Many Pāla land charters addressed to royal officers and the rural population use the term *mataṁ-astu* to signify the consent of the village community, but at a later stage even this euphemism is given up, and the term used is *viditam-astu* indicating thereby that the people concerned are just informed of the land or revenue transfers.

This change in the position of the king proved to be of great significance. Because of their well-recognised position as owners of land the kings in most parts of the country made large-scale land grants. The process created new property relations in land, though under the overall royal authority, and gave rise to a substantial class of landlords armed with fiscal and administrative rights and even with powers of private justice. On the other hand, the same process produced a class of servile peasantry overburdened with all kinds of imposts, and generally placed at the mercy of the newly created landed barons who could eject the peasants, compel them to stick to the soil and could even subject them to fresh levies not warranted by law or custom.

Chapter XV

TAXATION AND STATE FORMATION IN NORTHERN INDIA IN PRE-MAURYA TIMES

Whether the state is symbolized by a monarchy or an oligarchy, its overarching authority and the final verdict in vital matters becomes ultimately effective because of its capacity to compel the people to abide by its decisions. The decisions are enforced by officials recruited on account of their abilities or nearness to the seat of power. But in spite of a long, well-established tradition of obedience to the clan, tribal or family chief, in the ultimate analysis the state has to invoke the help of some coercive authority such as army or police to implement its decisions. In many tribal societies all able-bodied men are mobilised for animal hunting; the same thing applies to man hunting, which is another name for war. And since war is an important and legitimate source of livelihood in archaic and primitive societies, some anthropologists call it a source of booty production. The chief and elders enjoy judicial authority, but do not require any elaborate mechanism to enforce it. This is so because tribesmen willingly submit to whosoever represents the judicial power.

As pointed out elsewhere, a full-fledged state maintains a taxation system, a professional army, and a cadre of officials.[1] All these elements are listed and explained by ancient Indian thinkers whose ideas are strongly similar to those of Engels.[2] Some scholars add the law enforcing or law maintaining authority represented by the judicial organ to the list. As an organ manifesting the final and supreme authority the judicial and law-keeping organisation may be considered indispensable. The ancient Indian thinkers regarded territory (*rāṣṭra/janapada*) and the fortified capital (*durga*) as important ingredients;[3] both stress the territorial aspect, which is regarded as an important element in the modern definition of the state. Anthropologists notice

1. Supra, Ch. III.
2. Ibid.
3. Ibid.

temporary territorial demarcation even among groups of hunters and more so among those of herders. But in such modes of subsistence it is really the band of the kin-based solidarity that commands allegiance; the territory is a very weak claimant. The territory really assumes importance when people discover its potentialities for regular food production and use it for permanent habitation. At this stage, notwithstanding their immediate allegiance to various tribal units, sedentary people develop deeper attachment to the territory.

The territory is exploited through its producers by making them pay taxes. In fact, of the various elements of the state the revenue system is the most critical. Without a regular supply of resources in cash or kind it is not possible to maintain the central establishment comprising the king or the ruling aristocracy, the professional army, the executive and judicial officials. Hence in our opinion the origin and growth of the taxation system determines the rise and development of the state. It is interesting to note that this was realised by Kauṭilya. According to him *vārttā*, comprising agriculture, cattle rearing and trade, is beneficial because it brings in cereals, cattle, cash and labour power. Through it, by means of the treasury and the army, the king controls his own subjects as well as those of others.[1] Kauṭilya states clearly that the treasury is the source of the army. He adds that the relative importance of the two differs according to time and place, but he holds that while the treasury may be obtained and preserved through the army, the treasury can multiply itself and preserve itself, and it can also acquire and preserve the army.[2] Kauṭilya reiterates his basic thesis by stating that the army exists because of the treasure, and that the state territory, of which the treasure is the ornament, is won by the treasury and army.[3]

It is argued by some that the consensual factor plays the decisive role in the formation of the state.[4] Such an inference can certainly be drawn from the contract theories of the state which

1. *vārttā dhānyapaśuhiraṇyaviṣṭipradānādaupakarikī, tayā svapakṣam parapakṣañca vaśīkaroti kośadaṇḍābhyām. AŚ*, 1.4.
2. *AŚ*, VIII, I.
3. *AŚ*, II, 12.
4. *The Early State*, Henry J.M. Claessen & Peter Skalnik (ed.), Mouton, 1978, pp. 612-13.

speak of taxation in lieu of protection. But it is equally certain that these theories were put forward by state ideologues not only in India but also in other countries in order to justify the functioning of the state and to assert and legalise its right to collect taxes. Even the contract theories, propounded in Pāli and Sanskrit texts, suggest that it was found necessary to protect the institutions of property and patriarchal family which were naturally the chief concerns of the members of the upper varṇas. Whatever that may be, there is little doubt that ancient India had a class of ideologues who justified the authority of the state in various ways. Apart from providing 'secular' justification they resorted to myth-making and religious validation. They invented costly coronation ceremonies for the purpose of impressing the people with the power, prestige and majesty of the king, and they indoctrinated the common people in the divine attributes and even incarnation of the king. Therefore, though some tradition of consensus may have survived as a tribal legacy, deliberate efforts were made to win consent and acceptability. It seems that almost the whole priestly class was engaged in this ceaseless exercise which brought constant gains to it. The priests even found it necessary to invent superstitious practices for replenishing the royal exchequer. The ideological and communicative role involving downright propaganda was performed by the brāhmaṇas, who in turn had to be supported by the state through payment of handsome gifts. Apparently a resourceless chief could not meet the demands of the brāhmaṇas or even of Jain and Buddhist monks whose preachings also kept the state and society going by promoting 'consensus'. Hence resource raising was essential not only for the maintenance of the professional army, and of the executive and judicial officers, but also of those who promoted 'consensus'. At least this seems to be the experience of the ancient Indian state.

Since in our opinion the state assumes real shape in the age of the Buddha, especially in the middle Gangetic plains, we will try first to examine in terms of Kauṭilya's *vārttā* the material conditions that prepared the way for the production of the surplus and indicate the methods adopted to collect it, especially in the form of taxes. Our second attempt would be to look for links, as emphasised by Kauṭilya in his own way, between the taxation system on the one hand and the formation and preservation of the other state organs such as the army, territory, etc., on the other.

The period with which we are concerned is noted for the rise of a large number of territorial states, mostly located in northern India and numbering more than fifty, if we take into account the 28 states mentioned by Alexander's historians.[1] Of course the idea of territory was not completely absent even in the hunting and grazing stage of the tribal people, who claimed certain stretches of territory as their sphere of influence and operation. In the *Ṛg Veda* the terms *pastya*[2] and *vṛjana*[3] are used frequently, and they stand for enclosures or pasture grounds. In the *Ṛg Veda* even the term *rāṣṭra*[4] is used, and *rājya*[5] occurs in later texts. In later Vedic texts the idea of territory or *rāṣṭra*[6] is expressed repeatedly. But for the greater part of the Vedic period people seem to have been more attached to their clan or similar kin-based institutions than to the territory which they used for grazing and cultivation. It was really with the end of the Vedic period, and particularly in post-Vedic times, that field agriculture based on the use of the iron ploughshare enabled the people to set up their farms and households and tied them down firmly to the soil.

The discussion of the *janapadaniveśa*, founding of rural settlements or large territorial units, in the *Arthaśāstra* of Kauṭilya (II. I) does indicate the general process of migration and colonisation, and underlines the crucial importance of agriculture and land distribution. The ultimate object of setting up settlements is the collection of taxes levied according to the carrying capacity of the soil and its cultivators. This point is clearly made in the *Mahābhārata*, which states that the state is based on the treasury and the treasury is based on settlements.[7] The Kauṭilyan *janapada* consisted of 3200 villages,[8] and apparently a *mahājana-*

1. *Sixteen mahājanapadas* including republics are mentioned in the *Aṅguttara Nikāya*, six republican states are also mentioned in Pāli texts, and twenty-eight states are mentioned by Alexander's historians. H.C. Raychaudhuri, *Political History of Ancient India*, University of Clacutta, 1972, pp. 85, 169-74, 216-29.
2. *VI*, i, 512-13.
3. *VI*, ii, 320.
4. *VI*, ii, 223.
5. *VI*, ii, 220-21.
6. *VI*, ii, 223.
7. *...rāṣṭram ca kośabhutaṃ syat kośo veśmagatastathā.*
8. *AŚ*, II.I read with II.35.

pada comprised several *janapadas* accounting for several thousand villages. Bimbisāra called the meeting of 80,000 *grāmikas*,[1] which may be a conventional number; in such a case his state would consist of 250 *janapadas*. But at any rate the *mahājanapada* was a large settled territorial unit capable of bearing taxes and various impositions.

Certain material conditions favoured the rise of the *mahājanapadas*. In Punjab and the upper Gangetic plains the process of large-scale settlements had started much earlier, but in the middle Gangetic plains large states were the products of the material culture associated with the phase of the Northern Black Polished Ware. So far nearly 570 NBPW sites have been counted in northern India, central India and the Deccan, but most of them are located in eastern U.P. and Bihar. They suggest beginnings of large-scale settlements in the alluvial soil since the sixth century B.C. or so. The use of iron for crafts and agriculture was an essential feature of the NBPW culture, although iron was also associated with some other types of pottery. The two factors which made iron, a cheaper and convenient metal to use were its availability in large quantities and the technological skill to make it more carburised. We have evidence for both these things. Some iron artifacts, recovered in excavations from Rajghat (Varanasi), contain the same iron ore impurities as are found in the ores from Singhbhum and Mayurbhanj.[2] This leaves little doubt that the users of iron in the middle Gangetic plains were familiar with the area containing the richest iron ores. Similarly an examination of iron artifacts belonging to early NBPW times shows that the smiths were capable of putting more carbon in them and thus making the tools lasting and more serviceable.[3] The second development that contributed to the material life of the period was the beginning of paddy transplantation.[4] With the large-scale clearance of the extremely fertile middle Gangetic zone and the introduction of new methods of cultivation, the production per hectare may have doubled. The farmers, therefore, were in a position to support their households and dependants

1. H.C. Raychaudhuri, op. cit., p. 155.
2. The results of the examination of these objects are available in H.C. Bharadwaj, *Aspects of Ancient Indian Technology*, Delhi, 1979.
3. Ibid.
4. R.S. Sharma, *Material Culture and Social Formations in Ancient India*, New Delhi, 1983, pp. 96-99.

and able to pay taxes to the state. The problem is to find out the stages by which taxation became a regular feature.

Archaeologically the existence of many *mahājanapadas* and some other states in the middle Gangetic zone and its periphery is supported by the finds of NBPW, punchmarked coins and many other signs of habitation and craft activities. The distribution of NBPW in these territorial states corroborates the Pāli evidence about their existence in respect of nearly half the *mahājanapadas*. It further suggests that practically every state in the middle Gangetic plains had an upper social crust which used this de lux pottery. This crust may have consisted of priests, warriors and substantial *gahapatis*, who appear as important elements in Pāli and Sanskrit texts. The formation of a ruling order with functions of fighting, administering, etc., legally assigned to it on a hereditary basis by the Dharmasūtras is almost peculiar to the Indian situation. In later Vedic texts the rājanya, a relative or kinsman of the rājā, played the diminutive role of a chief. Now he practically came to be replaced by the kṣatriya/khattiya order in the Dharmasūtras and Pāli texts. Later Vedic rituals reflect a long drawn-out struggle between the *viś* or the tribal peasantry on the one hand and the rājanya or the ruling chiefs who insisted on collecting tributes from the tribesmen. By the age of the Buddha this struggle seems to have been ideologically resolved in favour of the kṣatriyas, whose ruling functions were clearly defined and accepted in the Dharmasūtras, of course with the support of the priests/brāhmaṇas. The Jain and Buddhist monks, who had no place in the brāhmaṇical hierarchy, lent greater support to the emergent ruling order, for they accorded the khattiyas the first place in social ranking. Without going into the composition of the kṣatriya varṇa at any length, we may say that the kṣatriyas mainly comprised the chiefs of the ruling class and lineages,[1] although many poor cousins may have been included in this category.

1. Mainly on the basis of African analogy the terms tribe, clan, lineage, segment, etc., are being used increasingly in the Indian context by anthropologists, but the ancient kinship terms such as *jana*, *viś*, *gotra*, *vaṃśa*, *kula*, etc., carry their own nuances. In the Vedic context, *jana* is understood by Indologists as tribe, and *viś* as clan on the assumption that a tribe separates into clans. It is held by some anthropologists (viz. Mandlebaum) that in India lineage separates into clans, but whatever little idea I have of large kin-based units in north Bihar and elsewhere in

But whatever be their origin, legally and ideologically they were entitled to rule, and ruling meant primarily collection of taxes, and enforcement of decisions in disputes relating to patriarchal family and property, and of course protecting people against invasions. In course of time the legitimacy of the kṣatriya's function to rule became so well established that even brāhmaṇa rulers had to adopt kṣatriya titles and paraphernalia.

How and why certain segments of people came to claim taxes in the age of the Buddha is discussed in the Pāli texts in a theoretical manner. They present the picture of an ideal, collectivist, prestate society, which was distorted by the appearance of property in land and patriarchal family. This picture may reflect some reality, but how voluntary offerings evolved into mandatory payments is nowhere indicated. This process has not been treated even by modern scholars including U.N. Ghoshal. However the pioneer but excellent works of Fick and Mr and Mrs Rhys Davids, supplemented by those of B.C. Sen, A.N. Bose and R.N. Mehta, provide valuable information regarding the system of land revenue in about a couple of centuries preceding the establishment of the Maurya empire. Nevertheless their generalizations regarding the nature of the royal share collected from the peasants, and of the grants made by the king, need reappraisal. Fick and Rhys Davids hold that the royal share was a tithe levied upon the annual produce in kind,[1] but Bühler thinks that it was 'ground rent', which presupposes the measurement of the ground held by a peasant family and the calculation of the average yield on the basis of the produce extending over a number of years; the fertility of the soil may have also been taken into account. 'Ground rent' would appear therefore a kind of fixed tithe based on the area of the cultivable land. However the term rent is used in the context of landlords collecting their dues from the tenants. In modern terms ground

north India shows that the clan is larger than the "lineage". In a discussion of the Puranic account H.C. Raychaudhuri applies the word "lineage" to the ruling house of the Yadus in the sense of family (op. cit., p. 77 with fn. 3). He also speaks of the Yādava clans (Ibid., p. 447, fn. 3), and of the Licchavi clan (Ibid., p. 109). Although he did not take an anthropological view, it seems that he considered clan a larger unit than the lineage.

1. Richard Fick, *Social Organisation of N.E. India etc.*, pp. 118-19; *Cambridge History of India*, i, ed. E.J. Rapson, p. 177.

rent is understood in the sense of the rent which is fixed by the landlord on the basis of the market price and not on the basis of the yield in a harvest. But by 'ground rent' Bühler probably means land tax fixed on the basis of the produce and paid to the state.

Apparently the early Indologists saw no difference between tax and rent. As is well-known, in the case of oriental despotism Marx considers tax to be identical with rent. This is based on Bernier's view that in the seventeenth century India the king symbolizing the state was the landlord or the sole owner of the land. But the pre-Maurya tradition does not represent the king as the owner of land. On the other hand, the earliest law-books justify the king's claim to a share of the produce or tax on the ground that he protects the people. But even if the demand of the state from the agriculturists is called rent in place of tax, there is no doubt about its being regular and compulsory in the age of the Buddha.

How voluntary offerings were transformed into compulsory payments can be seen from an examination of the terms used for tax. In any case 'tithe' and 'ground rent' may be taken as two successive stages in the development of the ancient taxation system. Since we are dealing with a period of about 300 years such a development seems to be possible.

That the tithe system prevailed can be inferred from a Jātaka story in which a *seṭṭhi* feels guilty in conscience while plucking some blades from the untithed field.[1] On the other hand, the two references, which relate to the measuring of field by royal officers, are capable of being interpreted in a way which may suggest some sort of 'ground rent'[2]. Bühler compares the *rajjugāhaka-amacca* with the Land Revenue Settlement Officer of British India and suggests that measurement was used for assessing 'ground rent'[3]. But Fick surmises that land was measured either to form an approximate idea of the amount of rent payable by the subjects to the king or to determine the average produce to be brought to the king's store-room.[4] Never-

1. *Jāt.*, ii, 378.
2. Ibid., ii, 376; iv, 169.
3. Ibid., ii, 378; *ZDMG*, xlvii, 468-70.
4. Richard Fick, *Social Organisation of N.E. India etc.*, p. 149.

theless, the fact that in measuring the field the *rajjugāhaka-amacca* was conscious of doing nothing which might cause loss either to the rājā or to the *khettasamika* or *kuṭumba*[1] lends strength to Bühler's hypothesis that the land was measured for the purpose of levying rent on it. But whether this was the normal practice throughout the upper and middle Gangetic zones cannot be stated. Pāṇini, who belonged to north-western India, refers to officers called *kṣetrakara*, who divided the cultivable land into plots by survey and measurement and fixed their area.[2] It is not clear whether these plots were demarcated for purposes of taxation, although the possibility cannot be ruled out. Another reference in Pāṇini (vi.3.10) has been taken to mean that an impost of two or three *pada* coins was levied on every *hala* or plough-measure of land in eastern India.[3] This interpretation of the *Kāśikā* in its comment to *karanāmni ca prācām halādau* may be applied to the middle Gangetic zone in pre-Maurya times, but its mention of the three other taxes, in the same connection, levied respectively on households, individuals, and hand-mills[4] may perhaps be true of the conditions existing during the seventh century A.D., when this commentary was written.

Theoretically, as head and symbol of the clan or the community, the king could claim ownership of all the land, a position which developed out of the Vedic custom, according to which no land could be alienated without the consent of the *viś*. But neither the early Pāli texts nor the earliest law-books, called the Dharmasūtras, assert such a claim for the king. The functions of such royal officers as *kṣetrakaras*, *rājakammikas*,[5] etc., show that in many cases the king exercised his right of levying 'ground rent' effectively. But, as regards taxes on the general peasantry, the early Pāli texts never assert that the king levied taxes because he was the owner of the soil. The law-book of Gautama, however, states that the king was entitled to *bali* because of the protection afforded by him to the people.[6] Protection was a

1. *Jat.*, ii, 376.
2. V.S. Agrawala, *India as Known to Pāṇini*, Lucknow, 1953, pp. 142, 197.
3. Ibid., pp. 414-15.
4. Ibid.
5. *Jāt.*, iv, 169.
6. X.28 with the comm. of Haradatta (*ASS* edn.).

function inherited from the king from the stage of tribal chieftainship, but now it served as a good excuse for validating his authority. Commenting on Gautama, Maskarin (12th century) states that taxes are to be paid by the cultivators on the plots of land which they obtain from the king,[1] obviously this was a much later development, for many texts of early medieval times represent the king as the owner of land. Gautama adds that the rate of *bali* should be 1/6, 1/8 and 1/10,[2] which Haradatta, a commentator of about the 12th century, interprets as differing according to the fertility of soil. It is obvious, then, that there was no uniform rate irrespective of the nature of the yield. This might suggest that the idea of land rent was gradually developing. But the varying rates might also mark stages in the development of the capacity of the peasants to pay. The capacity would obviously depend on the nature of the tools they used, the crops they produced, and the fertility of the soil they cultivated. Apparently the carrying capacity of the soil to pay as much as 1/6 of the total yield presupposed production of sufficient surplus through cultivation based on the use of the iron ploughshare and practice of paddy transplantation; to this may be added advanced knowledge of weather conditions connected with the *nakṣatras* or lunar mansions. *Bali* stands for voluntary offering, religious or otherwise. Although the religious form continued in the post-Vedic period and also later, the non-religious form of tribute given to the tribal chief assumed a mandatory character. The term *bhāga* shows that the king was entitled to his share and the term *kara* shows that he could collect taxes from the people. *Bhāga* again was a remnant of the tribal stage of distribution system in which kinsmen were entitled to their shares. But what was received as a matter of custom by every kinsman came to be claimed compulsorily by the king, who no longer functioned in a tribal set-up. The same process applied to the presents offered by the kinsmen to their tribal chieftain. We may add that in ancient Assyria the term 'gift' was used for regular taxes for a long time in spite of the fact that the subjects were compelled to make these payments.[3] It would appear that what constituted gifts by clansmen at one stage became taxes later. In

1. Comm. to *Gautama*, X.24.
2. X.24.
3. Olmstead, *History of Assyria*, p. 516.

ancient India there continued for some time the contradiction between the tax terminology and its actual content. Thus although taxes were compulsory in pre-Maurya times, a more frequently used term in the Jātakas is *bali* and not *bhāga*.[1] But Gautama uses the term *kara*,[2] and Pāṇini a more emphatic word *kāra*.[3] Later the two terms *bhāga* and *kara* came to be used more frequently. In course of time *bhāga* came to be regarded as the principal form of land tax, and the king came to be known as *ṣaḍbhāgin*, with the result that in the *Arthaśāstra* of Kauṭilya *bali* figured as one of the several taxes connected with land.[4]

We have no idea about the traditional and customary rate of *bali*, coming down from the Vedic period; it may have varied from 1/16 to 1/10. But since the needs of the ruling class were increasing and the productive capacity of the peasants was developing, the rate was evidently raised. In spite of the exhortation that the king should levy taxes only in accordance with *dhamma*,[5] several instances of oppressive taxes appear in the Jātakas.[6] They suggest that the king could increase taxes, either in order to fill up his coffers or to harass the people. He could also remit taxes.[7] The fact that the king could enhance and remit *bali* shows that this was no longer treated as a voluntary or customary offering, but as a tax imposed on the people by the king. Thus *bali* became political in nature.

Initially *bali* was not collected in money, although we find that incomes of villages were estimated in terms of money, and in some cases even hired labourers were paid in cash. But the early Pāli texts do not know of tithe being commuted into money rent. Nevertheless, as shown earlier, it can be inferred from Pāṇini that in eastern India money rental was imposed on every plough-measure of land. In spite of numerous finds of hoards of punch-marked coins, mostly of silver, since *c.* 500 B.C. in the middle Gangetic zone, generally, money economy was not so advanced as to eliminate payment of the royal share in kind. That *bali*

1. *Jāt.*, ii, 378.
2. X.II.
3. Agrawala, op. cit., p. 415.
4. II.15.
5. *Jāt.*, iv, 399, 400.
6. Ibid., ii, 240; iv, 224; v, 98.
7. Ibid., iv, 169.

was synonymous with payment in kind can be deduced from the fact that at one place, in the same compound, *bali* and *kahāpaṇa* are mentioned as two separate impositions.[1] The term *nivāsa-vetana*, occurring in a Jātaka story,[2] can be taken in the sense of house rent, but here also payment is made not in cash but in oxen.

But the use of the term *kara* or *kāra* is significant, and Pāṇini's statement that money rental was imposed on every plough-measure of land in eastern India is significant. The practice may have prevailed around *c.* 400 B.C. or a little earlier. It is clearly linked with the appearance of metallic money generally in the form of punchmarked silver coins, which phenomenon does indicate commodity production (whatever be the scale) and long-distance transaction. Metallic money was a symptom of the weakening of the barter system or the mutual gift system, as the case may be, associated with the tribal economy. The significance of the advent of metallic money, especially of gold and silver in comparison with copper, is brought out by Karl Marx in these words:

> The precious metals last, they do not alter, they can be divided and then combined together again, they can be transported relatively easily owing to the compression of great exchange value in little space... The *precious* metals then split off from the remainder by virtue of being inoxidizable, of standard quality etc., and they correspond better, then, to the higher stage, in that their direct utility for consumption and production recedes while, because of their rarity, they better represent value purely based on exchange.[3]

Thus once money came into use it brought in the elements of private profit and accumulation at the cost of the gift system characterising kinship ties. It also made possible centralised fiscal collection and consequently helped to consolidate dispersed bits of authority into an integrated authority. Therefore, the role of punch-marked coins called *kārṣāpaṇa* or *kahāpaṇa* in facilitating the formation of a central power structure cannot be underestimated. The fact that *paṇa* was associated with *karṣa* (to cultivate) shows that metallic money was meant for measuring the

1. Ibid., ii, 240.
2. Ibid., i, 194.
3. Karl Marx, *Grundriss*, p. 166.

agricultural products, a part of which had to be made over to the state.

We hardly know of any machinery created for revenue collection during the Vedic period. It is very doubtful whether the term *bhāgadugha* used in later Vedic texts can be understood in the sense of milcher of the share or tax-collector.[1] Most probably, in view of the distributive functions of tribal societies, the *bhāgadugha* distributed the spoils, cattle, cereals, etc., received by the later Vedic chieftain, commonly called *rājan*. But in post-Vedic northern India, especially in the middle Gangetic basin, we come across half a dozen officers who worked as tax-collectors. The *gāmabhojaka* and a few other functionaries were connected with the work of assessment and measuring grain for storing it in the royal granary. The precise functions of the *gāmabhojaka* and royal collectors, and their mutual relations, cannot be determined. Fick's view that the *gāmabhojaka* was an official appointed to collect the revenue of a village for the king has rightly been questioned,[2] for he relies upon a solitary passage in the introductory episode of a Jātaka story.[3] But since the *gāmabhojaka* could impose and collect fines from the villagers in the case of minor disputes,[4] and in those of murder and other offences committed by drunkards,[5] it is likely that his main concern was the maintenance of law and order. However in the earlier stage we cannot expect much differentiation of functions, and it is no wonder if a magistrate and judge functioned as a tax-collector. Revenue administration came to be assigned exclusively to a set of officers, but the *gāmabhojaka* did not belong to this category. He collected royal dues, but he also settled local disputes, maintained law and order,[6] sometimes interdicted cow-slaughter,[7] and occasionally helped villagers in times of distress.[8] The institution of *gāmabhojaka* was almost universal, but his function as a royal tax-collector seems to have been occasional. Further, the *gāmabhojaka* should not be

1. *VI*, ii, 100.
2. B.C. Sen, *JDL*, xx, 165.
3. *Jat.*, i, 354.
4. Ibid., i, 483.
5. Ibid., i, 199.
6. Ibid., i, 199, 483.
7. Ibid., iv, 115.
8. Ibid., ii, 135.

understood as an enjoyer of the village. This office was not a device for providing revenues to favourites and brāhmaṇas. In fact, though this office formed the lowest rung in the ladder, it was an important part of the administrative machinery, which was headed by the commander-in-chief.[1] *Gāmaṇis* are also mentioned as village headmen, who seem to have been king's favourites living in luxury,[2] but there is no proof that they acted as regular royal collectors and enjoyed revenues raised from the villages.[3] Probably the office of the village headman, whether of the *gāmabhojaka* or the *gāmaṇi*, was elective in the beginning, but in course of time he came to be an officer of the king and became less representative of the interests of the local folk.

The *gāmabhojaka* was not an absentee landlord, as is wrongly suggested by a writer.[4] It cannot be proved that revenues were assigned to the village headman; in this respect the literal meaning of the term cannot be taken as indicating the real position of the *gāmabhojaka*. In several passages of the *Aitareya Brāhmaṇa*[5] the term *bhoja* seems to be used as king's title. The use of the word *bhoja*, therefore, in the *gāmabhojaka* may indicate that this functionary was an agent appointed by the king for performing a few essential administrative functions in the village. The evidence that the *gāmabhojaka* primarily collected royal dues from the peasants is not strong, but to regard him as the lord of the land of the village will be stretching the imagination too far.

Half a dozen royal collectors, mentioned in the Jātakas, hold different designations, but they were not placed in charge of different taxes. On the contrary, they all were clearly connected with the collection of *bali*, which was the chief royal tax. One of these, the *yutta*[6] can be identified with Pāṇini's *āyukta*, which was a general term for government servants engaged in routine work.[7] When they were specially commissioned for some job they were called *niyukta*;[8] they seem to be the same as the

1. Ibid., v, 484.
2. Ibid., iv, 310.
3. Cf. *JDL*, xxiv, 16.
4. A.N. Bose, *Social and Rural Economy of Northern India*, i, 39.
5. VIII. 12, 14, 17; VI, ii, 112.
6. *Jāt.*, v, 117.
7. Agrawala, op.cit., p. 498.
8. Ibid.

niyuktaḥ mentioned by Gautama.[1] The commentators take two views of the functions of this office. Haradatta points out that they were appointed among the cultivators for their protection, but he quotes another view that this officer was employed for collecting *bali* and other dues.[2] Theoretically the two views can be reconciled, because taxation and protection were supposed to go hand in hand. Explaining the term *balidāna*,[3] Maskarin states that royal dues known as *rājagrahaṇam* or *baligrahaṇam* should be paid annually to the *niyukta* by those who live on agriculture.[4] Thus *nityukta* and *niyukta* of Gautama stand for the same officer, and the interpretation of *nityukta* as tax-collector suits the text better, for the term is used in connection with *bali*. Another class of tax-collectors, the *tuṇḍiyas*, were not regular tax-officers but a special class of collectors, employed to collect *bali* from the people by subjecting them to beating and binding.[5] The *akāsiyas* were also oppressive tax-collectors,[6] who dispossessed the cultivators of their earnings. So the *tuṇḍiyas* and *akāsiyas* were special officers appointed to raise taxes on behalf of the king in times of emergency or to collect additional taxes. But this does not seem to have been the case with *balisādhakas*[7] and *niggāhakas*[8] who also are put in the commentary[9] as *balisādhakas*; these two probably were ordinary tax-collectors, normally collecting *bali* from the people. The term *balipaṭiggāhaka* is also interpreted as tax-collector,[10] but originally it may have meant receiver of offerings or oblations,[11] the *rājakammikas* were, however, regular tax-collector who measured land and collected taxes.[12] Pāṇini mentions a class of officers known as *kārakaras*, who were entrusted with the raising

1. X.29.
2. Comm. to *Gautama*, X.29.
3. Ibid., X.23; *balidāna* is even now used in the sense of sacrifice of animals for religious purpose.
4. *Dharmakośa*, ed. L.S. Joshi, i, Pt. 3, 1661.
5. *Jāt*., v, 102-3, *gāthā* with comm.
6. Ibid., vi, 212. *gāthā*.
7. Ibid., v, 106.
8. Ibid., iv, 362.
9. Ibid.
10. Fick, op. cit., p. 120.
11. PTS *Pali-English Dictionary*, s.v. *balipaṭiggāhaka*.
12. *Jāt*., vi, 169.

of taxes in eastern India,[1] but the work of measuring land was done by the *kṣetrakaras*. Another officer connected with land revenue work was the *rajjugāhaka-amacca*, who may have been primarily an assessor of taxes rather than a collector. We may not have clear idea about the precise functions of each of these collectors, but in the age of the Buddha we find a fairly organised fiscal system free from the dominating influence of the kinsmen of the king. It was certainly a significant advance on the ad hoc, irregular, ceremonial collections of later Vedic times when some kinsmen of the chief collected such dues and the others (probably the distant ones) were persuaded to pay these.

The relation between different categories of tax-collectors in pre-Maurya times needs to be examined. Fick points out that taxes were paid to the official who represented the king in the province allotted to him.[2] But he does not make it clear who these officials were and how they were connected with the royal collectors noticed above. Similarly, he states that in the village revenues were given to the *gāmabhojakas*.[3] But if this official collected taxes from the cultivators in all cases what was the necessity of employing three or four other officers for the purpose? Besides, how did they function in relation to the village superintendent? Unfortunately for lack of further data these questions cannot be answered satisfactorily.

It may be asked whether there existed any considerable class of landed intermediaries in this period. Sometimes the *gāmabhojakas* are looked upon as a powerful class of intermediaries, somewhat analogous to the modern landlords.[4] In our opinion this statement can be applied in some measure to those brāhmaṇas who were granted land by the king and not to the *gāmabhojakas* who were either representatives of the local folk or regular officers appointed by the king and dismissed by him when occasion demanded it.

Whether there were manorial lords during this period depends upon the correct interpretation of certain terms such as *brahmadeyya* and *rāja-bhoggam*. The explanation of Buddhaghoṣa that the grants mentioned in the early Pāli canons carried with them

1. Agrawala, op. cit., p. 415.
2. Op. cit., p. 120.
3. Ibid.
4. Bose, op.cit., i, 38.

administrative and judicial rights[1] may be true of the conditions existing in the fifth century A.D. when the commentator flourished, but may not suit the state of affairs in the pre-Maurya period. Therefore, the inference of Rhys Davids that the practice of the grant to local notabilities of local government can be traced back to the time of the Buddha[2] cannot be sustained by evidence. Since the states were comparatively smaller in area, even the local affairs could be managed by the officers of the king. Although there are several instances of *brahmadeyya* grants in Kosala and Magadha, mentioned in the *Dīgha Nikāya*,[3] significantly enough neither the term *akara* nor any other term indicating immunity of taxes is found in the string of adjectives qualifying the land granted. The absence of the list of exemptions naturally leads us to think that the grantees had to pay some tribute to the king[4] although in general the brāhmaṇas/priests did not have to pay taxes. And hence, compared to the grants of post-Maurya and Gupta periods, the pre-Maurya grants conferred very limited advantages on the beneficiaries. The *brahmadeyya* grants of this period did not carry the privileges which appear in the early centuries of the Christian era.

The term *rāja-bhoggam* occurring in the grants of the *Dīgha Nikāya* is interpreted in different ways. In the opinion of T.W. Rhys Davids *rāja-bhogga* was a form of tenure, and its holder was empowered to exact all dues accruing to the government within the boundaries of the district or estate granted to him. He could hold his own courts, and occupied in many ways the position of a baron, or lord of the manor, except that he could draw no rent.[5] But, in the cluster of adjectives qualifying such grants, the term *rāja-bhoggam* should be taken in the sense of 'royal', or that enjoyed by the king; and not in the sense of "a grant to be enjoyed by the grantee in the same way as the king does it", as is done in the translation of this term by Rhys Davids.[6] In the grants occurring in the *Dīgha Nikāya*, the form of tenure is

1. *Sumaṅgala Vilāsinī, i*, 246.
2. *CHI*, i, 159.
3. i, 87, 111, 114, 131, 224.
4. Cf. Sen, *JDL, XX*, 106.
5. *CHI*, i, 159.
6. *SBB*, ii, 108.

indicated not by the term *rāja-bhoggam* but by the term *brahmadeyya*, which is a well recognised form of tenure in brāhmaṇical texts and inscriptions of the later periods. Fick cites several references to show that the *rāja-bhoggas* were a class of officers in the pay of the king, and equates them with the rājanyas.[1] This may hold good of the references he quotes.[2] But it may not apply to all such references found in the *Dīgha Nikāya*. The commentary explains *rāja-bhoggam* as *rāja laddham bhoggam*, i.e., the meal or domain acquired by the king[3] which evidently refers to royal possession. How the king came to acquire the domain or estate for his enjoyment is a matter of conjecture. The tribal analogy and examples from ancient Greek societies would show that the tribal chief was originally given a large parcel of land for the maintenance of his family; or he may have seized it with the support of the close circle of his kinsmen. In any case such acquisition is important in bolstering the authority of the chief over the rank and file of the people. Once he acquired a piece of land he could make grant out of it to win support and strengthen his political authority. Thus *brahmadeyya* grants were made out of the royal domain or the crown land, and not out of the land held by the communities of peasant proprietors. Holders of such grants evidently were priests who consolidated the state power by communicating prostate social and religious ideas to the producing masses. There is nothing to show that the grantees performed administrative functions.

Bhogagāma, which often occurs in the Jātakas, apparently means a village given by the king to his favourites for enjoyment; apparently such a village was not granted to people for rendering administrative or other services to the state. In one instance a barber happened to be the beneficiary of such a favour.[4] A passage from the Jātakas[5] has been interpreted to mean that the *amacca* was the *bhojaka* of a village, which was given by the king for his enjoyment as remuneration for his office.[6] But the passage in question makes it very clear that this was not the case.

1. Op. cit., p. 153.
2. Ibid., p. 152.
3. *Sumaṅgala Vilāsinī*, 245.
4. *Jāt.*, i. 138.
5. Ibid., 1, 354.
6. Bose, op. cit.

In reality this particular *amacca* was asked to collect royal revenues (*rājabali*) from this village. We learn that when he conspired with the robbers to carry off the taxes collected for the king, he was heavily punished. Another reference,[1] on the basis of which it has been stated that a monarch could endow a minister with the contributions of the *gāmas*[2] (villages), should not create the impression that the grant was made to the minister in return for his administrative services. In this particular case, sixteen excellent villages (probably conventional in number) were granted to a minister as a reward for his ability to provide the right solution to a philosophical question, namely, the definition of an ascetic; and further in this case the minister was the Bodhisatta. The reward was made for religious and philosophical services. The view that the minister got as their chief remuneration villages together with cows, chariots, elephants, etc.,[3] and that salaries and food were additional payments,[4] does not seem to be sound. In fact, they were given *bhattavetana* primarily as their remuneration, and villages were an additional favour occasionally bestowed on them when the king so pleased. The specific purpose for the grant of villages mentioned in the Jātakas is the reward for wise or religious instruction imparted to the king by the Bodhisatta,[5] although such instruction could be used for political purposes. Most *bhogagāmas* were enjoyed by the *purohita*[6] (priest) and some by the *seṭṭhis* (merchants). According to the Jātakas generally such villages were granted to the chief advisers and religious instructors to the king, and not to the *amātyas*. In spite of the fact that the grantees enjoyed the revenues of these village, it is obviously wrong to render *bhogagāmas* as zamindaris, as is done in several Jātaka translations, for the donees enjoyed no proprietory rights whatsoever in the villages granted to them.

Considered as a whole the grants suggest certain general points. First, although the king had the power to make grants, he was not under the obligation to do so, as seems to have

1. *Jāt.*, vi, 261.
2. *CHI*, i, 177.
3. De, *JDL*, xxiv, 10; *Jāt.* vi, 363.
4. Ibid.
5. *Jāt*, 365; ii, 229; vi, 344.
6. Ibid., ii, 428-9, *gāthā* 117; iii, 105; iv, 473.

become the practice in the early centuries of the Christian era. Secondly, in many instances a part of the royal domain or the crown land was granted. Thirdly, grants were made for spiritual and religious services. Fourthly, these were probably tenable for lifetime. This inference is, however, not based on the wrong translation of a Jātaka passage,[1] in which the term *gāmavaram* means prosperous village, and not 'for life', as Rouse understands. Further, the grants were not made in perpetuity. They give neither any indication of being passed on to the descendants of the grantees nor of the obligation imposed by the donor on his successors to maintain these grants under threats of imprecations. Fifthly, there is nothing to show that the *bhogagāmas* were free from tributes to the king. The dominant role of the kṣatriyas during this period might suggest that they perhaps collected taxes even from the brāhmaṇa donees. Lastly, even in the Jātakas, which are sometimes placed in the third or the second centuries B.C., grants had not become a common practice. It would, therefore, appear that revenue and other officers who manned the state apparatus were paid out of the taxes collected for the king rather than through the grants of land or revenues.

We have some idea about the usual mode of payment made to the officers and other employees of the king, and it seems that most payments were made out of the taxes collected by the royal agents. The common term used for remuneration is *bhattavetana*. At one place it has been translated as food-money.[2] But Horner renders *rañño bhattavetanāhāro* as "living on a salary and food from a king"[3] and probably this is correct. In what form the salary was paid is not clear; we can well presume that there was no necessity of paying the officers again in kind if they were already given provisions. Therefore, wherever the term *vetana* is compounded with *bhatta*, it may be taken in the sense of cash payment. Accordingly, the statement that elephant troops and chariotmen, royal guards and infantry were given *bhattavetana*[4] should mean that, besides provision for maintenance, they were paid cash salary by the king. We also learn of the rise in the pay (*vetana*) of his elephant-driver, or his life-guardsman,

1. Ibid., ii, 428-9, *gāthā* 117.
2. Ibid., iv, 132; Tr. *Jāt.*, iv, 84.
3. *The Book of Discipline*, ii, 67.
4. *Jāt.*, iv, 134, *gāthā* 100.

his chariot-soldier or his foot-soldier allowed by the king,[1] which may suggest that in such cases salaries were paid in cash. The armymen were not paid through land grants, as we find it in Assyria. In the Pāli texts soldiers were not allotted land for subsistence. In some cases even hired labourers were paid in cash.[2] Moreover, whether it is the income of a village,[3] or payment to a youth skilled in tracking footsteps[4] or an archer,[5] or gift to the Great Being,[6] the amount stated in each instance is a thousand pieces of money. Obviously this figure is conventional, as is inevitable in folk literature, but all this undoubtedly points to the probability of payment in cash to the officers and employees of the king. The finds of punch-marked coins between *c.* 500 and *c.* 300 B.C. suggest that taxes could be collected in metallic money and payments could be made through the same medium. This facilitated fiscal centralisation which helped the formation of large and strong polities. But initially revenues were mainly collected in kind, and so officers may have been paid in kind supplemented by cash.

The taxation system including the sources of tax and items of expenditure and also the state machinery, given in the *Arthaśāstra* of Kauṭilya,[7] when compared with the early Pāli evidence, shows a rapid development in both the financial and governmental mechanisms. We gather a good deal of information about the types of taxes and the mechanism for their levy and collection from the early Pāli texts, the Dharmasūtras and some other sources. But they do not specify the items on which the taxes were spent. This information is supplied by Kauṭilya, whose budgeting principles may have originated in pre-Maurya times. According to him expenditure (*vyaya-śarīra*) is incurred on gifts meant for the worship of gods and ancestors and for the chanting of auspicious mantras.[8] Thus the upkeep of the priests accounted for a good portion of what the state spent.

1. Ibid., vi, 295.
2. *Jāt.*, iii, 26.
3. Ibid., i, 138.
4. Ibid., iii, 505.
5. Ibid., v, 128.
6. Ibid., ii, 462.
7. For a general survey see Infra, ch. XXII.
8. Here the text constructed by R.P. Kangle (*AŚ*, II.6.11) has been followed.

Another item of expenditure covered the royal harem and the kitchen.[1] Apparently it was too early to draw a line between state expenditure and the private household expenditure of a king. The storehouse, the armoury, the house of commodities, the storehouse of raw materials, artisanal workshops (*karmānta*), and use of labour power (*viṣṭi*) appear as items of expenditure.[2] This would suggest that a large number of staff employed in fiscal, military and administrative activities had to be paid out of the state income. As many as eleven *adhyakaṣas*[3] or superintendents came under the items on which expenditure was to be incurred. But strangely enough no term is used to signify many categories of officers, whose salaries in cash are prescribed in Kauṭilya under *bhṛtyabharaṇīyam*.[4] Kauṭilya provides for the payment of various categories of royal agents by using the term *dūtapravartimam*[5] or the cadre of the *dūtas*. The *dūta* served not only as envoy/messenger but also as news carrier and executor of royal order; perhaps he also worked as spy. The *dūta* in the lowest grade was paid as little as ten *paṇas*. However it has to be stressed that the four wings of the military organisation, for which payment in cash is provided in *AŚ*, V.3, constitute a clear demand on state income.[6] In addition to all this, expenditure is provided for herds of cows, enclosures of beasts, deer, birds and rogue elephants and for storage of firewood and fodder.[7] An analysis of the items of expenditure would show that the vital organs[8] were maintained through taxes of various kinds.

It is, therefore, clear that the growth of the state apparatus was

1. Ibid.
2. Ibid.
3. These are *akarādhyakṣa, koṣṭāgārādhyakṣa, paṇyādhyakṣa, kupyādhyakṣa, āyudhāgārādhyakṣa, go'adhyakṣa, aśvādhyakṣa, hastyadhyakṣa, rathādhyakṣa, pattyadhyakṣa,* and *vivītādhyakṣa*, Ibid. II.1.
4. *AŚ*, V.3.
5. R.P. Kangle (ed.), *AŚ*, II.6.11.
6. Ibid.
7. Ibid. Śhamasastry takes *paśumṛgapakṣivyālavāṭaḥ* in the sense of the museum of these creatures, but the phrase should be understood in the context of the duties of the *kupyādhyakṣa*.
8. Salaries in cash are provided for the different types of priests and teachers in *AŚ*, V.3. *The purohitapuruṣāḥ(s)* are specified as *kārtāntika, naimittika, mauhūrtika, paurāṇika, sūta* and *māgadha* (ibid.) The learned *ācārya* was entitled not only to pay but also to *pūjā* (ibid.)

closely connected with the increasing supply of various taxes. But taxes were fewer in pre-Maurya times, and consequently the state machinery in this period was not as developed as in Maurya times. A good many revenue officials such as *akāsiya, balipaṭiggāhaka (bali-)niggāhaka, balisādhaka, kārakara, kṣetṛakara, nityukta* or *niyukta, rajjugāhaka-amacca,* and *tunḍiya* are mentioned in Pāli and other texts; the *rājakammika* was another official of this type, and the *grāmabhojaka* or *grāmakūṭa* was also assigned fiscal functions. A class of *mahāmātras* was also appointed for the levy of the tithe on produce. It is doubtful whether every state was equipped with all these officials in the age of the Buddha. But officers connected with the assessment and collection of *bali* may have served in most states. The existence of these worthies shows considerable advance in the differentiation of governmental functions, but they may also have acted as judge, police and magistrate.

The revenue officers were evidently backed by a number of other officers called *rājabhaṭa.*[1] They performed executive, military and judicial functions. Thus we hear of the *sabbathaka* or the officer in charge of general affairs,[2] the *sena-nāyaka mahāmattas*[3] or generals, the *vohārika mahāmattas*[4] (judicial officers). A class of *mahāmattas* also looked after the levy of the tithe.[5] Thus the institution of the *mahāmātra*, whose different categories were employed by Aśoka, appear in the *Vinaya Pitaka,*[6] which may belong to *c.* 300 B.C.

However the *amaccas* or *amātyas* who figure prominently in the Pāli texts appear in the early law-books and the *Arthaśāstra* of Kauṭilya but not in Aśokan inscriptions. They acted as members of the *parisā* or the council mentioned in the *Vinaya Pitaka*[7] and Aśokan inscriptions. They could depose the ruling prince and elect another in his place.[8] They also acted as judicial

1. The Mahākhandham of the *Mahāvagga* contains a section called Rājbhaṭavatthu. The term *rājabhaṭa* is rendered as 'high offer' (H.C. Raychaudhuri, op. cit., p. 184), but *bhaṭa* seems to have been derived from *bhṛtya.*
2. H. Oldenberg (ed.), *Vinaya Pitaka*, p. 207.
3. Ibid., p. 74.
4. Ibid.
5. H.C. Raychaudhuri, op.cit., p. 184.
6. H. Oldenberg (ed.), op.cit., p. 74.
7. Ibid., p. 348.
8. H.C. Raychaudhuri, op.cit., p. 155.

officers[1] connected with survey operations. Thus apparently in the *Vinaya Piṭaka* and the Jātakas the *amātyas* formed a cadre of officers, who were appointed in different posts with different functions, as is the case in the *Arthaśāstra* of Kauṭilya. This is also evident from the fact that one Jātaka mentions as many as 80,000 *amaccas.*[2] This number may be conventional, but we hear of a king who gathered his *amaccas* by beat of drum through the city.[3] This shows that a large number of these functionaries was employed on payment, and the administrative machinery was not kin-based.

It is held that the *parisā* or *parisad* was perhaps the most important institution in the republic.[4] This organ was obviously the same as found in the kingly states of the Upaniṣads, of which the principal ones were near in point of time to the early Pāli texts. If we go by the Kauṭilyan and Aśokan analogy[5] it would appear that the Pāli *parisā,* at least in the monarchical states, probably consisted of wholetime paid members. But the *pariṣad* described in the Dharmasūtras consisted only of vipras or brāhmaṇas.[6] One Pāli passage may be interpreted to mean that only the *amātyas* served in the *pariṣad* in monarchical states.[7] In any case such institutions as the *pariṣad* and various administrative positions mentioned above could be maintained only out of the taxes collected by the king.

Was the composition of the *pariṣad* or the recruitment of the *amātyas* kin-based? If we rely on the Dharmasūtra provision, the *pariṣad* consisted of the brāhmaṇas; they were evidently not the kinsmen of the king but religious and ideological leaders recruited from the priestly order. Some *amātyas* (literally companion) may have been kinsmen of the king. But if we look at the rules for recruitment of this cadre of officials in the *Arthaśāstra* of Kauṭilya their qualifications include high birth which could

1. Ibid., p. 184, fn. 1.
2. The terms used is *asiti amaccasahassāni. Jāt.,* v, 178.
3. Ibid., iii, 11.
4. H.C. Raychaudhuri, *Political History of Ancient India,* p. 173.
5. Supra, ch. X.
6. Ibid.
7. *brahmadatto kāsirājā vārānasim pavisitvā amacce pārisajje sannipātāpetvā etad avoca,* Herman Oldenberg (ed.), op. cit., p. 348.

equally cover the brāhmaṇas and could not be restricted only to the clansmen of the ruling princes.

The literary texts of the pre-Maurya period indicate the family antecedents of the chief advisers of the kings of Kosala and Magadha. Generally they did not belong to the family of the head of the state. Bandhula and Dīrghacārāyaṇa, the two important officials of Prasenajit of Kosala, were Mallas.[1] The generals of Kosala comprised the Crown Prince and some Malla chiefs.[2] This suggests collaboration and integration of the dominant with the defeated chiefs. It is well-known that Vassakāra, the prime minister of Magadha, who disrupted the unity of the Licchavis and brought about the fall of Vaiśālī, was a brāhmaṇa.[3] Of course the Vedic chiefs were aided by their priests, but these were not wholetime ministers, for such posts did not exist. The big Vedic chief called *rājan* really functioned with the assistance of his kinsmen called the rājanyas. The rājanya acted as both magistrate and tax-collector in later Vedic times. The appearance of regular institutions of councils, ministers and a good many officials was a post-Vedic phenomenon. These may be regarded as secondary, regular formations as compared with the *sabhā*, *samiti*, *gaṇa*, *vrāta*, *vidatha*, etc., which may be called primary, occasional formations based on the dominance of the kinsmen. Only when the tribes disintegrated into unequal social classes, the majority engaged in production and the minority in managing the social, economic, political and religious affairs, the old simple institutions were found inadequate. Two non-producing classes which lived on the social surplus found it necessary to evolve not only the ideological mechanism of the varṇa division but also a bureaucracy, a professional soldiery and other organs of the state apparatus to perpetuate the new order. Needless to repeat that every such institution as was not directly engaged in production and did not pay its own way had to be supported by gifts, taxes and tributes. In the Marxist view the origin of the state is heralded by the advent of the classes, and the state is considered to be an instrument of the propertied classes. But in the age of Buddha classes should not be seen as the owners of the means of production, except that the three higher varṇas were

1. H.C. Raychaudhuri, op.cit., p. 76.
2. Ibid., p. 178.
3. Ibid., pp. 186-89.

supposed to control the labour power broadly represented by the śūdras. We notice some big landowners and even millionaires possessing 800 million (80 *koṭis*) employing slaves and hired labourers; these could be rich vaiśyas/*gahapatis*, and some of them could be *mahāsāla* brahmaṇas. But basically we hear more of the privileges of the priests and warriors than of their property. Members of the two higher varṇas were exempted from payment of taxes, which were the main charge on the vaiśyas or *gahapatis*. The privileges were based on a social system which reserved primary production for the vaiśyas and sūdras. Similarly the social surplus was distributed according to the rules of the same system. This system was crystallised in the varṇas whose upkeep and elaboration needed the support of some authority backed by ideological propaganda.

Since our evidence regarding the nature of the taxation system and the other state organs is based on the Jātakas, one may question its validity for pre-Maurya times. Of course we cannot settle here the stratification of a Buddhist birth story divided into the present story, the past story and the versified sermon (*gāthā*); the last is considered to be the most ancient. But it is known that these stories are represented in the reliefs of around *c.* 200 B.C., and hence the floating kernel may be dated around *c.* 300 B.C. or earlier. In largely illiterate societies, particularly in the Indian context, the tradition of oral communication or *śruti* has persisted for long and still holds the ground in many pockets of the country. Of course those portions of the Jātakas which show a wide geographical horizon including south India, refer to various sea ports, and speak of active and distant commerce may belong to the end of the Maurya rule or to a later period. This may also apply to such stories as speak of the grant of villages to ministers. But the fiscal and administrative pattern reflected in several Jātakas clearly lags behind the one provided by Kauṭilya. Even if the Maurya date of Kauṭilya is doubted, the state organisation deducible from the classical Greek accounts and Aśokan inscriptions is far more developed than that represented in the Jātakas. Although a few technical terms of fiscal, judicial and administrative import used in the Jātakas survive in Aśokan inscriptions, other disappear, and new terms are introduced to indicate the organs and functions of the state. We can, therefore, ascribe a good deal of the Jātaka material on state organisation to the pre-Maurya period.

The evidence supplied by Alexander's historians may be considered to be more reliable. For several states, including the state of the Nandas in Magadha, they provide some statistics about the composition of the army. Curtius states that Agrammes, King of the Gangaridae and the Prasii, who had their capital at Palibothra or Pāṭaliputra, kept in the field for guarding the approaches to his country 20,000 cavalry and 200,000 infantry, besides 2,000 four-horsed chariots, and a troop of 3,000 elephants. Diodorus and Plutarch give similar accounts, but the first raises the number of elephants to 4,000 and the second to 6,000.[1] If we assign 2 men to every horse, their cavalry would account for 40,000 men. Similarly 2,000 four-horsed chariots might require 8,000 men, and 6,000 elephants would require at least 12,000 persons. Thus the total number of men employed in the professional army would come to about 260,000 men. If 10 per cent of people were recruited in the army, the total population of the Gangaridae, identical with the people of middle Gangetic plains and of the Prasii identical with the Prācyas, would come to nearly 2,600,000. The calculation can be verified in another manner. It is evident that the major portion of the agricultural surplus collected by the state was consumed by the army totalling 2,60,000, but in addition to this there may have been another 1,30,000 administrative personnel and members of the royal household, priests, etc., not engaged in primary production. We may, therefore, suggest a round number of 400,000 non-producing people. If these people were supported by a 6th of the produce, the total population would come to 2,400,000, which figure is not far removed from the one calculated according to the formula applied to the numerical strength of the army. On the basis of the land under cultivation in the time of Akbar it has been calculated that Bihar could not then have more than 1,4/1,500,000 people.[2] Our estimate, therefore, for the middle Gangetic plains as a whole may not be wrong. Considering the conditions of the age of the Buddha, when almost every city had some forest or the other in its vicinity, the middle Gangetic plains seem to have been settled in patches.

1. H.C. Raychaudhuri, *Political History of Ancient India*, pp. 208-9.
2. I owe this calculation to Chandra Prakash Narayan Singh.

At this state a population of $2\frac{1}{2}$ million would not be inconsiderable even for the state of Magadha.

It is obvious that taxes raised from the peasants of this state enabled the Nandas to maintain their longterm service army. Tax-collection may have been one of the reasons for which the Nandas standardised weights and measurements in their kingdom. "The accumulation of an enormous amount of wealth by the Nanda kings probably implies a good deal of financial extortion."[1] The system of assessment and collection of taxes and the organisation of the taxation machinery, which we have discussed on the basis of the Pāli texts, may have been true of the conquering Magadhan state, so far as regular taxes are concerned. But the oppressive tax-collectors such as *tuṇḍiyas* and *akāsiyas* may have been employed by the Nandas and similar rulers to supplement their income from regular taxes. In any case the maintenance of a large professional army was made possible because of a well-organised taxation system just as the collection of taxes was facilitated because of the existence of a coercive authority. This interconnection is stressed by Kauṭilya also.

The state system was well established in the north-western part of the subcontinent. We hear of nine nations and 5,000 cities lying between the Beas and the Jhelum.[2] Information about the figures of the professional army is available from Alexander's historians about five states in this area. The kingdom of Assakenos (part of Swat and Bunner)[3] possessed 20,000 cavalry, more than 30,000 infantry and 30 elephants.[4] The term Assakenians probably stands for the Sanskrit Aśvaka 'land of horses.'[5] This accounts for the large number of the cavalry. However if we apply the earlier formula to the calculation of the total population, the latter would come to nearly 700,000, who apparently paid for the maintenance of this professional army.

Further, the kingdom of Elder Poros, which lay between the Jhelum and the Chenab, was an extensive and fertile district

1. H.C. Raychaudhuri, op. cit., p. 209.
2. John W. McCrindle, *Ancient India as Described in Classical Literature*, Reprint, New Delhi, 1979, pp. 39-40.
3. H.C. Raychaudhuri, op.cit., p. 217.
4. Ibid. According to a fourth century A.D. classical version the Accae tribes, identical with the 'Assacanians' had 40,000 men under arms (John W. McCrindle, *Ancient India as Described in Classical Literature*, p. 151 with fn. 5).
5. H.C. Raychaudhuri, op. cit., p. 217.

containing nearly 300 cities.[1] According to Diodoros, Poros had an army of more than 50,000 foot, about 3,000 horses, 1,000 chariots and 130 elephants.[2] Here also according to the formula adopted above the total population would not exceed 600,000. Interestingly enough, urbanism appears a very important factor in the state of Elder Poros. Urbanism was also an important element in the state of a people called Glauganikai, whose tract lay to the west of the Chenab and bordered the dominion of Poros.[3] It included no less than 37 cities, the smallest of which had the minimum population of 5,000, and many cities contained more than 10,000.[4] It is needless to stress that urbanism presupposes a strong agricultural base and intensifies social differentiation so important to state formation.

Near the kingdom of the Siboi, who lived below the junction of the Jhelum and Chenab,[5] were located the Agalassoi.[6] They could mobilise an army of 40,000 foot and 3,000 horse.[7] It is not clear whether they maintained this force all the year round or mustered it in times of war from amongst their tribesmen. If it were a professional army, then our formula would suggest a total population of about 460,000.

The largest state in north-western India seems to have been that of the Mālavas and Kṣudrakas, taken together. The Mālavas seem to have occupied the right bank of the lower Ravi,[8] and the Kṣudrakas occupied part of the territory below the confluence of the Jhelum and Chenab.[9] According to Curtius the Sudracae and the Malloi had an army comprising 90,000 foot soldiers, 10,000 cavalry and 900 war chariots.[10] This would imply that the two ruling oligarchies collected taxes from more than one million people.

Finally we may refer to the military strength of the Abastanoi

1. McCrindle, *Ancient India etc.*, p. 25.
2. Ḥ.C. Raychaudhuri, op. cit., p. 220.
3. Ibid., p. 221.
4. Ibid.
5. Ibid., p. 223.
6. Ibid., p. 224.
7. Ibid.
8. Ibid., p. 225.
9. Ibid., p. 224.
10. J.W. McCrindle, *Invasion of Alexander*, p. 234, quoted in H.C. Raychaudhuri, op. cit., p. 225.

or the Ambaṣṭhas, who were settled on the lower Chenab.[1] Described as farmers,[2] they had probably an oligarchical form of government. Their army consisted of 60,000 foot, 6,000 cavalry and 500 chariots.[3] Their total population might come to about 850,000.

Thus, apart from the state of the Nandas in Magadha, at least five states in the north-western part of the subcontinent possessed well-organised military systems. These systems could be fed and oiled only by well-established taxation systems. From the Pāli texts, especially the Jātakas, we have sufficient indication of the tax mechanism in north-eastern India. But Pāṇini's grammar, which seems to have been composed in the north-western part, speaks not only of *kāra* in the sense of tax but also of *kṣetra-karas*, who divided the arable land into plots by survey and measurement and fixed their area. It is not necessary to add that changes in material life triggered off by the use of iron in the middle Gangetic plains also affected the north-western part, although different climatic conditions may have favoured different cereals. Although only a few sites have been excavated in this area, an incidental mention of 300 cities in one kingdom and of 37 cities in another in classical accounts suggests solid agricultural support. We can therefore infer that compared to earlier times production increased substantially and enabled the people to spare a good part of their produce for the payment of taxes.

It is therefore possible to establish some kind of link between the advent of taxes and the emergence of the state in pre-Maurya times. Of course neither the taxation system nor the other organs of the state such as bureaucracy, judicial system, etc., were as developed in pre-Maurya times as they were in Maurya times. But there is no doubt about the building of the state systems in this period. As stated earlier, altogether we know the names of at least 50 states, some of them being conquering or incorporative. Mostly these states, oligarchies or kingships, bear ethnic names, which imply that the dominant section of the tribe, clan, or lineage, as the case may be, managed to acquire the headship of the state. But once it was formed, to the state belonged different

1. H.C. Raychaudhuri, op. cit., p. 225.
2. *Jāt.* iv.363 quoted ibid.,p. 226.
3. *Invasion of Alexander*, p. 252, quoted in H.C. Raychaudhuri, op. cit., p.

racial units incorporated in the same territorial unit. The rulers established control over their own near and distant kinsmen, who were thrown out of the circle of equality and reduced to inferior and subordinate positions. Thus while the terms *Mālava* and *Kṣudraka* convey ruling status, the terms *Mālavya* and *Kṣaudrakya* convey non-citizenship.[1] More or less a similar distinction is drawn between the ruling Śākyas and Koliyas on the one hand and their slaves and workmen on the other.[2]

The state in such cases is not formed by those who own the means of production and constitute it for protecting their property. Protection of property against theft may be an important state concern, but it covered both who had more property and less property. We certainly notice differential access to the resources of production. Land is occupied unequally, and in quite a few cases revenues of villages are given to brāhmaṇas in grant and sometimes even to the seṭṭhis, but this unequal distribution is not carried too far. The real inequality lies in the collection and distribution of taxes. The state is formed and run by those who collect the surplus from the peasants and spend it mainly on the maintenance of the army, various fiscal and executive officials, and renouncers and ideologues. There is a great discrimination in the levy of taxes inasmuch as the brāhmaṇas and kṣatriyas are exempted from tax, but otherwise no sharp distinction is made between various categories of taxpayers, unless it be the one between artisans, traders and peasants. What is further important in the context is the fact that the taxes which are collected from the people in the name of affording protection to them are mainly consumed by the state and very little of it percolates as feedback to the taxpayers.

A good share of the state income goes to *bhikṣus* (Jain and Buddhist) and brāhmaṇas, who play the role of priests, renouncers and ideologues. Some of these are active statists, but even others generally support the political order; opposition on their part is seen rarely. The unique thing about these religious men is that they are supported not only by the state but also by the artisans, peasants, traders and substantial men in society. In fact peasants are subjected to two kinds of taxes, one paid to the state and the other paid to those who uphold the authority of the

1. Supra, ch. IX.

state. Various kinds of gifts by the householders to monks and priests on different occasions may not be technically placed in the category of tax, but the social backing and the Dharmasūtra sanction behind this practice acquired such authority that a householder could not dare defy them easily. The Dharmasūtras clearly enjoined the twice-born to perform sacrifices and make gifts. Of course the rule embraced the brāhmaṇas, but in our sources they hardly figure as givers; they mainly appear as acceptors of gifts. If the tribal analogy is stretched it will have to be assumed that at an early stage of social development, when kin-based relations and obligations were universally binding, gifts were bilateral and multilateral and served the cause of mutual exchange in society. But how eventually gifts came to be unilaterally monopolised by monks, brāhmaṇas, and similar people remains to be still explained satisfactorily. The brāhmaṇas may indeed have given blessings and good wishes in return and offered prayers, but such religious returns were more symbolic than real; these were empty formalities devoid of any concrete gains accruing to the sacrificing householders. On the other hand the householders were asked to accept the existing order and the ruling authority of the kṣatriyas.

The origin of taxes raises three important questions. Why and how did voluntary presents called *bali* become obligatory? Why and how did a particular chiefly family or group of families come to be considered the exclusive receivers of various offerings and then of taxes? Why and how did the "redistribution" of gifts and presents become infrequent and their accumulation and consumption by fewer people—officials and armymen—far more important?

In a good part of the Vedic phase kinsmen and defeated clans and tribes paid *bali*. The practice was solemnised and validated through association with religious ceremonies such as the *rājasūya* sacrifice, which was prescribed for making a rājā. The idea that the tribesmen (*viṭ* or *viś*) constituted the food of the chief or the ruler[1] was propagated by priests. Religious exhortation was cleverly coupled with some coercion. The *Śatapatha* rituals ensure that the *viś* pays *bali* to the *kṣatriya*.[2] All the

1. The king or chief is called *viśāmattā*. We also find: *annaṃ vai kṣatrasya viṭ*, *Śatapatha Brāhmaṇa*. III, 3.3.2.8.
2. *Śat. Br.* I, 3.1.15.

same until *c.* 600 B.C., to which the *Śatapatha Brāhmaṇa* may be assigned, there was no fixity or regularity about the payment of *bali*. This text states that the *vaiśya* (derived from the term *viś*) secretly stores property (*nihita*), and the *kṣatriya* (chief or ruler) asks the *vaiśya* to deliver it to him whenever he so wishes it.[1]

Bali became regular when sufficient surplus was made available in the age of the Buddha as a result of the use of the iron ploughshare and other iron tools and also because of the introduction of paddy transplantation. Evidently agriculture made a great leap in the middle Gangetic plains in this period, and the flow of surplus for tax was assured on a continuing basis. The availability of surplus was a necessary condition but not sufficient in itself. Coercion had to be applied to get the surplus. The element of coercion and compulsion is clearly visible in dealing with the recalcitrant tribal peasantry (*viś*) and the people in general (*prajā*) in the *Śatapatha Brāhmaṇa*. This text states that when in a sacrifice the people (*prajā* or *viś*) are asked to descend by the kṣatriya or the ruler they submit to him.[2] Apparently the coercive aspect of later Vedic times was later strengthened by the installation of collectors backed by professional soldiers and priestly propaganda. The *somayāga* portion of the *Śatapatha Brāhmaṇa* mentions several ritualistic attempts to bring the recalcitrant *viś* under control.

In the age of the Buddha those who received taxes belonged to the kṣatriya order, but all the kṣatriya families, though exempt from taxes, were not entitled to receive them. Taxes were the preserve of certain families/dynasties such as those of Mahākosala of Kosala, Bimbisāra of Magadha, etc. Of several collateral families why and how did a particular chiefly family acquire validation and come to claim larger shares in the social surplus? How did it come to hold exclusive claim to taxes? The view that membership of a 'lineage' determines social status and control over economic resources[3] is broadly supported by the customary (*laukika*) law and by written texts on rules of inheritance in the Dharmaśāstras. According to the customary law the eldest

1. *tasmādyadota kṣatriyaḥ kāmayate athāha vaiśya mayi yat te paro nihitiṃ tadāhareti*, I.3.2.15.
2. *tasmādu kśatriyamāyantam imāḥ prajā viśaḥ pratyavarohanti*, *Śat.Br.* III.9.3.7.
3. Romila Thapar, *Presidential Address*, 44 Indian History Congress, Burdwan, 1983, p. 3.

son becomes the owner of the estate and the younger sons get their maintenance. In the Dharmaśāstras, the eldest son is entitled to more share (*jyeṣṭhāṃśa*) or the best share.[1] He occupies a high social status, which in the view of ancient Greek thinkers, consists of ancient wealth and good birth. The history of several estates from medieval times onwards shows that in course of time the family of the eldest son comes to be looked upon as the family belonging to the senior line. When these rules operate in a much developed stage of society and property they are meant to preserve large landed estates.[2] The preference given to age, seniority, and experience in production, in a proto-state society may have helped the heads of some chiefly families not only to acquire special shares in the spoils and the produce but also to attain positions of preeminence.

The right to receive taxes exercised by the head of the state called monarch was a continuation of the practice to receive voluntary or ceremonial presents by the chief from his kinsmen. But how did chiefdom arise? Indra was elected the head or king of the gods because he was 'the most vigorous, the most strong, the best in carrying out work'.[3] Evidently it was because of these physical and other qualities that a tribal was elected chief. It seems that a successful chief could claim a larger share because of his qualities of head and heart, because of the leadership provided in war, because of his successful protection of the cattle or the grazing ground. His son could ask for a similar share on the ground of hereditary skill and experience in production and conduct of tribal affairs. In the case of several sons the eldest would always be preferred because of his age and because of possessing more information and experience. Eventually there arose the tendency to perpetuate chiefship in the same family whose members, though bereft of these qualities, may have manipulated things in such a manner as to retain the chiefship. The *Śatapatha Brāhmaṇa* refers to a ten-generation (*daśapuruṣa*) rule.[4] But even in this text the law of primogeniture is not

1. Manu, IX, 112. Generally the Hindu law prescribes equal shares. About the whole estate or special share for the eldest son. See P.V. Kane, *History of Dharmaśāstra*, iii, Poona, 1973, pp. 522-31, 543, 566.
2. In Bihar they applied to many landed estates including that of Darbhanga.
3. *AB*, VIII.12-17.
4. *ŚB*, XII.9.3.1 and 3.

established.[1] Of his different sons the king would elect his dearest son, thinking that the son would perpetuate the vigour of the father.[2] The *Śatapatha Brāhmaṇa* does not refer to the regular practice of passing on the "state" to the eldest son, although it may have been taken for granted.

As a device meant to perpetuate vested interests, posts, privileges and property were regulated by birth in ancient societies, but the genealogical right became entrenched in India because of the varṇa system. Once the post became hereditary the law of primogeniture worked, as can be seen from many instances in the *Ādi Parva* of the *Mahābhārata.* The son of the eldest brother, although much junior to a son of the younger brother, got the chiefdom. Force of tradition and convenience of exploitation paved the way for hereditary succession. The demand for stability in exploitation gave rise to the practice of primogeniture, and the primogeniture first limited to a member of a large family extended to the descendants of smaller families arising out of it. What has been stated may be called a hypothesis unless the stages in the process are attested by more textual references.

Whatever be the reasons for the perpetuation of the predominance of some chiefly families, voluntary offerings were converted into taxes and appropriated by them only when necessary conditions for more production were created in post-Vedic times in the Gangetic plains. Earlier, sacrifices provided the occasions for offering gifts and presents to the chief, who redistributed them and held great feasts to feed one, and all.[3] Relics of "redistributions" are still associated with many Hindu sacraments or saṃskāras. In later Vedic times numerous Vedic sacrifices became possible because of the production of cereals. In the *Śatapatha Brāhmaṇa*, *yajña* or sacrifice is considered identiful with a cart full of cereals.[4] Various types of sacrifices involved animal slaughter, particularly that of cattle, on an enormous scale. But all the same the process of gifts and feasts associated with these religious festivities held by the chief helped to level down the

1. The case of the *daśapuruṣa* refers to a family which lost its power even after ten generations of rule. Ibid.
2. Ibid., V.4.2.8.
3. These instances are found in the *Rāmayaṇa* and *Mahābhārata.*
4. *yajño vā anaḥ*, *Śat.Br.*, I.1.2.7.

disparity between him and his common tribesmen. However towards the end of the Vedic period some kṣatriya princes questioned the utility of the *yajña* probably because it benefited the brāhmaṇas more. A far more powerful protest was raised by the Buddhists, who strongly opposed the slaughter of animals, particularly that of cattle. All this may have drastically reduced the frequency of sacrifices and consequently the occasions for redistribution. Frequent sacrifices accompanied by redistribution were needed so long as elections of the chiefs or kings continued. The chief's power could be preserved through constant renewal of the support of tribesmen through feasts and fanfire. But by the end of the Vedic period we find widespread heredity so much so that even a ten-generation rulership is mentioned in the *Śatapatha Brāhmaṇa*. Stability became an important feature of the big chiefdoms. Hence they did not require too many sacrifices for maintaining and reinforcing their positions. Naturally what the chief or the king received came to be consumed mainly by his establishment or by his officials and armymen, who became his firm supporters because of the new bonds of payment and maintenance which superseded kinship bonds. The pattern of new relationships became far less personal. The infrequency of "redistribution" therefore rendered the flow of taxes to the chief more and more unilateral. The one-way traffic immensely contributed to the resources of the ruler and materially helped state formation.

Chapter XVI

VARṆA IN RELATION TO LAW AND POLITICS

(c. 600 B.C.—A.D. 500)

The character of the post-Vedic polity cannot be fully comprehended without a consideration of the relation between the varṇa system on the one hand and law and politics on the other. From the 5th century B.C. onwards caste, which played a vital part in the rise of the state power, largely conditioned its growth at various stages as well as shaped its organs and moulded its laws.

The Purāṇic speculation establishes causal connection between the rise of varṇas and the origin of the state.[1] It is stated in half a dozen Pūrāṇas that, although the duties of different varṇas were settled, they did not perform their respective functions and came into mutual conflict. In order to put an end to this state of affairs Brahmā prescribed coercion (*daṇḍa*) and war (*yuddha*) as the profession of the kṣatriyas.[2] Such speculations may have been made in the Gupta period when the Purāṇas and the didactic portions of the *Mahābhārata* were put into their final shape. But these ideas could not possibly have occurred to the thinkers unless there was a basis for them in age-old traditions, or unless such a process went on in some of the contemporary tribes breaking into classes. Further, the Dharmaśāstras, the *Arthaśāstra* and the other brāhmaṇical works enjoin the head of the state to maintain the social order based on the varṇas.[3] According to Kauṭilya the king, as the promulgator of *dharma*, is there to protect the fourfold caste system.[4] The *Śānti Parva* clearly states that the duties pertaining to one's caste or social class (*jātidharma* and *varṇadharma*) rest upon the state power (*kṣātradharma*).[5] Manu declares that the kingdom can prosper only so long as the

1. Supra, pp. 53-54.
2. *Vāyu Purāṇa*, i, VIII.160.
3. Cf. supra, p. 61.
4. *AŚ*, III.1.
5. 64.1-2; cf. 24-25 and 65.5-6.

purity of varṇas is maintained. If the bastard people of the mixed castes sully it, the state will perish together with its inhabitants.[1] In fact Manu can hardly think of the royal functions without being connected with the caste system in one way or the other. As Hopkins puts it: "Incidental mention of the king standing without particular relation to the other castes can only be sparingly quoted."[2] According to brāhmaṇical authorities if anybody deflects from his caste duties, it is nothing short of a calamity. As Nārada, a lawgiver of about the fifth century A.D., states: "If the king does not dictate punishments to any caste, when they have left the path, the created beings of the world would perish."[3] The *Śānti Parva* identifies the institution of kingship with the preservation of the varṇa system. It prescribes the same punishment for rebellion against the king as for causing confusion in the social orders.[4] In respect of the support of the class system by the state we find broad agreement between the views of the ancient Indian thinkers and those of Plato and Aristotle,[5] although class was considered not so rigid in Greece as varṇa in India.

The Dharmaśāstra insistence on royal responsibility to uphold the varṇa system is corroborated by epigraphic evidence, which, although conventional in some cases, throws light on the actual position. Asoka's officers are appointed to work among the warriors (*bhaṭamayeṣu*), brāhmaṇas and the ibhyas (*i.e.* vaiśyas).[6] The term *dāsabhataka* in Aśokan inscriptions[7] may stand for the śūdras. Broadly speaking, Aśoka took the existing social order for granted and appointed his officers to work amongst the four social classes. Proceeding further, the Nasik Cave Inscription of the brāhmaṇa Sātavāhana ruler Vāsiṣṭhiputra Puḷumāvi (middle of the second century A.D.) informs us that the king, who was hostile to the kṣatriyas, was a preventor of confusion in the

1. *yatratveteparidhvaṃsājjāyante varṇadūṣakāḥ rāṣṭrikaiḥ sahatadrāṣṭraṃ kṣiprameva vinaśyati. Manu,* X.61; cf. VII.35, VIII.41.
2. *Mutual Relation of Four Castes*, pp. 75-76.
3. *Nārada Smṛti*, XVIII.14.
4. *rājño vadhaṃcikīrṣedyastasya citro vadho bhavet, ājīvakasya stenasya varṇasaṃkarasya ca.* 86.21.
5. *Republic*, iii, 434; *Politics*, pp. 274-75.
6. R. E. V. For the term *bhaṭamaya* the interpretation of Sénart seems to be correct.
7. R. E. IX. XI, XIII and P. E. VII.

fourfold varṇa system.[1] The near contemporary Śaka ruler Rudradāman, although of foreign extraction, is described as being approached (or elected?) by the varṇas.[2] An inscription, of A.D. 529, of king Samkṣobha of the Parivrājaka family describes him as devoted to the establishment of the *varṇāśrama dharma.*[3] Again, the Mandasore Stone Inscription, of A.D. 532, of Yaśodharman mentions one of his predecessors Abhayadatta as acting to the advantage of those who belonged to the four castes.[4] It is claimed therein that Dharmadoṣa made the kingdom free from the intermixture of all the castes.[5] Reference may also be made to the Banskhera Inscription of Harṣa, in which his father Prabhākaravardhana is described as a regulator of the system of orders and stages.[6] The epigraphs of the Guptas and their successors, refer to some of the most distinguished rulers of the age as "employed in settling the system of castes and orders" and "in keeping the castes confined to their respective sphere of duty."[7] The inscriptional evidence[8] shows that in both theory and practice the preservation of the varṇa divided society was the main function of the state.

As to the caste of the king himself, he was to be a kṣatriya. In the early literature the terms rājanya and kṣatriya are synonymous. But there are instances of the members of other castes also becoming kings. The Jātakas furnish at least four examples of brāhmaṇa kings.[9] Later, in post-Maurya and Gupta periods, we find the famous examples of the Āndhras, Śuṅgas, Kāṇvas, Vākāṭakas, Gaṅgas and Kadambas founding ruling dynasties. Some of these may have been of brāhmaṇa origin; others, especially in the Deccan and south, may have been local dynasties elevated to the rank of the highest social class. At any rate the emergence of brāhmaṇa ruling houses is a new development, for which there seems to be hardly any parallel in earlier times. It

1. *khatiya-dapa-māna-madanasa vinivatita-cātuvaṇa-saṇkarasa. Sel. Inscr.*, II, no. 86, 1.6.
2. *Sel. Inscr.*, II, no. 67, 1.9.
3. *varṇāśrama-dharma-sthāpanā-niratena*, Ibid., p. 375, 1.10.
4. *CII*, iii, no. 35, 11.15-17.
5. Ibid., 11.18-19.
6. *EI*, iv, 29, 1.3.
7. H.C. Raychaudhuri, *Advanced History of India*, p. 195.
8. Beni Prasad, *The State in Ancient India*, p. 500.
9. R.N. Mehta, *Pre-Buddhist India*, p. 104.

is not found necessary to confer the status of kṣatriya on these rulers. This is, however, needed in the case of those who originally belonged to the śūdra caste. The Purāṇic prophesy that most kings in the Kali age would be śūdras[1] probably refers either to the Buddhist and heretic rulers or to such rulers of foreign stock as failed to conform strictly to the brāhmaṇical pattern of life. Perhaps the line of demarcation between the foreigners and śūdras was as thin as between slaves and barbarians in ancient Greece.[2] According to Manu and Viṣṇu a *snātaka* (one who has finished the period of his studentship) should not stay in the land of a śūdra ruler, which obviously admits the possibility of the existence of a śūdra ruler.[3] But historically there are very few examples of śūdra rulers. The available instances show that after accession to the throne the rulers did not continue to behave or to be treated as śūdras. Candragupta Maurya, who, according to the Jain tradition, was the son of a peacock tamer, came to be glorified in medieval inscriptions as a descendant of the solar race.[4] Gupta kings, whose title according to the Dharmaśāstra regulations should make them vaiśyas, came to be connected by marriage alliance with the kṣatriya Licchavis and the brāhmaṇa Vākāṭakas, and in a Javanese text, came to be described as belonging to the kṣatriya race.[5] It has been suggested that Harṣavardhana was a vaiśya, but Hsüan Tsang informs us that he was a Rājput, and Bāṇa states that he was a kṣatriya. All this demonstrates a tendency on the part of the brāhmaṇical society to absorb tribal heads and rulers of lower castes into the kṣatriya fold. If we look at small and big rulers in the period under review, most of them will be found to be kṣatriyas and many of them brāhmaṇas. The view that orthodox opinion was more outraged by brāhmaṇa kingship than by vaiśya or śūdra sovereignity[6] does not seem to be sound. From post-Maurya times onwards the way for the exaltation of the rich foreign rulers

1. *rājānaḥ śūdrabhūyiṣṭhāḥ*. *Vāyu P.*, ii, 58.40; *Kūrma P.*, Ch. 30, p. 303.
2. Aristotle, *Politics*, pp. 27, 36.
3. *Manu*, IV.61; *Viṣṇu*, LXXI.64.
4. The different views regarding the caste of the Mauryas have been summarised in an article by K.C. Ojha "Original Home and the Family of the Mauryas" in *Journal of the Ganganath Jha Research Institute*, Vol. ix, 1951.
5. H.C. Raychaudhuri, *PHAI*, 5 edn., p. 258.
6. Rangaswami Aiyangar, *Rājadharma*, p. 213.

or the wealthy members of the lower castes to higher social status may easily have been paved by the importance of wealth existing in the consciousness of the people. It was stated in the *Pañcatantra* that it is wealth which makes a person powerful or learned.[1] In other words, wealthy people might be considered as good as kṣatriyas and brāhmaṇas. If enterprising individuals from the lower classes rose to the throne either on a wave of reaction against the ruling class, or on account of their growing wealth, the brāhmaṇical ideologues were prudent enough to assimilate them to the kṣatriya caste by recasting the old genealogical legends and thus causing the least dislocation in the existing social system. This process is going on even in recent times.[2] Much has been made of the Roman virtue of maintaining the basic social structure by admitting into the fold of the ruling class the leading members from the unprivileged classes and keeping out the rest. This virtue, it would seem, was cultivated in no small measure by the ruling class of ancient India.

Next to the heads of the state its most important organ was the army. The right to bear arms—to exercise coercive power based on *daṇḍa*—was an exclusive privilege of the kṣatriyas. According to Manu, in times of emergency this right could be extended to the brāhmaṇas and the vaiśyas but never to the śūdras.[3] In view of the disabilities imposed upon the vaiśyas, and particularly the sūdras, there was a legitimate apprehension that the latter might turn their arms against the state which upheld the privileges of the upper classes. Kauṭilya alone holds that the army made up of vaiśyas and śūdras is important on account of their numerical strength. He seems to hold a low opinion of the army of brāhmaṇas, who, to his mind, can be won over by persuasions.[4] While defining the army as an indispensable element of the state, Kauṭilya expressly declares that the best army is purely composed of the soldiers of the kṣatriya caste.[5] This is corroborated by Megasthenes, who refers to the fighting

1. *arthena balavān sarvo' pyarthādbhavati paṇḍitaḥ. yasyārthāḥ sa pumāṃlloke yasyārthāḥ sa hi paṇḍitaḥ*, *Pañcatantra*, II.30-31.
2. D.D. Kosambi, "Ancient Kosala and Magadha", *JBBRAS*, xxvii (1952), 184.
3. *Manu*, VIII.348.
4. *bahulasāraṃ vā vaiśyaśūdrabalamiti*. *AŚ*, IX.2.
5. Ibid., VI.1.

men (in our opinion corresponding to kṣatriyas) as forming the fifth class of the Indian population, maintained at the expense of the state and leading a life of ease in times of peace.[1] The *Kāmandakanītisāra*, which draws heavily upon Kauṭilya, states that the kṣatriyas make the most excellent material for the army.[2] All this may indicate that at least in the Maurya period the kṣatriyas generally constituted the standing army paid by the state. Kauṭilya states that even the vaiśyas and śūdras could be considered for enlistment, but Megasthenes does not agree with him. Megasthenes clearly notes that the husbandmen (obviously the vaiśyas and śūdras of Kauṭilya, agriculture being their common occupation)[3] are exempted from military service and the soldiers are meant to protect them.[4] This means that in face of foreign attacks and internal oppression the vaiśyas and śūdras were completely disarmed, so that even the wild beasts and fowls damaging their crops were to be scared away by a special class of hunters and not by them.[5]

The key post in the army was that of the *senāpati* (commander). Later authorities confine it either to the brāhmaṇa or the kṣatriya caste.[6] Kāmandaka states that the priest, ministers and nobles are the principal leaders of the army.[7] As will be shown later, the ministers were either brāhmaṇas or kṣatriyas. The early Buddhist and Jain texts inform us that, besides the kṣatriyas, the brāhmaṇas also filled the office of the *senāpati* and *yodhājīvas* (warriors).[8]

Bureaucracy, which was an important instrument of the state apparatus and which was covered by the term *amātya* in the *saptāṅga* theory of the state, seems to have been organised on caste basis. In the Jātakas the *amātyas* play a vital role as companions, councillors, and generals of the king.[9] The repeated

1. Megasthenes, XXXIII, J.W. McCrindle, *Megasthenes and Arrian*, p. 85.
2. IV.65-67.
3. R.S. Sharma, *Some Economic Aspects of the Caste System in Ancient India*, p. 14.
4. Megasthenes, XXXIII, McCrindle, op. cit., pp. 43-44.
5. Ibid.
6. *senāpatiḥ kāryo brāhmaṇaḥ kṣatriyo' thavā. Agni Purāṇa* (BI), 220, I.
7. *KNS*, XV, 20.
8. B.C. Law, *India as Described in Early Texts of Buddhism and Jainism*, p. 155.
9. R.N. Mehta, op. cit., p. 136.

mention of the term *amaccakulam* (family of ministers) precludes the possibility of lower class people becoming ministers.[1] Fick states that these ministers like the khattiyas were characterised by "a specially developed class consciousness."[2] He, however, does not clarify their caste.[3] But an examination of references to *amaccas* would suggest that they were occasionally brāhmaṇas and frequently kṣatriyas.[4] There is no case of *gahapati* (householder) or artisans acting as the minister of the king. It appears that even during the pre-Maurya period the elasticity of the caste system was not so great as to permit the members of the lower classes to rise to high posts. The Dharmasūtras hardly give any idea of the caste of the *amātyas*, although Āpastamba states that men of the first three castes should be appointed to protect the people in towns and villages.[5] In the chapter on *amātyotpattiḥ* Kauṭilya does not clearly assign any caste to the *amātyas*, but a close study of their qualifications may give some idea about this. An obvious item common to the list of requisites laid down by Kauṭilya and other thinkers whom he quotes is noble birth. This is expressed variously as "father and grandfather being amātyas", "*abhijana*" and "*jānapado'bhijātaḥ*."[6] It is doubtful whether noble birth could be an attribute of anybody else than the members of the upper two varṇas.[7] As Aristotle puts it, good birth is nothing but ancient wealth and virtue,[8]—an attribute which can hardly be expected of the lower classes. Again, the enumeration of the other qualifications constituting the *amātya-sampat* leaves little doubt that the minister was to belong to the higher classes.[9] That the avenues to higher positions were closed to members of the lower castes is borne out by the statement of Megasthenes. He mentions the professional class of the councillors and assessors, who monopolise the highest posts of government, executive and judicial.[10] On his basis a later authority states

1. Ibid.
2. Fick, *The Social Organization of N.E. India etc.*, p. 143.
3. Ibid., p. 143.
4. Ibid., p. 144; R.N. Mehta, op. cit., p. 136.
5. II.10.26.4.
6. *AŚ*, I.8-9.
7. *AŚ*, I.9.
8. Aristotle, op. cit., p. 163.
9. *AŚ*, I.9.
10. Megasthenes, XXXIII, J.W. McCrindle, op. cit., p. 85.

that the noblest and richest take part in the direction of state affairs, administer justice, and sit in council with the kings.[1] That theirs was an exclusive caste is obvious from the rules that its members could not marry outside their own caste, exchange one profession or trade for another, or follow more than one business.[2]

The same position seems to have continued in the Gupta period. The lawgiver Kātyāyana insists that the *amātya* should belong to the brāhmaṇa caste.[3] An example is found in the Udayagiri Cave Inscription of Candra Gupta II, which speaks of a brāhmaṇa minister holding his position acquired by hereditary descent.[4]

Since Hopkins mentioned the *Śānti Parva* passage recommending twenty-one rich vaiśya *amātyas* out of a total council of thirty-seven, too much notice has been taken of this fact.[5] The passage does not find place in the critical edition of the *Śānti Parva*; it may have been interpolated in the post-tenth centuries when the traders regained some of the importance they had lost in the post-third centuries. The *Śānti Parva* also recommends a body of eight *mantrins*, of whom four should be brāhmaṇas, three loyal, disciplined and obedient śūdras, and one a *sūta*.[6] The appointment of three obedient śūdras as *mantrins* could be an ideal worth trying and is in keeping with the liberal attitude of the *Śānti Parva* towards the śūdras in other matters. However the term *mantrin* means the possessor of a magic formula, which implies a brāhmaṇa.[7]

The post of envoy or ambassador (*dūta*) was of considerable importance because of ally being an organ of the state. It was laid down that the candidate should belong to the aristocratic family (*kulīnaḥ*) and should be devoted to the duties of a kṣatriya (*kṣātradharmarataḥ*).[8] Speaking of the epic ambassador, Hopkins says that "he may be either a priest or an officer of military

1. Arrian, LVI, Ibid., p. 138.
2. Megasthenes, XXXIII, Ibid., pp. 85-86.
3. Verse 11.
4. *CII*, iii, no. 6, ll. 3-4.
5. Hopkins, "Position of the Ruling Class in the Epic", *JAOS*, xiii (1889), 95; K.P. Jayaswal, *Hindu Polity*, p. 319.
6. *ŚP*, 85, 7-10.
7. Kosambi, *JBBRAS*, NS, xxii, 47.
8. *ŚP*, 86, 26-27; *Manu*, VII.63ff.

caste."[1] The early Buddhist and Jain texts show that members of the Śrotriya class of brāhmaṇas were occasionally employed as *dūtas.*[2]

In the Gupta period some important posts were probably filled by vaiśyas. A Gupta inscription of A.D. 493-4 refers to an initiated householder named Śarvadatta, who acted as an *uparika* (provincial governor) and a *dūtaka* (executor of grants).[3] Since this officer is described as the master of masons (*sthapatisamrāṭ*)[4] perhaps he was a vaiśya or a śūdra.

The influence of caste is to be also seen in such collective institutions as the *pariṣad, paura* and *jānapada*. The post-Vedic *pariṣad* decided not only disputed points of law but also tendered advice to the king. It was undoubtedly an influential body of brāhmaṇas.[5] Thus in his comment to Gautama's passage, providing for the composition of the *pariṣad*, Maskarin holds that only the brāhmaṇas have the right to expound the law, and quotes Vasiṣṭha in his support.[6] Baudhāyana makes it clear that the ten members of this body should be *vipras.*[7] Elsewhere the details of qualifications laid down for the membership of the *pariṣad* lead us to the conclusion that it was almost entirely confined to the priests.

We have no definite information about the caste composition of the Jātaka *parisā*. It is suggested that it consisted of ministers, *uparājan* (deputy king), *senāpati* (commander), *seṭṭhi* (head merchant)[8] and the *purohita* (chief priest). The *mantripariṣad* of Kauṭilya, generally regarded as an inner cabinet, consisted of the *mantrins* recruited out of the *amātyas*, whose varṇa character has been discussed earlier. The Aśokan inscriptions do not indicate the structure of the *parisā*. Under the influence of Buddhist ideology it may have been closed to the brāhmaṇical priests. But, as would appear from Manu and Yājñavalkya, in

1. *JAOS*, xiii, (1889), p. 163.
2. B.C. Law, op. cit., p. 155.
3. *CII*, iii, no. 26, ll. 23-24.
4. Ibid.
5. Hopkins, in *JAOS*, xiii (1889), p. 148, footnote; *HCIP*, i, *The Vedic Age* pp. 484-85.
6. *brāhmaṇa eva dharmapravacane teṣāmevādhikārāt. Gautama.* XXVIII. 50-51; cf. *Vas. Dh. S.*, III.20.
7. *Baudh.*, I.1.8.
8. R. N. Mehta, op. cit., p. 135.

the post-Maurya period the *pariṣad* was entirely manned by the brāhmaṇas.[1]

It is difficult to reach any precise conclusion about the caste composition of the *paura* and *jānapada*, the existence of which itself is a matter of controversy.[2] There seems to be no basis for the theory that there was a central assembly of the *paura-jānapada*, but Jayaswal's arguments in favour of the prevalence of the separate bodies of *paura* and *jānapada* cannot be entirely ignored. Literally the term *paura* means an inhabitant of the city, and the term *jānapada* an inhabitant of the countryside. Assuming that in some cases the *paura* and *jānapada* were corporate bodies consulted by the king, our problem is to determine their caste representation. On the basis of a passage from the *Gautama Dharmasūtra* Jayaswal suggests that the śūdra could be a member of the *paura* body. But Maskarin's commentary on the said passage interprets *paura* as *samānasthānavāsī*, an inhabitant of the same place.[3] We are on more secure ground about the vaiśya membership of the *paura*, which is implied by merchants acting as president of that body.[4] There are several instances of the *gahapatis* (vaiśyas and śūdras according to Jayaswal) acting as members of the *naigama*, which probably was a substitute for the *paura* in the period represented by the Jātakas.[5] The near contemporary account of Megasthenes states that husbandmen (mainly vaiśyas and also śūdras) do not go to town to take part in its tumult for any other purpose,[6] which may imply that the *paura* was confined to the people of the town. In the Pāli texts princes also appear as *negamas*,[7] but their number does not seem to be great.

Regarding the membership of the *jānapada* body there are two sets of evidence. The Buddhist sources inform us that the brāh-

1. *Manu*, XII.110-4; *Yāj.*, 1.9.
2. Jayaswal, op. cit., Chs. XXVII and XXVIII; V.R.R. Dikshitar, *Hindu Administrative Institutions*, pp. 156-58; A.S. Altekar, *State and Government in Ancient India*, pp. 101-9; Dikshitar, "Notes on the Paura Jānapada" and "Reply of N.N. Law" *IHQ*, vi (1930), pp. 181, 183-84.
3. *Gautama*, VI.10.
4. Jayaswal, op. cit., p. 275.
5. Ibid.
6. Megasthenes, XXXIII. *McCrindle*, op. cit., p. 85.
7. Jayaswal, op. cit., p. 273.

maṇas and kṣatriyas were called *jānapadas*.[1] The *Śānti Parva* refers to the *mantrin* as a *jānapada*, which shows that probably in early times even important ministers attended it.[2] But a passage from the *Rāmāyaṇa* excludes brāhmaṇas and a section of the kṣatriyas (called *balamukhyas*) from the membership of the *jānapada*.[3] Perhaps the Buddhist references indicate an earlier stage of development. In later times as class distinctions became rigid, there grew a tendency to exclude the two upper classes from the meetings of the *paura* and *jānapada*, where the members of the lower castes could meet them on equal terms.

The functions of the *paura* and *jānapada* may throw some light on the nature of their composition. Since consideration of taxation was regarded as an important function[4] of the *paura* and *jānapada*, in all probability the tax-free brāhmaṇas and kṣatriyas could not be their members. Their membership in later times was perhaps confined to the vaiśyas and śūdras, whose important representatives assembled and deliberated over matters which affected them. Judged in this light, the *paura* and *jānapada* would appear to be territorial orders of the vaiśyas and perhaps of free śūdras, not having any real voice in the affairs of the state but summoned by the king or his agents for the collection of taxes. The Jain sources inform us that there was a *parisā* (an assembly) of the *gāhāvais* (vaiśyas and śūdras),[5] but whether it had to do anything with the collection of taxes is not known. Arguing on this basis of the nature of the *paura* and *jānapada*, it would appear that members of the lower classes were sounded on matters of taxation but ignored in matters of administration.

The maintenance of order and the administration of justice were the primary functions of the early state, but the machinery framed for the purpose was a superstructure raised on relations existing between the four social orders. In fact the effect of the varṇa system is to be seen most clearly in the organization of the judicial system and the legislation framed by the brāhmaṇical lawgivers. Judges were to be recruited on caste basis. Manu and

1. Ibid.
2. *kṛtaprajñaścamedhāvī budhojānapadaḥ śuciḥ sarvakarmasu yaḥ śuddhaḥ sa mantraṃ śrotumarhati*. *ŚP*, 84.38.
3. *brāhmaṇābalamukhyāśca paurajānapadaiḥ saha*. *Ayodhyā Kāṇḍa*, II.19-20.
4. Jayaswal, op. cit., pp. 262-63.
5. J.C. Jain, *Life in Ancient India*, p. 71.

Yājñavalkya give the first preference to the brāhmaṇas; failing them, members of the next two classes could be appointed judges, but on no account could a śūdra be permitted to hold this office.[1] Viṣṇu (about A.D. 300) provides that the administration of justice should be entrusted to well-instructed brāhmaṇas, either accompanying the king or alone.[2] Kātyāyana also repeats the injunction of the previous authorities and affirms that in no case should a śūdra be appointed as judge (*prāḍavivāka*).[3] According to him, a few merchants, who are men of high family, could be present in the court (could act as *sabhyas*).[4]

A very little known[5] but prominent feature of the brāhmaṇical law code is its class legislation. It is to be found in the law of evidence and in the penalties prescribed for offences against person, property, reputation, etc. To begin with the law of evidence, the outcast, one fallen from his varṇa duties, could not act as a witness,[6] and members of one caste could not appear as witnesses for persons of the other castes. It was laid down that a brāhmaṇa shall act as a witness for a brāhmaṇa, a kṣatriya for a kṣatriya, a vaiśya for a vaiśya, a śūdra for a śūdra, and a woman for a woman.[7] It was further provided that *dāsas* (slaves) or *bhṛtakas* (servants), obviously recruited from the śūdra varṇa, must not be examined as witnesses.[8] While deposing, members of different castes were to be administered different kinds of oath and shown different kinds of treatment.[9] The same discrimination obtained in matters of ordeal. Yājñavalkya lays down the ordeals of weight, fire, water, and poison, respectively for the four varṇas.[10]

Like the code of Hammurabi or the Anglo-Saxon code, the

1. *Manu*, VIII.20-21; *Yāj.*, 2-3 with Vijñāneśvara's commentary.
2. *Viṣṇu*, III.72-73.
3. *brāhmaṇo yatra na svāttu kṣatriyaṃtatra yojayet, vaiśyaṃ vā dharmśāstrajñāṃ śūdraṃ yatnena varjayet*. Verse 67.
4. *Kātya.*, Verse 58.
5. B.N. Dutt was the first to emphasise this aspect in his work *Studies in Indian Social Polity*.
6. *Viṣṇu*, VIII.2.
7. *strīṇāṃ sākṣinaḥ striyaḥ kuryāddvijānāṃ sadṛśaḥ dvijāḥ, śūdrānāṃ santaḥ śūdrāsca antyāṇāmantyayonayaḥ*, *Vas. Dh. S.*, XVI, 30; *Manu*, VIII.18; *Yāj.*, II.19.
8. *Manu*, VIII.70.
9. *Gautama*, VIII.20-23; *Manu*, VIII.88-89.
10. II.98.

Dharmaśāstras prescribe different punishments for different varṇas for the same offence. The value of the compensatory fine in the case of death varies from caste to caste. Two lawgivers of about the fifth century B.C. lay down that for slaying a kṣatriya the offender has to give to the king one thousand cows and a bull in expiation of his sin, for slaying a vaiśya one hundred cows and a bull, and for slaying a śūdra ten cows and a bull.[1] Four later lawgivers provide for similar discriminatory rules.[2] It sounds shocking to the modern democratic mind to learn that Baudhāyana, Āpastamba and Manu prescribe the same fine for killing a śūdra as for killing a dog.[3] Several lawgivers ordain that, if a man of lower caste strikes a man of higher caste, he shall be deprived of the limb which he uses.[4] Such laws relate to defamation,[5] stealing,[6] inheritance,[7] etc., also. Indeed there is hardly any conceivable sphere of life, economic, political or social, free from legal discrimination between the different varṇas. The Dharmaśāstra, and the *smṛti* section of the epics and the Purāṇas, are replete with such discriminatory regulations. The law-books of the Gupta period softened some of these provisions, leading to some improvement in the legal status of the fourth varṇa.[8] A somewhat similar trend appears in the Byzantine empire of Justinian (527-65), under whom procedure was simplified in manumitting slaves,[9] but class distinctions ruled in the penalties of criminal law. Thus if a rich man forged, he was deported, if a poor man did he went to the ghastly toil of the mines.[10] In Gupta India, however, legal discrimination was not directly based on economic distinctions but on varṇa divisions, which were closely connected with economic status.[11]

1. *Baudh.*, 1.10.19. 1 and 2; *Āpastamba*, 1.9.24.1-4.
2. *Gautama*, XXII.14-16; *Vas. Dh. S.*, XX.31-33; *Manu*, XI.130-31; *Viṣṇu*, L. 1-7 and 14.
3. *Baudh.*, 1.10.19.6; *Āpastamba*, 1.9.25.13; *Manu*, XI.132.
4. *Manu*, VIII.279; *Yāj*, II.215; *Gautama*, XII.1.
5. *Gautama*, XII.11-13.
6. *Viṣṇu*, IX.11-14.
7. *Baudh.*, II.2.3.10; *Vas. Dh. S.*, XVII.48-50; *Viṣṇu*, III.32; *Gautama* X.31; *Manu*, IX.151; *Yāj.*, II.125; *AŚ*, III.6.
8. *Śūdras*, pp. 250-51.
9. Cf. Ibid., pp. 228-29.
10. Jack Lindsay, *Byzantium into Europe*, p. 111.
11. This has been discussed in the author's *Some Economic Aspects of the Caste System in Ancient India*.

Between the beginning of such discriminatory laws with the early law-books and their climax with Manu, Kauṭilya's legislation introduces a liberal interlude, its object being to provide a scheme of imperial laws overriding petty considerations of caste. In consonance with his view that moderation is the essence of the administration of justice,[1] Kauṭilya tries to lessen the rigours of class legislation. According to him in certain cases capital punishment could be inflicted even upon the brāhmaṇas,[2] and in others his face could be branded so as to mark him as a criminal.[3] For giving false evidence he possibly prescribes the same fine for members of all the castes.[4] While the law-books prescribe different rates of interest for different classes, Kauṭilya only states that an interest of a *paṇa* and a quarter per month is just.[5] It seems that Kauṭilya considers a section of the śūdras as Āryas and hence does not agree to their enslavement.[6] Aśoka expresses a similar attitude when he ordains that kindness should be shown to the serfs and slaves. In spite of all this there is hardly any fundamental difference between Kauṭilya and the authors of Dharmaśāstras on questions of class legislation. An illustration of the point is his law regarding sexual relations, according to which, for adultery with a brāhmaṇa woman, a kṣatriya shall be subjected to the highest fine, a vaiśya deprived of his property, and a śūdra burnt alive wound in mats.[7] Further examples of this type can be produced from Kauṭilya's laws regarding defamation, assault and offence of eating forbidden food.[8]

How far did class legislation work in practice? The very fact that it forms a common feature of all the law-books shows that it must have its roots in the actual life. As Hopkins says in another connection: "the unanimity of the legal works in most of these particulars would point to their universal custom."[9] Corroborative evidence from early Jain literature also points to the same

1. *yathārhadaṇḍaḥ pūjyaḥ*. *AŚ*, I.4.
2. *brāhmaṇaṃ tamapaḥ praveśayet*. *AŚ*, IV.9.
3. *tasyābhiśastāṅko lalāṭe*. *AŚ*, IV.8.
4. *AŚ*, III.9.
5. *sapādapaṇā dharmyā māsavṛddhiḥ paṇaśatasya*. *AŚ*, III.9.
6. *Śūdras*, pp. 163-66.
7. *AŚ*, IV.13.
8. Ibid., III.18-19; IV.13.
9. *JAOS*, xiii (1889), p. 104.

direction. A Jain text of about the fourth century A.D. refers to four kinds of *parisā* (orders) in the administration of justice. We learn that for the same crime an offender from the *khattiya* order was beheaded, the offender from the *gāhāvai* (vaiśya and śūdra) order was burnt to death on a pile of bark, the offender from the *māhaṇa* order was either branded on the body as a criminal or was banished, and the offender who was an *isi* (*ṛṣi*) was admonished mildly.[1] Another Jain text informs us of a case in which a brāhmaṇa killed a washerman and dyed his body with the blood. When the guild of washermen went to the king's court, they returned disappointed without getting justice because they found the brāhmaṇa sitting there.[2] These references from the Jain literature of the early centuries of the Christian era show that class legislation was not a paper business, but actually worked in practice. The whole thing, as embodied in the brāhmaṇical law-books, may not have been applied literally, but unless sufficient evidence to the contrary is forthcoming it is difficult to believe that it was merely normative.

A superficial review of the varṇa in relation to law and politics may create the impression that in all administrative and judicial matters the brāhmaṇa got the first place, the kṣatriya came second, the vaiśya followed next, and the śūdra got the last place. But there are good reasons to think that the kṣatriya was nearer to the brāhmaṇa and the vaiśya nearer to the śūdra.[3] U.N. Ghoshal cites a number of examples, which show the existence and importance of close political alliance between the two vital social forces, the brāhmaṇas and the kṣatriyas, during the later Vedic period.[4] More instances are found in post-Vedic times. If the brāhmaṇical literature emphasises the primacy of the brāhmaṇas, the Buddhist and Jain literature, although a little biased in favour of the *seṭṭhis* (merchants) and *gahapatis* (peasant householders) because of their financial support, lays

1. Quoted in J.C. Jain's *Life in Ancient India*, p. 71.
2. Ibid., p. 65.
3. Hopkins was the first to make this suggestion more than sixty years ago in his works *Relation of the Four Castes in Manu and Position of the Ruling Caste in the Epic*. It was further pursued by G.S. Guhrye in *Caste and Race in India* and utilised by S.A. Dange to draw new conclusions in his book *India from Primitive Communism to Slavery*. The various aspects of this central point need further examination.
4. *A History of Hindu Public Life*, pt. 1, pp. 73-80.

stress on the primacy of the kṣatriyas. None of these, or no other branch of ancient literature, pleads for the primacy of the vaiśyas or śūdras. In the Jātaka stories whenever the kṣatriya loses his throne, he does it to the brāhmaṇas.[1] They mention several anti-royal revolts engineered by the combined leadership of the brāhmaṇas and kṣatriyas. The same idea is expressed by Kauṭilya in these words: "Royal power (*kṣatra*) triumphs even without arms and ever remains invincible when it is held up by the brāhmaṇas, is sanctioned by the counsels of ministers (*mantrins*), and follows the precepts of *śāstra*."[2] The later Dharmaśāstras dilate upon the necessity of having a common front of the two upper orders and in doing so they relegate the vaiśyas to the position of the śūdras. Manu clearly states that kṣatriyas cannot prosper without brāhmaṇas and brāhmaṇas without kṣatriyas, but being closely united they prosper in this world and the next.[3] He naturally enjoins the king to carefully compel the vaiśyas and śūdras to do their work otherwise the whole world would become chaotic (*vyākula*).[4] The measure recommended here is similar to the one we find in the Roman empire, where in the third century A.D. an attempt was made to compel the slaves and lower orders to stick to their functions.

In the *Brahmavaivarta Purāṇa*, a work of early medieval period, cow slaughter by a vaiśya or a śūdra is regarded as an offence of the same nature.[5] It further states that a vaiśya who kills a vaiśya or a śūdra is equally sinful,[6] so that the same value is attached to the life of persons of both the lower classes.

Except the Jātakas, the sources quoted above may represent the theoretical position. But the political combination and importance of the two upper classes is generally confirmed by literary and epigraphic sources. Such a situation obtained in the republican as well as in the monarchical states. We have already referred to the correlation of class forces in the republic of about the sixth to the fourth century B.C., in which the kṣatriya aristo-

1. Jātaka. iii, 513-14.
2. *brāhmaṇenaidhitaṃ kṣatraṃ mantrimantrābhimantritam, jayatyajitamatyantaṃ śāstrānugamaśastritam*. *AŚ*, I.9.
3. *Manu*, IX.322.
4. Ibid., VIII.418.
5. *Kṛṣṇajanmakāṇḍa* (Allahabad, 1920), LXXXV, p. 407.
6. Ibid., pp. 418-19.

cracy ranked higher in the social scale than the brāhmaṇas and *gahapatis*, not to speak of inferior classes.[1] As regards post-Maurya republics, the prohibition of the use of the terms Mālavya and Kṣaudrakya for the non-brāhmaṇas and non-kṣatriyas by Patañjali shows that at least in the republics of Mālavas and Kṣudrakas the two upper classes lorded it over the lower classes.[2]

In the case of the monarchies epigraphic records of the Gupta period suggest political combination between the brāhmaṇas and kṣatriyas made through marriage. There is the well-known example of the marriage of the Vākāṭaka brāhmaṇa prince with a kṣatriya princess of Bhāraśiva Nāga family.[3] The Poona Plate of Prabhāvatī Gupta, daughter of Candra Gupta II, shows that she was married to the Vākāṭaka brāhmaṇa ruler Rudrasena II in the fourth century A.D. The Mandasore inscription of Yaśodharman of Malwa mentions the brāhmaṇa Ravikīrtti as the husband of Bhānuguptā, sister of the Gupta ruler Bhānugupta (A.D. 501-11).[4] Kākutsthavarman, the brāhmaṇa king of the Kadamba family, got his daughter married to Gupta and other rulers. We also learn that Hastibhoja, a brāhmaṇa minister of the Vākāṭaka *mahārāja* Devasena, was descended from a kṣatriya lady married to his ancestor, the brāhmaṇa Soma.[5]

Although throughout the period under review there seems to have been the combined domination of the brāhmaṇas and kṣatriyas it seems that until Maurya times the principal role in the combine was that of the kṣatriyas, influenced by the heterodox ideology of the Buddhists and Jains. But in post-Maurya and Gupta times the mantle fell on the brāhmaṇas or brāhmaṇical rulers bred in the orthodox Dharmaśāstra ideology. Later texts generally give the first place to the brāhmaṇas. Kṣatriya domination meant more authority to the state probably in a limited territory such as the middle Gangetic plains, but brāhmaṇical domination set in motion the process of its feudalisation. The power and influence of the brāhmaṇas rested mainly on gifts of land or land revenues made to them. A brāhmaṇa, whether learned or ignorant, deserved to be a donee and could

1. Supra, p. 132, fn. 3.
2. Patañjali on Pāṇini, IV.1.168 and *Kāśikā* on Pāṇini, V.3.114.
3. *CII*, iii, no. 56, lines 2-7.
4. Ibid., p. 152.
5. Ibid.

accept gifts without any scruples.[1] Further, in early medieval times, the people were required to pay to the brāhmaṇas a regular tax called *brāhmaṇaviṃśati*,[2] comparable to the tithe collected by the Church in medieval Europe. This shows that the producing population was brought under the obligation to support the priests, for this tax, which accounted for a 20th part of the produce, was recognised and hence indirectly sanctioned by the state. But the most important factor that contributed to the growth of the brāhmaṇical power was the practice of land grants, the virtues of which were extolled in the Dharmaśāstras and the didactic portions of the epic and the Purāṇas. The early Buddhist texts seem to suggest that the process of land grants to the brāhmaṇas had begun as early as the fourth century B.C., but it assumed serious proportions by Gupta times. The political results of such a process, as would appear from epigraphic evidence, were bound to prove fatal to the organization of a centralised state.

Notwithstanding the difference in the character of the kṣatriya-dominated centralised Maurya state on the one hand, and the brāhmaṇa-dominated decentralized Gupta state system on the other, there seems to be hardly any alteration in the position of the vaiśyas and śūdras so far as their exclusion from the high offices of the state is concerned. It seems that the brāhmaṇas and kṣatriyas constituted the ruling class and the vaiśyas and śūdras formed the ruled class, and this in spite of the fact that the latter two accounted for the overwhelming majority of the population. Some merchants who acted as heads of corporate bodies or were sufficiently rich may have received special favours, but on the whole the two lower classes were excluded from important political bodies and higher public offices. This seems to be more true especially in the case of the śūdras. Although Yājñavalkya, who otherwise adopts a liberal attitude towards the śūdra, declares him to be without rights (*adhikāra-hīna*) in religious matters,[3] it is pretty certain that he was also excluded from high public offices.

Aristotle states that, if many poor men are excluded from

1. Kane, *History of Dharmaśāstra*, ii, 117.
2. *IA*, vii, 75, 79, 85; *pūrvapradattadevabrahmadeyabrāhmaṇa viṃśatirahitam*. *EI*, viii, no. 20A (A.D. 639-40), l.45; 20B (A.D. 640-41), l.48.
3. *Yāj.*, III.262.

office, the state would be necessarily full of enemies.[1] Similar views were not expressed by ancient Indian thinkers, and it is difficult to find out the reaction of the lower classes to the discriminatory measures because of lack of literature written from the standpoint of the vaiśyas and śūdras. The scattered references in the Jātakas, Dharmasūtras, Kauṭilya's *Arthaśāstra*, later portions of the *Mahābhārata*, *Manu Smṛti* and the *Viṣṇu Smṛti* are meagre and unsatisfactory. Still something can be said on their basis. To begin with the Jātakas, in a course of revolt against the plundering rule of the king and the priest the *negamas* and the *jānapadas* (obviously including the vaiśyas and śūdras)[2] do play their part, but theirs is the role of acting as auxiliaries, the principals being the brāhmaṇas and kṣatriyas. The people beat the plundering priest and the king to death, and the Bodhisatta, who is a brāhmaṇa, is raised to the throne.[3] In another case, the people hasten to kill the tyrannical king with sticks and stones, but he is saved by divine intervention and banished out of the city.[4] These stories provide evidence of the kingly and priestly collusion for the oppression of the common folk, whose revolts results in the transfer of power from one faction of the upper classes to another faction. The traditional account in the *Mahābhārata* states that the śūdras and vaiśyas went out of control and violated brāhmaṇa women during the period of anarchy, which followed the slaughter of the kṣatriyas by Paraśurāma.[5] It is difficult to assign this account to any definite period, but it seems to be a reflection of the advent of the Kali age around the third-fourth centuries A.D. and justifies Manu's ordination that the king should compel the vaiśyas and śūdras to work. We have some indication of the anti-state activities of the śūdras in the period under review, although they cannot be compared in any way with the revolts of slaves in Rome and those of helots in Sparta.

1. F.W. Coker, *Readings in Political Philosophy*, p. 66.
2. *suṇantu mejānapadā negamā ca samāgatā...rājā vilumāate rāṭṭam brāhmaṇo ca purohito*. *Jātaka*, iii, 513-14.
3. Ibid.
4. *Jāt*., vi, 156ff.
5. *tataḥ śūdrāśca vaiśyāśca yathāsvairapracāriṇaḥ, avartanta dvijāgryāṇām dāreṣu bharatarṣabha*. *ŚP*, 49-61.

Chapter XVII

RELIGION AND POLITICS IN THE ARTHAŚĀSTRA OF KAUṬILYA

I. Influence of Religion on the Policy of the State

In addition to varṇa, religion appears as an important factor in the development of ancient Indian polity. The Vedic rituals give us the first clear indication of close connection between religion and politics in ancient India. When monarchy is established on a firm footing in post-Vedic times this connection takes on a different shape. The Vedic rituals tended both to strengthen and restrict royal power, but the religious measures of the state, as known from the *Arthaśāstra* of Kauṭilya, were more intended to strengthen royal power than limit it. Although Kauṭilya's *Arthaśāstra* does not contain any independent section on religion and politics, numerous references to this subject lie scattered throughout his treatise. They show how considerations of religion shape the internal policy of the state and how religion is used as an effective instrument, especially in relation to external enemies.

As regards internal policy the Kauṭilyan state upholds the brāhmaṇical social order and follows the brāhmaṇical religious practices. Brāhmaṇism, as developed on the basis of the Vedic religion, may be regarded as the bedrock of the *Arthaśāstra* polity; what is *dharma* (righteous) and what is *adharma* (unrighteous) is learnt from the three Vedas.[1] The *varṇāśrama dharma*, which in post-Vedic times had become the foundation of the social structure, is expounded by Kauṭilya[2] in such terms as we find it in the early law-books. He requires every varṇa to perform its functions, and, at the end of this exposition, concludes that the person who observes his duty attains heaven and infinite bliss. In case he violates his duty, the world is destroyed on account of the confusion of castes.[3] What is more significant,

1. *AŚ*, I.2.
2. Ibid., I.3.
3. Ibid.

Kauṭilya instructs the king that he should never allow the people to deviate from their duty. For if human society adheres to the practices befitting the āryas, is based on the law of the four social classes and stages, and is maintained in accordance with the precepts of the three Vedas, it will prosper and never perish.[1] Thus the king is required to maintain a society which is supposed to derive its ultimate sanction from the Vedas. At one place the Kauṭilyan king is called *dharmapravartaka,* which is taken to mean that he is the promulgator of a new *dharma.* From this it cannot be inferred that *dharma* does not place any limitation on the powers of the king who enjoys absolute authority in this respect.[2] The context in which this epithet is applied to the king does not warrant this inference. It is stated that, if the *varṇā-śrama dharma* perishes, the king should act as the founder of the *dharma,*[3] which clearly leaves no freedom to the king to establish the social order of his liking but merely enjoins him to restore and revive the order which is destroyed. Evidently Kauṭilya wants the head of the state to preserve and enforce the brāhmaṇical social organization, which rests for its validity on the Vedas.

The external policy of the Kauṭilyan state is guided by religious considerations. In the pacification of the conquered peoples the king is asked to pay attention to their religious practices and susceptibilities. Kauṭilya states that the king should show his devotion to the territorial and religious festivals and the amusements of the conquered people.[4] He should worship the local gods and favour the orators and religious and intellectual leaders with gifts of land and money, and remission of taxes.[5] It is further said that he should do away with the unrighteous practices (*adharmiṣṭam*) and establish righteous practices in their place. He should prohibit the slaughter of animals for half a month during the period of *cāturmāsya* (a season of four months), for four nights during the periods of the full moon, and for a night on the day of the birth star of the conqueror or of the national

1. Ibid.
2. Cf. H.N. Sinha, *Sovereignty in Ancient India*, pp. 149, 199.
3. *caturvarṇāśramasyāyam lokasyācārarakṣaṇāt naśyatāṃ sarvadharmāṇāṃ rajā dharmapravartakaḥ. AŚ*, III.1.
4. *AŚ*, XIII.5.
5. *sarvatrāśramapūjanaṃ ca vidyāvākyadharmaśūrapuruṣāṇāṃ ca bhūmi-*

star. The king should also interdict the slaughter of females as also the castration of young ones.[1] In the enemy country the life of an ārya and the property belonging to gods, brāhmaṇas and ascetics should not be enjoyed by the king.[2] According to the provisions, the king is required to respect the religious sentiments of the conquered people not only by following a policy of toleration, but also by positively observing their religious practices and enforcing the main tenets of the brāhmaṇical social order in which the priests enjoyed several immunities.

Kauṭilya's attitude towards the brāhmaṇas, who were the ideological custodians of the existing social order and were mainly concerned with religious affairs, deserves careful consideration. The later Vedic texts allow three important privileges to the brāhmaṇas, exemption from physical torture, and the right to honour and gifts. All these concessions are generally recognised by Kauṭilya. According to him, the brāhmaṇa is described as *apīḍanīya*[3] which implies his immunity from physical punishment, but in the *Śānti Parva* he is repeatedly described as *adaṇḍya*[4] which seems to suggest his exemption from all kinds of punishments. Exception in the *Arthaśāstra* is, however, made in the case of rape with the wife of a teacher, selling liquor and committing theft, for all of which the face of the brāhmaṇa convict has to be branded.[5] There is at any rate no doubt about the highest place of honour being accorded to the brāhmaṇas in the *Arthaśāstra*, which states that they occupy the same position among human beings as gods occupy in heaven.[6] This view of the status of the priestly class is perhaps corroborated by epigraphic evidence, for Aśoka seems to have exposed the brāhmaṇas who were considered deities on the earth.[7] Similarly Kauṭilya unequivocally recognises the brāhmaṇas' special privileges to officiate at the sacrifices and to receive gifts in return. These are not only retained but sanctified by the laws enforced

1. *AŚ*, XIII.5.
2. *paraviṣayādvā vikrameṇānītaṃ yathāpradiṣṭaṃ rājñā bhuñjita anyatra āryaprāṇebhyo devabrāhmaṇatapasvidravyebhyaśca*. *AŚ*, III.16.
3. *AŚ*, IV.8.
4. 56.22; 59, 69, 114.
5. *AŚ*, IV.8.
6. *ye devā devalokeṣu ca brāhmaṇāḥ*. Ibid., XIV.3.
7. Here the interpretation of Sènart and H.P. Śāstri has been followed,

by the state. We have detailed regulations about the payment of the sacrificial fee. Thus in case the priest dies, the fee as fixed according to the nature and importance of the sacrifice, big or small, is to be paid to the heir of the priest.[1] If a sacrificer dismisses a priest before the completion of the sacrifice, he is to be punished with the first amercement.[2] Like other lawgivers, Kauṭilya is, however, in favour of sending out those priests who do not maintain the prescribed standards.[3] The real significance of these provisions lies in the fact that they are incorporated in the section which deals with the wages of the labourers and those engaged in co-operative undertakings, which implies that *dakṣiṇās* (sacrificial gifts) are not voluntary but obligatory inasmuch as they are to be enforced by the state.

More important evidence of the intimate connection of the state with the brāhmaṇical religion is to be found in the regulations, which provide for the state patronage of several gods and their worship. In connection with the construction of the capital Kauṭilya lays down that the northern area of the city should be reserved for the tutelary deity of the city (*nagaradevatā*) and for the brāhmaṇas.[4] In the centre of the city are to be located half a dozen divinities.[5] Deities of architecture are to be established in the corners, and guardian deities of quarters in quarters appropriate to them. The principal gates of the capital should be named after gods and be called Brāhma, Aindra, Yāmya and Saināpatya, and places of worship and pilgrimage should be constructed inside the capital.[6] The section dealing with the duties of the treasurer provides that the three-storey treasury should be graced with the presence of a guardian deity. All the various buildings connected with the treasury should be furnished with necessary means to worship the appropriate guardian gods.[7] Similarly, while dealing with the duties of the superintendent of agriculture, Kauṭilya prescribes that at the time of sowing seeds a

1. *AŚ*, III.14.
2. Ibid.
3. Ibid.
4. Ibid., II.4.
5. Ibid.
5. Ibid.
6. Ibid.
7. Ibid., II.5.

formula should be recited in saluting God Prajāpati Kaśyapa and invoking the blessings of Sītā Devī.[1]

The *Arthaśāstra* prescribes several rituals for warding off providential visitations such as fire, flood and similar other natural calamities. Although it is not stated whether these are to be performed on behalf of the state, this can be inferred from the qualifications laid down for the office of the royal *purohita,* who is assigned the highest pay of 48,000 paṇas. It is ordained that the chief priest should be capable of preventing calamities, providential or human, by performing such expiatory rites as are provided in the *Atharva Veda.*[2] Probably his office is intended to be used in the worship of Indra, Gaṅgā, Parvata and the Mahākacchapa in case of drought; in the worship of rats against rat menace;[3] in the worship of snakes against snake menace; in the worship of the Parvata against the menace of tigers and in the worship of the *caityas* (funeral mounds, or sanctuaries) against the menace of demons (*rākṣasas*).[4] Further, the chief priest seems to have been required to officiate in the performance of oblations and the making of offerings to gods on ordinary and full moon days.[5] The obligation of the state does not cease with the appointment of the *purohita* for the purpose of obviating bad days. Kauṭilya further enjoins the king to honour and settle in his kingdom such accomplished ascetics as are expert in magical arts and consequently able to ward off providential visitations.[6] His indication of royal responsibility for the protection of the people against natural calamities is in tune with the primitive view of the similar functions of the king, but the *Arthaśāstra* provision for the office of the chief priest, one of the three highly paid posts in the state, shows that the king was not expected to exercise this function himself, as in the case of the primitive chief, but through an independent religious functionary appointed for the purpose.

In some provisions Kauṭilya affords special protection to wealth owned by the temples. He lays down that the village

1. Ibid., II.24.
2. *AŚ*, I.9.
3. Ibid., IV. 3; additional reading found in the Munich ms.
4. Ibid.
5. Ibid.
6. Ibid.

elders should augment the property of the temples along with that of the minors.[1] Provision is also made for the protection of the *devapaśu*, which term is taken to mean certain animals left in the name of the god for the use of the community.[2] But if we rely on the comment of T. Gaṇapati Śāstrī to another passage of the *Arthaśāstra*, it would appear that this term probably stands for animals owned by the gods and temples. For it is laid down that those who steal or take possession of images, animals, employees, fields, houses, gold, gold coins, precious stones and crops belonging to the gods are either to be beheaded or have to pay the highest amercement.[3] The severity of this provision indicates special concern about the protection of the property belonging to gods and temples.[4] Particular favour is shown by Kauṭilya to sacred places in general. It is stated that, if hindrance is caused to the forests of brāhmaṇas, *soma* plantations, temples, places of gods, sacrifice and pilgrimage, steps shall be taken to remove it first and then to take care of the lands belonging to ordinary peasants.[5] Several rules are intended to secure the sanctity of the images of gods. It is ordained that when a senseless person indulges in sexual intercourse with the idols of goddesses, he shall be fined twenty-four paṇas.[6] Another law relates to the protection of the sacred trees, which are the objects of worship by the common people. If these trees are felled, the offenders are made liable to fines double the amount meant for felling ordinary trees. Similar fine, however, is recommended in the case of cutting trees, which mark the boundaries or which are grown in the king's forests.[7] This law reminds us of the provision of Hammurabi, who prescribes the same punishment for stealing the property belonging to the temple or the palace.

Persons and things associated with religious worship are

1. Ibid., II.1.
2. *AŚ*, IV.13; Tr. p. 263.
3. Ibid., IV.10; *TGS*, ii, 166.
4. Manu (IX.280) broadens the scope of this rule by providing that those who break into a royal storehouse, an army, or a temple, and those who steal elephants, horses or chariots, should be slain by the king without any hesitation.
5. *AŚ*, III.9.
6. Ibid., IV.13.
7. Ibid., III.19.

granted some concessions. Commodities intended for sacrificial performance, worship of gods and any religious rite are allowed exemption from toll.[1] A śrotriya, a brāhmaṇa learned in the Veda can take flowers, fruits, and part of barley and wheat as *agrāyaṇa* (first fruits), and obviously he shall not be held guilty.[2] All such references sufficiently demonstrate that the policy of the Kauṭilyan state is influenced by religious considerations, involving preferential treatment of the priests, gods, temples and sacred trees. At one place in the *Arthaśāstra* the king is made responsible to divine power. It is stated that, if the king punishes an innocent man, he shall throw into water, dedicating to Varuṇa, a fine equal to thirty times the unjust imposition, and afterwards this amount shall be distributed among the brāhmaṇas. Kauṭilya adds that by this act the king shall be free from the sin of unjust imposition; this is because Varuṇa is the ruler of sinners among men.[3] The present ordinance of Kauṭilya involves three important points. First, the king is not considered accountable to any human agency for his acts of commission and omission. Secondly, if Varuṇa is the *śāstā rājā* (ruling king) among men who commit wrongs, where is the room for the jurisdiction of the earthly king? Since the king is considered responsible to Varuṇa, it is obvious that he is supposed to derive his competence from that god. Thirdly, how is this responsibility to be exercised in effect? On behalf of the god this can be done only by some human agency which is represented by the brāhmaṇas, who in fact collect the fines from the king and thus exercise *de facto* power over the king. Strikingly enough the idea that the king has to pay a fine for the miscarriage of justice is to be found in Yājñavalkya, a law-book of the Gupta period.[4] Whether the idea of the ruler's responsibility to divine power was borrowed by the Gupta lawgiver from Kauṭilya or whether this was incorporated in the *Arthaśāstra* at a later stage is difficult to determine in the present state of the textual study of Kauṭilya.[5] This idea is expressed in a slightly different form by

1. Ibid., II.21.
2. *AŚ*, II.24.
3. *adaṇḍyadaṇḍane rājño daṇḍastriṃśadguṇe ambhasi, varuṇāya pradātavyo brāhmaṇebhyastataḥ param. AŚ*, IV.13.
4. II.307.
5. Progress in the study of the *Arthaśāstra* will mainly depend on the determination of its stratification on the basis of an inscriptional study

Manu, who declares that Varuṇa is the lord of fines inflicted on the great sinners just as, being the wielder of *daṇḍa*, he is also the lord of the kings.[1] But he does not state whether in case of miscarriage of justice the king should pay any fines to Varuṇa. At any rate if we accept the crucial passage of Kauṭilya at its face value, it will mean that our author imparts a theocratic character to the state.

How far Kauṭilya thinks in terms of divine kingship is difficult to say. One of his measures for winning the allegiance of the people is to depute spies for the propagation of the king's divinity among them. The folk in the town and countryside have to be convinced about his special visible quality, which entitles the king to burden them with fines and punishments. Therefore the spies are instructed to tell the people that kings who dispense rewards and penalties occupy the position of Indra and Yama. He who disregards them is afflicted with divine punishment. Such is the argument to be used in dispelling the doubts of the people of 'low type.'[2] This view of the divine element in the king is different from Kauṭilya's earlier statement, which implies that the king is ultimately responsible to Varuṇa, and indirectly through him to the brāhmaṇas. The present idea, however, seems to have been developed in Manu and the *Śānti Parva*, which ascribe the attributes of about half a dozen divinities to the king. But, unlike these post-Maurya texts, Kauṭilya nowhere states that the king is a great deity functioning in the form of a human being. Besides, his present view is dissimilar to the idea of the divine character of kingship prevalent in near contemporary Hellenistic monarchies. When Alexander conquered Egypt, he found it politically useful to accept the native idea that Pharaoh was a deity. In subsequent times this conception was inherited and welcomed by the Hellenistic monarchies of Egypt, Bactria, etc., which arose on the ruins of the Alexandrine empire.[3] They officially encouraged emperor-worship. In any case the Kauṭilyan comparison of the king with some gods could serve the purpose of strengthening royal power, and not

1. IX.243-45.
2. *AŚ*, I.13.
3. W.W. Tarn, *Hellenistic Civilization*, p. 49ff. Tarn's view that the idea of the divinity of the king was borrowed by Alexander from Asia also does not apply to the case of India.

priestly power which stood to gain by the theory that the king was responsible to Varuṇa.

In contrast to the favours extended to the brāhmaṇas Kauṭilya exhibits an attitude of antipathy towards the sects opposed to the brāhmaṇical system of life. Particularly the Pāṣaṇḍas, who included the Buddhist monks and were outside the pale of the Vedic system, are marked out for discriminatory treatment. The Pāṣaṇḍas and caṇḍālas are required to live on the border burial grounds.[1] Further, if the Pāśupatas, Śākya monks, etc., come to stay in charitable institutions, information to that effect has to be sent to the local officials called *gopa* or *sthānika.*[2] No such intimation is considered necessary if ascetics and śrotriyas of known character come to reside there.[3] Kauṭilya thinks that the abodes of the Pāṣaṇḍas provide shelter to suspicious characters, and hence spies are instructed to make a search for them in such places.[4] Possibly the Pāṣaṇḍas were associated with anti-state activities, for Kauṭilya lays down certain regulations regarding crimes committed by the Pāṣaṇḍas and the Kṣapaṇakas. It is provided that in lieu of paying fines they may perform penances or oblations or a ritual called *mahācchavardhana* in the name of the king for as many nights as the number of paṇas imposed on them. No such exemption, however, is to be granted if they are guilty of theft, assault, defamation, and abduction of women.[5] Further, the Pāṣaṇḍas are not given any security of property. Kauṭilya ordains that spies can confiscate the property of the church of the Pāṣaṇḍas and of temples, provided it is not enjoyable by the brāhmaṇas. It implies that the property of the brāhmaṇas is free from such attachment.[6]

Kauṭilya shows similar antipathy towards some classes of ascetics, whose movement is to be regulated by the state.[7] Only the *vānaprasthas* are permitted to settle in the countryside and not other kinds of *pravrajitas.*[8] An omnibus rule prohibits all

1. *AŚ*, II.4.
2. Ibid., II.36, on the basis of the commentary of T. Gaṇapati Śāstrī.
3. Ibid.
4. Ibid.
5. Ibid., III.16.
6. Ibid., V.2.
7. Ibid., II.1.
8. Ibid., III.20.

kinds of heretical sects from participation in the feast meant for gods and ancestors. According to this, if the Śākyas, Ājīvikas and śūdra ascetics are invited at the feast, a fine of hundred paṇas shall be imposed on the guilty.[1] Further, those ascetics who indulge in unseemly conduct shall be prevented from doing so under penalty by the king, for such a practice amounts to *adharma*. And when *adharma* overwhelms *dharma*, ultimately it destroys the ruler himself.[2]

The references cited above bear witness to the intolerant policy of the Kauṭilyan state. This policy, however, does not amount to rank persecution, for the rigour of intolerance is relieved by a number of redeeming features. In several cases no distinction is made between the Pāṣaṇḍas and other sections of people. It is stated that the Pāṣaṇḍas and people of four castes can fix their abode in a large area, without offering any obstacle to one another.[3] This can be compared with the harsh attitude of Manu, who provides for the immediate expulsion of the Pāṣaṇḍas (understood as Buddhists, etc., by Sarvajñanārāyaṇa) from the capital or town (*pura*), along with some other undesirable elements,[4] on the plea that because of their unrighteous conduct they disturb the loyal subjects.[5] Moreover, according to Kauṭilya, the problems of the Pāṣaṇḍas, like that of all the other classes of people including the śrotriyas, should receive the attention of the king. Equality between heretics and others is ensured by the rule that kinsmen, śrotriyas or Pāṣaṇḍas cannot acquire the right of possession over the building of others, during the absence of the king, by mere occupation thereof.[6] Hence as regards residence and attendance to their business the same law applies to the orthodox and heretical sects. But strict vigilance is to be kept over the movements and dwelling places of the heretics, who are prevented from mixing with the people of the countryside, perhaps the apprehension being that they

1. Ibid., III.16. Shamasastry gives a different translation of this passage, which is construed in *TGS*, ii, 99 as *pravrajyāsu vṛthācārā rājā daṇḍena vārayet, dharmo hyadharmopahataḥ śāstāraṃ hantyupekṣitaḥ.*
2. Ibid., III.16.
3. Ibid.
4. IX.226. In the parallel verses in *ŚP*, 89.13-14 the Pāṣaṇḍas are not mentioned.
5. Ibid., I.19.
6. Ibid., III.16.

might incite the people against the brāhmaṇical social order, a suspicion which is clearly shared by Manu. The present exposition of Kauṭilya's view of the religious policy clearly establishes the religious, especially the brāhmaṇical, character of the state. But this runs counter to some other pieces of evidence according to which the interests of the state override considerations of religion and priestly privileges. Thus it is stated that of the four legs of law, *carita* (custom), *vyavahāra* (agreement), *dharma* (the provisions of the law-books) and *rājaśāsana* (royal edicts) the succeeding item overrides the preceding one.[1] This clearly implies that royal edict supersedes all the other sources of law. Moreover, it is explicitly stated that whenever *śāstra* (the brāhmaṇical law-book) comes into conflict with a royal decree based on the customs of the people (*dharmanyāya*), the latter shall prevail.[2] Thus in so far as priestly power is made subordinate to royal power this reflects the non-religious character of the state.

Further evidence of the non-religious character of the state is found in Kauṭilya's emphasis on the unquestioned loyalty of the officials to the head of the state. He does not like the high officials to be divided in their allegiance; their primary loyalty should be to the king and not to religious practices. This can be inferred from the nature of tests laid down for the examination of the character of those *amātyas* who are appointed in government departments. Thus only those *amātyas* who prove themselves above religious allurement deserve to be appointed to the post of judges. The test laid down for such appointment begins with the dismissal by the king of a priest who, when ordered, refuses to teach the Veda to a person who is without right to sacrifice. In such a situation, if in spite of the instigation of the king's spies, the *amātyas* refuse to be provoked into action against the king, they are considered fit for employment in civil and criminal courts.[3] This suggests that high officials of the state such as judges are required to tender their primary allegiance to the king, even in violation of prevalent religious practices laid down by the brāhmaṇical religion, which does not permit the teaching of the Veda to one who is not entitled to the perform-

1. *AŚ*, III.1.
2. Ibid., based on the commentary of *TGS*, ii, 10.
3. *AŚ*, I.10.

ance of the Vedic sacrifice (*ayājya*). This is another proof of the exaltation of state power. It implies that the king may appoint as judges only such persons as can override religious considerations if necessary and faithfully execute royal orders in the administration of justice.

There seems to be some indication of the state control of even brāhmaṇical institutions. Kauṭilya provides for an officer known as the superintendent of temples (*devatādhyakṣa*), who is charged with the function of collecting at one place various kinds of property of the gods of the capital and countryside and depositing them in the royal treasury.[1] It is not made clear whether the temples have to pay any regular dues to the state or their property is forcibly confiscated by the state. But since the functions of the *devatādhyakṣa* are mentioned in the section on the replenishment of treasury, obviously the property of the temple is intended to be used for state purposes. This policy is, however, clearly to be followed only in relation to the property of the non-brāhmaṇical sects. But the comment of Patañjali to a passage of Pāṇini that the Mauryas sold the images of gods[2] might suggest that even the brāhmaṇical temples were not intended to be exempt from the policy of expropriation, which may have been adopted in emergent situations.

The foregoing analysis of the influence of religion on the policy of the state leaves no doubt that on many points, in the opinion of Kauṭilya, the policy of the state can hardly be conceived independently of religious considerations. But the relation between the two expresses itself in two contradictory ways. The Kauṭilyan state upholds the brāhmaṇical mode of life in so far as it is in consonance with its main objective, the maintenance of the *varṇāśrama dharma*, but discards the religious practices which stand in the way of the expansion of the state. This also seems to be the view of a school in the ***Śānti Parva***, which states that if the teacher or friend acts against the interests of the seven element state he should be killed.[3] The same text, however, adds that the teacher should be abandoned.[4]

1. *AŚ*, V.2.
2. *mauryairhiraṇyārthibhirarcāḥ prakalpitāḥ*...Pat. on *Paṇini*, V.3.99; cf. V.S. Agrawala, *India as Known to Pāṇini*, pp. 361-62.
3. 57.5.
4. 57.6-7.

The Kauṭilyan state does care for gods and temples, and mostly confirms the privileges claimed by the priestly class. At the same time it adopts a policy of discrimination towards the heretical sects, a policy which is in line with the attitude of Manu but seems to have been modified by the lawgivers of Gupta times. Both Yājñavalkya[1] and Nārada[2] refer to the guilds of Pāṣaṇḍas and enjoin the king to enforce their rules and customs. This betokens a liberal attitude towards the heretical sects, which is well in accord with a similar view of the religious position of the śūdras during this period.[3] Although Kauṭilya does not allow the heretics semi-autonomous existence, his policy of discrimination is not carried to such extremes as appear in the idea of the state cult expounded by Plato in the *Laws*. For the sake of maintaining the integrity and unity of the state Plato introduces the state cult, which implies that certain religious beliefs and practices have to be enforced among all sections of people. Those who violate them are either to be imprisoned or even put to death. But such persecution does not vitiate the policy of the Kauṭilyan state. Although Kauṭilya emphasises that the dharma based on the three Vedas has to be observed, the policy that he recommends towards the dissenters outside the Vedic fold is to keep watch on their dwelling places, to ban their entries into villages and to confiscate their property in order to meet the needs of the state treasury. They are to be punished when they commit crimes such as theft, assault, defamation and abduction of women. Such provisions do not bear comparison with the type of sectarian intolerance in the *Laws*, which adduces the first reasoned defence of religious persecution.

The Kauṭilyan state is comparatively tolerant, but not secular, as has been suggested by some scholars. Secularism implies complete elimination of religious influence from the organised policies of the state, which is far from true in the case of Kauṭilya. In Indian tradition the special importance of Kauṭilya lies in the fact that in many ways his text overrides religious considerations to serve the cause of the state. In this sense he made the first serious attempt to reconstruct the science of polity

1. *śreṇinaigamapākhaṇḍigaṇānāmapyayaṃ vidhiḥ, bhedaṃ caiṣāṃ nṛpo rakṣet pūrvavṛttiṃ ca pālayet*. II.192.
2. X.1-2.
3. *Śūdras*, pp. 268-78.

superstitions which should be exploited by the king to serve his interests.

Advantage is to be taken of this policy in dealing with the internal enemies of the state. It is provided that when a seditious person (*dūṣya*) is engaged in a sacrificial performance in a forest, fiery spies may murder him and carry away the corpse as that of an outcast.[1] Moreover, spies are instructed to lure the seditious person into the purchase of rich offerings to be made to the god to acquire a vast amount of treasure. When he brings out his newly-acquired wealth for the purpose, he may be caught red-handed in the very act of the purchase[2] and his whole property confiscated. Hence Kauṭilya does not believe in the performance of sacrifice by the opponents of the state whom he regards as condemnable and irreligious.[3] On the contrary he considers religious engagements of the seditious person to be suitable opportunity for punishing him.

But it is especially in dealing with the external enemies of the state that Kauṭilya makes use of sacrifices and worship. He lays down a number of contrivances for destroying the enemy in those places of worship and pilgrimage which he frequents out of faith.[4] To enumerate these contrivances, a wall or stone may be let fall on the head of the enemy when he has entered a temple.[5] Stones or weapons may be showered on his head from the topmost storey.[6] An outdoor panel or a huge rod may be made to fall on the enemy.[7] Weapons concealed inside the body of an idol may be hurled at his head.[8] It is also laid down that when the enemy visits a temple or ascetics, spies hidden in underground chambers or somewhere else may strike him.[9] Kauṭilya also provides that poisoned rice and water may be served in feeding the enemy's people in honour of gods or ancestors, and in conspiracy with traitors to his enemy he may strike the enemy

1. *AŚ*, V.2.
2. Ibid.
3. Ibid.
4. *daivatejyāyāṃ yātrāyām amitrasya bahūni pūjyāgamasthānāni bhaktitaḥ. tatrāsya yogamubjayet. AŚ*, XII.5.
5. *AŚ*, XII.5.
6. Ibid.
7. Ibid.
8. Ibid.
9. *AŚ*, XIII.2.

with his concealed army.[1] Further, if the fort is surrounded by the enemy, the ruler may lie concealed in a hole bored in the body of an idol.[2]

Another masterly method recommended by Kauṭilya is that the enemy may be manoeuvred into the performance of certain sacrifices by the spies of the king, who should kill him in the act of performing the sacrifice.[3] In order to delude the enemy the ruler intent on conquest may himself undertake the performance of expiatory rites to stay the calamity, and thus may snare his enemy into the celebration of sacrifices.[4] The measures show that in contriving the end of the enemy the ruler should profit by the latter's religious preoccupations.

Kauṭilya recommends the use of religious camouflage for doing harm to the enemy in other ways. Thus he states that spies disguised as ascetics may serve the sacrificial beverage mixed with an intoxicant to the cowherds of the enemy, and thus may carry off their cattle.[5]

In an invasion of the enemy's country Kauṭilya thinks it of primary importance that the people should be convinced of the omniscience and divinity of the king intent on conquest. Such a ruler should enthuse his people and overawe his enemy's people by giving publicity to his power of omniscience and close association with gods.[6] Kauṭilya lays down several artifices for the purpose, in which spies play a vital part. As to his omniscience, acting on the information brought by the spies about the activities of chief officers and seditious people the king should create the impression that he knows everything because of his supernatural power.[7] He should attribute his knowledge of foreign affairs to his power of reading omens, although he actually gets

1. *daivatopahāraśrāddhaprahavaṇeṣu vā rasaviddhamannapānamavasṛjya kṛtopajāpo dūṣyavyañjanairniṣpatya gūḍhasainyo'bhihanyāt. AŚ*, XII.5.
2. *AŚ*, XII.5.
3. *AŚ*, XIII.2.
4. *etān vā yogānātmani darśayitvā pratikurvīta. pareṣāmupadeśārtham. tataḥ prayojayedyogān. AŚ*, XIII.2.
5. *AŚ*, XIII.2.
6. *vijigīṣu paragrāmamavāptukāmaḥ sarvajñadaivatasaṃyogakhyapanābhyāṃ svapaksaṃ uddharṣayet parapaksaṃ ca udvejayet. AŚ*, XIII.1.
7. *sarvajñakhyāpanaṃ tu gṛhaguhyaprāvṛttijñāne mukhyānāṃ pratyādeśo kaṇṭaskaśodhanāpasarpāgamena prakāśanaṃ rājadviṣṭakāriṇaṃ. AŚ*, II. XI 1. Jolly's edn. of the *AŚ*, p. 242, prefers *jñānena* in place of *jñāne*.

people of their earnings but also to mobilise them for furthering the aggrandizing schemes of the conqueror and for destroying the enemy. The way in which Kauṭilya lays down these measures shows that he does not believe in them and regards them as superstition. Since they exert tremendous hold on the minds of the masses, he turns them into an instrument for serving the interests of the state. Indeed he earnestly desires that the common people should put their faith in these superstitious practices. To achieve this object he proposes methods of organized persuasion and indirect coercion. Perhaps the most important function of the propaganda machinery of the Kauṭilyan state is to sow the seeds of illusion in the masses of the people about the supernatural powers of his ruler. Kauṭilya seems to have acted according to the principle that as a result of ceaseless and effective propaganda even falsehood can be made to appear as truth. If the people refuse to be credulous, they are to be subjected to practical indoctrination and physical torture at the hands of the agents of the king. The Kauṭilyan king should not believe in the performance of sacrifices or worship of gods, because whenever the occasion demands they are to be violated with impunity. Kauṭilya's attitude on the whole question can be perhaps summed up by stating that what is superstition for the ruler is true faith for the masses.

In times of distress (*āpaddharma*) the brāhmaṇical canons such as the *Manu Smṛti* and the *Śānti Parva* permit the ruler to override religious cansiderations. The latter, however, also recommends the use of superstitious practices on the part of the king for misleading the people. In a section, in which Bhīṣma instructs the king to behave as a veritable opportunist, he lays down that a ruler desirous of wealth should pose as a religious pretender, appearing with a tuft of hair.[1] Clearly the measure is intended to capitalize on the superstitious beliefs of the masses in order to extort contributions from them. The difference between the *Śānti Parva* and Kauṭilya lies in the fact that the latter prescribes many other measures of this type.

This is, however, not to single out Kauṭilya as an exponent of superstitions in ancient politics, because it is precisely this idea which is to be found in *The Republic of Plato* which propagates

1. *arthakāmaḥ śikhāṃ kuryāddharmadhvajopamām*. *ŚP*, 120.9.

the lie and fiction that God placed gold in the philosophers, silver in the warriors, and brass and iron in the husbandmen and artisans.[1] He feels that it is not possible to pass this myth as fact among the masses in one generation, but they may be made to believe in the tale in the second, third and the succeeding generations.[2] Widely separated in point of distance, although not in point of time, Plato and Kauṭilya[3] give expression to the view that the ruling class should foster superstitions for the preservation and extension of its power. This view found favour also with the politicians in Rome. In spite of the influence acquired by the priestly colleges of Rome, "it was never forgotten—least of all in the case of those who held the highest position—that their duty was not to command, but to tender skilled advice."[4] The Roman statesmen submitted to these transparent tricks rather from considerations of political expediency than from religious scruples; and the Greek Polybius might well say that "the strange and ponderous ceremonial of Roman religion was invented solely on account of the multitude which, as reason had no power over it, required to be ruled by signs and wonders."[5] A similar trick was exercised by statesmen in early India and sometimes exposed by bold and penetrating thinkers. Thus "Bāṇa had the temerity to reject the whole rigmorale of royal divinity as the work of sycophants who befuddled the minds of weak and stupid monarchs, but did not fool the strong and wise."[6]

We have assigned an independent section to superstition and politics in Kauṭilya in order to draw attention to a feature which has generally been ignored. But really we cannot draw any sharp line between the first and second sections of our study. Taken as a whole our examination of the relation between religion and politics in the *Arthaśāstra* reveals three major trends. First, basically the Kauṭilyan state upholds the brāhmaṇical ideology

1. *The Republic* (Jowett's Tr.), pp. 126-27.
2. Ibid.
3. The writer is inclined to agree with the theory that Kauṭilya was a contemporary of Candragupta Maurya, though his work was considerably retouched afterwards.
4. Mommsen, *History of Rome*, i, 179, quoted in *SBE*, xii, pt. I, Introd., x. p.
5. Mommsen, op.cit., iii, 455, quoted in *SBE*, xii, pt. I, Introd., x. p.
6. Basham, *Wonder That Was India*, pp. 86-87.

found so far, and some of them bear names ending in *bhadra* and *mitra*.[1] Naturally some elements of the Aśokan government continued under the Sātavāhanas in the western Deccan. Like Aśoka the early Sātavāhana kings were called raja.[2] Although Gautamī Balaśrī, the mother of Gautamīputra Śātakarṇi, claims that her son and grandson were *mahārājas*,[3] actually this title is adopted neither by Gautamīputra nor by Vāsiṣṭhīputra Puḷumāvī; these rulers did not assume those grandiloquent titles which distinguish the names of Kuṣāṇa princes. Further, the Sātavāhana kings conveyed their orders to subordinate officers called *amātyas*,—and not *kumāra*, *āryaputra*, or *mahāmātra* as in Aśoka's reign,—in the same idiom and in the same language Prakrit as were prevalent under Aśoka.

The Sātavāhana kingdom was divided into *āhāras* (literally 'food') or districts, which were also called *rāṣṭras*. *Āhāras* are not named in Aśokan inscriptions. But the Sātavāhana inscriptions frequently mention Govardhana-*āhāra* and some others. This administrative unit continued in the Vākāṭaka kingdom, and obtained in Mahārāṣṭra and Gujarat according to inscriptions of Gupta and post-Gupta times dated in the Kalacuri era.[4] A Sātavāhana epigraph of the first quarter of the third century A.D. suggests that the *āhāra* was indentical with the *janapada*,[5] which is mentioned in both the *Arthaśāstra* of Kauṭilya and Aśokan inscriptions. But the similarity in nomenclature may not imply the same size because the Aśokan *janapada*, consisting of probably 3200 villages according to Kauṭilya,[6] was a far wider unit.

Mahāmātras, although rarely mentioned by Kauṭilya, formed under Aśoka a cadre of officers meant for multipurpose work. They also occur in Sātavāhana inscriptions, and in one case a

1. Information from A.M. Shastri.
2. *Sel. Inscrr.*, II, no. 86, 1.10.
3. Ibid.
4. H.C. Raychaudhri thinks that the *āhāra* tends to disappear after the Sātavāhana age (G. Yazdani, ed., *The Early History of the Deccan*, Pts. I-IV, p. 45), but this is not supported by inscriptions.
5. ...*janapade sātavahaṇihāre*, *Sel. Inscrr.* II, no. 90, 1.2.
6. The *sthānīya* consisted of 800 villages (*AŚ*, II.2.1) and formed a part of the *janapada* (II.2.3), which was divided into four units for revenue purposes (II.2.34), and these may have been identical with *sthānīyas*.

mahāmātra seems to have been in-charge of Buddhist monks,[1] thus roughly comparable to the *dhammamahāmātra* of Aśoka. But clearly this institution was not so widespread and important in the Sātavāhana kingdom. The Sātavāhana substitute for the Aśokan *mahāmātra* seems to have been the *amātya* or *amacca* to whom all royal orders regarding gifts of land or caves are communicated. *Amātyas* appear as advisers or ministers in the Jātakas, but the most detailed information about them is available in the *Arhaśāstra* of Kauṭilya, in which they constitute a class of officers from which all other functionaries are recruited. Oddly enough this very important class of officers is not mentioned in Aśokan inscriptions. They figure for the first time in Sātavāhana inscriptions, which show that the post of the *amātya* was not hereditary, as was the case in Gupta times. We know of at least three persons, Viṣṇupālita,[2] Śivadatta[3] and Śyāmaka,[4] who held this post within a period of 6 years at Govardhana in the reign of Gautamīputra Śātakarṇi. Again in A.D. 152 in the reign of Vāsiṣṭhīputra Puḷumāvi we hear of the *amātya* Śivaskandila working at the same place.[5] The names of these four officers working within a range of 28 years at the same place suggest that they did not even belong to one family. References to several other *amātyas* such as Parigupta probably under Gautamīputra Sātakarṇī,[6] and Sateraka,[7] Sarvākṣadalana and Viṣṇupāli under Vāsiṣṭhīputra Sātakarṇī[8] do not disclose any hereditary pattern. A few inscriptions speak of the *rājāmātya*, but the *kumārāmātya* of Gupta times does not appear as yet. By and large the *amātyas* formed a predominant element in the Sātavāhana polity, and they enjoyed the same position in it as the *mahāmātras* in Aśokan and the *kumārāmātyas* in Gupta polity. As regards their functions there is nothing to show that they acted as advisers or ministers; they functioned as governors, treasurers and executors of land grants. The *rājukas*[9] mentioned

1. Ibid., no. 75, ll. 1-2.
2. *Sel. Inscrr.*, II, no. 83, l.2.
3. Ibid., l. 5.
4. Ibid., no. 84, l. 1.
5. Ibid., no. 87, l. 2.
6. *Luders List*, no. 1105.
7. Ibid., 994.
8. *Collected Works of R.G. Bhandarkar*, ii, 242.
9. *Lüders' List*, nos. 416, 1195.

donors. If the merchants gave so liberally in the cause of religion the state would not permit them to be stingy in the cause of politics. Direct evidence on the royal income from artisans and merchants is little, but the use of the term *kāru-kara* would show that even artisans living in villages had to pay taxes. Ferry dues, which were remitted in some cases by Uṣabhadāta,[1] may have been mainly paid by merchants. Customs officers may have been appointed to look after custom-houses in various seaports of the Sātavāhana kingdom, but we have no means of finding out the real position.

Possibly the Sātavāhanas gave high government posts to merchants. The names of their *amātyas*, Śivagupta and Parigupta, would show them to be vaiśyas. Merchants seem to have been closely associated with the management of towns, whose number was evidently the largest in the Sātavāhana territory. Inscriptions mention Broach, Sopara, Kanheri, Kalyāṇa, Paithan, Tagara (Ter), Junnar, Karle, Govardhana, Nasik and Dhānyakataka. Excavations reveal the existence of many of these and other urban settlements. These are Maski, Brahmagiri, Chandravalli, Brahmapurī (Kolhapur), Jorwe, Kondapur, Bahal, Sangankullu, Amarāvatī, Nagarjunikonda, etc; we might include Arikamedu also.[2] The Ariake Sadenon of Ptolemy, identifiable with the Sātavāhana kingdom, contained five ports and eighteen inland towns[3] and in all likelihood many of these are covered by those mentioned in inscriptions or unearthed by excavations. While disclosing their identity the merchants seem to be more particular about stating the names of their towns than those of their parents. Several *negamas* state that they hailed from Kalyāṇa.[4] We also hear of a *negama* from Sopara,[5] a blacksmith from Kalyāṇa,[6] and also of a carpenter from Dhenukākaṭaka.[7] Some people merely call themselves *nigamaputra*, inhabitant of town. These instances

1. *Seḷ. Inscrr.*, II, no. 59, l. 2.
2. For details see R.S. Sharma, *Urban Decay in India* (c. 300-1000), Delhi, 1987, Chs. 4 and 5.
3. *JAHRS*, xxii (1952-54), 69.
4. *Lüders List*, nos., 1000-1, 1024, etc.
5. No. 995.
6. No. 1032.
7. No. 1092.

are not exhaustive, but they clearly tell of the pride that artisans and merchants took in their cities and perhaps in their civic life to which they contributed their mite. Numerous examples of this type demonstrate that the merchants considered urban or territorial affiliations far more important than tribal or family identities.

At least some of these towns were managed by the *nigamasabhā*, in which Uṣabhadāta proclaimed and got registered his deed of gift according to custom.[1] Sometimes the inhabitants of a town made donations as a corporate body, and there are several references to the gifts made by the town of Dhānyakaṭaka in Amarāvati sculptures.[2] Members of the *nigamasabhā* were apparently merchants, although some *gahapatis* also served in this capacity.[3] The popular element in local administration has been underlined by several writers. What needs emphasis is that perhaps at no other time in ancient history do epigraphic records and excavations reveal so many towns in the Deccan, especially in Mahārāṣṭra, as in the first two centuries of the Christian era. Apparently merchants did not participate in civic life on such a scale in ancient India as they did in the Deccan during this period. With the evidence from the guilds of traders and artisans, commonly mentioned as *seni* or *śreṇi* and *nikāya* in inscriptions,[4] the whole thing adds up to an unprecedented burgeoning of civic life under the Sātavāhana rule. In what relation did the guilds of traders and artisans stand to the *nigamasabhā* is unknown, and so is the nature of the relation between the guilds and the state. But evidently the guilds constituted a great source of economic stability to the king and may have helped him in the administration of towns. Curiously enough such merchant bodies are not heard of under the successors of the Sātavāhanas till the end of the sixth century A.D.

Another element that did not survive the end of the Sātavāhana rule for long is that of matrilineal inheritance, which

1. *Sel. Inscrr.*, II, no. 58, l. 4.
2. C. Sivaramamurti, *Amaravati Sculptures in the Madras Government Museum* (*Bulletin of the Madras Government Museum*, N.S. General Section, IV, Madras, 1956), 275, 285.
3. V.S. Bakhle, "Sātavāhanas and the contemporary Kṣatrapas", *JBBRAS*, N.S., iv, 57 quoted in the *Early History of the Deccan*, pts. I-IV, p. 135.
4. *Lüders' List*, nos. 1137, 1180, 1133, 1165.

can be inferred from metronymics and other similar traces. Gupta and post-Gupta kings are represented as devoted to the feet of father (*pitṛ-pādānudhyāta*), but Gautamīputra Śātakarṇi is described as one who rendered uninterrupted service to his mother (*avipanamātususuka*)[1]. It is significant that Gautamīputra Śātakarṇi, Vāsiṣṭhīputra Puḷumāvi,[2] Vāsiṣṭhīputra Śātakarṇi, Gautamīputra Śri-Vijaya Śātakarṇi and Gautamīputra Śri-Yajña Śātakarṇi do not mention their father's names, which is in sharp contrast to the Gupta practice in north India where princes make it a point to refer to their father and also describe their exploits, real or imaginary, with gusto.

Since Simuka and Kṛṣṇa, the earliest Sātavāhana kings known from inscriptions, appear without metronymics, it has been thought that matriarchal practices appeared in the Sātavāhana dynasty later. But the stratigraphical position in which the coins of Vāsiṣṭhīputra Viḷivāyakura, Māḍharīputra Sivalakura and Gautamīputra Viḷivāyukura have been found at Brahmapurī in Kolhapur district in Mahārāṣṭra[3] attests that the matriarchal practices prevailed in the Deccan even before the advent of the Sātavāhanas. This also obtained among the Mahāraṭhīs, who were the contemporaries and vassals of the Sātavāhanas. Metronymics were common even among the ordinary folk, as would appear from the name of the household (*gṛhapati*) Kaunta (apparently son of Kuntī) Sāmba.[4] Matrilineal inheritance seems to be the likely explanation of the metronymics, and since in the dynastic rule the state was a larger version of the family the same system of inheritance prevailed there. The exact mode of succession in the Sātavāhana dynasty cannot be determined, but metronymics suggest that princes did not owe their throne to their father. Among the Nayar community property inherited by the daughter is managed by her brother and failing him by her son. Probably this analogy applies to the case of Gautamīputra Śātakarṇi, who evidently looked after the kingdom inherited by his mother. Occasionally

1. *Sel. Inscrr.*, II, no. 86, l. 4.
2. Vāsiṣṭhiputra Puḷumāvi however, donated a village 'out of love for his father'. *Sel. Inscrr.*, II, no. 86, l. 11.
3. P.L. Gupta, "Coins from Brahmapuri Excavations (1945-46)", *The Bulletin of the Deccan College Research Institute*, vol. 21, pp. 45-47.
4. *Sel. Inscrr.*, II, no. 90, l. 3.

the queen asserted her legal rights, as she did in the 24th year of her son's reign when she directly conveyed her orders to the governor of Govardhana regarding the grant of a field. Only the rightful occupant of the throne could function in this manner, for in Aśokan or in other Sātavāhana inscriptions orders were sent to the governors only by the king.

The long and impressive list of Vedic sacrifices performed by Nāganikā is an indication of the matriarchal influence over the Vedic and brahmaṇical patriarchal tradition which did not permit sacrifices to women. The argument that she did it in company with her royal consort[1] is based on a forced reading of the inscription. The exalted religious status, which involved huge gifts in villages, money and animals[2] and consequently an immense drain on royal treasury, undoubtedly reflects the high political position of Queen Nāganikā, whose imąge seems to have been put up publicly. Although the two queens Nāganikā and Gautamī Balaśrī[3] give their antecedents in full, their land grants are not endorsed by the king. These queens held villages not as maintenance grants, as under the Cāhamānas, but probably as portions of matrilineal inheritance.

Wives of the officials and vassals of the Sātavāhanas bore the administrative designations held by their husbands, which shows that they claimed similar prestige and influence; the titles *mahāsenāpatnī*[4] and *mahātalavārī*[5] bear witness to this. We have also the peculiar example of a woman doorkeeper who drafted a land charter.[6] All these facts are sufficient to demonstrate the important role of women in the Sātavāhana system of government.

Although mothers of kings are mentioned in Gupta records, except for Prabhāvatī, the daughter of Candra Gupta II who acted as regent in the Vākāṭaka kingdom, none played any noticeable part in administration. Obviously the Sātavāhana legacy

1. D.C. Sircar, *Sel. Inscrr.*, (2nd edn.) p. 97, fn. 1.
2. *Sel. Inscrr.*, II, no. 82.
3. Ibid., no. 86.
4. Ibid., no. 89, l. 2.
5. Ibid., no. 98, l. 9; it is an Ikṣvāku inscription of the second half of the third century A.D.
6. *Sel. Inscrr.*, II, no. 84, l. 6; based on the reading of D.C. Sircar and his fn. 1 on p. 201 in the second edn.

did not make any serious impression on the Gupta or post-Gupta system of government, although women played an important part in administration in early medieval Orissa.

But several elements in the Sātavāhana polity proved to be durable. We may begin with the supernatural and superhuman attributes assigned to Gautamīputra Śātakarṇi. He is compared in prowess and lustre to some legendary figures and supernatural forces such as Rāma, Keśava, Arjuna, Bhīma, Nābhāga, Nahuṣa, Janamejaya, Sagara, Yayāti, Ambarīṣa, Pavana, Garuḍa, Siddha, Yakṣa, Rākṣasa, Vidyādhara, Bhūta, Gandharva, Cāraṇa, Candra, Divākara and planets.[1] This analogy tends to bring out divine aspects of kingship, which come out prominently in the epigraphic descriptions of Gupta kings.

The Sātavāhana political functionaries provide one of the earliest instances of the use of the title *mahā* or great, which came to be widely associated with the designations of the Gupta princes and officials and feudatories. The Sātavāhana kings call themselves rājā, although the term *mahārāja* is mentioned in their inscriptions. There occur other designations such as *mahāsenāpati*, *mahārathī*, *mahābhoja*, *mahātalavāra*, etc., which are considered to be the epithets of the feudatories of the Sātavāhanas. Some feudatories such as the Mahārathīs not only bore metronymics like the Sātavāhanas but also enjoyed hereditary status,[2] enabling them to issue coins[3] and grant villages in their own rights.[4] Some of these titles are found among the Ikṣvākus, Cuṭus, Viṣṇukuṇḍins, etc., and also among some branches of the Sātavāhanas, who were evidently the feudatories of the main branch. The use of the prefix *mahā* introduces graded and unequal relationships and marks the beginning of the titles which became popular in feudal hierarchy in the early medieval period.

But the significant element, which was adumberated later, in the Sātavāhana system was the rural administration in which people were committed either to the care of police and soldiers or of religious beneficiaries. In the rural areas there is no indica-

1. *Sel. Inscrr.*, II, no. 86, ll. 7-9.
2. *Sel. Inscrr.*, II, no. 85, ll. 2-3.
3. P.L. Gupta, *The Bulletin of the Deccan College Research Institute*, vol. 21, 42-45.
4. *Sel. Inscrr.*, II, no. 85, ll. 2-3.

tion of any popular element, as has been sometimes thought.[1] On the basis of Hāla's *Gāthā Sattasai* it has been suggested that the jurisdiction of the *grāmaṇī* extended to five or even ten villages.[2] But the mention of the term *rahaṭṭaghaḍiya* in Chapter V of that text would suggest that it was compiled some time in the ninth century A.D. when the Persian device of *araghaṭṭa* irrigation is mentioned in northern inscriptions. Although many villages are named in connection with the religious gifts of the Sātavāhanas, their headmen and elders do not come in for notice as they do in later charters. On the strength of an inscription of the first quarter of the third century A.D.[3] it is suggested that the village was managed by the *gāmika* or *grāmika*, but the crucial term seems to be *gumika*, the Prakrit form of *gaulmika*.[4] This fits the context in which the *gaulmika* Kumāradatta is represented as subordinate to the *mahasenāpati* Skandanāga. who held charge of Sātavāhaṇihāra. A century later a Pallava copper-plate charter from the same area includes the *gumika* or *gaulmika* in the list of royal officers to whom the grant is addressed.[5] The *gaulmika*[6] was head of a *gulma* consisting, according to the sources of the first four centuries of the Christian era, of 9 *pattis*, amounting to 9 chariots, 9 elephants, 27 horse and 45 foot in all.[7] Most probably chariots had gone out of use in war at this stage, but it is evident that the *gulma* was an army platoon. Manu states that the *gulma* should be stationed in the midst of two, three, five or hundred villages.[8] These police-cum-military contingents obviously lived off the countryside, where they were the chief symbols of royal power. The earliest evidence for this development appears in Bellary district, south of the Krishna in Karnataka, during the third century A.D. and may not be true of the earlier period and the western Deccan, to which most of the

1. G. Yazdani, ed., *Early History of the Deccan*, pts. I-IV, p. 135.
2. Ibid.
3. *Sel. Inscrr.*, II, no. 90.
4. *EI*, XIV, 155, fn. 5.
5. Ibid., III, no. 65, l. 5.
6. *Sel. Inscrr.*, II, no. 90, l. 3. D.C. Sircar reads *gamika*, but Sukthankar suggests *gumika- gaulmika* (*EI*, XIV, 155, fn. 5). This is accepted by D.D. Kosambi, *An Introduction to the Study of Indian History* p. 276.
7. *Mbh.* I.2.15-17 and *Amarakośa*. II.8.10-11 quoted in Kosambi, op. cit., 276.
8. VII.114.

early Sātavāhana inscriptions belong. Even in the second century A.D. the *mahāsenāpati* performed some civil functions such as drafting land charters,[1] but it is not known whether he held charge of large territorial units. Sukthankar suggests that these military officers were feudal lords of the lands, holding them as *jagirs*. This may or may not be true, but the practice of having military officers as governors is in sharp contrast with the administration of the Aśokan *janapada* which was placed under a high civil functionary called *rājuka*. Though Aśoka was obsessed with the problem of maintaining peace among the frontier peoples, yet he did not place them under military rule.

That coercive elements are prominent in the Sātavāhana rural administration can also be made out from the nature of concessions granted to religious beneficiaries. Gifts of both cultivated fields and villages are rendered free from molestation and entry of policemen and soldiers and also from the interference of royal officials. Since the charters pay chief attention to these privileges and not to taxes from whose payment the beneficiary was exempted, they create the impression that royal police, soldiers, retainers and officials freely operated in the rural areas and formed an effective agency of exploitation. The practice was continued with vigour by the Vākāṭakas, who clearly enumerated the provisions that the villagers had to supply to various types of royal retainers, and it became a general feature of early medieval polity in the countryside.

The military character of the Sātavāhana rule is also evident from their common use of such terms as *kaṭaka* and *skandhāvāra*, meaning military camps. It seems that every *āhāra* had its *kaṭaka*; the situation of Benakaṭaka in Govardhana-*āhāra*[2] is an example, although Dhenukākaṭaka or Dhānyakaṭaka may have held a similar position in another *āhāra*. The Sātavāhanas originated the practice of issuing land charters from victory camps, which became widespread in early medieval times.

Land grants formed a significant trait of the Sātavāhana rural administration. Inscriptions show that the Sātavāhanas started the practice of granting fiscal and administrative immunities to brāhmaṇas and Buddhist monks. Perhaps the

1. *Sel. Inscrr.*, II. no. 87, l. 4.
2. *Sel. Inscrr.*, II, no. 83, l. 1.

earliest epigraphic grant of land is found in the Nānāghat Cave Inscription of Nāganikā, who bestowed villages (*grāma*) on priests for officiating at Vedic sacrifices,[1] but it does not speak of any concessions in this context. These appear first in grants made by Gautamīputra Śātakarṇi in the first quarter of the second century A.D. and include the surrender of royal rights to the procurement of salt from cultivated fields, which in actual practice may not have been found in every field. What is further important is that royal officials,—apparently policemen, retainers and soldiers,—are asked not to interfere with the administration of the donated field or village, which is thus left completely in the hands of religious beneficiaries.

The Sātavāhana inscriptions of the second century A.D. speak of exemptions of all kinds granted to the beneficiaries by using the phrase *sarva-jāti-parihāra*.[2] *Parihāra* in the sense of royal charter is defined by Kauṭilya as an act of royal favour done to special castes, towns, villages or countries.[3] In the sense of remission of taxes it is recommended for cultivators in new settlements,[4] and for sailors and merchants[5] in special cases; remission for five years is also prescribed for those who renovate irrigation works.[6] In the *Arthaśāstra* we hear of villages which enjoyed remissions[7] and also of royal favourites who lived on such remissions.[8] Kauṭilya's main objective in recommending *parihāra* is purely secular, to eventually augment royal resources. But the Sātavāhana inscriptions speak only of *parihāras* granted for religious reasons, and specify only four or five[9] items from which immunity was granted. Eighteen items (*aṣṭādaśajātiparihāra*) are mentioned separately in a fourth century A.D. Pallava inscription[10] which refers to their prevalence in the Sātavāhana *rāṣṭra*;[11] but we are not quite sure whether the peasants were

1. *Sel. Inscrr.*, II, no. 82.
2. Ibid., no. 83, l. 4.
3. *AŚ*, II.10.
4. Ibid., II.1.
5. Ibid., II.16.
6. Ibid., III.9.
7. Ibid., II.35.
8. Ibid., II.37.
9. *Sel. Inscrr.*, II, no. 83, ll. 3-4.
10. Ibid., III, no. 65, ll. 31-36.
11. Ibid., l. 27.

subjected to all these impositions since the early third century A.D. when this area was occupied by the Sātavāhanas.

Nor was the transfer of fiscal and administrative rights made absolute and permanent. A village granted to one set of Buddhist monks seems to have been taken away and granted to another set by Vāsiṣṭhīputra Puḷumāvi.[1] Further, Gautamīputra seems to have resumed the grant of a field from the monks on the ground that it was not being cultivated and the village was not being inhabited. Instead of this the monks were granted another piece of land on the boundary of the town.[2] In any case perpetual grants of land were not made in the Sātavāhana kingdom. Although we hear of the *akṣayanīvi*[3] tenure, yet at this stage it implied the inexhaustible character of the benefice and not its grant in perpetuity.

Evidently the Sātavāhanas supplemented the coercive method of maintaining their authority in the countryside by grants to monks and priests. The Buddhist monks, who seem to have been one of the earliest landed beneficiaries according to inscriptions, must have preached peace and rules of good conduct, obviating the occasions for defiance of the royal authority and social order. A similar service may have been rendered by the brāhmaṇas, who would be interested in enforcing the rules of the varṇa system. In an inscription Gautamīputra Śātakarṇi is called the sole brāhmaṇa and credited with the prevention of the fusion of four varṇas. The Sātavāhanas seem to have been improvised brāhmaṇas, which accounts for their zealous support of the brāhmaṇical order. Perhaps all the four varṇas mentioned in the Sātavāhana inscriptions were not equally well established in their dominions, and in actual practice royal task may have been confined to the disciplining of the śūdras, although Gautamīputra claims to have disgraced the kṣatriya princes. The role which this king takes upon himself is commended to the king by Kauṭilya. Later this claim is made in inscriptions by Gupta kings, Harṣavardhana and others. But the royal responsibility for maintaining the existing social order was first stressed by the Sātavāhanas.

The picture of the Sātavāhana political system that emerges

1. Ibid., II, no. 87, ll. 2-4.
2. Ibid., no. 84, ll. 3-5.
3. Ibid., no. 87, l. 2.

from this study is incomplete. We do not have any information about their judicial system, very little about their civil administration, and not enough about their fiscal and military system. Inscriptions of the second and third centuries show that their kingdom was divided into *rāṣṭras*, *āhāras* and *grāmas* in hierarchical order. It was governed by an official hierarchy of *āmātya* or *mahāsenāpati*, and *gaulmika*. The two later officials as heads of territorial units appear in the third century A.D. in Bellary district. Hence it is difficult to visualise this neat territorial arrangement uniformly for the whole period and the entire kingdom of the Sātavāhanas. Numerous epigraphic references suggest that the Sātavāhana polity was sustained by monks and merchants, but we cannot assess their exact contribution to administration. Probably the first preached peace in return for the rich grants they received, and the second provided the necessary resources for the expenditure of the state.

Not the least striking feature of the Sātavāhana rule was its coercive, military character. It seems that cavalry had an important place in the Sātavāhana military organisation. The importance of the coercive element can be inferred from the importance attached to freedom from visits of the police and soldiers to the countryside and from the names of such administrative functionaries as *mahāsenāpati* and *gaulmika*.

Because of the presence of Aśokan elements in it the Sātavāhana polity is sometimes seen as an example of secondary state formation. But the megalithic material legacy, contact with the Tamil states of the Coḷas, Ceras and Pāṇḍyas, and the stimulus from the Roman trade should not be ignored. The Maurya model may have inspired the Sātavāhana state builders, but it should not be considered to be a new version of the Maurya state.

The Sātavāhana system of administration appears to be a significant link between the Mauryas and Guptas, and between the North and the South. The Sātavāhanas retained a few elements of the Aśokan administration, but they introduced several important ones which were continued by the Vākāṭakas and Guptas. The role played by women and merchants in their government did not last long, but the practice of placing rural districts under military rule and granting fiscal and administrative immunities spread both northward and southward. In this respect the Pallava system of administration was the southward extension of the Sātavāhana legacy. It retained the *gulma* system of government as well as the practice of granting to the landed beneficiaries exemptions, which counted eighteen *parihāras* in the fourth and as many as thirty-five in the sixth century.

CHAPTER XIX

THE KUṢĀṆA POLITY

The basic facts that formed the background of the Kuṣāṇa polity were the expansion of trade and the needs of administration created by conquest in an unfamiliar area. The Kuṣāṇa dominions extended from the Aral sea to the Ganga, and Indian merchants profited from silk trade carried on the silk route passing through the Kuṣāṇa empire in Central Asia. The Indian gold coins issued by the Kuṣāṇas owed much to the supply of gold from Central Asia. What is more important, they issued the largest number of copper coins which must have affected at least the urban economy and added to the importance of artisans and merchants.

Attempts have been made to read foreign influence in the Maurya polity, but this exercise should prove more fruitful in the study of the Kuṣāṇa polity. The Scythians brought in ideas of kingship and administration from Central Asia and China and tried them in India. Foreign rulers as they were, their high officers had to be their compatriots, and they had to evolve some kind of feudatory organisation for the government of the newly conquered lands in which the military element had to be given an important place.

After more than two centuries of disintegration following the fall of the Maurya empire the Kuṣāṇas restored the partial political unity of northern India and maintained it for about more than a century. But the Kuṣāṇa political organization did not possess that rigid centralisation which characterised the Maurya administrative machinery. Inscriptions and, to some extent, coins, which form the chief source of our study of the Kuṣāṇa polity, do not indicate numerous state officials, who are known from the epigraphs of Aśoka and the *Arthaśāstra* of Kauṭilya. The one striking difference between the Maurya and the Kuṣāṇa rulers is the use of grandiloquent titles by the latter. In the beginning Kujūla Kadphises, the founder of the Kuṣāṇa power in India, is described as a small chief (*yavuga*), but, with the expansion of their power, he and other Kuṣāṇa rulers use such titles as *mahārāja*, *rājātirāja*.[1] Both these titles were used by the Parthian[2] rulers Gondopharnes and Azilises, who flourished in the first half of the first century A.D.,[3] although in comparison with the Kuṣāṇa successors their power was very limited. The earliest epigraphic mention of the title *mahārāja* appears in the first century B.C. Hāthīgumphā Inscription of Khāravela, where his ancestor Mahāmeghavāhana is described as *mahārāja*,[4] although coins show the use of this term for Indo-Greek Kings of earlier times. But the title *rājātirāja*, although Indian in form, was of foreign extraction and was apparently derived by the Kuṣāṇas from their Parthian predecessors, who adopted it from the Achaemenians. The first Parthian king to use the title 'King of Kings' was Mithridates II, 123-88 B.C.[5] This seems to have been imitated by the Śaka chief Maues[6] after 88 B.C., and was also used by the Parthian rulers now and then. A Jain text, the *Kālakācāryakathānaka*, which seems to contain genuine traditions about the first appearance of the Śakas in India,[7] uses the prakritised form *rāyāhirāya* for a Śaka ṣāhi.[8] Since lesser rulers such as the Śaka, and especially the Parthian, styled themselves *rājātirāja* and *mahārāja*, these titles should not be taken to betoken greater royal authority. This also applies to the case of the Kuṣāṇas. Undoubtedly Aśoka's empire was far wider and his authority far stronger, yet he remained satisfied with the simple title of *rājā*. Therefore these Kuṣāṇa titles perhaps betray a tendency towards tributary arrangement rather than the real exaltation of royal authority, as has been suggested by some scholars.[9] Such titles take notice of the existence of lesser kings and chiefs who stood in the relation of feudatories to the sovereign power, for the king is called *mahārāja* or the great king in relation to other kings (*rājās*), who do not enjoy that position. Similarly he is called *rājātirāja* or the supreme king of kings in

1. *Sel. Inscrr.*, II, no. 51, l. 2; cf. p. 124.
2. Ibid., II, no. 29, l. 1.
3. Ibid., II, no. 23, l. 1.
4. L. 1.
5. *CII*, ii, pt. I, p. xxix.
6. Ibid.
7. Ibid., pp. xxvi-vii.
8. Ed. H. Jacobi, *ZDMG*, 1880, verse 62.
9. Raychaudhuri, *PHAI*, 5th edn. p. 518; Ghoshal, in *The Mauryas and Sātavāhanas* p. 344.

relation to other subordinate kings in his kingdom. Thus these titles indicate a feudatory or tribute paying organization consisting of tributary states or chiefs.

The rulers belonging to the Kaniṣka group generally prefixed to their names a title ṣāhi.[1] The title appears as *shaonano shao* on the coin-legends of Kaniṣka and his successors.[2] The sanskritised form of the title, *ṣāhānuṣāhi*, appeared in the Allahabad Inscription of Samudra Gupta. Although this epithet was ultimately derived from the Persian source, we are not certain about the intermediary from whom the Kuṣāṇa rulers adopted this title. Since the title on the coin-legends is written in pure Khotanī Śaka language[3] and ascribed in its prakritised form, *sāhāṇusāhi*, to the Śakas by the *Kālakācāryakathānaka*,[4] most probably the Kuṣāṇas adopted it from their Śaka predecessors, whom they supplanted in the area near about Mohenjo-daro. The administrative and political significance of this title can be brought out from the context in which it is used in the abovementioned Jain text. It informs us[5] that the Jain teacher, Kālaka, whose sister was abducted by Gardabhilla, King of Ujjayinī, went to the *Śaka Kula*. There the feudatories (*sāmanta*) were called *ṣāhi* and their overlord (*sāmantāhivai*) *ṣāhāṇuṣāhi*. Kālaka stayed with one of the ṣāhis, and as this chief together with ninety-five other ṣāhis fell into disgrace with the *ṣāhāṇuṣāhi*, he induced them to proceed to Saurāṣṭra, which they divided among themselves. When the autumn came, the Jain teacher led them on to Ujjayinī, where Gardabhilla was made a prisoner. A ṣāhi was established as overking (*rāyāhirāya*), and this led to the establishment of the Śaka dynasty. This story reveals three distinct elements in the Śaka polity, which seem to have been adopted by the Kuṣāṇas. First, the ṣāhis were not independent kings who had been subjugated but chiefs who stood in the relation of feudatories to the great lord (*sāmantāhivai*). Secondly, the ṣāhis belonged to the same clan as the *ṣāhāṇuṣāhi*, and, hence the overlord was only the first among the equals. Thirdly, since the ṣāhis were the kinsmen of their overlord because of the

1. *Lüders' List* nos. 21, 69a, 72, 149a, 161; *Sel. Inscrr.*, II, no. 49, l. 10.
2. *CCIM*, i, 69, 75-79, 84.
3. *CII*, ii, pt. I, p. liii.
4. *ZDMG*, 1880, p. 262, lines 33-36.
5. Ibid., p. 267ff.

feelings of equality at the slightest provocation they could withdraw their fealty from him and seek their fortunes independently. We have some information about the nature of the obligations of the ṣāhis towards their overlord. In A.D. 90 the Yue-chi sent their viceroy Sie, according to M. Sylvain Lévi, a ṣahi, to attack Pan-chao, who, however, succeeded in defeating him.[1] This shows that to render military aid to the overlord was an important obligation of the ṣāhi. Unfortunately the existing data neither mention the names of the lesser rajās, ṣāhis, etc., nor indicate the nature of their relations with their Kuṣāṇa overlord. But for an external conquering minority the feudatory organization was apparently a suitable form of political system.

The feudatory character of the Kuṣāṇa political system can also be inferred from some other titles. Thus the title *mahīśvara* adopted by Wema Kadphises II[2] means the great lord. The title *sarvaloka-īśvara*[3] means the lord of the whole world. Although these titles were not adopted by the Kaniṣka group of Kuṣāṇa rulers, similar epithets were assumed by Indian rulers in later centuries. Significantly enough the generally prevalent Kuṣāṇa titles such as *rājātirāja* and *ṣāhi* were not adopted by indigenous rulers, but the term *īśvara* associated with the titles of the Kadphises group came to be common with post-Gupta rulers, who styled themselves as *parmeśvara*, the supreme lord. Curiously enough *ṣāhi* continues as the title of some affluent landed castes in eastern U.P. and in north Bihar.

The Kuṣāṇas were influenced by the Roman system of administration inasmuch as Kaniṣka adopted the title of *Kaiser*,[4] which was obviously used to challenge the Roman power. But this was a superficial imitation. They were not influenced by the Roman system of provincial administration, which was an important Roman achievement. The Kuṣāṇas could not evolve any sound provincial system either on Maurya or Roman lines. We do not know whether they exercised any direct administrative control over a sizable part of their territories. The Sārnāth Buddhist Image Inscription of the year 3 of Kaniṣka I (A.D.

1. Quoted in *CII*, ii, pt. p. lxxii.
2. *Sel. Inscrr.*, i, II, no. 31, l. 1.
3. Ibid.
4. Ibid., II, no. 51, ll. 1-2.

81?)[1] refers to the rule of two kṣatrapas, Vanaspara and Kharapallāna, ruling over the easternmost province, including the Banaras region of Kaniṣka's empire.[2] That there prevailed the system of dual kingship in some parts of northern India in earlier times is known from Greek and Jain sources. But the Kuṣāṇas seem to have introduced the curious practice of dual governorship in a province. Apparently it was intended that one kṣatrapa would act as a check on the power of the other. But probably Vanaspara and Kharapallāna could not remain on the same footing for long, since in another inscription the former is mentioned as a *kṣatrapa* and the latter as a *mahākṣatrapa*.[3] What led to this change is difficult to say. Perhaps this was more in keeping with the hierarchical organization in the feudatory system than with the equal position of the two kṣatrapas. The *mahākṣatrapa* (the great satrap) was made, as it were, the overlord of the *kṣatrapa*, who assisted him in the work of administration. The names of Vanaspara and Kharapallāna clearly show that they were foreigners. It is suggested that they were the descendants of the *mahākṣatrapa* Ṣoḍāsa of Mathurā and retained in their position by the Kuṣāṇas.[4] If we accept this suggestion, it would mean that even the kṣatrapas were not directly appointed by the Kuṣāṇa king but were reinstated in their position as vanquished chiefs. This may have been true in some cases; in other cases the kṣatrapas may have been appointed directly. At any rate it is clear that generally the scions of the ruling family were appointed to this post; thus in one case the son of a mahārāja was appointed a kṣatrapa, probably in north-western India.[5] We have no exact idea of the number of satrapies in the Kuṣāṇa empire. It has been suggested that the empire was divided into five, perhaps seven, satrapies.[6] But we do not know how long and how regularly this division functioned, nor can we easily classify these satrapies into any well-defined categories.

Inscriptions do not give us sufficient idea about the functions

1. Ibid., II, no. 37, ll. 1-10.
2. Ibid., fn. 4.
3. Ibid., II, no. 38, ll. 1-2.
4. S.K. Chattopadhyaya, *Early History of Northern India*, p. 84.
5. *Sel. Inscrr.*, II, no. 36, l. 2.
6. B.N. Puri, "Provincial and Local Administration in the Kuṣāṇa Period", *Proc. IHC*, 1945, p. 64.

of the kṣatrapas. As individuals they erected images of the Buddha as Vanaspara and Kharapallāna did, or established several relics of the Buddha as in the case of Kṣatrapa Veśpasi,[1] who had appointed a donation master for the purpose. Except this they do not throw any light on the civil functions of the kṣatrapa as a governor. The analogy of the Achaemenian satraps,[2] who were the predecessors of the Parthian and Kuṣāṇa satraps, might not help much, for the Kuṣāṇas were distant in point of time from the Persians by about five centuries. Nevertheless, as can be inferred from the designation *grāmasvāmī* (lord of the villages) of a kṣatrapa in a late Kharoṣṭhī inscription of the Peshawar area,[3] probably the officer acted as an intermediary between the village headman on the one hand and the king on the other, perhaps collecting royal dues from the villages.[4] That this particular kṣatrapa enjoyed considerable personal influence verging on independence from his sovereign (*mahārāja*) can be deduced from the fact that a novice paid homage to him by erecting a *saṅghārāma* and *stūpa* in his honour,[5] in the same manner as many people honoured the Kuṣāṇa *mahārājas* by making religious donations for the spiritual well-being of these rulers.[6]

The military system of the Kuṣāṇas is not reflected in their records. The frequent use of the term *daṇḍanāyaka* in its different forms in their inscriptions suggests the importance of the military element in their polity. But how far they changed the character of the conventional fourfold Indian army has yet to be found out. Undoubtedly they were skilled horsemen using stirrups, which, judging from the sculptures of the period, were introduced by the Scythians. In this period horses were sent from India to China, and a Han law said that those who used horses must use trousers, which practice was true of the Indian Kuṣāṇas. The Mathura statue of Kaniṣka clearly shows that boots and trousers formed the essential equipment of the Kuṣāṇa horsemen

1. *Sel. Inscrr.*, II, no. 43, ll. 2-4.
2. Herodotus, *The Histories* (Penguin), pp. 214-15.
3. *EI*, xxiv, p. 10.
4. There may be another possible interpretation of the title *grāmasvāmī* applied to this *kṣatrapa*. Perhaps in return for his services he was remunerated by the grant of a village by his suzerain. But we have no corroborative evidence for this.
5. *EI*, xxiv, p. 10.
6. Infra, p. 308.

who seem to have been good archers. Unfortunately we know neither about the strength of the Kuṣāṇa army nor about its organisation and distribution.

The kṣatrapas exercised their powers through semi-military officers known as *daṇḍanāyaka* and *mahādaṇḍanāyaka*, who seem to have occupied an important position in the Kuṣāṇa polity. During the reign of Kaniṣka we hear of *daṇḍanāyaka* Lala, who served Kṣatrapa Veśpasi as his donation master.[1] This military officer was a scion of the ruling family, for he is described as "the increaser of the Kuṣāṇa race."[2] Besides, a Mathurā inscription apparently ascribable to Kuṣāṇa times mentions a *mahādanḍanāyaka* Valina.[3] Another Mathurā inscription mentions a *mahādaṇḍanāyaka* whose son served under Huviṣka.[4] Still another Mathurā inscription of the fourth year of Kaniṣka refers to *mahādaṇḍanāyaka* Hummiyaka Caṅyakka, whose name was given to a Buddhist monastery.[5] Some of these references suggest that these officers occasionally performed non-military functions also, but in a conquest state their military duties may have been far more important. It is difficult to accept the view that the *daṇḍanāyaka* was a feudatory chief who rendered civil and military aid to the king.[6] Apparently this interpretation has been suggested to account for the military, magisterial and judicial functions attributed to this office by different authorities. But all these could well have been performed by a royal officer under an alien rule at a time when there was not much separation of functions. In course of time the military and coercive aspect of this office may have receded into the background, and its judicial aspect may have come to the forefront. It is this which explains its meaning as judge or rod-applier in later lexicons. Thus on the civil side, if we may so call it, we hear of *rājā* and *mahārāja*, *kṣatrapa* and *mahākṣatrapa*, and on the military side we hear of *daṇḍanāyaka* and *mahādaṇḍanāyaka*,

1. *CII*, ii, pt. I, no. 76, ll. 2-3. For various interpretations of the term *daṇḍanāyaka* and *mahādanḍanāyaka* see Ghoshal, *Indian Historiography and Other Essays*, pp. 177-79. Ghoshal rightly concludes that the term *mahādaṇḍanāyaka* means commander-in-chief. Ibid., p. 179.
2. *CII*, ii, pt. I, no. 76, l. 2.
3. *Lüders' List*, no. 60.
4. *JRAS*, 1924, p. 402, l. 5.
5. K.D. Bajpai, *Proc. IHC*, 1958, p. 68, l. 2.
6. B.N. Puri, *India Under the Kushāṇas*, p. 84.

a feature which seems to be in tune with the prevalent hierarchy. Thus the names of the Kuṣāṇa functionaries do not suggest any territorial or functional associations, as we find in the case of Maurya officials, but indicate a graded hierarchy of the same type of officers, the one being superior and the other subordinate. How royal officers were paid is nowhere stated. Probably they received salaries in cash, as can be inferred from cash donations made for feeding the brāhmaṇas and from the use of gold and copper coins on a large scale in the Kuṣāṇa dominions. Further, since the Kuṣāṇas had a small administrative establishment, this payment would not have been difficult.

As regards territorial units of administration under the Kuṣāṇas, the Allahabad Inscription of Samudra Gupta speaks of *viṣaya* and *bhukti* in their dominions.[1] The prevalence of the *bhukti* is not corroborated by any source and hence may have been a projection of Gupta units into Kauṣāṇa times, but that of the *viṣaya* is attested by a Buddhist Mahāyānist text of the third century A.D., which, while defining a *devaputra*, refers to kings ruling in *viṣayas*.[2] In the post-Maurya and Gupta inscriptions such units are generally mentioned in connection with land grants, which have not been found so far in the case of the Kuṣāṇa kings. We have practically no infor nation about urban administration in the Kuṣāṇa dominions. Although literary evidence for the existence of guilds in north-eastern India can be inferred from early Pāli texts and certainly from Buddhist texts of post-Maurya times, we get the earliest epigraphic evidence in Kuṣāṇa times. Four seals of the Kuṣāṇa period from Bhīṭā speak of the *nigama*,[3] and an inscription refers to two guilds (*śreṇis*), of which one was that of wheat-flour dealers, at Mathurā.[4] The two Mathurā guilds, which received endowments in cash for feeding the brāhmaṇas, were surely capable of taking care of their members and possibly of managing the affairs of the town. Though inscriptions do not refer to as many guilds in northern India as in western India and the Deccan, they undoubtedly mark the beginnings of the activities of the *nigama* which continued in Vaiśāli and other towns in the Gupta age.

1. Lines 23-24.
2. *JA*, 1934, p. 3.
3. *ASR*, 1911-12, p. 56.
4. *Sel. Inscrr.*, BK II, no. 49, ll. 12-13.

The lowest territorial unit was undoubtedly the village, under the *grāmika*, who seems to have been a regular part of the Kusāṇa system of administration in the Mathurā region. A *grāmika* is expressly mentioned in a Mathurā Jain inscription of the time of Vāsudeva;[1] another Jain votive image epigraph from the same place, which mentions two generations of an apparently local *grāmika*,[2] should also be ascribed to Kusāṇa times. This village institution was obviously taken over by the Kuṣāṇas from their predecessors and retained by them, for the office of *grāmika* was as old as the time of Bimbisāra, whose kingdom is credited with the existence of 80,000 *grāmikas*. The post continued in Maurya times, as is known from the *Arthaśātra* of Kauṭilya. But the continuity in name does not necessarily suggest continuity in status and functions. We do not know precisely how far the *grāmika* of post-Maurya times continued to perform the duties of the *gāmabhojaka* of pre-Maurya and *grāmika* of Maurya times. Some indication of the position and functions of the *grāmika* can, however, be obtained from references to that officer in Manu. Maintenance of law and order, for purposes of which in cases of necessity he could approach the lord of ten villages, and collection of royal dues in the form of grain, drink, fuel, etc., were his chief duties,[3] and in these respects he does not seem to have been different from the earlier village headman. Nor does there seem to have taken place any change in his mode of appointment, since like the *gāmabhojaka* the *grāmika* was appointed by the king. But we notice two important changes in the office of the village headman in Manu. First, he was no longer trusted with the defence of the village, a function which seems to have been exercised by the *gāmabhojaka* in the pre-Maurya period and undertaken by the *gāmika* and the villagers in Maurya times.[4] This was now transferred to the *gulma* or military cantonments stationed by the king in two, three or five villages in the countryside.[5] Apparently in post-Maurya times the foreign rulers did not consider it safe to leave the old village headmen in possession

1. *Lüders' List*, no. 69a.
2. Ibid., no. 48.
3. Manu, VII.116-18.
4. Altekar, *State and Government in Ancient India*, p. 226; *AŚ*, III.10.
5. Manu, VII.114.

of arms. Secondly, the *grāmika* was paid not in the shape of fines gathered from the villagers as in pre-Maurya times, or in cash salary as the *grāmabhṛtaka* in Maurya times, but in grant of a piece of land, probably during the second century A.D. and later.[1] Thus the first tended to decrease and the second to strengthen the power of the headman. But on the whole the hereditary character of the post coupled with the grant of land for the office tilted the balance in favour of the growing importance of the village headman, which development can be inferred from the use of the title *grāmasya adhipati* (lord of the village) for the *grāmika*.[2] We also hear of an officer called *padrapāla*,[3] who may have been the head of the common uncultivated land attached to the village.

On the basis of Manu it can be said that the *grāmika* of Kuṣāṇa times had something to do with revenue collection, but we have no information about the other revenue officers of this period. Nor have we any idea about the different kinds of tenure. We get, however, some indication of the revenue system of the Kuṣāṇas from the prevalence of the *akṣayanīvi* tenure during this period. The Mathurā Stone Inscription of Huviṣka (year 28—A.D. 106 ?) refers to two gifts, one of *puṇyaśālā*[4] and the other of 500 *purāṇas*,[5] according to the *akṣayanīvi* system, which means that these endowments were made on a permanent basis. During this period endowments of money were also made in Mahārāṣṭra according to the same system, as we learn from the Nāsik Cave Inscription of the time of Nahapāna,[6] who was probably a kṣatrapa under Kaniṣka in the early part of his satrapal rule. Land grants according to this system, which meant numerous exemptions in revenue, became frequent in the Gupta period. From the first century B.C. onwards we have epigraphic evidence of land grants made by the Sātavāhana rulers, but we have no such epigraphic examples in the case of northern India. It seems that under the Kuṣāṇas the practice of the *akṣayanīvi* tenure covered only money endow-

1. Ibid., VII.119.
2. Ibid., VII.115-16.
3. B.N. Puri, *India Under the Kuṣāṇas* p. 84.
4. *Sel. Inscrr.*, II, no. 49, ll. 1-3.
5. Ibid., ll. 11-12.
6. Ibid., II, no. 58, l. 1.

ments; it was extended to land/grants under the Guptas. Money endowments, according to this system, in both the north and the Deccan, suggest that during the first two centuries of the Christian era the use of monetary transactions were widespread. Moneylending seems to have been sanctioned by religion, for religious needs were to be met out of interest on cash endowments. This fact together with the large number of copper coins attributable to Kuṣāṇas may lead us to think that revenues were largely collected in cash. In spite of money economy, which could have enabled the Kuṣāṇas to maintain a professional soldiery and hold their authority over the lesser lords, the feudatory organization was bound to lead to the formation of a tributary system of government over a good part of the country.

Perhaps the centrifugal forces were counterbalanced by the proclaimed association of divine elements with the ruler. Despite the fact that most Kuṣāṇa rulers were Buddhists, they tried to deify themselves by adopting the title of *devaputra* (son of God) and instituting the dead king's cult. The deification of the king was alien to the Buddhist theories of the origin of kingship as enunciated in the *Dīgha Nikāya* and but not completely out of tune with the early brāhmaṇical theories. Although the coronation formulas of the later Vedic period refer to prayers to various gods for conferring their respective qualities on the king, they nowhere describe him as the son of God. On the contrary the Vedic coronation formulas clearly mention the human parents of the king. The *Śatapatha* Brāhmaṇa, however, respresents the king as the manifestation of Prajāpati.[1] A similar idea is found in the *Atharva Veda*, which describes Vaiśvānara Parīkṣit as the king who rules over all peoples, the god who is above mortals,[2] but this portion of the collection is a later addition. At any rate it is clear that such a view of the divinity of the king did not appear forcefully during the Vedic period. In subsequent times the *Arthaśāstra* makes skilful use of religion for strengthening royal authority,[3] but it does not lend divinity to the office of the king. The Buddhist ruler Aśoka prided himself on being called *devānām-*

1. V.1.5.14.
2. XX.127.7-10.
3. Supra, ch. XVII.

priya, dear to gods, a title which was continued by Daśaratha, the grandson of Aśoka,[1] but it was abandoned in post-Maurya times when the title *devaputra*, mentioned in 21 Brāhmī (according to *Lüders' List*) and 3 Kharoṣṭhī (according to Konow's List) inscriptions, seems to have been as popular with the Kuṣāṇa rulers as *devānāmpriya* with Aśoka; the title *devavrata*, devoted to God, was confined to the Parthian king Gondopharnes.[2]

Once the title *devaputra* had been adopted by the Kuṣāṇa rulers, theoretical justification came to be provided in a near contemporary Mahāyānist Buddhist text, *Suvarṇaprabhāsottamasūtra*, to which attention was first drawn by Sylvain Lévi.[3] Here the question is asked why a king born as a human being is called God (*deva*) and why he is styled the son of God (*devaputra*).[4] The answer is that before being born as a man he was living among the gods, and that, because the thirty-three gods (each) contributed to his substance, therefore he is called "God-son"[5]. A similar explanation of the divine origin of the king in the *Manu Smṛti*[6] and the *Śānti Parva* was probably inspired by Kuṣāṇa associations. Unlike the *Suvarṇaprabhāsottamasūtra*, Manu does not use the term *devaputra* for a king but states that the king is vested with the respective attributes of eight gods,[7] and asserts that even if the king is a child he should not be disregarded, for he functions as a great divinity in the form of a human being.[8] The *Śānti Parva*, which has many verses in common with Manu and which poses the question regarding

1. *Lüders' List*, nos. 954-56.
2. *Sel. Inscrr.*, II, no. 29, l. 1.
3. *JA*, 1934, p. 1 ff.
4. *kathaṃ manuṣyasaṃbhūto rājā devas tu procyate, kena ca hetunā rājā devaputras tu procyate*. Quoted by F.W. Thomas in *B.C. Law Volume*, ii, 313.
5. *devendrāṇām adhiṣṭhāne mātuḥ kukṣau pravekṣyati. purvaṃ adhiṣṭhite devaiḥ paścād garbhe prapadyate. Kiṃ cāpi mānuṣe loke jāyate śrīyate nṛpaḥ; api vai devasambhūto devaputraḥ sa ucyate. trayastriṃśair devarājendrair bhāgodatto nṛpasya hi; putrāstvaṃ sahadevānāṃ nirmito manujeśvaraḥ JA*, 1934, pp. 3-4.
6. The law-book of Manu is generally assigned to the period 200 B.C.—A.D. 200; probably the extracts dealing with *rājādharma* were compiled in the first two centuries of the Christian era or later.
7. VII.7.
8. VII.8.

the origin of kingship practically in the same manner as the Mahāyānist Buddhist text, represents the original king to be the descendant of God.[1] Thus these three texts, one Buddhist and the other two brāhmaṇical, impart such a divine character to the king as he never enjoyed before, and in all these the inspiration seems to have come from the Kuṣāṇa side. But the Kuṣāṇa royal title *devaputra* was not in accord with the Indian tradition, and hence it did not find favour with other Indian rulers, contemporary or subsequent.

It has been contended by F.W. Thomas that *devaputra* was not an official title of the Kuṣāṇa rulers but a complimentary epithet given to them by their subjects, a view accepted by U.N. Ghoshal.[2] Taking the hint from Lévi, Thomas establishes that *devaputras* are mentioned in earlier Indian literature and that they form a class of divinities.[3] But the use of the term in earlier literature as "god-son" or as "a class of divinity" does not preclude it from being used in a special sense by the Kuṣāṇa rulers. That the title *devaputra* was used to underline the divinity of the Kuṣāṇa rulers can be inferred from its justification given in the *Suvarṇaprabhāsottamasūtra* and the explanation of the divine origin in near contemporary texts on polity. Thomas argues that this title cannot be regarded as official, for it does not occur in Kuṣāṇa coins which contain the official titles such as *mahārāja* and *rājātirāja*. On the basis of his consultation with Allan he holds that Cunningham's reading of *devaputra* on a coin of Kuyala Kara Kaphsa (Kadphises II) is an error.[4] Even if this is conceded we may note that all the titles cannot be accommodated in the coins due to lack of space. Perhaps *devaputra* was not considered so important a title as to find place in the coins to the exclusion of such other official titles as *mahārāja* and *rājātirāja*. Thomas' contention that in India the term *devaputra* was never used as an appellation of royalty except in reference to the Yueh-chih[5] does not lend support to his theory. Several other Kuṣāṇa titles such as *rājātirāja*, *ṣāhi*, *ṣāhānuṣāhi* were also not used by Indian rulers, but for

1. Ch. 59.
2. *The Mauryas and Sātavāhanas*, p. 345.
3. *B.C. Law Volume*, ii, 306-10.
4. Ibid., 307.
5. Ibid., 319.

that reason they cannot be dismissed as unofficial epithets of the Kuṣāṇas. Thomas points out that direct communications in Kharoṣṭhī from Chinese Turkestan mention *mahanuava* and *maharaya* as the titles of the king but omit *devaputra.*[1] But this line of argument does not sustain his thesis since the other Kuṣāṇa official titles *rājātirāja* and *ṣāhānuṣāhi* are also not mentioned in the preliminary to these communications. In face of Thomas' negative arguments, which only refer to the omission of *devaputra* in some sources, we have positive evidence to show that the title was used not only in India, but also in Central Asia, where it occurs in the Khotanese documents in Kharoṣṭhī, especially in datings.[2] In Kuṣāṇa inscriptions *devaputra* is mentioned along with the other official titles, and hence it cannot be treated on a separate footing from them. Besides, it is applied to Huviṣka by a state official, who held the title or designation of *bakanapati* and who was the son of a *mahādaṇḍanāyaka.*[3] It is natural that the officers would prefer to use only official titles. Further, the title *daivaputra* appears along with the other official titles in the famous Allahabad Inscription, which was drafted by Hariṣeṇa, the official scribe of Samudra Gupta. He could not have probably adopted an appellation which was invented by and confined to the subjects and not officially favoured by the Kuṣāṇa rulers. Finally, the evidence of a Buddhist text of the third century A.D., translated into Chinese in A.D. 392, in which the king of India and the king of the Yueh-chih each is described as "*Son of Heaven*",[4] and the testimony of a Chinese source of the third century A.D., in which the king of the Yueh-chih is described as the Son of Heaven,[5] are decisive; and Thomas himself finds it difficult to refute their testimony.[6] Thus it is pretty clear that the title *devaputra* was officially adopted by the Kuṣāṇas. But perhaps Thomas is right in suggesting that this title was not of Chinese origin. If with

1. Ibid., 308.
2. *CII*, ii, pt. I, p. lxxiv. Unfortunately I have no information about the contents of the coins of Kaniṣka and Vāsudeva, which have been discovered in Russian Central Asia.
3. *JRAS*, 1924, pp. 402-3.
4. *B.C. Law Volume*, ii, 314-15.
5. Ibid., 318.
6. Ibid., 319.

Allan and Thomas we reject the reading *devaputra* on a coin of Wima Kadphises, it would appear that this title was peculiar only to the Kaniṣka group of Kuṣāṇa rulers, who completely supplanted the Parthian rule in north-western India in the second half of the first century A.D. Whatever might have been the source, Semitic or Hellenistic, it is undoubted that the two Parthian rulers Pharates II and III, who flourished in the first half of the first century A.D. and were the immediate predecessors of the Kuṣāṇas, had adopted the title of "*god-fathered.*"[1] Apparently when Parthia had been conquered by the early Kuṣāṇas the Parthian titles and dominions alike were appropriated by Kaniṣka and his successors. As the explanations given in contemporary texts show, in course of time the title came to be used as an important legitimatising device.

The Kuṣāṇas followed the practice of erecting *devakulas*, in which the statues of the dead rulers were housed. The term *devakula* is recorded in the inscription on the colossal image of Wima,[2] and we have also a reference to the repair of the *devakula* of the grandfather of Huviṣka during the reign of the latter.[3] On the basis of the *Pratimānāṭaka* of Bhāsa the term *devakula* has rightly been interpreted to mean the place where statues were erected in honour of dead potentates.[4] Further on the strength of the same source it is argued that this structure was a temporal temple and not a place of worship.[5] But the fact that the temple in the drama bore no flag, had no divine weapons and other signs of an ordinary temple,[6] merely suggests that it was not as important as regular temples. Much should not be made of the fact that in the drama the brāhmaṇa keeper prevents Bharata from bowing before the images of his ancestors. Here we have to bear in mind the argument of the keeper that a brāhmaṇa should not bow down before kṣatriya sovereigns taking them to be gods.[7] The plea is obviously inspired by his class prejudice and is irrelevant to the kṣatriya Bharata.

1. Ibid., 305.
2. D.R. Sahni, *JRAS*, 1924, p. 402.
3. Ibid., pp. 402-3.
4. Jayaswal, *JBORS*, 1923, pp. 98-99; H.P. Sāstrī, ibid., pp. 558-61.
5. Jayaswal, *JBROS*, 1919, pp. 98-99.
6. Ibid.
7. Ibid., p. 960.

The term *devakula* clearly means "deity-house", and, what is more important, the Mathurā Inscription of Huviṣka shows that the repair of the dilapidated *devakula* of his grandfather by a state official was an act of religious merit intended for the increase of the life and strength of the *mahārāja rājātirāja devaputra* Huviṣka.[1] The prevalent method of seeking the physical and spiritual well-being of the king was to erect some *stūpa* over the relics of the Buddha or to perform similar other acts of piety. Obviously in this case also the physical welfare of the king was to be achieved by performing the religious act of the repair of the *devakula* of his ancestor. Moreover, the last line of this inscription[2] suggests that something was done for the daily guests, and brāhmaṇas[3] who were evidently attached to the *devakula* as priests. Such priests are found in the *devagaḍhas* of Rajputana.[4]

From where did the Kuṣāṇas derive the practice of setting up *devakulas*? It is suggested that this system was taken over from the Romans on the bank of the Tiber.[5] But the cult of the dead king was in vogue not only in ancient Mesopotamia, but also in Egypt where mortuary temples were built to enshrine the statues of the Pharaohs. Probably the Romans imbibed this idea from these predecessors and passed it on to the Kuṣāṇas either through direct commercial contacts or through some intermediaries. On the basis of the pre-Kauṭilyan date of Bhāsa it would be wrong to suppose that the practice prevailed in India from pre-Maurya times onwards,[6] and therefore was adopted by the Kuṣāṇa rulers. The correct position seems to be different. Reference has been made to *devapitṛpūjā* (worship of gods and ancestors) in Kauṭilya[7] but this does not imply that the statutes of the forefathers were worshipped. Besides, Kauṭilya does not specifically refer to the worship of the dead kings. Obviously this practice was introduced by the Kuṣāṇa rulers who have left several royal statues. The writings of Bhāsa, who seems to have flourished

1. *JRAS*, 1924, p. 402, ll. 2-5 of the inscription.
2. Ibid., l. 6.
3. Ibid., p. 403.
4. *JBORS*, 1919, p. 559.
5. *PHAI*, 5th edn., p. 519.
6. *JBORS*, 1919, p. 560.
7. II.6; *PHAI*, 5th edn., p. 517, fn. 2.

during the period, merely reflect the existing practice. Clearly the practice of erecting *devakulas*, was in keeping with the official title of *devaputra,* and both contributed to the apotheosis of the Kuṣāṇa kings. That the adoption of the title *devaputra* and establishment of *devakulas* by the Kuṣāṇas were deliberate devices to deify the kings can be deduced from the representation of divine aura round the busts of the kings on their coins. On the gold pieces of Kadphises II the shoulders of the king are surrounded by luminous rays of flames, and his bust appears to issue from the clouds like the gods of Greece. The nimbus appears on some pieces of Kaniṣka, but is much more frequent on certain gold pieces of Huviṣka, who is at once ornamented with nimbus, flames and clouds. Vāsudeva has simply the nimbus round his head.[1] We know that the nimbus or *prabhā-maṇḍala* was especially associated with the divinities represented on the coins of Kaniṣka and Huviṣka.[2] Therefore it was in order to propagate their celestial origin that the Kuṣāṇa kings got themselves represented on their coins with the nimbus, aureole, clouds or flames.[3]

In contradistinction to the theory of Divine Right in England, where it developed as a logical sequel to the ideas of absolutism and centralisation prevalent in the Tudor period, the wide-ranging activities of the state of Maurya India did not emphasise the divinity of royal power. The divine theory was sharply enunciated in post-Maurya times, when legitimatisation was needed for alien dynasties. The high-sounding titles of the Kuṣāṇa rulers indicated nothing more than the reality of need for stability and their recognition by the people and lesser rulers. The device of deification was an attempt to conceal and remove their political weakness. Although the idea of the divintiy of the king could lead to royal absolutism at the cost of priestly and other elements, it was eagerly seized and sharpened by the brāhmaṇas as a weapon in defence of the existing social order.[4]

1. M.E. Drouin, "The Nimbus and Signs of Deification on the Coins of the Indo-Skythian Kings", *Revue Numismatiqe*, 1901, pp. 154-66, tr. *IA*, 1903, p. 427.
2. *IA*, 1903, p. 428.
3. Ibid., p. 432.
4. The current interpretations of the Dharma*śāstra* ideas on the king's divinity are summarised and examined in Ghoshal, *A History of Indian Political Ideas*, pp. 566-67, fn. 20.

The deification of the Kuṣāṇa king served to secure him the allegiance of the subjects, of which we have enough evidence in the religious gifts made by officers and individuals. Thus a Kharoṣṭhī inscription from Taxila refers to the establishment of the relics of the Buddha in the Dharma-rājikā *stūpa* of Taxila by a Bactrian for the bestowal of health on an unnamed Kuṣāṇa emperor, who is described as *mahārāja, rājātirāja* and *devaputra.*[1] Similarly another Kharoṣṭhī inscription from Afghanistan speaks of the institution of the relics of Śākya Muni for the spiritual merit of *mahārāja rājātirāja* Huviṣka.[2] The practice of making gifts by individuals and state officers for the spiritual and physical benefit of the rulers never took root in northern India, but it continued among the later Kuṣāṇas of the north-west frontier. Thus a monastery (*vihāra*) was erected by a *vihārasvāmī* named Roṭa-Siddha-Vṛddhi not only for the benefit of his relatives but also for that of the queen, princes and princesses of Mahārāja Toramāṇa Shāh Jaūvla.[3]

The Kuṣāṇa claim to divine power was accompanied by the unambiguous declaration of the religion they professed. The coins, which are considered an important insignia of sovereignty, broadly indicate the faith to which they belonged. Thus the Kuṣāṇa *yavuga* Kujala Kasa, identified with Kadphises I, calls himself *dhramathidasa*,[4] a title which also occurs as *sacadhramaṭhitasa* on the other coins of the Kuṣāṇas. This apparently refers to their devotion to the *dharma* of the Buddha. Besides, we have representations of Śiva on their coins.[5] But in spite of their proclaimed preference for Buddhism or Śaivism the Kuṣāṇas never adopted a policy of religious persecution. On the other hand they seem to have worshipped numerous gods, Greek, Iranian and Indian, who are represented on the coins of Huviṣka.[6] The variety of gods on their coins may also suggest the policy of the Kuṣāṇas to respect the religious sentiments of their subjects. Under their rule Mathurā was a noted centre of Jainism, as would appear from numerous gifts of Jain images

1. *Sel. Inscrr.*, II, no. 34, l. 3.
2. Ibid., II, no. 55, l. 2.
3. *Lüders' List*, no. 5.
4. *Sel. Inscrr.*, II, no. 19, l. 1.
5. Ibid., p. 125, fn. 3; p. 155.
6. Ibid., p. 155, fn. 5.

made there by lay and clerical votaries in the reigns of Kaniṣka and Huviṣka. Similarly the brāhmaṇical sacrificial religion was also tolerated. An inscription mentions the erection of the sacrificial post (*yūpa*) by a brāhmaṇa of the Bhāradvāja gotra after having performed a *sattra* of twelve nights.[1] Apparently it was a policy of live and let live. But since the Kuṣāṇas showed preference for Buddhism this may have contributed to brāhmaṇical resurgence under the Guptas, who replaced the Kuṣāṇas in northern India within half a century of the end of their rule.

The sketch of the Kuṣāṇa polity, though inadequate on account of lack of material, would show that the Kuṣāṇas introduced certain new elements in Indian polity. Some of them such as the practice of making gifts for the spiritual or physical well-being of the king by his subjects, and the dual governorship in the provinces, did not find suitable soil in India. But the idea of the divinity of the king made some impression on later rulers, for Samudra Gupta is compared to four different gods. Again, the office of the *mahādaṇḍanāyaka* came to function in the eastern, southern and northern provinces of the Gupta empire,[2] and the practice of the *akṣayanīvi* cash deposits for religious purposes was replaced with the *akṣayanīvi* or perpetual tenure system of land grant in Gupta times. Above all, the main characteristic of the Kuṣāṇa political structure, namely the organization of the hierarchical feudatory system, seems to have been adopted by Samudra Gupta in his imperial system. For the rest, the Kuṣāṇa continued the old pattern of village administration by the *grāmika*, with the probable change that this officer was paid for his services by assignment of some land revenue but relieved of his responsibility for the defence of his village. Probably they encouraged the guilds of artisans and merchants which continued in Gupta times.

1. *Lüders' List*, no. 149a.
2. Ghoshal, *Indian Historiography and Other Essays*, p. 178.

CHAPTER XX

KUṢĀṆA ELEMENTS IN THE GUPTA POLITY

The two large kingdoms that preceded the foundation of the Gupta empire were those of the Sātavāhanas and Kuṣāṇas, whose political systems could not be ignored by their successors. The Guptas did not directly rule in the former dominions of the indigenous Sātavāhanas in the Deccan, but in those of the Kuṣāṇas in northern India. The time gap between the end of the Kuṣāṇa kingdom in about A.D. 230 and the foundation of the Gupta rule in about A.D. 275 was less than fifty years, which was possibly filled in by the Yaudheyas in north-western India and the Muruṇḍas in the area around Pāṭaliputra in north-eastern India. Naturally, the Guptas inherited many elements of Kuṣāṇa culture, which had evolved as an amalgam of indigenous and Central Asian ingredients. The Kuṣāṇa influence can be seen not only in Gupta art and coinage but also in political organisation.

The evidence for tracing Kuṣāṇa survivals in the Gupta polity is mostly derived from coins and inscriptions. Several titles, offices and institutions known from Kuṣāṇa sources have their Gupta counterparts. But sources do not give a complete picture of the system of administration. Not all officers and administrative practices are mentioned in Aśokan, Kuṣāṇa and Gupta epigraphs, and the lacuna cannot be easily filled in by literary sources, because of the difficulty of dating them. So the continuity or otherwise of institutions has to be discussed under this limitation.

Compared with the Sātavāhanas, the Kuṣāṇas seem to have been a exclusively patriarchal community. Although Kuṣāṇa records mention several religious gifts made by women, there is no evidence of any matriarchal element in their inheritance. On the other hand, the Kuṣāṇas practised patriarchal inheritance, which was further strengthened in Gupta times. The Guptas did not set up *devakulas* for worshipping dead kings, although they described themselves as devoted to father. Nor did they adopt the practice of the joint rule of two male members, which seem to have been the Kuṣāṇa custom.[1]

A conspicuous feature of the Kuṣāṇa polity was the divinity of kingship emphasised by the adoption of the royal title *devaputra* (son of the god) by the deification of royal statues in the *devakulas* and by the representation of kings in divine surroundings on coins. Statues of Kuṣāṇa kings have been found not only in Mathurā but in the Swat valley and Surkh Kotal.[2] In the case of the grandfather of Huviṣka, it is said that the kingdom was conferred on him by Sarva and Caṇḍavīra,[3] a practice found in some other post-Maurya kingdoms. All this did not make much impression on Gupta kings, who permitted themselves to be compared to different gods like the Sātavāhanas, but did not claim divine descent in spite of the fact that the Kuṣāṇa kings continued to hold the title *devaputra* in the Gupta period.[4] However Samudra Gupta,[5] Candra Gupta II[6] and Kumāra Gupta[7] were called *deva* (god) possibly in the same manner as teachers, parents and brāhmaṇas were called gods in early times.

The tolerant religious policy of the Kuṣāṇas indicated by the association of Indian, Greek, Roman and Iranian deities with their coins and by their donations to both Buddhist and brahmanical sects was certainly continued by the Guptas, whose empire was inhabited by followers of different races, creeds and sects. Mostly Śaivites, the Kuṣānas patronised Buddhism and other Indian religious sects. Perhaps it was necessary to respect the religious sentiments of numerous petty princes whom the Kuṣāṇas had subjugated and organised into a feudatory system. Their titles *mahārāja, rājātirāja, ṣāhānuṣāhi, shaonano shao* and *basileus basileon*, some of them borrowed from the

1. B.N. Mukherjee, *The Kushana Genealogy*, Calcutta, 1967, p. 79.
2. It is suggested that the statue of Huvishka was worshipped in his lifetime (*Mathurā Inscriptions* by H. Lüders, ed. K.L. Janert. Göttingen, 1961, p. 145).
3. *Mathurā Inscriptions*, pp. 138-39.
4. Allahabad Stone Pillar Inscription of Samudragupta, 1.23.
5. Ibid., 1. 28.
6. A.S. Altekar, *Corpus of Indian Coins*, vol. IV. *The Coinage of the Gupta Empire*, Banaras, 1957. pl. XX.
7. Ibid., pl. XXIII.

Bactrians and Parthians,[1] emphasise the supremacy of the Kuṣāṇa kings over lesser princes, rulers and vassals, whose existence is also indicated independently. Aśoka also may have established some feudatory organisation, although his titles do not betray it. But the Kuṣāṇa titles make this explicit, and the practice was continued by the Gupta kings. The Guptas did not call themselves *rājātirāja* and *ṣāhānuṣāhi*, but they assumed the titles *mahāraja*, and also some new titles, such as *mahārājādhirāja*, *parmeśvara* (the supreme lord) and *paramabhaṭṭāraka*. Such attributes, old or new, were undoubtedly in line with the Kuṣaṇa practice and were elaborated in post-Gupta times.

However, the characteristic Gupta system of transferring fiscal and administrative functions to religious beneficiaries, especially in the principalities of the feudatories in central India, is derived from the Sātavāhana practice. In the Kuṣāṇa system, a faint trace can be found at Mathurā in the bestowal of certain cash deposits in the reign of Huviṣka according to the *akṣayanīvi* (perpetual tenure) system,[2] which came to be applied to land grants in Gupta times. The gift of *harmya*,[3] temple or cottage, and the construction of tanks and monasteries (*vihāras*) might imply donation of land for religious purposes, but this is not specified in any Kuṣāṇa record. Some forms of royal income known as *praṇaya* (extra imposition), *kara* (royal share of the produce) and *viṣṭi* (forced labour), mentioned in the Junagadh inscription of Rudradāman, continued in Gupta times, but we are not quite sure whether they first orginated in the Śaka dominions.

The Kuṣāṇa use of cavalry was their most significant contribution to the military system of India. The Mauryas seemed to have owed their success to the use of elephants, whose overwhelming importance in the military machine is stressed by Kauṭilya;[4] the Kuṣāṇas seemed to have owed their success to the use of cavalry. The Scythians were excellent horsemen, and so close was their association with horses that in Central Asia sometimes as many as 14 horses were buried, along with

1. Supra, Ch. XIX.
2. D.C. Sircar, *Select Inscriptions*, II, no. 49.
3. Ibid., no. 40.
4. *AŚ*, II. 2.

all their trappings, with their warrior owners.[1] The Kuṣāṇas were skilled horsemen, using reins, saddles and above all stirrups. Saddled horses are represented on their coins, and Indian sculptures around the beginning of the Christian era show that strirrups were introduced into the country by the Scythians. In the beginning only rope and not metal stirrups seem to have been used. Horse-riding had been introduced into China earlier, and to facilitate it a Han law of 122 B.C. required horsemen to wear trousers. The Kuṣāṇa coins and sculptures clearly show that boots, tunics and trousers formed the essential equipment of the Kuṣāṇa horsemen, who were good archers. Their love of horses is indicated by the coins of Maues.[2] Soter Megas, Kaniṣka I[3], Huviṣka[4] and Vāsudeva.[5] According to the Chinese account, the king of the Yueh-chih raised an army of 70,000 horsemen under the order of Viceroy Hsieh to fight against the Chinese general Pan-ch'ao[6]. The Śaka and Parthian coins[7] demonstrate that their chiefs were heavily armoured and mostly fought with spear from horseback; this may have been also true of the Kuṣāṇa captains. Although the Kuṣāṇa kings cannot be called equestrian, even on the basis of their coins the importance of horsemanship in their military system cannot be underestimated.

From the Kuṣāṇa period onwards cavalry assumed a dominant role in the Indian polity. Some Gupta rulers are represented as excellent, unrivalled chariot warriors, and horsemen figure frequently on their coins. The outfit of the Gupta horse-riders, as deducible from their coins, consisted of tunics fastened by belts, of helmets, of trousers and of buttoned-up boots, and all these evidently formed part of the Kuṣāṇa legacy. Possibly, the Gupta soldiers learnt the use of long swords fitted with scabbards from the Kuṣāṇas. The Guptas also used armoured, caparisoned horses fitted with rope stirrups, which were borrowed

1. Rahul Sankrtyayana, *History of Central Asia*, Calcutta, 1964, p. 14.
2. Bhaskar Chattopadhyay, *The Age of the Kushāṇas—A Numismatic Study*, Calcutta, 1967, p. 50.
3. Ibid., pp. 50-51.
4. Ibid., pp. 60-61, 63-66.
5. Ibid., p. 76.
6. Ibid., p. 94.
7. *Indian Antiquary*, vol. 32, 1903, p. 422.

from their Central Asian predecessors. Their seals and inscriptions speak of *aśvapati*,[1] *mahāśvapti*[2] and *bhaṭāśvapati*, which stand for captains of horsemen and testify to the growing importance of cavalry. To my knowledge, the early Gupta records do not mention any officer connected with the management of elephants, although the term *pilupati* occurs in a sixth-century inscription from Bengal, and although the use of elephants is attested by Kuṣāṇa coins.

The Kuṣāṇas ruled over a conquest kingdom, and hence coercive elements seem to have occupied a more important place in their government. Leaving aside the *kṣatrapas* (provincial satraps) and *mahākṣatrapas*, the *daṇḍanāyakas* and *mahādaṇḍanāyakas* figure as prominent officials even in donative and votive records. Although military, magisterial and judicial functions are attributed to them by different authorities and lexicons,[3] at the intial stage the military aspect seems to have been far more important. The common device of the rod of punishment in the form of a mace or a standard on Kuṣāṇa coins attests the high position of the *daṇḍa* and its bearers in their polity. This is also reflected in many verses common to the *Manu Smṛti* and the *rājadharma* section of the *Śānti Parva*, which were evidently compiled in the early centuries of the Christian era. The element of *daṇḍa* continued to dominate the political scene in the reign of Samudra Gupta, whose standard-bearer type coins were most popular.[4] The *daṇḍa*[5] and the officials who wielded them continued to enjoy importance under his successors. In the areas conquered by the Guptas, the office of the *mahādaṇḍanāyaka* functioned in their eastern, southern and northern provinces,[6] and formed a regular feature of their polity.

Another military official, *balādhika* appears in a Kuṣāṇa record,[7] but the use of the terms *balādhikṛta* and *mahābalādhi-*

1. John M. Rosenfield, *The Dynastic Arts of the Kushans*, University of California Press, 1967, pp. 124-29, *Archaeological Survey, Reports*, 1911-12, pp. 52-53.
2. Ibid.
3. For details, see supra, Ch. XIX.
4. Altekar, op.cit., p. 40.
5. Ibid., p. 141.
6. U.N. Ghoshal, *Indian Historiography and Other Essays*, p. 234.
7. *Mathurā Inscriptions*, pp. 161-63.

kṛita[1] in Gupta inscriptions shows that the old office acquired more importance.

Of the civil functionaries, the *amātya*, mentioned in Śaka and Kuṣāṇa records, may be regarded as Maurya. Although mentioned by Kauṭilya, this post does not occur in Aśokan inscriptions, where *mahāmātras* appear as the counterpart of the *amātyas*. *Amātyas* were an important element in the Sātavāhana polity, but satraps seem to enjoy the corresponding position in the Kuṣāṇa system. The cadre of the *amātyas*, however, continued under the Guptas with the change that the *kumārāmātyas* emerged as the most important civil functionaries. Moreover, the office of *saciva*, mentioned in the Junagadh inscription of Rudradāman, also continued to exist in Gupta times.

Another functionary, the magistrate or *vyavahārika*, to which the first epigraphic reference is found in Aśokan edicts,[2] appears in the sense of elder or manager in a Mathurā inscription,[3] possibly of Kuṣāṇa times. In both these references, the *vyavahārin* appears in an urban setting, for while the Aśokan inscription speaks of the post of the *nagaravyavahārika* held by *mahāmātra*, the Mathurā inscription refers to more than eight merchants acting as the commissioners of the saṅgha,[4] apparently for managing its property. Another Mathurā inscription of the time of Kaniṣka I speaks of *vyavahārin* Matsya Gupta,[5] who was evidently a merchant and whose surname suggests that at least some Guptas had their apprenticeship in administration under the Kuṣāṇas. The *vyavahārins* also appear in Gupta records but not in an urban context. The Begram copper-plate inscription of A.D. 448 uses the term *saṃvyavahāripramukhān*[6] in the sense of village elders connected with the general management of the village.

The village headman seems to have acquired more authority in Kuṣāṇa times, as can be inferred from the epithet *grāmasvāmī*, owner of the village, applied to a *kṣatrapa*.[7] This is in

1. *Select Inscriptions*, III, no. 17, 1. 8.
2. First Separate Rock Edict, Dhauli version, 1. 1.
3. *Mathura Inscriptions*, etc., p. 101.
4. Ibid.
5. *Select Inscriptions*, II, no. 45 A, 1. 1.
6. Ibid., no. 41, 1. 2.
7. *EI*, XXIV, p. 10.

keeping with the use of the term *gramasyādhipati* in the law-book of Manu, who prescribes payment of this officer by grant of a piece of land.[1] The term *grāmādhipati* is used in the *Śānti Parva*,[2] and it seems that the village headman added to his power in Gupta times. A passage from the *Kāmasūtra* of Vātsyāyana suggests that at least in western India, where this work was composed, the village headman, called *grāmādhipati āyuktaka*, compelled peasant women to fill up his granary, to carry various articles, to clean and decorate his residence, to work in his fields and to spin various types of yarn for his clothes.[3]

The guilds seem to have played an important role in town administration in Kuṣāṇa times, and this position did not undergo much change in the Gupta period. The profitable silk trade in which the Kuṣāṇas participated and the use of gold coins must have stimulated the growth of towns and merchants. North Indian epigraphs first refer to guilds of artisans and merchants in Kusāṇa times. Four seals of the Kuṣāṇa period from Bhita, near Allahabad speak of the *nigama*,[4] and an inscription mentions two Mathurā guilds (*śreṇis*), including that of wheat dealers.[5] These two guilds received endowments in cash for feeding the brāhmaṇas, and if they could administer donations, they could surely look after their own affairs as well as those of the towns to which they belonged. Although more of such guilds existed in western India, their influence in northern India was not inconsiderable. They certainly mark the beginnings of the activities of the *nigama*, which continued to function in Vaiśalī in the Gupta age.

Separate guilds of artisans (*kulika*) and of merchants (*śreṣṭhi*) existed in Vaiśālī, but as many as 274 seals belong to the combined guild of the merchants, itinerant traders (*sārthavāhas*) and artisans.[6] Obviously, this body carried on not only economic activities, but also looked after the administration of the town. In addition to Vaiśālī, guilds of artisans and traders continued

1. VII.115-16.
2. 88.3-9.
3. V.5.5; cf. *Indian Feudalism*, pp. 51, 52.
4. *ASR*, 1911-12, p. 56.
5. *Select Inscriptions*, II, no. 49, ll. 12-13.
6. *ASIR*, 1903-04, p. 110.

to function at Bhita, and were found at Indor in Bulandshahr and Mandasor in Malwa. In Indor, the guild of oilmen administered the donation made by a brāhmaṇa.[1] That of silk weavers in Lāta (Nausari-Broach region) were engaged in silk-weaving, possibly since Kuṣāṇa times, when this craft may have first appeared on account of contact with the Chinese; but they no longer found it paying in the Gupta period, possibly on account of decline in silk trade. However, on the analogy of Vaiśālī it appears that various groups of artisans and traders participated in urban administration, which fact is also supported by the Damodarpur copper-plate inscription with regard to the headquarters of the Koṭivarṣa *viṣaya* (district) in Puṇḍravardhanabhukti[2] in Bangladesh. Naturally, the law-books of the Gupta period not only enjoin the king to observe the laws of the guilds but also to enforce them.

It would be wrong to think that the Gupta polity was entirely based on the Kuṣāṇa polity. Like the state control of activities under the Mauryas, the satrapal system practised by the Kuṣanas was an interlude in the history of India. The Kuṣāṇa practice of having a dual rulership or governorship did not find suitable soil in India, but the Śaka-Parthian system of having the joint rule of two brothers was adopted with modification by the Maitrakas of Valabhi, among whom succession passed from elder brother to younger brother. Many officers of the Kuṣāṇa period, such as *rāṣṭriya* (head of 100 villages), *gañjavara* (treasurer), *dānapati* (manager of donations) *bakanpati* (officer in charge of temples), *vaiśvāsika* (confidential agent), etc., are not mentioned in Gupta records although officers called *paramaviśvāsin* and *mahāparamaviśvāsin* appear in later inscriptions.

But the idea of the divinity of kingship was not alien to the Indian ethos. It made some impression on Gupta rulers, who were compared to different gods and even addressed as god. Similarly, the office of the *mahādaṇḍanāyaka* came to function in the eastern, southern and northern parts of the Gupta empire, and the practice of making religious grants according to the *akṣayanīvi* or perpetual tenure, which was confined to cash donations in the earlier period, came to be applied to land dona-

1. *Select Inscriptions*, III, no. 27.
2. Ibid., no. 36, 11. 1-4.

tion system in the Gupta period. The Kuṣāṇa system of having a strong cavalry was adopted by the Guptas, whose horsemen were equipped in the Central Asian fashion. An obvious influence can be seen in the Gupta feudatory system. The Kuṣāṇas had introduced a hierarchical feudatory system for administering their empire, and this pattern was followed by Samudra Gupta and his successors. Decentralisation was further encouraged by the full-fledged recognition given to the guilds of artisans and merchants in the Gupta age. Thus, there is no doubt that several Kuṣāṇa elements continued in the Gupta system of administration.

Chapter XXI

THE GUPTA POLITY

I

The chief element in the economic background of the Gupta polity was the excessive preoccupation of the people with land. It was an age of agricultural expansion, evidenced by land grants to brāhmaṇas in backward areas. The period saw the pronounced beginnings of the growth of private rights in land, of the sale and purchase of which for religious purposes we have the first epigraphic instances in north Bengal. The law-books had to take notice of this important phenomenon, and in both law and fact we hear of many devices for resolving land disputes. Land grants affected the administrative structure in a way they had never done before. Grants of villages to religious beneficiaries led to new fiscal and administrative arrangements.

Although the volume of foreign trade decreased in the Gupta period, arts and crafts continued in northern India. Individual artisans, merchants and traders and their guilds are frequently mentioned in seals and inscriptions, and emerge as a leading factor at the local levels of Gupta government at several places. The fact that the Guptas seem to have been vaiśyas might explain this development as well as the appointment of non-brāhmaṇa and non-kṣatriya governors and officials in different parts of the empire.

What makes the Gupta period spectacular from the economic point of view is the abundance of gold coins issued by its rulers. It is in this sense that this period should be regarded as a golden age. Gold coins were exchanged in land transactions, and may have been collected as revenue and disbursed in payment to high officers. But the paucity of copper coins would suggest that minor officers were not maintained in large numbers.

The capital fact in the political situation of Gupta times was the victorious march of Samudra Gupta followed later by the campaigns of Candra Gupta II in western India. This made it necessary to evolve some kind of relation with the subjugated princes.

Finally we may take note of the dominance of the brāhmaṇical ideas. The privileges of the priestly caste enunciated in the law-book of Manu are expounded with force by Nārada in this period. The didactic texts of the period preach the merits accruing out of land grants, and the idea of securing spiritual merit for the ancestors works as a great lever leading to large-scale land gifts and consequent administrative problems.

Changes in the nature of kingship in the Gupta period are difficult to detect. In contrast to the Sātavāhana practice under the Guptas royal succession was purely patriarchal. Although the Gupta emperors mention the names of their mothers, women did not play any effective part in administration. Prabhāvatī Guptā, daughter of Candra Gupta II, acted as regent in the Vākāṭaka kingdom, but we have no such instances in the Gupta kingdom. However, the law of primogeniture was not firmly established, and sometimes elder sons were passed over in favour of younger sons, and according to one theory after the death of Skanda Gupta in A.D. 467 the empire had to be partitioned between two contending princes. The curious practice of younger brother succeeding the elder, which prevailed among the Maitrakas of Valabhī, the feudatories of the Guptas, did not obtain in the Gupta dynasty.

Coins and inscriptions represent the Gupta king primarily as a fighter and general who took delight in hunting and fighting. The king appointed ministers, commanders, governors, etc. He received the obeisance of his vassals and princes, and his pompous titles *parameśvara*, *mahārājādhirāja*, *paramabhaṭṭāraka* indicate the existence of lesser princes and chiefs with whom he had to come to terms in his empire.

As in the case of Gautamīputra Sātakarṇi, the maintenance of the *varṇāśrama dharma* appears as an important royal duty in Gupta inscriptions. Protection of the subjects is another major obligation imposed upon the king, who is described as the giver of thousands of gold coins. The old theory that the king was entitled to taxes in lieu of protection is repeated in some Gupta legal texts. But it is no longer emphasised; on the other hand we notice a significant new trend. Kātyāyana states that the king is entitled to taxes because he is the owner of the land.[1]

1. Verse 16.

This theory lends feudal character to the state and enables it to make land grants, although in actual transactions parties having interests in the land need to be consulted and informed.

The second change noticeable in the Gupta kingship is not qualitative but quantitative and relates to its divine associations. Like the Sātavāhana Gautmīputra Sātakarṇi, the Gupta kings are repeatedly compared to different gods such as Yama, Varuṇa, Indra, Kubera, etc. They are compared to Viṣṇu as regards their function of preserving and protecting the people, and Lakṣmī, wife of Viṣṇu and goddess of prosperity, appears on many Gupta coins. The Vaiṣṇavite affiliations of the Gupta kings therefore may have served some political purpose. But the striking thing is that they are called *deva*[1] which clearly represents them as god, although not the son of the god as in the case of the Kuṣāṇa kings.

Despite the divine elements attributed to the Gupta king it would be wrong to envison him as a despot in law. Theoretically he laboured under the obligations of observing the rules laid down by the Dharmaśāstras. In practice the brāhmaṇas, who acted as the chief custodians and interpreters of these laws, exercised a great check on royal power. The king had to further share power with the guilds and corporate bodies, whose decisions he had to ditto and whose usages he had to enforce. Above all, the king had to reckon with the beneficiaries and feudatories who enjoyed enormous powers. In fact royal power was more circumscribed in Gupta times than in Maurya or pre-Gupta days.

Ministers called by different names such as *mantrin*, *amātya* or *saciva* may have restrained the despotic activities of the king, although inscriptions give very little idea of their functions and no idea of their corporate existence. The term *mantrimaṇḍala* is used in the *Kāmandaka Nitisāra*, a text of about the 8th century A.D., but not in inscriptions. Undoubtedly some individual ministers such as Hariṣeṇa were rendered powerful because of having combined the offices of the *mahādaṇḍanāyaka*, *kumārāmātya*, *sāndhivigrahika* in the same person. And then the post was hereditary in the same family for several generations. Such families must have played an important part in politics.

1. *Sel. Inscrr.*, III, no. 2, l. 28. The term *paramadaivata* (ibid., no 16, l. 2) probably means the great devotee of the god.

Ministers or advisers formed part of the higher bureaucracy of the Guptas. Among the other high officers we may take special notice of the *kumārāmatya* and the *sāndhivigrahika*, who are not known to earlier inscriptions. Like the *mahāmātras* under Aśoka and the *amātyas* under the Sātavāhanas, the *kumārāmātyas*[1] formed the chief cadre for recruiting high functionaries under the Guptas. The office of the *kumārāmātya* is repeatedly mentioned as existing in the headquarters of the *bhuktis* of Magadha or Nagara and Tīra.[2] We also hear of *kumārāmātyas* attached to the emperor[3] or to the heir-apparent.[4] The district of Pañcanagarī *viṣaya* in Bengal was presided over by a *kumārāmātya*. Although the holders of this title appear as district governors, they are also known as *mantrins*, *senāpatis*, *mahādaṇḍanāyakas*,[5] *sāndhivigrahikas*,[6] and even *mahārājas*.[7] Some of the *kumārāmātyas* functioned in their own rights and maintained their regular office called *kumārāmātyādhikaraṇa*. The literal meaning, minor *amātya* or the *amātya* attached to the prince, does not indicate the functions of the officer which differed according to the additional office he held. Towards the end of the Gupta empire some *kumārāmātyas* such as the *mahārāja* Nandana[8] asserted independence and issued land charters.

Literally translated as the minister of peace and war, the *sāndhivigrahika* first appears under Samudra Gupta, whose *amātya* Hariṣeṇa holds this title. But in the lesser feudatory state of Śarvanātha such an officer is known as the *mahāsāndhivigrahika*, and hence it would be wrong to think in terms of any hierarchy of these officers. The need for such an office can be well understood in the context of the relations subsisting between the many warring principalities from Gupta times onwards, but his function of issuing land charters to brāhmaṇas needs to be

1. Curiously the literary texts of Gupta times do not throw any light on the office of the *kumārāmātya*.
2. The term is *tīra-kumārāmāty ādhikaraṇakasya*; the word *bhukti* is not mentioned. *ASIR*, 1903-4, p. 109.
3. Ibid., p. 108.
4. Ibid., pp. 107-8.
5. *Sel. Inscrr.*, III, no. 2, l. 32.
6. Ibid.
7. *JASB, NS,v* (1909), 164.
8. *EI*, X, p. 49.

explained. The practice began with the Gupta period and gained currency in early medieval times. Altekar thinks that because the foreign office possessed detailed knowledge of the family tree of the grantors the *sāndhivigrahika* was asked to draft land charters. But perhaps the main duty of this officer was to deal with the feudatories who may have been granted charters for military services. And hence he may have been empowered to issue charters to religious parties also.

Considerations of caste[1] and family certainly played an important part in the recruitment of officers. We have some examples of higher governors belonging to the royal family, and certain families contributed a good number of *amātyas* and provincial governors known as *uparikas*. The growing hereditary character of the ministers, divisional and district officers is very evident. Although Kauṭilya lays down that officials (*amātyas*) and soldiers should be hereditary, we are unable to cite actual cases from the Maurya period. However, the inscriptions of the Gupta period show that the posts of the *mantrin* and the *saciva*, who served with the Gupta emperor, were hereditary,[2] so was the post of the *amātya* in central India[3] and Vaiśālī.[4] In one case, in central India we find five generations of office-bearers in one family, of whom the first was *amātya*, the second *amātya* and *bhogika*, the third *bhogika*, and the fourth and the fifth *mahāsāndhivigrahika*.[5] The same region also furnishes other instances of two[6] and sometimes three[7] generations of *bhogikas*. These officers however served the feudatories of the Guptas and not the Gupta kings directly. But the surname *datta* of the *uparikas* in charge of the *bhukti* of Puṇḍravardhana[8] suggests that they probably belonged to the same family. The officials owed their tenure to the discretion of the emperor, but in practice they and their descendants continued to be in office because of their local strength. They gained in power and influence by combining

1. Supra Ch. XVI.
2. *Sel. Inscrr.*, III, no. 17, ll. 6-7; *CII*, iii, no.6, ll. 3-4.
3. *CII*, iii, no 22, ll. 28-30.
4. *ASR*, 1913-14, p. 134.
5. *CII*, iii no. 22, ll. 28-30; no. 23, ll. 18-20.
6. Ibid., no. 27, ll. 21-22.
7. Ibid., no. 26, ll. 22-23,
8. *Sel. Inscrr.*, III, no. 18, l. 3; no. 34, l. 2; no. 36, l. 2.

several offices in the same person. We have the famous example of Harişeṇa, who held several important portfolios. We hear of a *kumārāmātya* who held the offices of the *mahāśvapati* and *mahādaṇḍanāyaka*.[1]

We have no precise idea of the mode of payment to the officers under the Gupta empire. The discovery of numerous Gupta gold coins and their use in land transactions in Bengal coupled with the prevalence of the tax known as *hiraṇya* would suggest that at least higher officers were paid in cash. The Chinese evidence on this point is not quite clear. Legge's translation of a passage from Fa-hsien informs us that "the king's body-guards and attendants, all have regular salaries."[2] But Beal translates the passage differently: "The chief officers of the king have all allotted revenues"[3]; and a Chinese scholar translates the crucial passage thus: "The king's attendants, guards, and retainers all receive emoluments and pensions."[4] If we accept the last rendering, it would appear that the term emoluments, having a wider context, might include grants of revenues. Thus it would appear that members of bureaucracy were paid in cash and also by grants of revenues.

In addition to the high echelons, inscriptions reveal more than a dozen other officers of high and low grades, engaged in managing military, fiscal and rural matters. Although the Gupta establishment was not as larger as the one provided in the *Arthaśāstra* of Kauṭilya, it was neither negligible nor powerless. Records of land transactions shows that no land could be sold unless the recordkeepers or the *pustapālas* certified that it was available for sale and unless the district governor or the *viṣayapati* endorsed it. The hereditary character of the officers and decreasing payment in cash would suggest that the Gupta functionaries could develop vested interests with less difficulty than their Maurya predecessors.

II

In spite of the whirlwind conquests of Samudra Gupta and the

1. *ASR*, 1911-12, p. 52.
2. *A Record of Buddhistic Kingdom*, Tr., p. 45.
3. *Travels of Fah-hien etc.*, p. 55.
4. Ho Chang-Chun, "Fa-hsien's pilgrimage to Buddhist Countries", *Chinese Literature*, 1956, no. 3, 154.

campaigns of Candra Gupta II and Skanda Gupta the information about the military system of the Guptas is meagre. About the composition of the army we can draw a few inferences from Gupta coins and inscriptions. A few Gupta kings are described as excellent, unrivalled chariot warriors, and horsemen are usually represented on their coins. Archers are also depicted on coins which testify to the importance of horse archery and cavalry. The growing importance of cavalry is supported by seals and inscriptions which speak of *aśvapati,*[1] *mahāśvapati*[2] and *bhaṭāśvapati,*[3] evidently the commander of horsemen. The early Gupta records do not mention any officer connected with the management of elephants. The term *pilupati* occurs in a sixth century inscription from Bengal, and we are not quite sure whether the office was important under early Gupta Kings. Designations for the commanders of the other wings of the army are so far not known from inscriptions. The other military officers are *mahābalādhikṛta*, *mahāpratīhāra* and *gaulmika*. The last two are known to pre-Gupta inscriptions, but the first appears as a new military functionary in this period.

Civil officials such as *amātyās, kumārāmātyas*, etc., performed military functions or were promoted to the rank of high military officers. A minister hailing from Pāṭaliputra accompanied Candra Gupta II on his campaign to western India. Similarly military officers may have performed civil functions.

We have some idea about the stationing of troops in important cities such as Vaiśālī. The discovery of a seal bearing the legend *śrīraṇabhāṇḍāgārādhikaraṇa*[4] from there attests the existence of some military store which may have been needed for the army stationed there. We also hear of the war office attached to the royal heir apparant[5] and of the head of the infantry and cavalry.[6] The head of the palace guard was also stationed at Vaiśālī.[7]

1. *ASR*, 1911-12, pp. 52-53.
2. Ibid.
3. Ibid., 1903-04, p. 109. The *mahāpilupali* mentioned in the spurious Nālandā plate of Samudra Gupta does not appear in earlier records.
4. Ibid., p. 108.
5. *yuvarāja-bhaṭṭārakapādīya-balādhikaraṇasya*. Ibid.
6. Ibid., p. 109.
7. Ibid., p. 108.

III

The taxation system of the Guptas was not so elaborate and organised as we find it in the *Arthaśāstra* of Kauṭilya. The villagers paid in kind certain customary miscellaneous dues, which could be measured, but these are not specified.[1] They also paid *hiraṇya*[2] or gold, but what it actually meant cannot be said. The artisans also had to pay some imposts,[3] and traders were subjected to customs on commodities of trade, which were levied and collected by the customs officer.[4] Probably he had to deal with the corporation of bankers, merchants and artisans which was active in Vaiśālī, Bhīṭā, Indor (Bulandshahr), Mandasor, etc.

We have some idea of the officials working in the district or *viṣaya* in connection with land transactions. The officer known as *pustapāla*[5] maintained records of land sale, and the village accountant (*grāmākṣapaṭalādhikṛta*[6]) preserved records of land in the village. It is difficult to make out the meaning of *pāditarika*, who is addressed in the Bihar grant of Skanda Gupta,[7] but the *gaulmika*[8] mentioned therein was a minor military officer in charge of a small detachment of soldiers. Probably he stood by the civil authorities in times of disturbances caused by peasants or unsocial elements.

The list of taxes enumerated in the *Arthaśāstra* of Kauṭilya is much longer than that found in Gupta inscriptions, which would suggest that the burden of taxation decreased in Gupta times. The Greek accounts suggest that peasants had to pay one-fourth of their produce as tax, but if we rely on the legal texts of the Gupta period and land sale transactions in Bengal, the royal share did not exceed one-sixth of the produce. Of the emergency taxes recommended in the *Arthaśāstra* there is no trace in Gupta times. In fact the principles of taxation which enjoin the

1. *CII*, iii, no. 60, l. 12.
2. *EI*, xxiii, no. 8, l. 3.
3. Ibid.
4. Ibid., no. 12, l. 20.
5. *EI*, xxiii, no. 8, l. 8.
6. *CII*, iii, no. 60, l. 15.
7. Ibid., no. 12, l. 28.
8. Ibid., l. 29.

king to leave enough subsistence to the producer were the products of the early centuries of the Christian era and may have influenced the fiscal policy of the rulers of this period. Since the Guptas did not maintain a large administrative establishment they did not require as many taxes as the Mauryas did. Curiously enough more taxes are mentioned in Vākāṭaka inscriptions than in their Gupta counterparts.

Most revenue officers mentioned in land grants seem to have been connected with the assessment and collection of land revenue. *Āyuktaka* and *viniyuktaka* from both Bengal and Gujarat were connected with land transaction. For transfer of land in Bengal the *āyuktaka* had to undertake suitable steps. Land records were maintained by the *gramākṣapaṭalādhikṛta* or the *deśākṣapaṭalādhikṛta*, who possibly acted as accountants and paṭwārīs. Scribes called *divira*, *karaṇika*, kāyastha, etc., were employed chiefly in the revenue office, and Yājñavalkya advises the king to protect the subjects against the oppression of the kāyasthas.

Revenues may have been collected mostly in kind; probably rich peasants paid in cash, for gold coins have been discovered in large quantities and were certainly used in purchasing land. The officer who collected dues in cash is called *hiraṇyasāmudāyika* and is mentioned in a Bengal inscription of the first half of the sixth century.[1] Since this officer appears along with the *audraṅgika*, who collected the royal share in kind, it is apparent that he did the same thing in cash.

The only officer connected with the collection of tolls on commodities seems to have been the *śaulkika*, although we hear of an officer in Bengal connected with the department of trade. During the first half of the sixth century in the territories held by the feudatories of the Guptas we come across the *aurṇasthānika*,[2] who had something to do with the regulation of the wool-market in Bengal; in Gujarat during the same period we hear of *draṅgika*, who collected customs in border towns.

IV

The Gupta kings evolved, as we learn from inscriptions, the

1. *Sel. Inscrr.*, III. no. 46, l. 4.
2. Ibid.

first systematic provincial and local administration, which was primarily concerned with the collection of revenues and maintenance of law and order. The core of the empire directly controlled by the Guptas was divided into a number of provinces, smaller than a Maurya province but much larger than a modern division.

The *bhukti* seems to have been the largest administrative unit under the Guptas, and there were at least six such divisions spread over Bengal, Bihar, Uttar Pradesh and Madhya Pradesh. It was placed in charge of an *uparika*.[1] The exact connotation of this high officer is obscure; probably in origin it had something to do with the collection of *uparikara*, an additional impost on the peasants in addition to the fixed annual share of the produce. The officer was undoubtedly a governor appointed by the Gupta king, but the literal meaning of the term *bhukti* suggests that the territory placed under his charge was intended to be enjoyed rather than governed by him in its own interest. It is a pity that we have no information regarding the functions of the head of the *bhukti*.

The *bhukti* was divided into *viṣayas* or districts, whose number is not known. The *viṣayas* of Rājagṛha, Pāṭaliputra and Gaya were included in Magadhabhukti which, if we believe the geographical details in the spurious Nalandā grant of Samudra Gupta, also included Krimilā *viṣaya*,[2] roughly corresponding to Munger and Begusarai districts and extending over both the north and south of the Gaṅgā. In Tirabhukti Vaiśalī was important enough to be the headquarters of a *viṣaya*, although it is mentioned as such in only one seal,[3] and here too the reading is doubtful. In Puṇḍravardhanabhukti now in Bangladesh, the *viṣaya* of Koṭivarṣa was a famous administrative unit. The *viṣaya* was in charge of the *kumārāmātya* in early times, but later it came to be placed under the *viṣayapati*, Ordinarily in Bengal and Bihar the *viṣayapati* was the head of the *viṣaya* where he carried on administration with the help of the local office or *adhikaraṇa*. But in one case in western U.P. he was placed in charge of a district called *bhoga*. We have some idea

1. *ASIR*, 1903-4, p. 109.
2. *EI*, xxv, no. 9, l. 5.
3. *ASIR*, 1903-4, p. 110.

of the way the district governor maintained his power in the *viṣaya* of Koṭivarṣa. He based his authority on the force consisting of elephants, cavalry and infantry, whose cost was defrayed probably out of the revenues supplied by the district.[1] Perhaps every district had a strong military contingent to back civil authority in times of need.

The *viṣaya* was divided into *vīthīs*. In Bihar we know of Nandavīthi,[2] whose headquarters lay 2 miles to the north-west of Surajgarha in south Munger. But several *vīthīs* are known from Bengal, and in one case we have full information about the composition of the committee which took part in its government. According to the Mallasârul copper-plate inscription of the time of Gopacandra, ascribable to the first half of the sixth century A.D., altogether eleven rural settlements, mostly villages, are specifically represented on the *adhikaraṇa* of the *vīthī* Vakkattaka situated in Vardhamānabhukti, so that it is not an eight-member body or a decimal unit as recommended by the law-books. Some representatives owe their headship of the villages to their *agrahāra* grants, others to their important military position as swordsmen or perhaps transport organisers; the remaining are unspecified. Thus landed and military interest—all connected with the king—are well represented on the committee. Whether the *vīthī adhikaraṇa* was an *ad hoc* body constituted according to the nature of the business it transacted or a regular committee cannot be said. We may note that of the eleven villages mentioned in this list two form part of the boundaries which enclose the land to be transferred with the consent of the committee. At any rate the functioning of the *vīthī* managing body with landed beneficiaries and military personnel as its members was a reality, and probably they had something to do with the maintenance of law and order and settlement of local disputes.

The *vīthī* consisted of villages, which formed the lowest units of administration; several of these are mentioned in Gupta inscriptions and seals. The leading part in managing the affairs of the village was taken by its *grāmika* and elders known as the *mahattama*, *mahattaka* or *mahattara*. Inscriptions speak of

1. R.S. Sharma, *Indian Feudalism*, p. 18.
2. *EI*, xxiii, no. 8, l. 3.

grāmika in Bengal[1] and central India. In the latter region his post seems to have become hereditary, for in one instance the name of his father and grandfather is mentioned.[2] He may have assisted in the collection of taxes, but in this case he had set up a boundary pillar on the limits of the kingdom of his prince.[3]

In north Bihar the head of the village called *mahattara* was important enough to have his seal. From this designation has been derived the term *mahto* prevalent in many parts of this province and still understood in some areas as the head of the village. The term is widely used as a title of members of the Koeri, Kurmi and other peasant castes.

Land grants from Bengal provide some welcome information on the position of the *mahattaras*. Generally they did not belong to the brāhmaṇa community, for in land grants brāhmaṇas and *mahattaras* are addressed separately. In the Baigrām copper-plate inscription of A.D. 448 these elders are addressed as *samvyavahāripramukhān*,[4] but *mahattara* is the usual term for them. In north Bengal no land, even for religious purpose, could be sold without the consent of the *mahattaras*, some of whom also sold their lands for the same reason. The Mallasārul copper-plate mentioned above specifically names some of these *mahattaras* and similar other important elements from several villages. Three *mahattara-āgrahāriṇas* are each attached to one village,[5] which would suggest that the *mahattara* was the head of the village granted to him as an *agrahāra*. But in two villages two such elders are named in every case,[6] which would imply that in each village these two functionaries shared the management between them. The names of these *āgrahāriṇas* ending in *datta* and *svāmin*[7] suggest that some were brāhmaṇas and others kāyasthas who had been granted revenue-free villages for some services rendered to their king. In addition to these, the inscription also mentions a *mahattara* head of a village who is not an *āgrahāriṇa*.[8]

1. *Sel. Inscrr.*, III. no. 34, l. 3.
2. *CII*, iii, no. 24, ll. 4-6.
3. Ibid.
4. *Sel. Inscrr.*, III, no. 41, l. 2.
5. Ibid., no. 46, ll. 5-6.
6. Ibid., ll. 6-7.
7. Ibid., ll. 5-7.
8. Ibid., l. 5.

The inscription also mentions three *khāḍgīs*, swordsmen, each from one village,[1] suggesting thereby that villages were held by them for some kind of military service, and finally we hear of the *vāhanāyaka* Hari, etc., who represent one village.[2] Perhaps Hari presided over a village which supplied porters and carriers to the king. In Bengal village elders called *mahattaras* seem to have been organised into corporate bodies at the district level as well as the village level. The body at both the stages was called *aṣṭakulādhikaraṇa,*[3] a corporate organisation comprising eight leading families. Eight may well be a conventional number, whose origin is not known to us. Whether the families belonged to the same caste or represented the eight leading castes and professions in the locality is not known. Most probably all the families represented the same caste, but they should not be taken in the sense of small units as they are today but as wider circles of agnates. The Bengal inscriptions make it clear that no land transactions could be effected without their consent, and we can well presume that they wielded an effective voice in the management of other local affairs.

In some areas in central India local affairs in the rural areas were managed by a committee of five known as the *pañcamaṇḍalī*, which is greeted by a donor while making a religious donation. In this case we have the forerunner of the later *pañcakula* in Rajasthan and Gujarat and of the subsequent panchāyat throughout the country. How the *pañcamaṇḍalī* was constituted is not known, but there is no doubt about its corporate character.

Finally we have to take note of the various *janapadas*, which issued their seals and coins. It is evident that although many of them were affiliated to Nālandā for fiscal and administrative purposes, they were important and autonomous enough to have their seals which testify to their corporate existence. For larger *janapadas* committees of five are recommended, and the practice seems to have started long before the Gupta period.

Some kind of *pariṣads* functioned in the neighbouring towns or villages of Vaiśālī. We hear of a *pariṣad* flourishing in Udānakūpa.[4] But it cannot be said whether it was a panchāyat

1. Ibid., l. 7.
2. Ibid., ll. 7-8
3. Ibid., no. 34, ll. 2-3; *EI*, xvii, no. 23, ll. 5-6.
4. *ASIR*, 1903-4, p. 109.

managing the affairs of that village or a council of learned brāhmaṇas concerned with the interpretation of the laws laid down by the Dharmaśāstra. Yājñavalkya enjoins the king to make the people obey the laws of their families, castes, guilds, associations, or villages (*janapadān*),[1] and Manu takes into account such laws.[2] All this indicates that the *janapadas* in the Nālandā region had their own laws which were respected by the king.

The existence of these bodies should not be confused with the democratic participation of the rural people in administration. At best these indicate diffusion of authority in a limited circle whose support to the administration could not be easily dispensed with. The term *grāmādhipati* and *grāmasyādhipati* used in contemporary texts[3] would suggest that the village headman was treated as the lord of the village. If we rely on a passage from the *Kāmasūtra* of Vātasyāyana, perhaps in western India, where this text was composed, the village headman called *grāmādhipati āyuktaka* tended to become all-powerful. He compelled peasant women to fill up his granary, to carry various articles into or out of his office, to clean and decorate his residence, to work in his fields and to spin yarn of cotton, wool, flax or hemp for his clothes.[4]

The expanding scope of the village administration is a significant aspect of the Gupta polity. This came to happen because the state neither raised too many taxes to maintain a large official apparatus nor had too many copper coins to pay minor employees. Naturally many of the functions once performed by the central government devolved on the village administration, which was not a homogenous, egalitarian community but one dominated by landed and influential elements.

V

Towns in the Gupta empire were placed under an officer called *purapāla* at least in Bengal, but leading local elements were associated with the work of administration. In parts of north and central India, as seals and inscriptions would suggest, the

1. I. 361.
2. VIII. 41; cf. SBE, xxv, 260, fn. 41.
3. *ŚP*, 88.3. For heads of multi-village units the terms *pati, adhipati* and *adhyakṣa* are used in *Manu*, VII.115-19 and *ŚP*, 88.3-9.
4. V.5.5; cf. *Indian Feudalism*, pp. 51, 52.

Gupta period was a flourishing age for the guilds of artisans and traders functioning in such towns as Vaiśālī, Bhīṭā near Allahabad, Indor in Bulandshahr and Mandasor in Malwa. They evidently bore a good bit of responsibility for urban administration.

Vaiśālī in Bihar is an important town about whose administration we get some idea in Gupta times. We hear of the separate guilds of artisans (*kulika*) and of merchants (*śreṣṭhi*) in that town. But the most numerous seals, as many as 274, found there belong to the *nigama* guild of the *śreṣṭhis*, (merchants) *sārthavāhas* (itinerant traders) and *kulikas* (artisans).[1] The *nigama* has been compared to the modern Chamber of Commerce,[2] but the inclusion of artisans shows that it was a somewhat different and wider body which carried on not only economic activities but also looked after the administration of the town. We do not possess any precise information about the constitution of the *nigama*, whose members seem to have been the leading persons from every profession either elected or hereditary. The titles *dāsa*, *datta*, *nandī*, *pāla*, *sena*, *siṁha*, etc., show that members of different castes were admitted in to the guild. The *nigama* probably performed municipal functions in regard to bankers, traders and artisans whom it represented, and also in relation to the employees of various civil and military offices whose headquarters were situated in Vaiśālī. We learn from a contemporary lawgiver that the *nigama* framed its own rules known as *samayas*,[3] and that the king was under the obligation to maintain the usages settled among them in both open and fortified settlements.[4] This suggests that *nigamas* in Vaiśālī enjoyed a large measure of autonomy.

In regard to north Bengal the Damodarpur copper-plate inscriptions give clear indication of the participation of representatives of traders and artisans in the municipal management of those towns. According to them affairs at the headquarters of the Koṭivarṣa *viṣaya* (district) in Puṇḍravardhanabhukti were not the sole responsibility of the district governor but of the local merchants and traders who were possibly recognised for

1. *ASIR*. 1903-4, p. 110.
2. Ibid., p. 104.
3. *Nārada*, X.1.
4. Ibid., X.2.

the purpose by the *uparika*.[1] Thus we hear of the *nagaraśreṣṭhi* Ṛbhupāla, the *sārthavāha* Vasumitra, the *prathamakulika* Varadatta and the *prathamakāyastha* Viprapāla.[2] All these served on the district committee at least for four years, for which epigraphic records are available. This period should not be taken as the length of their tenure. Along with the *āyuktaka* the functionaries counted five, which number was coming into use in both the rural and urban areas. It is clear that elements of trade and industry were fairly represented in local administration. The titles *pāla, mitra, datta* are still common in Bengal, and on this basis we could not tell that only brāhmaṇas and kṣatriyas manned the district managing committee.

VI

Probably the coercive role of the state had become far more important in Gupta times because of the widespread social disturbances as reflected in the Kali Age descriptions of about the third-fourth centuries A.D. The machinery for maintaining law and order in this period was based on the office of the *daṇḍanāyaka*, the *dāṇḍika* and the *daṇḍapāśika*. The first seems to have been a high executive officer in command of sufficient force. This office was especially popular in Bihar and U.P. As many as eight Gupta seals of these *daṇḍanāyakas* have been discovered from Bhīṭā.[3] Seals of *mahādaṇḍanāyaka* have been found at both Bhīṭā[4] and Vaiśālī.[5] Some holders of this post inherited it from their father, as can be seen in the case of Hariṣeṇa. Essentially the *dāṇḍika, daṇḍapāśika* and *daṇḍanāyaka*, all seem to have performed police and magisterial functions. The emphasis on the role of the *daṇḍa* and *dāṇḍika* given in the law-book of Manu would suggest that their functions were negative, to punish those who broke the established laws. The police work was performed by the *daṇḍapāśika*, whose office *adhikaraṇa* is mentioned in a Vaiśālī seal.[6] The Orissa *daṇḍausī*, literally derived from *daṇḍapāśika*, functions as a village watchman who

1. *Sel. Inscrr.*, III. no. 36, ll. 1-4.
2. Ibid., ll. 3-4.
3. *ASR*, 1911-12, pp. 54-55.
4. Ibid.
5. Ibid., 1903-4, p. 109.
6. *ASR*, 1903-4, p. 108.

seems to be a poor survival of his Gupta predecessor. Another officer charged with this duty in the rural areas was the *caurod-dharaṇika,* the predecessor of the medieval *chaudharī* who maintained law and order as one of the leading landed magnets. The title still prevalent in north India is shorn of all prestige and power. In towns the magisterial function was discharged by the *vinayas-thitisthāpaka,* who had certainly his office in the headquarters of Tīrabhukti, and possibly in other provincial headquarters.

Most officers mentioned above appear in late Gupta land grants. Since land disputes would disturb the peace and stability of the villages they were notified of all important changes in its transfer and possession.

The Gupta period marks a landmark in the history of the administration of law and justice in early India. It produced a rich corpus of legal literature which reflects a distinct advance in the legal system. For the first time the lawgivers of the period draw a clear line between what may be regarded as civil and criminal law. Bṛhaspati enumerates eighteen titles of law and adds that fourteen of these have their origin in property (*dhanamūla*) and four in injury (*hiṃsāmūla*)[1]. The first might be compared to the *dharmasthīya* section of Kauṭilya and the second to his *kaṇṭakaśodhana* section. But the administration of criminal law seems to be important in Kauṭilya and of civil law in Bṛhaspati. On account of the growth of private property in land[2] which was sold for money in Gupta times, we find very detailed laws about partition, sale, mortgage and lease of land in Gupta law-books. All this shows considerable progress of rational trends, but curiously enough superstitions invade the judicial procedure. Manu[3] prescribes only two types of ordeal, Yājñavalkya[4] and Nārada[5] raise the number to five, and Bṛhaspati[6] to nine. Whether this was done deliberately or to accommodate tribal peoples with their beliefs in different ordeals cannot be said, but the development will strike anybody who cares to glance through the law codes. Many of these

1. II, 5.
2. R.S. Sharma, *Indian Feudalism*, pp. 145-52.
3. VIII.114.
4. II.95.
5. I.252.
6. X.4.

ordeals may not have been used, because the criminal would break down in defence and thus help the course of justice.

The legal texts of Gupta times lay down detailed rules about the constitution of court and the law of evidence. The king is asked to decide suits with the help of at least three *sabhyas*, his preference being not limited to brāhmaṇas alone; however, śūdras are to be carefully excluded. Unfortunately land grants do not throw any clear light on the composition of these courts. But the term *adhikaraṇa* used to describe in inscriptions a managing committee of eight at the district (*viṣaya*) headquarters (*adhiṣṭhāna*) or at the village level, or a committee at the *vīthī* level, is also understood in the sense of a judicial court in the literary texts of the 7th century. The *Mṛcchakaṭika* describes a judicial court consisting of the *adhikaraṇika*, the *śreṣṭhi* and the kāyastha, which partly answers to the epigraphic description of the committee which not only mentions its *nagara-śreṣṭhi* and *prathamakāyastha* members but also its *sārthavāha* and *prathamakulika*. It is therefore likely that the local bodies of five, eight or eleven, as the case may be in the *viṣaya*, the village or the *vīthī*, also decided disputes relating to land and other matters.

Civil courts seem to have functioned at important administrative centres. Two seals from Nālandā containing the term *dharmādhikaraṇa* (in one case the name Śrī Śīlāditya is also mentioned)[1] seem to be of this type and indicate that Nālandā was the headquarters of some kind of civil court.

The law-books provide for a hierarchy of local courts, which are to be recognised but not established by the king. Yājñavalkya and Bṛhaspati mention three grades of local courts, *kula, śreṇi* and *puga*, and Bṛhaspati adds that the appeal shall lie to the higher court in the same order.[2] Kātyāyana introduces *gaṇa* in place of *puga* and adds in the same ascending order two other courts, namely an authorised person and the king.[3] According to the law-book farmers, artisans, traders, etc., can

1. *MASI*, no. 66, p. 53. Except the seals of the Gupta kings which can be clearly identified, Gupta and post-Gupta seals of Nālandā have been uncritically mixed up in *MASI*, no. 66. The two can be separated from one another on the basis of palaeography.
2. *Bṛhaspati*, I. 28-30.
3. Verse 82.

have their courts, which are empowered to decide on all matters relating to these groups of people. Kātyāyana advises artisans, farmers, etc., to get their disputes decided by their *mahattaras*, who are repeatedly mentioned as elders or village headmen in Gupta inscriptions. The epigraphic *aṣṭakulādhikaraṇa* relating to villages was evidently the counterpart of the *kula* court mentioned in the Gupta law-books. At any rate the legal texts leave the impression that professional associations functioned as courts of justice, which obviated the necessity of providing justice through the state machinery.

Towards the end of the Gupta period corporations of merchants were granted considerable autonomy by royal charters. This is illustrated by the charters of Viṣṇuṣena issued in A.D. 592 in western India. It exempted the traders from various dues, left them free to deal with labourers, herdsmen, etc., and authorised them to impose forced labour on certain artisans.[1] The traders were allowed immunity from the entry of royal officials in their area and from payment of dues and rations for supporting these officials.[2] Such charters are not known to northern India, but may not have been altogether absent.

VII

The system of administration underwent several changes under the Guptas, but the most striking developments related to the grant of fiscal and administrative immunities to the beneficiaries and to the establishment of relations with the subjugated princes called feudatories. In grants, from the time of Pravarasena II Vākāṭaka (5th century A.D.), onwards, the ruler gave up his control over almost all sources of revenue, including pasturage, hides and charcoal, mines for the production of salt, forced labour, and all hidden treasures and deposits.[3] The *Raghuvaṁśa* states that, among other things, mines constitute the wages (*vetana*) of the king for protecting the earth.[4] According to some grants of the 4th and 5th centuries A.D. the brāhmaṇas were granted the right of enjoying the hidden treasures

1. *EI*, xxx, 163-81; *JESHO*, ii, 281-93.
2. *EI*, xxx, no. 36, l. 6
3. *Sel. Inscrr.*, III, no. 62, ll. 26-29.
4. XVII. 66.

and deposits of the village;[1] this meant the transfer of royal ownership over mines, which was an important sign of the king's sovereignty.

Equally important is the fact that the donor abandoned the right to govern the inhabitants of the villages that were granted. The Gupta period shows at least half a dozen grants of apparently settled villages made to the brāhmaṇas by the big feudatories in central India in which the residents, including the cultivators and artisans, were expressly asked by their respective rulers not only to pay the customary taxes to the donees but also to obey their commands. In two other land grants of post-Gupta times royal commands were issued to government officials employed as *sarvādhyakṣa* and also to regular soldiers and umbrella-bearers that they should not cause any disturbance to the brāhmaṇas.[2] All this provides clear evidence of the surrender of the administrative power of the state.

Till the 5th century A.D. the ruler generally retained the right to punish thieves, which was one of the main bases of the state power. Devolution of power reached its logical end when in later times the king made over to the brāhmaṇas not only this right, but also his right to punish all offences against family, property person, etc. In central and western India some royal donors conferred upon the grantees the right of trying cases in the donated villages. Their grants use the term *abhyantara-siddhi*,[3] which has been interpreted variously.[4] It makes sense if we take it as adjudication of internal disputes in the village,[5] which is thus made completely self-dependent. Apparently this technical expression is the counterpart of *sa-daṇḍa-daś=āparādhaḥ* used in north Indian grants. But while the later limits the grantee's jurisdiction to criminal cases,[6] the former extends it to civil cases, so that armed with such powers the donees could turn the benefices into practically independent pockets.

1. *CII* iii, no. 41, l. 8; *Sel. Inscrr.*, III, no. 62, l. 29.
2. R.S. Sharma, "*Politico-Legal Aspects of the Caste System*", *JBRS*, xxxix, 325.
3. *abhyantara siddhikāḥ*, *CII*, iv, no. 431, l. 1.
4. *CII*, iv, 154 fn. 1.
5. Ibid.
6. Ibid., iii, 189-90, fn. 4.

The Maurya state is credited with "comprehensive competence based on centralised control", which may have been true of its rule in the core area of the middle Ganga plains. The Gupta period shows the process of the devolution of the state authority. The functions of the collection of taxes, levy of forced labour, regulation of mines, agriculture, etc., together with those of the maintenance of law and order, and defence, which were hitherto performed by the state officials, were now step by step abandoned, first to the priestly class, and later to the warrior class.

Gupta grants from Bengal and central India confer the right of enjoying the revenues from land in perpetuity on the beneficiary, but they do not authorise him to alienate or grant his rents or land to others. Perhaps the earliest record of this type comes from Indore in central India where an inscription of A.D. 397 records the consent of one Mahārāja Svāmidāsa, probably a feudatory of the Imperial Guptas, to the grant of a field by a merchant.[1] The fact that Svāmidāsa was empowered to endorse the religious grant made by an individual in his jurisdiction suggests that as a feudatory he himself could make religious grants without royal consent. But neither in this case nor in that of other Gupta feudatories such as the Parivrājaka and Ucchakalpas, who granted several villages, is there anything to show that they held land of the king. Thus these grants do not illustrate true subinfeudation. However, the Indore grant authorises the grantee to enjoy the field, cultivate it and get it cultivated so long as he observes the conditions of the *brahmadeya* grant.[2] This leaves clear scope for creating tenants on the donated land and provides perhaps the earliest epigraphic evidence of the subinfeudation of the soil. Although early examples of this type are not found in other parts of the country, we have here the beginning of the process of subinfeudation which continued in the western part of central India in the 5th century A.D. and characterised the grants of the Valabhī rulers to their donees in the 6th and 7th centuries.

Significantly enough the heart of the Gupta empire, which covered the modern states of Uttar Pradesh, Bihar and Bengal, hardly knows of any grant of village or land made by any feuda-

1. *EI*, no. 16, ll. 1-9. It is not quiet clear whether the merchant was the donor.
2. *ucitayā brahmadeyabhuktyā bhuñjataḥ kṛṣatah kṛṣāpayataś ca*. Ibid., ll. 6-7.

tory chief without royal consent; all such grants are confined to the periphery of this area in the outlying regions whose chiefs owed only nominal allegiance to the Imperial Guptas. Only towards the end of the rule of the Imperial Guptas such practices appeared in the kernel of their empire. The *kumārāmātya-mahārāja* Nandana granted a village located in Gaya district in the middle of the 6th century A.D.[1] although this seemed to have been a royal prerogative of the Imperial Guptas in earlier times. However, we hear of some *āgrahārikas,* who seem to have been religious beneficiaries enjoying revenue-free villages. They are mentioned in a Gupta grant of the late 5th century, and we also hear of a brāhmaṇa *āgrahārika*, being granted some land in south Munger[2] in the sixth century. Apparently the *āgrahārika* maintained some staff for collecting various dues from the inhabitants of the gift villages, although even the forged grants of Samudra Gupta assignable to the 7th century do not allow any administrative functions to the grantees in Magadha, as is the case with religious grants made by the feudatories of the Guptas in Madhya Pradesh. The jurisdiction of the *āgrahārika* in Bihar was far more limited than that of his counterpart in central India. An important condition imposed on him was that he would not introduce any tax-paying peasants and artisans from another village in his *agrahāra* otherwise it would constitute an infringement of the endowment. The beneficiary of the *agrahāra* enjoyed a free hand in the management of the affairs of the village so granted to him, for in one case it is laid down that no trouble should be caused to him by the descendants of the grantee.[3]

Land grants giving rise to feudal conditions are typical in Gupta times of those areas which were forested and mountainous and hence less exposed to commerce and the use of money. Most coins issued by the Gupta kings have been found in the plains and only a few in Madhya Pradesh. If the Parivrājaka and Uccakalpa princes could issue land charters without the consent

1. *JASB*, NS, v (1909), 164; EI, x, 12.
2. *EI*, xiii, no. 8, l. 3. The charter is couched in the same terms as the land grants of north Bengal, but the donee was local, and so also seems to have been the donor for he describes himself simply as *viṣayapati* Chhatramaha suggesting thereby that he is well-known in the area to which the donee bolongs.
3. Ibid., x, no. 12, l. 6.

of the Gupta sovereign, they could surely issue coins as did the vassals of the Sātavāhanas. But none of their coins have been found so far. Evidently religious or other services were paid by land grants mainly in those areas which suffered from lack of money.

According to the charters in return for land grants the priests were obliged to render religious services, which might secure the spiritual welfare of the donors or their ancestors. The secular obligations of the priestly beneficiaries are rarely laid down; an example is the Chammak copper-plate of the Vākāṭaka king Pravarsena II, which imposes certain obligations on one thousand brāhmaṇas who are granted one village.[1] It enjoins that they shall not conspire against the king and the kingdom, commit theft and adultery, slay brāhmaṇas, and poison kings, etc.; further they shall not wage war and do wrong to other villages.[2] All these are negative obligations, which imply that the priests enjoyed the land on condition that they would not act in opposition to the established social and political system. These were probably taken for granted on the part of the religious beneficiaries in other charters. But it is natural to expect that the brāhmaṇas more than repaid their generous donors and patrons by maintaining law and order in the areas under their charge and impressing upon the people the sacred duty of carrying out their varṇa functions and of obeying the king, who in the Gupta period and later was represented as embodying in his person the attributes of various gods. Hence whatever may have been the intentions of the donors, it would be wrong to think that these grants served only religious purposes. Certainly the priests prayed for the spiritual well-being of the donors and their ancestors, and never supplied any soldiers as the bishops did in England, but where was the need for military service if the people could be persuaded to behave themselves and to acquiesce in the existing order?

Epigraphic land grants made to officers for their military and administrative services are lacking, although such a possibility cannot be entirely ruled out. Manu's recommendation for the payment of fiscal officers by grants of land[3] is repeated by the

1. *CII*, iii, no. 55.
2. Ibid., ll. 39-43.
3. VII.115-20.

lawgivers of Gupta times. In the 5th century Bṛhaspati, while defining *prasāda-likhita*, a writing of favour, states that such a grant is made by the king when, pleased with the services, valour, etc., of a person, he grants him a district or the like.[1]

Some inscriptions of the Gupta period show that villages were granted to secular parties, who administered them for religious purposes. Under the Sātavāhanas and Kuṣāṇas cash endowments were made to the guilds of artisans for meeting religious needs, but under the Guptas land endowments were made to officials and others for the same purpose. A very early instance is found in central India in A.D. 496-7 in a grant made by the Uccakalpa *māhārāja* Jayanātha.[2] A village was granted as an *agrahāra* to a scribe (*divira*) and his son and two grandsons, who were to manage it for religious purposes.[3] The inhabitants were asked to pay *bhāga*, *bhoga*, *kara*, *hiraṇya*, etc., to the beneficiaries and to carry out their orders, but the donor retained the right of punishing the thieves.[4] These concessions may not have been always utilised by the secular trustees in the interests of religion, and less so by the scribes whose oppressions were proverbial. Whether the scribe was placed in charge of the endowment to supplement his remuneration for secular services is not clear, but in practice he may not have missed the opportunity of lining his pockets.

In the same area several other similar grants were made by Śarvanātha, the son of Jayanātha. Thus in A.D. 512-3 Śarvanātha granted a village in four shares, two of which belonged to Viṣṇunandin, another to the merchant Śaktināga and another to Kumāranāga and Skandanāga.[5] The village was given with *udaṅga* and *uparikara* and was not to be entered by the irregular or regular troops[6]—an important administrative immunity which does not occur in the grant cited above. It is obvious that here the immediate beneficiaries were the secular parties, whose descendants were authorised to enjoy the grant in perpetuity.[7]

1. Quoted in *Vyavahāramayūkha* (tr. P.V. Kane & S.G. Patwardhan), pp. 25-7.
2. *CII*, iii, no. 27.
3. Ibid., ll. 5-11.
4. Ibid., ll. 11-14.
5. Ibid., no. 28, ll. 1-17.
6. Ibid., ll. 9-10.
7. Ibid., ll. 12-13.

But the ultimate beneficiaries were the two gods for whose worship and for the repairs of whose shrines this grant was made with the agreement between the donor and the donee.[1] At any rate it is clear that the fiscal and administrative rights were to be exercised by the secular beneficiaries, and only the proceeds were to be enjoyed by the temples. A grant of half of a village on similar terms was made by the same king to a person called Choḍugomika, again a secular party, who agreed with the donor that the endowment would be utilised for the worship of the goddess Piṣṭapurikādevī and the repairs of her temple.[2] All these grants give the impression that secular parties functioned as managers of the villages which were to be enjoyed by the temples.

But a charter of A.D. 533-34 made by the same king leaves no doubt that land grants were made even independently to secular parties. According to it two villages were bestowed as a mark of favour in perpetuity with the fiscal and administrative rights mentioned above upon a person called Pulindabhaṭa,[3] who seems to have been an aboriginal chief; it is certain that before their transfer Pulindabhaṭa held the two villages on the strength of a purely secular charter. Other secular assignments may have been made in the Gupta period, but since they were not connected with religious donations they were not recorded on lasting material such as stone and copper.

Certain designations of the administrative officers and units of the Gupta period suggest that land revenues were granted for remunerating government services. The titles *bhogika* and *bhogapatika* suggest that these officers were assigned offices not so much for exercising royal authority over the subjects and working for their welfare as for enjoying the revenues. Sometimes the *bhogika* held the office of *amātya* also.[4] We wonder whether in such a case the office of the *bhogika* was meant to remunerate its holder for his functions pertaining to the other office. Further, the office of the *bhogika* was generally hereditary, for at least three generations of *bhogikas* are mentioned in

1. Ibid., ll. 13-16.
2. Ibid., no. 29, ll. 1-12.
3. Ibid., no. 31, ll. 1-10.
4. Ibid., no. 23, ll. 18-20; 26, ll. 22-23.

several cases.[1] All these factors must have naturally rendered the *bhogika* a powerful overlord, comparatively free from the control of the central authority. The *bhogapatika* is mentioned as one of about a dozen officers stationed in Vardhamāna *bhukti* when the *mahārāja* Vijayasena was ruling there as a vassal of the *mahārājādhirāja* Śrī Gopacandra about A.D. 507.[2] It has been rightly suggested that this officer was probably a *jāgīrdār*.[3]

The process of conquest, by which smaller chiefs were reduced to subordination and reinstated in their positions provided they paid regular tributes and did homage, contributed to the growth of feudal polity. It reached its culmination with Samudra Gupta, whose whirlwind conquests of vast areas led to the establishment of feudal relations on a much wider scale and provided a pattern for his successors. The obligations of the feudatories towards the sovereign are clearly set forth in the Allahabad Inscription, which shows that in return for being restored to their thrones the conquered and subjugated princes were expected to pay all tributes, to carry out royal orders, to give their daughters in marriage, and to render homage to the conqueror.[4]

The term *sāmanta* is not used for the conquered feudatories of Samudra Gupta. In the *Arthaśāstra* of Kauṭilya and the inscriptions of Aśoka[5] this term meant independent neighbours. In post-Maurya law-books it was used in the sense of a neighbouring proprietor of land.[6] It was from the fifth century A.D. onwards that the term *sāmanta* was used in the sense of vassal in south India, for the phrase *sāmanta-cūḍāmaṇayaḥ* appears in a Pallava inscription of the time of Śāntivarman (*c.* A.D. 455-70).[7] The term occurs in some grants of southern and western India of the same century in the sense of vassals.[8] In north India the earliest uses of the term in a similar sense seem to have been in a Bengal inscription, and in the Barabar Hill Cave Inscription

1. *CII*, iii, no. 26, ll. 22-23.
2. *Sel. Inscrr.*, III, no. 46, ll. 3-4.
3. Ibid., p. 360, fn. 9.
4. Ll. 22-24.
5. *AŚ*, I, 6; P.E. II. l. 5.
6. *Manu* [SBE], VIII. 286-9; *Yāj*, II. 152-53.
7. R.B. Panday, *Historical and Literary Inscriptions* no. 29, l. 31.
8. These instances have been collected by L. Gopal, in "Sāmanta—its varying Significance in Ancient India", *JRAS*, pts. 1 & 2, April 1963.

of the Maukhari chief Anantavarman, in which his father is described as *sāmanta-cūḍāmaṇiḥ* ("the best among feudatories").[1] Paleographically this inscription is placed earlier than A.D. 554, the date of the Harahā Inscription,[2] and hence the date of Anantavarman's father may be put around A.D. 500, when the Maukharis served as the *sāmantas* of the Imperial Guptas. The term *sāmanta* is also found in the Mandasor Stone Pillar Inscription of Yośodharman (*c.* A.D. 525-535), in which he claims to have subjugated the *sāmantas* (feudatories) in the whole of northern India.[3] During the 6th century A.D. the rulers of Valabhī bore the title of *sāmanta-mahārāja* and *mahāsāmanta*. Gradually the application of the term *sāmanta* was extended from defeated chiefs to royal officials. Thus, in the inscriptions dated in the Kalacuri-Cedi era, from A.D. 597 onwards *rājās* and *sāmantas* took the place of *uparikas* and *kumārāmātyas*.[4] In the sixth century A.D. several inscriptions from northern and western India know of the *sāmanta* as a vassal. Although the term does not occur in the records issued by the Gupta emperors, we may certainly assume that the *sāmanta* was an important link in the feudatory organisation of the later half of the Gupta period.

The contrast between the Maurya and the Gupta system of administration is evident. In spite of divine elements being attributed to him the Gupta king was not so powerful as his Maurya counterpart. His army, bureaucracy and taxation machinery were not as elaborate as that of the Mauryas. Officials tended to be hereditary and strong through occasional grants of land revenues. The Gupta rulers in both rural and urban areas initiated the first systematic provincial and local administration, with which landed, military and professional interests were associated. The period marked the sudden elevation of the village administration to a high position of authority. This was a necessary concomitant of the reduction of the bureaucratic staff. Local elements also played an important part in the administration of law and justice which seem to have been far more organised in this than in an earlier period.

1. *CII*, iii, no. 49, l. 4.
2. R.G. Basak, *The History of N.E. India*, p. 105.
3. *Sel. Inscrr.*, III, no. 54, verse 5.
4. *CII*, iv, Introd., p. clxi.

The two most striking developments of the period were the grants of whole villages to religious beneficiaries by the feudatories of the Guptas in central India with fiscal and administrative concessions and the establishment of unilateral contractual relations with the conquered princes by the Gupta emperors. On the whole we notice distinct feudal traits in the Gupta system of administration which prepared the way for a complete feudal structure in subsequent times.

CHAPTER XXII

STAGES IN ANCIENT INDIAN POLITY: VEDIC AND POST-VEDIC

I

The Ṛg Vedic Phase: Tribal Military Democracy

The political organisation of Ṛg Vedic times cannot be followed in isolation from the material and social life of the people who evolved it. Unfortunately the archaeological chasing of the Āryans in India has proved to be futile, and no material remains unearthed so far can be attributed with confidence to the Ṛg Vedic people. In spite of diligent digging since 1950 or so our main source for the reconstruction of the picture of the material life of the earliest Āryans in India continues to be literary.

If we rely on the *Ṛg Veda* the chief material element which distinguished the new comers from the Harappa people or their other predecessors was the possession of horse and chariots. Those who possessed and fought from chariots drawn by horses obviously constituted the ruling aristocracy, as was the case in Western Asia with the Mitannis and the Hyksos. On the other hand ordinary soldiers in possession of horse formed the rank and file of society.

Chariot-makers play an important part in the social organisation of Vedic times, but we have no idea of the material of which the chariots were made; their metal fiittings, if any, have not been discovered so far.

The Ṛg Vedic people knew the use of a metal called *ayas*, but whether it was copper or bronze cannot be said. It is thought that they used bronze, and this may be expected in view of the use of this metal on a large scale in Persia from about 1200 B.C. onwards. But only one or two objects found in the land of seven rivers can be ascribed to the period of the *Ṛg Veda*, and as such they are not sufficient to establish the use of bronze on any considerable scale. Since the colour of *ayas* is described as reddish, it seems to have been copper. It seems that their arrows were made of copper (*ayomukham*), and on the whole in spite of their possession of horse their tools and weapons would not enable them to form large empires, leading to developed state organisation.

The Ṛg Vedic people were a semi-nomadic people more in the pastoral stage, and without the knowledge of iron did not practise effective plough cultivation. They probably used hoes (*vṛka*) made of stone and shares (*sīra*) made of wood. Cattle rearing was a more important source of livelihood than agriculture, and cattle and bullocks formed their most valued possessions. The influence of cattle-rearing is writ large upon their social and military organisation. Thus people who lived with their cows under the same cowshed came to belong to the same *gotra*, which did not indicate descent from the same ancestor in the age of the *Ṛg Veda*. Again, since cattle formed the main bone of contention in tribal wars, the word for fight came to be known as *gaviṣṭhi*, a search for cows.

Because of their living in the semi-nomadic stage and constantly engaged in fighting for the sake of cows they had to be mobile. This naturally prevented them from forming stable kingdoms and at the same time did not allow their social relations to be rigid and stratified. Under the circumstances small tribal or clan principalities had to be the rule of the day.

The social organisation of the Ṛg Vedic people had not transcended the tribal stage. Kinship formed the basis of the social structure. The predominance of the tribal life is indicated by the frequent use of two terms *jana* and *viś* in the *Ṛg Veda*. The first occurs about 275 times in that text, and the second about 170 times. We also come across the term *pañcajanāḥ* in the sense of five tribes. The Vedic *jana* was the highest social unit, and it corresponded to the Roman *gens* and Greek *genos*.

The *jana* was split up into *viś*; the former stood for the whole tribe and the latter for the clan. We do not have its duplicate in Indo-European languages. We are not quite sure whether the Vedic *viś* corresponded to the Roman *tribus* and the Greek *phylae*. But there is no doubt that the *viś* was a fighting unit similar to the fighting groups of kinsmen in Homeric Greece and ancient Germany.

It is suggested that the *viś* was divided into *grāmas*, but this division was not widely prevalent because *grāma* figures only 13 times in the *Ṛg Veda*. In this period *grāma* is not ordinarily used in the sense of village but in that of small tribal fighting groups, which were mobilised together for purposes of war (*saṃ-grāma*).

Family may have been the lowest tribal unit, but it was not a well-rooted institution and certainly not a small monogamous unit as we understand it today. The word *kula*, family, is not mentioned in the *Ṛg Veda* independently. It however forms part of the term *kulapā*, head of family, which occurs only once in the *Ṛg Veda*. But even *kulapā* is represented as a fighter and not as an ordinary householder. *Gṛha* is mentioned in the *Ṛg Veda* several times in the sense of family or household. We have no idea of the size to which the Ṛg Vedic family could grow and keep together. It was a large patriarchal family in which probably members of three generations lived under the same roof.

The patriarchal aspect of the Ṛg Vedic family does not need any emphasis. Desire is expressed for *prajā*, which might include both boys and girls. But really people were keen on having brave sons (*suvīrāḥ*) who might fight their wars. However, it would be wrong to exaggerate the patriarchal character of the Ṛg Vedic society. Although the term father or *pitā* is mentioned 335 times in the *Ṛg Veda*, the term mother or *mātā* is mentioned 234 times. Further, we have several goddesses which suggests the importance of woman. In some cases a woman could freely carry on love affairs. She could take part in sacrifices along with her husband, and some women are credited with the authorship of the Vedic mantras. Clearly in Ṛg Vedic times mother-right was not completely submerged by father-right, and women sat on several tribal assemblies.

Social classes either based on hereditary occupation or on the appropriation of the surplus produced by the peasants and artisans had not clearly emerged in the age of the *Ṛg Veda*. Members of the same family followed different occupations. In one case the father was a priest, the mother a grinder of corn, and the son a physician, and yet all lived together happily. The term *varṇa* is mentioned only 23 times in the *Ṛg Veda*, but not always in the sense of social class. Although warriors and priests tended to separate from the tribal fraternity the four varṇas did not exist as well-defined social classes. In the *Ṛg Veda* the term brāhmaṇa is mentioned 15 times and kṣatriya 9 times, and vaiśya and śūdra each only once. Although the power of the *rājanyas* is reflected in later Vedic texts, the term *rājanya* occurs only once in the *Ṛg Veda*, and that too in the tenth book. Naturally the political structure of the period is tribal, free from discrimination based on varṇa.

The subjection of defeated peoples caused inequality in Ṛg Vedic society. The conquerors acquired and maintained a large number of *dāsas*, especially women, whom they gave away to priests. The conquerors were possibly divided into the chiefly group equipped with chariots and the common tribal kinsmen who just followed their elders. This disparity contributed to the growth of the power of chiefs and was occasionally reflected in the structure of the Ṛg Vedic assemblies.

Given their material life and tribal structure, the Ṛg Vedic people were not capable of developing any advanced political system which can be called state either in the ancient Indian or the modern sense of the term. The land of the seven rivers, covering the area of the Punjab and parts of western U.P., was held by small tribal principalities, five of whom are known by the name of *pañcajanāḥ*. Although the term *rājan* is used for the Ṛg Vedic chiefs, the nature of the Ṛg Vedic kingship was basically the same as chiefship. It was not a territorial monarchy in which all the inhabitants of territory, rich or poor, high or low, regard the monarch as the symbol of authority over the country to which they belong. The Ṛg Vedic chiefs fought for cows and not for territory. The terms for territory are not common in that text. Although the term *jana* is used 275 times, the term *janapada* is not used even once. The term *rājya* occurs only once, and the word *rāṣṭra* figures 10 times in all. Only in the latest portions of the *Ṛg Veda*, in BK X, the king is asked to uphold the *rāṣṭra* or kingdom,[1] which suggests that the territorial idea appears at the end of the period. The term *grāma* occurs 13 times in the *Ṛg Veda*, but not in the sense of village. It meant a tribal unit mobilised for fighting, so that the *vrājapati*, who was in charge of the pasture grounds held in common by the tribe and who naturally led family heads to battle for capturing cows, became later identical with the *grāmaṇi*. The *grāmaṇi* was originally not the head of the village but of the tribal unit called *grāma*. He cannot be identified with any official whose title may suggest any territorial administration. All this is sufficient to demons-

1. *RV*, X.173.1 and 2.

trate that the Ṛg Vedic chiefs did not think in terms of territorial states.

The Ṛg Vedic kingship was primarily a tribal institution. The king or the *rājan* is repeatedly connected with the tribe. Basically he rules over his people or *jana* and is therefore called their protector, *gopa janasya* or *gopati janasya*. The terms *gopa* or *gopati* signify that human headship over the herds of cattle was gradually extended over the tribe or the people.

The tribal character is also disclosed by the application of Caidya to Kasu, of Sṛñjaya to Daivavāta, and of Uśīnarāni to the queen of Uśīnaras.[1] Princes and princesses were therefore known by the tribes to which they belonged.

The Ṛg Vedic king was one of the equals whose hereditary position was not beyond question. Several passages suggest that the king owed his office to the choice of his people. A passage from the tenth Book of the *Ṛg Veda* uses the simile "like subjects choosing their king."[2] The coronation hymn from the same Book suggests the acceptance of the king by all the tribe (*viśaḥ*).[3] Most references to the election of the king by the tribesmen are found in the *Atharva Veda*,[4] but it is obvious that the practice must have begun much earlier. The fact of formal sanction implied by the hymn shows that at the earlier stage the tribe elected its chief.

On the other hand some references suggest that kingship or chiefship was confined to certain families.[5] Trasadasyu inherited the kingship of his tribe from his grandfather, his father having lost his throne through an enemy attack. The family of Sudās had enjoyed chiefly authority for three generations. Thus actual examples do not confirm the practice of royal succession in one family for more than three generations. Evidently the principle of heredity from father to son, based on the law of primogeniture, was not established in the oldest period.[6] A similar situation obtained among the Grecian *genos* in the Homeric age. Clearly

1. Bandyopadhaya, *Development of Hindu Polity and Political Theories*, p. 85, fn.
2. X.124.8.
3. *viśastvā sarvā vāṃchaṃtu*, X.173. 1ff.
4. Quoted in K.P. Jayaswal, *Hindu Polity*, ch. XXIII, and Bandyopadhaya, op. cit., pp. 88-91.
5. Bandyopadhaya op. cit., p. 85.
6. Ibid., p. 86.

the law of primogeniture was not sharply defined in the age of the *Ṛg Veda*, and if it is not defined it is as good as none at all.

Lack of strong hereditary succession did not allow the chief to gather too much power. Royal or chiefly authority was circumscribed by the tribal assemblies, especially the *sabhā* and the *samiti*.[1] The *rājan* had also to reckon with the power and prestige of the *purohita* who accompanied him to battle and boosted his morale with spells and prayers. Several passages in the *Ṛg Veda* advise the king to give special attention and protection to the brāhmaṇa or priest, so that everything goes well with him and he wins the riches of his enemies and his kinsmen. But these pious wishes do not necessarily indicate royal dependence on priestly support; the days of priestly domination were yet to come.

But constant wars added to the power of the tribal chief, who consequently commanded the services of a large number of slaves (*dāsas*). Out of the spoils of war the *rājans* offered to the priests rich and varied presents consisting of cows, horses, chariots, blocks of gold and beautifully dressed women slaves. On their part the priests developed the system of a formal consecration and composed laudatory hymns called *dānastuti*, which enhanced the prestige of their patron and spread the myth of his supremacy among the conquered subjects and the fellow tribesmen alike.

Acquisition of cattle and slaves enabled the chiefs to live better than their clansmen. Perhaps they lived in good houses, but in spite of literary hyperboles we cannot visualise any grand buildings unless we come down to the Maurya period, which ushers in the use of burnt bricks in the country after their disuse for about 1500 years.

The resources and the technological knowledge of the Ṛg Vedic people could not support a large administrative machinery. Pastoral communities in the main, their primitive agriculture could not afford too many officials. The only surplus that could be disbursed for the maintenance of the king and his officials was received in the form of *bali*, literally offering. This term occurs several times in the *Ṛg Veda* in the sense of tribute to a prince or offering to a god.[2] In the former sense it forms part of

1. Supra, Ch. VIII.
2. I.70.9; V.1.10.

the compound *balihṛt*, paying tribute, which is applied to (king) Nahuṣa in the earlier portion and to the tribes in the latest portions of the *Ṛg Veda*.[1] The tribute was received in kind, probably from the conquered peoples as well as the clansmen of the chief. Hostile tribes defeated in battle were forced to pay *bali* or some kind of tribute. By its very nature this was obligatory, but there is nothing to show that it was regular. Tribesmen led to victory by their chiefs may have offered in gratitude voluntary presents to the latter, but these cannot be regarded as taxes which are assessed and collected regularly. The *Ṛg Veda* does not mention any official meant for collecting taxes, which form a vital organ of the state. Since the people were mainly pastoral, a part of the agricultural produce could not be regularly available.

Similarly although we come across a functionary called *senānī*, evidence for a regular standing army supported by the taxes collected by the king is lacking. The term *senā* is mentioned 20 times in the *Ṛg Veda*, but it seems to have been an *ad hoc* institution mobilised out of the tribesmen whenever occasion demanded it. Military functions were the main concern of the Vedic assemblies, attended by members of the tribe. Evidently tribal people were generally armed and mustered in times of need. Some of them who possessed chariots and possibly bronze weapons were better armed, but otherwise the distinction was not sharp. Those engaged in comparatively peaceful occupations such as *vrājapati*, head of the pasture ground, and *kulapā*, head of family, appear as military functionaries; the former led the latter to battle. The *grāmaṇī* also carried out a similar responsibility. The state therefore did not have permanent military officials to meet its military needs. Perhaps *purpatis*, commanders of mud forts or strongholds, would have some permanent responsibility for defence, otherwise the military organisation would be very simple.

Because of certain crimes arising out of the encroachment on private property it was necessary to have a few police officials. Forcible occupation of other's land is not mentioned, but cases of theft, burglary, highway robbery, cheating at grambling, and above all cattle lifting are reported. The king employed spies called *spasa* to keep an eye over the conduct of the people. *Ugra*[2]

1. VII.6.5; X.173.6.
2. *RV*, VII.38.6.2; X.97.11.

and *jīvagṛbha*[1] were probably officials meant for dealing with the criminals, and the *madhyamaśī* seems to have acted as a mediator in disputes.

However, punishments were not attended with such severity as appeared in later times. A wergeld of 100 cows had to be given for killing a man, and in cases of theft also the principle underlying the penality was to secure the satisfaction of the person who was wronged. In post-Vedic times theft was punished even with death, but in the Ṛg Vedic age the sanctity of private property had not reached the stage which would warrant such a drastic step. In short the coercive apparatus was not so well organised and oppressive in this period.

State officials whom we may describe as civil were not too many. About half a dozen functionaries such as the crowned queen known as *mahiṣī* (the powerful one),[2] the *purohita*, treasurer, the charioteer who originally distributed royal goods and favour, the *takṣan* (the carpenter whose implement was the axe)[3] and the *dūta*[4] or messenger are mentioned. All these appear in the list of *ratnins* in the later Vedic period. This also includes the Ṛg Vedic *senānī*, who was not without some civil functions. In view of the importance of chariots in the Ṛg Vedic state the charioteer occupies a high place even in the kernel of the *Ṛg Veda*. Nevertheless in this period we have a rudimentary apparatus to meet the bare minimum needs of government. We do not hear of any code of laws, which came to be embodied in the Dharmaśāstras in post-Vedic times; nor do we meet with any class of officers to administer justice. In spite of all talk of *ṛt* and *vrata* the Ṛg Vedic chief did not enforce any civil code overriding customary tribal law. Since the tribal assemblies functioned with vigour and looked after the tribal affairs, not much was left to the royal responsibility, and this accounts for a small number of officials.

As shown earlier, such tribal assemblies as the *sabhā*, *samiti*, *gaṇa* and *vidatha* played an important part in the life of the early Vedic people. The first two had definite political functions to perform, and the *rājan* could not run the government without

1. *RV*, X.97.22.
2. *RV*, V.37.3.
3. *VI*, i, 297.
4. Ibid., 371.

their support and co-operation. The third assembly was also not without political significance, but the political role of the fourth, namely the *vidatha*, cannot be precisely determined. In any case these tribal bodies practised a kind of direct democracy in which members made speeches and reached unanimous decisions. The need for organising successful wars dominated their deliberations. Every member was obviously a fighter who provided his own equipment and lived on a share of the spoils of war. Fighting wars was evidently the most important function of tribal assemblies, and Ṛg Vedic terms such as *grāma, grāmaṇi, senā, senānī*, etc., also underscore this aspect. The *gaṇa*, and particularly the *vidatha*, distributed the booty and whatever else was gathered and produced among the tribesmen. This prevented accumulation in the hands of the chief who could not grow very strong.

The political system deducible from a study of the *Ṛg Veda* does not measure up to the definition of the state. At best it was a tribal chieftainship, without the halo of monarchy, lacking in firm territorial basis, and devoid of taxation, standing army and permanent public officials, which all constitute the essential ingredients of the state in both the ancient Indian and modern sense. The chieftain owed his power to the support of the clan assemblies whose military functions forcibly strike our attention. In spite of primitive equipment and lack of standing army the Ṛg Vedic society was predominantly military in character.

II

The Later Vedic Phase: Transition to Class and Territorial Government

In some ways the material basis of the later Vedic society was strikingly different from that of Ṛg Vedic society. The Vedic people now shifted their scene of activity to western U.P., where they displaced, and imposed themselves on a copper-using people whose tools and weapons spread over this area are ascribed to 1700-1000 B.C. They may also have encountered some late Harappan and ochre-coloured pottery using people. Their expansion was facilitated by the use of iron tools and weapons, which have been discovered in good numbers at Atiranjikhera in Eta district of western U.P. and belong to the period around 1000 B.C. and are not later than 800 B.C. The later Vedic texts composed in the land of Kuru Pañcāla or western U.P. use the term *śyāma ayas* for iron. Iron technology enabled the Vedic people to spread as far as Videha in north Bihar by the end of the Vedic period. Although initially iron was used for war, it may also have helped jungle clearance and agriculture.

In association with iron objects at Atiranjikhera, and independently at many sites in western U.P. and the adjoining areas of the Panjab, Haryana, Delhi region and Rajasthan, numerous sherds of Painted Grey Ware have been found. Now there are nearly 700 PGW sites, indicative of settled communities inhabiting this area in 1000-500 B.C.

In association with iron objects at Atranjikhera, and independently at many sites in western U.P. and the adjoining areas of the Panjab, Haryana, Delhi and Rajasthan, and the two together occupied the whole of western U.P. The rulers no longer depended on uncertain tributes, but probably claimed a portion of agriçultural produce. Secure in their regular income they could support a good number of priests, who developed rituals that constitute our only important source for the profile of later Vedic polity.

Settled life created conditions for the differentiation of the Vedic people into four varṇas. Brāhmaṇas who originally formed one of the 16 classes of priests came on top, and, in the Vedic ritual texts they composed, claimed both social and political privileges. Śudras comprising both Āryan and pre-Āryan elements occupied an ambiguous position, which was echoed in both society and politics. Kṣatriyas functioned as rulers, and vaiśyas as the unwilling tribute payers. The influence of varṇa distinctions and that of the brāhmaṇas first comes to the fore in the political organs during later Vedic times.

In the early Vedic age women lost in importance because of constant fighting in a stage of mounted pastoralism. In the agricultural stage their inability to handle the plough driven by bullocks, though wooden ploughshares were used, made them all the less important. Family became more and more patriarchal. There appeared gotra restrictions on marriage with relations from father's side. Mother-right tended to be more and more undermined, and princes became polygamous; the

Aitareya Brāhmāṇa speaks of the hundred wives of king Hariścandra. The influence of the new family relations can be traced in the composition of the public bodies and the organs of the state.

The nature of kingship was transformed in this period. Rituals outlined in later Vedic texts resound with conflicts between the tribal and the territorial facets of the emerging kingship. The territory was thought to be fluctuating, and so the king was announced to the deities and the people by name, parentage and clan. Such rites as chariot-race, cattle-raid and game of dice are intended to demonstrate the supremacy of the royal candidate over his kinsmen. And the assembly (*pariṣad*) of the Pañcālas presided over by the king or the chiefs is named after the people and not after the country.

But gradually the territorial element asserted itself. The song of election from the *Atharva Veda* wishes that the *rāṣṭra* or the territory be held by the king and be made firm by the king Varuṇa, the god Bṛhaspati, Indra and Agni.[1] In later texts the very fact of performing an elaborate coronation ritual called *rājasūya* extending over two years shows the necessity of having a fixed place. In the Kuru-Pañcāla country the place where the royal seat was situated came to be known as the capital or *āsandīvat*. In the *ratnahavīṃṣi* ceremony the king had to approach dignitaries who lived in permanent dwellings. Several coronation formulas represent the king to be conscious of the territorial aspect of his position. According to a passage from the *Taittirīya Saṃhitā*, an early *Yajus* collection, the king is announced "in this tribe (*viś*)", "in this kingdom (*rāṣṭra*)"[2], which shows that the tribe and the geographical region occupied by it were becoming coeval. The same text adds that the partial performance of a ritual enables the king to attain the people (*viś*) but not the *rāṣṭra*, which can be achieved only by its full performance.[3] Further, a ceremony occurring in four versions of the *Yajus* collection symbolises the sovereignty of the king over the four quarters and the zenith.[4]

The latest Vedic texts have no doubt about the territorial

1. VI.88.2.
2. I.8.12.
3. II.3.1.
4. *VS*, X.10-14; *TS*, I.8.13; *KS*, XV.7; *MS*, II.6-10.

character of government. The *Aitareya Brāhmaṇa* enumerates ten forms of government or chieftainship prevalent in different parts of the country,[1] which shows that power was established in fixed areas. Some of these forms of government may have obtained among the non-Āryan tribal people not yet brought under Vedic influence. Though most terms used for these forms cannot be precisely defined for the Vedic period, *ekarāja* may mean a ruler whose authority was undisputed in his domains.[2] We may also note that the *Śatapatha Brāhmaṇa* calls the king *rāṣṭrabhṛt* or sustainer of the kingdom.[3]

Towards the end of the later Vedic period the territorial idea generated a sense of possession over the land. Hitherto the chief or the king distributed only the spoils of war, mainly cattle and women slaves, among the priests. Now he claimed to grant a part of the land with the consent of the clan.[4] Though this was rarely done in this period it is symptomatic of the new character of chiefdom or kingship.

The emergent social structure naturally left its stamp on polity. Since the territory was not always identical with the *viś* to which the king belonged but was inhabited by brāhmaṇas, rājanyas/kṣatriyas, vaiśyas and śūdras emerging out of the disintegration of the Vedic tribes and assimilation of non-Vedic peoples, it was found necessary to enlist the support of these social groups by means of a coronation ritual.[5] It is clear that the king now belonged to the kṣatriya class, and what really mattered to him was the support of the priests for domination over the mass of the people. The king is called the protector of the brāhmaṇas and the eater of the people.[6] Some rituals stress the supremacy of priests, and others the supremacy of warriors. But finally by means of a compromise both appear as the upholders of the existing order. The king has to give a pledge of standing by the law to the brāhmaṇa priest, and the *Śatapatha Brāhmaṇa* states that the king and the *śrotriya* together uphold the *dharma*.[7]

1. VIII.12 and 13.
2. *AB*, VIII.15.
3. IX.4.1.1.
4. *ŚB*, VII.1.1.4.
5. *VS*, X.10-14; *KS*, XV.7.
6. The terms used are *viśāmattā* and *brāhmaṇānāṃ goptā*. *AB*, VIII.17.
7. V.4.4.5.

Though coronation rituals recall the original election of the king, the *Aitareya Brāhmaṇa* prescribes formulas for securing kingship for one, two and three generations.[1] A formula from the *Śatapatha Brāhmaṇa* extends it to ten generations.[2] We also come across the term *rājaputra*, which can be interpreted as the king's son in many cases. Examples of kingship for several generations can be produced. Thus kingship or chiefship had become hereditary in this period.

The other feature that developed in this age was the association of divine elements with the king. There is hardly any piece of evidence of the type in the *Ṛg Veda*, but the consecration ceremonies of the later Vedic texts invoke different gods to endow the king with their respective qualities, and sometimes even represent him as a god.

The later Vedic polity marks the firm beginnings of two important organs of the state, taxation system and administrative machinery. Stable agriculture made available moderate surplus in kind. The term devourer of the people (*viśāmattā*)[3] used for the king shows that he lived on tributes collected from his kinsmen and others. We hear of an official called *bhāgadugha*, who distributed shares on behalf of the chief. In western U.P. this would be a portion of wheat, rice and other cereals mentioned in the later Vedic texts. The association of this functionary with Puṣan, the god of the herdsmen who later became agriculturists, may suggest that these shares were given to the peasants, probably in ceremonial feasts.

Availability of tributes led to an increase in the number of administrative functionaries during this period. At least 12 of the ratnins seem to have been officials, who were evidently supported out of the taxes collected by the state. They were not concerned with the prevention of crimes but with certain positive functions possibly inherited from tribal bodies. Thus they looked after metal working, chariot making, meat supplying, chariot driving, etc. Such artisanal and other functions can be better appreciated in the context of the material basis of the society whose part they formed. Further, several of them were associated with the distribution of game, cattle, land, cereals,

1. VIII.7.
2. *SB*, XII.9.3.1 and 3.
3. *AB*, VIII.17.

etc. The continued practice of distribution cut down social inequality and hence obstructed the strengthening of the chiefly authority. Perhaps the ratnins were members of the chief's entourage and did not constitute what may be called public servants independent of it. They included the *purohita* or the chief priest, who occupied the first place in several lists.

For the greater length of the later Vedic period the *senānī* seems to have been a minor functionary, which would mean that the standing army remained in the background. But since the *senānī* heads the list of the ratnins in the *Śatapatha Brāhmaṇa* it shows that the army emerged as an important element towards the end of the Vedic period, a fact also supported by the inclusion of the makers and drivers of chariots in the list of the ratnins. However, even at this stage the army was confined to the kinsmen. The Kuru king is surrounded by sixty-four ever-ready warriors who are his sons and grandsons.[1] But when the Pañcāla king performs a rite, there arise six thousand and thirty-three warriors clad in mail.[2] This conventional figure might include soldiers outside the royal kin. In this sense the later Vedic period perhaps marks the beginning of royal body guards.

Of the development of the internal coercive machinery such as the police system the later Vedic texts give no idea. Probably the police officers of the Ṛg Vedic period continued to function. The king's claim to banish the brāhmaṇa, to overpower the vaiśya and to beat the śūdra could not materialise without a coercive apparatus. It is thought that references to the *sthapati* and *śatapati* indicate the beginnings of a regular system of provincial administration,[3] but these officials find no place in the list of ratnins nor does the *adhikṛta* who is regarded as a village officer appointed by the king.[4]

The rise of territorial states made it difficult for the popular assemblies to function in the old way. People from different parts of the kingdom would find it very much inconvenient to come together. Only those who could afford and lived at the capital could gather easily. The rulers were also faced with the difficulty of giving place to non-Vedic peoples. All this gave an

1. *AB*, III.48 (sons and grandsons of Vṛddhadyumna).
2. *ŚB*, XIII.5.4.16.
3. H.C. Raychaudhuri, *An Advanced History of India*, i (1958), 44.
4. *Praśna Upaniṣad* quoted, ibid., 45.

aristocratic tinge to the *sabhā* and *samiti*, which came to be monopolised by the male gender; women were now completely excluded from these bodies. The popular assemblies lost some of their activities to new officials and became attenuated in both functions and composition.

In retrospect the later Vedic polity, although far more developed in royal power and administrative structure than the Ṛg Vedic polity, fell sort of the *saptāṅga* theory of the state. Really it represents a phase of transition from tribal organisation to varṇa and territorial organisation, under male domination; the process was nearing completion towards the end of the Vedic period.

III

The Pre-Maurya Phase : Territorial Monarchies and Tribal Oligarchies

The available sources for the period relate either to north-east or to north-west India. Their comparative silence about the land of the Kuru-Pañcālas or western U.P., which played a prominent part in the politics of later Vedic times, suggests that it lapsed into abscurity in the age of the Buddha. The widespread use of iron in eastern U.P. and western Bihar, as evidenced from excavations at Rajghat (Banaras), Chirand (Chapra) and Khairadih (Balia) led to the formation of large territorial states which were better equipped militarily and in which the warrior class played the main role. New agricultural tools and implements enabled the peasants to produce a good amount of surplus, which not only met the needs of the ruling class but also supported numerous towns. Excavations show Rajgir, Vaiśālī, Rajghat, Chirand, and Kauśāmbī to be urban settlements of the sixth century B.C., although Śrāvastī belongs to a later period. Thus around 500 B.C. we notice a modest beginning of town life in north-eastern India, giving rise to new problems of administration. Further, these material sinews helped the expansion of Ujjain, Kosala and Magadha, which incorporated non-Vedic areas and peoples into their kingdoms with the result that they became less homogenous.

The period introduced the earliest use of coins, made of copper or silver. From around 500 B.C. onwards the punch-marked coins came definitely into use, which naturally facilitated internal transactions and trade. An important commodity for the market was the Northern Black Polished Ware, evidently fashionable with the upper classes of society. On the one hand trade and industry constituted a profitable source of income to the state, and on the other it gave rise to a class of merchants, called seṭṭhis, who could not be ignored in society and politics.

The rise of large states with towns as their base of operations strengthened the territorial idea. A passage from Pāṇini shows that people owed allegiance to the *janapada* or the territory to which they belonged. Later the term *janapada* becomes an important qualification for the recruitment of high officials in the *Arthaśāstra* of Kauṭilya.

The new material and social situation led to the rapid development of such state organs as army and taxation system. But it also gave rise to some abortive reaction in favour of the old tribal order, leading to the republican experiment.

Most kingdoms of the period, of which Kosala and Magadha were the most powerful, were ruled by hereditary monarchs belonging to the kṣatriya varṇa. The term "kingmaker" is used in Pāṇini, and some Jātaka stories refer to the expulsion of the king and his chief priest by the people, but occasions of election or dismissal were rare. The king enjoyed the highest social status and special protection of his person and property. He yielded ground to only such religious leaders as the Buddha.

We hear of officials, both high and low. High functionaries were called *mahāmātras* in the early Pāli texts. Employed in different capacities as multipurpose officers *mantrin*, *senānāyaka*, judge, chief accountant (*gaṇaka*), and head of the royal harem, they formed a cadre of officers. Although the designation *mahāmātra* is not known to the law-books, *āyuktas*, and *amātyas* may have discharged corresponding functions in the Dharmasūtra set-up.

The office of the advisers or the ministers of the king first appears in this period, and Vassakāra of Magadha and Dīrgha Cārāyaṇa of Kosala were effective and influential advisers. There is nothing to show that high officers or ministers belonged to the clan of the king; from the beginning the priestly community formed the recruiting ground for these offices.

In both Kosala and Magadha revenues of villages were granted not only to influential brāhmaṇas but also to seṭṭhis. This did not require the consent of the clan, as we find in later Vedic texts.

But administrative rights, which become subjects of grants in inscriptions of north India since the 3rd or the 4th century A.D., were not conferred on the beneficiaries at this stage.

In the countryside things were managed by the village headman. Originally functioning as leaders of tribal regiments, the *grāmaṇī* was called *vaiśya-grāmaṇī* in late Vedic texts. Once tribal contingents settled down to agriculture the *grāmaṇī* was naturally transformed into a village headman. Really the period marked the beginnings of the village organisation presided over by the village headman, called variously as *gāmabhojaka*, *grāmaṇi* or *grāmika*. 80,000 *grāmikas* are said to have been summoned by Bimbisāra. Although conventional, this number suggests the widespread prevalence of the institution and the importance of the village headman, who was directly linked with the king. Apparently village headmen were responsible for the assessment and collection of taxes and maintenance of law and order in their locality, and sometimes oppressive headmen were taken to task by the villagers.

The real increase in statepower in the period is not so much indicated by the elaboration of the administrative apparatus for civil functions as by the formation of a standing army on a solid basis. The growing prominence given to army is suggested by the exalted place of the *senānāyaka* in the list of high functionaries. At the time of Alexander's invasion the king of the Gangaridae and Prasii, obviously the Nanda ruler of Magadha, kept 20,000 cavalry, 200,000 infantry, 2,000 four-horsed chariots and 3,000-6,000 elephants. Chariots were gradually losing their importance not only in north-eastern but also in north-western India where they were introduced by the Āryans.

The most striking difference in the composition of the army between Magadha and north-western India lay in the use of elephants, of which fewer are mentioned in the later case. As regards cavalry the king of Assakenos (part of Swat and Buner) possessed 20,000 cavalry, as many as the Magadhan king did. It is therefore evident that the possession of elephants gave an edge to the Magadhan monarchy.

How this Magadhan army was organised and supported we have no means to tell. Apparently this large standing army was financed by the enormous wealth of the Nandas for which they were traditionally famous. But we have no idea of the specific measures which brought money. Doubtless the fiscal system was now established on a firm basis. Warriors and priests—kṣatriyas and brāhmaṇas—were exempted from payment of taxes, and the main brunt was borne by the peasants, mainly vaiśyas. Gautama makes us assume that in the beginning the royal share was 1/12th of the produce, but gradually it settled down to 1/6th. Members of the upper varṇas could use the labour power of the śūdras. Taxes were collected directly by royal agents with the help of the village headman, and discoveries of numerous hoards of punch-marked coins would suggest considerable payment in cash. In north-eastern India payment was made in paddy, as would appear from Buddhist texts. Peasants were further subjected to corvée for royal work.

In addition to peasants, we find taxpayering artisans and traders. According to the law-books the first were made to work once a month for the king, and the second had to pay taxes on the sale of their commodities, which were collected by the toll officer known as *śaulkika* in the Dharmasūtras and *śulkādhyakṣa* in the Pāli texts. The new arrangement was a natural sequel to the rise of urban economy.

The Indian legal and judicial system originated in this period. The old tribal custom was found inadequate to deal with the problems arising out of the differentiation of the relatively egalitarian community into sharply-defined social ranks with privileges and disabilities. So the Dharmasūtras laid down the duties of each one of the four varṇas and based a great deal of civil and criminal law on varṇa division. Civil law was administered by the *vyāvahārika mahāmātra* and criminal by royal agents, who inflicted rough and ready punishments such as scourging, beheading, tearing out the tongue, breaking ribs, etc. The police and magistracy set up for dealing with offences against person and property seem to have been rudimentary, and village headmen performed both fiscal and police functions.

But the development did not quite supplant the old tribal and family law although it superseded the old in many respects. Further, non-Vedic tribal groups and regions incorporated into the brāhmaṇical social order and the monarchical set-up were on the one hand given fictitious social origins and on the other conceded the right to be governed by their own customs, some of which are quoted in the *Baudhāyana Dharmasūtra*. This recognition served as a precedent for new urban occupations organised into guilds, which, though of not the same nature as tribal groups, were permitted to observe their own laws.

Whether guilds had any important hand in urban administration in this period cannot be said. The evidence of the Jātakas might refer to a later period, and the earlier Pāli texts such as the Nikāyas and *Vinaya Piṭaka* contain very little on this point. In spite of the rise of towns since c. 500 B.C. no reliable picture of their administration can be reconstructed until we come to the Maurya period.

The monarchies of the period no longer enjoyed assistance of the *sabhā* and *samiti*. The disappearance of popular assemblies in post-Vedic times needs a word of explanation. Essentially tribal in their origin, these bodies decayed and disappeared as tribes and clans disintegrated into varṇas and lost their identity. The process started with the end of the Vedic period when these assemblies were already in a state of decline. Now their place was taken by caste associations, whose laws and customs came to be taken into account by the writers of law-books but whose activity was confined to social matters. No effort was made to place the tribal assemblies on a territorial basis, as was done by Cleisthenes in Athens in the 5th century B.C. Popular assemblies could succeed only in small territories such as those of the Vedic period. With the emergence of the large states of Kosala and Magadha and the difficulty of communications regular meetings became impossible. Being tribal the old assemblies could not accommodate many non-Vedic peoples who lived in the new kingdoms. The changed circumstances therefore did not favour the continuance of the old political order. So although we hear of the *samiti* of the Pañcālas in later Vedic times, we do not hear of any popular assembly of their successors. Instead the Dharmasūtras provide for a new small body called *pariṣad* consisting exclusively of the brāhmaṇas. Assemblies there were, but in the smaller republican states of the Śākyas, Licchavis, etc.

The republican experiment is a distinctive feature of the pre-Maurya polity. The republics are found either in the Indus basin or in the foothills of the Himalayas in U.P. and Bihar. The first may have been remnants of Vedic tribes, although in some cases monarchies or chiefdoms seem to have been followed by republics. The second may have been breakaway states from parent chiefdoms or monarchies in U.P. and Bihar. Their defection may have been inspired by the old ideal of tribal equality, which may have been fostered by smaller chiefs and their kinsmen.

In all cases real power lay in the hands of tribal oligarchies, which had assumed caste characteristics. In the republics of the Śākyas and Licchavis the ruling class belonged to the same clan and same varṇa. It is doubtful whether the brāhmaṇas sat on the republican assemblies which met in the motehalls. But in post-Maurya times in the republican states of the Mālavas and Kṣudrakas, they also were given citizenship from which slaves and hired labourers were excluded. Alexander's companions noticed a state on the Beas, whose membership was restricted to those who could supply at least one elephant to the state. This may be taken as the most typical example of an oligarchy in the Indus basin.

The administrative machinery of the Śākyas and Licchavis was simple and rudimentary, consisting as it did of a *rājā*, *uparājā*, *senāpati* and *bhāṇḍāgārika*. A fifth century A.D. allusion in a Buddhist commentary to a hierarchy of seven courts meant for trying the same case is too late and too idealised to carry credence.

Several differences marked out the republics from the monarchies. In Magadha and Kosala the king claimed to be the sole recepient of revenue from the peasants, but in the republics this claim was advanced by every tribal chief, by each one of the 7707 Licchavi kings who maintained their store-houses. According to a Jātaka this may also have been the case with 60,000 khattiyas in the capital of the Ceta state, all of whom were styled princes (*rājāno*).[1] Similarly a monarchy maintained its regular standing army to the exclusion of armed rivals or competitors within its borders, but in a tribal oligarchy each *rājā* felt happy with his own little army under his *senāpati* or with his elephants and competed with the other. Brāhmaṇas had no place in the early republics nor did they recognise these states in their law-books. Finally, what evidently distinguished the republics was the functioning of assemblies, which languished and disappeared in the new monarchies.

1. *Jāt.*, vi, 513-17; cf. V.S. Agrawala, "The Janapada and the Greek City-State", *IHQ*, xxx, 46.

The republican tradition became feeble from the Maurya period onwards. Even in pre-Maurya times the monarchic factor was far stronger. The significance of the pre-Maurya period lay in evolving the military, fiscal and judicial organs to meet the new social, economic and political situation in the large territorial kingdoms in Bihar, Uttar Pradesh and the adjacent areas.

CHAPTER XXIII

STAGES IN ANCIENT INDIAN POLITY: MAURYA AND LATER

I

The Maurya Phase: Centralised Bureaucratic Interlude

The archaeology of the Maurya period shows the flowering of towns on a large scale in north India. To this period belong most urban settlements with the usual complex of Northern Black Polished Ware and punch-marked coins, in whose history the Maurya age marks a period of culmination. The punch-marked coins account for the largest number of hoards associated with any coin series in ancient India, and although these range from *c.* 500 B.C. to *c.* 100 B.C. most coins can be attributed to Maurya times. This naturally gave a great impetus to trade and industry, whose problems occupied the attention of the Maurya state and also enabled the government to pay its employees in cash. The Maurya settlements show considerable use of burnt bricks, which, although as old as Harappa in north-western India, are not noticeable in north-eastern India before the Maurya age.[1] Obviously this new housing material facilitated widespread urban settlements and lent them stability. Discoveries of iron ploughshare, sickles and other implements demonstrate the advanced technological knowledge, which was employed in erecting free-standing monolithic polished pillars. Kauṭilya speaks of reclamation of virgin land, opening of new trade routes and control of trade and industry, and Megasthenes testifies to the interest of the Maurya state in agriculture, irrigation, and in the regulation of economic activities in the capital. Aśokan inscriptions suggest the large-scale employment of masons, artisans and labourers all over India for hewing out pillars, polishing them and carrying them to the right place. Thus whatever might be the reasons the vast economic activities of the government are evident. These naturally left their impact on administration, leading to the creation of an elaborate establishment.

1. Claims are made for their find in Kauśāmbī in pre-Maurya times.

The capital fact of the Maurya political history was the establishment of the Magadhan empire covering the whole of India except the far south. Won by force it could be maintained by force, which was necessary for external defence and internal peace. Internal peace may have been threatened from above by the supporters of old dynasty and from below by the new elements in urban population. The state also faced the wrath of the peasants because the term *prakṛti-kopa* is used by Kauṭilya. Tribal peoples living within and on the frontiers of the empire were a source of constant headache. All this required a huge professional army and an efficient system of criminal administration, for supporting which new sources of revenue had to be tapped.

The *Arthaśāstra* of Kauṭilya exalts royal power. According to a verse from it royal order supersedes all the other sources of authority including *dharma*. Royal order has to be in accordance with the *dharma*, for the king has to promulgate *dharma*, when the organisation based on the four varṇas perishes. This teaching of Kauṭilya may not belong to the Maurya period, but Aśoka's edicts give clear proof of the all-pervading character of royal orders touching even the social and religious life of the people.

The state tried to control all spheres of life because of the long arms given to it by its vast bureaucracy. If we rely on the *Arthaśāstra* of Kauṭilya the establishment of a large and complex bureaucracy would appear to be a remarkable feature of the Maurya government. At one place Kauṭilya mentions 18 *tīrthas* who are probably called *mahāmātras*[1] or high functionaries. Although the term *mahāmātra* is used only on a few occasions in the *Arthaśāstra* its real counterpart being *amātya* it is familiar enough in Aśokan inscriptions. A few classes of *mahāmātras* are known to the *Vinaya Piṭaka*, but their number is multiplied by Aśoka in whose empire they served in every great city and district. They were employed in both urban and rural administration and in the border administration. But above all they functioned as *dharmamahāmātras*, enforcing the social and political order ushered in by Aśoka.

In addition to the 18 *tīrthas* Kauṭilya provides in some detail for 27 superintendents (*adhyakṣas*) concerned mostly with

1. *AŚ*, I.13.

economic functions and some military duties though social functions are not ignored. There is nothing common between the officers in this list and those occurring in the list of the *tīrthas*, which suggests that two different traditions have been put together. The other possibility is that *tīrthas* are higher functionaries and do not include *adhyakṣas*, for the pay roll mentions most *tīrthas* but only a few *adhyakṣas*. Further, we hear of several other officers such as *gopa sthānika*, *dharmastha*, *nāgaraka*, etc., who do not find place in any of the three lists mentioned above, and yet they are assigned important functions. How far the *Arthaśāstra* lists reflect the real state of officers is difficult to say. But surely the various lists indicate a tendency to increase the number of officials, which is also broadly supported by the mention of several magistrates by Megasthenes and of a dozen categories of officials in Aśokan inscriptions.

Although Megasthenes and Aśokan inscriptions have nothing to say on rules of recruitment, Kauṭilya lays down certain qualifications for the cadre of high officers known as *amātyas*, the emphasis being on noble birth. From this cadre are to be selected such high officers as *samāhartā*, *sannidhātā* and *dharmastha*, provided they pass certain tests. Thus although no competitive examinations are recommended rules of recruitment do suggest some kind of bureaucratic organisation.

That this bureaucracy was highly hierarchical is suggested by the pay scale for different categories of employees. The highest functionaries such as the *mantrin*, *purohita*, *senāpati* and *yuvarāja* are paid generously as much as 48,000 paṇas, paṇa being a silver coin with a silver content equal to 3/4th of a tolā.[1] In contrast the lowest officials are recommended 60 *paṇas* in the consolidated pay list given in the section on *bhṛtyabharaṇīyam* (V. 3), but at other places they are given as small a pittance as only 10 or 20 paṇas. The ratio therefore would work out at 1:4800, which indicates an enormous gap between the highest and the lowest class of government servants. What is more important for us is that it shows a pyramidical bureaucratic structure. All told the Mauryas created a singular bureaucratic machinery, which does presuppose a large empire and a considerable amount of surplus in cash and kind for its support. It may not be regarded rational

1. R.P. Kangle, *The Kauṭilya Arthaśāstra*, iii, 208.

in the modern sense of the term, but it is not patrimonial either for it was not a part of the royal household.

Bureaucracy formed the arm of the royal power, but the crucial factor that contributed to it was the development of the coercive power of the state on an unprecedented scale. According to Justin Candragupta Maurya possessed 600,000 troops, which was thrice the number of infantry possessed by the Nandas. The usual limbs, the infantry, the cavalry, the chariots and the elephants were strengthened by the addition of two wings, the navy, and transport and commissariat,—a development suggested by both Megasthenes and Kauṭilya. The power of sword was strengthened by the royal monopoly of arms and control over artisans who produced weapons.

The army may have been occasionally used to put down internal revolts, but if we rely on the *Arthaśāstra* of Kauṭilya the Mauryas developed the first efficient system of police and criminal administration buttressed by an elaborate system of espionage. The *kaṇṭakaśodhana* was organised to deal with a large number of economic crimes typical of an urban environment. Many of its provisions are directed against the activities of artisans and traders who used false weights and measures and demanded high prices. The organisation of criminal administration, so characteristic of Kauṭilya, does not show any trace of external influence, and was evidently an indigenous phenomenon. Similar is the case with various categories of spies, who were employed to keep an eye and report on the criminal and anti-government activities of the people.

However, the officers who were charged with the administration of criminal law and investigation of crimes were not exclusively police officers in the modern sense of the term. The nearest approach to a modern police-cum-magisterial officer was the *pradeṣṭā*, but he had also some revenue functions. On the other hand the *samāhartā*, the *sthānika* and the *gopa*, who had mainly fiscal functions, were also assigned some police and magisterial duties.

The growing economic activities of the state and needs of urban settlements led to the creation of a machinery for town administration, of which we do not hear much in pre-Maurya times. The municipal administration of Pāṭaliputra described by Megasthenes does show the concern of the government for certain basic urban problems such as sanitation, care of foreigners, registration of births and deaths, etc., which also receive the attention of Kauṭilya. Kauṭilya does not give any indication of the association of the local elements with town administration, which is imposed from above. He lays down in detail the duties of the *nāgaraka*, probably identical with the *nagaravyāvahārika* of Aśokan inscriptions. The *nāgaraka* is charged with the maintenance of law and order and with the supervision of sanitation arrangements. In view of the widespread use of wooden structures, remnants of which have been discovered at the Maurya sites at Patna, an important duty of the *nāgaraka* was to take measures against outbreaks of fire.

The *nāgaraka* had under him subordinate officials called *sthānika* and *gopa*, who were placed in charge of the wards into which the town was divided and maintained records of the number of houses. These two officials are first mentioned in connection with the rural revenue administration. Apparently the rural system of administration was projected on to the urban areas to meet their needs, the *nāgaraka* being the only officer typical of the urban areas.

The Maurya rural administration, as can be inferred from the *Arthaśāstra* of Kauṭilya, was mainly designed to meet the needs of revenue administration. The *samāhartā*, head of the *janapada*, was primarily responsible for assessment of revenue, in which he was assisted by the *sthānika* and *gopa* who carried out an elaborate census for the purpose. These officials not only assessed and collected revenues but also enforced law and order. Along with the *pradeṣṭā* they combined in their hands revenue, police and magisterial functions.

Aśoka introduced an element of moderation in his border administration and in his dealings with the tribal peoples. The *antamahāmātras* were asked to persuade the border peoples to conform to *dharma*, rules of peaceful social conduct such as obeying the king and elders and desisting from violence. But if they did not observe those rules they were threatened with punishments. It is claimed by Aśoka in his Kandhar inscriptions that this policy really succeeded with the people.

The Maurya period constitutes a landmark in the evolution of the system of taxation in ancient India. Kauṭilya introduces us to new taxes to be collected from the rural and urban areas, from peasants and from artisans and traders. All this required a strong and efficient machinery for assessment, collection and storage. An Aśokan inscription mentions tax concession and some other Maurya epigraphs indicate the presence of rural store-houses. These granaries stored taxes in kind, and helped people in times of distress. However Kauṭilya considers assessment more important than storage and depositing. The harm done to the state by the *samāhartā*, the highest officer in charge of assessment, is thought to be more serious than that caused by the *sannidhātā*, the chief custodian of the state treasury and storehouse. Thus the assessment machinery really seems to have appeared in the Maurya period.

The list of taxes and imposts in the *Arthaśāstra* is impressive, and if these were really collected they must have proved oppressive. But even all these were not considered adequate to meet the needs of the exchequer, which had to finance the vast military and bureaucratic establishments. These therefore had to be supplemented by the reclamation of the virgin land, exploitation of mines and the running of goldsmith's shops, liquor shops and weaving concerns, all done under the aegis of the state.

What has been stated above will show that the Maurya government was highly centralised. We have no direct evidence of the functioning of the village councils in this period, although guilds enjoyed some autonomy and some local elements may have participated in the administration of Pāṭaliputra. Probably Aśoka shared powers with the *pariṣad* and so did some of his provincial governors, but all this did not result in much decentralisation. However, the *Arthaśāstra* of Kauṭilya shows a few traits of decentralisation. In new settlements tax-free lands are to be granted to priests, preceptors, the *purohita* and other learned brāhmaṇas as well as to superintendents and some village servants of lower classes.[1] Nevertheless such gift lands are inalienable,[2] and the grant of a whole village to an officer is not recommended.[3] Again, the detailed provisions regarding *parihāras* or remissions from various kinds of revenue in gift villages to be allowed to peasants, etc., have in view the augmentation of the state revenue and not the reward of religious

1. *AŚ*, II.1.
2. Ibid.
3. Ibid., V.3.

beneficiaries as characterised the *parihāras* of the early centuries of the Christian era under the Sātavāhanas and Pallavas. However, the one single factor that worked for decentralisation in the later part of the Maurya empire was large executive and judicial powers granted by Aśoka to the *rājukas*, who were placed over hundreds and thousands of people.

Elements of decentralisation have a subordinate place in the Maurya polity. Our sources convey the impression of centralised bureaucratic control, which is consistent with the vast empire and expanding economic activities of the Mauryas. This together with a well organised police and military system and revenue machinery helped to strengthen royal power, which manifested itself in *śāsana*. Kauṭilya instructs the king to keep the power of the treasury and army in his own hands.[1] Since these two vital organs seem to be very well-established in the Maurya age, they would give enormous powers to the king who wielded them.

Several reasons suggest that royal control penetrated a very large area, at least in the core of the empire. This was because of the strategic position of Pāṭaliputra, from where royal agents could sail up and down the four directions. Besides this, the royal road ran from Pāṭaliputra to Nepal through Vaiśālī and Champaran. We also hear of a road at the foothills of the Himalayas. It passed from Vaiśalī through Champaran to Kapilavastu, Kalsi (in Dehradun district), Hazara and eventually to Peshawar. Megasthenes speaks of a road connecting north-western India with Patna. Roads also linked Patna with Sasaram and from there they went to Mirzapur and central India. The Aśokan pillars were manufactured in the sandstone quarry of Chunar near Banaras, and transported from there to the different parts of the empire. The Maurya capital was connected with Kalinga by a route through eastern Madhya Pradesh, and Kalinga in its turn was linked with Andhra and Karnataka. All this facilitated transport in which horses may have played an important part. In the northern plains the Ganga and other rivers were routes of communication.

The location of Aśokan inscriptions on important highways suggests that Maurya control over the settled parts of the country may have matched that of the Mughals and perhaps of the East

1. *AŚ*, VIII. 2.

India Company. Medieval transport improved due to more settlements on the highways and the use of stirruped horses. The Company had the advantage of better guns which was reinforced by steam navigation from early 1830s onwards.

It is argued that the Mauryan polity was based on the Achaemenid and Ptolemid model. Borrowings in Aśokan architecture and inscriptions and the Persian rule on the north-western borders of India may suggest the possibility of the Achaemenid influences on the Indian system of government. But it would be too much to think that the absolutist, internal government outlined in the *Arthaśāstra* was a ready-made import from outside. Really it was the culmination of forces and processes visible in pre-Maurya times. Even if the inspiration was exogenous the change was induced from inside. Āpastamba, a pre-Maurya lawgiver, advises the king to found the capital city, and Vasiṣtha asks him to appoint officers to look after the harem. This reminds us of the colonisation policy and the appointment of *strīadhyakṣa* recommended by Kauṭilya.

The Jātakas hold the king responsible even for such things as want of rain, non-availability of bridegroom for the daughter and calamity befalling the oxen of a farmer. These are obviously things over which the king had no control, but as head of the community he was seen as a performer of all those functions which once pertained to the office of a tribal chief. From this the state control of various activities recommended by Kauṭilya was not a far cry.

The main reason for the exaltation of royal power lay in the growing importance of the warrior class from pre-Maurya times onwards. The consistent policy of aggrandisement followed by Magadha steeled the warriors and brought them to the fore. The new situation is recognised by Kauṭilya and Aśoka, both of whom try to undermine brāhmaṇical influence in politics, religion and society. Since priestly power was the only important check on royal authority, what it lost was a gain to royal power.

II

The Post-Maurya Phase: Divinity and Decentralisation

The initiative taken by the Maurya state in opening new regions to trade and agriculture bore fruition in post-Mauyra times. The real significance of the Maurya rule lay in spreading the use of coins, Northern Black Polished Ware, and advanced knowledge of iron technology in the Deccan and other peripheral areas outside the pale of the brāhmaṇical culture. This paved the way for the rise of a large number of towns in the Deccan, as is borne out by excavations and inscriptions. People used coins of lead, potin and silver, which have been discovered in large quantities. This facilitated internal transactions and promoted foreign trade with Central Asia, South-East Asia and above all with Rome, whose gold coins have been discovered in large hoards south of the Vindhyas. In the north we have the gold coins of the Kuṣāṇas, and, what is more important for ordinary transactions, we have a large number of their copper coins. Naturally never before and after inscriptions speak of so many guilds of artisans and merchants in ancient India, especially in the Deccan. All this left its mark on the Śaka-Sātavāhana polity.

The social and religious setting of the post-Maurya period cannot be ignored. The indigenous ruling houses of the Śuṅgas, Kaṇvas and Sātavāhanas appear to have made it an age of triumphant brāhmaṇism, although with the artisans and merchants in the Deccan and with some rulers from outside such as the Greeks and Kuṣāṇas Buddhism seems to have been popular. Land grants had to be made to both brāhmaṇas and Buddhists to keep them going. By ascribing divine attributes to the king the brāhmaṇas created a fertile soil for the germination of foreign ideas on divinity brought by the Scythians. They also converted some indigenous kings into zealous champions of the social and political order advocated by the early law-books. Moreover, they compiled the law-book of Manu which not only served as their Magna Carta but also legalised the wide proliferation of the caste system. According to Manu the mixed castes numbered around sixty, nearly five times more than their number in Maurya times. Since the caste absorbed and governed a large area of the activities of its members little was left for the government to take care of unless it concerned itself with inter-caste conflicts or certain criminal offences of which the caste could not take cognizance.

The fall of the Maurya empire led to the revival of a few republics in Rajasthan and the Punjab, but their coins show a progressive tendency towards monarchisation. Essentially it was an age of small monarchies or chieftainships, the Sātavāhanas and the Kuṣāṇas being the only two large kingdoms, which entered into feudatory relations with smaller kings. Such an organisation was needed by the Sātavāhanas, who were improvised brāhmaṇas ruling over semi-brāhmaṇised or non-brāhmaṇised chiefs in the Deccan and South. For the Seythians, who came from Central Asia, it was all the more natural. The Sātavāhanas therefore had several feudatories such as the Mahārathīs, Ikṣvākus, etc., who set up their independent states on the ruins of the rule of their overlord. The titles adopted by the Kuṣāṇa kings indicate the existence of many lesser kings and *ṣāhis*, who paid homage and tribute to the paramount power and rendered it military service. Clearly the Sātavāhanas and Kuṣāṇas did not exercise effective direct control over such a large part of the country as the Mauryas did.

A second facıor leading to decentralisation was the grant of fiscal rights to Buddhist and brāhmaṇa beneficiaries. This was typical of the Sātavāhana rule in the Deccan, for although the term *akṣayanīvi*, inexhaustible deposit, is used in Kuṣāṇa inscriptions, land grants according to this tenure are found only later in Gupta times. Lands or villages granted for religious purposes enjoyed *parihāras*, or concessions which included exemption from the entry of royal agents, policemen and soldiers. To this extent the beneficiaries were free to manage village affairs and to maintain law and order there. They formed semi-independent administrative pockets in the countryside and probably also impressed upon the rural people the necessity of observing social laws and obeying the king, who was credited with some divine attributes.

The post-Maurya polity is distinguished by the functioning of almost autonomous governments in nearly a dozen cities in the second and first centuries B.C. Guilds of traders belonging to these cities issued coins (although of copper), which is ordinarily done by sovereign powers. The term *nigama* is clearly mentioned in five pre-Indo-Greek coins, 4 of them bearing the names of the different quarters of Taxila,[1] and the term *pañca-nigama* is found in a sixth coin[2] from Taxila. It is evident that on

1. John Allan, *Catalogue of the Coins of Ancient India*, pp. xxcvii, 214-16.
2. Ibid., p. 216.

the eve of the Greek occupation of Taxila its government was carried on either by a single corporation of artisans and merchants or by a joint body comprising five corporations. The practice also prevailed in Kauśāmbī which is known as *nigama* on one of its coins.[1] Coins of the guild of the *gandhikas*, literally perfumers but really general merchants, have been also found in the region around Kauśāmbī.[2] In such cities as Tripurī, Māhiṣmatī, Vidiśā, Eran, Bhagilā, Mādhyamikā, Vemaka, Vārāṇasī, etc., whose names occur on their copper coins, the corporate existence of each one is evident, but how they were governed is not clear. Although the term *nigama* does not occur in their coins, the cities probably emerged as autonomous entities on the disintegration of the Maurya empire and before the rise of the Śaka and Kuṣāṇa power. At no stage in early Indian history do we find cities or its guilds issuing coins as we find them in the post-Maurya period in northern and central India.

When the Sātavāhanas and the Kuṣāṇas established their kingdoms in the first two centuries of the Christian era, these towns lost their autonomous character, but their civic life did not lose its vigour. The rulers had to reckon with merchant corporations called *nigama sabhā* in the towns of the Deccan and with the guilds of artisans in the Kuṣāṇa territory. Inscriptions show that they administered donations in towns in north India and western India; especially in the latter region this was done on a large scale. Clear proof of the participation of merchants in town administration is lacking. But if they were thought competent enough to take care of rich donations made by princes, why could not they be trusted with the responsibility of urban administration? The fact that many merchants proudly associate their names with the towns to which they belonged betrays a high degree of civic sense, possibly born of their actual involvement in the government of their towns. Thus the Maurya town administration was a mechanism imposed from above, but the post-Mauryan counterpart seems to have been an experiment emanating from below. In any case the internal affairs of the guilds were regulated by its customs and laws,

1. K.D. Bajpai, "Authority of minting coin in ancient India", *JNSI*, xxv 1963, 20.
2. Ibid., 19.

although they were not granted any special charters by the state, as came to be the case in the 6th century A.D.

At several points the old centralised system of administration was continued and even strengthened by the accession of new elements. The Aśokan system of dividing the kingdom into *āhāras* and placing them under the charge of royal officers continued in the Sātavāhana kingdom, the only difference being that now the officer was called *amātya* in place of *mahāmātra*. A passage from the *Sabhā Parva* suggests that their posts were hereditary.[1] The *amātyas* are not heard of in the Kuṣāṇa system although they were commonly employed by the Śaka rulers of western India where they functioned as both advisers (*mati-saciva*) and administrators (*karma-saciva*). Their counterpart in the Kuṣāṇa dominions was provided by the *daṇḍanāyakas* whose military duties outweighed their civil functions.

We do not find traces of the Maurya system in the territories ruled by the Indo-Greeks and their successors from outside India. The Śakas and Parthians introduced the practice of joint rule, the heir apparent sharing powers equally with the reigning king, and the Śakas and Kuṣāṇas brought in the satrapical system borrowed from the Achaemenids via the Parthians. The Kuṣāṇas also introduced the curious practice of double governor-ship in the provinces which was a reflection of the old practice at the centre. In the Kuṣāṇa dominions administration at the village level continued to be carried on by the *grāmika* or the *grāmasvāmī* appointed by the king. Apparently the village head-man continued to discharge police and revenue functions.

The system of taxation seems to have been rendered simpler in post-Maurya times, perhaps because of the smaller size of the states. Many taxes and revenue officers mentioned by Kauṭilya are not supported by inscriptions of post-Maurya times. *Bali*, *bhāga*, *bhoga* and *kara* occur in inscriptions of western India and the Deccan, but what part of the produce they formed is not known. In the Śaka dominions in western India the emer-gency tax called *praṇaya* and forced labour called *viṣṭi* seem to have been in operation. *Viṣṭi* was imposed on the subjects in general and not confined to slaves and wage earners. Largescale use of coins would suggest assessment and collection in cash in the territories held by the Śakas, Kuṣāṇas and Sātavāhanas.

1. 5.33.

A significant development in the fiscal system is indicated by Manu and the Śānti Parva. They recommended the arrangement of the fiscal units on the basis of the decimal system, 1, 10 and 100 villages. The largest unit consisted of 1,000 villages and was held by the *sahasrapati*, who was probably identical with the *rāṣṭrīya*.[1] The *rāṣṭrīya* is to be paid in cash and kind not directly by the king but out of the revenues of a branch town assigned to him.[2] Thus the officers charged with the collection of taxes in the decimal units are allowed payment in revenues from a piece of land, a village or a town, as the case may be. In this case the Maurya payment in cash is partly substituted by payment in kind derived from assignments of revenues to officers, which may be regarded as a feudal practice. However, the relevant verses which suggest this practice could also be attributed to a period beyond A.D. 300.

Although we have no information about the military strength of the Sātavāhanas or the Kuṣāṇas, it seems that the latter owed their power to the use of cavalry who used rope stirrups, represented in the sculpture of the period. An important development of the period seems to have been the militarisation of government in both the Sātavāhana and Kuṣāṇa dominions. An *āhāra* was placed under the *mahāsenāpati* and a village under a *gaulmika*, head of a small military unit. Similarly under the Kuṣāṇas semi-military officers known as *daṇḍanāyaka* and *mahādaṇḍanāyaka* looked after local units of administration. The Kuṣāṇas being alien rulers, their system is understandable; in the Sātavāhana dominions military rule may have prevailed in the newly conquered areas.

In one sense the religious aspect of the kingship was weakened in post-Maurya times, for the *purohita*, who appears as a very high functionary in all early texts right from late Vedic to Maurya times, figures neither in Sātavāhana nor in Kuṣāṇa inscriptions; nor does he appear in Gupta inscriptions.[3] It is argued that with the disappearance of Vedic sacrifices the *purohita* lost his position. But even the revival of sacrifices under

1. *ŚP*, 88.8-9.

2. Ibid. cf. B.P. Roy, "Political Ideas and Institutions in the Mahābhārata', (Ph.D. thesis, Patna University, 1967), p. 487.

3. But the fact that the *purohita* appears in Gāhaḍavāla inscriptions of the 11th and 12th centuries will have to be explained.

the Sātavāhanas did not elevate the political status of the priest. The Sātavāhanas may have acted as their own priests. No similar explanation can be offered for the non-existence of the chief priest in the Kuṣāṇa and Gupta polity, which would suggest less of religious influence. However, the absence of the priestly office was more than made up by the ascription of divine attributes to the king.

A typical feature of the period was the stress on divine aspects of the kingship. Formerly gods were compared to princes. Now the emphasis shifted the other way about and rulers began to be compared to gods. This appears in an inscription in which the Sātavāhana king Gautamīputra Śātakarṇi is compared to several gods in prowess. But a conspicuous development takes place among the Kuṣāṇa rulers, who are called *devaputra*, son of the god. Aśoka is described as *devānāṃpriya*, dear to gods. But the Kuṣāṇa kings adopted a title known only to the Chinese and the Romans. They also started the practice of setting up *devakulas*, deification of the statues of the dead kings in temples. In contrast to the Greek rulers of Egypt who adopted the practice of the emperor worship under local influence the Kuṣāṇa rulers introduced this in India under foreign influence. For lack of an indigenous base none of these practices survived the Kuṣāṇa rule. On the other hand the Sātavāhana practice of comparing the king with the gods was continued in Gupta inscriptions, which accredit the Gupta king with the attributes of different gods.

On the indigenous side the coins reveal that some tribal republican states came to be headed by their gods in whose name the coins were issued. The Kuṇīndas and Audumbaras issued coins on behalf of their gods.[1] A typical example is that of the Yaudheyas who ruled in the name of their god Brahmaṇya.[2] This practice is also supported by a seal from Bhīṭā which refers to the offer of a kingdom to the god Mahāsena.[3] All this would suggest that in some post-Maurya republics and monarchies of north India the rulers functioned as the regents of god, reminding us of a similar practice in the medieval Deccan where some

1. P.L. Gupta, "Bearing of the numismatics on the history of the tribal republics in ancient India", *IHQ*, xxvii, 204-07.
2. Ibid., 207.
3. Ibid., fn. 51a.

rulers reigned as the leaseholders of their gods. But perhaps the wishes of the presiding deities of these states were not interpreted by the priests as happened under priestly and theocratic rule in Egypt. Probably the rulers only made a formal surrender of their kingdoms to their patron gods and received them back in the same manner as a devotee receives back the offerings made to the god and uses them for his own purpose. At best the practice shows the tendency to treat the state as an item of property on the part of the king who was the symbol of the governing class.

From about the fifth century B.C. onwards religious sanction in the form of penances was invoked for the maintenance of social stability. Remarkably enough their number shoots up in the law-book of Manu, which provides 267 verses on the *prāyaścitta dharma*. The penances mentioned therein have a comprehensive scope and include not only murder and abuse but also purely social offences such as violation of caste rules of which the modern law does not take cognizance. The possible agency for enforcing the penances were the brāhmaṇas who mobilised the conscience of the community for the purpose. The sudden spurt to brāhmaṇical activities in politics and society from post-Maurya times onwards ties up with their role in implementing the penances. Possibly they collected gifts imposed upon the offenders and administered the necessary penances to them. Penances therefore played an important role in maintaining law and order, especially in the rural communities.

The deification of the king, the militarisation of administration, the attempts at provincial administration, collection of taxes and imposition of forced labour through royal agents, all these factors helped maintain the old centralised system. But there were fewer officials to promote it, certainly not as many as the Mauryas had. Since kingdoms were smaller and taxes few it was not possible to support a large administrative establishment. Most economic activities now devolved on guilds and individuals, which obviated the necessity of having too many officials engaged for this purpose in the Maurya empire. Further, a good part of administration was handled by the guilds of merchants in the urban areas and by religious beneficiaries in the rural areas. The beneficiaries also taught the people the rules of *varṇāśrama dharma* and non-violence, which led to peace and stability in society. The feudatories also played an important role. On the whole we notice several elements of decentralisation in the Saka-Sātavāhana polity, which naturally paved for the feudal traits of the Gupta polity.

III

The Gupta Phase : Proto-Feudal Polity

The Gupta age was a period of economic expansion promoted by grants of land to enterprising brāhmaṇas in inhospitable and virgin tracts in central India, Deccan and south India. The period saw a marked growth of private property in land recognised by the law-books and attested by actual sale and purchase of land with gold coins. The economic prosperity of the ruling class is indicated by so many gold coins as do not belong to any other dynasty of ancient India. The use of gold currency strengthened traders and rich artisans, with whose guilds cash endowments in gold were occasionally deposited. Despite decrease in foreign trade and urban decline, guilds continued to take part in the economic and administrative set-up of Gupta times in several towns.

For a total picture of political organisation in Gupta times we have to bear in mind the presence of numerous dynasties throughout the length and breadth of the country. Allowing for an element of exaggeration in the account of Hariṣeṇa, a good many of them were subjugated by Samudra Gupta, and certainly western India was conquered by Candra Gupta II. Conquests of distant regions made it necessary to evolve some kind of feudatory organisation.

In contrast to the Mauryas the Gupta kings adopted pompous titles such as *parameśvara*, *mahārājadhirāja*, *paramabhaṭṭāraka*, which signify the existence of lesser kings in their empire. Although kingship was hereditary, royal power was limited by the absence of the firm practice of primogeniture. Nārada stresses the supremacy of *rājaśāsana* over all the other sources of law, but the Gupta king had to reckon with his ministers, feudatories and above all the brāhmaṇas, who claim many privileges in the law-book of Nārada and who were certainly the chief custodians and interpreters of the law embodied in the Smṛtis. Although the *purohita* or the chief priest is not mentioned as a high functionary in Gupta records, in return for munificient gifts the grateful brāhmaṇas, who evidently composed Gupta inscriptions, compared the Gupta kings with different gods, thus maintaining the Sātavāhana tradition and projecting it on to north India.

Despite the glowing account of the all-round conquests of Samudra Gupta we do not have much information about the military apparatus of the Guptas. Unfortunately Fa-hsien does not state the numerical strength of the Gupta army as classical writers do in the case of the Nandas and Mauryas and Hsüan Tsang in the case of Harṣavardhana. But evidently the troops supplied by the feudatories accounted for a good portion of the Gupta army. Chariots receded into the background, cavalry came to the fore, and horse archery became prominent in military tactics. But the state no longer enjoyed monopoly over the possession of horses and elephants, which now came to be owned by powerful private individuals.

Taxes mentioned in Gupta inscriptions are not as many as enumerated by the *Arthaśāstra* of Kauṭilya. But land taxes increase in number, and those on trade and commerce decrease. The two chief land taxes typical of the Gupta period are *udraṅga* and *uparikara*, but what portion of the peasant's produce they covered is not known. Richer peasants seem to have paid in cash, preferably in gold, which was known by the name of *hiraṇya*. In central and western India the rulers imposed forced labour or *viṣṭi* on the peasants. In addition to this, in the territories held up by the Vākāṭakas and others in central India the peasants had to supply animals, foodgrains, furniture, etc., for the maintenance of royal officers and retainers on duty in the rural areas.

Although land grants mention quite a few officials surely the number of officers associated with the fiscal and economic activities was not as large as in Maurya times. The Gupta bureaucracy was not as elaborate and as organised as its Maurya counterpart. The widely prevalent cadre which supplied superior officers was that of the *kumārāmātya*, corresponding to the *mahāmātya* of Aśokan and *amātya* of Sātavāhana inscriptions. Most high officers were directly appointed by the king in the home provinces and possibly paid in cash. Since the Guptas were of vaiśya origin recruitment was not confined to the two upper varṇas. But several offices came to be combined in the hands of the same person and posts became hereditary. This naturally weakened central control over the administrative machinery.

For the first time inscriptions give us an idea of systematic local and provincial administration in the Gupta period. The empire was divided into *bhuktis*, each of which was placed under the charge of an *uparika*; we know of at least half a dozen *bhuktis* in Bengal, Bihar, U.P. and Madhya Pradesh. The *bhuktis* were divided into *viṣayas* placed under the charge of the *viṣaya-pati*. In eastern India the *viṣaya* was divided into *vīthīs*, and the *vīthī* into villages. This pattern, however, obtained mainly in the territories directly governed by Gupta kings. Elsewhere we hear of different fiscal and administrative units such as *deśa*, *maṇḍala*, *bhoga*, etc., especially in central and western India.

The village administration assumed new dimensions in the Gupta period. The state did not exercise any close supervision as the *gopa* did on its behalf in Maurya times, and households were not registered. Village affairs were now managed by the village headman with the assistance of elders, *mahattara*, who were sometimes also associated with the government of the *viṣaya*. The Gupta inscriptions refer to the participation of leading local elements in the administration of the village or small towns called *vīthīs*. No land transactions could be effected without their consent, and this may have been also true of other important affairs. Thus while villages in Maurya times were managed from above those in Gupta times seem to have been managed from below.

The urban set-up of north India is no longer marked by the existence of such towns as issued coins in post-Maurya times. They now issued only seals to enforce their authority. The seals from Vaiśālī clearly show that artisans, merchants and bankers served on the same corporate body, and in this capacity obviously managed the affairs of the town; corporations of artisans and bankers existed separately too. In addition to this we hear of numerous separate guilds of artisans, traders, etc., at Bhīṭā and Vaiśālī. The guild of silkweavers in Mandasor and that of oilpressers in Indor (Bulandshahr) are celebrated in Gupta inscriptions. The professional guilds were different from family organisations and showed considerable mobility, as can be inferred from the example of the Mandsor silkweavers. Guilds were guided by their customs and usages observed by their officers without any interference from the state. Although guilds are mentioned in the pre-Gupta law-books, the most detailed laws regarding their functioning and regarding business partnerships are laid down by the lawgivers of Gupta times. Undoubtedly corporate bodies had now become so prominent as to attract the special attention of the jurists, who enjoined the king not only to respect the laws and customs of the guilds but also to implement them. The managers of the guilds could naturally invoke the coercive authority of the state if their members did not behave well. A concrete example of how the guilds of merchants enjoyed immunities and exercised control over artisans is found in the charter of Viṣṇuṣena granted in A.D. 592. It would therefore appear that in Gupta times guilds looked after the affairs of their members as well as of the towns in which they were situated. Consequently the state was partly relieved of the burden of administering the towns, and inscriptions do not speak of any state officers who may have been specifically charged with such responsibilities.

Corporate bodies played an important part in the administration of justice. The law-codes provide a hierarchy of three such courts from which the final appeal lay to the king. We have no idea of the law they administered. But the general legal system was the handiwork of brāhmaṇical lawgivers who produced a rich collection of legal texts in the Gupta age. In several directions the legal system registered a distinct advance. First, the law of inheritance, because of the introduction of partition of landed property, received an elaborate treatment in the law-book of Yājñavalkya. Secondly, Nārada and Bṛhaspati drew a line between two types of law, 14 titles relating to property and 4 to injury. Thirdly, the law-books of Nārada, Bṛhaspati and Kātyāyana tell us in detail about the constitution of courts, the judicial procedure and the law of evidence. The lawgivers generally prefer judges and assessors of the brāhmaṇa varṇa, failing which those of the two lower varṇas can be entertained, but in no case the śūdras are to be recruited. The judicial officers or courts mentioned in the law-books are not attested by inscriptions. On the other hand the only important judicial officer, *vinayasthiti-sthāpaka*, mentioned in a Vaiśālī seal is not known to the Smṛtis of the period. The judicial procedure of the Gupta law-books prescribe too many ordeals for establishing the guilt of the persons on trial. Their number is nearly doubled, which shows increasing belief in divine dispensation evidently fostered by the priests. The fear of ordeals may have extorted confessions from the criminals and helped the administration of justice.

Although north Bengal, Bihar and U.P. were ruled directly by the officers appointed by the Gupta king, the major part of the empire was held by such feudatories as the Parivrājaka and Uccakalpa princes and many others subjugated by Samudra Gupta. The vassals, who evidently lived in the outer fringe of the empire, carried out their obligations in three ways. They offered homage to the sovereign by personal attendance in his court, paid tributes to him, and presented to him daughters in marriage. The Allahabad Inscription of Samudra Gupta mentions all these practices, but in addition the vassals apparently supplied troops to their overlord, who extended protection to their protégés in times of war. The leading feudatories of the Guptas included the Maitrakas of Valabhī, the Vardhanas of Thaneser, the Maukharis of Kanauj, the Later Guptas of Magadha, the Candras of Bengal, etc., who set up independent states on the ruins of the Gupta empire.

But the real feudal development in the Gupta empire was the conferment of fiscal and administrative immunities on priests and temples as a result of land grants. The practice started with the Sātavāhanas in the Deccan and became widespread in central India in the territories held by the feudatories of the Guptas and in those held by the Vākāṭakas, although the Gupta emperors made very few grants. The new fiscal concessions embraced transfer of royal rights over salt and mines, which were royal monopolies and evident signs of sovereignty. The religious beneficiaries were granted villages for ever and were entitled to all the taxes accruing to the benefactor without any responsibility of paying any portion of it to the grantor in north India and the Deccan. What distinguished the land charters of the Gupta period was the administrative privileges conferred on the beneficiaries. They enjoyed freedom from the entry of royal agents, retainers, etc., which is also found in Sātavāhana charters. But now they were empowered to punish the criminals.

guilty of ten offences. In other words they were vested with magisterial and police powers. Further, the inhabitants of the villages placed under the charge of the beneficiaries as a result of gifts made to them were asked by the king to obey their new masters and to carry out their orders.

The avowed purpose for which lands were granted to priests and temples was religious and spiritual. In one case, however, the brāhmaṇas are granted land on the condition that they commit no wrong against the state and maintain good behaviour. In practice the beneficiaries exclusively bore the burden of administration in the areas granted to them and exercised a salutory and stabilising influence over the rural communities by teaching them the duties of castes, prescribing penances, and presenting to them the divine image of their princely benefactors.

Whether state officials were paid by grants of land in Gupta times is not clear. Abundance of gold coins would suggest that high officers were paid in cash. But the law-books of the period lay down clear provisions for remuneration of revenue officials by land grants and for reward of officers by the same mode. Inscriptions from central India show that lands granted to temples were placed under the management of scribes and merchants, and sometimes aboriginal chiefs were assigned land for their maintenance. But the practice of service tenures had not become widespread.

Since a considerable area of imperial administration was managed by feudatories and beneficiaries the Gupta rulers did not require as many officials as the Mauryas did; officials were also rendered redundant because of the absence of state economic activities on any big scale. Nor was a large standing army needed on the same scale as was maintained by the Mauryas. The need for an elaborate administrative establishment was further lessened by the participation of artisans, merchants, elders, etc., in rural and urban administration—a feature not noticeable in Maurya times. Villages assumed more authority leaving less for the centre to do. The Guptas therefore neither needed nor possessed the elaborate bureaucracy of the Maurya type, and in spite of the strong arms of the Gupta kings institutional factors working for decentralisation were far stronger in the Gupta age than in pre-Gupta times. In many ways the Gupta rule marked the beginnings of the feudal polity, which became typical of early medieval India.

APPENDIX TO CHAPTER XXIII. I

It is held that at no point of time the traditional empires such as the Maurya and Mughal exercised central control. In all such empires the king had to share power with his equals in the realm.[1] We are not concerned herewith the Mughal empire,[2] but will consider the view that the Maurya empire was not an integrated and organised political entity and that its bureaucracy did not exercise effective control.[3] Absence of chains of command, reporting system, delegation of power and above all a mechanism to monitor the activities of departmental heads is adduced as an important ground.[4] Emphasis is laid on difficulties of communication and consequent mobilising of the resources.[5]

Heesterman argues that although Kauṭilya mentions numerous departments he does not speak of chains of command and delegation and communication.[6] It is true that Kauṭilya does not provide any systematic mechanism for supervising the activities of nearly thirty superintendents of the departments. But most superintendents are assigned economic functions, and the general collector of revenue called *samahārtā* is tied up with almost all of them. It is his responsibility to collect taxes from both the fortified city (*durga*) and the countryside (*rāṣṭra*). In the town he is to deal either with various kinds of superintendents such as *laksaṇādhyakṣa, mudrādhyakṣa* and *devatādhyakṣa* and also to collect taxes from customs (*śulka*), weights and measures (*pautava*), liquor (*surā*), slaughter house (*sūnā*), spinning (*sūtra*), sale of commodities (*paṇya*), prostitutes (*veśyā*), etc.

1. J.C. Heesterman, *The Inner Conflict of Tradition*, pp. 16-18, 129, 132-33, 139-40, 142-43, 260 with fns. 20-21.
2. On this see the refutation by Irfan Habib of A. Wink's views regarding lack of centralisation (*Indian Economic and Social History Review*, vol. XXV, no. 4 (1988), pp. 527-31; XXVI, no. 3 (1989), pp. 363-72; also his paper on Mapping the Maurya Empire submitted to the Fiftieth Session of the Indian History Congress at Gorakhpur, 1989.
3. J.W. Mabbett, *Truth, Myth and Politics in Ancient India*, New Delhi, 1971.
4. J.C. Heesterman, op. cit., p. 129.
5. Romila Thapar, *The Mauryas Revisited*, Calcutta 1985.
6. *The Inner Conflict of Tradition*, pp. 18, 129.

Each one of these taxpaying items is managed exclusively by a superintendent or *adhyakṣa*.[1] Further, the monitoring responsibility is also given to the treasurer called *saṃnidhātā*, who looks after the establishments connected with commodities (*paṇya-saṃsthā*), treasures (*koṣṭhāgāra*), forest produce (*kupya*), etc.[2] Each one of these items is given a separate superintendent. Thus both the collector and the treasurer are given the supervision of the economic activities of the superintendents.

Special instructions are given about the appointment of superintendents. It is stated that all superintendents should be endowed with the excellence of a minister (*amātya*) and appointed for various functions depending on their ability. The *pradeṣṭṛ* (understood as magistrate or inspector) is provided to constantly inspect their works. The superintendents are expected to carry out the tasks according to orders. Obviously the inspector sees to it that they do not act in concert otherwise they could swallow up the fruits of the undertakings. They are also enjoined not to quarrel among themselves, for this might prove ruinous. Further, the superintendents are asked not to commence any work without informing the king; however they may go ahead with measures against calamities. It is further laid down that if a superintendent neglects his work a fine double his daily wage and other expenses shall be imposed on him. All these provisions[3] detailed under the duties of the *pradeṣṭṛ* ensure a tight control over the superintendents.

When Kauṭilya provides for several heads of a department,[4] he is not really concerned with ensuring equality of the peers,[5] which is more a feature of the kin-based society, but with preventing them from being detrimental to the state. Kauṭilya faces a dilemma. On the one hand he wants the work to be done, for which he provides that the departmental heads should not quarrel. On the other he wants that these heads should not act in concert for they may grab the income from the undertakings.[6]

1. II.6.2. The *gaṇikādhyakṣa* obviously looks after the *vesyā*. All the *AŚ* references in the Appendix are from R.P. Kangle's text.
2. II.5.1.
3. II.9.1-8.
4. II.31; Heesterman (op. cit., p. 237, fn. 58) wrongly refers to II.10.31.
5. Heesterman, op. cit., pp. 133, 140.
6. *AŚ*, II.9.6.

At the same time two provisions, occurring at separate places, are meant to keep an eye on the activities of the superintendents (*adhyakṣas*) or of the departments (*adhikaranas*). The (*samāhartā*) or the collector general deputed an agent in the guise of an ascetic to ascertain *inter alia*, the honesty or dishonesty of the departmental heads.[1] More importantly, the accountant general (*akṣapaṭalamadhyakṣa*) maintained control over all the departments called *adhikaraṇa*.[2] The audit system may not have been effective,[3] which may have been typical of pre-capitalist governments, but Kauṭilya makes detailed arrangements for accounting and the punishment of those who either embezzle or misuse government money.

Kauṭilya provides for sufficient general control over all the departments, and BK IV. 9 deals with this problem. According to R.P. Kangle the *samahaṛtṛ* with the *pradeṣṭṛs* working under him is ultimately responsible for clean administration, and even the judges are under his servillance.[4] The relevant passage[5] has been translated thus: "The Administrator and the magistrates should first keep in check the heads of departments and their subordinates." This seems to be correct except that the *samahartā* may be rendered as collector.

It would be ridiculous to apply the *maṇḍala* theory or the idea of circle of kings enumerated by Kauṭilya to the Maurya empire and consider it a little kingdom, as is sometimes implied.[6] Really the *maṇḍala* theory reflects 'some sort of feudal relationship'[7] and seems to have been inserted in the *Arthaśāstra* in early medievel times. Significantly enough the term *maṇḍala* is not known to ancient inscriptions. The *maṇḍala* theory speaks of a *nāyaka* being placed over ten *senāpatis*[8] though the *senāpati* is very high in the list of the eighteen important officials enumerated in the earlier portions of the *Arthaśāstra*; the pay

1. *AŚ*, II.35.13.
2. *AŚ*, II.7.3.
3. Heesterman, op. cit., pp. 132-33.
4. *The Kauṭilīya Arthaśāstra*, pt II, p. 321, fn. 1.
5. *samāhartṛpradeṣṭāraḥ purvam adhyakṣānām adhyakṣapuruṣānāṃ ca niyamanaṃ kuryuḥ*, *AŚ*, IV, 9.1.
6. Heesterman, op.cit, pp. 16-18, 149-50.
7. R.P. Kangle, *The Kauṭilīya Arthaśāstra*, pt III, 262.
8. *AŚ*, X.6.45 cf. X.2.4.

prescribed for him is 48,000 paṇas in contrast to that of the *nāyaka* who is to be given 12,000 paṇas.[1]

It is rightly held that a modicum of monetisation would ensure payment of salaries in cash to state officials which would consequently make the central control effective, but it is wrong to attribute a low degree of monetisation to the Maurya period.[2] The cash payment provided by Kauṭilya[3] should not be considered conventional. Payment may be linked to the pan-Indian series of punch-marked silver coins which are also called the 'imperial' series. There were also numerous local coins, and nearly 550 types of punch-marked coins have been identified. Whatever may be the date of the *Arthaśāstra* of Kauṭilya that metal money circulated in a large volume around 300 B.C. is clear. Considering references to the use of cash money for sale, purchase, fines, etc., in the brāhmaṇical and Buddhist texts there is no doubt that the prescription for salary payment in money worked, though payment in kind may not have been negligible.

Because of its prescriptive nature, stratification and uncertain date the *Arthaśāstra* of Kauṭilya may not really indicate the extent of control exercised by the Maurya empire. For an idea of the actual position the account of Megasthenes and Aśokan inscriptions may be preferred. Pillar Edict IV of Aśoka, with its versions found at many places, clearly speaks of the large judicial and magisterial powers delegated to the *rājukas* or *lājukas* who were placed over hundreds of thousand of people in the countryside. They were empowered not only to punish the law-breakers but also to reward the law-abiding.[4] Similarly, as shown by Rock Edict V, the *dhammamahāmātras* were authorised to establish and promote *dhamma* and to look after the welfare and happiness of the followers of *dhamma* in all sects (*pāṣaṇḍa*), śūdras, vaiśyas, brāhmaṇas, *ibhyas* (affluent people) destitutes, etc. They were appointed in Pāṭaliputra and outer towns, in all the harems of king's brothers, sisters and of all his other relations. Further, for promoting *dhamma* they were

1. *AŚ*, V.3.4 and 8.
2. Heesterman, op.cit., p. 139.
3. *AŚ*, V.3.
4. Delhi—Topra Version, lines 2-6, D.C. Sircar, *Sel. Inscrr.*, i, BK I, no. 27.

appointed among the Yavanas, Kambojas, Gandhāras, Riṣṭrikas, Petenikas and others who inhabited northern Konkan.[1]

We can detect at least three links in the chain of command emanating from the head of the state. Thus in one case we find that a dignitary, whose official identity cannot be established, was asked to communicate the royal order to the *āryaputra* and *mahāmātras* of Suvarnagiri who in their turn had to communicate orders to the *mahāmātras* of a district or divisional headquarters at Isilā. The *rājuka*, who was delegated by the king wide powers in his jurisdiction in the countryside, was asked to order the *rāṣṭrikas* or administrators of the smaller units (*rāṣṭra*) of the countryside.[2] Further on the basis of the royal command, orders issued most probably by the *mahāmātra*, were communicated to the elephant-riders, scribes (*kāraṇakān*), chairot-riders and brāhmaṇas.[3]

More importantly the *mahāmātras*, who are charged with varied functions, are authorised to constitute a council or *parisā*, and if there is a difference of opinion among them the matter has to be immediately reported to the king. To quote from Rock Edict VI :

"And if in the council (of Māhāmātras) a dispute arises, or an amendment is moved, in connection with proclamation I am myself ordering, or (in connection with) an *emergent matter delegated to the Mahāmatras*, it must be reported to me immediately, anywhere, (and) at anytime."[4]

We therefore see a clear provision for communication between the head of the government and the functionaries to whom he had delegated powers. For this purpose the *prativedakas* or reporters were appointed. They were asked to report to the head of the government not only on disputes in the council of the *mahāmātras* but also on all general matters. To quote again from what Aśoka states in Rock Edict VI, lines 3-5.

"Reporters (*paṭivedika*) are posted everywhere (with instructions), to report to me the affairs of the people at any time while I am eating, in the inner apartment, in the harem, even at the

1. Manshera Version, lines—1-8, Ibid., no. 10.
2. MRE: Yerragudi version, *Sel. Inscrr.*, i, BK I, no. 23, lines 12-14.
3. Ibid., lines 18a-19.
4. Rock Edict VI, lines 5-8.

cowpen, in the palanquin, and in the parks. And everywhere I am disposing of the affairs of the people."

Royal orders could be communicated to the provincial governor called the *kumāras*[1] or *āryaputras*.[2] They could be also directly sent to the other provincial functionaries called *prādeśikas*[3] and *mahāmātras*.

As regards reporting the *duta*[4] played an important part in it. He acted not only as an envoy but he also communicated the royal order to various officers. Because of this function he is called *śāsanahara* by Kauṭilya.[5] The *prādesika*, who is asked by Aśoka to go on circuit along with the *rājukas* and the *yutas*, may have been a reporter. Although the term *prādeśika* is taken to mean a local chief and governor, according to F.W. Thomas this term is derived from the word *pradiś* which means to report.[6] Further, though the elaborate system of espionage provided by Kauṭilya[7] indicates lack of trust in the officials appointed by the central government and in the people over whom they rule, it also shows a well-organised mechanism to collect intelligence about the maintenance of law and order which was the crucial responsibility of the king. If anything went amiss obviously the royal hand would come heavily over the officers. Moreover, the classical writers refer to a class of functionaries called *epiakopoi* who oversee what happens throughout the country and in the cities and report to the king in a monarchy and to the magistrates in a non-monarchical state.[8] Strabo calls this class of men the *ephori* and informs us that they are asked to keep an eye on all that goes on and report privately to the king. It is significant that according to Strabo only the best and the most

1. Separate Rock Edict I. Both Dhauli (ll. 23 and 24) and Jaugada (l. II) mention the *kumāra* of Ujjain and that of Taxila. SRE II (Dhauli), l.1 mentions the *kumāra* of Tosali.
2. Minor Rock Edict I (l. 1) of Brahmagiri, Siddapura and Jatinga-Ramesvara mentions the *āryaputra*.
3. Rock Edict III: Girnar Version, *Sel. Inscrr*, i, BK I, no. 8, line 2.
4. Rock Edict XIII: Shahbazgarhi Version, *Sel. Inscrr*, i, BK I, no. 17, line 10.
5. *AŚ*, II.28.18.
6. *JRAS*, 1950, p. 97 quoted in H.C. Raychaudhuri, *Political History of Ancient India*, 1972, p. 283, fn. 4.
7. *AŚ*, I.11 and 12.
8. Chinnock, *Arrian*, p. 413, quoted in H.C. Raychaudhuri, p. 258 with fn. 3.

faithful persons were appointed inspectors, and posted both in the city and the camp, and in both the cases they took the help of women.[1]

At the local level Strabo mentions six bodies, each of which looks after a department in the city, and speaks of their functioning in a collective capacity. The six bodies have charge both of their special departments and of matters affecting the public welfare, such as the repairs of public works, the regulation of prices, and the care of markets, harbours, and temples.[2] How the officials of the six bodies coordinated their efforts is not known to us. But if there could be coordination at the local level, it may not have been wanting at the central level.

The use of the terms *kumāra* and *āryaputra* do not necessarily mean that the viceroys located at provincial capitals were princes of the royal blood. In fact such titles may merely recall earlier practices when kinsmen really played an important part in government. These titles may be similar to Aśoka addressing his subjects as his children. Even if we concede an element of equality between the king and his provincial governors this would be more ritualistic than real. Further, the *mahāmātras* were posted in the harems of king's brothers, sisters and of all his relations to establish and promote *dhamma*; this may have meant some watch on the close kinsmen of the king. In any case there is nothing to show that the *mahāmātras* were related to the king. Kauṭilya does not prescribe kin-based qualifications for the selection of the *amātyas*[3] from whose cadre all the officials were to be appointed. Nor are such qualifications laid down for the appointment of the *mantrin* and *purohita*.[4] The officers are not necessarily the kinsmen of the king; they come from a caste-divided society and seem to be mainly brāhmaṇas and kṣatriyas. Thus the tribal order is not strong enough to obstruct the development of the bureaucratic orders.[5]

The 'impressive bureaucracy' of the Mauryas is considered 'more of a machinery for the diffusion of resources than for

1. John W. McCrindle, *Ancient India as Described in Classical Literature*, Reprint, p. 53 with fn. 3.
2. John W. McGrindle, op.cit., p. 54.
3. *AŚ*, I.8.
4. *AŚ*, I.9.
5. But Heesterman, op.cit., p. 134. thinks otherwise.

their pooling and husbanding'[1]. But how could resources be distributed unless they were mobilised? Such a view betrays total ignorance of the taxation system provided by Kauṭilya.

The Aśokan inscriptions indicate that autonomous regions and tributaries existed in the Maurya empire. Aśoka himself makes a distinction between the areas which were directly conquered by the state and were therefore called *vijita* and those which were just subdued and were therefore called *avijita*.[2] Clearly the Maurya control over the subjects could not be as effective as the British control, but certainly it could not be much less than that of the Roman emperors. That we are not able to precisely determine the different degrees of control in various regions is because of the limitations of our sources. But it is going too far to say that the Indian rulers were only the masters of roads.[3]

The central government of the Mauryas took steps to look into the complaints of oppression made by the provincial subjects and put down revolts even in distant areas. The *Divyāvadāna* tells us that Aśoka was despatched to suppress the revolt at Taxila during the reign of Bindusāra.[4]

At present it is not possible to clearly identify a central zone in which the Maurya state control operated effectively from Pāṭaliputra.[5] It is not clear whether nearly thirty superintendents provided in Book II of the *Arthaśāstra* of Kauṭilya functioned in the hinterland of the capital or in a wider area. But by *c.* 300 B.C. settlements had appeared on a considerable scale in the northern plains including the great Indo-Gangetic Divide, the upper Gangetic plains, the middle Gangetic plains and the lower Gangetic plains, and hence there could not be much difficulty in transportation from Bengal to Punjab. It is held on linguistic grounds that certain word formations found in the pillar edicts of Aśoka show similarity and therefore the language

1. Heesterman, op. cit., p. 132.
2. Rock Edict XIII: Shahbazgarhi Version, *Sel. Inscrr*, i, BK I, no. 18, lines 3, 7.
3. Heesterman, op. cit., p. 20.
4. E.B. Cowell and R.A. Neil, ed., *The Divyāvadāna*, p. 371f.
5. An attempt has been made to divide the Maurya empire into the metropolitan, core and peripheral areas. Romila Thapar, op.cit., p. 4ff.

spoken in this area was of one variety.[1] We may note that almost all the inscribed and uninscribed pillars of Aśoka, except one in Amaravati, have been found in the northern plain whose altitude is below 200 meters. It has been argued that the Aśokan pillars were quarried, chiselled and made cylindrical in Chunar,[2] from where they were taken to various destinations. If such huge pillars could be transported, probably by river, there was no reason why men and material could not be moved.

It may further be noted that nearly 500 sites showing sherds of Northern Black Polished Ware have been found in the middle Gangetic plains and its periphery.[3] Nearly 30 excavated sites in this area have yielded not only NBPW but also a type of silver punch-marked coins which carry the same symbols and also uninscribed cast coins which both types give clear indications of supralocal provenance. Excavations give proof of urban settlements at many sites in the northern plains around 400-300 B.C. though urbanism really flourished during the period 200 B.C.-A.D. 300.[4] More importantly, similarities in coins, teracottas and types/techniques of NBPW presuppose constant contact between the various town settlements. All this also demonstrates that by *c.* 300 B.C. almost the whole of the northern plains was more or less at the same stage of material culture which made it possible for the Maurya empire to extract taxes and tributes from the people.

Of course in later centuries communications improved in the northern plains because of increasing number of settlements on the highways which may have helped the movement of troops, officials and merchants in the Mughal empire. But the system of transportation under the Mauryas was not fundamentally different from that under the East India Company till 1830s when the first steam boat appeared on the Ganges. If the Company could control the plains, the Mauryas could also do it

1. Irfan Habib has underlined this similarity in his paper entitled Mapping the Mauryan Empire in *Papers on Indian History* submitted to the Indian History Congress, Golden Jubilee Session, 1989, Gorakhpur.
2. P.C. Pant and Vidula Jayaswal, "Chunar Stone Quarries: Raw Material for Sculpture and Architecture". *Mārg*, xlii, no. 1, 59-61.
3. R.S. Sharma, *Material Culture and Social Formations in Ancient India*, pp. 104-105.
4. R.S. Sharma, *Urban Decay in India* (*c. A.D.* 300-*c. A.D.* 1000); chs. II-III.

although they lacked the hand guns of the Mughals and the Company.

The term empire applied to the Maurya dominions should be distinguished from the same term applied to the political entities founded by the British and other colonial European powers. The Magadhan state maintained itself on the taxes directly collected from the peasants and also on the spoils of plunder made in the course of its conquest. It did not face the problem of moving huge quantities from one country to another distant country. The British empire did not gain so much in the form of taxes as through the operation of its colonialist economic system. As a consequence of the Industrial Revolution the British factory owners manufactured numerous articles which were sold in the Indian market. India was made to supply raw material for the needs of the British industry. Such an economic imperative for obtaining raw material and exporting finished products neither worked in the case of the Roman nor in that of the Magadhan empire. Again, ancient empires were much smaller in extent and therefore much simpler in administrative organisation. In the ancient context we may talk of chiefdoms, kingdoms, principalities, etc., which were comparatively smaller and whose boundaries were more flunctuating. States with large territories are called empires in order to distinguish them from smaller political entities with simpler instruments of exercising power. Obviously large states had to collect taxes and tributes from distant places for which they needed taxation system and had also to evolve a large, better-organised coercive apparatus to maintain law and order in their territories. This was done through a large army and an organised judiciary, for both of which we have evidence under the Mauryas. The Indian king who conquered a large area outside his paternal kingdom was called *cakravartin*, though even princes with smaller kingdoms could claim this title.

Similarly the concept of modern bureaucracy, which is open to merit and competition and operates effectively in a set-up in which time and distance are annihilated, is different from that of its ancient counterpart. It could be nobody's argument that the bureaucratic hierarchy in Maurya times was qualitatively of the modern type. But we cannot overlook the fact that the orders issued by the central government operated even in distant areas, though guilds, caste/kin organisations and local potentates also managed the local administration. Both in modern and ancient times bureaucracy serves as an important instrument of the ruling class in enforcing its basic policies and protecting its interests. However the ancient bureaucracy seems to have been dominated by the brāhmaṇas and kṣatriyas.

APPENDIX TO CHAPTERS XXII AND XXIII: I(A)

From Jana to Janapadaniveśa
(A note on polity and settlement)

Jana

The term *jana* occurs 234 times in the *Rig Veda.* It means people, band or tribe. No other term in this sense appears in the earliest Veda so many times. The term *viś*, which means tribe or dwelling, occurs 170 times. Probably the *jana* was a wider and the *viś*, a smaller unit. We repeatedly hear of five peoples that is Anu, Yadu, Druhyu, Pūru and Turvaśa. They are frequently called *pañcajanāḥ* (*Aspects,* 160[1]. VI, I, 467) or sometimes *pañcakṛṣṭyaḥ*. The later term indicates that some tribal people practised agriculture. The *Rig Veda* refers frequently to cattle rearing but much less to agriculture. It appears that the earliest Vedic people were primarily cattle keepers and therefore mainly semi-nomadic. But a few who were agriculturists had to be sedentary. Archaeologically these people may be placed in the Gandhara area.

Janapada

But the term *janapada* which indicates tribal settlement does not occur in the *Rig Veda.* It seems that many of the earliest Vedic people were organised in bands of various types not based on kinship but on collective efforts needed for hunting, food gathering and cattle rearing.

The term *janapada*, which denotes tribal or territorial settlement, does not occur in the *Rig Veda*. It first appears in later Vedic texts comprising the Brāhmaṇas (*VI*, I, 273), which were composed in the upper Gangetic plains around the eighth-seventh centuries B.C. Recently settlements found in this area have been studied archaeologically and classified according to their sizes[2]. The *janapadas* may represent the later Vedic settlements belonging to

1. R.S. Sharma, *Aspects of Political Ideas and Institutions in Ancient India*, Delhi, 1996.
2. George Erdosy, *Urbanisation in Early Historic India*, Oxford 1988; Makkhan Lal, *Settlement History and the Rise of Civilisation in the Ganga-Yamuna Doab,* Delhi, 1984.

the Painted Grey Ware phase when iron weapons were used for war and hunting. Most probably the ruling class in the *janapadas* used these weapons. But the Vedic texts do not use any term for the head of the *janapada*.

We find various terms for the heads of the *janapada* in post-Vedic times, when many *janapadas* appear. The post-Vedic *janapada* was a political unit with its own dialect and culture. These *janapadas* were mostly Indo-Aryan speaking. The grammarian Pāṇini, who lived in the Gandhara area around 450 B.C. according to V.S. Agrawala[3], mentions 19 *ekaraja* (single-ruler) *janapadas*. They cover not only a good part of north India but also include parts of Afghanistan and south Central Asia. The *mahājanpada* called Kamboja in Pali texts represents modern Tajikistan lying in south Central Asia. It lies in the Pamir plateau area, which mainly covers Tajikistan. Between 1500 and 1000 B.C. Tajikistan shows remains of horse, chariots and spoked wheels, cremation and swastika, all associated with the Indo-Aryan speakers. Around 500 B.C. both Sanskrit and Pali were spoken in Kamboja, which was connected with Pāṭaliputra by the *uttarapatha* or northern route.

Pāṇini mentions two types of *janapadas* or territorial units. He calls the head of the *janapada janpadin* which means the holder of the *janapada*. (The epics also mention some titles for headship of the *janapada*). The *Mahābhārata* speaks of *janapadeśvara* and *janapadasya īśa*, and the *Rāmāyaṇa* mentions *janapadādhipa* (*Aspects*, p. 189). These titles may have been in use around 400 B.C. Although we find several terms used for the head of the *janapada*, we do not find any term for the head of the *mahājanapada*.

Janapadin

Pāṇini notices two types of rules in the territorial settlement called *janapada*. They are called *ekaraja*[4] and *saṃgha*[5]. *Ekarāja* means

3. Vasudevasharan Agrawal first wrote in English *India as known to Pāṇini*, Lucknow, 1953. Then he wrote in Hindi a larger book *Pāṇinikālīna Bhāratavarṣa*, Varanasi, 1969, which has been used in this Appendix.
4. Agrawal, p. 429.
5. Ibid.

one-man rule, and *saṃgha* indicates group rule. The *ekaraja* number 19[6]. There were many *āyudhajīvī saṃghas*[7], but their number is not known. We have no clear idea about the number of the ancient *janapadas.* Ancient texts mention 32 *janapadas*, but the Purāṇas enumerate 175 *janapadas.* However, their dates cannot be given[8].

Generally some territorial units or *janapadas* were managed by a single ruler and others by multi-rulers (*saṃgha*) similar to the republic of Vaishali.

Mahājanapada

The *janapadas* or territorial states were made possible because of the use of the low carbon steel from about the sixth century B.C. onwards. Iron tools caused the clearance of forests and promoted cultivation and settlement in the Gangetic plains on a wide scale. Because of the use of iron weapons and collection from agriculturists some kings of the *janapada* conquered other kings, and this process produced sixteen *mahājanapadas*. Although we find several terms used for the head of the *janapada*, we do not notice any such term for the head of the *mahājanapada.*

The sixteen *mahājanapadas* covered almost the whole of northern India, north-western India, a part of the Deccan and even parts of Afghanistan and south Central Asia. Eventually a *mahājanapada* called Magadha conquered several other large counterparts including Kośala and Avanti and turned into a tax and tribute collecting empire. This empire developed almost all the organs of the state which are first discussed by Kauṭilya. These organs included seven elements such as kingship, army, territory, taxation, fortification, etc. (*Aspects,* Ch. 3). Though treasure or *kośa* and *daṇḍa* or army are considered essentials of polity, the first is more important than the second.

Janapadaniveśa

It seems that the *janapada* system continued under the Mauryas, for it is mentioned in Asokan inscriptions. But the existing

6. Ibid.
7. Ibid., p. 57.
8. Ibid., p. 413.

janapadas did not provide adequate tolls, taxes, tithes and tributes to the rulers. Therefore Kauṭilya, who is ascribed to this period, recommends the policy of founding new settlements in the countryside. This is called *janapadaviniveśa* (AŚ, I.2.1). New settlements were villages. When urbanisation began, in contrast to town (pura or nagara) the *Janapada* came to be considered a village. Since his main objective was to enrich the treasury, Kauṭilya lays down various measures for increasing production. According to him the new *janapada* should consist primarily of śūdra and *karṣaka* (cultivator) settlers (AS, II. 1.2)[9]. It means that the śūdras would have served as slaves and labourers, and the *karṣakas* would work as agriculturists. Kauṭilya states that the king should allot arable land to taxpayers for life, and unarable land should not be taken away from those who are making it arable (AŚ, II. 1.8). The settlement should be inhabited by families ranging from 100 to 500 *kulas*. *Kula* generally means family, but it also means field. This would imply that a *janapada* should cultivate an area comprising 100 to 500 fields, but the *janapada* was really a much larger unit comprising many villages.

Those who do not cultivate should be deprived of their fields which should be given to others. Cultivation should be carried on by village labourers and merchants. Those who do not till should meet the loss of the treasury (Ibid., 12). Kauṭilya discards such settlers as have renounced active life and turned ascetics (*vānaprastha*). They are considered a liability for production. Similarly he also does not welcome people who are engaged in various types of entertainments. He says that actors, dancers, singers, musicians, and professional story tellers, etc., should not obstruct the work of the people; he does not like parks or recreation halls in the *janapada* (AŚ II, 1. 83-84). Only people who are engaged in the field work add to the treasury (*kośa*), forced labour, metallic money, food grains and various types of liquids (Ibid., 85).

The whole idea behind founding a new *janapada* lies in attaining *kośavṛdhikara* or in arranging taxes raised for increasing the treasury. Kauṭilya advises the king to help the cultivators with grains, cattle

9. The Sanskrit term is *śūdrakarṣakaprāyam*. Since the Dharamasūtras attributed to 500-200 BC do not represent śūdras as cultivators, the term used by Kauṭilya may be treated as *dvandva samāsa*.

and money, which should be paid back when possible. The king should bestow such favours and exemptions as would add to the treasury and not diminish it. (AŚ, II. 1. 13-15). The king is asked to protect agriculture against the troubles caused by fines, and by taxes on labourers. He should also save herds of cattle oppressed by thieves, wild animals, crocodiles, poison and diseases (AŚ. II. 1.37). He is also asked to keep the trade routes free from the difficulties created by royal favourites, robbers, frontier chiefs and even by herds of cattle (Ibid. II. 1.38).

Administrative arrangements for the *janapada* are recommended by Kauṭilya. According to him the king should establish a *sthānīya* in the middle of 800 villages, a *droṇamukha* in 400 villages, a *karvaṭīka* in 200 villages, and a *saṃgrahaṇa* in a group of 10 villages (AŚ, III. 1.4). These hierarchical offices seem to be located in towns for revenue collection. It is estimated that altogether a *janapada* consisted of 3200 villages (*Aspects*, p. 200). Thus it was a fairly large territorial unit, and many such units formed a *mahājanapada*. The *Janapadaniveśa* gives an idea of administration, but this may not have been all pervasive in the Maurya dominions.

The social structure in the *janapada* seems to be caste oriented. Priests, preceptors and those learned in the Vedas (śrotriyas), etc. are to be welcomed in the *janapada* and granted tax-free land without the right of sale and mortgage (AŚ. 1.7). The concession made to the brāhmaṇas is also recommended for heads of departments, accountants, local officer called *sthānika,* horse-trainers, persons looking after cattle (*gopa*), physician and some other employees (Ibid). But in the country as a whole Kauṭilya provides for general payment of the employees in cash. We may recall that śūdras and vaiśyas are the main inhabitants. Others including the caṇḍālas are settled on the frontier of the *janapada* fortification outside the main settlement. In addition to the caṇḍālas these include some tribals, called Śabaras, Pulindas, and forest people who are asked to defend the settled territory.

A person with means is held responsible for the support of his parents, widows, children and other non-working members of his family. He is fined if he cannot support them (AŚ, II. 1.28). However, rise in production was the main objective. The king was expected to make people work. Kauṭilya states that slaves, persons kept under pledge and even kinsmen should be made by the king to work (AŚ, II. 1.25)[10]. It was his responsibility to check the loss in agricultural production. Thus the tribal character of the *janapada* had been completely undermined by Kauṭilya's time. By his time the proto-state had become a full fledged state with its seven organs. The early *janapada* or the territorial state did not have much of inequities in terms of gender and social classes. But all this became prominent by the time of Kauṭilya.

Evidence from Aśokan Inscriptions (based on *Sel. Inscr.*, 1, pp. 51-52, 57-58)

The terms *jana, janapada* and *jānapada,* all appear in Aśokan inscriptions of the 3rd century BC.

The *rajukas* were given the charge of the *janapada*. They were asked to look after the welfare of the people and also introduce *vyavahāra samatā* and *daṇḍa samatā* in the territory under their charge. The term *samatā* shows prevalence of social inequality in legal terms. This is clear from instructions given by Kauṭilya in the *janapadaniveśa.* Inequality in possession of property and provision for punishment for different varṇas was a peculiarity of the Dharmasūtras or the earliest brahmanical legal texts. Aśoka tried to remove this discrimination in the *janapadas* through the functions of *rajukas.* This may have contributed to the decline of his empire because of brahmanical reaction.

Conclusion

Though several terms such as *jana, viś, gaṇa, vrāta, śarddha, kṛṣti,* etc., occur in the RV, only *jana* came to the associated with a territorial unit. The term *janapada* is used even in the sense of community in later Vedic times, but generally it came to be used in the sense of an organised political unit, which meaning is given to it even now in north India. The term *rāṣṭra* occurs in the *Rig Veda* and later Vedic texts, and is called 'kingdom' in the *Vedic Index,* but it could not be as current as *janapada* in post-Vedic texts.

The early Buddhist *janapada* or territorial state of Pāṇini's times was transformed into a full-fledged state by Kauṭilya's time. But

10. All reference to AŚ in this article belong to R.P. Kangle. *The Kauṭilīya Arthaśāstra,* part II, University of Bombay, 1963.

the state was called *maṇḍala* which included several *janapadas*. By Maurya times production had increased so much that the king could afford to provide food grains, cattle and money to new cultivators for founding settlements in the countryside. The *janapadaniveśa* plan was intended to add to the treasury which was considered the basis of polity and society. People were asked to follow the rules of patriarchal family system. They were fined if they did not. On the other hand slaves, labourers, pledgemen and even non-working kinsmen were punished for negligence of their duties in the new *janapada*. Thus the *janapadaniveśa* may represent a tax-based and varṇa based pre-capitalist colonisation.

CHAPTER XXIV

RECAPITULATION

The independent chapters assigned to political ideas in this book occupy a comparatively minor place, but that is no measure of their importance. Some of the ideas, such as the *saptāṅga* concept of the state, are marked by considerable coherence and systematization, and can rightly be placed in the category of theories. Indeed, keeping in view the other ancient notions of the state, the seven-element theory of the state must be reckoned as a unique contribution of the ancient Indian thinkers to political philosophy. It not only shows a happy blending of theory and practice but also holds certain elements in common with the modern definitions of the state.

As regards the theories of the origin of the state, references to the contract theory in ancient Indian texts seem to be very attractive from the Western point of view. The various stages in the development of the theory, extending over more than a thousand years, mark progressive enlargement of the obligations of both the contracting parties, especially of the ruled, for payment of various taxes. Thus in ancient India the contract theory was intended to emphasise the power of the king rather than that of the people. From the Indian point of view, considerations of preserving family, property and varṇa system played the most vital part in the origin of the state. The traditional account of the state of nature and the circumstances leading to the rise of coercive authority, the conditions obtaining in a kingless society, the concept of the main duties of the monarch,—all point to the same conclusion.

Theoretical discussions about the state do not appear in the *Ṛg Veda*. In the later Vedic texts some kṣatriya princes speculate on the nature of relation between God and the soul, but they have nothing to contribute to political ideas. The Vedic period, especially the early part of it, was essentially an age of primordial collectivities which cannot be considered political in the modern sense. These institutions such as the *gaṇa*, the *vidatha*, the *sabhā*, the *samiti* and the *pariṣad* were mainly tribal in character. Of these the *vidatha* seems to have been of the greatest antiquity among the Indo-Āryans and contains memories of even pre-Ṛg Vedic times. The presence of women on it negates the view that from the very beginning the Āryan society was patriarchal. However, the woman membership of the *pariṣad* may have been a pre-Āryan trait. In the Vedic *gaṇa* this feature is not prominent, although the epic and purāṇic allusions associate women with this body also. The *gaṇa*, though not as old as the *vidatha*, shares with it the traits of communal ownership and distribution of spoils and other froms of property. It provided a pattern of republican government to some oligarchic states, which supplanted monarchies or chiefdoms in the age of the Buddha. The purely political functions of these Vedic assemblies cannot be easily isolated from their other activities, which again bespeaks of their primitive, communal identity. Political functions mark the *sabhā* and *samiti* more prominently, although it is difficult to ascribe these bodies to any precise period or area. Vedic assemblies were mostly local congregations dealing with local problems; it would be far-fatched to regard them national assemblies covering all the Vedic peoples.

The assemblies of the early Vedic period indicate an extremely rudimentary administrative organization. But in the later Vedic age the jewel-offering ceremony suggests its develoment. The tribal order was undermined by the growing importance of the brāhmaṇa and rājanya, who came to occupy higher positions in the ratnin list. Nevertheless, in so far as the body of the ratnins was predominantly military in character and similar to the council of twelve among early Indo-European peoples, it retained certain primitive traits. Such rituals as cow-raid, game of dice, chariot-race, etc., betray the tribal remnants of the later Vedic polity. At bottom the various consecration ceremonies were either so many ordeals intended to test the qualifications of the candidate for the chieftainship of the tribe, or initiation rites to signalise a new phase in the life of the sacrificer. But these were reduced to formalities divested of all reality; in practice the later Vedic polity had become largely non-tribal and territorial because of the spread of agriculture among the Vedic peoples.

In post-Vedic times, from *c.*600 B.C. onwards varṇa or social class superseded tribal elements and emerged as an important factor in law and politics. Considerations of varṇa apparently influenced the various organs of the state such as the king, ministers or high functionaries, the *pariṣad*, the *paura*, the *jānapada* and army. The origin and growth of the Dharmaśāstra law were conditioned by the varṇa system, and civil and criminal laws discriminated between one social order and another. The need for combination and co-operation between the two upper orders is emphasised, although in actual politics sometimes the kṣatriyas, and, at other times the brāhmaṇas, enjoyed the upper hand. As a social order the vaiśyas or the śūdras never acquired any dominant role in politics.

The main stages in the history of ancient Indian polity can be identified. The earliest stage was that of tribal military democracy in which tribal assemblies, which had some place for women, were mainly preoccupied with war. The age of the *Ṛg Veda* was primarily a period of assemblies. The second stage saw the break-up of the tribal polity under the stress of constant kin conflicts between the rājanya kṣatriya and his ordinary kinsmen called the *viś*. The chiefs were helped by the priests called the brāhmaṇas. This stage saw the beginnings of taxes and classes or varṇas which came to be firmly established in the third stage. The third stage was marked by the formation of the full-fledged state. There arose large territorial monarchies of Kosala and Magadha and tribal oligarchies in north-western India and in the foot of the Himalayas. For the first time we hear of large standing armies and organised machinery for the collection of the land revenue. But the class of landed intermediaries was small and did not enjoy any administrative concessions. The fourth or the Maurya phase saw bureaucratic centralisation based on the expanding economic activities of the state. The state control of various spheres of life could have been effective in the middle Ganga plains. In the Maurya period religion was cleverly exploited for serving political ends. Since Kauṭilya supports the brāhmaṇical social order and opposes heretical sects the state policy recommended by him cannot be regarded as secular. But he does not hesitate to override brāhmaṇical professions wherever and whenever they are at odds with the interests of the ruler intent on conquest. Kauṭilya makes bold and deliberate use of superstition to secure the loyalty of the masses to the state by hoodwinking them. But by way of genuine deification of the king there is little in his treatise.

The fifth stage was marked by the process of decentralised administration in which towns, feudatorise and military elements came to the forefront in both the Deccan and north India. This was partly neutralised by the emphasis on the divinity of the king. The Kuṣāṇa princes assumed the official tittle of *devaputra* and instituted the cult of the worship of the dead king, and the Sātavāhana princes came to be compared to deified epic heroes. The last stage, identical with the Gupta period, may be called the period of proto-feudal polity. The land grants now played an important part in the formation of the political structure, and those made by the Gupta feudatories conferred fiscal and administrative privileges on priestly beneficiaries. It is problematic whether civil officers were allotted land for their services to the state, and the grant of land for military service, so characteristic of European political fedudalism, was absent in the India of Gupta and post-Gupta times. On the other hand from the first century A.D. onwards decentralised administration was sustained by a marked growth in the powers of the caste and professional guilds and also of village headmen and elders.

The present study would show that the development of polity and political ideas in ancient India cannot be isolated from social and economic processes. The tribal set-up seems to have been an important element in Vedic times, but because of the availability of agricultural surplus and kin conflicts social classes and territorial states emerged as important elements in post-Vedic days. Economic activities and the needs of a vast empire determined the Maurya mechanism for administration. Although the impact of trade on polity was felt in post-Maurya times, in the Gupta period land grants conditioned the formation of administrativa structure. A few foreign features appeared in the post-Maurya polity, but by and large developments continued on indigenous lines. The influence of religion is perceptible throughout, though it becomes more important in post-Maurya and Gupta times when deliberate attempts are made to attribute divine powers to the head of the state.

BIBLIOGRAPHY

VEDIC TEXTS

Aitareya Brāhmaṇa, *BI*, 1895-1906.

Āpastamba Śrautasūtra with the comm. of Rudradatta, Ed. Richard Garbe, 3 vols., *BI*, Calcutta, 1882-1902. Tr. W. Caland, 3 vols., Göttingen-Leipzig-Amsterdam, 1921-28.

Atharva Veda Saṃhitā (School of the Śaunakas), Ed. C.R. Lanman, Tr. W.D. Whitney, *HOS*, vii and viii, Harvard, University, 1905. Ed. R. Roth and W.D. Whitney, Berlin, 1856. With the comm. of Sāyaṇa, Ed. S. Pāṇḍurang Paṇḍit, 4 vols., Bombay, 1895-98. Tr. R.T.H. Griffith, 2 vols., Banaras, 1916-17.

Baudhāyana Gṛhyasūtra, Ed. R. Shamasastry, Oriental Library Publications, University of Mysore, 1920.

Bṛhadāraṇyaka Upaniṣad with the *Prakaśikā* of Ranga Ramanuja, ASS, No. 64, Poona, 1911.

Chāndogya Upaniṣad, Text, Tr. and Annotation, Emile Sénart, Paris, 1930.

Gobhila Gṛhyasūtra, Tr. H. Oldenberg, *SBE*, xxx, Oxford, 1892.

Gopatha Brāhmaṇa, Ed. Deinke Gaastra, E.J. Brill, Leiden, 1919.

Kāṭhaka Saṃhitā, Ed. Leopold von Schroder, F.A. Brockhaus, Leipzig, 1900-10.

Khadira Gṛhyasūtra, Mysore, 1913. Tr. H. Oldenberg, *SBE*, xxix, Oxford, 1886.

Jaiminīya or Talavakāra Upaniṣad Brāhmaṇa, Ed. Rama Deva, D.A.V. College Research Department, Lahore, 1921.

Kātyāyana Śrautasūtra with the comm. of Karkācārya, Ed. Madanmohan Pathak, Banaras, 1904.

Maitrāyaṇī Saṃhitā, Ed. Leopold von Schroder, Otto Harrassowitz, Leipzig, 1923.

Nighaṇṭu and Nirukta, Ed. and Tr. Lakshman Sarup, Text, University of Panjab, 1927. Eng. Tr. and Notes, Oxford, 1921.

Pañcaviṃśa Brāhmaṇa, Tr. W. Caland, *BI*, Calcutta, 1931.

Pāraskara Gṛhyasūtra, Ed. M.G. Bakre, The Gujarati Printing Press, Bombay, 1917.

Ṛg Veda Brāhmaṇas: *Aitareya* and *Kauṣītaki Brāhmaṇas*, Tr. A.B. Keith, *HOS*, xxv, Harvard, 1920.

Ṛg Veda Saṃhitā with the comm. of Sāyaṇa, 5 vols., Vaidika Samshodhan Mandal, Poona, 1933-51. Tr. of the first six Maṇḍalas, H.H. Wilson, London, 1850-7, German Tr. K.F. Geldner, Cambridge, Massachusetts, 1951.

Sāmavidhāna Brāhmaṇa, Ed. Satyavrata Samasrami, Mahendranath Sarkar (Satyayantra), 2nd edn, Calcutta, 1895.

Taittirīya Brāhmaṇa, i, Ed. H.N. Apte, ASS, No. 37, 1898.

Taittirīya Saṃhitā, Ed. A. Weber, *Indische Studien*, Band 11 and 12, Leipzig, 1871-2. Tr. A.B. Keith, *HOS*, xviii and xix, Harvard, 1914.

(*The*) *Taittirīya Saṃhitā* of the *Kṛṣṇa Yajur-Veda* with the commentary of Bhaṭṭabhāskara Miśra, Ed. A.M. Sastri and K. Rangacharya, Government Oriental Library Series, Mysore, 1895.

DHARMAŚĀSTRA AND ALLIED LITERATURE

Āpastambīya Dharmasūtra, Ed. G. Bühler, Government Central Book Depot, Bombay, 1892-94.

Arthaśāstra of Kauṭilya, Ed. R. Shamasastry, 3rd edn., Mysore, 1924 (unless otherwise stated references in this work refer to this text.) Tr. R. Shamasastry, 3rd edn., Mysore, 1929. Ed. with comm. by T. Gaṇapati Śāstri, 3 vols., Trivandrum, 1924-25. Ed. J. Jolly and R. Schmidt, vol. i, Lahore, 1924. *Arthaśāstra ili Nauka Politiki*, Tr. in Russian, V.I. Kalyanov, Moscow, 1959. R.P. Kangle, *The Kauṭilīya Arthaśāstra*, Ed. and Tr., 3 pts, University of Bombay, 1960-65.

Commentaries on the *Arthaśāstra*.

(i) *Jayamaṅgalā* (runs up to the end of BK I of the *AŚ* with gaps), Ed. G. Harihara Sastri, *JOR*, xx-xxiii.

(ii) *Pratipada-pañcikā* by Bhaṭṭavāmin (on BK II from sec. 8), Ed. K.P. Jayaswal and A. Banerji-Sastri, *JBORS*, xi-xii.

(iii) *Nayacandrikā* by Mādhava Yajva (on BKs. VII-XII), Ed. Udayavira Śāstrī, Lahore, 1924.

(iv) *Nītinirṇīti* of Āchārya Yoggham alias Mugdhavilāsa, a fragment of the commentary on *A Fragment of the Kouṭalya's Arthaśāstra* alias *Rājasiddhānta*, Ed. Muni Jina Vijaya, Bombay, 1959.

Abhilaṣitārthacintāmaṇi or *Mānasollāsa*, Ed. G.K. Shrigondeker, GOS, xxviii and lxxxiv, Baroda, 1925-29.

Bārhaspatya-sūtram (*Arthaśāstra*), Ed. F.W. Thomas, Punjab Sanskrit Series, Lahore, 1922.

Baudhāyana Dharmasūtra, Ed. E. Hultzsch, F. A. Brockhaus, Leipzig, 1884.

Bṛhaspati Smṛti, Ed. K.V. Rangaswami Aiyangar, GOS, lxxxv, Baroda, 1941. Tr. J. Jolly, *SBE*, Oxford, 1889.

Gautama Dharmasūtra, Ed. A.S. Stenzler, London, 1876, with the comm. of Maskarin, Ed. L. Srinivasacharya, Government Oriental Library Series, Mysore, 1917.

Kāmandakīya Nītisāra, Ed. R.L. Mitra, Bl, Calcutta, 1884. (The Chowkhamba Sanskrit Series text, Banaras, has been followed in Ch. III). Tr. M.N. Dutt, Calcutta, 1896.

Kāmandaka Nītisāra, Trivandrum Sanskrit Series, Trivandrum, 1912.

Kātyāyana Smṛti on Vyavahāra (Law and Procedure), Ed. with reconstituted text, Translation, Notes and Introduction by P.V. Kane, Published by the Author, Bombay, 1933.

Manu Smṛti or Mānava Dharmaśāstra, Ed. S.N. Mandlik, Ganpat Krishnaji's Press, Bombay, 1886, Tr. G. Bühler, *SBE*, xxv, Oxford, 1886.

Nārada Smṛti with extracts from the comm. of Asahāya, Ed. J. Jolly, *BI*, Calcutta, 1885. Tr. J. Jolly, *SBE*, xxxiii, Oxford, 1889.

Samarāṅgaṇa Sūtradhāra, 2 vols., Ed. T. Gaṇapati Śāstrī, GOS, Baroda, 1924-5.

Śukranītisāra, Ed. Jībānanda Vidyāsāgara, Calcutta, 1890.

Tirukkuṛal, Tr. V.R.R. Dikshitar, The Adyar Library, 1949.

Vasiṣṭha Dharmaśāstra, Ed. A.A. Führer, Government Central Book Depot, Bombay, 1883.

Viṣṇu Smṛti or Vaiṣṇava Dharmaśāstra, (with extracts from the comm. of Nanda Pandita), Ed. J. Jolly, BI, Calcutta, 1881. Tr. J. Jolly, *SBE*, vii, Oxford, 1880.

Vajñavalkya Smṛti with Vīramitrodaya and Mitākṣarā, Chowkhamba Sanskrit Series, Banaras, 1930.

Tr. of the Dharmasūtras of Āpastamba, Gautama, Vasiṣṭha and Baudhāyana by G. Bühler in *SBE*, ii and xiv, Oxford, 1879-82.

EPICS, PURĀṆAS AND ALLIED WORKS

Ādi Parva, Critical Edn., Bhandarkar Oriental Reseaıch Institute, Poona, 1933.

Agni Purāṇa, *BI*, Calcutta, 1882. This text has been used in chapters other than Chapter II.

———Ed. Hari Narain Āpte, ASS, 1900 (this text has been used in Ch. II. In other Chapters the *BI* Calcutta text has been used).

Ayodhyā Kāṇḍa of the *Rāmāyaṇa*, Bombay, 1913.

Bāla Kāṇḍa of the *Rāmāyaṇa*, Bombay, 1912.

Bhāgavata Purāṇa, Kumbakonam, 1916.

Brahma Purāṇa, ASS, 1895.

Brahmāṇḍa Purāṇa, Venkatesvara Press, Bombay, 1913.

Bṛhannārdīya Purāṇa, *BI*, Calcutta, 1891.

Kālakācārya-Kathānaka, Ed. H. Jacobi, *ZDMG*, 1880.

Kūrma Purāṇa, *BI*, Calcutta, 1890.

Kṛṣṇajanmakhaṇḍa of the *Brahmavaivarta Purāṇa*, Allahabad, 1920.

Mahābhārata, Calcutta Edn. Ed. N. Siromani and others, *BI*, Calcutta, 1834-9. Tr. K.M. Ganguly, published by P.C. Roy, Calcutta, 1884-96. Kumbakonam Edn. Ed. T.R. Krishnacharya and T.R. Vyasacharya, Bombay, 1905-10. Critical Edn. Ed. Various hands, Poona, 1927-1966. (*The*) *Jaya Saṃhitā*, i.e. *The Ur Mahābhārata*, 2 vols., redacted by Keshavram K. Shastree Gujarat Research Institute, Ahmedabad, 1977. *Śānti Parva*, Chitrashala Press, Poona, 1932.

Mārkaṇḍeya Purāṇa, Ed. Rev. K.M. Banerjee, *BI*, Calcutta, 1862. Tr. F.E. Pargiter, Calcutta, 1904.

Mṛcchakaṭika of Sūdraka, Ed. and Tr. R.D. Karmarkar, Poona, 1937. Tr. R.P. Oliver, Illinois, 1938.

Padma Carita, Bombay, Vikrama Saṃvat, 1885.

Pancantantra, Ed. F. Edgerton, Poona, 1930; Tr. F. Edgerton, American Oriental Society, New Haven, Connecticut, 1924.

Vāyu Purāṇa, Ed. R.L. Mitra, 2 vols., *BI*, Calcutta, 1880.

Viṣṇu Purāṇa, Gita Press Edn., Gorakhpur, Tr. H.H. Wilson, 5 vols., London, 1864-70.

BUDDHIST TEXTS

Dīgha Nikāya, Ed. T.W. Rhys Davids and J.E. Carpenter,

3 vols. PTS, London, 1890-1911. Tr. T.W. Rhys Davids, 3 vols., *SBB*, London, 1899-1921.

Dīgha Nikāya (Hindi), Tr. Rahula Sāṅkṛtyayana and Jagadisa Kasyapa, Banaras, 1936.

Divyāvadāna, Ed. E.B. Cowell and R.A. Neil, Cambridge, 1886.

Jātaka with commentary, Ed. V. Fausböll, 7 vols. (vol. 7, Index, by D. Anderson), London, 1877-97. Tr. Various hands, 6 vols., London, 1895-1907.

Mahāvastu, Ed. E. Sénart, 3 vols., A.L. Impremerie National (Societe Asiatique Series, no. 2), Paris, 1882-97.

Milindapañho, Ed. V. Trenckner, London, 1928, Tr. T.W. Rhys Davids, *SBE*, Oxford, 1890-4.

Sumaṅgala-Vilāsinī (comm. to *Dīgha Nikāya*), Ed. T.W. Rhys Davids and others, 3 vols., PTS, London, 1886-1932.

Sutta-Nipāta, Ed. V. Fausböll, 2 vols., PTS, London, 1885-94.

Vinaya Piṭaka, Ed. H. Oldenberg, 5 vols., PTS, London, 1879-83. *The Book of Discipline*, Tr. I.B. Horner, 5 pts, *SBB*, London, 1938-52.

W.W. Rockhill, *The Life of the Buddha*, Trübner's Oriental Series, London, 1907.

TECHNICAL WORKS

Amarakośa, Ed. H.D. Sharma and N.G. Sardesai, Oriental Book Agency, Poona, 1941.

Kāmasūtra of Vātsyāyana with the comm. Jayamaṅgalā of Yaśodhara, Ed. Gosvami Damodar Shastri, Banaras, 1929.

Mahābhāṣya of Patañjali, Ed. F. Keilhorn, 3 vols., The Department of Public Instruction, Bombay Sanskrit and Prakrit Series, Nos xxviii-xxx, Bombay, 1892-1909.

Pāṇini-Sūtra-Pāṭha and Parisiṣṭas with Word Index, compiled by S. Pathak and S. Chitrao, Bhandarkar Oriental Research Institute, Poona, 1935.

COINS AND INSCRIPTIONS

A.S. Altekar, *Corpus of Indian Coins*, vol. IV; *The Coinage of the Gupta Empire*, Banaras, 1957.

J.F. Fleet, *Inscriptions of the Early Gupta Kings*, *CII*, iii, London, 1888; Reprint, Indological Book House, Varanasi,

1963; Sten Konow, *Kharoṣṭhī Inscriptions, CII*, ii, Part I, Government of India, Central Publication Branch, Calcutta, 1929.

Heinrich Lüders, *Mathura Inscriptions*, unpublished papers ed. Klaus L. Janert with an Introductory note by E. Waldschmidt, Göttingen, 1961.

Lüders' List of Inscriptions, *EI*, x.

V.V. Mirashi, *Inscriptions of the Kalacuri-Cedi Era, CII*, iv, two parts, Government Epigraphist for India, Ootacamund, 1955.

D.C. Sircar, *Select Inscriptions Bearing on Indian History and Civilisation*, i, Calcutta University, 1942.

——*Indian Epigraphical Glossary*, Motilal Banarsidass, Delhi, 1966.

V.A. Smith, *Catalogue of the Coins in the Indian Museum, Calcutta*, Oxford, 1906.

FOREIGN SOURCES

(i) Greek

Aristotle, *Politics*, Tr. B. Jowett, Oxford, 1905.

Herodotus, *The Histories*, Tr. Aubery de Selincourt, Penguin Books, 1954.

J.W. McCrindle, *Ancient India as Described by Megasthenes, and Arrian*, Chukerverity, Chatterjee Co., Calcutta, 1926.

Ancient India as Described in Classical Literature, Reprint, Eastern Book House, Patna, 1987.

Plato, *Laws*, Tr. R.G. Bury, 2 vols., The Loeb Classical Library, London, 1926.

——*The Republic*, Tr. B. Jowett, New York, 1946.

(ii) Chinese

Samuel Beal, *Travels of Fah-hian and Sung Yun* (Tr.), London, Trübner, 1869.

——, *The Life of Hiuen Tsiang*, London, 1888.

Ho Chang-Chun, "Fa-hsien's Pilgrimage to Buddhist Countries", *Chinese Literature*, 1956, No. 3.

H.A. Giles, *The Travels of Fa-Hsien or Record of Buddhistic Kingdoms* (Tr.), Cambridge, 1923.

James Legge, *A Record of Buddhistic Kingdoms* (being an account of the Chinese monk Fa-hien's Travels), Tr., Oxford, 1886.

T. Takakusu, *A Record of Buddhist Religion*, The Clarendon Press, Oxford, 1896.

T. Watters, *On Yuan Chwang's Travels in India*, Ed. T.W. Rhys Davids and S.W. Bushell, 2 vols., Royal Asiatic Society, London, 1904-5.

REFERENCE BOOKS

Karl Brugmann, *Elements of the Comparative Grammar of the Indo-Germanic Languages*, Tr. from German, Various hands, 4 vols., New York, 1888-95.

V.R.R. Dikshitar, *Puranic Index* (incomplete), Madras, 1952.

Laxmanshastri Joshi, *Dharmakośa*, i (in three parts), iv (in six parts), Wai, Dist. Satara, 1937-41 and 1973-79.

A.A. Macdonnel and A.B. Keith, *Vedic Index of Names and Subjects*, 2 vols., Indian Text Series, London, 1922.

Monier Monier-Williams, *A Sanskrit-English Dictionary*, Oxford, 1951.

T.W. Rhys Davids and W. Stede, *Pali-English Dictionary*, PTS, London, 1921.

Viswabandhu Shastri, *Vedic Padānūkrama Kośa*, In five vols. subdivided into 14 parts, V.R.R. Institute, Lahore, 1944.

SECONDARY WORKS ON ANCIENT INDIAN POLITY AND ALLIED SUBJECTS

V.S. Agrawala, *India as Known to Pāṇini*, University of Lucknow, Lucknow, 1953.

S.K. Aiyangar, *Ancient India*, Lurac, London, 1911.

———*Evolution of Hindu Administrative Institutions in South India*, University of Madras, 1931.

A.S. Altekar, *State and Government in Ancient India*, Motilal Banarsidass, Banaras, 1949; second edn., Delhi, 1955; third edn., Delhi, 1958.

———*Sources of Hindu Dharma*, Institute of Public Administration, Sholapur, 1952.

Perry Anderson, *Lineages of the Absolutist State*, New Left Books, Verso, London, 1974.

K.D. Bajpaiyi, "New Finds of the Kushana Period from Mathura", *Proc. IHC*, Vallabh Vidyanagar, 1957, pp. 68-70.

A. Barth, *Religions of India*, Routledge & Kegan Paul, London, 1882.

N.C. Bandyopadhaya, *Development of Hindu Polity and Political Theories*, R. Cambray, Calcutta, 1927.

———*Kauṭilya or an Exposition of His Social and Political Theory*, National Publishing House, Calcutta, 1927.

P.N. Banerjea, *International Law and Custom in Ancient India*, Reprint from Journal of Department of Letters, xx, Calcutta University, 1920.

———, *Public Administration in Ancient India*, Macmillan, London, 1916.

L.D. Barnett, *Antiquities of India*, Philip Lee Warner, London, 1913.

A.L. Basham, *The Wonder That Was India*, Sidgwick & Jackson, London, 1954.

Emile Benveniste, *Indo-European Language and Society*, Faber and Faber, London, 1973.

D.R. Bhandarkar, *Carmichael Lectures*, Calcutta University, 1918.

———, *Some Aspects of Ancient Hindu Polity*, Banaras Hindu University, Banaras, 1929.

H.C. Bhardwaj, *Aspects of Ancient Indian Technology*, Motilal Banarsidass, Delhi, 1979.

Sibesh Bhattacharya, "Political Authority and Brahman Kshatriya Relationship in Early India—An Aspect of the Power Elite Configuration", *IHR*, Vol. 10, no. 1-2, 1984, pp. 1-20.

G.M. Bongard-Levin, Ed., "Republics in Ancient India" in G.M. Bongard-Levin, *A Complex Study of Ancient India (A Multi-Disciplinary Approach)*, Ajanta Publications, Delhi, 1986.

Atindranath Bose, *Social and Rural Economy of Northern India* (*cir.* 600 B.C.—200 A.D.), 2 Vols, Firma K.L. Mukhopadhayay, Calcutta, 1945.

H.M. Chadwick, *The Heroic Age*, Cambridge, 1912.

Bhaskar Chatterjee, "Religion and Polity in the Kushan Age" *JIH*, 1976, pp. 511-15.

S.K. Chattopadhyaya, *Early History of Northern India*, Academic Publications, Calcutta, 1958.

B. Chattopadhayay, *Kushan State and Indian Society—A Study in Post-Maurya Polity and Society*, Punthi, Pustak, Calcutta, 1975.

B.D. Chattopadhayay, "Transition to the Early Historical Phase in the Deccan. A Note" in B.M. Pande and B.D. Chattopadhayay (Ed.), *Archaeology and History*, Agam Kala Prakashan, Delhi, 1987.

V. Gordon Childe, *Man Makes Himself*, Watt, London, 1948.

H.J.M. Claessen and P. Skalnik, Eds, *The Early State*, Mouton, The Hague, 1978.

H.J.M. Claessen and Pieter Van De Velde, Eds, *Early State Dynamics*, E.J. Brill, Leiden, 1987.

F.W. Coker, *Readings in Political Philosophy*, Macmillan, New York, 1938.

H.T. Colebrooke, *Miscellaneous Essays*, Ed. E.B. Cowell, Higgin Botham, London, 1871-2.

S.A. Dange, *India From Primitive Communism to Slavery*, PPH, Bombay, 1949.

A.C. Das, "Limited Monarchy in Ancient India", *Modern Review*, ii, 1907.

P.S. Deshmukh, *Religion in Vedic Literature*, Oxford University Press, London, 1933.

Premkumari Dikshit, *Mahābhārata men Rājyavyavasthā*, Archana Prakashan, Lucknow, 1970.

V.R.R. Dikshitar, *The Gupta Polity*, University of Madras, 1952.

———, *Hindu Administrative Institutions*, University of Madras, 1929.

———, *Mauryan Polity*, University of Madras, 1932.

———, "Notes on the Paura-Janapada", *IHQ*, VI, 1930.

Charles Drekmeier, *Kingship and Community in Early India*, Oxford University Press, Stanford University Press, California, 1962.

M.E. Drouin, "The Numbus and Signs of Deification on the Coins of the Indo-Skythian Kings", *Revue Numismatique*, 1901, pp. 154-66, Tr. IA, 1903, p. 427ff.

L. Dumount, "The Conception of Kingship in Ancient India", *CIS*, Vol. 6, 1962, pp. 407-77.

Will Durant, *The Story of Civilization*, i, Our Oriental Haritage, Simon & Schuster, New York, 1942.

B.N. Dutta, *Dialectics of Hindu Ritualism*, Pt. I, Gupta Press, Calcutta, 1950; Pt II, Gupta Press, Calcutta, 1956.

———, *Hindu Law of Inheritance*, Nababharat Publishers, Calcutta, 1957.

———, *Studies in Indian Social Polity*, Purabi Publishers, Calcutta, 1944; New Edn., Nababharat Publishers, Calcutta, 1983.

R.C. Dutta, Civilization in the Brahmana Period", *Calcutta Review*, lxxxv, 1887.

F. Engels, *The Origin of the Family, Private Property and the State*, Moscow, 1948.

August Fick, *Indogermanischen*, Göttingen, 1871.

Richard Fick, *The Social Organisation in North-East India in Buddha's Time*, Calcutta University, 1920.

James George Frazer, *The Golden Bough*, Third Edn, 2 Vols, Macmillan, London, 1922.

U.N. Ghoshal, "The Constitutional Significance of Samgha-Gana in the Post-Vedic Period", *Indian Culture*, vii, 1945.

———, *Contributions to the History of Hindu Revenue System*, Saraswat Library, Calcutta, 1929.

———, *Hindu Political Theories*, OUP, Calcutta, 1923.

———, *A History of Hindu Public Life*, Ramesh Ghoshal, Calcutta, 1945, ii (*A History of Indian Public Life*), OUP, Bombay, 1966.

———, *A History of Indian Political Ideas*, OUP, Bombay, 1959.

———, "The Statue of the Brahmanas in the Dharmasutras", *IHQ*, xxiii, pp. 83-92.

Jan Gonda, *Ancient Indian Kingship from Religious Points of View*, E.J. Brill, Leiden, 1969.

Lallanji Gopal, "The Śukranīti—a Nineteenth Century Text", *BSOAS*, xxv, 524-26.

G.S. Ghurye, *Caste and Class in India*, Bombay, 1950; Popular Book Depot, Bombay, 1961.

———, *Caste and Race in India*, London, 1932; Popular Prakashan, Bombay, 1979.

Alexander Goldenweiser, *Anthropology*, New York, 1946.

Jack Goody, *The Oriental, the Ancient and the Primitive*, Cambridge University Press, 1990.

R.A.L.H. Gunawardana, "The Analysis of Pre-Colonial Social Formations in Asia in the Writings of Karl Marx", *IHR*, ii, 365-88.

Irfan Habib, "An Examination of Wittfogel's Theory of

Oriental Despotism", *Studies in History*, Asia, Bombay, 1969, pp. 378-92.

H.R. Hall, *The Ancient History of the Near East*, Methuen, London, 1936.

R.C. Hazra, *Studies in the Puranic Records in Hindu Rites and Customs*, Dacca, 1940; Motilal Banarsidass, Delhi, 1975.

———, *Studies in the Upapuranas*, Vol. I, Sanskrit College Research Series, Calcutta, 1958.

J.C. Heesterman, *The Ancient Indian Royal Consecration*, Mouton, The Hague, 1957.

———, *Inner Conflict of Indian Tradition*, OUP, Delhi, 1985.

———, "The King's Order", *CIS*, Vol. 20, No. 1, 1986, pp. 1-13.

G.W.J. Hegel, *Philosophy of History*, Tr. J. Sibree, New York, 1949.

Barry Hindess and Paul Q. Hirst, *Pre-Capitalist Modes of Production*, Routledge & Kegan Paul, London, 1975.

E.W. Hopkins, *The Mutual Relations of the Four Castes According to the Manavadharmasastram*, Parlour, Delhi, 1976; Leipzig, 1881.

———, "Social and Military Position of the Ruling Caste in Ancient India", *JAOS*, xiii, 57-376; Bharat Bhariti, Varanasi, 1972.

Jagdish Chandra Jain, *Life in Ancient India as Depicted in the Jain Canons*, New Book Company, Bombay, 1947.

K.P. Jayaswal, *Hindu Polity*, 2 pts., Butterworth, Calcutta, 1924.

———, *Hindu Polity*, The Bangalore Printing & Publishing Company, Bangalore, 1943 (Unless specified otherwise, references correspond to this edition).

———, *Manu and Yājñavalkya*, Butterworth, Calcutta, 1930.

D.N. Jha, *Revenue System in Post-Maurya and Gupta Times*, Punthi Pustak, Calcutta, 1967.

Rev. Richard Jones, *An Essay on the Distribution of Wealth and on the Sources of Taxation*, Reprint, New York, 1956.

P.V. Kane, *History of Dharmasastra*, ii, Bhandarkar Oriental Research Institute, Poona, 1941.

Richard S. Kennedy, "The King in Early South India, As Chieftain and Emperor", vi, *IHR*, Vol. 3, No. I, 1976, pp. 1-15.

A.B. Keith, *A History of Sanskrit Literature*, Oxford, 1928.

———, *Religion and Philosophy of the Vedas*, OUP, London, 1925.

D.D. Kosambi, "Ancient Kosala and Magadha", *JBBRAS*, NS, xxvii.

——, *An Introduction to the Study of Indian History*, Popular Prakashan, Bombay, 1956.

——, *The Culture and Civilization of Ancient India in Historical Outline*, Routledge & Kegan Paul, London, 1965; Vikas, Delhi, 1970.

Gunnar Landtman, *The Origin of the Inequality of Social Classes*, London, 1938.

B.C. Law, *India as Described in Early Texts of Buddhism and Jainism*, Luzac, London, 1941.

N.N. Law, *Aspects of Ancient Indian Polity*, Orient Longman, Bombay, 1921;

——, "Reply to Mr. Dikshitar's Note on Panura-Janapada", *IHQ*, vi, p. 183ff.

R. Lingat, *The Classical Law of India*, tr. from French with additions by J. Duncan M. Derrett, University of California, 1973.

I.W. Mabbett, *Truth, Myth and Politics in Ancient India*, Thomsons Press, Delhi, 1972.

A.A. Macdonell, *Vedic Mythology*, Encyclopedia of Indo-Aryan Series, Verlag Von Karl J. Trübner, Strassburg, 1897.

T.V. Mahalingam, *South Indian Polity*, Madras University, Madras, 1955.

S.K. Maity, *The Economic Life of Northern India in the Gupta Period*, World Press, 1957; Motilal Banarsidass, Delhi, 1970.

R.C. Majumdar, *Corporate Life in Ancient India*, Firma K.L. Mukhopadhayay, Calcutta, 1969.

——, Ed., *History of Bengal*, i, Dacca University, Dacca, 1943.

——, and A.S. Altekar, Ed., *The Vakataka-Gupta Age*, Motilal Banarsidass, 1967.

——, and A.D. Pusalkar, Ed., *History and Culture of the Indian People*, i, *The Vedic Age*, Bharatiya Vidya Bhawan, Bombay, 1951.

——&——, ii, *The Age of Imperial Unity*, Bharatiya Vidya Bhawan, Bombay, 1951.

Karl Marx, *Historical Writings*, i, PPH, Bombay, 1944.

——, *Pre-Capitalist Economic Formations*, Ed. and introd., E. Hobsbawm, Lawrence and Wishart, London, 1964; *The Grundrisse*, Ed. M. Nicolaus, Penguin, Harmondsworth, 1973.

——, *Capital*, i, Progress Publishers, Moscow, 1965; *Capital*, iii, Progress Publishers, Moscow, 1962.

B.N. Mukherjee, *The Kushana Genealogy*, Calcutta, 1967.

F. Max Müller, *A History of Ancient Sanskrit Literature*, Oxford University Press and IBH, Delhi, 1970; Allahabad, 1917.

E.M. Medvedev, "K Voprosu o Formakh Jemlevaldeniya Severnoi Indii, v, VI-VII vekakh", *Problemi Vostokovedeniya*, 1959, i, pp. 49-61.

R.N. Mehta, *Pre-Buddhist India*, Examiner Press, Bombay, 1939.

B.B. Mishra, *Polity in the Agni Purāṇa*, Punthi Pustak, Calcutta, 1965.

K.N. Mishra, *State Sponsored Public Welfare Plans in the Mahābhārata*, Bharat Manisha, Varanasi, 1972.

S.C. Mishra, An Inscriptional Approach to the Study of the Arthaśāstra of Kauṭilya, Ph.D. Thesis, University of Delhi, 1984.

S.N. Mishra, *Ancient Indian Republics from the Earliest Times to the Sixth Century* A.D., Upper India Publications, Lucknow, 1976.

Yogendra Mishra, *An Early History of Vaiśālī*, Motilal Banarsidass, Delhi, 1962.

William P. Mitchell, "The Hydraulic Hypothesis: A Reappraisal", *Current Anthropology*, xiv, Dec. 1973, 532-34.

Montesquieu, *The Spirit of Laws*, Tr. T. Nugent, The Hafner, New York, 1949.

Lewis H. Morgan, *Ancient Society*, Reprint, K.P. Bagchi, Calcutta, 1982.

Hirendranath Mukherjee, *India Struggles for Freedom*, PPH, Bombay, 1946.

R.K. Mookerjee, *Aśoka*, Motilal Banarsidass, Delhi, 1962; London, 1928.

——, *Local Government in Ancient India*, Oxford, 1920.

Shobha Mukerji, *The Republican Trends in Ancient India*, Munshiram Manoharlal, Delhi, 1969.

A.K. Narain, "The Kushan State: A Preliminary Study" in Henri J.M. Classen and Peter Skalnik (Ed.) *The Study of the State*, Mouton Publishers, The Hague 1981, pp. 251-73.

Pran Nath, *Economic Conditions of Ancient India*, Royal Asiatic Society, London, 1929.

S.L. Pande, *Bhīshma Kā Rājadharma*, Arya Nagar, Lucknow, 1955.

K.A. Nilakanta Sastri, Ed., *A Comprehensive History of India*, ii, *The Mauryas and Satavahanas*, Orient Longman, Bombay, 1957.

——— "The Place of Arthasastra in the History of Indian Polity", *ABORI*, xxviii, 1941.

———, "Address of the General President", *Proceeding of the 16th Session of the All-India Oriental Conference*, i, Lucknow, 1951.

K.C. Ojha, *Original Home and the Family of the Mauryas*, *JGJRI*, ix.

F.E. Pargiter, *Indian Historical Tradition*, London, 1922; Motilal Banarsidass, Delhi, 1972.

N.E. Parry, *A Monograph on Lushai Customs and Ceremonies*, Aizwal, Mizoram, 1973.

D.R. Patil. *Cultural History from the Vāyu Purāṇa*, Deccan College, Postgraduate & Research Institute, Poona, 1946.

Beni Prasad, *Theory of Government in Ancient India*, Central Book Depot, 1986; Allahabad, 1928.

———, *The State in Ancient India*, The Indian Press, Allahabad, 1928.

B.N. Puri, *India in the Time of Patanjali*, Bharatiya Vidya Bhawan, Bombay, 1968.

———, "Ideology and Religion in the Kushan Epoch", *Central Asia in the Kushan Period*, Vol. II, UNESCO, Mockba, 1975, pp. 183.

———, "*Provincial and Local Administration in the Kusana Period*", *Proceedings IHC*, Annamalai, 1945, pp. 62-66.

———, *India Under the Kushanas*, Bharatiya Vidya Bhawan, Bombay, 1965.

R. Rajalakshmi, *Post-Sangam Tamil Polity*, Madras, 1983.

K.V. Rangaswami Aiyangar, *Indian Cameralism*, Adyar Library, Madras, 1949.

———, *Rajadharma*, Adyar Library, Madras, 1941.

E.J. Rapson, Ed., *The Cambridge History of India*, i, Cambridge, 1922.

Wilhelm Rau, *Staat und Gesellschaft im alten Indien*, Wiesbaden, 1957.

H.C. Ray, "Position of the Brahmanas in the Arthaśāstra", *Proceedings of the All-India Oriental Conference*, 1924.

H.C. Raychaudhuri, *Political History of Ancient India*, Seventh Edn, University of Calcutta, Calcutta, 1972.

John M. Rosenfield, *The Dynastic Arts of the Kushans*, University of California Press, 1967.

B.P. Roy, *Political Ideas and Institutions in the Mahābhārata*, Punthi Pustak, Calcutta, 1975.

W. Ruben, "Some Problems of the Ancient Indian Republics", H.K. Krüger (Ed.), *Kunwar Md. Ashraf—An Indian Scholar and Revolutionary 1903-62*, PPH, Delhi, 1969, pp. 5-29.

Rahul Sankrityayana, *History of Central Asia*, Calcutta, 1964.

B.K. Sarkar, *Political Institutions and Theories of the Hindus*, Chukerverti Chatterjee, Calcutta, 1939.

B.C. Sen, *Some Historical Aspects of the Inscriptions of Bengal*, University of Calcutta, 1942.

Emile Sénart, *Caste in India*, Tr. Denison Ross from the French reprinted by ESS Publications, Delhi, 1975.

Sudarshan Seneviratne, "Kalinga and Andhra: The Process of Secondary State Formation in Early India", *IHR*, Vol. 7, No. 1-2, pp. 54-69.

H.C. Seth, "The Spurious in Kauṭilya's AŚ", *A Volume of Eastern and Indian Studies Presented to Professor F.W. Thomas.*

M.K. Sharan, *Tribal Coins—A Study*, Abhinav Prakashan, New Delhi, 1972.

Dasharatha Sharma, "Disarming of the Peasants under the Mauryas", *Enquiry*, No. 5, 114-19.

J.P. Sharma, "The Question of Vidatha in Vedic India", *JRAS*, 1965, Pts. 1 & 2, 43-56.

———, *Republics in Ancient India*, Leiden, 1968.

R.S. Sharma, *Śūdras in Ancient India*, 3rd edn. Motilal Banarsidass, Delhi, 1990.

———, *Indian Feudalism*, University of Calcutta, 1965.

———, "Disarming of the Peasants Under the Mauryas", *Enquiry*, No. 6, 129-33.

———, *Material Culture and Social Formations in Ancient India*, Macmillan, Delhi, 1985.

———, *Urban Decay in India* (*c.* 300-*c.* 1000), Munshiram Manoharlal, Delhi, 1987.

———, *Origin of the State in India*, University of Bombay, 1989.

———, *Ancient India*, NCERT, New Delhi, 1990.

———, "Stages in State Formation in Ancient India", *Social Science Probings*, Vol. 2, No. I, March 1985, pp. 1-19.

Jagdish Lal Shastri, *Political Thought in the Puranas*, Published by the Author, Lahore, 1944.

S.D. Singh, *Ancient Indian Warfare with Special Reference to the Vedic Period*, E.J. Brill, Leiden, 1965.

H.N. Sinha, *Sovereignty in Ancient Indian Polity*, Luzac, London, 1936.

N.K.P. Sinha, *Political Ideas and Ideals in the Mahabharata* (A Study of First Two Parvans), Oriental Publishers and Distributors, New Delhi, 1976.

D.C. Sircar, *Studies in the Political and Administrative Systems in Ancient and Medieval India*, Motilal Banarsidass, Delhi, 1974.

William Smith, *A Smaller History of Rome From the Earliest Times to the Death of Trajan*, John Murray, London, 1887.

J.W. Spellman, *Political Theory of Ancient India*: A Study of Kingship from the Earliest Times to Circa A.D. 300, Clarendon Press, London, 1964.

Mrs. Sinclair Stevenson, *The Heart of Jainism*, OUP, London, 1915; Munshiram Manoharlal, 1970.

N. Subrahmaniam, *Sangam Polity*, Ennes Publication, Madurai, 1980.

W.W. Tarn, *Hellenistic Civilisation*, 3rd Edn. Revised by the Author and G.T. Griffith, Edward Arnold and Company, London, 1952.

Romila Thapar, *A History of India*, Vol. I, Penguin, 1966.

———, *Ancient Indian Social History*, Orient Longman, Delhi, 1978.

———, *From Lineage to State: Social Formations in the Mid-First Millennium* B.C. *in the Ganga Valley*, OUP, Delhi, 1984.

———, *The Mauryas Revisited*, K.P. Bagchi, New Delhi, 1987.

George Thomson, *Aeschylus and Athens*, London, 1946.

———, *Studies in Ancient Greek Society*, i, London, 1949.

B.G. Tilak, *The Arctic Home in the Vedas*, Tilak Bros. Poona, 1925.

A.A. Vigasin and A.M. Samozvantsev, *Society, State and Law in Ancient India*, Sterling Publishers, New Delhi, 1985.

K.J. Virji, *Ancient History of Saurashtra*, Bombay, 1952.

S.V. Viswanath, *International Law in Ancient India*, Longman Green, London, 1925.

Heinrich Zimmer, *Altindisches Leben*, Berlin, 1879.

INDEX

SUBJECT

(Matter covered by the Contents is generally left out in the Index)

Abhaya Datta, 235
absolutism, 307
Aditi, 120, 146
Ādityas, 120, 127, 178
administration, Aśokan 289; border 372; civil and criminal 21, 33, 289; Coḷa 3; criminal 372, 374; decentralised 406; in Gupta period 388; Indo-Persian system of 30; judicial 26; Maurya rural 375; post-Maurya militarization of 385; municipal 28, 374; of justice 24, 243-44; 246-47, 264, 337, 390; provincial 362, 385; rural 284, 286; self 4; town 75; urban 25; urban and rural 372; village 309, 334
administrative units, 27, under the Guptas 330-31; under the Kusāṇas 295; under the Sātavāhanas 276
Afghanistan, 15, 308
Agalassoi, 225
Agni, 90-6, 98, 106, 112, 124, 134, 178, 359
Agni Vaiśvānara, 151
Agora (Homeric assembly), 111
agriculture 85, 130-31, 183, 238, 350; as basis of the state 225-26; iron and 358; iron ploughshare based 132; invention of 194; and later Vedic state 361; Mauryas opening new regions to 378; operations 34; pre-plough 103, 121; promotion of 166; spread among Vedic peoples 404
agrarian resources, transfer of, 82
Aindra, 256
Ajātaśatru of Kāśī, 151
Ajīvikas, 262
akṣayanīvi (perpetual tenure), nature of, 288; under the Kuṣāṇas 300, 380; under the Guptas 309
Alexander, 28, 223-24, 260, 365, 368
Allahabad, 317, 335
Ambarīṣa, 284
Amarāvatī, 280-81, 400
Ambaṣṭhas, 178, 226
anarchy, 56, 251; and election of Manu 68; and agreement 72
Aṅga, 46, 128
Andhra(s), 235, 278, 377
Anantavarman, 347
Anushilan samiti, 4
amātya(*s*) (ministers or high officers) 18, 21, 27, 30-32, 38-42, 44, 47, 215, 219, 220, 238, 240, 277, 280, 289, 323-25, 327, 345, 364, 372-73, 382, 387, 393, 398; distinguished from *mantrins* 33-34; functions of 276, 278; qualifications of 33-34, 263; in Śaka and Kuṣāṇa records 316. See also *mantrin*
Aral sea, 291
Arikamedu, 280
Arjuna, 284
army, as coercive power 36; composition of 37; composition of Maurya army 374; in later Vedic period 362; in pre-Maurya period 365; in Gupta period 391; and *varṇa* considerations 224-25. See also *daṇḍa*.
aristocracy, compared with Greek and Roman, 10-11; ruling 349
artisans, 38, 83, 152-53, 227, 273; activities of 84; administrative role of 281, 381; and merchants 279, 281, 319, 391; and traders in urban administration 318; areas set apart

for 36; importance of 291; important in post-Maurya period 380-81; imposition of forced labour on 339; income from 280; lost mobility 84; outside kin structure 174; taxpaying 366
āryas, 253, 255
āryan(s), 131, 133, 139, 145, 347, 365; influence 128; non- 131, 156-57, 275; political organization of 143; pre- 127; tribes 150; Vedic 166
āryanisation, 16
Asia, 7, 30, 77-78
Aśoka, 20, 26-27, 67n, 70, 130, 219, 234, 246, 255, 276-77, 291-92, 301-02, 313, 324, 372, 375-77, 384, 397-400
Assakenos, 224, 365
Asiatic mode of production, 77, 78
assemblies, comparison with other Indo-European institutions 90; disappearance of popular 367; kin based 105; kin-ordered 97; Licchavi 110; popular 5, 6, 89, 363; primitive 88, 91, 92; Ṛg Vedic 352, 355; republican 8, 131; Roman 122; tribal 88, 116, 351, 356; Vedic 87, 102; and woman 90
Assyria, 217
Asuras, 63, 121, 127, 133, 136, 138, 177-78
astronomy, 25
astrology, 25
astrologer, 82, 270
Aśvapati Kaikeya, 151
Aśvins, 148
Athens, 367
Atranjikhera, 357-58
Audumbaras, 386
Australia, 150
autarchy, 83
authority, assertion of royal 162; central 26, 78; check on royal 85; coercive 17, 131, 197, 224; diffusion of 334; of brāhmaṇas 177; exaltation of 21, of the council 155; priest as check on royal 378; sacredotal 274; validation of 206
autocratic, form of government 3; institutions 9; measures 3; rule 1
Āyogava, 171, 173
Azilises, 292

Babylon, 168
Bactria, 260, 313
Bahal, 280
bali (offerings, taxes), 179, 182, 189, 205-08, 210-11, 228-29, 354-55, 382
balidāna, 211
Banaras, 295, 377
band, as kin-based solidarity, 198
Barabar Hill, 347
Basārh, 130
Beas river, 224, 368
Benakaṭaka, 286
beneficiaries, administrative rights and 365; conferment of administrative privileges on 390; in post-Maurya period 380, 385; landed 85; priestly 406; religious 286-87, 313, 342-43, 348; secular 345
Bengal, 321, 324, 326-27, 329-30, 332-36, 341
Bhadrāśva, 45
Bhagilā, 381
Bhānugupta, 249
Bharhut, 279
Bhāraśiva Nāga, 249
Bharata, 94, 305
Bharatas, 145, 147, 155, 160
Bhīma, 284
Bhīṣma, 273
Bhīṭā, 130, 298, 317-18, 328, 335-36, 384, 388
Bhūtas, 128, 284

Bihar, 16, 29, 317-18, 328, 335-36, 384, 388
Bimbisāra, 201, 229, 299, 365
Bindusāra, 399
Bodhisatta, 215, 257
Brahmā, 46, 52-53, 73, 136-37, 233
Brahmagiri, 206, 280
brāhmaṇas, allowed to bear arms 37; and kṣatriyas exempted from tax 277; as custodians of social order

255; as a class 40, 102; as *dūtas* 241; as *ratnin* 145; authority of 23; contract with 72; important in post-Maurya and Gupta times 72; in *Ṛg Veda* 351; non-Aryan origin of 160; pretensions of 18, 151; privileged status of 161; tax-free 243
brāhmaṇical, culture 379; influence in politics 378; law 243-46; patriarchal tradition 283; school 37; tradition 49
Brāhmaṇism, 253
Brahmaṇya (Yaudheya god), 384
Brahmapuri (Kolhapur), 280, 282
Brāhmī, 26, 302
Broach, 280
Buddha 23, 31, 58, 64-69, 71, 76, 85, 132, 213, 223, 229, 296; administrative machinery in the age of the 220; age of the 202, 212, 221, 363, 404; dharma of the 308; relics of the 306, 308; taxes in the age of the 203
Buddhaghoṣa, 212
Buddhism 29, 68, 379
Buddhist, monks 202, 275, 277, 285; political thought 8
bureaucracy, 85, 132, 226, 238, 402; as an arm of royal power 374; beginnings of a 156; complex Maurya 372; Gupta 347, 387, 391; higher 324; in Asiatic mode of production 78; in Maurya times 79, 83, 347, 392, 398; in pre-Maurya period 226; modern 401; paid in cash and also by grants 326

Cāhamānas, 283
caṇḍālas, 216
Candellas, 84
Candra Gupta II, 240, 249, 283, 312, 321-22, 327, 386
Candragupta Maurya, 28, 236, 374
Candras of Bengal, 390
cash, 25, 198; dues paid in 329; endowments in 317; endowments to guilds 344, 386; grants in 275; high Gupta officers paid in 326, 387, 391; payment to officers in Maurya period 383, 395; payment in 217, 278; post-Maurya assessment and collection in 382; richer peasants paid in 387; revenue collected in 301; salaries in 216, 298; taxes in 279
caste(s), 11, 33, 402; and rise of state power 233; associations 367; brāhmaṇical 322; composition of *pariṣā* 241; composition of *paura* and *jānapada* 242; confusion of 61, 253; considerations in the recruitment of officers 325; and recruitment of judges 243; duties of 52, 391; in the origin of the state 55; intermixture of 56-57, 59, 61, 71, 235; laws of 334; and guilds 335; mixed 148, 152, 234; of *amātyas* 239; origin of 24; proliferation in post-Maurya period 379; representation in the appointment of high functionaries 157
Celts, 155
Central Asia, 291, 304, 313, 379-80
centralisation, 20, 79; and despotism 78; bureaucratic 405; in the Kuṣāṇa period not rigid 291; in the Maurya period 250, 341, 376-77
Ceras, 289
Ceylon, 23
Chammak, 343
Champaran, 377
Chandravalli, 280
chariot, makers 178; race 165-66, 169
Chenab, 224
chiefdom, 232
China, 77, 291, 296, 313
Chinese accounts, 28-29
Chirand, 363
cities/city, 224-26; tyrannical king banished out of the 251. See also urban.
clan, 95, 105, 127, 135, 200, 228, 359; assembly 88, 107; comprising kinsmen 187; *gaṇa* as armed organization of 123; grant of land with the consent of the 360; king

elected by the 169; kṣatriya 126; loyalties 180; members of the 131, 165; oligarchic 129; peasantry 172; principalities 350; solidarity 120; support of the 357
clansmen, 100, 134, 164, 174, 206, 221, 354; of the chief 355
class legislation, 244, 246; Jaina literature and 247
Cleisthenes, 367
code, Anglo-Saxon, 244; of Hummurabi 244
coercion, apparatus of 43; and surplus 229; usefulness of 46
coercive, apparatus 356, 401; authority 403; power 45. See also authority.
coins, copper 301; gold and copper 298; Gupta 26, 311, 321, 323, 327; Gupta copper 334; Gupta gold 321, 326, 329, 391; imperial series of 25-26, 395; inscribed 275; *janapada* 333; Kuṣāṇa 303, 307, 308, 311-12, 317; Kuṣāṇa copper 291; local 395; Maurya 278; of guilds 381; made of lead, potin and silver 379; of Śakas and Parthians 314; of Wima Kadphises 305; *pada* 205; punch-marked 25, 202, 207-08, 217, 363, 366, 371, 400; saddled horses on Kuṣaṇa 314; Sātavāhana 278-79; spread in Maurya period 379; uninscribed cast 400
Coḷa, 3, 4, 289
Comitia Centuriata 113
conflict, between *viś* and *rājanya* 202; in Vedic times 177; kin 173, 175, 405-06
constitution, 2; city-state 28; German 116; Licchavi 24; Śākya 24
constitutional method, 4
contract theory, 37, 67-68, 76, 199; brāhmaṇical exposition of 68; Buddhist 65, 68; of the origin of kingship 69, 70; of the origin of the state 63-64, 71, 198, 403
coronation, 114
coronation, ceremony, 199; hymn 353; ritual 359-60; in Vedic period 64
corporate, bodies 323; organization 333
corporation(s), 21; of artisans and bankers in Gupta period 388; of merchants 339. See also guilds
council of ministers, 19
crafts and arts, 279
Cuṭus (dynasty), 284

Daityas, 121, 128, 136
Damodarpur, 318, 335
daṇḍa (coercive power), 38, 41, 45, 53-54, 57, 233, 237, 260; as an element of the state, 31, 36-37; in *Arthaśāstra* 44, 270; in Kuṣāṇa polity 315; in *Manu-smṛti* 17-18, 45; role of 336; in *Śānti Parva* 71; in Yājñavalkya 46; wielded by kṣatriyas 39-40
Daśaratha, 59, 302
Deccan, 20, 84, 201, 235, 275-76, 279, 281-82, 285, 298, 301, 311, 379-81, 384, 390, 406
decentralisation, 20, 319, 376; institutional factors working for 391; in Maurya period 377; in post-Maurya period 380; in Śaka-Sātavāhana polity 386
Delhi, 358
democracy, 11; Vedic direct 357; tribal 128; tribal military 349, 405
despotism, Asiatic 79, 85; oriental 82, 86, 204; royal 82, theory of hydraulic 78
Devāpi, 94, 186
Devasena, 249
Dhanvantari, 137
Dhānyakaṭaka, 280-81, 286
dharma (law, duty, social order), 23, 25, 46, 59, 61, 65, 68, 82, 108-09, 233, 253-54, 262-63, 265, 308, 372, 375; brāhmaṇical 60; canons of 38; *daṇḍa* as custodian of 45; inscriptions 26; king as upholder of 60; limiting role of 85
Dharma-rājikā *stūpa* of Taxila, 308
Dhārṣṭaka Kṣattra, 116
dice, 149; game of 164, 169; vaiśya

and śūdra excluded from game of 176
Dīrghacārāyaṇa, 221, 364
Divākara, 284
divinity of kingship, 6, 7, 165, 261, 383-84; in *Arthaśāstra* 270-71; in Manu 17; in *Śānti Parva* 18. See also king, kingship.
divorce, between mental and physical labour 180; between production and management 180
donee, 249, 340, 345. See also grantee.
Draupadī, 106
dual governorship in Kuṣāṇa polity, 295, 318
dual kingship, 295, 318
durga (fort), as an element of the state 35-6, 44; in the *Arthaśāstra* 31, 36, 41, 43; in the Maurya period 83, 197, 392; in the *Śānti Parva* 40
Duryodhana, 194

Egypt, 260, 306, 384-85
empire, 1, 26, 29; Alexandrine 260; British 401; Byzantine 245; core of the 330; disintegration of Maurya 381; Gupta 311, 319, 321, 326, 334, 387, 390; kernel of Gupta 342; Magadhan 372; Maurya 28, 373, 377, 379, 385, 392, 394, 399, 400; Mughal 392, 400, 406; Roman 248; traditional 392
England, 343
Eran, 381
Eta district, 357
Europe, 5, 11, 30, 77-78

family, creation of 66; establishment of 70; identity 281; institution of 50-1; laws regarding 16; monogamous 50; patriarchal 101, 202, 351, 358; peasant 203; preservation of 58; role in origin of the state 52
farmer(s), 226. See also peasants.
ferry dues, 280
feudal, conditions 342; landholders 80; polity 346, 392; property 80-2; structure 348; traits 386
feudalisation, brāhmaṇical domination and 249; of the state apparatus 45. See also land grants.
feudatory/feudatories, 43, 323, 339; Gupta 284, 341, 348, 390, 406; in central India 340; in post-Maurya period 386; Kuṣāṇa 292-93; obligation of 346; organization 313, 347, 386; principalities of the 313; relations of Sātavāhanas and Kuṣāṇas 380; *sandhivigrahika* to deal with the 326; supplied troops in Gupta times 387; system of the Kuṣāṇas 312
fiscal, centralisation 217; rights to beneficiaries in post-Maurya period 380; system of the Sātavāhanas 278, 289; system free from the influence of kinsmen of the king 212; units 27; decimal units in the post-Maurya period 383
forced labour 37; levy of 341. See also *viṣṭi* and peasants.

gaṇa 15, 19, 90-92, 119-32, 138, 188, 221, 356, 403-04; as collection of families 127; as local court 338; as tribal republic 128; association of women with 121; commercial vaiśya 130; kin-based 132; Mālava 119; Marut 119, 124-25; matriarchal 126, 136, 138; of kṣatriyas 126, 130; of *mlecchas* 128; organization 120; post-Vedic 125; *Śiva*- 136, 138; transforming into monarchy 125; tribal 121; tribal character of 120; women membership of 126
Gandak, 16
Gandhāras, 396
Gaṅgā, 183, 257, 291, 330, 405
Gangaridae, 223, 365
Gaṅgas, 235
Gardabhilla, 293
Garuḍa, 284

Gautama, 16, 31, 141, 205-07, 211, 241, 365
Gautamī Balaśrī, 276, 283
Gautamīputra Śātakarṇi, 276-77, 282, 284, 287-88, 322, 384
Gautamīputra Śrīvijaya Sātakarṇi, 282
Gautamīputra Viḷivayakura, 282
Gaya, 330, 342
gens, 89, 350; council of 104; Iroquois 93-4; Latin 120
genos, 350, 53
gentile society, 39
Germany, 350
gift(s), 206, 228, 255, 309; according to custom 281; by artisans and merchants 281; in village, money and animals by queens 283; mutual 208; of cave 277; of cultivated fields and villages 286; offering 231; of *harmya* 313; of land 249, 254, 277, 376; redistribution of 228, 231; to Buddhist monks 279; villages 342; voluntary 125
Glauganikai people, 225
Gondopharnes, 292, 302
Gopacandra, 331, 346
gotra (clan) 99. See also clan.
Govardhana, 276-77, 280, 283, 286
government; art of 23; Aśokan system of 275; central 9; forms of 16, 360; centralised Maurya 376; republican form of 5, 119; theory of 11
granaries, in the Maurya period 376
grantee 341-42; secular 85. See also donee.
Great Britain, 5
Greece, 15, 166, 168, 236-37, 307
Greek *phylae*, 350
guild(s), 21, 36, 279, 321, 402; autonomy of 376; in town administration 281, 317; in urban administration in post-Maurya period; king had to share power with 323; laws in Gupta period 389; laws of 334; of traders issued coins in post-Maurya period 380; power grew in the Gupta period 406; relationship with the state 281
Gujarat, 276, 329
Gupta(s), 311-19, 321-48; administration 289, 347; bureaucracy 387; coinage 311; empire 311; feudatories 341; feudatory system 319; political institutions 19; rulers as chariot warriors 314

Haihayas, 126
Hammurabi, 244, 258
Haradatta, 206, 211
Harappa, 349, 371
Hariścandra, 94, 359
Hariṣeṇa, 304, 324, 326, 386
Harṣavardhana, 29, 235-36, 288, 387
Haryana, 178
Hastibhoja, 249
Hathigumpha, 27, 292
helots, in Sparta 251
heretical sects, and authority of the state 274; discrimination towards 265
Hindu(s) 2, 5, 7; institutions 12; psychological make up of 86; revivalism 4; sacraments 231; state 29
homage, and tribute to paramount power in post-Maurya period 380; to the conqueror 346
Homeric Greece, 111
Hummiyaka Cañyakka, 297
Huviṣka, 297, 300, 304-09, 312, 314
Hyksos, 349

ideologue(s), 227; brāhmaṇical 237
ideology, 12, 23; and varṇa-divided society 23; brāhmaṇical 131, 273; Buddhist 241; colonialist 2; Dharmaśāstra 249; genealogical 179; heterodox 249; imperialist 2; nationalist 2
Ikṣvākus, 284, 380
Indo-Āryan(s), 87, 90, 120; history 93; kin-based assembly 103
indoctrination, of people in Maurya period 272
Indo-European, institutions 113; lan-

guage 90, 103, 105, 128; peoples 13, 91, 97-8, 103, 143, 155, 159, 166, 169, 404; texts 15
Indology, 4
Indological knowledge, 29
Indologist, 202, 204
Indo-Greeks, 275, 292, 382
Indore, 318, 328, 335, 341
Indra, 63-64, 73, 93-96, 98, 101, 106, 108, 110, 122-23, 125-27, 133, 145, 172-74, 178-79, 230, 257, 260, 323, 359
infantry, 36-37, 374. See also army.
inheritance, law of 389; matriarchal 311; matrilineal 281-83; problem of 17
institution(s), of family and property 65; of marriage 56; of property, family and caste 57, 59; of property, family and social classes 55
international law 9, 10, 12
international politics 12
interstate relations 18, 21
Iran, 15
iron, absent in the *Ṛg Veda* 350; advent of 178; for craft and agriculture 201; ploughshare 189, 206; ploughshare and tools 229; spread during Maurya period 379; technology 358; use of 226, 275
Iroquois, 89, 93-94, 115
irrigation, 28, 79, 86; arrangements 45; in arid zones 78; under Mauryas 79; works 287
Isilā, 396

Jaina, images 308; literature 247; monks 202
Jainism, 308
Jambūdvīpa, 45, 128
Janamejaya, 284
Jayanātha, 344
Jhelum, 224-25
Jorwe, 280
judicial court, composition of Gupta 338-39
judicial procedure, 17
judiciary, effect of *varṇa* on 243, 273-74; role of corporate bodies in 389
Junnar, 279-80
justice, miscarriage of 259

Kadamba(s), 235, 249
Kadphises I, 308
Kadphises II, 303, 307
Kaiser, 294
Kākutsthavarman, 249
Kalacuri, 276
Kali Age, 52, 191, 236, 251, 336
Kali social crisis, 191
Kaliṅga, 377
Kalsi, 377
Kalyāṇa, 280
Kambojas, 396
Kanauj, 390
Kandhar, 375
Kanheri, 280
Kaniṣka, 294, 296-97, 300, 307, 309, 314, 316
Kāṇvas, 72, 235, 379
Kapilavastu, 377
Karle, 280
Karnataka, 275, 285, 377
Kārtikeya, 120, 136
Kāsī, 141
Kaśyapa, 128
Kaunta, 282
Kauravas, 181
Kauśāmbī, 363, 381
kayastha(s), 329, 332, 338; grant of *agrahāra* to 332
Keśava, 284
Khairadih, 363
Khāravela, 27, 292
Kharoṣṭhī, 26, 27, 296, 302, 304, 308
kin, aristocracy, 174; assembly 90, 97, 103; based society 228, 393; based solidarity 198; conflicts 173, 405-06; equality 129, 131-32; groups 179; ordered character of *sabhā* 117; ordered society 164; secondary ties of 182; structures 176
king, acquired the status of god 167; acquisitive aspect of 189; and the

sabhā 109-111; authority of 23; as agriculturist 194; association with god 269-70; and brāhmaṇa 235; companions and courtiers of 34; compared with gods in Gupta period 387; divine attributes of 384; divinity of 18, 165, 269, 405; duties of 16, 17, 19, 24, 57, 58; election by *samiti* 109; election of 66, 73; exempted from judicial punishment 163; expulsion of 364; functions of 21; god- 166; guaranteed social welfare 69; ideal 12; identified with state 43; national 10; as owner of the land 205; 322; as protector 56, 59; as protector of brāhmaṇa 360; as protector of property 57; as protector of *varṇa* 191; responsible to Varuṇa 259; 261; as upholder of dharma 60-61, 360
kingship, and varṇa system, 234; contractual origin of 69; divine 17, 73, 260, 302, 312; divinity of 7, 260, 284, 318; evolution of 138, 187; feudal character of 322-23; hereditary 131, 168; in Buddhist and Jaina texts 24; Manu accepted 54; origin of 16, 24, 63, 70, 71, 132, 303; religious aspect of 383; Ṛg Vedic 353; tax-enjoying aspect of 190; tribal 352; tribal basis of later Vedic 162; tribute collecting aspect of 188-89; Vedic, 64, 160, 169
Kinnara, 128
kinship, bond 182, 232; conflict within 172; institution of 180; structure 172
kinsmen, 172-73, 178, 206, 214, 262, 293, 350, 352, 354, 368; chief's close 171; control over 227; distribution among 181; of king 145, 164; presents from 230; tributes from 361
Kolhapur, 208
Koliyas, 120, 227
Kondapur, 280
Konkan, 396
Kosala, 19, 23, 31, 213, 221, 229, 363-64, 367-68, 405
Koṭivarṣa, 318, 331, 335
Krimilā viṣaya, 330
Krishna river, 80
Krivis, 358
Kṛṣṇa, 181, 282
Kṛta age, 49, 50, 55, 127
Kṣapaṇakas (unorthodox sects), 261
kṣatriya(s), and *gaṇa* 126-27; and brāhmaṇa domination 172; as a class 67, 102; as a kin-ordered group 171; as material for the army 37; *bali* for the 228; brāhmaṇa support to 202; clan 126; composition of 202; contempt for labour 152; function of 52-53; *gaṇas* of 126; in *Ṛg Veda* 351; oligarchs 67; privilages of 237; protects the brāhmaṇa 72; relationship with the brāhmaṇa 247-50; the state and 132
Kṣaudrakya, 119, 227, 249
Kṣudrakas, 119, 225, 227, 249, 368
Kubera, 323
Kujula Kadphises, 291
Kumāradatta, 285
Kumāranāga, 344
Kuṇindas, 26, 384
Kuru, 15, 50, 145, 147, 155, 160, 180-81, 358, 362
Kuru-Pañcāla, 143, 358-59, 363
Kuṣāṇas, 275-76, 291-309, 311-19, 344, 379-84, 406; Roman influence on 294; Śaka influence on 293

labour, contempt for 152; division of 99, 103, 121, 152; manual 147; power of śūdra and women 176
labourer, hired 35, 131, 207; hired agricultural 120; paid in cash 217; reproduction of 165; wages of 256
land, growth of private property in 386; of Kuru-Pañcāla 143; of peasants 258; ownership 29, 81; possession over 360; proprietary rights to 79; reclamation under Mauryas 371, 376; royal ownership

of 86, 194-95, 322; sale, mortgage and lease of 326, 337; sale and purchase of 386; tax-free 376; titles to 82, tenure 80
land grants, drafting of 278; executors of 277; affected the administrative structure 321; from Bengal 332; gave rise to feudal conditions 342; Gupta 337; in inhospitable and virgin tracts 386; merits accruing from 322; Sātavāhana 286; to brāhmaṇas 66, 250; to brāhmaṇas and Buddhists in post-Maurya period 379
Lakṣmī, 323
Lāṭa (Nausari-Broach region), 318
Late Harappan people, 357
Later Guptas of Magadha, 390
law, and customs of guilds 389; and order 342-43; brāhmaṇas as custodians of 323; class character of brāhmaṇical 243-46; code 337; civil 21; criminal 17, 21, 245; customary 229; customary tribal 356; enforcing authority 197; four legs of 263; Gupta period distinguished between civil and criminal 337; Han 314; levies not warranted by 195; of evidence 244, 338; of inheritance 245, 389; of primogeniture 230-31; on varṇa division 366; role of penances in maintaining 385; tribal 114; varṇa considerations in 244; Welsh 90
legal system, in the Gupta period, 389-90
Licchavi(s), 24, 110, 126, 131-32, 221, 236, 367-68
lineage(s), 178, 202 with n; and control over economic resources 229; noble 33
Lushais, 180

Māḍharīputra Sivalkura, 282
Madhyadeśa, 29, 145
Mādhyamikā, 381
Madhya Pradesh, 23, 31, 213, 221, 223-24, 226, 229, 342, 363-65, 367-68, 390, 405
Magadhabhukti, 324, 330
Magna Carta, 379
Mahākacchapa, 257
Mahāmeghavāhana, 292
Maharashtra, 80, 276, 278, 281-82, 300
Mahāsena, 384
Mahāvīra, 132
Māhiṣmatī, 381
Maitrakas of Valabhī, 318, 322, 390
Mālava, 26, 119, 225, 227, 249, 368
Mālavya, 119, 227, 249
Mallas, 120, 221
Mallasārul, 331-32
Malwa, 249, 318, 335
Manasdeva (god of harmony), 173
maṇḍala theory (circle of kings), 394
Mandasore, 318, 328, 335, 388-89
Manu Svāyambhuva, 54
Manu Vaivasvata, 68
Marduk, 168
marriage, ceremony, 89; institution of 56; political combination through 249; subjugated princes gave daughters in 346
Marutta Āvikṣita (Āyogava), 171
Maruts, 90-91, 95-97, 119-20, 125-27, 138, 164, 172-74, 178, 181
Maski, 206
Mathura, 296-300, 306, 308, 312-13
matriarchy, 90, 138
matriarchal, practices 282
matrilineal, inheritance 281-82; traces 275
Maues (Śaka chief), 292, 314
Maukharis of Kanauj, 347, 390
Maurya(s), administration 347; and elephants 313; army 387; province 330
Maurya state, 341; acquisitive character of 69; centralised 250; character of 392-402
Mayurbhanj, 201
megalithic legacy, 275
merchant(s), gifts made by 279-80; associated with the management

of towns 280; participation in civic life 281
Mesopotamia, 306
metronymics, 120, 280, 282, 284
military system, in the *Arthaśāstra* 20, 37; in the *Śānti Parva* 26; under the Mauryas 26; under the Kuṣāṇas 296-97, 315; under the Guptas 327; under Harṣa 28
ministers, importance of 43; caste of 238-40; in the Gupta period 323-24. See also *mantrin, amātya, saciva*
Mirzapur, 377
Mithridates II, 292
Mitannis, 349
Mitra-Varuṇa, 91, 95, 114
Mizoram, 149
Mlecchas, 128
Mohenjodaro, 293
monarchy, 6, 12, 23, 32, 119, 129, 197; constitutional 5, 6, 159; despotic 8; hereditary 71; limited 3, 12; territorial 352; to republic 131; tribal 169. See also kingship.
money, economy, 207; endowments under the Sātavāhanas and Kuṣāṇas 279, 301; -lending 301; in less use in the Gupta period 342-43; misuse of government 394; payment in 207
Monghyr, 315, 330, 342
movements, nationalist 3-5, 12; revolutionary 5; social 2; political 2
Mughals, 377
Muruṇḍas, 311
Muslims, 12

Nābhāga(s), 126, 130, 284
Nāgas, 270
Nāganikā, 278, 285, 287
Nahapāna, 300
Nahuṣa, 284, 355
Nalanda, 330, 334, 338
Nanaghat, 278, 287
Nandas, 223-24, 226, 365, 387; infantry of the 374
Narmada, 16
Nasik, 234, 279-80
nationalism, and research in ancient Indian polity 2-13
nationalists, 9
nationality, 8
nationhood, 2
Nayars, 282
Nepal, 29, 376
Niṣāda, 173
Northern Black Polished Ware, 201-02, 364, 371, 400; spread during Maurya period 379
Nṛṣad, 133

Ochre Coloured Pottery, 357
officer(s), for drafting of charters 278; for civil and criminal administration 336-37; payment to 278, 326, 345-46, 373; family background of 325-26; hierarchy of 297-98; in the *Ṛg Veda* 355-56; in later Vedic times 361-62; in the pre-Maurya period 364-65
oligarchies, 67, 131, 197, 226; of Videha and Vaiśālī 131; of Mallas and Koliyas 120; in north-eastern India 77-8; ruling 225; tribal 363, 368
Olympia, 166
Oraons, 121
organic theory of state, 46, 47, 48
oriental despotism, 82, 86, 204; features of 77; in Maurya period 83; theory of 77-8, 85
oriental scholars, 8
orientalist(s) 2, 86
Orissa, 29, 336
ownership of land 66-7; communal 80; royal 66, 80, 82

paddy transplantation, 201, 206, 229
Pahlavas (Parthians), 18, 63
Painted Grey Ware, 178
Paithan (town), 280
Pālas, 84
Pallava(s), 191, 285, 287, 290, 377
Pañcāla(s), 15, 111-13, 135, 145, 147,

155, 160, 181, 358, 362; *samiti* of 112
Pan-ch'ao 314
Pañcanagarī *viṣaya*, 324
Pāṇḍyas, 289
paper, introduction of, 27
Paraśurāma, 251
Parivrājaka (dynasty), 235, 341-42, 390
Parthians, 18, 275, 292, 296, 313-14, 382
Pāṣaṇḍas (unorthodox sects), 261-62, 265, 395; Kauṭilya's attitude to 262; Manu on 262
pastoral economy, 107-08; of the Vedic period 125, 350
Pāśupatas, 261
Pāṭaliputra, 28, 273, 311, 327, 330, 376-77, 395; municipal administration of 374
Patna, 375, 377
patriarchal house, 98, 100, 105
patriarchy, 90
Persia, 349
Peshawar, 296, 377
Petenikas, 396
Pharaoh, 260, 306
Pharates, II and III, 305
Piṣṭapurikādevī (goddess), 345
plough cultivation, 350
ploughshare, iron 189, 200; wooden 183, 358
political institutions, compared with those of the West 11, 13
political science, 8, 22; *Arthaśāstra* and 22
political theory, Hindu 5; history of 38; Indian 6, 8, 11
political thought, in the Purāṇas 19-20
polity, foreign influence on 291, 306, 378; Hindu 9, 12; influence of religion on 7, 8, 26, 253, 273; in the *Rāmāyaṇa* 18-19; material background of 349-50, 357-58, 363-64, 371; military character of 158; religious aspects of 12; tribal character of 351-52
power, coercive 1, 57: despotic 10, 78; judicial 197; structure 158; superstition, ruling class and 273
Prabhākaravardhana, 235
Prabhāvatī Gupta, 249, 283, 322
Prajāpati, 63, 116, 165, 254, 301
Prajāpati, Kaśyapa 257
Prakrit language, 20, 26, 275-76
Prasenajit of Kosala, 221
Prasii, 223, 365
Pravāhaṇa Jaivali, 112, 151
Pravarasena II, 339, 343
pre-state society, 24, 49, 283
priest, chief 362; as check on royal authority 378; conferment of fiscal and administrative immunities on 390, high position of 40. See also *purohita*
primitive, character of *sattra* sacrifice 99; institutions 128; society 94; tribal organization; tribes 125, 150
primogeniture, 180, 230-31, 353-54; absence of the practice in Gupta times 386; not firmly established 322
property, private 49, 51, 202, 355; collective ownership of 404; confiscation of 268; contract for the protection of 73; establishment of 70; its role in the origin of the state 53, 55; king's duty of protecting 57; offences connected with 58; partition of landed 389; penalty for offences against 244; protection of 199, 227; sanctity of 356; violation of 60
Pṛthu, 54, 56, 71-72
Pṛthu Vainya, 71, 194
public opinion, role of the priest in moulding 270
Pulindabhaṭa, 345
Puṇḍravardhana *bhukti*, 318, 325, 330, 335
Punjab, 358, 379, 399
punishment, in the *Ṛg Veda* 356; varying according to caste 244-45
Pūṣan, 93, 122, 136, 148, 181, 361

Rajghat (Varanasi) 201, 363

Rajasthan, 358, 379
Rajgir (Rājagṛha), 330, 363
Ravi river, 225
Ravikīrtti, 249
religion, as a force in politics 385-86; and politics 7, 12, 22, 26, 107, 253, 273, 406; influenced political ideas and institutions 12; moneylending sanctioned by 301; polity emancipated from 265-66; Vedic 253
rent, ground 203-05; and tax 204
republics, 5-6, 26, 367-68, 379; compared with Greek city-states 28; *gaṇas* as 128; in the Age of the Buddha 124; Mālava and Kṣudraka 119-20; of Licchavis and Śākyas 132; of Mallas and Koliyas 120; pariṣad important in 220; post-Maurya 249; post-Vedic 130; tribal character of Vedic 119-22; transformed into monarchies 129-30; features of 367-68; revival of 279-80
revenue, concessions in villages for religious purposes 278; from land in perpetuity 341; in pre-Maurya times 203
revenue officers, 215, in the Gupta period 329
revenue system, in the Gupta period 328, under the Kuṣāṇas 300-01; under the Sātavāhanas 278-79. See also taxes, taxation
revolts, anti-royal 248, peoples' 251; popular in Buddhist and brāhmaṇical texts 85
rex 185
rights, delegation of fiscal and administrative 195; denial of 131; mother 358; mother and father 351; private land 321; śūdras without 250, to the throne 168
rituals, coronation 188, 359-60; elaboration and explanation of 177; indicate conflict 176; later Vedic 172; primitive character of 163; private and public 15; symbolised emerging kingship 359; to ensure control over the peasantry 173; to win support 173
Rome, 97, 251, 273, 379
Roṭa-Siddha-Vṛddhi (a *vihārasvāmī*), 308
royal, authority circumscribed by tribal assemblies 354; command 26; charter 27; control of economic activities 21; despotism 85; divinity 273; immunity from punishment 163; lordship of land 81; ownership over mines 340; proprietorship of land 80, 193; share of the produce 29, 366. Also see king.
Rudra, 91, 119-20, 127, 134-35, 137, 174, 178
Rudradāman, 34, 79, 192, 235, 313, 316
Rudrasena II, 249
ruling class, 12, 48; and superstition in the *Arthaśāstra* 271-72; in the *Republic* of Plato 272-73

sabhā, 15, 17, 87-88, 90-91, 102-03, 105-111, 116-117, 120, 128, 134, 138, 141, 157, 221, 354, 356, 363, 403-04; character of 105-07; clan character of 107; compared to other Indo-European institutions 107; judicial functions of 109-10; in the epics 111; compared to early Greek assemblies 110-11; and *samiti* 116-17; women and 105-06
sacrifice(s), brāhmaṇas officiated at 255; collective nature of 97, 99; communal nature of 98, 100; later Vedic 183; *sattra* 99; *vajapeya* and *rājasūya* 100; Vedic 98, 283, 287, 383; women and 351
Śakadvīpa, 45
Śakas, 18, 235, 275, 292-93, 313-14, 379, 381-82
Śaktināga, 344
Śākya Muni, 308
sale transactions in Bengal, 328
samiti, 15, 16, 87-88, 90-91, 94, 102, 105, 109, 111-17, 123, 128, 141, 179, 221, 354, 356, 363, 368, 403-04; compared to the Greek Agora 111;

tribal character of 111-12; compared to early Indo-European institutions 113; compared with the assembly of Iroquois 115; compared with German institutions 114-15; military functions of 112-13
Samudra Gupta, 27, 74, 293, 298, 304, 309, 312, 315, 321, 324, 326, 330, 342, 346, 386-87, 390
Sanchi, 279
Sangankullu, 280
Sanskrit, 20, 24-25
Śantanu, 94, 186
Śāntivarman, 346
saptāṅga theory of state, 31-48, 238 403; importance of 403; Vedic polity fell short of the 363
Sārnāth, 294
Śarvanātha, 344
Sasaram, 377
satarpal system, 318
Sātavāhanas, 27, 72, 234, 275-90, 300, 312-13, 322, 324, 344, 377, 380, 382-84, 406; as champions of the varṇa system 275; matrilineal inheritance of 281-83; their familiarity with the Maurya administration 275-77; vassals of the 343
Saurashtra, 79, 293
Scythians, 291, 296, 313-14, 379-80
secular, character of the state 13; Kauṭilyan state was not 265
self-government, 2, 12; local 3, 9, 12
self-rule 9
settlement, of new territories 35 ; tribal 34
Simuka, 282
Sind, 28
Śiva, 128, 135-36, 138-39, 308
Śivadatta, 277
Skanda, 120-21, 128, 135-39
Skanda Gupta, 322, 327-28
slaves, and barbarians 236; and serfs 246; and workmen 227, excluded from political power 120; in Rome 251; manumitting 245; in the Mālava and Kṣudraka states 119-20
social contract, in *Dīgha Nikāya* 66; theory of 72
social order, brāhmaṇical, 255
social organization brāhmaṇical 254; of Vedic times 349-50
social structure, kinship as the basis of 350; *varṇāśramadharma* as foundation of 253
Ṣoḍāsa, 295
Soma, 97, 106-07, 110, 126, 258
soma (drink) 97, 114, 125-26, 171-72
Somadeva Sūri, 25
Someśvaradeva, 60
Sopara, 280
sovereignty, 38, standard of 43; territorial 160-62
Sparta, 251
Śrāvastī, 363
Sri Lanka, 23
Śrī Śilāditya, 338
state, apparatus 215, 218; brāhmaṇical character of the 263; breakaway 131; centralised 48, 250; class character of the 38; contract theory of the 64, 75; decentralized Gupta 250; dedicated to God 26; democratic 28; elements of the 36, 38, 41-3, 68; enemies of the 268; functions of the early 243; family, property and *varṇa* in the origin of the 53; ideologues 199; kingless 19; Magadhan 224, 226, 401; Marxist conception of the 40, 221; monarchical 132; non-monarchical 32; non-religious character of the 263; offences against the 58; organs of the 39, 222, 226; origin of the 24, 38, 55, 71-2; republican 367; secular character of the 13; structure of the 39; system in pre-Maurya times 224; territorial 353; theocratic character of the 260, theories of the 63, 74, 403; treated as an item of property 385; tribal character of the 162; varṇas in the origin of the 52, 233
state control, and ascetics, 261-62;

and brāhmaṇical institutions 264; in the Maurya period 69, 372
state formation, and consensual factor 198; fullfledged 405; history of 30; preconditions for Sātavāhana 275; role of family, property and varṇa in 61; social differentiation and; tax and 232
state of nature, 50-1, 61, 64; early 49; in Buddhist sources 49, 55
stirrups, 314; in the Kuṣāṇa period 383
subinfeudation, growth of 341-42; of the soil 341
Sudarśana lake, 79
Sudās, 353
śūdra(s), 85, 130, 234, 236; as *senānī* 146; functions 52; in *Ṛg Veda* 351; intra-tribal war gave rise to 175; labour power of 222; not allowed to bear arms 37; not recruited as judges 389; *ratnins* 157; ruler 236; their exclusion from public officers 250-51; to be enlisted in the army according to Kauṭilya 37
Śuṅgas, 17, 72, 379
Surajgarha, 331
Surkh Kotal, 312
Suryā, 89
Suvarṇagiri, 396
Svāmidāsa, 341
Śvetaketu, 112
Swat region, 224, 312, 365
Sweden, 97, 116, 165
Switzerland, 5
swordsmen, villages held by 333
Śyāmaka (Sātavāhana *amātya*) 277

Tacitus, 113, 116
Tagara (Ter), 280
taxation, and the development of the state 198; exemption from 21; in lieu of protection 11, 67, 75, 199; laws regarding 16; machinery 224, 347; Maurya system of 375, oppressive 67, 224; principles of 11, 17, 19, 75, 328; rate of 67; self—4; system 132, 197, 328, 361, 364, 401; voluntary in the Vedic gaṇa 124-25. See also taxes, revenue
taxes, and the rise of the state 226; as a feature of the state 37; according to the carrying capacity of the soil 200; collection and distribution of 227; customary 340; declining burden of 328-29; exemption from 21, 227; in Gupta inscriptions 387; in lieu of protection 190, 204, 322; in metallic money 217; on forest inhabitants 69; on grain 69, 74; on commodities 69, 71; on metals 69; on artisans 279, 366, 376; on traders 366, 376; on households 206; on land increased in the Gupta period 387; origin of 228, 231; regular 67, 224; remission of 41, 207, 254, 287; proper and improper 81; were fewer in Gupta times 219. See also taxation and revenue.
Taxila, 308, 380-81, 399
technology, in the early Vedic period 349-50; in the later Vedic period, 357-58; in the pre-Maurya period 363-64; in the Maurya period 371
temples, conferment of fiscal and administrative immunities on 390; deification of dead king in 384; Kauṭilyan state does not care for 265; land grants to 391; not exempt from expropriation 264; proceeds enjoyed by the 345
peasant(s) and forced labour 387; *bhoga* from 81; clan 172, 174; capacity to pay 206; castes 332; disturbances caused by 328; eviction of 82, 195; gifts from 169; in actual possession of land 193; kept disarmed 40; made surplus available 132; periodical supplies by 81; power over 131; productive capacity of 207; property 82; rent from 368; servile 195; subjected to corvée 366; subordinate rights of 79; surplus from 227, 351; taxes from 83, 131, 210, 376; taxpaying 342;

tenants 84; tribal 131, 229; tribute paying 172; wrath of 372
Teutons, 107
Thaneser, 390
Tirabhukti, 324, 330, 337
Timmes of Sierraleone, 163
toll, commodities exempted from 259, 273. See also taxes, taxation, revenue
town(s), administration under the Mauryas 374, 375, 581; administration in Sātavāhana kingdom 281; administration in Kuṣāṇa kingdom 317; administration in Gupta period 334, 389; artisans and traders in 84; decline of 84, 86; merchants in administration of 375
trade, and local administration 336; expansion of 291; Mauryas opened new regions to 378; officers regulated 69
traders, administrative role of 335-36; exempted from dues 339; subjected to customs on commodities 328
tribal assemblies, 15; in the Vedic period 356-57
tribe(s), broke into peasant households 190; chieftainship of the 404; disintegrated into classes 167, 233; *gaṇa* as 119; Himalayan 149; Lushai 149; primitive 13, 39, 125, 135, 168; Vedic 93, 360
tribesmen, 98, 104, 107, 119, 124, 197, 232, 354-55, 357; Greek 123-24; tributes from 202
tribute, frequent collection of 156, 182-83; payment of 346
Tripurī, 381
Turvasas (warriors), 181
tyrannical rule of Vena, 71
tyrant, 7

Ucchakalpas, 341-42, 390
Ujjain, 293, 363
urban, administration 298, 335, 347; decline in Gupta period 386; economy 291, 366
Uṣabhadāta, 280-81
Uttānapāda, 53
Uttarakurus, 129
Uttaramadras, 129
Uttar Pradesh, 16, 29, 178, 201, 294, 330, 341, 352, 357-58, 361, 363, 367-69, 388, 390

Vaiśālī, 131, 221, 298, 317-18, 325, 327-28, 330, 357, 363, 377, 388-89
vaiśya(s), allowed to bear arms 37; as *amātyas* 240; as unwilling tribute payers 358; functions of 52; *gaṇas* of 130; identified with *bala* 181; in the *Ṛg Veda* 351; membership of the *paura* 242; right to fight in emergency 237; struggle with kṣatriya 171
Vajji state, 58
Vākāṭakas, 72, 235-36, 249, 276, 283, 286, 289, 322, 329, 331, 390
Valabhī, 24, 341, 347, 390
Vardhamānabhukti, 331, 346
Vārāṇasī, 201, 381
Vaiśvānara Parīkṣit, 301
Varāha, 128
varṇa(s), and organs of the state 404-05; duties of 59, 190, 233; functions of 343; importance of 52; in relation to law and politics 233, 247; legal discrimination between 244-45; organization 363; social order based on 45. See also varṇa system
varṇa system, and the rise of the state 52-3, rules of the 288; absent in the Kṛta age 50; formation of 174, 176
Varuṇa, 95, 101, 147, 178, 259-61, 323
Vāsiṣṭhīputra Puḷumāvi, 234, 276-77, 282, 288
Vāsiṣṭhīputra Śātkarṇi, 282
Vāsiṣṭhīputra Viḷivāyukura, 282
Vasskāra of Māgadha, 221, 364
Vāsudeva, 299, 314
Vasus, 127, 178
Vātsyāyana, 334

Vedic polity, matriarchal element in 146; tribal aspect of 166; class and territorial aspects of later 169
Vena, 56, 61, 71
vidatha, 15, 87-104, 123, 128, 134, 138, 148, 157, 221, 356-57, 403-04; association of woman with 88-90; clan character of 91; functions of 91-96; antiquity of 102-03; and the old European popular assemblies 89-90; and the council of Iroquois 89, 93-94; and the Anglo-Saxon Witenagemot 101; and the Gothic *vitoth* 103
Videgha Māthava 150-51
Videha Janaka, 150-51
Videha(s), 113, 131, 145, 150, 155, 358
Vidiśā, 381
Vijayasena, 345
Vijñāneśvara, 17
Vidyādharas, 128, 284
Vighna, 137
village(s), administration 309, 334, 347, 388; as lowest unit of administration 331; gift of 340, 342, 390; laws of 334; managers of 345; rent from 35; revenue concessions in 278; revenue of 227, 364; self-sufficiency of 82-83, 86
village, elders, 333, 365-66
village government, under the Coḷas 4
village headman, functions of 334. See also *grāmika*, *grāmādhipati*
village panchayats, 4
Vindhya, 136, 379
Viṣṇu, 71, 137, 323
Viṣṇukuṇḍins, 284
Viṣṇunandin, 344
Viṣṇupālita, 277
Viṣṇuṣena, 339, 389

wealth, political power and 12; distribution of 91-92; communal appropriation of 92
weights and measures, standardization of 224
Wema Kadphises II, 294, 305
Western Asia, 349
Witenagemot, 101, 107
women, abduction of 53, 58, 261, 265; administration and 284, 322; as *sabhāvatī* 105; driving out enemy 121; door-keeper 283; *gaṇa* and 121, 126; members of *pariṣad* 138; military assemblies of 121; *pariṣad* and 137; post-Vedic deterioration in position of 152; peasant 317, 334; sacrifices and 283; *sabhā* and 106; *samiti* and 111; in later Vedic period 358; *vidatha* and 88, 90, 103; their voice counted in the consecration of the king 90; in the list of *ratnins* 157-58

Yādava contingents, 181
Yama, 109, 260, 323
Yakṣa, 94, 112, 128, 284
Yaśodharman, 235, 249, 347
Yaudheyas, 26, 311, 384
Yaśas, 106
Yavanas, 395
Yayāti, 284
Yudhiṣṭhira, 190
Yue-chi, 294, 303-04, 314

PĀLI, SANSKRIT AND ALLIED TERMS

abhiṣecanīyam (sprinkling ceremony), 161
abhyantara-siddhi (right to settle civil disputes), 340
ācārya (teacher), 40
adaṇḍya (exempted from punishments), 255
adharma (unrighteousness), 61, 253, 262
adharmiṣṭam (unrighteous practices), 254

adhikaraṇa(s) (local body, department), 21, 330-31, 338, 394
adhikaraṇika (member of the *adhikaraṇa*), 338
adhikṛta (village officer), 362
adhiṣṭhāna (headquarters), 338
adhyakṣas (superintendents), 218, 372, 373, 393
agrahāra (grant for religious and educational purposes), 331, 326, 342, 344
āgrahārikas (holders of educational and religious grants), 342
āgrahārikas (holders of educational and religious grants), 342
āgrahārin(s) (holders of educational and religious grants), 332
agrāyaṇa (first fruits), 259
āhāra(s) (administrative unit, district), 276, 286, 289, 382-83
akara (non-taxable), 213
akāsiyas (oppressive tax collector), 211, 219, 224
akṣapaṭalamadhyakṣa (accountant general), 394
akṣaśālā (state accounts officer), 149
akṣāvāpa (dice thrower), 146, 149, 152, 156-57
amacca(s) (high state officers/ministers), 33, 214, 219, 237, 277
amaccakulam (family of ministers), 239
amātyasampat (qualifications of a minister), 239
antamahāmātras (border officers), 375
āpaddharma (duties in emergencies), 272
apīḍanīya (exempt from physical punishment), 255
araghaṭṭa (Persian water-wheel), 258
arājaka (kingless state), 19, 55
araṇya (forest), 117
artha (wealth), 23, 61
ārya, 176
āryaputra, 27, 276, 396-98
āsandīvat (capital), 359
āśramadharma (duties pertaining to stages in life), 54
aṣṭādaśa-jāti-parihāra (exemptions of eighteen types), 287
aṣṭakulādhikaraṇa (body of eighteen leading families), 333, 339
aṣṭāṅga (eight organs), 45
aṣṭāṅga bala (army comprising eight elements),
aṣṭāṅgika rājya (state of eight organs), 32
aśvamedha (horse sacrifice), 74, 178, 181
aśvapati (cavalry officer), 315, 327
audraṅgika (collector of royal share in kind), 329
aurṇasthānika (regulator of the wool market), 329
avanīndra (lord of the earth), 193
avanīśa (lord of the earth), 193
avijita (subdued), 399
ayājya (not entitled to Vedic sacrifice), 264
ayas (metal, copper or bronze), 349
ayomukham (copper arrows), 349
āyuktaka(s) (revenue officers), 210, 329, 336, 364

bakanpati (Kuṣāṇa official in charge of temples), 304, 318
bala (force), 181-82
balādhika (Kuṣāṇa military official), 315
balādhikṛta (Gupta military official), 315
bali (offerings, taxes), 179, 182, 189, 205-06, 354-55, 382
baligrahaṇam (royal dues), 211
balihṛt (collector of *bali*), 189, 355
balipaṭigāhaka (collector of taxes), 219
baliṣaḍbhāgahārin (king, enjoyer of *bali* and a sixth part of the produce), 190
balisādhaka (collector of taxes), 211, 219
basileus basileon (Kuṣāṇa title), 312
bhāga (land tax), 206-07, 344, 382
bhāgabhuj (king as enjoyer of taxes), 190
bhāgadugha (distributor of shares),

146, 148, 152, 156, 157, 181, 209, 361
bhāṇḍāgārika (storekeeper), 124, 368
bhaṭamayeṣu (among warriors), 234
bhaṭāśvapati (commander of horsemen), 315, 327
bhatta vetana (remuneration), 215-16
bhoga (royal share of the fruits, district), 81, 194, 279, 330, 344, 382, 388
bhogakara (enjoyment of agrarian resources), 81, 194
bhogagāma (donated village), 214-16
bhogapatika (district officer, fief holder), 345-46
bhogika (district officer, fief holder), 325, 345-46
bhoja (a form of kingship), 189, 210
bhojaka, 214-15
bhṛtakas (servants), 244
bhṛtya (servant), 192
bhūbhuj (king as enjoyer of land), 193
bhukti(s) (administrative divisions), 298, 324, 325, 330, 388
bhumeradhipati (lord of the soil), 191
bhūmīśvara (lord of the land), 193
bhūpa (king as protector of landowner), 193
bhūpati (owner of the land), 193, 195
bhūsvāmin (landowner), 81, 191-92, 195
brahma (priest), 85
brahmadeya (land grant to a brāhmaṇa), 212-14, 341
brāhmaṇaviṃśati (twentieth part of the produce paid to the brāhmaṇas), 250

caityas, 257
cakravartin (king of kings), 401
carita (custom), 82, 263
cāturmāsya (a season of four months), 254
cauroddharaṇika (police official), 337
chaudhurī (village head), 337
citta (thought), 114-15

daivaputra (son of god), 304
dakṣiṇās (sacrificial gifts), 256
dāna (charity), 31
dānapati (manager of donations), 318
dānastuti (hymn in praise of gift), 354
daṇḍanāyakas (commanders), 47, 296, 297, 315, 336; functions of 336; in the Kuṣāṇa period 382-83
daṇḍanīti (science of punishment), 22, 45, 171
daṇḍapāśika (police officer), 30, 336; function of 336
daṇḍausī (village watchman), 30, 336
dāṇḍika (magistrate or ruler), 336
dāsabhataka (slaves and servants), 234
dāsas (slaves), 192, 244, 352, 354
deśa, 388
deśākṣapaṭalādhikṛta (district accountant), 329
deva, 302, 313, 323
devagaḍhas (places of gods), 306
devakula(s) (temples with statues of dead kings), 305-07, 311, 384
devānāmpriya (dear to gods), 384
devapaśu (animals left in the name of god), 258
devapitṛpūjā (worship of gods and ancestors), 306
devaputra (son of god, a title applied to Kuṣāṇa kings), 298, 301-04, 306-08, 312, 384, 406
devasūhaviṃsi (offerings to gods in coronation), 159
devatādhyakṣa (superintendent of temples), 164
deya-meya (royal share of the produce), 279
dhamma (law, morality, social order), 207, 395, 398
dhammamahāmātra (high officer of *dhamma*), 20, 395
dhanamūla (civil law), 337
dharmādhikaraṇa (law-court), 338
dharmādhipati (upholder of *dharma*), 60
dharmadhvaja (standard bearer of *dharma*), 60
dharmaketu (standard bearer of law), 60

dharmamahāmātras (high officers of *dharma*), 227, 372
dharmamahārāja (king as upholder of *dharma* or law), 190
dharmanyāya (customs of the people), 263
dharmapravartaka (promulgator of *dharma*), 190, 254
dharmarāja (upholder of *dharma*), 190
dharmastha (judge), 373
dharmasthiya (civil court), 338
dharmathidasa (devoted to *dharma*), 308
dharmayuddha (fair fight), 10
dhārmikatvam (adherence to virtuous life), 267
dhīras (brave), 92
dīnāra (gold coin), 17, 28
dīvira (scribe), 329, 344
drāṅgika (customs officer), 329
digvijaya (universal conquest), 9
durgalambhopāya (method of capturing the fort), 271
durganiveśa (foundation of forts), 35-36
durgavidhāna (construction of fort), 35
dūṣya (a seditious person), 268
dūta (ambassador), 218, 240, 356, 397
dūtaka (executor of royal charters), 241
dūtapravartimam (royal agents), 218
dvandva (monogamous family), 52

ekarāja (world ruler), 360
ephori (overseers), 397
epiakopoi (overseer), 397

gahapati (householder), 190, 222, 239, 242, 247, 249, 281
gāhāvai (householder), 243, 247
gāma(s) (villages), 215
gāmabhojaka (village headman), 209, 210, 212, 299
gāmaṇi (village headman), 210
gāmavaram (prosperous village), 216
gāmika (village head), 285
gaṇadharas (sectional leaders in Jaina religious order), 132
gaṇaka (musician), 126, 364
gaṇakarmāṇi (duties of the *gaṇa*), 123
gaṇānāmpati (chief or king), 123
gaṇapatibhyaḥ svāhā (a formula recited before religious offerings to the *gaṇa* chief), 125
gaṇarājya (republic), 126
Gandharvas, 128, 284
gandhikas (perfumers, merchants), 279, 381
gaṇebhyah svāhā (a formula recited before religious offerings to the *gaṇa*), 124
gaṇeśvara (lord of the *gaṇa*), 188
gaṇī (leader), 132
gaṇikā (woman singer), 126
gañjavara (treasurer), 318
gāthā (versified sermon), 222
gaulmika (head of a military unit), 285, 289, 327-28, 383
gaviṣṭhi (search for cows, war), 164, 350
gopa (head of five or ten villages), 261, 353, 372, 374-75, 388
gopa janasya (ruler of the people or *jana*), 353
gopati (cowherd or chief), 185, 349
gopati janasya (protector of the people, tribe), 252
gotra (clan), 99, 350
govikartana (butcher, chief huntsman), 149, 150, 157
grāma (tribal unit, village), 173 287-89, 350, 357
grāmabhojaka (village headman), 219, 365
grāmabhṛtaka (village headman in Maurya times), 300
grāmādhipati (lord of the village), 317, 334
grāmādhipati āyuktaka (village headman), 334
grāmākṣapaṭalādhikṛta (village accountant), 329
grāmaṇī (village headman), 112, 146-47, 152, 156, 285, 352, 355, 357, 365; royal dues received through 147; vaisya 147, 157

grāmasvāmī (village head), 296, 316, 382
grāmasyādhipati (lord of the village), 300, 317, 334
grāmika (village headman), 201, 285, 299, 300, 309, 331-32, 365, in the Kuṣāṇa period 299, 300, 382; functions of 299, 300
grāmyavādin (village judge), 109
gṛha (household), 101
gṛhapati (householder), 282
gulma (smallest military unit), 285, 290, 299
gulmika (head of *gulma*), 285

hairaṇyika (treasurer), 279
hala (plough measure), 205
haṭṭa (periodical market), 85
hiṃsāmūla (offences involving violence), 337
hīnasippa (inferior crafts), 152
hiraṇya (gold, cash), 28, 69, 266, 326, 328, 344, 387
hotṛ (priest), 93-94, 96, 101

ibhyas (affluent people), 395
īkṣaṇikas (a type of astrologer), 270
Iśāṇa (president), 140
Iśvara (lord), 73, 182, 294

jāgīr (fief), 286
jāgīrdār (fief holder), 346
jajamānī, 83, 85
iama(s) (tribes, peoples), 34-35, 39, 99, 101, 186, 188, 350, 352
ianapada (kingdom, settlement), 5, 31, 34-36, 38-39, 41, 44, 180, 186, 189, 197, 200, 201, 276, 286, 333-34, 352, 405
janapadādhipa (king), 189
janapadaniveśa (founding of settlements), 200
janapadasthāmavīryaprāpta (one who has attained the security of his realm), 70
janapadeśvara (lord of the *janapada*), 189
janapadin (king), 189
janarājan (ruler of the people), 186
jānarājya (rule over the tribe), 15, 160
janasya gopā (head of the tribe), 186
janasya gopati (chief of the tribe), 195
janya, as śūdra, 161
jātidharma (duties pertaining to the caste), 233
jhum (slash and burn cultivation), 180
jīvagṛbha (police official), 356
jīvikā (livelihood), 266
jyāsvant (superiors), 124
jyesṭhāṃśa (eldest son's shares), 230

kahāpaṇa (a coin), 208
kalpavṛkṣa (wish fulfilling tree), 49
kaṇṭakaśodhana (criminal administration), 337, purpose of 374
kara (tax), 206-08, 226, 313, 344, 382
kārakaras (tax-collectors), 211, 219
karaṇika (scribe), 28, 329
karmāra (carpenter), 150
karma-saciva (executive minister), 34
karmānta (artisanal workshop), 218
karṣa (to cultivate), 208
kārṣāpaṇas (coins) 278
kāru-kara (taxes on artisans), 279-80
kāruka-rakṣaṇam (laws against undesirable activities of artisans), 84
kaṭaka (military camp, city), 286
khaḍgis (swordsmen), 338
khani (mining activities), 83
khattiya, 65, 202
khattiya-maṇḍala (community of the nobles), 67-68
khettasāmika (field owner), 205
kośa (treasury finance), 31, 36, 38, 40-41, 44, 73, 270
Krauñcadvīpa 45
kṛṣi (agriculture)
kṣatra (power), 85, 159, 171-72, 174-75, 248
kṣātradharmarataḥ (devoted to the duties of a kṣatriya), 240
ksattṛ, 146-47, 152, 157
kṣitīndra (lord of the earth), 81, 193
kṣitipati (suggests royal ownership of land), 193

kṣitiśa (suggests royal ownership of land), 81, 193
kṣiteradhipa (indicates land ownership), 193
kṣetrakara (officer in charge of land survey), 205, 212, 219
kṣetrasādha (distributor of land), 149
kula (family), 101, 357
kula (as local court), 338-39
kulapā (protector of the family), 100, 351, 355
kulika (artisan), 317, 335
kulīnaḥ (of a good family), 240
kumāra (provincial governors), 276, 397-98
kumāramātya(s) (high officers), 277, 316, 323-24, 326-27, 330, 347, 387
kumārāmatyādhikaraṇa (office of *kumāramātya*), 324
kuṭumba (peasant or householder), 205

lābhavighna (obstructions to profit), 267
madhyamasī (mediator in disputes), 356
maghavan(s) (rich men), 102, 111, 117
mahābalādhikṛta (chief commander), 315, 327
mahābhiṣekha (great coronation ceremony), 64, 167
mahābhoja (title of Sātavāhana feudatory), 284
mahācchavardhana (a penance performed for several nights), 261
mahādaṇḍanāyaka (chief commander), 297, 304, 309, 315, 318, 323-24, 326, 336, 383
mahājanapada (large territorial state), 200-02
mahākhattiya (protector of the fields), 52
mahākṣatrapa (the great satrap), 295, 297, 315
mahāmātra(s) (high officers), 20, 26, 219, 276-77, 316, 324, 364, 372, 382, 396, 398
mahāmātrīyam (the office of the *mahāmātra*), 20
mahāmātya (cadre of superior Aśokan officials), 387
māhaṇa (brāhmaṇa), 247
mahanuava (title of the Kuṣāṇa king in Kharoṣṭhī), 304
mahaparamaviśvāsin (Gupta official), 318
mahāpātra (ministerial title), 30
mahāpratīhāra (the great chamberlain), 327
mahārāja (the great king), 249, 284, 292, 296-97, 303, 306, 308, 312-13, 324, 346
mahārājādhirāja (the great king of kings), 313, 322, 346, 386
mahāraṭhis (title for Sātavāhana feudatories), 279, 282, 380
maharaya (title for the Kuṣāṇa king in Kharoṣṭhī), 304
mahāsammata (the elected chief), 65, 70, 347
mahāsāndhivigrahika (the great minister of peace and war), 324-25
mahāsenāpati (the great commander), 278, 283-86, 289, 383
mahātalavāra (title for Sātvāhana feudatories), 284
mahātalavārī (wife of *mahātalavāra*), 283
mahattaka (elder), 331
mahattama (elder), 331
mahto (elder), 332
mahattara(s) (elder), 331-33, 334-35, 339, 388
mahattara-āgrahārīṇa (head of the *agrahāra* village), 332
mahiṣī (the consecrated queen), 145-46, 152, 157-58, 356
manas (mind), 115
mangalatithinakṣatreṣṭitvam (faith in the auspiciousness of days and stars), 267
mantra (counsel), 34, 115, 137
mantrimaṇḍala (the council of ministers), 323

mantrin(s) (ministers), 18, 21, 33-34, 40, 240-41, 248, 323-25
mantripariṣad (the council of ministers), 141, 241
manujādhipa (signifies lordship over people), 190
mātā (mother), 351
mati-saciva (minister for counsel), 34, 382
mitra (ally), 31, 37, 39, 41, 336
mūrdhābhiṣikta (consecrated head), 70

nagaradevatā (presiding deity of the town), 256
nāgaraka (town magistrate), 373, 375
nagaraṣreṣṭhi (chief merchant of the town), 336, 338
nagaravyāvahārika (town official), 316, 375
naigama (merchant or town inhabitant), 242
nakṣatras (lunar mansions), 206
narādhipa (lord of the people), 190
narendra (lord of the people), 190
nareśvara (lord of the people), 190
nariṣṭā (a resolution that cannot be broken), 110
navakarmika (a class of overseer), 279
nāyaka (military title), 30, 394-95
negama(s) (merchants), 242, 251, 279-80
netā (leader), 45
nigama (town), 298, 317, 335, 380-81
nigamaputra (town inhabitant), 280
nigamasabhā (town body, merchant corporation) 281, 381
niggāhakas (tax collector), 211, 219
nikāya (guilds), 281
nivāsa-vetana (house rent), 208
niyukta (special government servant), 210-11, 219
nṛpa (king), 190
nṛpati (king, lord over people), 190

pāditarika (village revenue official), 328
padrapāla (head of the common land), 300
pālāgala (messenger), 150-51
paṇa(s) (metallic money), 208, 218, 246, 257, 261-62, 373, 375
pañcajanāḥ (five tribes), 160, 186, 188, 350, 352
pañcamaṇḍalī (a rural committee), 333
pañcavrātas (five races of men), 187
paṇya (commodities), 392
paṇya-saṃsthā (commodities), 393
paralokāpekṣā (desire for the other world), 267
paramabhaṭṭāraka (the supreme lord), 313, 322, 386
paramarṣayaḥ (the great sages), 72
paramaviśvāsin (Gupta official), 318
parameśvara (the supreme lord), 294, 313, 322, 386
parihāras (exemptions), 20, 21, 28, 287, 290; number of 289; in the Maurya period 376-77; in the post-Maurya period 377, 380
parisā (*pariṣad*, order), 26, 141, 219-20, 241, 243, 247, 396
pariṣad (council), 116, 133-41, 220, 241-42, 333, 367, 376, 403, 405
pāriṣada (member of the pariṣad), 18, 136
pāriṣadadāna (gift consisting of companions), 137
pariṣadbala (strength of the *pariṣad*), 140
pāriṣadpriya (fond of companions), 135
pariṣadvān(s) (members of the *pariṣad*), 133
pariṣadya (worthy of attending the *pariṣad*), 134-35, 140
parivṛkti (secondary queen), 90, 146, 151, 154-55, 158
pastya (enclosure), 200
paśupālana (cattle rearing), 130
paṭṭika-pālaka (keeper of records), 278
paṭwārīs (village revenue officials), 329
paura (inhabitant of town), 5, 241-42, 405
paura-jānapada (urban and rural people), 27, 242, 241-43

purāṇikas (story tellers), 270
pautava (weights and measures), 392
pilupati (head of elephant force), 315, 327
pitā (father), 351
pitṛ-pādānudhyāta (devoted to the feet of father), 282
prabhāmaṇḍala (nimbus), 307
prāḍavivāka (judge), 244
prādeśika(s) (district officers), 20, 278, 397
pradeṣṭā (police-cum-magistrate), 374-75
pradeṣṭṛ (magistrate, inspector), 393-94
prajā (progeny, subjects), 174, 229, 351
prakaraṇas (sections), 21
prakṛtis (people), 41
prakṛti-kopa (wrath of people), 372
pralaya (dissolution of the social order), 59
praṇaya (gift of affection, tax), 20, 28, 313, 382
prasāda-likhita (a writing of favour, grant), 344
praśastis (eulogies), 27
prathamakāyastha (chief scribe), 336, 338
prathamakulika (chief artisan), 336, 338
pratihāra (an officer), 278
pratyudyaminī (refractory), 175
pravrajita (ordinated), 261
prāyaścittadharma (the law of penance), 385
pṛthivī (the world), 72, 194
priyaḥ janaḥ (dear tribesmen), 98
puga (guild), 338
puṇyasālā (alms-house), 300
pura (capital town), 35, 36, 40, 262
purapāla (town administrator), 334
purapati (head of town, commander of forts), 355
purohita (priest), 40, 145, 151-52, 176, 188, 215, 241, 257, 354, 356, 262, 273, 276, 283
puruṣamedha (sacrifice of human being), 107
puruṣas (royal agents), 278
pustapāla(s) (record keepers), 326, 328

rahaṭṭa-ghaḍiya (Persian water-wheel), 385
rājā (king), 31-32, 40, 65, 67-68, 70, 72, 102, 110, 129, 172, 179, 202, 228, 276, 292, 297, 347, 368. See also rājan
rājabali (royal revenue), 215
rājabhaṭa (royal officer), 219
ṛajabhoggam (king's domain in the sense of possession), 212-14
rājabhoggas (royal officers), 214
rājadharma (duties of the king), 17-19, 63, 71, 139, 315
rājagrahaṇam (royal dues), 211
rājakaṃ-khetam (royal land), 80, 194
rājakammikas (royal officers dealing with rent), 205, 211, 219
rājakartṛs (king makers), 179
rājakīya-bhoga (land revenue/rent), 81, 194
rājāmatya (royal minister), 277
rājan (king), 15, 38, 101-02, 112, 123-24, 171, 185-88, 194, 209, 221, 354, 356 See also *rājā*
rājanya(s), 101-02, 164-65, 171-73, 175-76, 178-79, 182, 202, 214, 221, 235, 360, 404; as ratnin 145, 152, 156
rājanya-bandhu, 171
rājaputra (prince), 361
rājasaśāna (royal edict), 263, 386
rājasūya (coronation ceremony), 100, 143, 145, 152, 155, 159, 161-62, 164, 172, 176, 228, 359
rājātirāja (king of kings), 292, 294, 303-04, 306, 308, 312-13
rājjugāhaka-amacca (officer in charge of rent)
rajuka(s) (high royal officer), 20, 26, 67n, 277, 286, 377, 395-97
rājya (kingdom), 38, 200, 352
rākṣasas (demons), 257, 266, 284
rāṣṭra (kingdom, territory, district),

34, 40, 114, 156, 162, 180, 182, 188, 197, 200, 276, 287, 289, 352, 359
rāṣṭrabhṛt (upholder of the kingdom), 188-89, 360
rāṣṭrpāla (protector of kingdom), 188
rāṣṭra-gopa (protector of kingdom), 188
rāṣṭrapati (lord of kingdom), 188-89
rāṣṭrikas (administrator of *rāṣṭra*), 396
rāṣṭriya (head of *rāṣṭra*), 383
ratnin(s) (jewel-holders), 143-58, 157, 182, 356, 361-62, 404
rāyāhirāya (Śaka title), 292-93
ṛṣis (sages), 71, 100
ṛt (natural law), 356
ṛtvik (priest), 40

sabhācara (member of the *sabhā*), 108
sabhāpāla (protector of the *sabhā*), 105
sabhāpati (president), 109
sabhāsad(s) (members of the *sabhā*), 108-09
sabhāsaha (member of the *sabhā*), 106
sabhāvatī (women member of the *sabhā*), 105
sabhāyogya (worthy of the *sabhā*), 134
sabheya (distinguished member of the sabhā), 106
sabhyas (member of the *sabhā*), 18, 338
sachivatantra (constitutional monarchy), 6
saciva (minister), 18, 34, 40, 42, 316, 323, 325
sācivyakaras (companions of ministers), 270
sa-daṇḍa-daś=āparādhāḥ (with the right to collect fines for ten offences), 340
ṣaḍbhāgabhuk (enjoyer of taxes), 190
saḍbhāgin (a title of the king referring to the tax collection aspect), 207
sadhura (joint labour), 124
sahasrapati (head of one thousand villages), 383
ṣāhi (kinsmen of the overlord, feudatories), 292-94, 303, 380
ṣāhnuṣāhi (title of Kuṣāṇa kings), 293, 303-04, 312-13
sajāta (of the same kin), 165, 169, 173
sāma (pacification), 31
samāhartā (collector), 373-76, 392, 394
samānasthānavāsī (inhabitant of the same place), 242
sāmanta(s) (neighbour, vassal), 346-47; changing meaning of the term 346
sāmantabhūmiśvara (emphasises lordship over land), 93
sāmanta-cūḍāmaṇayaḥ (chief vassals), 346-47
sāmantāhivai (overlord), 293
sāmanta-mahārāja (feudatory), 347
samaya (contract, rules), 73, 335
saṃgrahītṛ (treasurer), 146, 148, 152, 157
saṃgrāma (collection of tribal units, battle), 112-13, 178, 351
samrāṭ (the great king), 102
saṃsad (council), 134
saṃskāras (rituals), 161, 231
samvyavahāripramukhān (village elders) 316, 332
sāndhivigrahika (officer dealing with peace and war), 28, 278, 323-25; functions of 324-25
saṅghas (corporations), 132
sannidhātā (treasurer), 148, 373, 376, 393
sārathi, 148
sārthavāha (caravan leader), 317, 335-36, 338
sarvādhyakṣa (Gupta officials), 340
sarva-jāti-parihāra (exemptions of all types), 287
sarvaloka-iśvara (lord of the whole world), 294
śāsana (charter), 82, 377
śasanahara (*duta*), 397
śāsitā (administrator), 45
śāstā rājā (ruling king), 259
ṣaṣṭhavṛtti (enjoyer of taxes), 190
ṣaṣṭika (a type of rice), 183
śatapati (head of one hundred villages), 362

sarthavāhas (carvan leaders), 279
sattra (collective sacrifice), 99-100, 309
śaulkika (collector of tolls), 329, 366
sautrāmaṇi ceremony, 171, 175
senā (army), 88, 181, 355, 357
senānāyaka (captain), 364-65
senānāyaka-mahāmattas (generals), 219
senānī (commander), 145-46, 151, 156, 355-57; importance of 362
senāpati (head of the army), 124, 238, 241, 324, 368, 373, 394
seṭṭhi(s) 204, 215, 241, 247, 279, 364
shaonano shao (*ṣāhanuṣāhi* title of Kuṣāṇa kings), 293, 312
sipp(e)a (tribal unit), 105
sīra (ploughshare), 350
sitā (crown land), 81, 83
skandhāvāra (military camp), 21, 84, 286
snātaka (student), 236
spasa (spies), 355
śreṇi (guild), 207, 281, 298, 317, 388
śresṭhi (merchant), 217, 235, 238
śrīraṇabhāṇḍāgārādhikaraṇa (department of military store), 327
śrotriya (one who knows the Veda), 241, 259, 261-62, 360
śruti (oral communication), 222
sthānika (revenue officer), 261, 373-75
sthāniya (a unit of 800 villages), 35
sthapati (architect), 147, 362
sthapatisamrāṭ (master mason), 241
strīadhyakṣa (superintendent of women), 378
stūpa, 296, 306
suhṛt (ally), 37
sujātāh (well born), 106
sulkādhyakṣa (superintendent of tolls), 366
sūnā (slaughter house), 392
sūtra (spinning), 392
surā (liquor), 171-72, 175, 392
sūta (messenger), 147-48, 152, 156, 240
suvīrāḥ (brave sons), 106, 351
svadharma, 54
svāmī (king or head of the state), 31-32, 38, 41, 46, 191; as an element of the state 31-33, 44; in Śāka inscriptions 32; qualities of 32-33; calamity affecting 41. See also king
svarājya (republic), 129
svaramaṇḍala (expert in the knowledge of sound), 126
śyāma ayas (iron), 358
swaraj, 4

takṣan (carpenter), 150, 152, 356
taradeya (ferry dues), 21
tirthas (high functionaries), 372-73
tuṇḍiyas (tax collector), 211, 219, 224

udraṅga (royal share of the produce), 344, 387
ugra (police officer), 355-56
upanayana (sacred thread ceremony), 153
uparājā (deputy king), 368
uparājan (deputy king), 124, 241
uparakṣita (overseer), 279
uparika(s) (provincial governor), 241, 325, 330, 347, 387; origin of 330
uparikara (additional impost on peasants), 330, 344, 387
vāhana (means of conveyance), 148
vāhanāyaka (head porter), 333
vairājya (non-monarchical state), 32, 51, 129
vaidehaka-rakṣanam (laws against the undesirable activities of traders), 84
vaiśvāsika (confidential agent), 318
vaiśya-grāmaṇī (head of the village people), 157, 365
vājapeya(sacrifice of drink to strength), 100, 159, 165-67, 175
vajjidharma (customs of the Vājjis), 58
vanalatā (creepers), 49
vānapı asthas, 261
vāṇijya (trade), 130
vappamaṅgala (tradition of king/chief ploughing the land), 194
vārttā (material conditions), 198-99
varṇadharma (duties pertaining to varṇas), 54, 233

varṇāśramadharma (duties pertaining to varṇas and to stages in life), 53, 235, 253-54, 264, 322, 385
varṇavyavasthā (the system of social divisions), 56, 60
vasudhādhipa (owner of the land), 193
vasudheśvara (lord of the earth), 87
vāvātā (women *ratnin*, chief wife of king), 90, 146, 151, 157
veśyā (prostitute), 392
vetana (wages), 339
veṭh (forced labour), 30
vihāra (monastery), 308
vihārasvāmī (head of the monastery), 308
vijita (conquered), 399
vinayasthitisthāpaka (magistrate), 337, 389
viniccaya (trials), 33
viniyuktaka (revenue officer), 329
vipra(s) (brāhmaṇas), 105-06, 141, 220, 241
vīra (brave son), 93
viś(aḥ) (people), 90, 101, 111, 150, 157, 162, 169, 173-75, 178, 181, 186, 228-29
viśāmattā (chief of men, king), 172, 187, 189, 361
viśāmiśvaraḥ (tribute collector, king), 187
viśāmpati (chief, *rājā*), 172, 179, 186-87
viṣaya (district), 31, 298, 328, 330-31, 338, 388
viṣayapati (head of the *viṣaya*), 326, 330, 388
viśpati (chief, *rājā*), 172, 179, 186-87
viṣṭi (forced labour), 20, 28, 30, 218, 313, 382, 387
vīthī(s) (fiscal divisions), 331, 338, 38;
vīthī adhikaraṇa (sub-divisional body), 331
vohāra (lawsuits), 33
vohārika mahāmattas (judicial officials), 219
vrājapati (head of the pasture grounds), 352, 355
vrata (way of life), 114-15, 356
vrata (vow), 137
vrāta (people), 187-88, 219
vrātapaḥ (protector, lord of the *vrāta*), 187
vṛjana (enclosure, pasture), 200
vṛka (hoes), 350
vyākula (chaotic), 248
vyavahāra (civil law), 46, 54-55, 57
vyavahārika (magistrate), 316
vyavahārika mahāmātra (civil judge), 366
vyvahārin, 316
yajamāna (sacrificer), 98-99, 173
yajña (sacrifice), 94-95, 99, 231-32
yavuga (small chief), 291, 308
yodhājivas (warriors), 238
yoṣā (young woman), 88
yuddha (war), 112, 233
yukta(s) (magistrates), 20, 278
yūpa (sacrificial post), 309
yutta (government servant), 210, 397
yuvarāja (crown prince), 373

AUTHORITIES

Abhilaṣitārthacintāmaṇi of Someśvaradeva, 60
Ādi Parva, 127, 231
Agni Purāṇa, 20, 30, 31n, 42
Agrawala, V.S., 140, 205, 207, 210n, 264n, 268n, 368n
Aiyangar, K.V., Rangaswami, 4, 6, 236n
Aiyangar, S.K., 3, 11
Aitareya Brāhmaṇa, 16, 66, 90, 123, 129, 167-68, 176, 359-61; on forms of government 359-60; on types of chieftainship 171
Altekar, A.S., vii-viii, 22n, 30n, 35n, 49n, 63n, 104n, 133n, 242n, 299n 312; on functions of *sāndhivigrahika*, 325
Allan, J., 303, 305, 380n

Ambaṭṭhasutta, 24
Ancient Kingship from the Religious Point of View Xn
Ancient Indian Republics from the Earliest Times to the Sixth Century A.D., XIVn
(*The*) *Ancient Indian Royal Consecration*, XIn
Ancient Society, vii
Anderson, Perry, 86n
Anquetil-Duperron, 86
Anuśāsana Parva, 18
Āpastamba, 16, 239, 245, 378
Arrian, 28, 129, 240n
Arthaśāstra of Kauṭilya, 4, 8, 17, 20-3, 25-26, 28, 30-33, 35, 38, 42, 63, 141, 148, 156, 192, 207, 219, 220, 233, 251, 253, 257-59, 270-71, 291, 299, 301, 326, 328-29, 372-74, 378; date of 20-21; on *amātyas* 33, 277. on *akṣaśālā* 149; on agriculture 200; on calamities affecting the organs of the state 41-44; on contractual origin of the state 68; on king as upholder of *varṇas* 233; bureaucracy in 372-74; *janapada* in 364; on origin of kingship 69; on law 246; police administration in 374; on *pariṣad* 133, 139; on payments in cash 278; on recruitment of officials 220; on rituals and state 253, 255, 257; *svāmī* in 32; on superintendants 399; town and rural administration in 375; taxes in 217, 376; on elements of decentralisation 376-77; See also Kauṭilya
Aristotle, 1, 22, 38, 42, 47, 75, 77
(*The*) *Asiatic Mode of Production*, 86n
Aspects of Ancient Indian Polity by N.N. Law, 7
Aṭānaṭiyasutta, 50
Atharvan collections, 90
Aṭṭakathā, 58
Auckland, Colvin, 3
Ayodhyā Kāṇḍa, 55-56

Bajpai, K.D., 297n, 381n
Bakhle, V.S., 281n
Bāṇa, 236, 273
Bandyopadhaya, N.C., 7, 10, 49n, 94n, 105-06, 110, 112, 113n, 117, 161n, 353n
Banerjea, P.N., 5, 9-10, 49n
Barth, A., 98
Basak, R.G., 347n
Basham, A.L., viiin, 129n, 273n
Baudhāyana, 16, 67, 137-38, 141, 241, 245
Baudhāyana Dharmasūtra, 16, 366; on *baliharaṇam*, 124
Beal, Samuel, 326
Benveniste, Emile, 185n, 186n, 192n
Bhandarkar, D.R., 2, 5, 8, 49n, 55n, 130
Bhandarkar, R.G., 2
Bhāradvāja, on ministers, 43
Bharadwaj, H.C., 201n
Bhāsa, 305-06
Brāhmaṇas, 16, 30-01, 63; anticipate social contract, 64; contract theory in 65, 75; coronation ceremonies in 94; on *ratnahiviṃṣī* 152; *vidatha* in 87
Bloomfield, 7, 8, 87, 90, 95, 97-98
Bose, A.N., 203, 210n, 214n
Brahmavaivarta Purāṇa, 248
Brhadāraṇyaka Upaniṣad, 130
Bṛhannāradiya Purāṇa, 59
Bṛhaspati, 17-18, 54-55, 74, 122, 123, 125, 127, 145, 337-38, 344, 359, 389; on titles of law 337
Bṛhatsaṃhitā of Varāhamihira, 25
Brugmann, Karl, 90n
Bühler, G., 17, 203-05
Buddhaghoṣa, 212

Chadwick, H.M., 97, 116, 155
Chāndogya Upaniṣad, 110
Chaudhary, Bijoy Kumar, 173n
Chattopadhyay, Bhaskar, 314n
Childe, G., 49n, 51n
Chattopadhyaya, S.K., 295n
Classen, J.M., 198
(*The*) *Classical Law of India*, xiin
Coker, F.W., 251
Colebrooke, 79

Contributions to the Study of the Hindu Revenue System, 11
Corporate Life in Ancient India, 6
Cousion, 7
Cowell, E.B., 399n
Critical Edition (of the *Mahābhārata*), 18
Cullavagga, 23
Cunningham, Alexander, 303
Curtius, 223, 225
Curzon, 3

dāna-stuti (in the *Ṛg Veda*), 183
Dange, S.A., 50n, 120n, 124n, 247n
Das, A.C., 3
Datta, B.N., 100
Davids Ryhs, T.W., 194n, on land revenue 203; on *rāja-bhoggam* 213
Derrett, J. Duncan M., xiin
Deshmukh, P.S., 98n
Development of Hindu polity and Political Theories, 10
Dharmakośa by L.S. Joshi, 28, 81
Dīgha Nikāya, 24, 50, 58, 215, on contract theory of the origin of the state 63-75; on origin of kingship 301
Dharmaśāstra, 16, 23, 24, 28-29, 54, 60, 133, 139, 190, 229-30, 234, 236, 245-46, 248, 250-51, 279, 323, 334, 405
Dharmasūtra(s), 14, 16, 20, 31, 109, 137, 140, 141, 152, 189, 202, 205, 217, 220, 228, 239, 364, 366-67
Digest of Hindu Law, 79
Dikshitar, V.R.R., 8, 11, 49n, 57n, 133n
Diodorus, 223, 225
Divyāvadāna, 399
Drouin, M.E., 307
Dunning, 7, 8
Dutt, R.C., 3

Early Kingship and Community, by Charles Drekmeier, vii
Engels, F., 39, 40, 48, 53, 77, 89, 90n, 111n, 115n, 197

Evolution of Hindu Administrative Institutions, 11

Fa-hsien, 29n, 326, 387
Fick, August, 103n
Fick, Richard, 33n, 212, 214, 239; on land revenue 203-04; on *gāma-bhojaka* 209
Fleet, 119

Gaṇapati Sastri, T., 43n, 258, 261n
Ganguly, K.M., 127n
Gāthā Sattasai, 285
Gautama, 16, 31, 141, 205-07, 211, 241, 366
Gautama Dharmasūtra, 242
Ghoshal, U.N., ix, 7, 8, 11, 20, 22n, 43n, 81n, 87n, 102, 112n, 146n, 149n, 154n, 163n, 164n, 169n, 176, 194n, 212, 214, 239, 247, 266n, 303, 307n, 309n, 315n, on distribution of land in Vedic times 114; on *gaṇa* 132; on *ratnins* 143; on *ratnahavīṃṣī* ceremony 143; on *rājasūya* 159; on royal power 68; on *sabhā* 117; on taxation and protection 75
Ghurye, G.S., 247n
Gibbon, 1
Gonda, J., x-xii
Gopal, Lallanji, 346n
Green, 1
Griffith, 95n, 110, 121, 133, 134n
(*The*) *Grundrisse*, xivn
Gunawardana, R.A.L.H., 80
Gupta, P.L., 282n, 384n

Habib, Irfan, 78n, 392n, 400n
Hāla's *Gāthā Sattasaī*, 285
Hall, H.R., 10, 127n
Harihara, 140
Hazra, R.C., 31n, 42n, 59n, 377
Heesterman, J.C., xi-xii, 152, 159, 160n, 161n, 164n, 165n, 392n, 395n, 398n, 399; on Maurya state 392-99; on *ratnahavīṃṣī* ceremony 152; on *rājasūya* 159
Hegel, 7, 77, 82, 83n, 86
Herodotus, 296n
Hillebrandt, 100, 116

Hindess, Barry, 79n, 85n
Hindustan Review, 5
Hirst, Paul, Q, 79n, 85n
History of Dharmaśāstra, 81
(*A*) *History of Hindu Public Life*, ix
A History of Political Ideas Ancient and Medieval, ix
Hobbes, 64, 69, 76
Ho Chang-Chun, 326n
Homer, 111
Hopkins, E.W., 2, 19, 40n, 105, 109n, 111, 141n, 234, 240, 241n, 246, 247n
Horner, I., 216
Hsüan Tsang, 29, 236, 387
Hulzsch, 137n
Hutington, 7

Indian Antiquary, 5
Indian Epigraphical Glossary, 281
Indika, 28
Indraji, Bhagwan Lal, 2
Inner Conflict of Indian Tradition, xn
(*An*) *Introduction to the Study of Indian History*, xivn
Inscription(s), Allahabad pillar 27, 294, 298, 304, 346, 390; Aśokan 20, 219, 222, 234, 275-76, 278, 283, 316, 346, 371-73, 375-77, 387, 395; Baigram copper-plate 316, 332; Barabar hill cave 346; Banskhera 235; *dharma* 26; Damodarpur copper plate 318, 335; defence of *varṇa* system in 191; Gupta 18, 26, 316, 383-84; Hāthīgumphā 292, Harahā 347; Junagadh 192, 313, 316; Junnar cave, 279; Kandhar 375; Kassite 127; Kharoṣṭhī 296; Kuṣāṇa 304, 383; Mallasārul copper plate 331; Mathura 297, 300, 306, 316; Mathura Jain 299; Mandasore stone 235, 249; Mitannian 127; Nanaghat cave 278, 287; Nasik cave 234, 279, 300; official 27; of the Deccan 21; of the 2nd-3rd century A.D. 20; Pallava 346; private 26; Śaka 21; Sarnath Buddhist image 294; Sātavāhana 21, 276-77, 283, 283, 387; Udayagiri cave 240; Vākaṭaka 329

Jain, J.C., 243n
Jaina Purāṇas, 24
Janet, 7
Jaiminīya Brāhmaṇa, 146
Jātaka(s), 24, 33, 34, 109, 139, 141, 204, 207, 214-15, 220, 222, 226, 235, 238, 242, 248, 251, 277, 367; on the expulsion of the king 364; on king's responsibility 378; on state organization 223
Jaya Saṃhitā, xn, 193
Jayaswal, K.P., 4, 9, 17, 51n, 88, 110, 116-17, 132n, 133n, 143, 145, 148n, 149n, 152n, 161n, 163n, 167, 240n, 242, 243n, 305n; indologist 4; on *grāmaṇis* 147; on *ratnins* 143, 154, 157; on republics 119, 129; on *sabhā* 108-09; on *samiti* 112-13, 115; on *saṅghas* 132; on *vidatha* 88
Jayaswal, Vidula, 400n
Jones, Richard, 77, 79
Joshi, L.S., 28, 193n
Justin, 374

Kāmanadaka, 22, 23, 34-35, 40, 44-45, 47, 59-60, 238
Kamandaka Nītisāra, 22, 238, 323
Kamasūtra of Vatsyāyana, 317, 334
Kane, P.V., 28, 31n, 44n, 99n, 190n, 191n, 230n, 250n, 344n
Kangle, R.P., 4n, 217n, 218n, 373n, 393n
Kāṭhaka Saṃhitā, 145, 149
Kātyāyana, 17, 18, 58; on the caste of the *amātya* 240; on individuals' possession of land 193, 322; on king's ownership of the soil 191-93; on the organization of the judicial system 244; on settlement of disputes 338-39
Kauṭilya, 4, 6, 10, 20, 22-23, 26, 28, 31-38, 40-44, 46-47, 61, 69, 73, 123, 199, 222, 237-39, 241, 246, 255, 260, 263-64, 274, 276, 287, 386, 371-72, 374, 378, 398-99; compared with

Greek philosophers 28; compared with Aristotle 42; compared with Bṛhaspati 337; compared with Plato 272; on the composition of the army 237-38; compared with Manu 262-63; on seven elements of the state 31-38; his brāhmaṇical views on internal policy 243-54; on external policy 254-55; on state capital 256-57; on rituals for averting calamities 257; on protection of temple wealth 258; on unjust punishments 259; on king's divinity 260; on exalted position of the king 42; on sources of law 263; on *amātyas* 34, 239, 263-64, 325; on replenishment of treasury 267; on the use of superstition in dealing with enemies 268-69; on king's supernatural powers 269-71; on *parihāra* 287-88; on organization of bureaucratic machinery 372-74; on town and rural administration 374-75; on town and rural administration 374-75; on accounting 349; on heads of departments 392-93; on rules of recruitment 373; on cash payment to officials 395; on revenue assessment 375, 376; on taxes 74, 81, 198; on taxes and coercion 224; on religion and the state 263-64; on superstition and superstitious practices 266-71, 273, 405; on importance of elephants in military machine 313; on *vairājya* 51

Keith, A.B., 7, 38, 99n, 100n, 148n, 186n

Konow's List, 302

Kosambai, D.D., xivn, 160n, 237n, 240n, 285n

Landtman, G., 129n

Law, B.C., 129n, 238n, 301n, 303n, 304n

Law, N.N., 7

Lawrence, 10

Legge, 326

Lindsay, Jack, 245n

Lingat, Robert, xii

Lingat, Robert, xiin

Locke, 69, 76

Lüders, H., 277n, 279, 280, 281n, 293n, 297n, 299n, 302n, 308n, 309n, 312n

Ludwig, 102, 106, 111, 117

Mabbett, I.W., 392n

Macdonell, 174, 181n, 186n

Maitrāyaṇi Saṃhitā, 88, 90, 109, 145, 149

Majumdar, R.C., 5, 6, 98n, 117, 130

Mānava-Dharmaśāstra, 17

Mandlebaum, 202n

Manu, 17, 18, 31n, 32n, 34n, 35, 37, 44-46, 53, 58-60, 69, 71, 73, 81, 137, 191, 233-34, 236-37, 241, 243, 245-46, 248, 260, 262-63, 285, 299, 322, 334, 336, 337, 379, 383; on king as upholder of varṇas 233-34; on the appointment of judges 243; on king's responsibility to Varuṇa 260; on *pāṣaṇḍas* 262; on *gulma* 285-86; on king's divinity 302-03; on penances 385; on land grants 343; on village headman 316-17

Manu Saṃhitā, 17, 251

Manu Smṛti, 17, 272, 315

Marx, Karl, 77, 78n, 80, 83, 86, 204, 208

Marxist Perspectives in Archaeology, xiv

Maskarin, 206, 211, 241-42

Matsya Purāṇa, 19, 136

Max Müller, 1, 2, 7, 8

Megasthenes, 21, 26, 28, 40, 69, 149, 240n, 374, 377, 395; on Maurya officials 373; on recruitment to the army and bureaucracy 237-39; on republics 129

McCrindle, John W., 129n, 224n, 225n, 398n

Mehta, R.N., 34n, 141n, 203, 235n, 238n, 241n

Meillasoux, C., 178n

Mill, J., 77

Mitchell, William P., 79n

Mishra, B.B., 20n, 42n
Mishra, S.C., 21n
Mitra, R.L., 2
Modern Review, 5
Mommsen, 273n
Monier-Williams, 147n, 183n, 185n, 190n
Montesquieu, 77, 78
Mookherji, R.K., 9, 133n
Morgan, Lewis H., 49, 50n, 94n, 104n
Mṛcchakaṭika, 338
Mudrārākṣasa, 271

Naighuṇṭa, 185
Nārada, 17, 18, 54-55, 74, 173, 234, 265, 289, 322, 337; on king as upholder of varṇas 234; on *rāja-śāsana* 386
Neil, R.A., 399n
Nighaṇṭu, 100
Nirukta, 101, 186
Nītisāra, 24
Nītisāra of Kāmandaka, 22
Nītivākyāmṛta by Somadeva Sūri, 25

Ojha, K.C., 236n
Oldenberg, 87, 91, 103, 219n
Q'Leary, Brendan, 79n, 86n
(*The*) *Origin of the Family, Property and the State*, vii

Pañcatantra, 57, 237
Pandey, R.B., 346n
Pandey, R.C., 192n
Pāṇini, 23, 25, 123, 140, 264, on taxes 208, 226; on tax officials 210-11; on the recruitment of officials 364; on land survey and measurement 205
Pant, P.C., 400n
Pāraskara Gṛhyasūtra, 140
Pargiter, J.E., 139, 160n, 177
Parry, N.E., 180
Patañjali, 25, 119, 249, 264, 266
Plato, 22, 23, 38, 47, 59, 68, 75, 77; on the use of superstition 272-73
Plutarch, on army size 223
Politics, 22
Political Ideas and Ideals in the Mahabharata, ixn
Political Ideas and Institutions in the Mahabharata, ixn
Political Theory of Ancient India, viiin
Polybius, 273
Pratimānāṭaka of Bhāsa, 305
Pre-Capitalist Economics Formations, xivn
Ptolemy, 280
Puri, B.N., 295n, 297, 300n

Raghuvaṃśa, 339
Rāmāyaṇa, 19, 59, 137, 186, 189, 243
Ray, H.C., 141n, 223n
Raychaudhuri, H.C., 181n, 200n, 201n, 219n-221n, 224n, 225n, 226n, 235n, 255n, 276n, 292n, 362n, 397n,
(*The*) *Republic*, 22-23, 38, 59, 68, 75, 272-73
Republics in Ancient India, vii
Rey, P.P., 178n
Ṛg Veda, 15, 87-88, 91, 98-99, 101, 106-07, 111, 113, 115, 119, 122-23, 133, 148-49, 156, 179, 183, 186-200, 349-57, 361
Rockhill, 49n, 51n
Rosenfield, John M., 315n
Roth, 88, 103
Rouse, 216
Rousseau, 64, 68, 76
Roy, B.P., 383n
Ruben, Walter, 131n

Sabhā Parva, 18
Sacred Books of the East, 1
Sahni, D.R., 305n
Śalya Parva, 136
Śānti Parva, 18-19, 22, 24, 32-33, 36-37, 40, 44-46, 50-53, 55, 60, 63, 66, 68, 71-75, 127, 139, 141, 233, 240, 243, 255, 260, 264, 272, 317, 383; date of the *rājadharma* section of 19; on *daṇḍa* 315; on divine origin of the king 302; on king as upholder of varṇas 233-34; on the use of superstition 272-73
Sarasvatīvilāsa, 31
Sarkar, B.K., 5, 7, 12n

Śatapatha Brāhmaṇa, 16, 106, 110, 114, 125, 135, 143, 135, 145-46, 149-52, 155, 161, 163, 165-66, 168, 173, 176, 178-79, 183, 185, 187, 229-32, 301, 360-61; on army 362; king exempted from punishment in 163; on kingship 187, 230-32, 361; on *pariṣad* 135; on the list of *ratnins* 143, 145-46, 149-52; subordination of the *viś* in 174, 229
Sāyana (commentrator), 96, 106, 110, 112, 123, 133, 134, 146
Schomann, 171
Sen, B.C., 203, 209n
Sénart, 2, 255n, 274n
Seth, H.C., 271n
Sharma, J.P. xiii, 104n
Sharma, R.S., 45n, 79n, 80n, 171n, 175n-77n, 178n, 201n, 238n, 245n, 331n, 337n, 340n, 400n
Shamasastry, R., 4, 6, 218n
Shastri, A.M., 276
Shastri, H.P., 255, 305n
Shastri, J.L., 31n, 35n, 56n, 57n, 59n, 61n, 84n
Shastri, L.S., 82n
Singh, C.P.N., 223n
Singh, P.N., 3
Sinha, H.N., 25n
Sircar, D.C., 28, 80n, 191n, 283n, 258n, 313n
Sivaramamurti, C., 281n
Skalnik, Peter, 198n
Smith, Adam, 77
Smith, V.A., 7, 12
Smith, William, 97n
Spellman, J.W., 104n
Spencer, Herbert, 47
Śrautasūtras, 16
State and Government in Ancient India, vii
Stevenson, S., 132n
Strabo, 397-98
Śukra, 22, 47
Śukranītisāra, 30
Sukthankar, 285-86
Suvarṇaprabhāsottamasūtra, on divine kingship 302, 303

Taittirīya Āraṇyaka, 87
Taittirīya Brāhmaṇa, 90, 125, 143, 146
Taittirīya Saṃhitā, 15, 162, 172, 359
Tarn, W.W., 260n
Thapar, Romila, xiv, 131n, 178n, 229n, 392n, 399n
Thomas, F.W., 119, 302n, on Kuṣāṇa titles 303-04; on *prādeśika* 397
Thomson, G., 114n, 124n, 135n, 161n, 163n, 166n
Tirukkuṟaḷ, 57

Upaniṣads, 16

Vājasaneyi Saṃhitā, 87
Varāhamihira, 25
Vasiṣṭha, 16, 141, 241, 378
Vātsyāyana, 334
Vāyu Purāṇa, 19, 52, 127
Vinaya Piṭaka, 23, 219, 220, 367, 372
Viṣṇu, 236; on varṇa and administration of justice, 244
Viṣṇudharmottara Purāṇa, 31, 32, 55
Viṣṇu Purāṇa, 56
Viṣṇu Smṛti, 17, 251
Viswanath, S.V., 10
Vyvahārakhaṇḍa, of Kātyāyana, 17

Weber, Max, 143, 159, 162n
Whitney, 95n, 110
Willoughby, 7, 8
Wilson, 134
Wittfogel, Karl, 78, 79n

Yājñavalkya, 17, 18, 46, 244, 259, 265, 334; on appointment of judge 243-44; on king's responsibility, 259-60, 334; on kāyasthas 329; on *pariṣad* 241-42; on ordeals and justice 337-38; law of inheritance in 389; Pāṣaṇḍas in 265; śūdra excluded from high office in 250
Yajur Veda, 134
Yajus, 14, 105,109, 117, 143, 149, 150, 152, 164, 173, 176

Zimmer, 102, 113, 116